SYMBOL SOURCEBOOK

SYMBOL

An Authoritative Guide

HENRY DREYFUSS

SOURCEBOOK

to International Graphic Symbols

A VNR Book

JOHN WILEY & SONS, INC.

New York Chichester Weinheim Brisbane Singapore Toronto

First published in paperback in 1984
Cloth edition published 1972 McGraw-Hill Book Company
Book design and sketches by Henry Dreyfuss

Published by John Wiley & Sons, Inc.

Published simultaneously in Canada.

Library of Congress Cataloging-in-Publication Data:

Dreyfuss, Henry, 1904-
Symbol sourcebook.
Reprint. Originally published: New York: McGraw-Hill, 1972.
Bibliography: p.
Includes index.
1. Signs and symbols. I. Title.
AZ108.D74 1984 001.056 83-12514
ISBN 0-471-28872-1

40 39 38 37 36 35 34 33 32 31

Paul Clifton headed the entire Data Bank and Sourcebook project with devotion and with constant regard for quality, concept, and detail. His efforts and concern have been boundless and my gratitude is beyond words.

H.D.

To Doris
for untold amounts of encouragement, imagination, industry, patience, and endurance.

CONTENTS

ENGLISH

FOREWORD—R. Buckminster Fuller 14
INTRODUCTION 16
SEMANTOGRAPHY—C. K. Bliss 22
ISOTYPE—Marie Neurath 24
BASIC SYMBOLS 26
DISCIPLINES
- Accommodations and Travel 34
  - including Terminals
- Agriculture 39
  - Agronomy, Livestock and Dairy Products, Farm Structure and Lands, Forestry, Implements
- Architecture 48
  - Drafting, Landscaping and Planning
- Astronomy 54
- Biology 55
  - including Botany, Molecular Biology
- Business 58
  - including Computers, Office Equipment, Shops and Services
- Chemistry 67
- Communications 70
  - including Movement and Dance, Non-graphic Alphabets
- Engineering 80
  - Chemical, Electrical, Mechanical
- Folklore 86
  - Alchemy, Astrology, Hobo Signs
- Geography 92
- Geology 96
- Handling of Goods 98
- Home Economics 100
  - including Appliances
- Manufacturing 104
  - including Heavy Duty Machinery
- Mathematics 111
- Medicine 113
  - including Equipment, Hospitals
- Meteorology 120
- Music 123
- Photography 126
- Physics 128
- Recreation 130
  - including Olympics
- Religion 138
- Safety 140
- Traffic 143
  - Road, Air, Marine, Rail
- Vehicle Controls 157
  - including 3-Dimensional Shapes

GRAPHIC FORM 166
COLOR 231
ACKNOWLEDGMENTS 248
BIBLIOGRAPHY 252
INDEX 268

ARABIC

تقديم — R. Buckminster Fuller 14
مقدمة 16
سمنتوغرافي — C. K. Bliss 22
Marie Neurath—ISOTYPE 24
الرموز الاساسية 26
نظم
- السفر ومحطات الانطلاق والعودة 34
  - كـاملـة وترتيبات الاقـامه
- الزراعـة 39
  - الهندسة الزراعيه ، ومنتجات الالبان والمواشى وتنظيم المزارع والاراضى ، علم الغابات والادوات الزراعيه
- الهندسة المعمارية 48
  - وضع الرسومات ، مسح الاراضى والتخـطيط
- علـم الفلـك 54
- علـم الاحيـاء 55
  - ويشمل علم النبات والخلايا الحيـة
- اعمـال 58
  - ويشمل العقول الالكترونيه وتجهيزات المكاتب ، والحوانيت والخـدمـات
- الكيميـاء 67
- وسائل الاتصال 70
  - ويشـمل الحـركة والرقص والرموز والاشارات
- الهندسة 80
  - الكيميائية والكهربائية والميكانيكيه
- التراث الشعبى 86
  - الكيمياء الشعبيه التنجيم والرموز المستعمله من المتجولين والمتشردين
- الجغرافيـا 92
- علم طبقات الاراضى 96
- تعبئة وشحن السلع 98
- التدبير المنزلى 100
  - ويشمـل الادوات المنزليـة
- التصنيـع 104
  - ويشمل الماكينات الثقيلة
- الرياضـة 111
- الـطب 113
  - ويشمل الادوات الطبيه والمستشفيـات
- الارصاد الجوية 120
- المـوسيقى 123
- التصويـر 126
- علم الطبيعـة 128
- الترفيـه 130
  - ويشمل الاولمبيات
- الديـن 138
- الامـن 140
- المـرور 143
  - الطرق ، الجو ، البحر ، السكك الحديديـه
- مراقبة المركبات 157
  - وتشمل اشكال ذات ابعاد ثـلاث

الشكل التخطيطى 166
لـون 231
اهـداءات 248
بيان المراجع 252
فـهرس 268

CHINESE

前言 —R. Buckminster Fuller 14
序論 16
語意圖解 —C. K. Bliss 22
ISOTYPE—Marie Neurath 24
基本符號 26
學科
- 供應和旅行 34
  - 包括終站
- 農業學 39
  - 農藝、家畜和乳類產品、農場建築和土地、森林、器具
- 建築學 48
  - 製圖、風景設計和計劃
- 天文學 54
- 生物學 55
  - 包括植物學、分子生物學
- 商學 58
  - 包括電子計算機、零售商店、採購和服務
- 化學 67
- 通訊 70
  - 包括動作和舞蹈、手語或旗語
- 工程學 80
  - 化學的、電機的、機械的
- 民俗學 86
  - 鍊金術、占星學、流動工人交通記號或標誌
- 地理學 92
- 地質學 96
- 貨品處理 98
- 家政學 100
  - 包括設備
- 製造 104
  - 包括重型機械
- 數學 111
- 醫學 113
  - 包括儀器、醫院
- 氣象學 120
- 音樂 123
- 攝影學 126
- 物理學 128
- 娛樂 130
  - 包括運動競技
- 宗教 138
- 安全 140
- 交通 143
  - 陸路、航空、航海、鐵路
- 車輛控制 157
  - 包括三度空間之形狀

圖解形式 166
顏色 231
銘謝 248
參考書目 252
附錄 268

DANISH

FORORD—R. Buckminster Fuller 14
INDLEDNING 16
SEMANTOGRAFI—C. K. Bliss 22
ISOTYPE—Marie Neurath 24
GRUNDSYMBOLER 26
DISCIPLINER
Lokaleforhold og Rejser 34
indbefattet Stasjoner
Landbrug 39
Agronomi, Kreaturer og Mejeriprodukter, Landbrugsbygninger og Løsøre exclusive Maskiner, Forstvæsen, Redskaber
Arkitektur 48
Udkast, Havearkitektur og Planlægning
Astronomi 54
Biologi 55
indbefattet Botanik, Molekylær Biologi
Forretninger 58
indbefattet Regnemaskiner, Kontorudstyr, forretning og Tjenester
Kemi 67
Forbindelser 70
indbefattet Bevægelse og Dans, Ikkegrafisk Alfabet
Ingeniørvirksomhed 80
Kemi, Elektrisk, Mekanisk
Folklore 86
Alkemi, Astrologi, Landstrygertegn
Geografi 92
Geologi 96
Varehusholding 98
Økonomisk Hjemmeerhverv 100
indbefattet Indredninger
Fabrikation 104
indbefattet Tungt-Maskineri
Matematik 111
Medicin 113
indbefattet Udstyr og Sykehus
Meteorologi 120
Musik 123
Fotografi 126
Fysik 128
Adspredelser 130
indbefattet Olympiske Lege
Religion 138
Sikkerhed 140
Færdsel 143
Landevej, Fly, Søfart, Jernbaner
Køretøj Kontrol 157
indbefattet Tredimensionale Former
GRAFISKE FORMER 166
FARVE 231
ANERKENDELSER 248
BIBLIOGRAFI 252
INDEKS 268

DUTCH

VOORWOORD — R. Buckminster Fuller 14
INLEIDING 16
WOORDKUNDE — C. K. Bliss 22
ISOTYPE — Marie Neurath 24
BASIS SYMBOLEN 26
STUDIE VAKKEN
Logies en reizen 34
met inbegrip van aankomst- en vertrek faciliteiten
Landbouw 39
Landbouwkunde, vee en zuivelproducten, landbouwconstructies en bouwlanden, bosbouw, landbouwgereedschap
Bouwkunde 48
Ontwerpen, landschaps-architectuur en ruimtelijke ordening
Sterrenkunde 54
Biologie 55
met inbegrip van plantkunde en moleculaire biologie
Handel 58
met inbegrip van computers, kantoorbenodigdheden, winkels en dienstverleningsbedrijven
Scheikunde 67
Communicatie 70
met inbegrip van beweging en dans, niet-grafische alfabetten
Ingenieurswetenschappen 80
Scheikundig, electrisch en werktuigbouwkundig
Folklore 86
Alchemie, Astrologie en tekens door landlopers gebruikt
Aardrijkskunde 92
Geologie 96
Behandeling van goederen 98
Huishoudkunde 100
met inbegrip van huishoudelijke apparaten
Fabricage 104
met inbegrip van zware machines
Wiskunde 111
Geneeskunde 113
met inbegrip van uitrusting en ziekenhuizen
Weerkunde 120
Muziek 123
Fotografie 126
Natuurkunde 128
Ontspanning 130
met inbegrip van Olympische Spelen
Godsdienst 138
Veiligheid 140
Verkeer 143
weg-, lucht-, scheeps- en spoorwegverkeer
Voertuig instrumenten 157
met inbegrip van 3-dimensionele vormen
GRAFISCHE VORM 166
KLEUR 231
MEDEWERKERS 248
BIBLIOGRAFIE 252
INDEX 268

FINNISH

ESIPUHE—R. Buckminster Fuller 14
JOHDANTO 16
MERKITYSOPPI—C. K. Bliss 22
ISOTYPE—Marie Neurath 24
PERUSMERKIT 26
LAIT
Majoitusmahdollisuudet ja matkailu .. 34
mukaanlukien pääteasemat
Maanviljelys 39
Maatalous, karja ja maitotuotteet, maatilan rakenne ja maat, metsätalous, maanviljelyskalusto
Arkkitehtuuri 48
Piirros, maisema ja suunnittelu
Tähtitiede 54
Biologia 55
mukaanlukien kasvitiede, molekyylibiologia
Kauppa 58
mukaanlukien tietokoneet, toimistovälineet, myymälät ja palvelu
Kemia 67
Kanssakäyminen 70
mukaanlukien liike ja tanssi, erikoismerkit
Insinööritaito 80
kemiallinen, sähkö, mekaaninen
Kansantietous 86
alkemia, astrologia, maankiertäjien merkit
Maantiede 92
Geologia 96
Tavaroiden käsittely 98
Kotitaloustiede 100
mukaanlukien kotitalouskojeet
Tehdastuotanto 104
mukaanlukien raskaat koneet
Matematiikka 111
Lääketiede 113
mukaanlukien välineistö, sairaalat
Ilmatiede 120
Musiikki 123
Valokuvaus 126
Fysiikka 128
Virkistys 130
mukaanlukien olympialaiset
Uskonto 138
Turvallisuus 140
Liikenne 143
Maantie, ilma, meri, rautatie
Ajoneuvojen valvonta 157
mukaanlukien kolmiulotteiset muodot
GRAAFFINEN MUOTO 166
VÄRI 231
TIEDOKSIANTOJA 248
BIBLIOGRAFIA 252
HAKEMISTO 268

FRENCH

PREFACE—R. Buckminster Fuller 14
INTRODUCTION 16
SEMANTOGRAPHIE—C. K. Bliss 22
ISOTYPE—Marie Neurath 24
SYMBOLES DE BASE 26
DISCIPLINES
- **Locaux touristiques et déplacements** . 34
  y compris stations terminales
- **Agriculture** 39
  Agronomie, Bétail et produits laitiers, Bâtiments agricoles et terrains, Sylviculture, Outils
- **Architecture** 48
  Dessins et plans, Aménagement des jardins et planification
- **Astronomie** 54
- **Biologie** 55
  y compris Botanique, Biologie moléculaire
- **Affaires** 58
  y compris Ordinateurs, Matériel de bureau, Magasins et services
- **Chimie** 67
- **Communications** 70
  y compris Mouvement et Danse, Alphabets non-graphiques
- **Etudes techniques d'ingénieur** 80
  chimique, électrique, mécanique
- **Folklore** 86
  Alchimie, Astrologie, Code des vagabonds
- **Géographie** 92
- **Géologie** 96
- **Manutention des marchandises** 98
- **Economie ménagère** 100
  y compris Equipement ménager
- **Fabrication** 104
  y compris Machines pour gros travaux
- **Mathématiques** 111
- **Médecine** 113
  y compris Equipement, Hôpitaux
- **Météorologie** 120
- **Musique** 123
- **Photographie** 126
- **Physique** 128
- **Recréation** 130
  y compris Jeux olympiques
- **Religion** 138
- **Sécurité** 140
- **Circulation** 143
  Routière, Aérienne, Maritime, Ferroviaire
- **Contrôle des véhicules** 157
  y compris code de la route en trois dimensions

FORMULAIRE GRAPHIQUE 166
COULEUR 231
REMERCIEMENTS 248
BIBLIOGRAPHIE 252
TABLE DES MATIERES 268

GERMAN

VORWORT—R. Buckminster Fuller 14
EINLEITUNG 16
SEMANTOGRAPHIE—C. K. Bliss 22
ISOTYPE—Marie Neurath 24
GRUNDSYMBOLE 26
FACHGEBIETE
- **Unterkunft und Reise** 34
  einschliesslich Endstationen
- **Landwirtschaft** 39
  Ackerbau, Viehzucht, und Milchwirtschaft, landwirtschaftliche Bauwerke und Boden, Forstwirtschaft, Geräte
- **Baukunst** 48
  Entwürfe, Landschaftsgestaltung und Planung
- **Astronomie** 54
- **Biologie** 55
  einschliesslich Pflanzenkunde, Molekularbiologie
- **Geschäft** 58
  einschliesslich Rechenmaschinen, Büroausstattung, Läden und Dienstleistungen
- **Chemie** 67
- **Nachrichtenwesen** 70
  einschliesslich Bewegung und Tanz, schriftlose Alphabete
- **Ingenieurwesen** 80
  Chemisches, Elektrisches, Maschinenbau
- **Volkskunde** 86
  Alchemie, Astrologie, Zeichen der Landstreicher
- **Erdkunde** 92
- **Geologie** 96
- **Güterbeförderung** 98
- **Hauswirtschaft** 100
  einschliesslich Haushaltsgeräte
- **Industrielle Produktion** 104
  einschliesslich Schwerindustrie
- **Mathematik** 111
- **Heilkunde** 113
  einschliesslich Ausrüstung, Spitäler
- **Meteorologie** 120
- **Musik** 123
- **Photographie** 126
- **Physik** 128
- **Erholung** 130
  einschliesslich Olympischer Spiele
- **Religion** 138
- **Betriebssicherheit** 140
- **Verkehr** 143
  zu Land, Luft, Wasser und auf Schienen
- **Fahrzeugkontrolle** 157
  einschliesslich dreidimensionaler Formen

GRAPHISCHE FORM 166
FARBE 231
DANKSAGUNGEN 248
BIBLIOGRAPHIE 252
INDEX 268

HEBREW

הקדמה—**R. Buckminster Fuller** 14
מבוא 16
סמנטוגרפיה—**C. K. Bliss** 22
Marie Neurath—ISOTYPE 24
סמלים יסודיים 26
לימודים
- אכסון ונסיעות 34
  כולל תחנות
- חקלאות 39
  אגרונומיה, מקנה ותוצרות חלב
  מבני משק וקרקעות
  יערנות, מכשירים
- אדריכלות 48
  שרטוטים
  שפור נוף ותכנון
- תורת הכוכבים 54
- ביולוגיה 55
  כולל בוטניה,
  ביולוגיה מולקולרית
- עסקים 58
  כולל מחשבים,
  מכשירי משרד,
  חנויות ושירותים
- כימיה 67
- תקשורת 70
  כולל תנועה ורקוד,
  אלפי־בית לא־ציוריים
- הנדסה 80
  כימית,
  חשמלית, מכנית
- פולקלור 86
  אלכימיה,
  אסטרולוגיה, סימני נודים
- גאוגרפיה 92
- גאולוגיה 96
- טפול בסחורה 98
- כלכלת הבית 100
  כולל מכשירי בית
- יצור 104
  כולל מכונות כבדות
- תורת החשבון 111
- רפואה 113
  כולל ציוד, בתי חולים
- מטאורולוגיה 120
- מוסיקה 123
- צלום 126
- פיסיקה 128
- בידור 130
  כולל המשחקים האולימפיים
- דת 138
- בטיחות 140
- תנועה 143
  כבישים, אויר,
  ים, מסלות ברזל
- פקוח רכב 157
  כולל צורות תלת־ממדיות

צורות ציור 166
צבע 231
הודאות 248
ביבליוגרפיה 252
מפתח 268

HINDI

प्रक्कथन —R. Buckminster Fuller 14
परिचय 16
चिह्न का प्रयोग —C. K. Bliss 22
ISOTYPE—Marie Neurath 24
आधारित चिह्न 26
अनुशासन
वास्थान और यात्रा 34
सीमांत सहित
कृषिशास्त्र 39
क्षत्रकर्म, पशुधन और गाव्य,
खेती क ढांचे और भूमि,
वानकी साधन,
वास्तुकला 48
प्रारुपांकनदशयांकन तथा योजना
खगोलशास्त्र 54
जीवविज्ञान 55
वनस्पतिशास्त्र व्यूहाणु-जीवज्ञान सहित
व्यपार (वणित) 58
संगणक, दफ़तरी सामान,
दुकानें और सेवायें सहित
रसायनशास्त्र 67
संचारण 70
गीत, नृत्य सहित
अनुनिन्दु रखीय वर्णमालायें
अभियान्त्रकी 80
रसायन, विद्युत, यान्त्रिक
लोकजन 86
रसूविद्या, फलित-ज्योतिष, होबो
Hobo चिह्न
भूगोल 92
भूगर्भशास्त्र 96
सामान का प्रयोग-प्रबन्ध 98
गार्हस्थयविज्ञान 100
उपकार्णां सहित
निर्माण 104
भारी उद्योग की मशीन सहित
गणित 111
चिकित्साशास्त्र 113
सामान चिकित्सालय सहित
फटतुविज्ञान 120
संगीत 123
भाचित्रणा 126
भौतिकशास्त्र 128
मनोरंजन 130
औलिमपिक्स सहित
धर्म 138
सुरक्षा 140
यातायात 143
सड़क, हवा, समुद्रीय, संयान
यान-नियन्त्रन 157
त्रि-विमा आकार सहित
रेखाचित्र 166
वंण 231
अभिस्वीकृति 248
ग्रंथसूची 252
अनुक्रमणिका 268

ITALIAN

PREFAZIONE—R. Buckminster Fuller 14
INTRODUZIONE 16
SEMANTOGRAFIA—C. K. Bliss 22
ISOTYPE—Marie Neurath 24
SIMBOLI PRINCIPALI 26
DISCIPLINE
Alloggi e viaggi 34
compresi terminali
Agricoltura 39
Agronomia, Bestiame e Prodotti Caseari, Edifici Agricoli e Terreno, Silvicultura, Attrezzi
Architettura 48
Disegno, Progettazione Giardini e Pianificazione
Astronomia 54
Biologia 55
comprese Botanica, Biologia Molecolare
Affari e Commercio 58
compresi Calcolatori Elettronici, Attrezzature per Ufficio, Negozi e Servizi
Chimica 67
Comunicazioni 70
compresi Movimento e Danza, Alfabeti Nongrafici
Ingegneria 80
Chimica, Elettrica, Meccanica
Folclore 86
Alchimia, Astrologia, Segni dei Girovaghi
Geografia 92
Geologia 96
Maneggio Merci 98
Economia Domestica 100
compresi Elettrodomestici
Industria 104
compreso Macchinario Pesante
Matematica 111
Medicina 113
compresi Attrezzature, Ospedali
Meteorologia 120
Musica 123
Fotografia 126
Fisica 128
Svaghi 130
compresi Giuochi Olimpici
Religione 138
Sicurezza 140
Circolazione 143
Stradale, Aerea, Marittima, Ferroviaria
Controlli Veicolari 157
comprese Forme a 3 Dimensioni
FORMA GRAFICA 166
COLORE 231
RINGRAZIAMENTI 248
BIBLIOGRAFIA 252
INDICE 268

JAPANESE

前文—R. Buckminster Fuller 14
序論 16
セマントグラフィー—C. K. Bliss 22
ISOTYPE—Marie Neurath 24
基本記号 26
部門
旅行及び旅行施設 34
ターミナルを含む
農業 39
農業、牧畜及び酪農製品
農園施設及び土地、森林、用具
建築 48
製圖、都市計畫及び造園、計畫
天文學 54
生物學 55
植物學、分子生物學を含む
ビジネス 58
計算機、オフィス機器、店及び
サービスを含む
化學 67
通信 70
運動及びダンス、非グラフィック
アルファベットを含む
工學 80
化學、電氣、機械工學を含む
民俗學 86
錬金術、占星術、ホボ・サイン
地理學 92
地質學 96
商品扱い 98
家庭經濟 100
家庭用品を含む
製造 104
重機械を含む
數學 111
醫學 113
器具、病院を含む
氣象學 120
音樂 123
寫眞 126
物理學 128
リクリエーション 130
オリンピックを含む
宗敎 138
安全 140
交通 143
道路、航空、海上、鉄道
車輛コントロール 157
3次元形体を含む
グラフィック・フォーム 166
色彩 231
あとがき 248
文献 252
索引 268

NORWEGIAN

FORORD—R. Buckminster Fuller 14
INNLEDNING 16
SEMANTOGRAFI—C. K. Bliss 22
ISOTYPE—Marie Neurath 24
GRUNN-SYMBOLER ... 26
DISIPLINER
Losji og Reiser ... 34
inklusive Terminer
Landbruk ... 39
Agronomi, Kreaturvesen og Meieri Produkter, Bondegård og Land, Forstvesen, Redskaper
Arkitektur ... 48
Grunnrissning, Landskap og Planering
Astronomi ... 54
Biologi ... 55
inklusive Botanikk, Molekyl Biologi
Forretningsvesen ... 58
inklusive Beregnings Maskiner, Kontor Utstyr, Forretning og Tjenester
Kjemi ... 67
Samband ... 70
inklusive Bevegelse og Dans, Ikkegrafiske Alfabeter
Ingeniörvitenskap ... 80
Kjemisk, Elektrisk, Mekanisk
Folkeminneforskning ... 86
Gullmakeri, Astrologi, Tater Tegn
Geografi ... 92
Geologi ... 96
Handtering av gods ... 98
Hjem Ökonomi ... 100
inklusive Innretninger
Fabrikasjon ... 104
inklusive Tungt-Maskineri
Matematikk ... 111
Medisin ... 113
inklusive Utstyr, Sykehus
Meteorologi ... 120
Musikk ... 123
Fotografi ... 126
Fysikk ... 128
Rekreasjon ... 130
inklusive de Olympiske Lekene
Religion ... 138
Sikkerhet ... 140
Trafikk ... 143
Veg, Luftfart, Marine, Jernbane
Kontroll av Kjøretøi ... 157
inklusive Tredimensjonale Former
GRAFISK FORMAT ... 166
FARGE ... 231
ANNERKJENNELSER ... 248
BIBLIOGRAFI ... 252
INDEKS ... 268

PORTUGUESE

PREFÁCIO—R. Buckminster Fuller 14
INTRODUÇÃO 16
SEMANTOGRAFIA—C. K. Bliss 22
ISOTYPE—Marie Neurath 24
SÍMBOLOS BÁSICOS ... 26
DISCIPLINAS
Acomodações e Viagem ... 34
incluindo estações terminais
Agricultura ... 39
Agronomia, Gado e Produtos de Laticínios, Estruturas Agrícolas e Terras, Silvicultura, Implementos
Arquitetura ... 48
Desenho, Paisagem e Planejamento
Astronomia ... 54
Biologia ... 55
incluindo Botânica, Biologia Molecular
Negócios ... 58
incluindo Computadores, Equipamento de Escritório, Lojas e Serviços
Química ... 67
Comunicações ... 70
incluindo Movimento e Dança, Alfabetos Não-Gráficos
Engenharia ... 80
Química, Elétrica, Mecânica
Folclore ... 86
Alquimia, Astrologia, Código de Vagabundos
Geografia ... 92
Geologia ... 96
Manuseio de Mercadorias ... 98
Economia Doméstica ... 100
incluindo utensílios
Manufatura ... 104
incluindo maquinária pesada
Matemática ... 111
Medicina ... 113
incluindo equipamento, Hospitais
Meteorologia ... 120
Música ... 123
Fotografia ... 126
Física ... 128
Recreação ... 130
incluindo esportes olímpicos
Religião ... 138
Segurança ... 140
Tráfego ... 143
Rodoviário, Aéreo, Marítimo, Ferroviário
Contrôles de Veículos ... 157
incluindo formatos tri-dimensionais
FORMA GRÁFICA ... 166
CÔR ... 231
CRÉDITOS ... 248
BIBLIOGRAFIA ... 252
ÍNDICE ... 268

RUSSIAN

ПРЕДИСЛОВИЕ—R. Buckminster Fuller 14
ВВЕДЕНИЕ 16
СЕМАНТОГРАФИЯ—C. K. Bliss 22
ISOTYPE—Marie Neurath 24
ОСНОВНЫЕ ОБОЗНАЧЕНИЯ ... 26
ОТРАСЛИ
Удобства и Путешествие ... 34
включая Вокзалы
Сельское Хозяйство ... 39
Агрономия, Скот и Молочные Продукты, Сельскохозяйственные Сооружения и Земли, Лесоводство, Инвентарь
Архитектура ... 48
Черчение, Пейзажное Зеленое Строительство и Планирование
Астрономия ... 54
Биология ... 55
включая Ботанику, Молекулярную Биологию
Коммерческая деятельность ... 58
включая Вычислительные Машины, Конторское Оборудование, Магазины и Обслуживание
Химия ... 67
Средства Коммуникации ... 70
включая Движение и Танец, Неграфический Алфавит
Инженерная проектировка ... 80
Химическая, Электрическая, Механическая
Фольклор ... 86
Алхимия, Астрология, Знаки Бродяг
География ... 92
Геология ... 96
Товароуправление ... 98
Домохозяйство ... 100
включая Бытовые Электроприборы
Производство ... 104
включая Высокомощные Машины
Математика ... 111
Медицина ... 113
включая Аппаратуру, Госпитали
Метеорология ... 120
Музыка ... 123
Фотография ... 126
Физика ... 128
Развлечение ... 130
включая Олимпийские игры
Религия ... 138
Безопасность ... 140
Движение ... 143
Путевое, Воздушное, Морское, Железнодорожное
Контроли двигающихся предметов ... 157
включая Трех-Пространственные Формы
ГРАФИЧЕСКИЕ ФОРМЫ ... 166
ЦВЕТ ... 231
ПОДТВЕРЖДЕНИЕ ... 248
БИБЛИОГРАФИЯ ... 252
ИНДЕКС ... 268

SPANISH

PRÓLOGO—R. Buckminster Fuller 14
INTRODUCCIÓN 16
SEMANTOGRAFÍA—C. K. Bliss 22
ISOTYPE—Marie Neurath 24
SÍMBOLOS BÁSICOS 26
DISCIPLINAS
Alojamiento y Viajes 34
inclusive Terminales
Agricultura 39
Agronomía, Ganadería y Productos Lácteos, Estructuras en la Granja y Tierras, Silvicultura, Implementos Agrícolas
Arquitectura 48
Dibujo, Diseño de Alrededores y Planificación
Astronomía 54
Biología 55
inclusive Botánica, Biología Molecular
Comercio 58
inclusive Calculadoras Electrónicas, Equipo para Oficinas, Tiendas y Servicios
Química 67
Comunicaciones 70
inclusive Movimiento y Danza, Alfabetos No Gráficos
Ingeniería 80
Química, Eléctrica, Mecánica
Folklore 86
Alquimia, Astrología, Símbolos Populares de Vagabundos
Geografía 92
Geología 96
Manipulación de Mercaderías 98
Economía Doméstica 100
inclusive Aparatos Domésticos
Fabricación 104
inclusive Maquinaria Pesada
Matemáticas .111
Medicina 113
inclusive Equipo, Hospitales
Meteorología .120
Música 123
Fotografía 126
Física 128
Recreación 130
inclusive Deportes Olímpicos
Religión 138
Protección 140
Tráfico 143
Por Carretera, Aéreo, Marítimo, Ferroviario
Controles para Vehículos 157
inclusive Formas Tridimensionales
CONFECCIÓN GRÁFICA 166
COLOR 231
RECONOCIMIENTOS 248
BIBLIOGRAFÍA .252
ÍNDICE 268

SWAHILI

UTANGULIZI—R. Buckminster Fuller 14
DIBAJI 16
SEMANTOGRAFIA—C. K. Bliss 22
ISOTYPE—Marie Neurath 24
ALAMA ZA MSINGI 26
MAFUNDISHO FULANI
Makao na Kusafiri 34
pamoja na Vituo
Ukulima 39
Utunzaji wa Ardhi ya Mashamba, Mifugo na Mapato yake, Mashamba na Majengo yake, Utunzaji wa Misitu, Vyombo
Ujenzi 48
Uchoraji, Bustani za Mapambo na Kufikiria Mipango
Elimu ya Nyota 54
Elimu ya Maisha (Bayoloji) 55
hata na Elimu ya Mimea (Botani), na Bayoloji ya Viini
Biashara 58
hata na Makompyuta, Vyombo vya Ofisini, Maduka na Mafundi
Elimu ya Madawa (Kemistri) 67
Upelekeano wa Habari 70
hata na Miendo na Dansi, Alfabeti zisizoandikwa
Ufundi wa Uinjinia 80
Wa Madawa (Kemikali), Wa Umeme (Elektrisiti), Wa Umekanika
Hadithi za Kale 86
Asili ya Elimu ya Dawa (Alkimia), Unajimu, Alama za Watembezi
Jiografia 92
Jiolojia 96
Utunzaji wa Bidhaa 98
Elimu ya Mambo ya Nyumbani 100
hata na Zana za Nyumbani
Uundaji 104
hata na Mashine za Kazi Nzito
Hesabu 111
Dawa za Utabibu 113
hata na Mahospitali, na Zana
Elimu ya Utabiri wa Hali ya Hewa 120
Muziki 123
Maarifa ya Kupiga Picha (Ufotografia) 126
Elimu ya Tabia na Nguvu za Vitu 128
Maburudi 130
hata na Michezo ya Olympics
Dini 138
Usalama 140
Trafiki 143
Barabarani, Hewani, Majini, Reli
Usimamizi wa Magari 157
hata na Viumbo vyenye Pande Tatu
MPANGO WA 'GRAF' 166
RANGI 231
MATOLEO YA SHUKRANI 248
ORODHA YA VITABU 252
YALIYOMO 268

SWEDISH

FÖRORD—R. Buckminster Fuller 14
INLEDNING 16
SEMANTOGRAPHI—C. K. Bliss 22
ISOTYPE—Marie Neurath 24
GRUNDBETECKNINGAR 26
ÄMNESOMRÅDEN
Hotell och resande 34
innefattande Stationer och términaler
Jordbruk 39
Agronomi, kreaturbesättnig, och mejeriprodukter, gårdsstruktur och land, forstväsen, redskap
Arkitektur 48
Ritning, och planering av omgivningen
Astronomi 54
Biologi 55
innefattande botanik, molekylbiologi
Näringsliv 58
innefattande datorer, kontors-utrustning, butiker och services
Kemi 67
Kommunikationer 70
innefattande rörelse och dans, icke-grafiska alfabet
Ingenjörskonst 80
Kemisk, Elektrisk, Mekanisk
Folkminnesforskning 86
Alkemi, astrologi, luffartecken
Geografi 92
Geologi 96
Behandling av varor 98
Hushållsekonomi 100
innefattande hushållsmaskiner
Tillverkning 104
innefattande tungt maskineri
Matematik 111
Medicin 113
innefattande utrustning, sjukhus
Meteorologi 120
Musik 123
Fotografi 126
Fysik 128
Rekreation 130
innefattande Olympiska grenar
Religion 138
Säkerhet 140
Trafik 143
Vägar, Flygtrafik, Sjöfart, Järnväg
Fordonskontroll 157
innefattande 3-dimensionella former
GRAFISK FORM 166
FÄRG 231
RÅDGIVARE 248
BIBLIOGRAFI 252
INDEX 268

FOREWORD
by R. Buckminster Fuller

There now looms into silent recognition a new exclusively visible language, that of roadside and street intersection signs, airport signs, and supermarket signs, etc., which accommodate the world-around motorist, air traveller and telephoner. The travellers' high speed needs of swiftly integrating solutions to traffic problem solving has induced the invention of a wide variety of new symbolic language forms. At the same time TV animation also tends to return to generalized conceptual modeling.

The fundamentally visual language which Ezra Pound esteemed in early peoples' ideography now trends to bringing communication tools back into universal use and comprehension.

No one human today has had more experience with the development of the new silent language supplement of travel and communication symbols than has had Henry Dreyfuss. For years he has been the leading product refinement designer for transportation on land, air and sea, as well as for the world's largest manufacturers of telephone, radio, automobile, farm machinery and camera. Henry Dreyfuss has evolved for those industries swiftly effective, exclusively visual, symbolic tools.

Because I know him well I know that he has been intuitively inspired in this visual communication development by a foresighted realization that graphic symbols could mean far more to humanity than the immediate facilitation of the business of his specific industrial clients. Henry Dreyfuss has confided his awareness of the swiftly evolving world-around human predicament, but he is too modest to declare, even to himself, that he may be opening up a whole new world of exclusively visual language in which deafness would not prevent communication and comprehension of delicately nuanced meanings.

In the great overall evolutionary trending of humanity's gradual learning to produce ever more with ever less, it is implicit that the present discoveries of the electromagnetic behaviors of the brain and its local nerve system controls by mind will eventuate in telepathy's being graduated from society's assessment of it as mystical-magical phenomenon to an everyday communication facility.

Henry Dreyfuss' contribution to a new world technique of communication will catalyze a world preoccupation with its progressive evolution into a worldian language so powerfully generalized as to swiftly throw into obsolescence the almost fatally lethal trends of humanity's age-long entrapment in specializations and the limitations that specialization imposes upon human thinking. Thus humans can be liberated to use their own cosmically powerful faculties to communicate what needs to be done in local Universe, as humans are uniquely capable of doing — and uniquely advantaged to do — by the phenomenon love and the truthfully thinking mind. □

INTRODUCTION

Here is a word
in Greek δηλητηριον
in Japanese 毒
in Russian отрáва
in Hebrew רעל

I could go on and write this word in every language in the world and literally fill several pages of this book. Yet in the interest of expediency, all I need do is substitute one simple drawing. The symbol means exactly the same as each one of these words: POISON. And it is equally intelligible whatever the language of the viewer – and perhaps even more so than the word itself. The viewer who can neither read nor write immediately recognizes the danger this symbol so graphically conveys.

My own interest in graphic symbols dates back two decades, but it is only during the past few years that we have been actively soliciting data. As a result of information pouring in daily from every corner of the world, our Data Bank now contains over 20,000 symbols. It is on this collection that our Sourcebook is based. It would be folly to assume that our files include all existing symbols, for the task of assembling so complete a record would tax both the capabilities and endurance of any man. But at least to some extent, it will serve to show the reader what *is* — which is a first step, and will be a guide to future evaluations of what *should be* in the world of standardized, universally understandable graphic symbols.

My name on the title page is not so much to take credit as to assume the responsibility for the book's organization and content. It is titled a SOURCEBOOK to explain that it is not a dictionary, which would imply completeness. Alphabets and numbers, trademarks, emblems, all of which are already well documented, are not included. Instead, we have limited ourselves, with few exceptions, to those graphic symbols currently in use that serve to give instructions, directions, and warnings. But within this limitation the selection had to be arbitrary, for it was necessary to evaluate and weed out many symbols to avoid compounding chaos and confusion. On the page introducing the Discipline Section I have explained the parameters we followed in selection. It was indeed a monumental task.

This Sourcebook has been put together to aid all who in reading, travelling, or working come across symbols and need to define them, as well as professionals and specialists in the varied fields the Disciplines cover. Among these are students; educators; manufacturers and engineers; retailers and wholesalers; those involved in safety precautions, international shipping, and marketing; farmers and technicians; government agencies and those concerned with standards. And certainly it is planned for designers who create new symbols, in the hope that its guidance will stimulate their creativity and make them aware of what already exists so that further duplication and contradiction can be avoided.

There are today some 5,000 languages and dialects in use throughout the world, of which perhaps a hundred may be considered of major importance. In most instances, intercommunication among them ranges from difficult to impossible. One solution, of course, would be to establish an international language, and hundreds of attempts have in fact been made in the last two centuries to develop an official second language that in time could be adopted by all major countries. Esperanto, Interlingua, Ido, Volapuk – all combining elements of existing languages – and Ro and Suma, both created artificially, are but six such attempts. However, among other drawbacks, they all rely, as does basic English, on the Roman alphabet. This restricts their usefulness to those countries which utilize the Roman alphabet, and these are actually a minority among nations.

If a system of symbols could be compiled that would be equally recognizable in Lagos and Lapland, perhaps the dream of a universal basic means of communication could be realized. I believe this is possible.

In no way do I propose that this system be yet another language, for it is not really a language at all. Rather it is a supplement to *all* languages to help create a better and faster understanding in specific areas. Symbols have already evolved to the point of universal acceptance in such areas as music, mathematics, and many branches of science. A Beethoven symphony sounds the same in Japanese as it does in the original German; a column of digits adds up identically in Polish and Spanish; and a Russian scientist easily deciphers equations discussed in an English scientific journal.

Semiology, or semiotics, is the scholarly term for the science of signs indicating ideas or symbols, and *The Oxford English Dictionary* defines symbols in two ways: one as "Something that stands for, represents, or denotes something else ... esp. a material object representing ... something immaterial or abstract ... ."

An example of this definition would be an advertisement for a deluxe automobile. The smooth, sleek lines are not only immediately recognizable as a car, but also as a symbol of one's status among his peers — at least according to the current popular mythology. The image is enhanced by a languorous blonde in a white mink coat who becomes part and parcel of the deal.

But status symbols I will leave to others and instead turn to the other definition of symbols: "A written character or mark used to represent something; a letter, figure, or sign conventionally standing for some object, process, etc." These are the functional, instructive graphic symbols that this book is all about. They are older than words; they are found in every culture however primitive; and in modern times they seem to be increasing almost as fast as the population itself.

In the beginning, man created the symbol — and pictures on cave walls were sufficient for a time to express his ideas about the relatively simple processes of procuring food and shelter. It was when man began to feel a need to express abstractions — differences in degree, nuances in definition, philosophical concepts — that symbols proved inflexible and inadequate. Then languages began to proliferate. It now appears that in some increasingly important areas we need an adjunct to our sophisticated speech and need to work our way back to the simple universality of an understandable, albeit limited, symbology. Symbols have multiplied to an alarming degree along much the same lines of divergence as languages. Today it is this very diversity and multiplicity of symbols in our international life that is a matter of such immediate concern. As the world grows steadily smaller, the need for easy communication becomes increasingly acute, and man has apparently come full circle — from prehistoric symbols, to sophisticated verbal communication, and now back to symbols, to help us all live together in today's Tower of Babel.

Years ago, as an industrial designer, I tried to persuade some of our clients to substitute symbols for written captions on their products. My first success as a protagonist of semiotics was in the field of farm machinery, where we developed an entire vocabulary of symbols for vehicle and equipment operation. Our primary concern was safety. A simple, quickly comprehended form or color, or combination of both, is translated to the brain far faster and more directly than a written word. In emergency or panic, the milliseconds saved in reaction time could save a man's fingers, his arm, his leg, even his life.

In addition to this primary human concern, there were other dividends as well. Symbols fit on small control buttons and knobs, where written instructions would be too small to be legible. Then too, manufacturers ship products all over the world, and translating various instrument identifications and instructions into the language of import countries is both expensive and time consuming. Imagine a German dealer, under the pressure of a harvest, urgently ordering 500 tractors and finding the nearest ones in Paris – with French instructions! Imagine further that in Germany, once the tractors were converted, they might occasionally have to be operated by a Swedish or Hungarian worker! Happily, symbols can cut across such language barriers.

Experts – in the manner of experts – do not agree on precise distinctions between different types of graphic symbols. But to me, it seems logical to consider them as being either representational, abstract, or arbitrary. *Representational* symbols present fairly accurate, if simplified, pictures of objects (a silhouette of a locomotive to denote a railroad crossing), or action (a man bicycling to direct one to a path reserved for cyclists). *Abstract* symbols reduce essential elements of a message to graphic terms. These may once have been representational but have become simplified by design or degrees over many years, to the point where they now exist only as symbolic indications. For example, the signs of the zodiac were once realistic representations of gods or animals, yet today they bear faint resemblance to their original concept. *Arbitrary* symbols are those that are invented, and accordingly must also be learned. The three triangle "pinwheel" directing one to a fallout shelter is a good example; also the familiar treble clef in music; and the mathematical plus and minus signs.

To make the Sourcebook a convenient reference tool we have divided it into distinct sections, and have organized the symbols in three ways:

By DISCIPLINE – a reference of symbols related to each given field of interest or application, with Subdisciplines for logical division of major groupings.

By GRAPHIC FORM — a unique compilation permitting the identification of symbols out of context, when unknown to the reader. This section also permits the designer to familiarize himself with existing uses and meanings of any given form.

By MEANING — a liberal alphabetical Index, including what we call "Design Categories," to make it possible to readily find all symbols relating to a basic design concept. These are fully described at the beginning of the Index section.

Color produces immediate reaction and is the exclamation point of graphic symbols, so it must be reckoned with. Therefore, color is indicated on the symbols themselves throughout the book, and a separate section on the meanings of color in various cultures is also included.

The Contents for this book appears in 18 languages so that readers the world over may easily find the area in which they are doing research and thus quickly locate a specific symbol.

Men on the moon looking back at this earth from which they came have an awesome view of our opalescent spinning sphere. They are among the few to see our world in its entirety.

Many of us dream of one world, devoid of geopolitical boundaries and futile bickering. Our astronauts, alone in outer space, must sense continually the importance of all men being brothers.

In an infinitesimal way, this book is an effort to help us bring that concept into fulfillment. Communication — people to people, nation to nation — is a vital ingredient to understanding. It would be presumptuous to imply that standardized graphic symbols will result in perfect intercommunication; but perhaps this is the first faltering step to convince us that it is imperative for man to be able to communicate with any other man no matter where he may live. This need, accented by jet travel, is felt universally today. In consequence new symbols are springing up daily. But as these symbols multiply, confusion, contradiction, and duplication become rampant. Hopefully, with this Sourcebook as a start, standard symbols will some day be understood by all, regardless of language or culture. □

SEMANTOGRAPHY

ONE WRITING FOR ONE WORLD

by Charles K. Bliss, B.Sc.

The great Leibnitz dreamed 300 years ago that someone will some day invent a Universal Symbolism, a simple system of pictorial symbols which could be read (like $1 + 2 = 3$) in all languages — without translation. It would also contain a simple symbolic logic and semantics (just as anyone can today recognize the lie in $1 + 2 = 4$). Now eminent scholars have agreed that I have done just this.

Semantography can be typed with an IBM ball typewriter, and printed by computerized typesetting. It operates with about 100 basic symbols which can be combined for any meaning needed in communication, commerce, industry and science, as proved in the 882 pages of my book (see Bibliography).

Of the 100 basic symbols the following 30 are already internationally used:

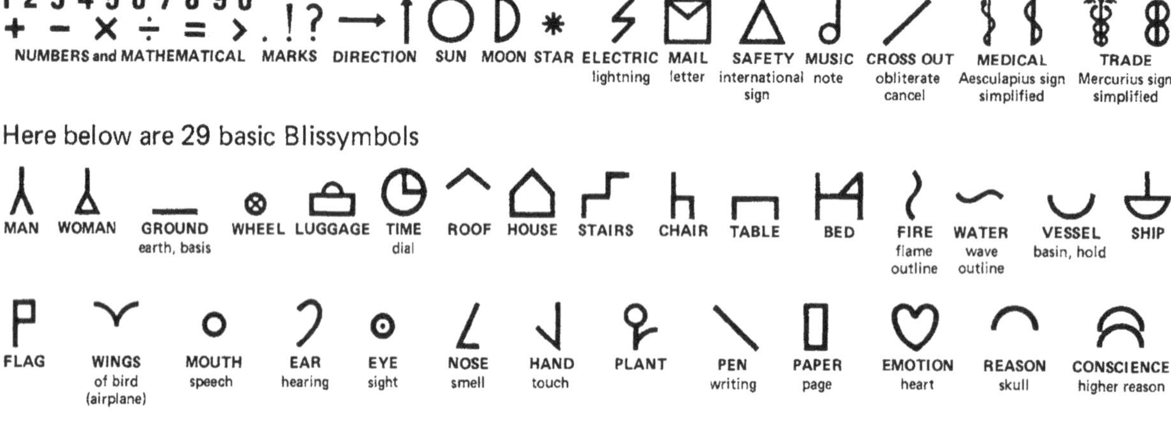
1 2 3 4 5 6 7 8 9 0
+ − × ÷ = > . ! ?
NUMBERS and MATHEMATICAL
MARKS
DIRECTION
SUN
MOON
STAR
ELECTRIC lightning
MAIL letter
SAFETY international sign
MUSIC note
CROSS OUT obliterate cancel
MEDICAL Aesculapius sign simplified
TRADE Mercurius sign simplified
Here below are 29 basic Blissymbols
MAN
WOMAN
GROUND earth, basis
WHEEL
LUGGAGE
TIME dial
ROOF
HOUSE
STAIRS
CHAIR
TABLE
BED
FIRE flame outline
WATER wave outline
VESSEL basin, hold
SHIP
FLAG
WINGS of bird (airplane)
MOUTH speech
EAR hearing
EYE sight
NOSE smell
HAND touch
PLANT
PEN writing
PAPER page
EMOTION heart
REASON skull
CONSCIENCE higher reason

By putting a small Action indicator on top of these symbols the verbs to hear, to see, to write, to feel, to reason, etc. are formed. With this, children learned to write whole sentences within the first hour and were able to read combinations they have never seen before.

Here below are some sample combinations from my book. But first, the "line letter" for the combination of outline symbols are for instance:

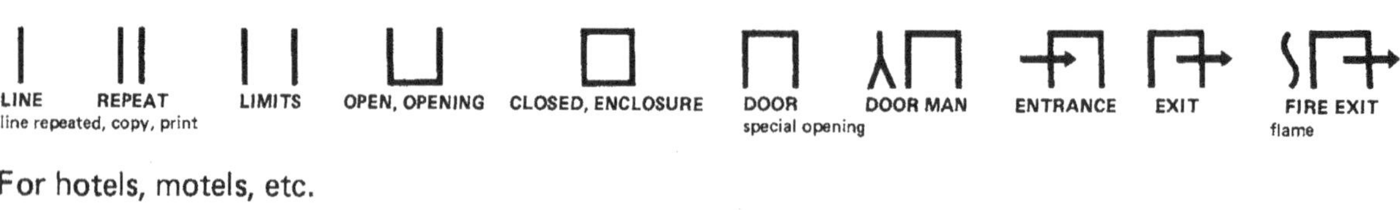
LINE
REPEAT line repeated, copy, print
LIMITS
OPEN, OPENING
CLOSED, ENCLOSURE
DOOR special opening
DOOR MAN
ENTRANCE
EXIT
FIRE EXIT flame

For hotels, motels, etc.

ROOM cabin
ROOM WAITER steward
ROOM MAID
LIFT
WAITING ROOM lounge (chair)
WRITING ROOM pen
ROOM WITH 2 BEDS
WATER wave
SHOWER coming down
BATHROOM tub

No book related to symbols would be complete without a bow to C. K. Bliss. In "Semantography," a word conceived by his fertile imagination, he has developed a complete system which crosses all language barriers. The lines and curves of his symbols, reminiscent of actual objects and actions, are translatable into all tongues. Mr. Bliss is an intrepid pioneer; his words and ideas are proudly included in this book. HD

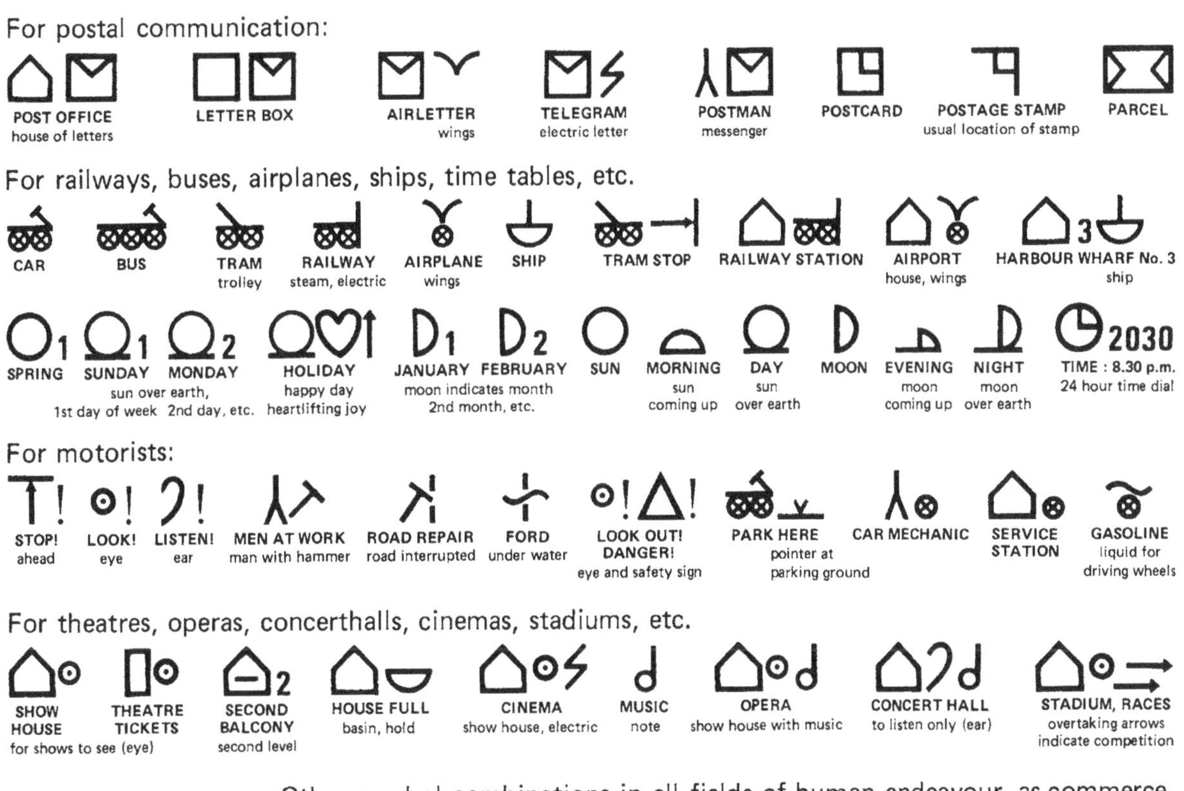

For postal communication:
POST OFFICE
house of letters
LETTER BOX
AIRLETTER
wings
TELEGRAM
electric letter
POSTMAN
messenger
POSTCARD
POSTAGE STAMP
usual location of stamp
PARCEL
For railways, buses, airplanes, ships, time tables, etc.
CAR
BUS
TRAM
trolley
RAILWAY
steam, electric
AIRPLANE
wings
SHIP
TRAM STOP
RAILWAY STATION
AIRPORT
house, wings
HARBOUR WHARF No. 3
ship
SPRING
SUNDAY
MONDAY
sun over earth,
1st day of week 2nd day, etc.
HOLIDAY
happy day
heartlifting joy
JANUARY
FEBRUARY
moon indicates month
2nd month, etc.
SUN
MORNING
sun
coming up
DAY
sun
over earth
MOON
EVENING
moon
coming up
NIGHT
moon
over earth
2030
TIME : 8.30 p.m.
24 hour time dial
For motorists:
STOP!
ahead
LOOK!
eye
LISTEN!
ear
MEN AT WORK
man with hammer
ROAD REPAIR
road interrupted
FORD
under water
LOOK OUT!
DANGER!
eye and safety sign
PARK HERE
pointer at
parking ground
CAR MECHANIC
SERVICE
STATION
GASOLINE
liquid for
driving wheels
For theatres, operas, concerthalls, cinemas, stadiums, etc.
SHOW
HOUSE
for shows to see (eye)
THEATRE
TICKETS
SECOND
BALCONY
second level
HOUSE FULL
basin, hold
CINEMA
show house, electric
MUSIC
note
OPERA
show house with music
CONCERT HALL
to listen only (ear)
STADIUM, RACES
overtaking arrows
indicate competition

Other symbol combinations in all fields of human endeavour, as commerce, banking, shipping, customs, menucards, shows, stores, ambulances, hospitals, as well as in all industries and in all sciences, including philosophy, religion and even poetry, are illustrated in the large chapters in my book.

But the symbols above belong only to Aspect 1 of my work. The other 5 aspects are even more fascinating. Aspect 2: a simple symbolic logic which even children can learn to use in their daily problems, and which would help them later as husbands and wives to avoid unnecessary quarrels. Aspect 3: a simple semantics which could help even children to recognize (and avoid) those dangerous words by which demagogues and dictators in the homes and nations threaten the peace of mankind.

By trying to find appropriate symbols for mankind's most important meanings like ethics, evolution, life, liberty, religion, God, etc. etc. I made some important discoveries already acknowledged by scholars. Aspect 4: a universal natural ethics encompassing all religions. Aspect 5: the biochemical discovery that cells act ethically in all creatures. Aspect 6: the archeological discovery that old stone age man was not a killer of his fellowman. Cannibalism and war began with new stone age man by the introduction of dangerous words. □

ISOTYPE
EDUCATION THROUGH THE EYE
by Marie Neurath

ISOTYPE was the original concept of Otto Neurath (1882–1945), the Austrian social scientist and teacher. His theory of education included the contention that, at least in the initial stages of acquiring new knowledge, pictures are a better means of communication than words. To translate complex figures into a form that would be both accurate and meaningful to a broad audience, he devised not only a series of refined pictographs, but also the techniques for their design and application.

He called them ISOTYPE, a name invented by borrowing the first letters from International System Of TYpographic Picture Education. Thus a large mouthful was reduced to an acceptable morsel.

Among these pictographs were ones representing different nationalities of the world, industries, and forms of communication. These pictorial "word supplements" (supplements, because they are an adjunct to any language), while being completely understandable in themselves, can assume other meanings through combination or other "grammatical" manipulations.

Men of the World   Commerce or Trade   Telegram   Air Mail

The graphic point of departure for all his pictures was always what the observer actually saw, rather than the spoken or written word associated with the object or person. However, the picture had to be so refined in its execution that it immediately presented the most important fact or characteristic first, less important ones second, and details last. The ISOTYPE grammar could impart further meanings or associations, either through color, texture, or additional pictographs.

Family   Water Bottle   Wine Bottle   Spring   Summer   Fall   Winter

Through hardship, success, war, economic depression, and eventual recognition all over again, Otto Neurath always had his wife Marie at his side. Today this unassuming lady carries on the work they began together through the Isotype Institute Ltd. We are indebted to her for this presentation. HD

At first, while searching for the best methods to communicate, we stammered; then we spoke; then we described how we spoke. Our system has a vocabulary – the symbols; and a grammar – the rules of our method.

The following signs illustrate a few basic pictographs and their combinations.

Shoe

Works

Shoe Works

Shoes Produced by Machine

Shoes Produced by Hand

Geographers and statisticians have used visual representations in a variety of methods, employing geometric shapes in sizes proportional to represented quantities. However, I believe no one has made statistics as easy to comprehend instantly, as does the system of ISOTYPE. In the modernized example below, it is readily apparent that the facts are clearer – and more likely to be remembered – than if the reader were confronted with a complex series of numerals or graphs. In presentations of statistical material in a comparative form, this technique is widely used today in newspapers, magazines, textbooks, financial reports, and business journals.

New Used

1969

1966

1963

1960

U.S. PASSENGER CAR REGISTRATION (Each symbol equals 6 million cars)

Otto Neurath firmly believed that the world needed a uniform, international visual system of expression that would work as an auxiliary language in complete accord with each of the world's spoken languages. He was wholeheartedly dedicated to this goal.

Just as ISOTYPE crosses all language barriers, so we, in an effort to continue our work, crossed the borders of many countries. We worked in Austria, Russia, Germany, Holland, England, Mexico, the United States, Nigeria; we fled, forced by circumstance or conviction, or traveled by choice, to expose and explain our system and promote its world wide acceptance. □

BASIC SYMBOLS

Certain symbols have become basic to semiotic communication. They appear and reappear, are consistent among disciplines, and their meaning remains constant. They reassure us in our interpretation of complex directions and are fundamental to the understanding of any symbol system. They are the foundation – the ABC's – of graphic symbols.

OR
PROHIBITION
RESTRICTION
WARNING
LEFT
RIGHT
UP
DOWN
ON
OFF
MALE
FEMALE
EMPTY
FULL
SMALL
LARGE

Although such symbols are not a clearly defined group like the 26 letters of the Roman alphabet, the following selection represents examples extracted from many disciplines which, in my personal judgment, can be called Basic.

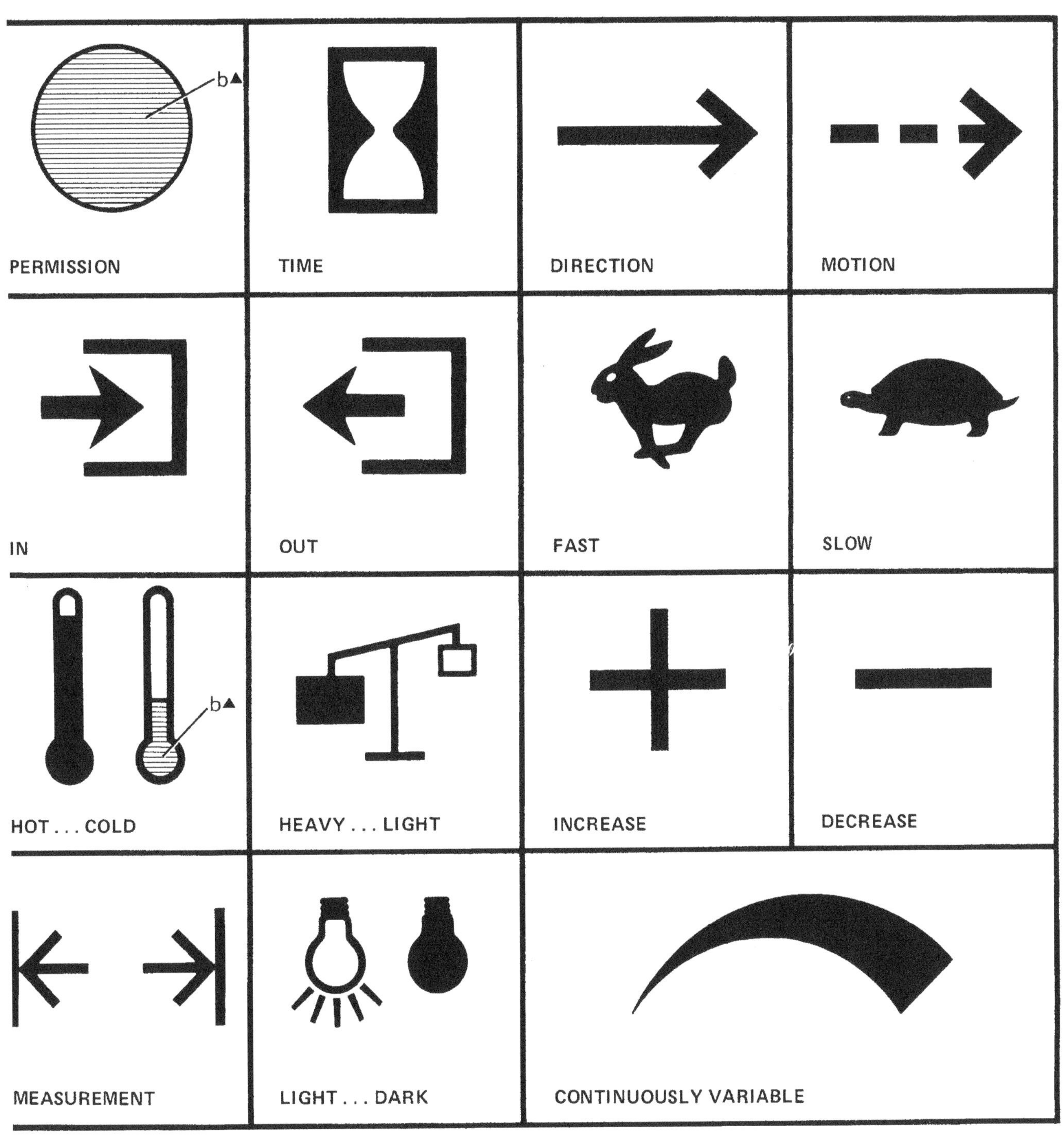
b▲
PERMISSION
TIME
DIRECTION
MOTION
IN
OUT
FAST
SLOW
b▲
HOT . . . COLD
HEAVY . . . LIGHT
INCREASE
DECREASE
MEASUREMENT
LIGHT . . . DARK
CONTINUOUSLY VARIABLE

▲ The letter b indicates color blue.

BASIC SYMBOLS *(continued)*

Basic Symbols, like the ones illustrated on the previous pages, are often combined with other symbols to develop more complex meanings and instructions. Thus a kind of *grammar* of semiotics evolves.

For instance, effective forms, reinforced by color, have been adopted by the United Nations for traffic guidance. Color is used for emphasis and instant recognition – red expressing prohibition or warning, and blue indicating permission. The meaning of the basic form is modified by what is placed within it:

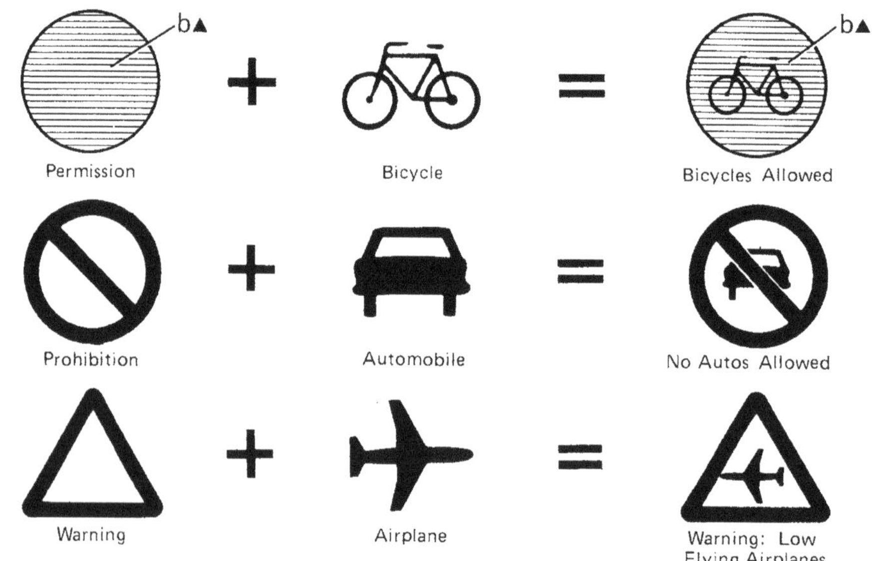

b▲
b▲
Permission
Bicycle
Bicycles Allowed
Prohibition
Automobile
No Autos Allowed
Warning
Airplane
Warning: Low Flying Airplanes

The much-used arrow can be modified to give more complex directions:

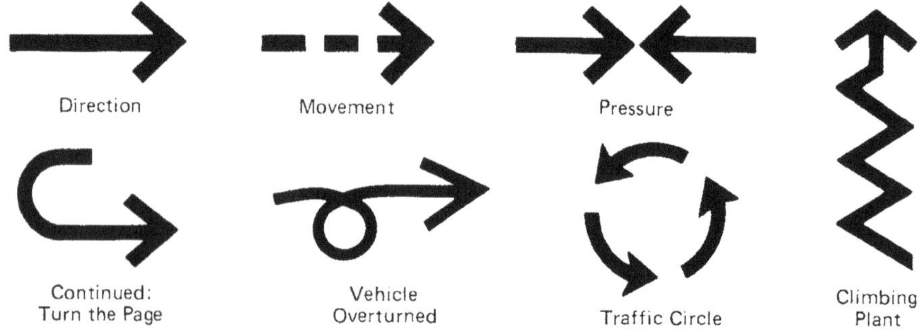

Direction
Movement
Pressure
Continued: Turn the Page
Vehicle Overturned
Traffic Circle
Climbing Plant

▲ The letter b indicates color blue.

Progression or intensity may be shown by size in relation to a fixed element:

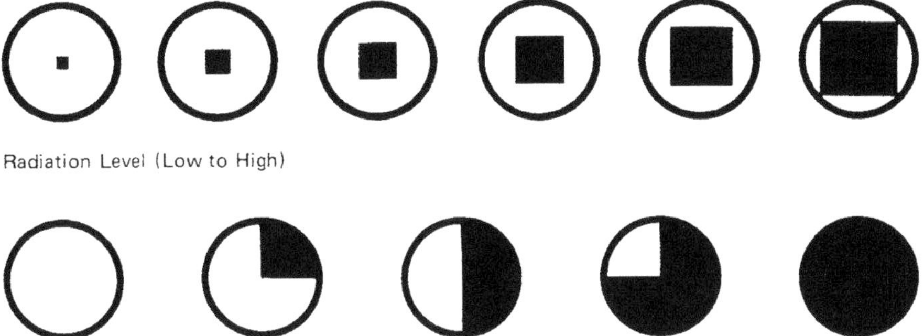

Radiation Level (Low to High)

Sky Coverage (Clear to Complete Overcast)

Progression may also be indicated by multiplication of a symbol, usually shown in a predetermined pattern:

Snowfall (Slight Intermittent to Heavy Continuous)

Powers of Ten (Unit to Ten-thousand)

This grammar concept is not limited to the symbols which we have selected as Basic. Some symbols have become well established in their own Discipline and are readily recognized. Thus, they can be combined to convey a clearly understandable message to anyone familiar with that Discipline:

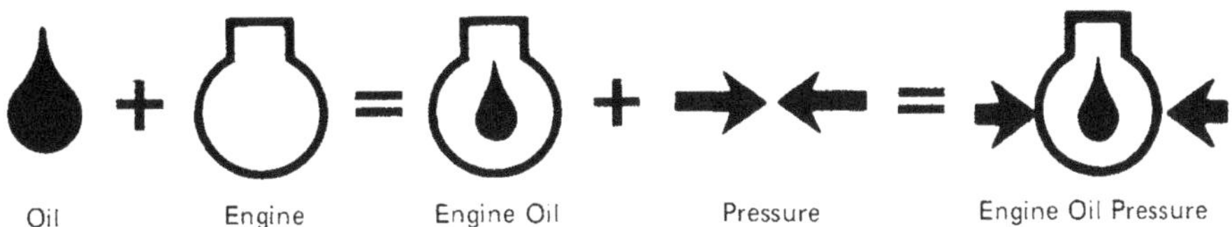
Oil
Engine
Engine Oil
Pressure
Engine Oil Pressure

Increase and Decrease can be related to a specific application by the following technique:

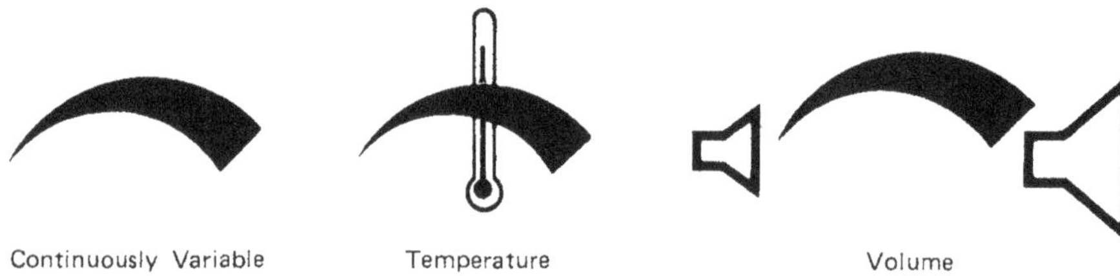
Continuously Variable
Temperature
Volume

Variations can be achieved simply by adding an "adjective" element to the basic symbol:

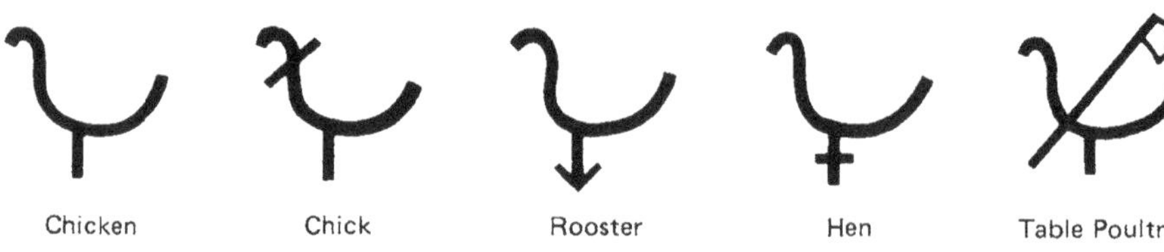
Chicken
Chick
Rooster
Hen
Table Poultry

THE SEARCH FOR PUSH AND PULL

As often happens, an elementary problem has become the most elusive to solve. It would appear easy to convey these simplest of actions: Push and Pull. But they defy obvious graphic delineation.

Certainly it is unfortunate that we can include no accepted symbols for these actions in our lexicon of Basic Symbols.

An internationally reprinted newspaper account of our symbol work reported our difficulty in finding satisfactory Push and Pull symbols. As a result, we received hundreds of suggestions.

Among these were a variety of drawings of hands. Although hands do indeed perform the act of pushing and pulling, these suggestions are all either closely related to STOP signs, or are limited in application or just plain confusing!

Using an established symbol, simple line changes — either in direction or length — can modify its meaning:

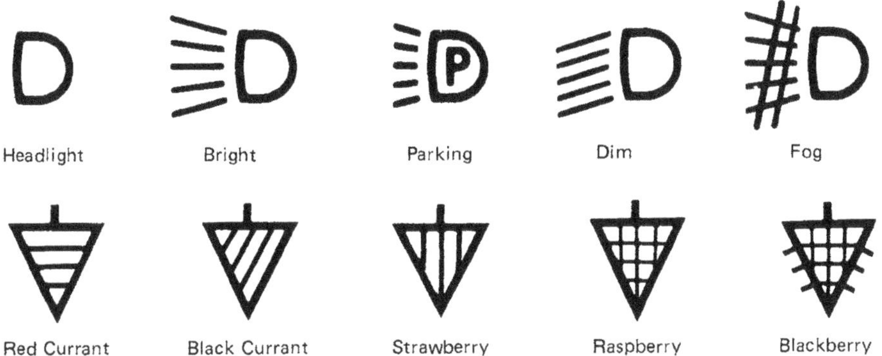
Headlight
Bright
Parking
Dim
Fog
Red Currant
Black Currant
Strawberry
Raspberry
Blackberry

These few examples show the emerging grammar of symbols and what can be conveyed by the consistent combination of familiar, simple forms to create a more complex message.

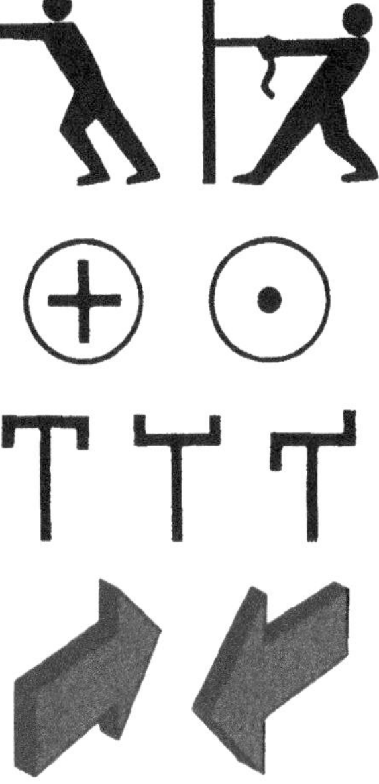

Most of the suggested symbols imply a sideways motion, which is fine for a sliding door, but in an emergency such instructions on a common hinged or swinging door could prove disastrous. They would be equally misleading on a control knob requiring an in-and-out motion.

Obviously, there are limitations to pictorial symbols; many signs and instructions do not lend themselves to this type of representation. So numerous contributors sent us strictly abstract designs.

DNA (Deutscher Normenausschuss), which is developing symbol standards for ISO (International Organization for Standardization), has proposed these very interesting diagrams for Push and Pull, and an adaptation for "turn."

Perhaps these isometric arrows would provide a solution?

DISCIPLINE SECTION

SELECTION – Frequently, several symbols exist for the same meaning. In those cases I have used my judgment in selecting one or more on the basis of clarity, common usage, or excellence of graphic presentation. But when there is only one symbol expressing a specific direction or instruction, it is included regardless of its quality. The inclusion of a symbol in no way indicates my approval.

In the strictly academic or technical Disciplines, we have enlisted the aid of experts in each field to select those symbols of maximum general interest. Most stringent editing has been used in these areas, as complete data is voluminously documented in readily available technical publications. Many of these are listed in the appropriate Discipline sections in the Bibliography, for those who require expanded information.

Initials, abbreviations, numerals, and Greek letters are included only when they are essential in the presentation of a Discipline and have an internationally accepted meaning; for example, abbreviations for chemical elements and Greek letter designations for units in physics.

EXCEPTIONS to our rule of including only two-dimensional graphic symbols have been made in special areas where no true graphic symbol exists. For example, in the Discipline of Religion, exclusion of three-dimensional symbols would have left the subject incomplete; we have therefore translated the major three-dimensional forms to simple definitive outline.

The three-dimensional shapes included in Vehicle Controls are another example of nongraphic directives serving for immediate transmission of information – adjuncts to the written word or symbol.

Light signals, as well as hand and arm signals, have been included in those few instances where they seemed essential in conjunction with or as alternates to graphic signs – such as traffic lights and semaphore codes.

GROUPING and sequencing of symbols are based, not on any academic or formal classification system, but rather according to what we considered the most logical arrangement of the material in our Data Bank.

DELINEATION – Symbols have been redrawn in order to present them with consistent delineation and with the amount of detail appropriate to the size of reproduction. Minor variations have occasionally been made to clarify the meaning. We have taken the liberty of standardizing some frequently used symbol components, such as arrows and human forms. In the case of arrows, we have also adopted a policy of using a broken line in the shaft whenever motion is to be expressed.

Color is indicated by consistent pattern codes and identifying lowercase letters as shown in the illustration below.

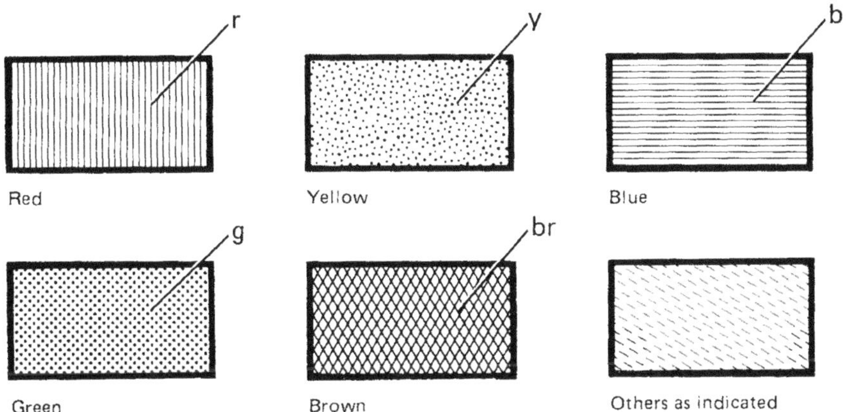

r
y
b
Red
Yellow
Blue
g
br
Green
Brown
Others as indicated

An exception to the above technique is made when a symbol has its own integral textural pattern; in such a case only a lowercase letter is used.

Very often the meaning of a symbol is dependent on its relationship to another graphic element. In such instances the point of reference is indicated by a light gray imprint.

ISO (International Organization for Standardization) footnote references have been made in the interest of promoting international standardization. "Recommendation" and "Draft" identification in footnotes are accurate as of the date of our publication; actual source documents are listed in the appropriate Discipline sections in the Bibliography.

ISO is composed of national member bodies concerned with general standardization. International and national standards organizations and their relationships are described at the beginning of the Bibliography.

ACCOMMODATIONS AND TRAVEL

OR
PARKING STRUCTURE
ENTRANCE
EXIT
NO ENTRY (Keep Out)
ESCALATOR, UP
ESCALATOR, DOWN
STAIRS, UP
STAIRS, DOWN
STAIRS, UP and DOWN
ELEVATOR
INFORMATION
INFORMATION
RENDEZVOUS POINT
STROLLERS
LOST CHILD
NURSERY
CLOAKROOM
MEN'S CLOAKROOM
WOMEN'S CLOAKROOM
LOST and FOUND
SAFE DEPOSIT BOXES
DELIVERY ENTRANCE
Facilities
WASHROOM
TOILETS
MEN'S TOILET
WOMEN'S TOILET
BATH and SHOWER

BATH
OR
OR
SAUNA BATH
SHOWER
OR
MEN'S SHOWER
WOMEN'S SHOWER
USED RAZOR BLADES
ELECTRIC RAZOR SOCKET
OR
220 V ~
FOOT PEDAL for WATER
SANITARY NAPKINS
NO FOREIGN OBJECTS in TOILET
TRASH
OR
OR
USED LINEN
USED TOWELS
USED CUPS
HOTEL RESERVATIONS
HOTEL
SINGLE ROOM
ROOM with TWIN BEDS
ROOM with DOUBLE BED
QUIET
BELLBOY
MAID
ROOM SERVICE
BARMAN
LAUNDRY
LIGHT SWITCH
0
MAXI
VENTILATION CONTROL
b
r
1/2
0
1/1
HEATING CONTROL
LOCK
UNLOCK
Food and Drink
RESTAURANT
OR
OR
SNACK BAR
COFFEE SHOP

ACCOMMODATIONS AND TRAVEL *(continued)*

GRILL

OR

VENDING MACHINE
(Automat)

OR

OR

BAR

DRINKING
FOUNTAIN

DRINKING
WATER

DON'T DRINK
the WATER

On-Board
Aircraft

FASTEN SEAT BELTS

OR

NO SMOKING

ASHTRAY

TOILETS AFT

TOILETS OCCUPIED

READING LIGHT

STEWARDESS
CALL

SEAT OCCUPIED

OR

PLACE LUGGAGE
on FLOOR

RETURN to SEAT

RETURN SEAT to
UPRIGHT POSITION

SICKNESS
CONTAINERS

O_2

OXYGEN

FIRE
EXTINGUISHER

REMOVE SHOES
on Evacuation Slide

MEGAPHONE

Terminals

OR
AIRPORT
HELIPORT
SHIP
FERRY
MONORAIL

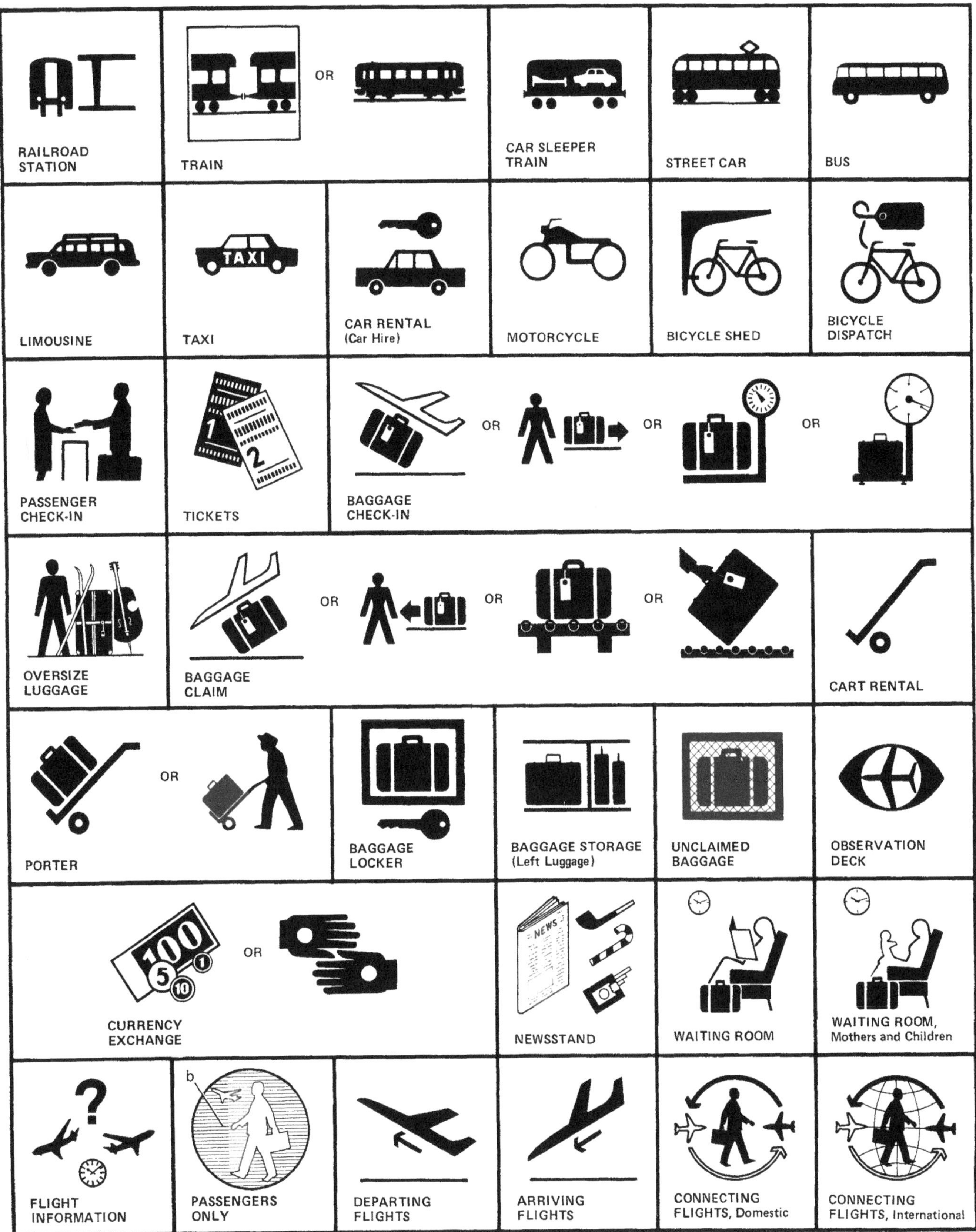

RAILROAD STATION
TRAIN
OR
CAR SLEEPER TRAIN
STREET CAR
BUS
LIMOUSINE
TAXI
TAXI
CAR RENTAL (Car Hire)
MOTORCYCLE
BICYCLE SHED
BICYCLE DISPATCH
PASSENGER CHECK-IN
1
2
TICKETS
BAGGAGE CHECK-IN
OR
OR
OR
OVERSIZE LUGGAGE
BAGGAGE CLAIM
OR
OR
OR
CART RENTAL
PORTER
OR
BAGGAGE LOCKER
BAGGAGE STORAGE (Left Luggage)
UNCLAIMED BAGGAGE
OBSERVATION DECK
100
5
10
1
OR
CURRENCY EXCHANGE
NEWS
NEWSSTAND
WAITING ROOM
WAITING ROOM, Mothers and Children
FLIGHT INFORMATION
b
PASSENGERS ONLY
DEPARTING FLIGHTS
ARRIVING FLIGHTS
CONNECTING FLIGHTS, Domestic
CONNECTING FLIGHTS, International

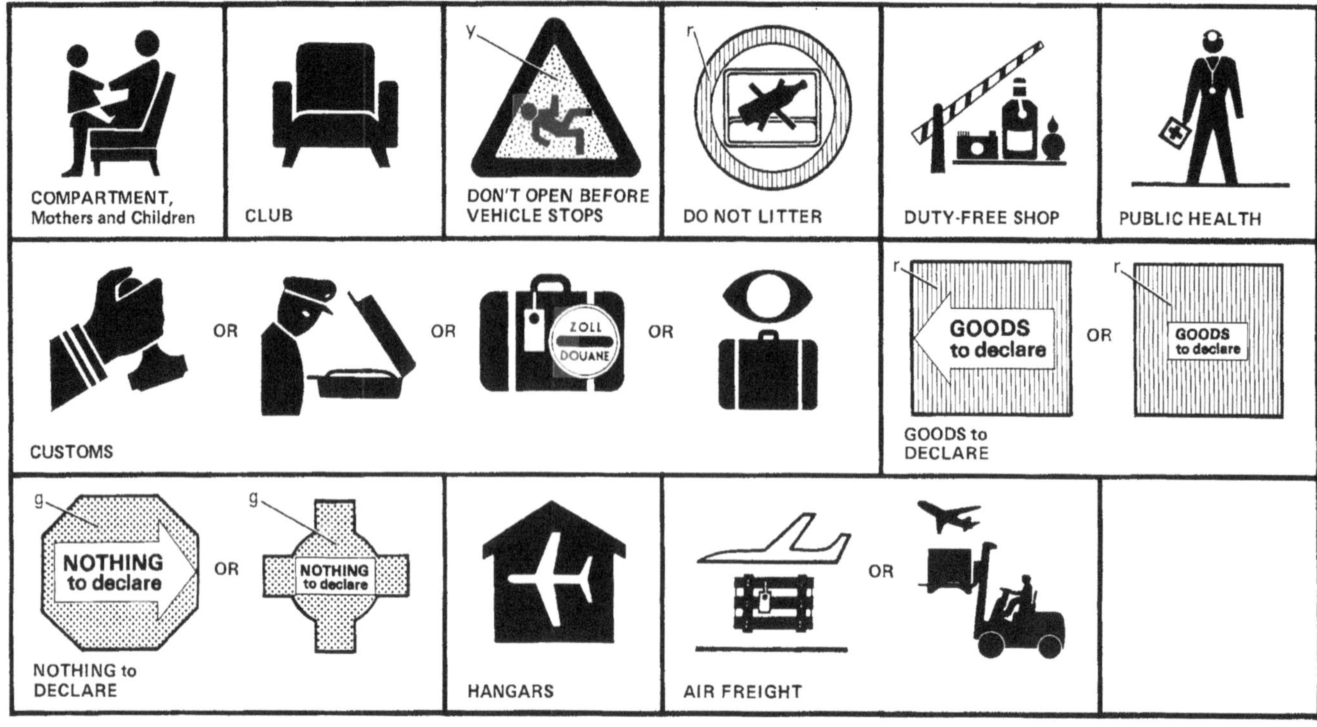
COMPARTMENT, Mothers and Children
CLUB
DON'T OPEN BEFORE VEHICLE STOPS
DO NOT LITTER
DUTY-FREE SHOP
PUBLIC HEALTH
OR
ZOLL
DOUANE
CUSTOMS
GOODS to declare
GOODS to DECLARE
NOTHING to declare
NOTHING to DECLARE
HANGARS
AIR FREIGHT

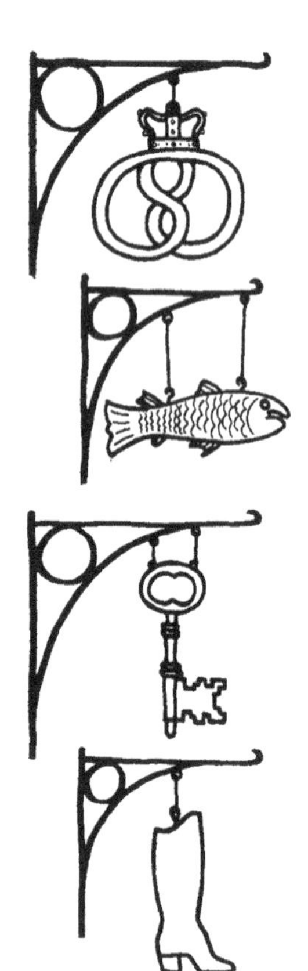

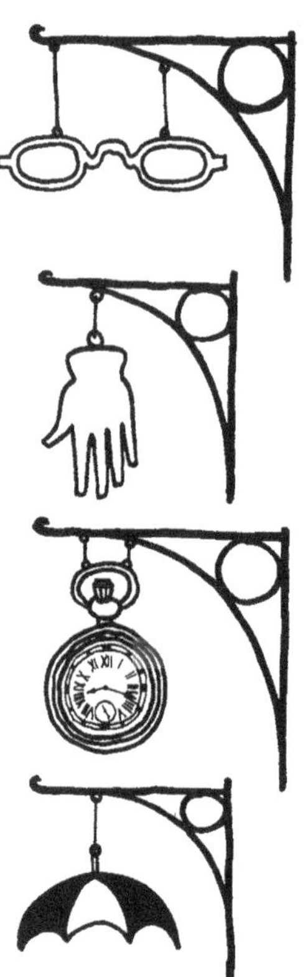

PRE-NEON

For centuries, shopkeepers and professionals the world over have displayed three-dimensional symbols on the outside of their premises.

Besides reminding regular customers of the services and merchandise offered, these indicators also informed tourists not familiar with the language, as well as local illiterates (who abounded before the last century), of what was available within.

These handcrafted symbolic sculptures are today much sought-after collectors' items. How far removed is today's excess of signs that visually pollute our streets and avenues.

AGRICULTURE

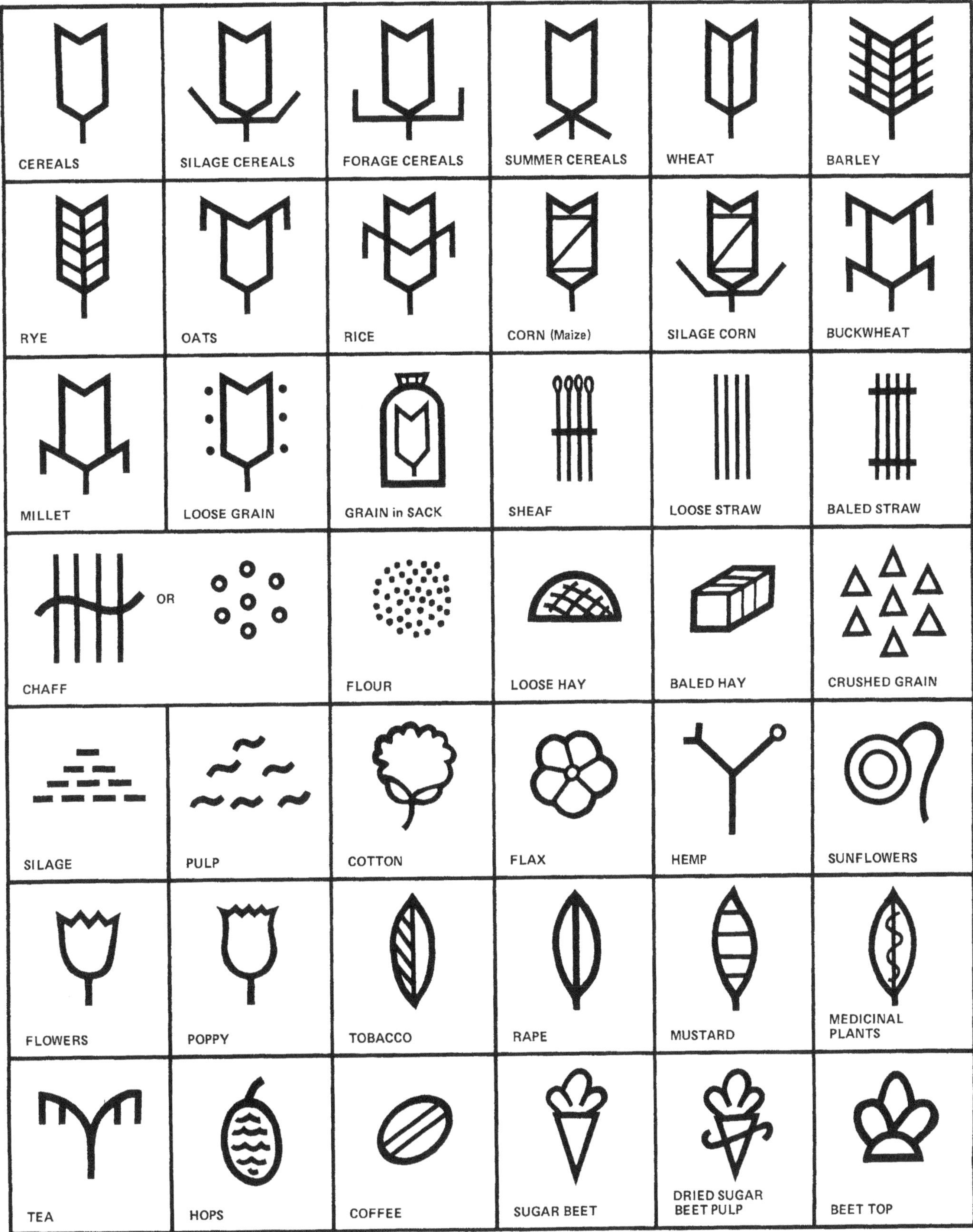
CEREALS
SILAGE CEREALS
FORAGE CEREALS
SUMMER CEREALS
WHEAT
BARLEY
RYE
OATS
RICE
CORN (Maize)
SILAGE CORN
BUCKWHEAT
MILLET
LOOSE GRAIN
GRAIN in SACK
SHEAF
LOOSE STRAW
BALED STRAW
OR
CHAFF
FLOUR
LOOSE HAY
BALED HAY
CRUSHED GRAIN
SILAGE
PULP
COTTON
FLAX
HEMP
SUNFLOWERS
FLOWERS
POPPY
TOBACCO
RAPE
MUSTARD
MEDICINAL PLANTS
TEA
HOPS
COFFEE
SUGAR BEET
DRIED SUGAR BEET PULP
BEET TOP

AGRICULTURE

Agronomy *(continued)*

MANGEL-WURZEL	CANE	CLOVER	ALFALFA (Lucerne)	SAINFOIN	SERRADELLA
WEED	GRASSES	Fruits and Vegetables	VEGETABLES	TOMATO	POTATO
CHITTED POTATOES	JERUSALEM ARTICHOKE	RUTABAGA	TURNIP	LEGUMES	BEAN
SOYBEAN	BROAD BEAN	LENTIL	VETCH	LUPINE	PEA
PEANUT	STANDARD	HALF STANDARD	BUSH	BUSH, spindle tree	FRUIT
CITRUS FRUIT	APPLE	PEAR	QUINCE	PEACH	APRICOT
PLUM	CHERRY	OLIVE	GRAPE VINE	VINEYARD	GOOSEBERRY

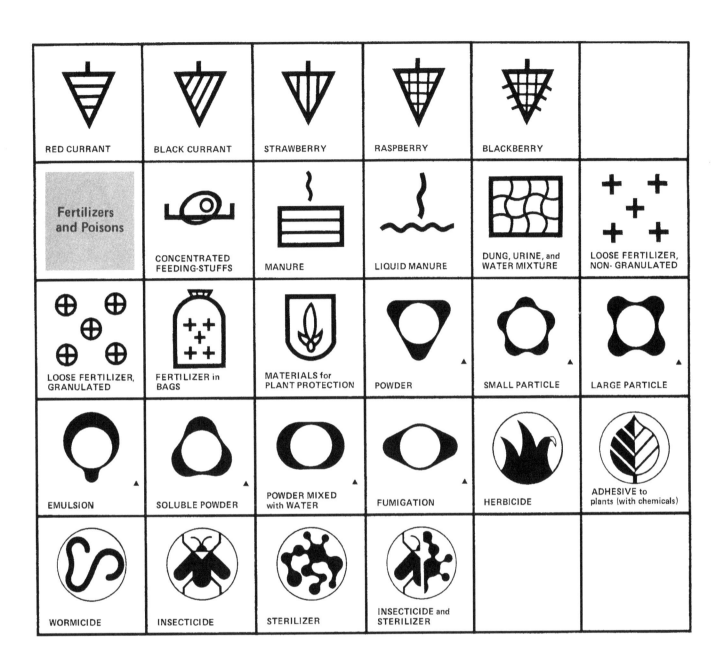

RED CURRANT	BLACK CURRANT	STRAWBERRY	RASPBERRY	BLACKBERRY	
Fertilizers and Poisons	CONCENTRATED FEEDING-STUFFS	MANURE	LIQUID MANURE	DUNG, URINE, and WATER MIXTURE	LOOSE FERTILIZER, NON- GRANULATED
LOOSE FERTILIZER, GRANULATED	FERTILIZER in BAGS	MATERIALS for PLANT PROTECTION	POWDER ▲	SMALL PARTICLE ▲	LARGE PARTICLE ▲
EMULSION ▲	SOLUBLE POWDER ▲	POWDER MIXED with WATER ▲	FUMIGATION ▲	HERBICIDE	ADHESIVE to plants (with chemicals)
WORMICIDE	INSECTICIDE	STERILIZER	INSECTICIDE and STERILIZER		

Livestock and Dairy Products

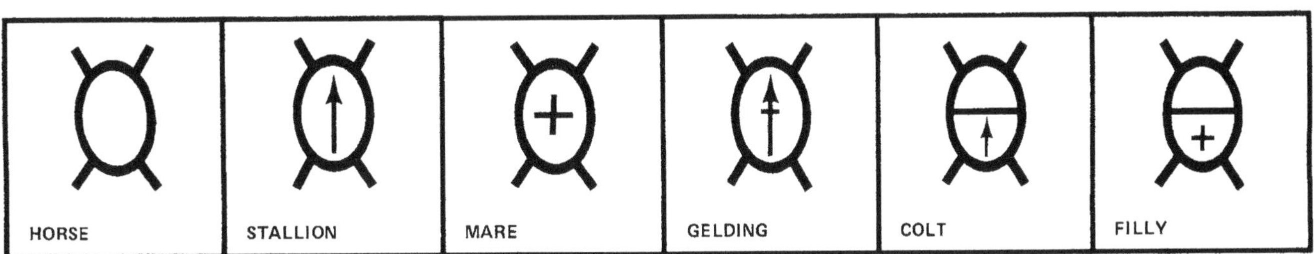
HORSE
STALLION
MARE
GELDING
COLT
FILLY

▲ May be combined with symbols indicating usage. **Example:** indicates Powdered Insecticide, indicates Sterilizer Emulsion.

AGRICULTURE

Livestock and Dairy Products *(continued)*

DONKEY (Ass)	MULE	HINNY	CATTLE	BULL	COW
BULL CALF	HEIFER	FATTENED CATTLE	OX	SWINE (Pig)	BOAR
SOW	PIGLING	FATTENED SWINE	PORKER	SHEEP	RAM
EWE	LAMB	GOAT	BILLY GOAT (Male)	NANNY GOAT (Female)	KID
RABBIT	SILKWORM	BEE COLONY	CHEESE	MILK	SKIMMED MILK; WHEY
Poultry	EGGS	ALBUMEN	POULTRY	TABLE POULTRY	CHICKEN
ROOSTER (Cock)	HEN	CHICK	TURKEY	TURKEY GOBBLER (Tom)	TURKEY HEN

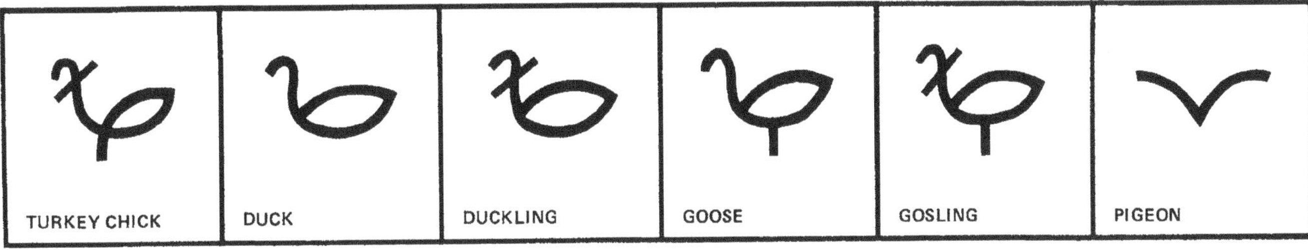
TURKEY CHICK
DUCK
DUCKLING
GOOSE
GOSLING
PIGEON

Farm Structures and Lands

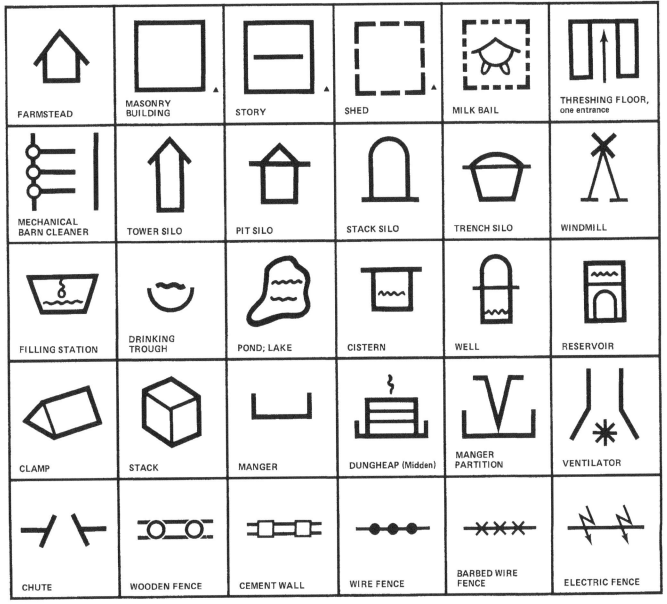

FARMSTEAD	MASONRY BUILDING ▲	STORY ▲	SHED ▲	MILK BAIL	THRESHING FLOOR, one entrance
MECHANICAL BARN CLEANER	TOWER SILO	PIT SILO	STACK SILO	TRENCH SILO	WINDMILL
FILLING STATION	DRINKING TROUGH	POND; LAKE	CISTERN	WELL	RESERVOIR
CLAMP	STACK	MANGER	DUNGHEAP (Midden)	MANGER PARTITION	VENTILATOR
CHUTE	WOODEN FENCE	CEMENT WALL	WIRE FENCE	BARBED WIRE FENCE	ELECTRIC FENCE

▲ These symbols may be combined with those from other Sub-Disciplines. **Example:** indicates Pig Shed; Repair Shop.

Farm Structures and Lands *(continued)*

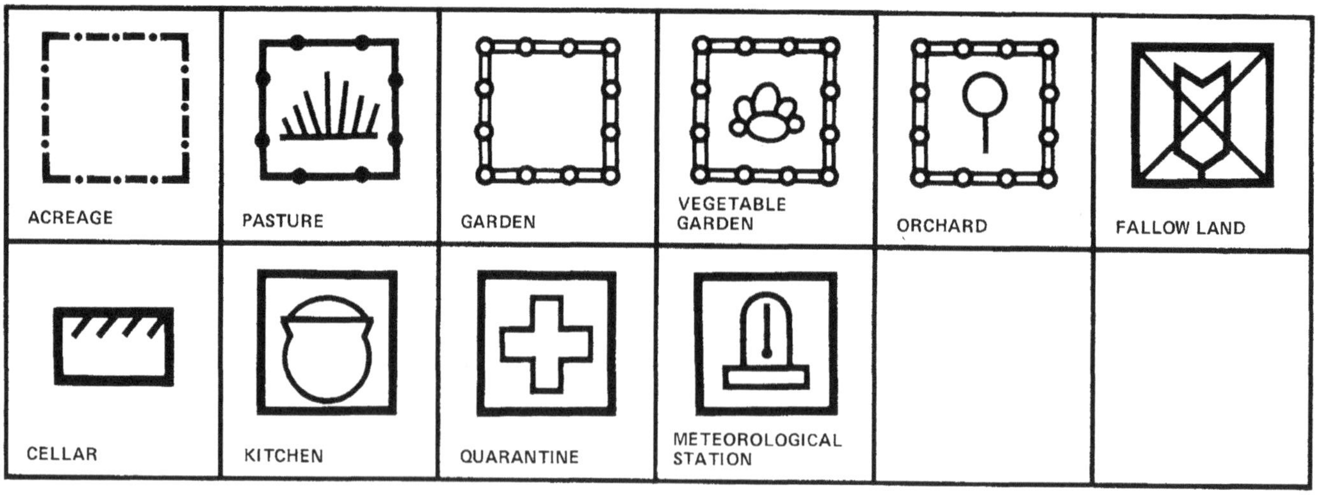

ACREAGE	PASTURE	GARDEN	VEGETABLE GARDEN	ORCHARD	FALLOW LAND
CELLAR	KITCHEN	QUARANTINE	METEOROLOGICAL STATION		

Forestry

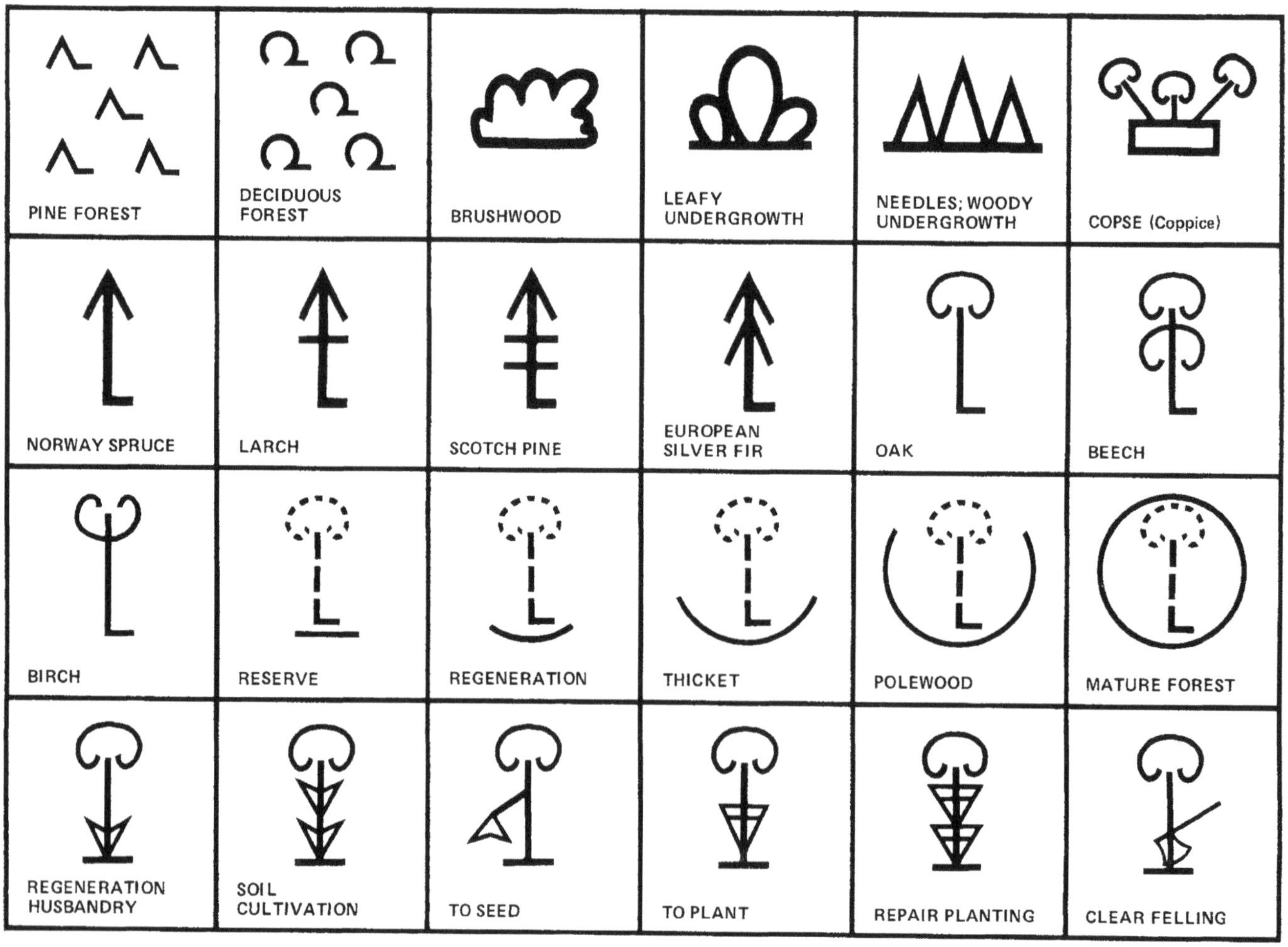

PINE FOREST	DECIDUOUS FOREST	BRUSHWOOD	LEAFY UNDERGROWTH	NEEDLES; WOODY UNDERGROWTH	COPSE (Coppice)
NORWAY SPRUCE	LARCH	SCOTCH PINE	EUROPEAN SILVER FIR	OAK	BEECH
BIRCH	RESERVE	REGENERATION	THICKET	POLEWOOD	MATURE FOREST
REGENERATION HUSBANDRY	SOIL CULTIVATION	TO SEED	TO PLANT	REPAIR PLANTING	CLEAR FELLING

CLEARING in YOUNG STAND
THINNING
TIMBER
FIREWOOD

Implements *

FORK	RAKE	SPADE; SHOVEL	HOE	SCYTHE	HATCHET; AXE
SCISSORS	DIBBLE	HANDTOOLS	SAW	CIRCULAR SAW	LADDER
RACK	PLOWSHARE	DISC	RAKE TINE	CULTIVATOR TINE	SUBSOILER
BEET LIFTING SHARE	POTATO DIGGING SHARE	DIGGING REEL	DISC DRILL COLTER	DRILL COLTER	KNOTTER
METAL WHEEL	PNEUMATIC TIRED WHEEL	CAGE WHEEL	MACHINE	DRAWBAR	RUT LOOSENER

* FOR MECHANIZED FARM EQUIPMENT, SEE **VEHICLE CONTROLS:** Agriculture, PAGE 160.

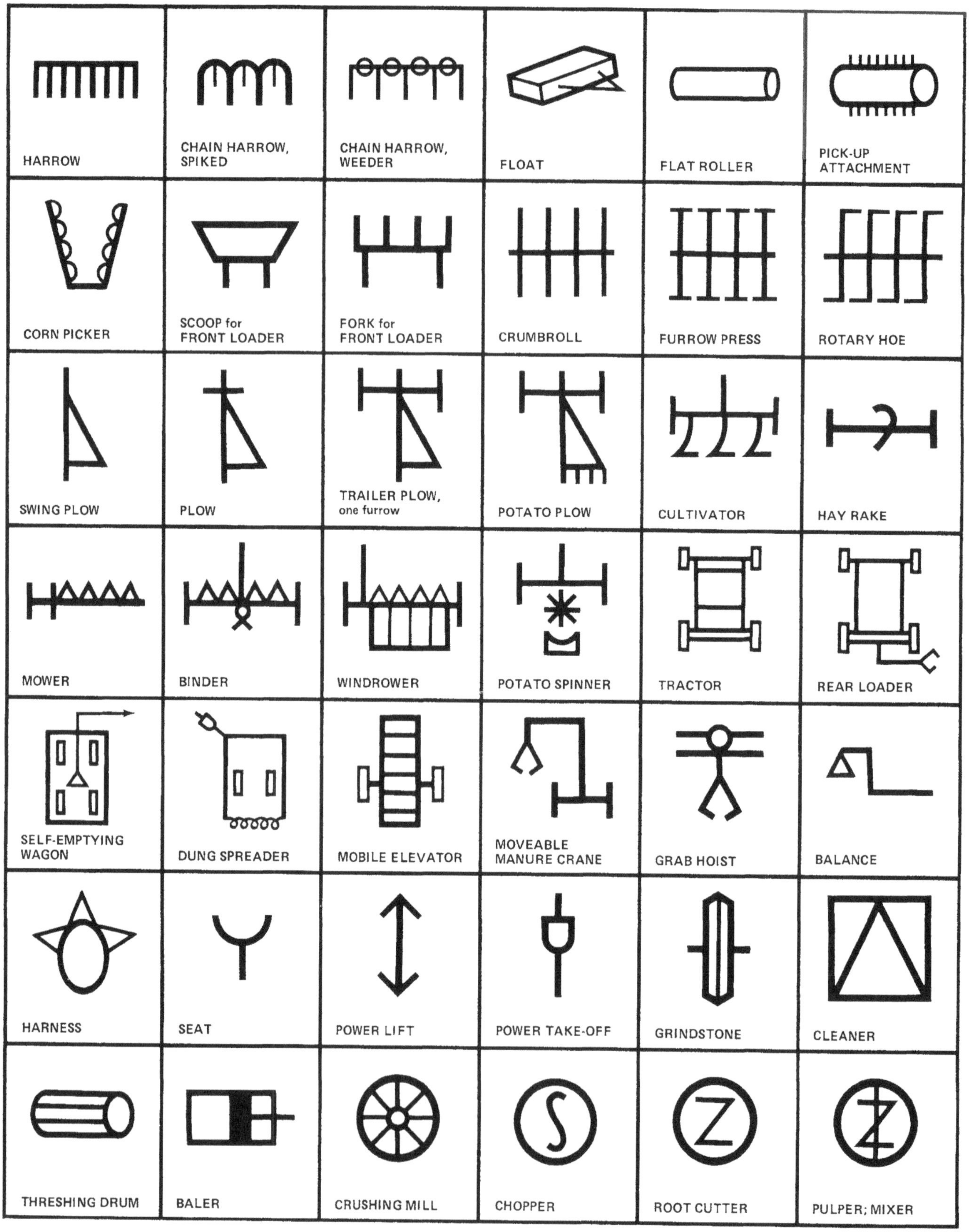

AGRICULTURE

HARROW	CHAIN HARROW, SPIKED	CHAIN HARROW, WEEDER	FLOAT	FLAT ROLLER	PICK-UP ATTACHMENT
CORN PICKER	SCOOP for FRONT LOADER	FORK for FRONT LOADER	CRUMBROLL	FURROW PRESS	ROTARY HOE
SWING PLOW	PLOW	TRAILER PLOW, one furrow	POTATO PLOW	CULTIVATOR	HAY RAKE
MOWER	BINDER	WINDROWER	POTATO SPINNER	TRACTOR	REAR LOADER
SELF-EMPTYING WAGON	DUNG SPREADER	MOBILE ELEVATOR	MOVEABLE MANURE CRANE	GRAB HOIST	BALANCE
HARNESS	SEAT	POWER LIFT	POWER TAKE-OFF	GRINDSTONE	CLEANER
THRESHING DRUM	BALER	CRUSHING MILL	CHOPPER	ROOT CUTTER	PULPER; MIXER

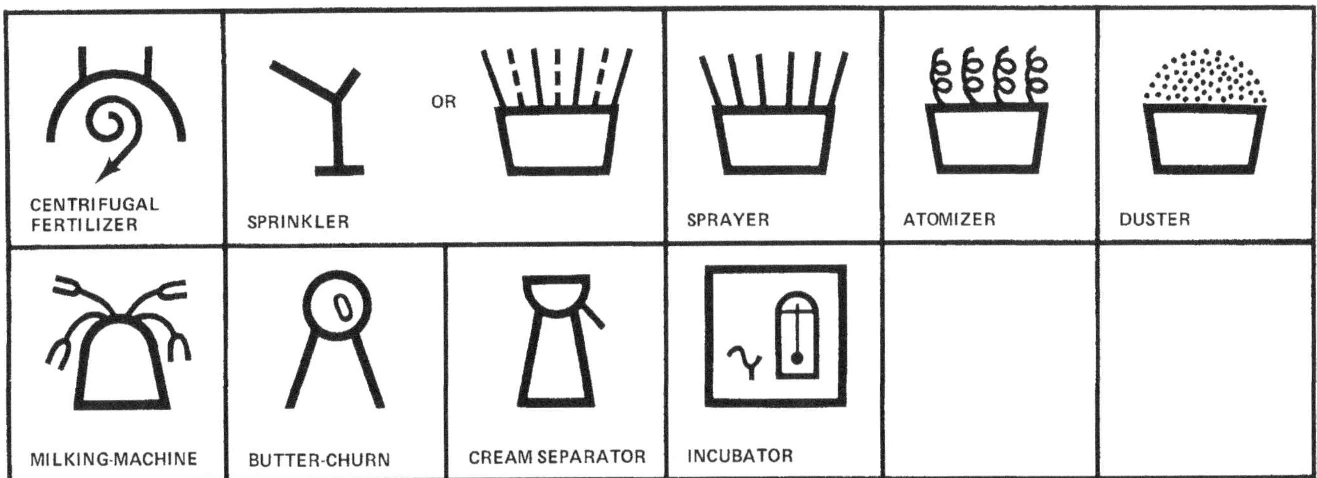
CENTRIFUGAL FERTILIZER
SPRINKLER
OR
SPRAYER
ATOMIZER
DUSTER
MILKING-MACHINE
BUTTER-CHURN
CREAM SEPARATOR
INCUBATOR

Justice

Against Lightning

Fertility

Sunshine

HEX

For centuries, though with little evidence of effectiveness, hex signs have been painted on barns to ward off trouble or attract good luck.

In the 17th century the faithful Amish and Mennonites brought the superstition from the Rhineland to the Pennsylvania Dutch countryside – and from there it spread to other parts of the country.

Magical powers have been claimed for these insignia of witchcraft. They are said to cause crops to grow, make the sun shine, bring on wet weather, summon fertility, or ward off cow fever.

Hex symbols can assume many forms, but most often appear as a star within a circle. In the Pennsylvania Dutch dialect they are referred to as "Schtanna," which means star, and each design variation indicates its own special meaning.

Even in this enlightened age farmers continue to enlist the services of the hex, though some admittedly use them for decoration rather than protection.

Rain

Wisdom

Good Luck

Against Demons

ARCHITECTURE *

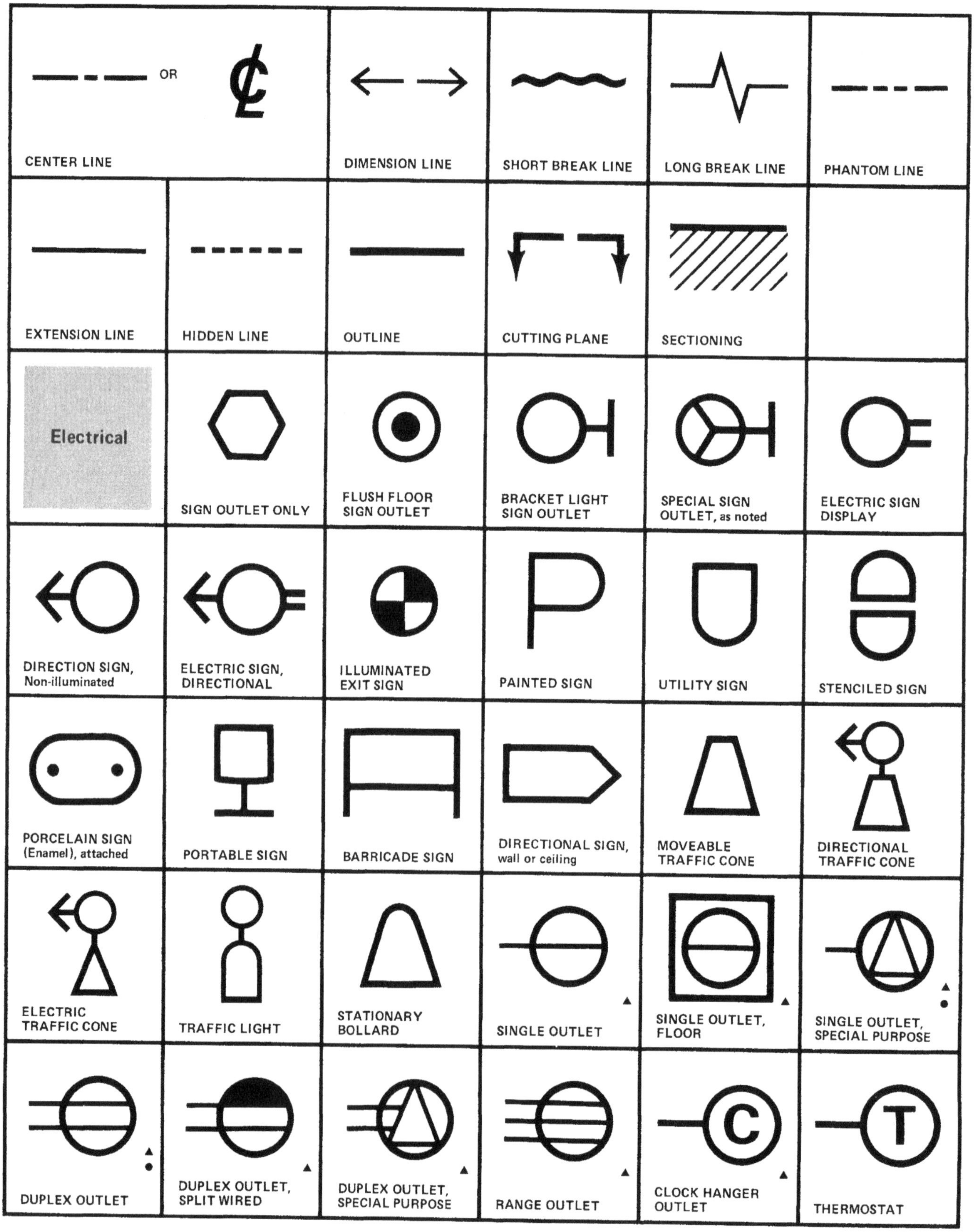

Drafting

OR CENTER LINE		DIMENSION LINE	SHORT BREAK LINE	LONG BREAK LINE	PHANTOM LINE
EXTENSION LINE	HIDDEN LINE	OUTLINE	CUTTING PLANE	SECTIONING	
Electrical	SIGN OUTLET ONLY	FLUSH FLOOR SIGN OUTLET	BRACKET LIGHT SIGN OUTLET	SPECIAL SIGN OUTLET, as noted	ELECTRIC SIGN DISPLAY
DIRECTION SIGN, Non-illuminated	ELECTRIC SIGN, DIRECTIONAL	ILLUMINATED EXIT SIGN	PAINTED SIGN	UTILITY SIGN	STENCILED SIGN
PORCELAIN SIGN (Enamel), attached	PORTABLE SIGN	BARRICADE SIGN	DIRECTIONAL SIGN, wall or ceiling	MOVEABLE TRAFFIC CONE	DIRECTIONAL TRAFFIC CONE
ELECTRIC TRAFFIC CONE	TRAFFIC LIGHT	STATIONARY BOLLARD	▲ SINGLE OUTLET	▲ SINGLE OUTLET, FLOOR	▲ ● SINGLE OUTLET, SPECIAL PURPOSE
▲ ● DUPLEX OUTLET	▲ DUPLEX OUTLET, SPLIT WIRED	▲ DUPLEX OUTLET, SPECIAL PURPOSE	▲ RANGE OUTLET	▲ CLOCK HANGER OUTLET	THERMOSTAT

▲ Subscripts are added to indicate a specific type of outlet; **G** (Grounded), **R** (Recessed), **WP** (Weather Proof), **VT** (Vapor Tight), **RT** (Rain Tight), **DT** (Dust Tight), **EP** (Explosion Proof). **Example:** $-\ominus_G$ means Grounded Single Outlet.

● Floor outlets are indicated by enclosing symbol in a square, as shown in Single Outlet, Floor.

* FOR SIGNS USED IN OR ON STRUCTURES, SEE **INDEX: Building Signage.**

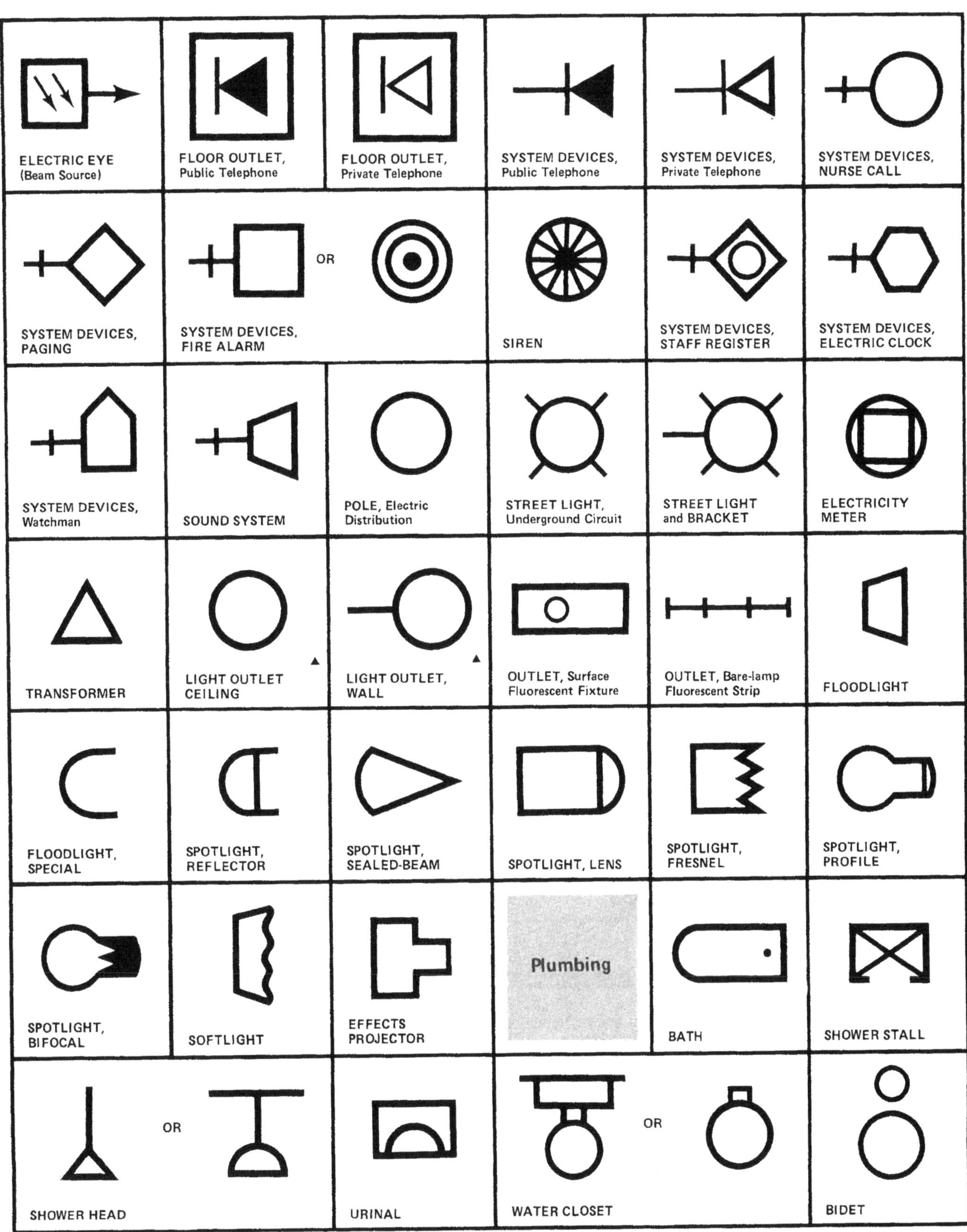
ELECTRIC EYE (Beam Source)
FLOOR OUTLET, Public Telephone
FLOOR OUTLET, Private Telephone
SYSTEM DEVICES, Public Telephone
SYSTEM DEVICES, Private Telephone
SYSTEM DEVICES, NURSE CALL
SYSTEM DEVICES, PAGING
SYSTEM DEVICES, FIRE ALARM
OR
SIREN
SYSTEM DEVICES, STAFF REGISTER
SYSTEM DEVICES, ELECTRIC CLOCK
SYSTEM DEVICES, Watchman
SOUND SYSTEM
POLE, Electric Distribution
STREET LIGHT, Underground Circuit
STREET LIGHT and BRACKET
ELECTRICITY METER
TRANSFORMER
LIGHT OUTLET CEILING ▲
LIGHT OUTLET, WALL ▲
OUTLET, Surface Fluorescent Fixture
OUTLET, Bare-lamp Fluorescent Strip
FLOODLIGHT
FLOODLIGHT, SPECIAL
SPOTLIGHT, REFLECTOR
SPOTLIGHT, SEALED-BEAM
SPOTLIGHT, LENS
SPOTLIGHT, FRESNEL
SPOTLIGHT, PROFILE
SPOTLIGHT, BIFOCAL
SOFTLIGHT
EFFECTS PROJECTOR
Plumbing
BATH
SHOWER STALL
SHOWER HEAD
OR
URINAL
WATER CLOSET
OR
BIDET

▲ Initials may be placed within the circle to indicate a special type of lighting outlet; e.g., **R** (Recessed Incandescent), **X** (Surface Exit), **B** (Blanked Outlet), **J** (Junction Box), **L** (Low Voltage Relay), **XR** (Recessed Exit).

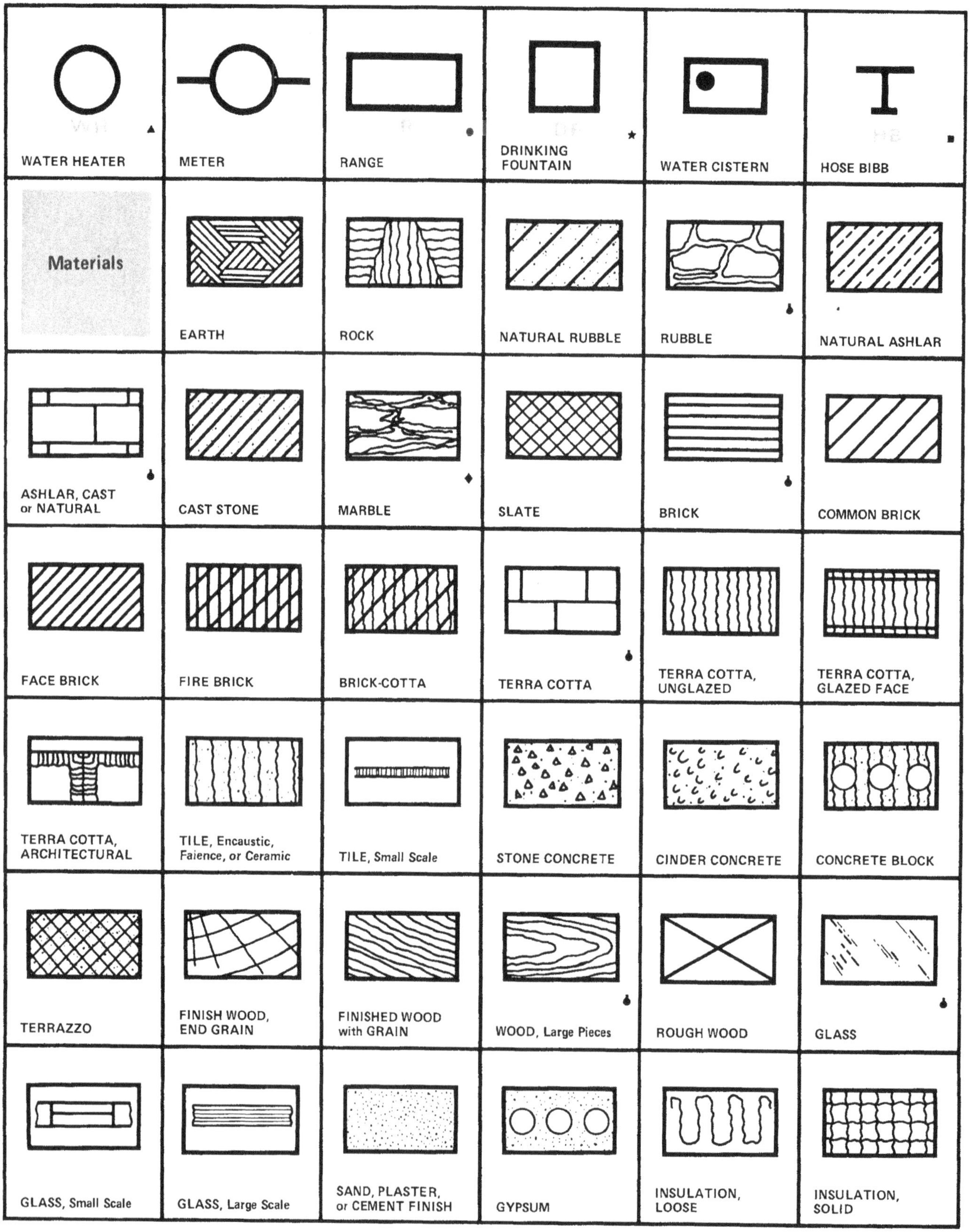

WATER HEATER ▲	METER	RANGE ●	DRINKING FOUNTAIN ★	WATER CISTERN	HOSE BIBB ■
Materials	EARTH	ROCK	NATURAL RUBBLE	RUBBLE 🌢	NATURAL ASHLAR
ASHLAR, CAST or NATURAL 🌢	CAST STONE	MARBLE ◆	SLATE	BRICK 🌢	COMMON BRICK
FACE BRICK	FIRE BRICK	BRICK-COTTA	TERRA COTTA 🌢	TERRA COTTA, UNGLAZED	TERRA COTTA, GLAZED FACE
TERRA COTTA, ARCHITECTURAL	TILE, Encaustic, Faience, or Ceramic	TILE, Small Scale	STONE CONCRETE	CINDER CONCRETE	CONCRETE BLOCK
TERRAZZO	FINISH WOOD, END GRAIN	FINISHED WOOD with GRAIN	WOOD, Large Pieces 🌢	ROUGH WOOD	GLASS 🌢
GLASS, Small Scale	GLASS, Large Scale	SAND, PLASTER, or CEMENT FINISH	GYPSUM	INSULATION, LOOSE	INSULATION, SOLID

▲ Different initials indicate different equipment; e. g., **DU** (Dental Unit), **HWT** (Hot Water Tank).
● Different initials indicate different equipment; e. g., **B** (Bath), **L** (Lavatory), **S** (Sink), **W** (Water Storage Tank), **DW** (Dishwasher), **LT** (Laundry Tray).
★ **DF** may be replaced by **FD** to indicate Drain.
■ **HB** may be replaced by **G** to indicate Gas Outlet.
🌢 Used in elevation drawings. All other Materials symbols shown are used in plan or section drawings.
◆ Used both in elevation drawings, and in plan or section drawings.

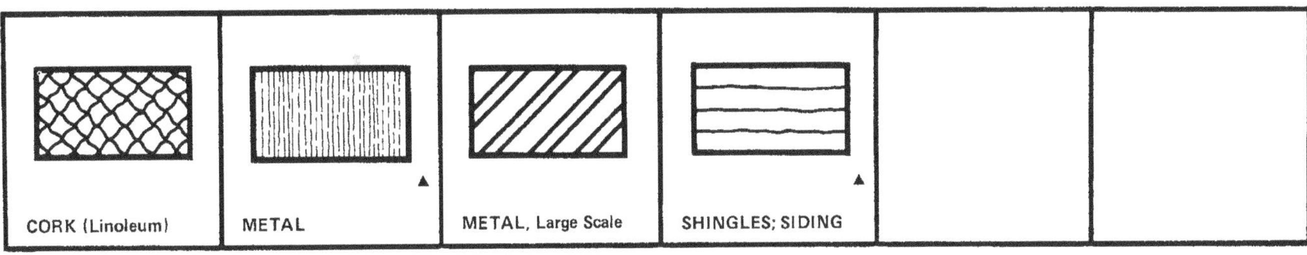
CORK (Linoleum)
METAL ▲
METAL, Large Scale
SHINGLES; SIDING ▲

Landscaping and Planning

PAVED AREA	GRASSED AREA	PLANTED AREA	NEW TREES	EXISTING TREES	EXISTING TREES REMOVED
TREE	SHRUB	HILL	MOUNTAIN	VALLEY	BODY of WATER
RUNNING WATER	FOUNTAIN	BELOW EYE LEVEL, Right	ABOVE EYE LEVEL, Left	FENCE	RAILING
UNDERPASS	BUILDING, HIGH	BUILDING, MEDIUM	BUILDING, LOW	GROUP of BUILDINGS	TOWER
HUMAN	BICYCLE	CAR	TRAIN	RANGE ●	USE ●

▲ Used in elevation drawings. All other Materials symbols shown are used in plan or section drawings.
● Basic element of the "HAMS" Code (Humanity, Artifacts, Mood, Space).

ARCHITECTURE

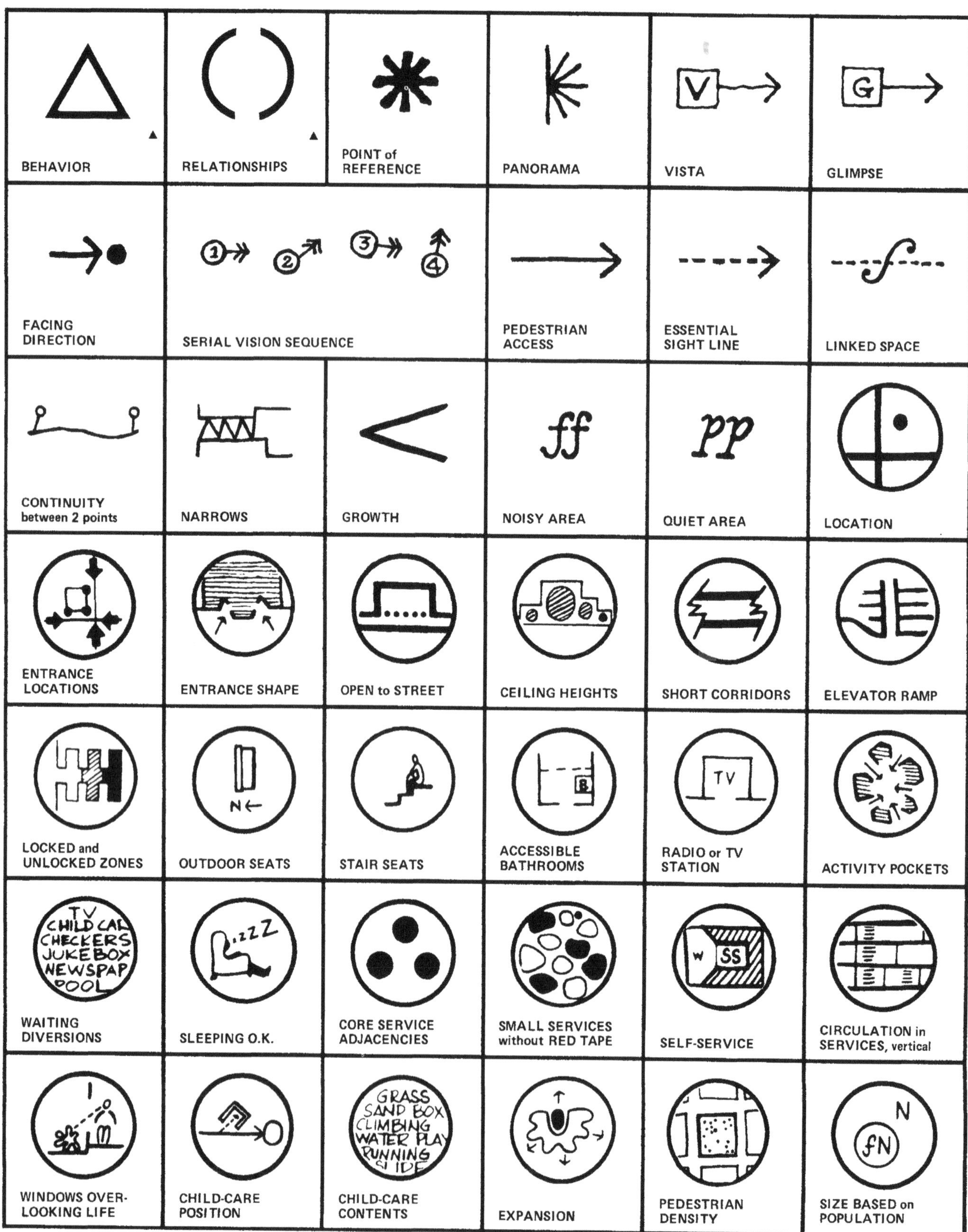
BEHAVIOR ▲
RELATIONSHIPS ▲
POINT of REFERENCE
PANORAMA
V
VISTA
G
GLIMPSE
FACING DIRECTION
1 2 3 4
SERIAL VISION SEQUENCE
PEDESTRIAN ACCESS
ESSENTIAL SIGHT LINE
LINKED SPACE
CONTINUITY between 2 points
NARROWS
GROWTH
ff
NOISY AREA
pp
QUIET AREA
LOCATION
ENTRANCE LOCATIONS
ENTRANCE SHAPE
OPEN to STREET
CEILING HEIGHTS
SHORT CORRIDORS
ELEVATOR RAMP
LOCKED and UNLOCKED ZONES
N←
OUTDOOR SEATS
STAIR SEATS
B
ACCESSIBLE BATHROOMS
TV
RADIO or TV STATION
ACTIVITY POCKETS
TV
CHILD CAR
CHECKERS
JUKEBOX
NEWSPAP
POOL
WAITING DIVERSIONS
zzZ
SLEEPING O.K.
CORE SERVICE ADJACENCIES
SMALL SERVICES without RED TAPE
W
SS
SELF-SERVICE
CIRCULATION in SERVICES, vertical
WINDOWS OVER-LOOKING LIFE
CHILD-CARE POSITION
GRASS
SAND BOX
CLIMBING
WATER PLAY
RUNNING
SLIDE
CHILD-CARE CONTENTS
EXPANSION
PEDESTRIAN DENSITY
N
fN
SIZE BASED on POPULATION

▲ Basic element of the "HAMS" Code (Humanity, Artifacts, Mood, Space).

POOLS of LIGHT	ARENA ENCLOSURE	ALL SERVICES OFF ARENA	ARENA THOROUGHFARE	DISH-SHAPED ARENA	ARENA DIAMETER
ARENA STORAGE	BUILDING Stepped Back from Arena	COMMUNITY WALL	TOWN MEETING	COMMUNITY TERRITORY	COMMUNITY PROJECTS TWO-SIDED
OFFICE FLEXIBILITY	MEETING ROOMS CLUSTERED	SEATS OUTSIDE MEETING ROOMS	WINDOW HEIGHT in Meeting Rooms	SECRETARY'S WORKSPACE	INFORMAL RECEPTION
INTERVIEW BOOTHS	SQUARE SEMINAR ROOMS	FORM-FILLING TABLES	STAFF LOUNGE	SMALL TARGET AREAS	STREET NICHES

PEACE

Controversy surrounds the origin of the ubiquitous peace symbol. It was introduced by pacifist Lord Bertrand Russell during Easter of 1958, when he marched at Aldermaston, England, campaigning for nuclear disarmament.

The most acceptable explanation of the design relates it to the international semaphore alphabet: N (for nuclear), D (for disarmament). These superimposed signals are surrounded by a circle indicating complete, world-wide, or total. Thus, total nuclear disarmament.

So today, this distinctive mark is universally a symbol for peace.

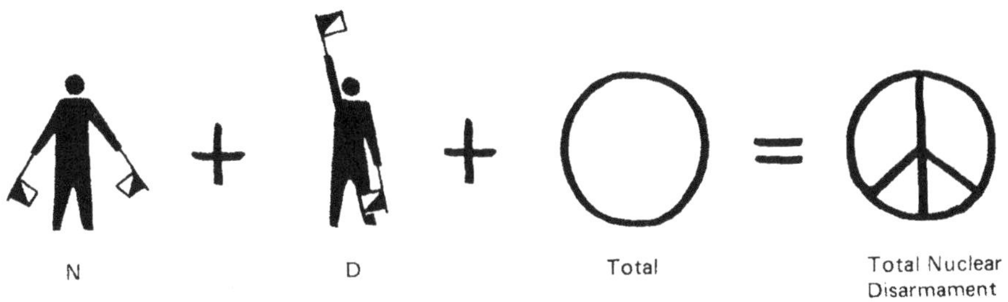
N
D
Total
Total Nuclear Disarmament

ASTRONOMY

SUN	NEW MOON	FIRST QUARTER MOON	FULL MOON	LAST QUARTER MOON	MERCURY
VENUS	EARTH; GLOBULAR CLUSTER	MARS	JUPITER	SATURN	URANUS
NEPTUNE	PLUTO	STAR	COMET	GALACTIC CLUSTER	PLANETARY NEBULA
GALAXY	CONJUNCTION	OPPOSITION	ASCENDING NODE	DESCENDING NODE	ARIES; VERNAL EQUINOX
TAURUS	GEMINI	CANCER	LEO	VIRGO	LIBRA; AUTUMNAL EQUINOX
SCORPIUS	SAGITTARIUS	CAPRICORNUS	AQUARIUS	PISCES	α RIGHT ASCENSION
δ DECLINATION	AU ASTRONOMICAL UNIT	μ PROPER MOTION	π ANNUAL PARALLAX	m APPARENT MAGNITUDE	M ABSOLUTE MAGNITUDE

Note: Stars in a constellations are designated by Greek letters assigned in order of brightness, followed by name of constellation (e.g., α Lyrae designates brightest star in constellation Lyra).

BIOLOGY

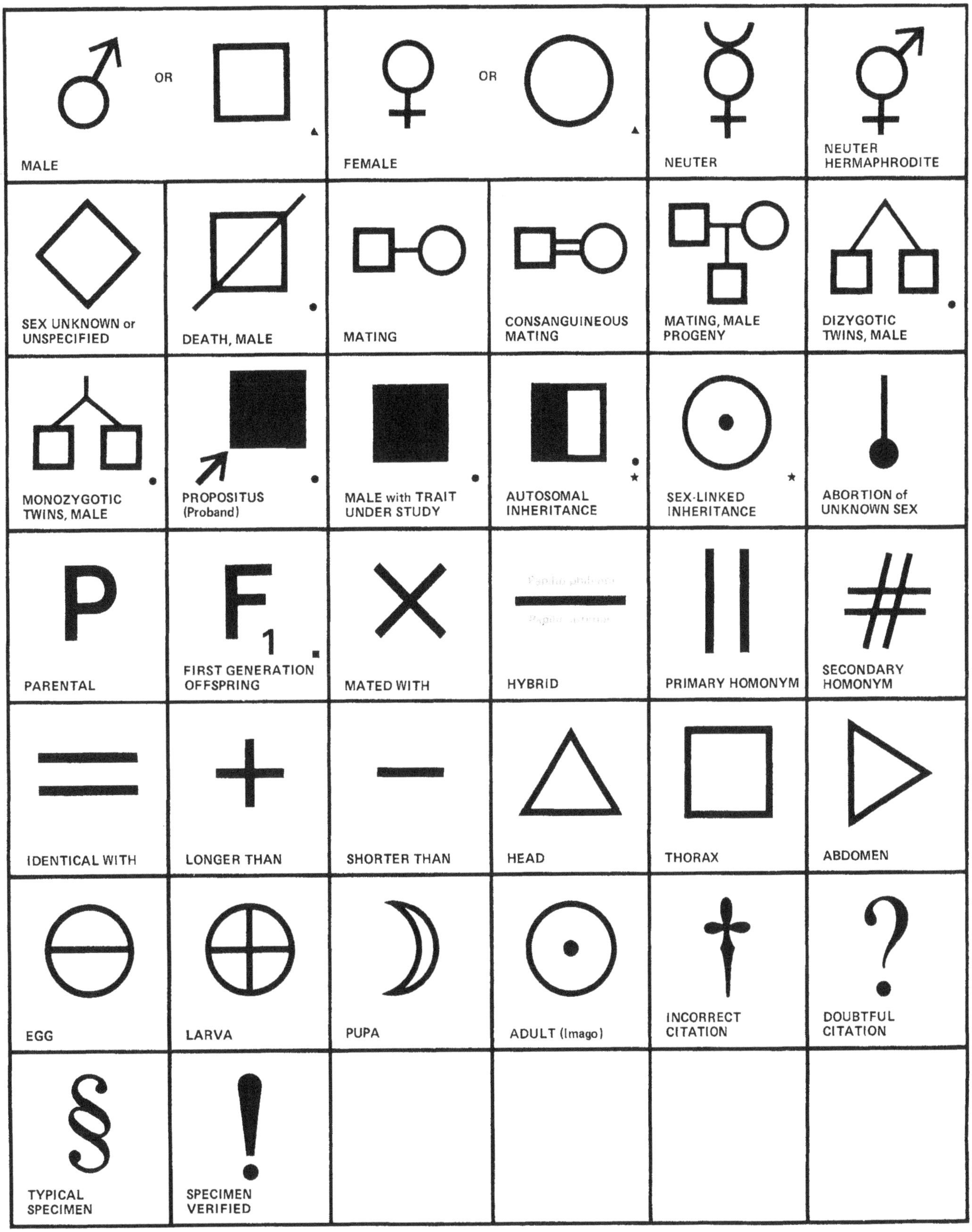

♂ OR ▲ MALE		♀ OR ▲ FEMALE		NEUTER	NEUTER HERMAPHRODITE
SEX UNKNOWN or UNSPECIFIED	● DEATH, MALE	MATING	CONSANGUINEOUS MATING	MATING, MALE PROGENY	● DIZYGOTIC TWINS, MALE
● MONOZYGOTIC TWINS, MALE	● PROPOSITUS (Proband)	● MALE with TRAIT UNDER STUDY	● ★ AUTOSOMAL INHERITANCE	★ SEX-LINKED INHERITANCE	ABORTION of UNKNOWN SEX
P PARENTAL	F_1 ■ FIRST GENERATION OFFSPRING	× MATED WITH	HYBRID	PRIMARY HOMONYM	# SECONDARY HOMONYM
= IDENTICAL WITH	+ LONGER THAN	− SHORTER THAN	HEAD	THORAX	ABDOMEN
EGG	LARVA	PUPA	ADULT (Imago)	INCORRECT CITATION	? DOUBTFUL CITATION
§ TYPICAL SPECIMEN	! SPECIMEN VERIFIED				

▲ A number indicating quantity may be placed within the figure.
● Female indicated when circle (○) is used instead of square (□).
★ Heterozygous recessive.
■ Number in subscript indicates generation. **Example:** F_2 would be second generation.

STAMINATE	OR	PISTILLATE	HERMAPHRODITE (Monoclinous)	DICLINOUS	MONOECIOUS
DIOECIOUS	POLYGAMOUS	ANNUAL ▲	BIENNIAL ▲	PERENNIAL	EVERGREEN
CLIMBING	WINDING to RIGHT	WINDING to LEFT	CLIMBING PLANT	HANGING PLANT	CREEPING PLANT
SWAMP PLANT	WATER PLANT	PLANT with WOODY STEM	SHRUB	TREE	PLANT USEFUL to WILDLIFE
SPORES with MALE NUCLEI	SPORES with FEMALE NUCLEI	CYSTOCARP	TETRASPORANGIA	ACTINOMORPHIC	ZYGOMORPHIC
HYBRID	GRAFT HYBRID	POLYBRID; NUMEROUS	CLONE	MERGED IN	DESCRIBED WELL in this SOURCE
NORTHERN HEMISPHERE	SOUTHERN HEMISPHERE	OLD WORLD	NEW WORLD	SUBGENUS; SECTION	OBSCURE SPECIES

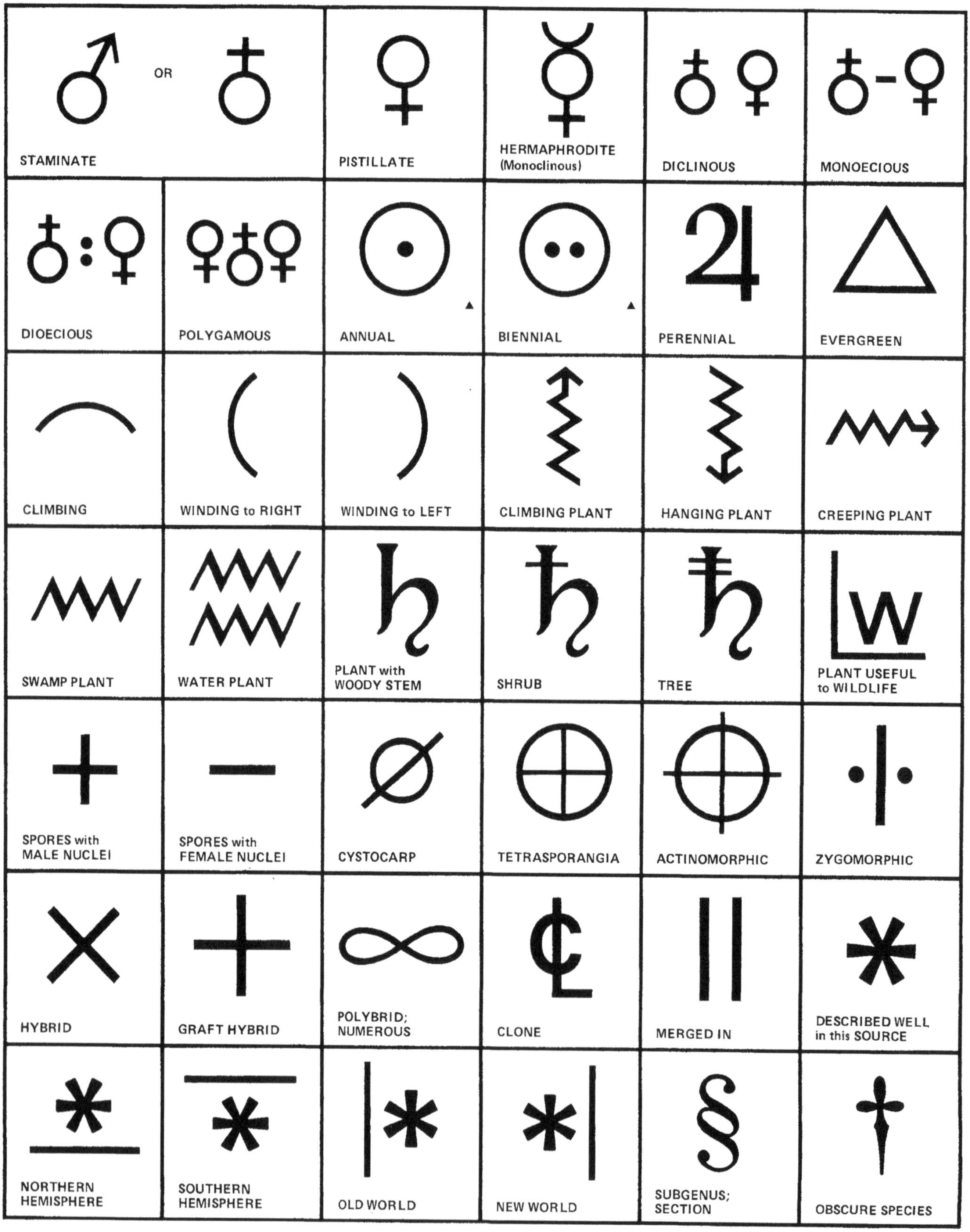

▲ A number may be substituted for dots. **Example:** ① for Annual, ② for Biennial.

CYS (C)	CYSTEINE
HIS (H)	HISTIDINE
ILE (I)	ISOLEUCINE
MET (M)	METHIONINE
SER (S)	SERINE
VAL (V)	VALINE
ALA (A)	ALANINE
GLY (G)	GLYCINE
LEU (L)	LEUCINE
PRO (P)	PROLINE
THR (T)	THREONINE
PHE (F)	PHENYLALANINE
ARG (R)	ARGININE
TYR (Y)	TYROSINE
TRP (W)	TRYPTOPHAN

ASP (D)	ASPARTIC ACID
ASN (N)	ASPARAGINE
GLU (E)	GLUTAMIC ACID
GLN (Q)	GLUTAMINE
LYS (K)	LYSINE
X (X)	UNDETERMINED or ATYPICAL AMINO ACID
RNA	RIBONUCLEIC ACID
DNA	DEOXYRIBONUCLEIC ACID
$S^{\circ}_{20,w}$	SEDIMENTATION COEFFICIENT
$[\alpha]_{\lambda}$	SPECIFIC ROTATION
$[\eta]$	INTRINSIC VISCOSITY
Π	OSMOTIC PRESSURE

pH	NEGATIVE LOGARITHM OF HYDROGEN ION CONCENTRATION
$\sim P$	HIGH ENERGY PHOSPHATE BOND
$\bar{v}$	PARTIAL SPECIFIC VOLUME
$\bar{M}_n$	NUMBER AVERAGE MOLECULAR WEIGHT
$\bar{M}_w$	WEIGHT AVERAGE MOLECULAR WEIGHT
$\bar{M}_z$	z AVERAGE MOLECULAR WEIGHT
γ	ACTIVITY COEFFICIENT
ϵ	MOLAR EXTINCTION COEFFICIENT
$\frac{\Gamma}{2}$	IONIC STRENGTH

OUR FRAGILE CRAFT

Adlai Stevenson said, "We travel together, passengers on a little spaceship; dependent on its vulnerable reserves of air and soil; all committed for our safety to its security and peace; preserved from annihilation only by the care, the work and . . . the love we give our fragile craft."

Today the whole world is concerned with the air we breathe, the water we drink, and what is happening to the flora and fauna that still survive.

At no other time has there been so concentrated an effort to protect our birthrights. A symbol for ecology has evolved: a circle, signifying wholeness, surrounded by an ellipse, indicating unity.

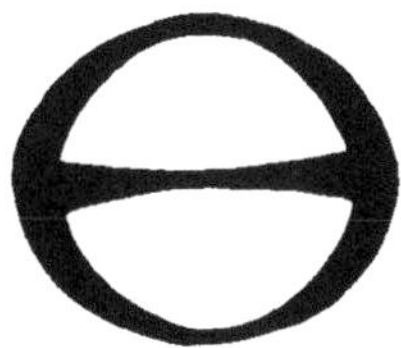

Additional symbols have been proposed to spotlight specifics, and these show the dangers we must control if we are to preserve the world in which we live.

Recycling

Noise

Air

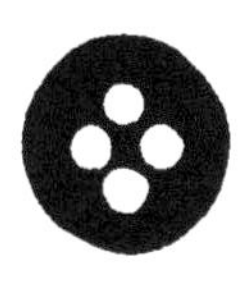

Population

Water

Land

BUSINESS

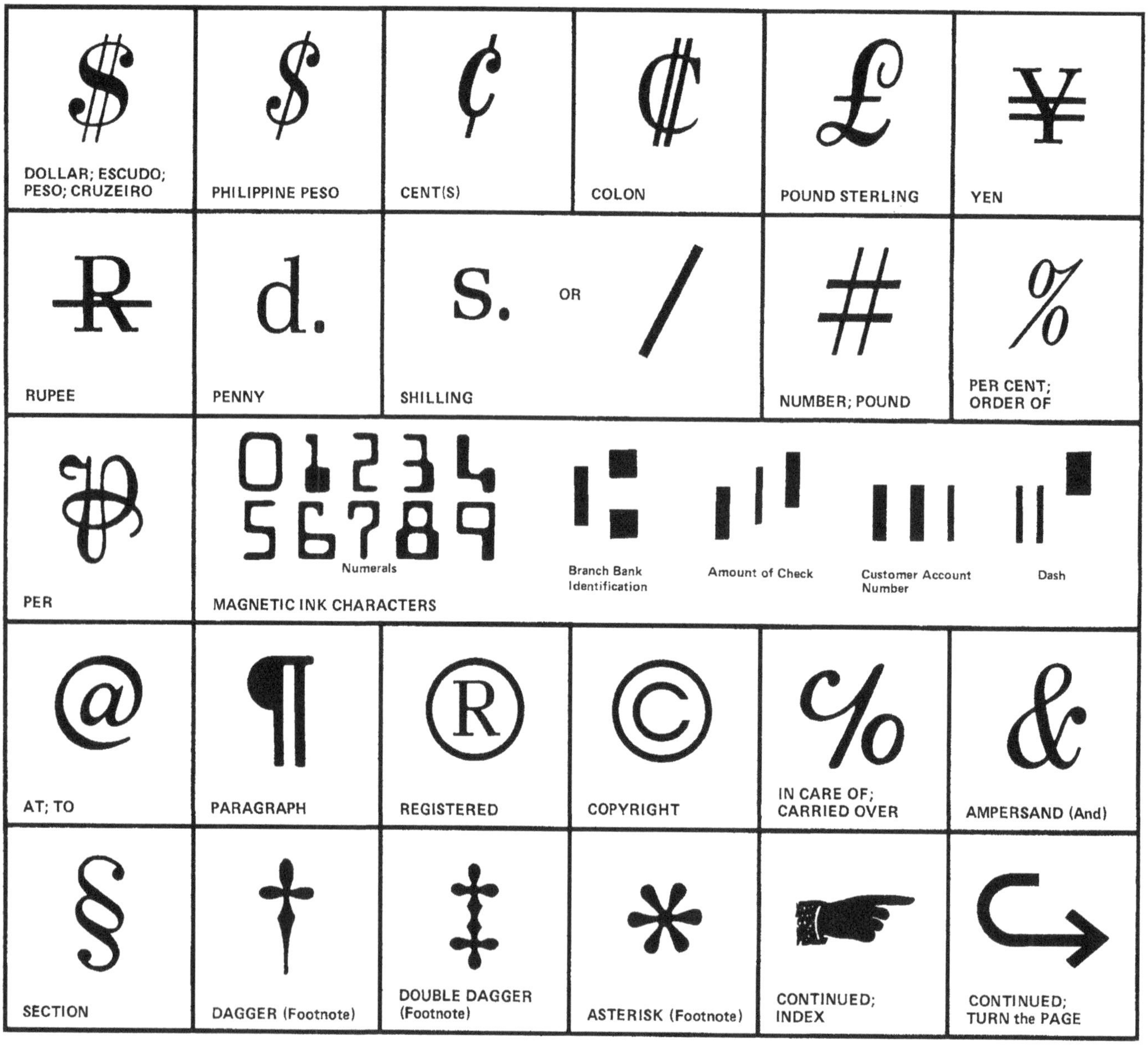

DOLLAR; ESCUDO; PESO; CRUZEIRO	PHILIPPINE PESO	CENT(S)	COLON	POUND STERLING	YEN
RUPEE	PENNY	SHILLING (OR)		NUMBER; POUND	PER CENT; ORDER OF
PER	MAGNETIC INK CHARACTERS: Numerals; Branch Bank Identification; Amount of Check; Customer Account Number; Dash				
AT; TO	PARAGRAPH	REGISTERED	COPYRIGHT	IN CARE OF; CARRIED OVER	AMPERSAND (And)
SECTION	DAGGER (Footnote)	DOUBLE DAGGER (Footnote)	ASTERISK (Footnote)	CONTINUED; INDEX	CONTINUED; TURN the PAGE

Computers

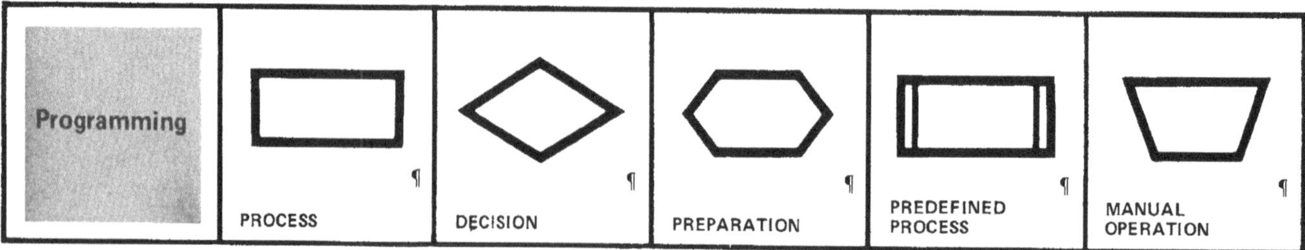

Programming
PROCESS ¶
DECISION ¶
PREPARATION ¶
PREDEFINED PROCESS ¶
MANUAL OPERATION ¶

¶ ISO Recommendation

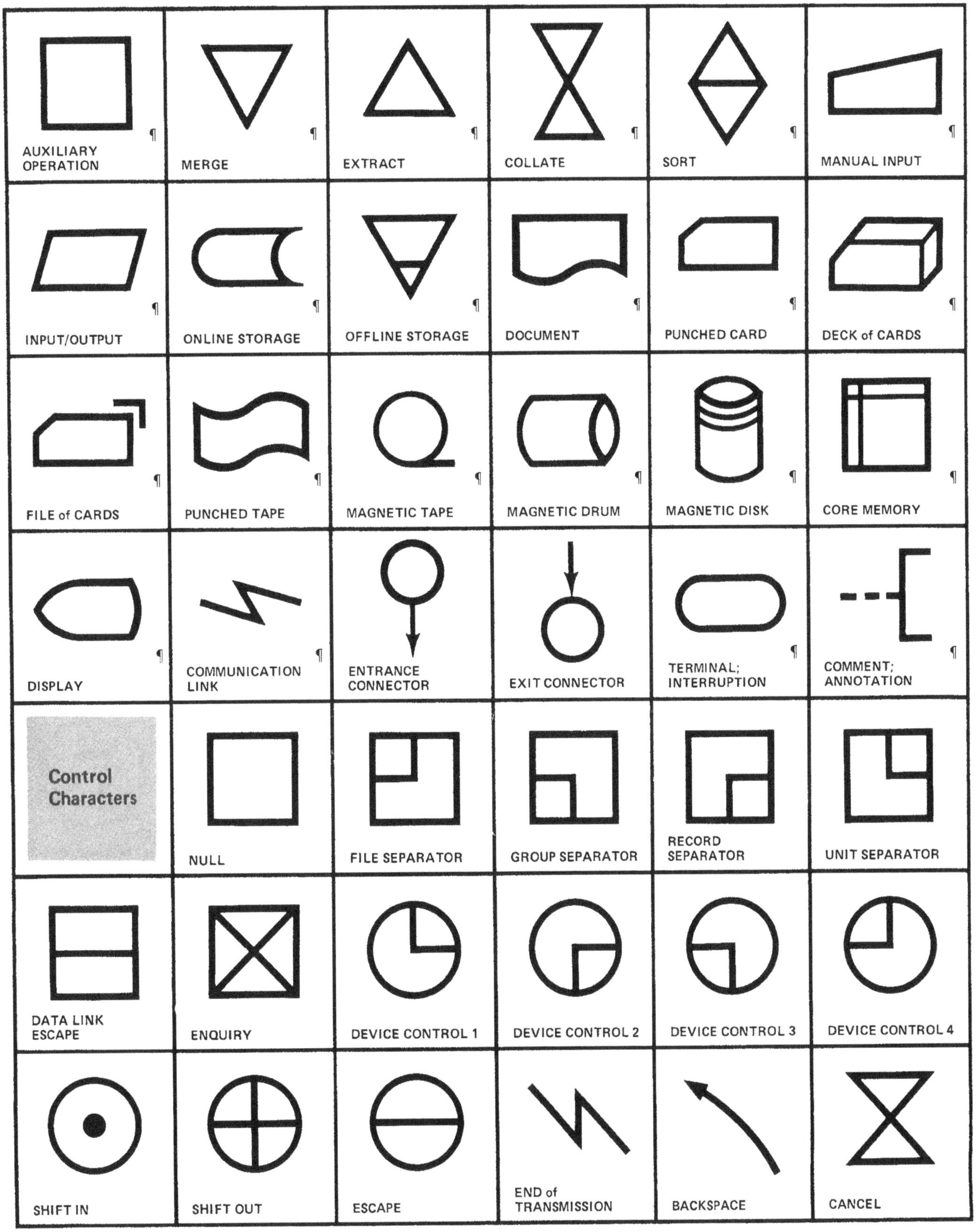

AUXILIARY OPERATION ¶	MERGE ¶	EXTRACT ¶	COLLATE ¶	SORT ¶	MANUAL INPUT ¶
INPUT/OUTPUT ¶	ONLINE STORAGE ¶	OFFLINE STORAGE ¶	DOCUMENT ¶	PUNCHED CARD ¶	DECK of CARDS ¶
FILE of CARDS ¶	PUNCHED TAPE ¶	MAGNETIC TAPE ¶	MAGNETIC DRUM ¶	MAGNETIC DISK ¶	CORE MEMORY ¶
DISPLAY ¶	COMMUNICATION LINK ¶	ENTRANCE CONNECTOR	EXIT CONNECTOR	TERMINAL; INTERRUPTION ¶	COMMENT; ANNOTATION ¶
Control Characters	NULL	FILE SEPARATOR	GROUP SEPARATOR	RECORD SEPARATOR	UNIT SEPARATOR
DATA LINK ESCAPE	ENQUIRY	DEVICE CONTROL 1	DEVICE CONTROL 2	DEVICE CONTROL 3	DEVICE CONTROL 4
SHIFT IN	SHIFT OUT	ESCAPE	END of TRANSMISSION	BACKSPACE	CANCEL

¶ ISO Recommendation

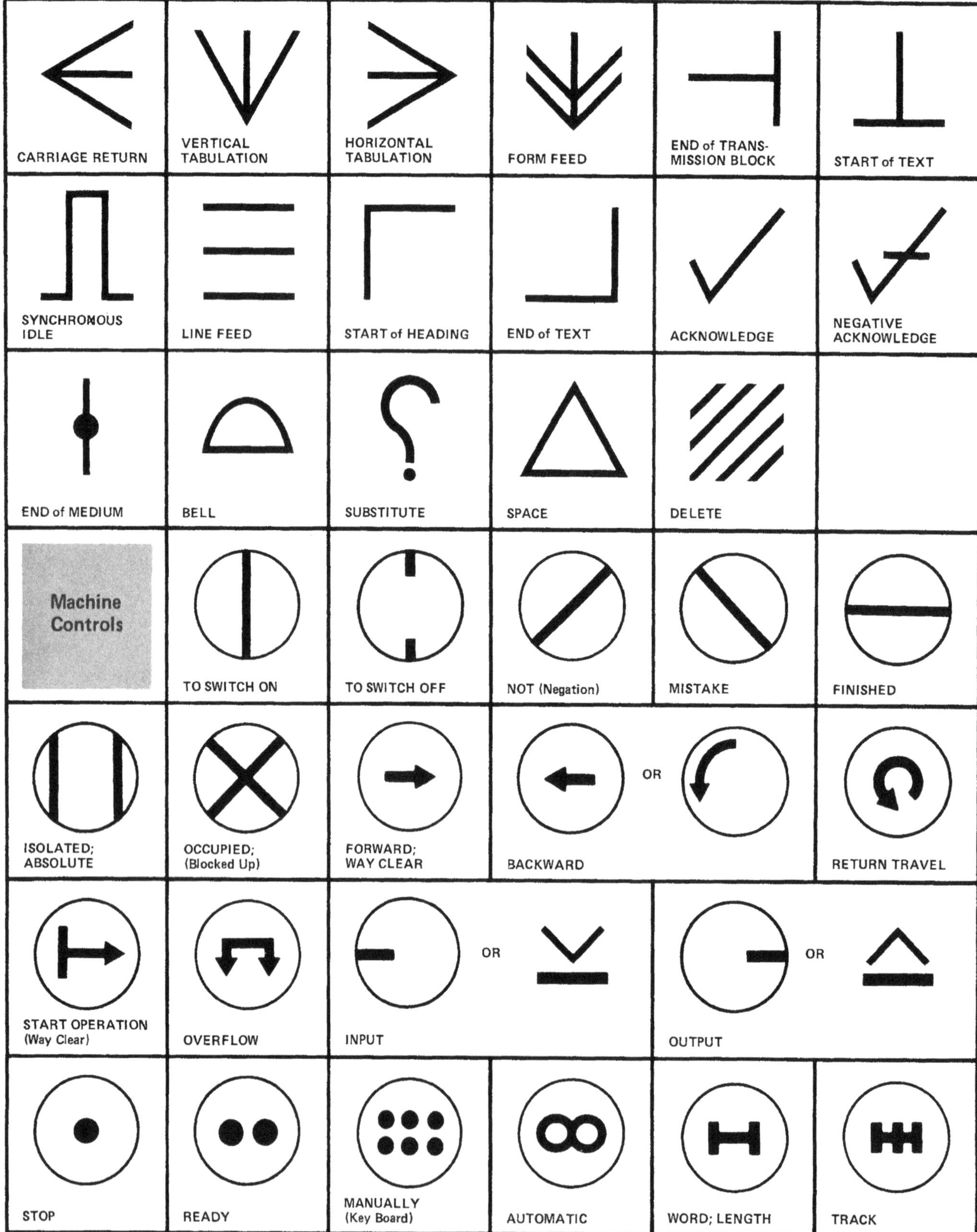
CARRIAGE RETURN
VERTICAL TABULATION
HORIZONTAL TABULATION
FORM FEED
END of TRANS-MISSION BLOCK
START of TEXT
SYNCHRONOUS IDLE
LINE FEED
START of HEADING
END of TEXT
ACKNOWLEDGE
NEGATIVE ACKNOWLEDGE
END of MEDIUM
BELL
SUBSTITUTE
SPACE
DELETE
Machine Controls
TO SWITCH ON
TO SWITCH OFF
NOT (Negation)
MISTAKE
FINISHED
ISOLATED; ABSOLUTE
OCCUPIED; (Blocked Up)
FORWARD; WAY CLEAR
OR
BACKWARD
RETURN TRAVEL
START OPERATION (Way Clear)
OVERFLOW
OR
INPUT
OR
OUTPUT
STOP
READY
MANUALLY (Key Board)
AUTOMATIC
WORD; LENGTH
TRACK

Note: The enclosing figure (usually a circle) is not part of the symbol but is used to contain the symbol and indicate scale.

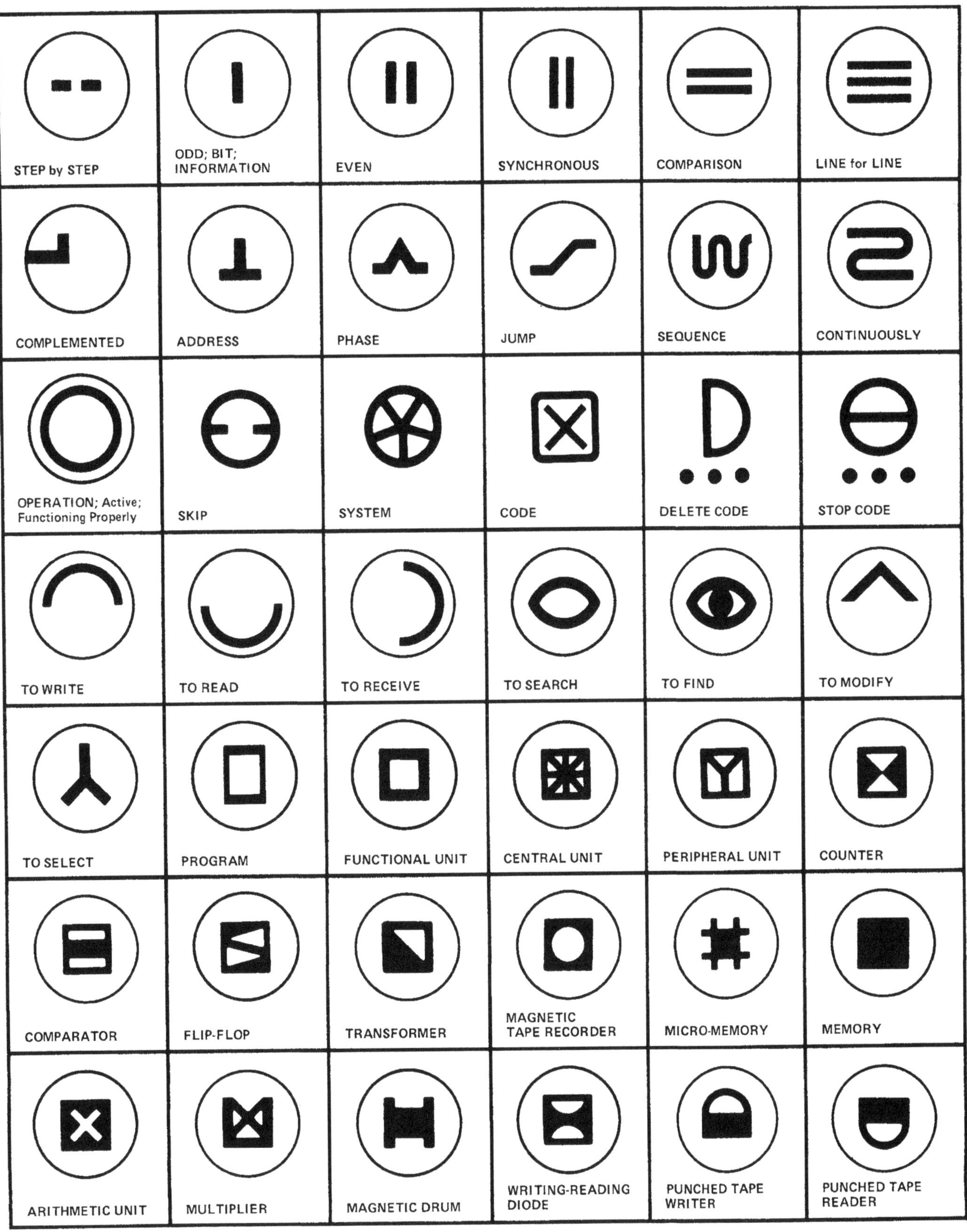

STEP by STEP
ODD; BIT; INFORMATION
EVEN
SYNCHRONOUS
COMPARISON
LINE for LINE
COMPLEMENTED
ADDRESS
PHASE
JUMP
SEQUENCE
CONTINUOUSLY
OPERATION; Active; Functioning Properly
SKIP
SYSTEM
CODE
DELETE CODE
STOP CODE
TO WRITE
TO READ
TO RECEIVE
TO SEARCH
TO FIND
TO MODIFY
TO SELECT
PROGRAM
FUNCTIONAL UNIT
CENTRAL UNIT
PERIPHERAL UNIT
COUNTER
COMPARATOR
FLIP-FLOP
TRANSFORMER
MAGNETIC TAPE RECORDER
MICRO-MEMORY
MEMORY
ARITHMETIC UNIT
MULTIPLIER
MAGNETIC DRUM
WRITING-READING DIODE
PUNCHED TAPE WRITER
PUNCHED TAPE READER

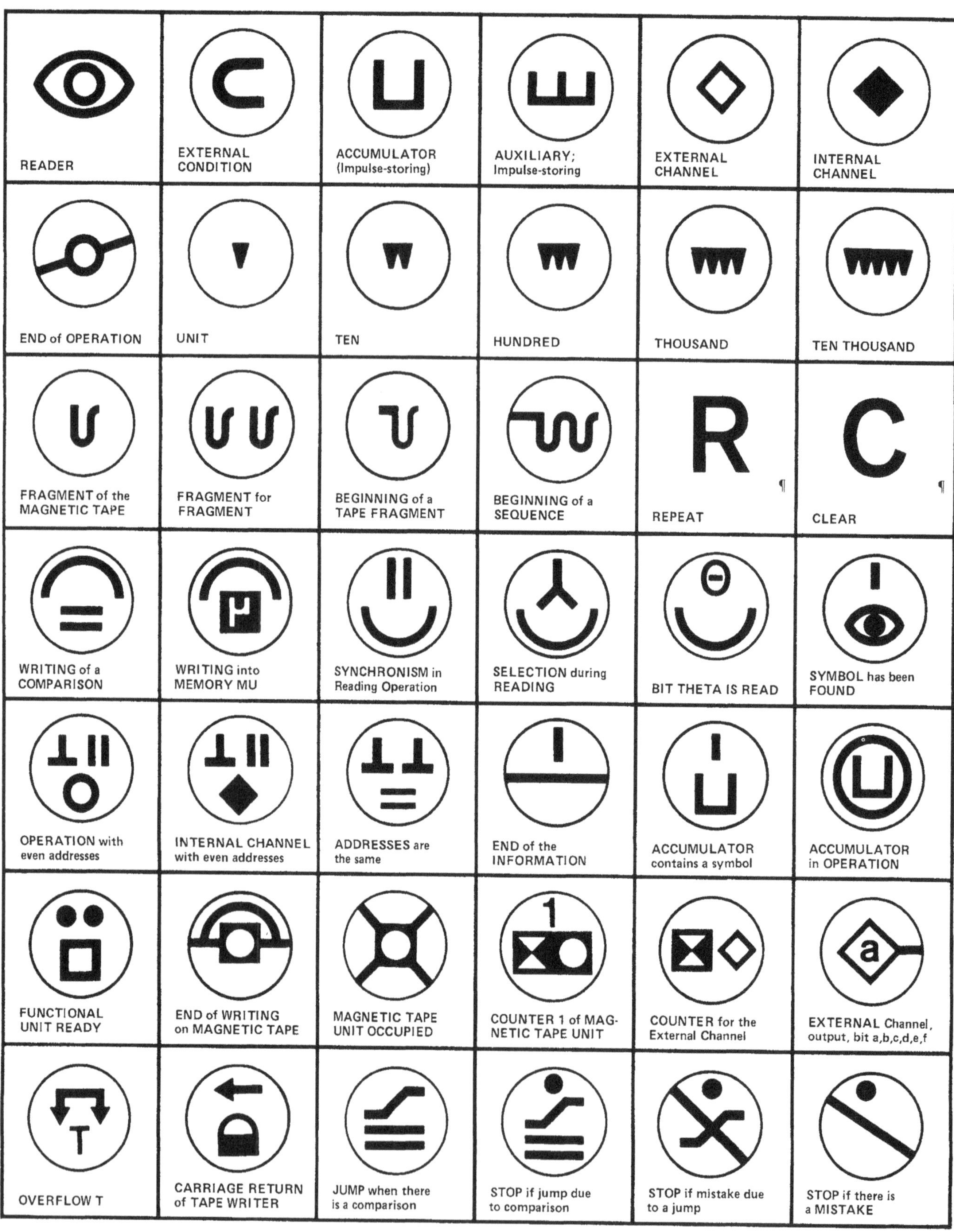
READER
EXTERNAL CONDITION
ACCUMULATOR (Impulse-storing)
AUXILIARY; Impulse-storing
EXTERNAL CHANNEL
INTERNAL CHANNEL
END of OPERATION
UNIT
TEN
HUNDRED
THOUSAND
TEN THOUSAND
FRAGMENT of the MAGNETIC TAPE
FRAGMENT for FRAGMENT
BEGINNING of a TAPE FRAGMENT
BEGINNING of a SEQUENCE
R
¶
REPEAT
C
¶
CLEAR
WRITING of a COMPARISON
μ
WRITING into MEMORY MU
SYNCHRONISM in Reading Operation
SELECTION during READING
BIT THETA IS READ
SYMBOL has been FOUND
OPERATION with even addresses
INTERNAL CHANNEL with even addresses
ADDRESSES are the same
END of the INFORMATION
ACCUMULATOR contains a symbol
ACCUMULATOR in OPERATION
FUNCTIONAL UNIT READY
END of WRITING on MAGNETIC TAPE
MAGNETIC TAPE UNIT OCCUPIED
1
COUNTER 1 of MAGNETIC TAPE UNIT
COUNTER for the External Channel
a
EXTERNAL Channel, output, bit a,b,c,d,e,f
T
OVERFLOW T
CARRIAGE RETURN of TAPE WRITER
JUMP when there is a comparison
STOP if jump due to comparison
STOP if mistake due to a jump
STOP if there is a MISTAKE

¶ ISO Recommendation

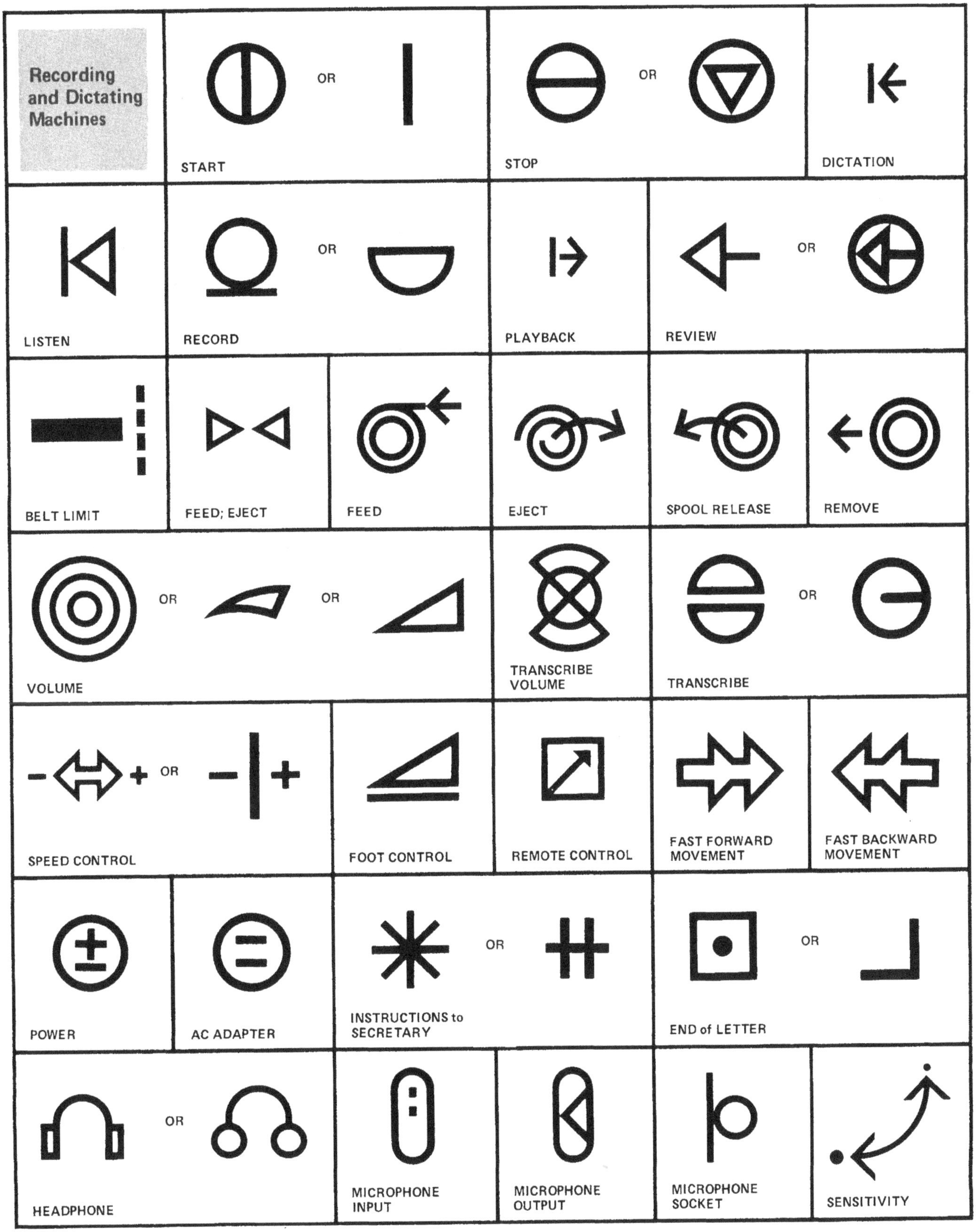

Recording and Dictating Machines	START (OR)	STOP (OR)	DICTATION
LISTEN	RECORD (OR)	PLAYBACK	REVIEW (OR)

BELT LIMIT	FEED; EJECT	FEED	EJECT	SPOOL RELEASE	REMOVE
VOLUME (OR, OR)			TRANSCRIBE VOLUME	TRANSCRIBE (OR)	
SPEED CONTROL (OR)		FOOT CONTROL	REMOTE CONTROL	FAST FORWARD MOVEMENT	FAST BACKWARD MOVEMENT
POWER	AC ADAPTER	INSTRUCTIONS to SECRETARY (OR)		END of LETTER (OR)	
HEADPHONE (OR)		MICROPHONE INPUT	MICROPHONE OUTPUT	MICROPHONE SOCKET	SENSITIVITY

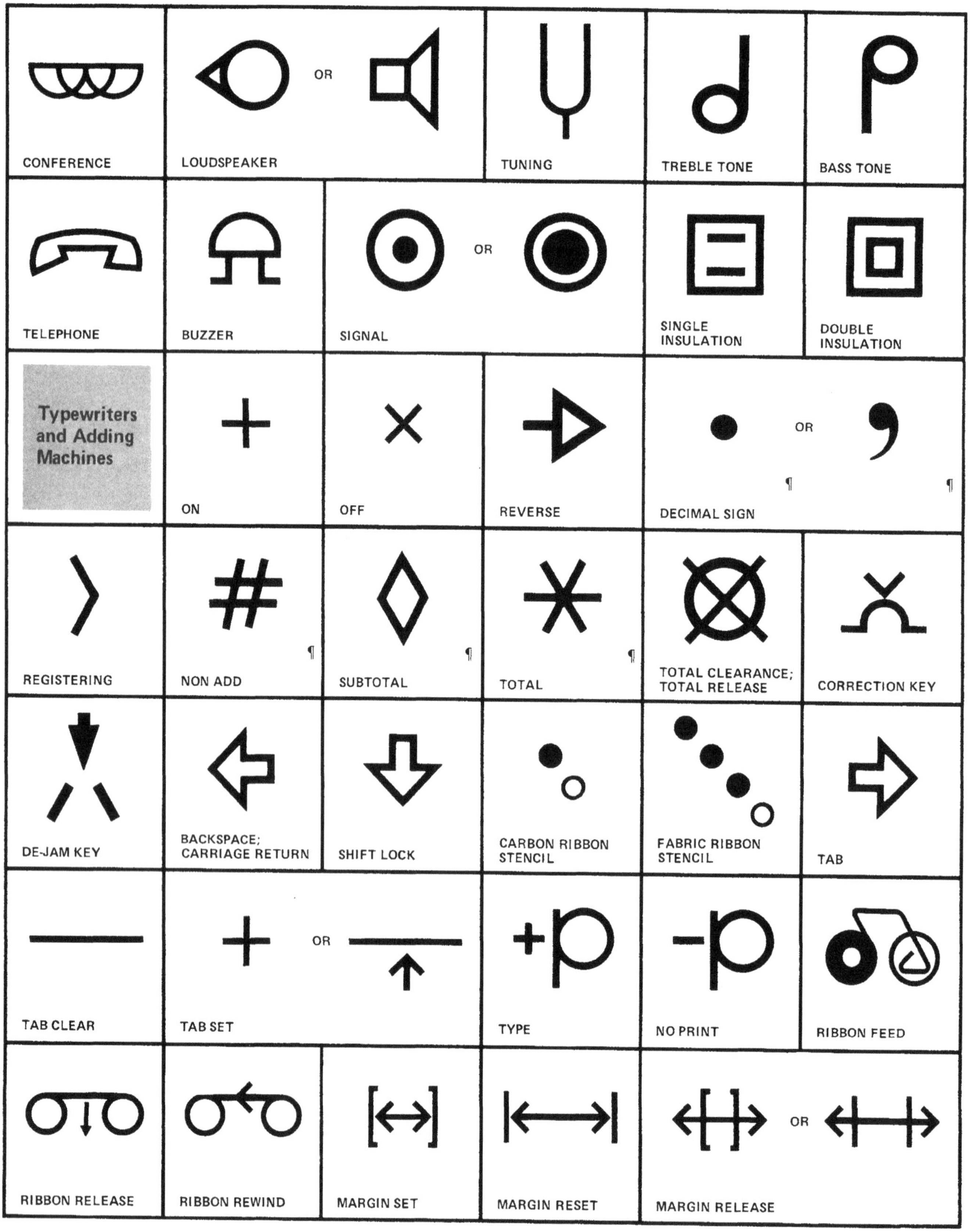

CONFERENCE	LOUDSPEAKER (OR)		TUNING	TREBLE TONE	BASS TONE
TELEPHONE	BUZZER	SIGNAL (OR)		SINGLE INSULATION	DOUBLE INSULATION
Typewriters and Adding Machines	ON	OFF	REVERSE	DECIMAL SIGN ¶ (OR) ¶	
REGISTERING	NON ADD ¶	SUBTOTAL ¶	TOTAL ¶	TOTAL CLEARANCE; TOTAL RELEASE	CORRECTION KEY
DE-JAM KEY	BACKSPACE; CARRIAGE RETURN	SHIFT LOCK	CARBON RIBBON STENCIL	FABRIC RIBBON STENCIL	TAB
TAB CLEAR	TAB SET (OR)		TYPE	NO PRINT	RIBBON FEED
RIBBON RELEASE	RIBBON REWIND	MARGIN SET	MARGIN RESET	MARGIN RELEASE (OR)	

¶ ISO Recommendation

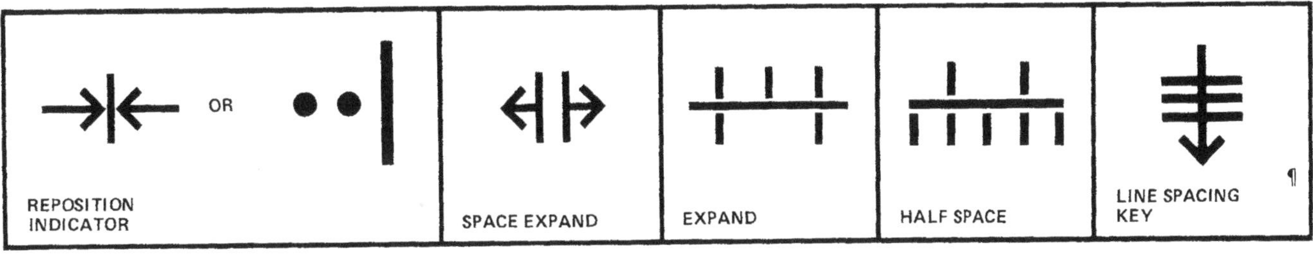

OR
REPOSITION INDICATOR
SPACE EXPAND
EXPAND
HALF SPACE
LINE SPACING KEY
¶

Shops and Services

BARBER (OR)		BEAUTY PARLOR	PHARMACY (OR … OR)		
MARKET; GROCERY (OR)		WINE and LIQUOR	TOBACCO	BOOK STALL (OR)	
PAWN SHOP (OR)		MECHANIC	CAR WASH	AUTOMOTIVE SERVICE	SUNDRIES
GIFT SHOP; SHOPPING CENTER	FLORIST	RECORD SHOP	CAMERA STORE	CANDY STORE	SNACK BAR
STATIONERY	PATTERNS	YARDAGE	NOTIONS	SEWING MACHINES	RAINGEAR

¶ ISO Recommendation

HARDWARE	ELECTRICAL SUPPLY	TELEVISION	LUGGAGE	COSMETICS	WATCHES
INDOOR GAMES	SILVERWARE	GLASSWARE	KITCHENWARE	BABY CLOTHES	GIRLS' CLOTHING
MEN'S SUITS	WOMEN'S WEAR	MEN'S WORK CLOTHES	MEN'S SWEATERS	MEN'S SHIRTS	LINGERIE
HOSIERY	SOCKS	LADIES' SHOES	MEN'S SHOES	HEADGEAR	GLOVES
STROLLER AREA	LUGGAGE LOCKER	STROLLER and LUGGAGE AREA			

SICHI

The Western world is indebted to the Medicis, that great money-lending family, for the crest from which we have borrowed the three golden balls that hang outside our pawnshops. But it took considerable digging to trace the origin of the very different pawn broker sign familiar to all Japanese.

When read in Japanese, the oriental calligraphy character indicating a pawnshop is pronounced "sichi," which also means "seven." Therefore the sign, a stylized 7, stands for pawnshop.

However, a Japanese friend tells me that his countrymen are embarrassed to mention a need for the sichi, so they refer to it as the "6 + 1 Bank."

CHEMISTRY

Elements

Ac	ACTINIUM	Co	COBALT	In	INDIUM	Os	OSMIUM	Sm	SAMARIUM
Ag	SILVER	Cr	CHROMIUM	Ir	IRIDIUM	P	PHOSPHORUS	Sn	TIN
Al	ALUMINUM	Cs	CESIUM	K	POTASSIUM	Pa	PROTACTINIUM	Sr	STRONTIUM
Am	AMERICIUM	Cu	COPPER	Kr	KRYPTON	Pb	LEAD	Ta	TANTALUM
Ar	ARGON	Dy	DYSPROSIUM	La	LANTHANUM	Pd	PALLADIUM	Tb	TERBIUM
As	ARSENIC	Er	ERBIUM	Li	LITHIUM	Pm	PROMETHIUM	Tc	TECHNETIUM
At	ASTATINE	Es	EINSTEINIUM	Lu	LUTETIUM	Po	POLONIUM	Te	TELLURIUM
Au	GOLD	Eu	EUROPIUM	Lr	LAWRENCIUM	Pr	PRASEODYMIUM	Th	THORIUM
B	BORON	F	FLUORINE	Md	MENDELEVIUM	Pt	PLATINUM	Ti	TITANIUM
Ba	BARIUM	Fe	IRON	Mg	MAGNESIUM	Pu	PLUTONIUM	Tl	THALLIUM
Be	BERYLLIUM	Fm	FERMIUM	Mn	MANGANESE	Ra	RADIUM	Tm	THULIUM
Bi	BISMUTH	Fr	FRANCIUM	Mo	MOLYBDENUM	Rb	RUBIDIUM	U	URANIUM
Bk	BERKELIUM	Ga	GALLIUM	N	NITROGEN	Re	RHENIUM	V	VANADIUM
Br	BROMINE	Gd	GADOLINIUM	Na	SODIUM	Rh	RHODIUM	W	TUNGSTEN
C	CARBON	Ge	GERMANIUM	Nb	NIOBIUM	Rn	RADON	Xe	XENON
Ca	CALCIUM	H	HYDROGEN	Nd	NEODYMIUM	Ru	RUTHENIUM	Y	YTTRIUM
Cd	CADMIUM	He	HELIUM	Ne	NEON	S	SULFUR	Yb	YTTERBIUM
Ce	CERIUM	Hf	HAFNIUM	Ni	NICKEL	Sb	ANTIMONY	Zn	ZINC
Cf	CALIFORNIUM	Hg	MERCURY	No	NOBELIUM	Sc	SCANDIUM	Zr	ZIRCONIUM
Cl	CHLORINE	Ho	HOLMIUM	Np	NEPTUNIUM	Se	SELENIUM		
Cm	CURIUM	I	IODINE	O	OXYGEN	Si	SILICON		

→	REACTION DIRECTION
⇄	REVERSIBLE REACTION
↑	GAS EXPELLED
↓	PRECIPITATION
△	APPLY HEAT
↻	ROTATION about the BOND
+ ▲	POSITIVE CHARGE
− ▲	NEGATIVE CHARGE
Mass Number 32, Ionization State 2+, Atomic Number 16, Atoms per Molecule 2: $^{32}_{16}S^{2+}_{2}$	NUCLIDE
Fe II	INDICATION of DIVALENCY
NO*	ELECTRONIC EXCITED STATE
$[NO_2]$	MOLAR CONCENTRATION
Solid Electrode (Anode), Ions in Solution, Solid Electrode (Cathode), Barriers: $Zn \mid Zn^{2+} \mid Cu^{2+} \mid Cu$ ●	ELECTROMOTIVE CELL (Battery)
Incoming Nuclide, Incoming Specie, Outgoing Specie, Outgoing Nuclide: N(n,p)C	NUCLEAR REACTION

▲ Progression is shown by adding number to basic symbol. **Example:** 2 +, 3 +; 2 -, 3 -, etc.
● When center barrier is double (II), means Idealized Reversible Cell.

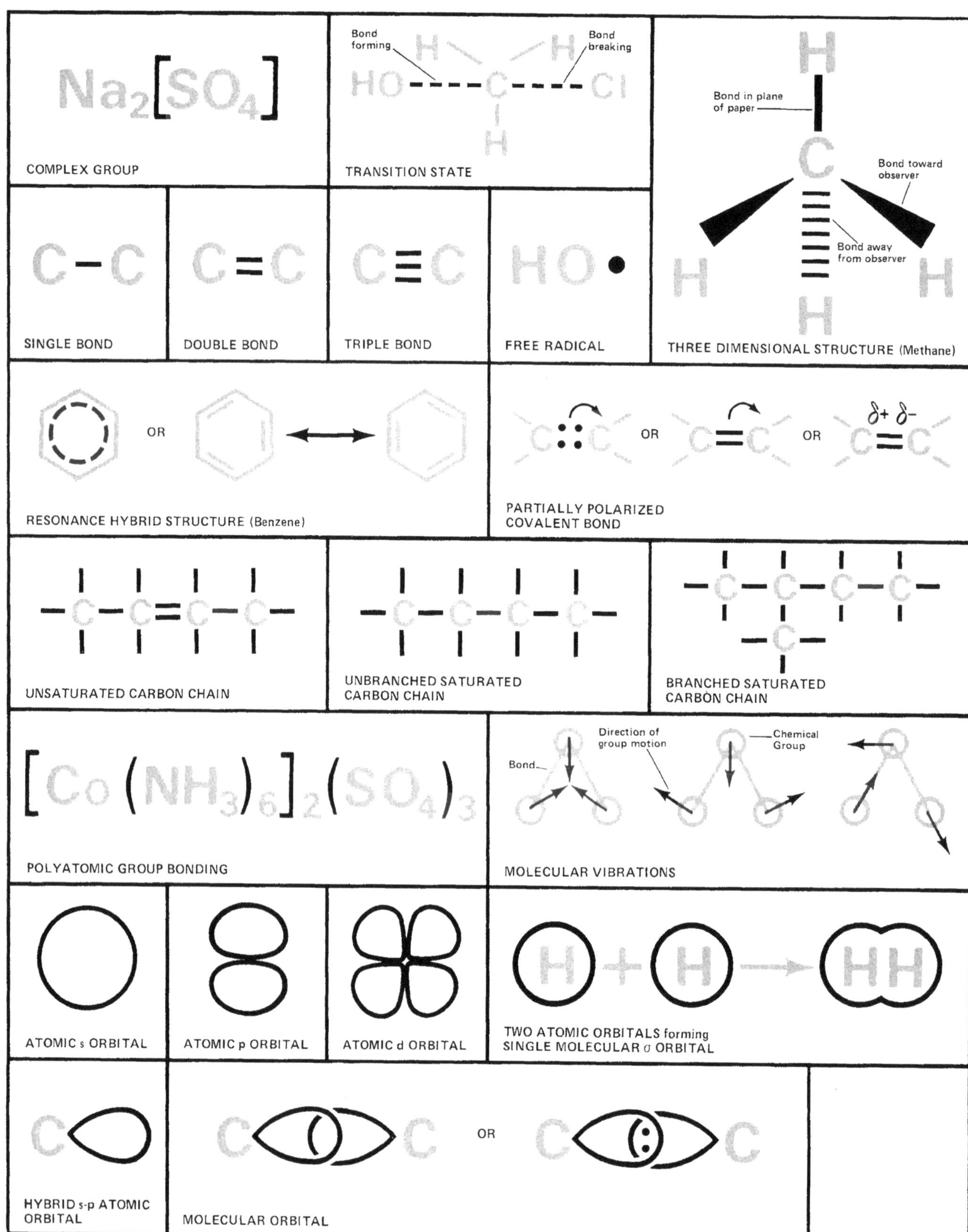

$Na_2[SO_4]$
COMPLEX GROUP
Bond forming
Bond breaking
HO- - - -C- - - -Cl
TRANSITION STATE
Bond in plane of paper
Bond toward observer
Bond away from observer
THREE DIMENSIONAL STRUCTURE (Methane)
C–C
SINGLE BOND
C=C
DOUBLE BOND
C≡C
TRIPLE BOND
HO•
FREE RADICAL
OR
RESONANCE HYBRID STRUCTURE (Benzene)
OR
OR
δ+ δ−
PARTIALLY POLARIZED COVALENT BOND
UNSATURATED CARBON CHAIN
UNBRANCHED SATURATED CARBON CHAIN
BRANCHED SATURATED CARBON CHAIN
$[Co(NH_3)_6]_2(SO_4)_3$
POLYATOMIC GROUP BONDING
Bond
Direction of group motion
Chemical Group
MOLECULAR VIBRATIONS
ATOMIC s ORBITAL
ATOMIC p ORBITAL
ATOMIC d ORBITAL
H + H → HH
TWO ATOMIC ORBITALS forming SINGLE MOLECULAR σ ORBITAL
HYBRID s-p ATOMIC ORBITAL
OR
MOLECULAR ORBITAL

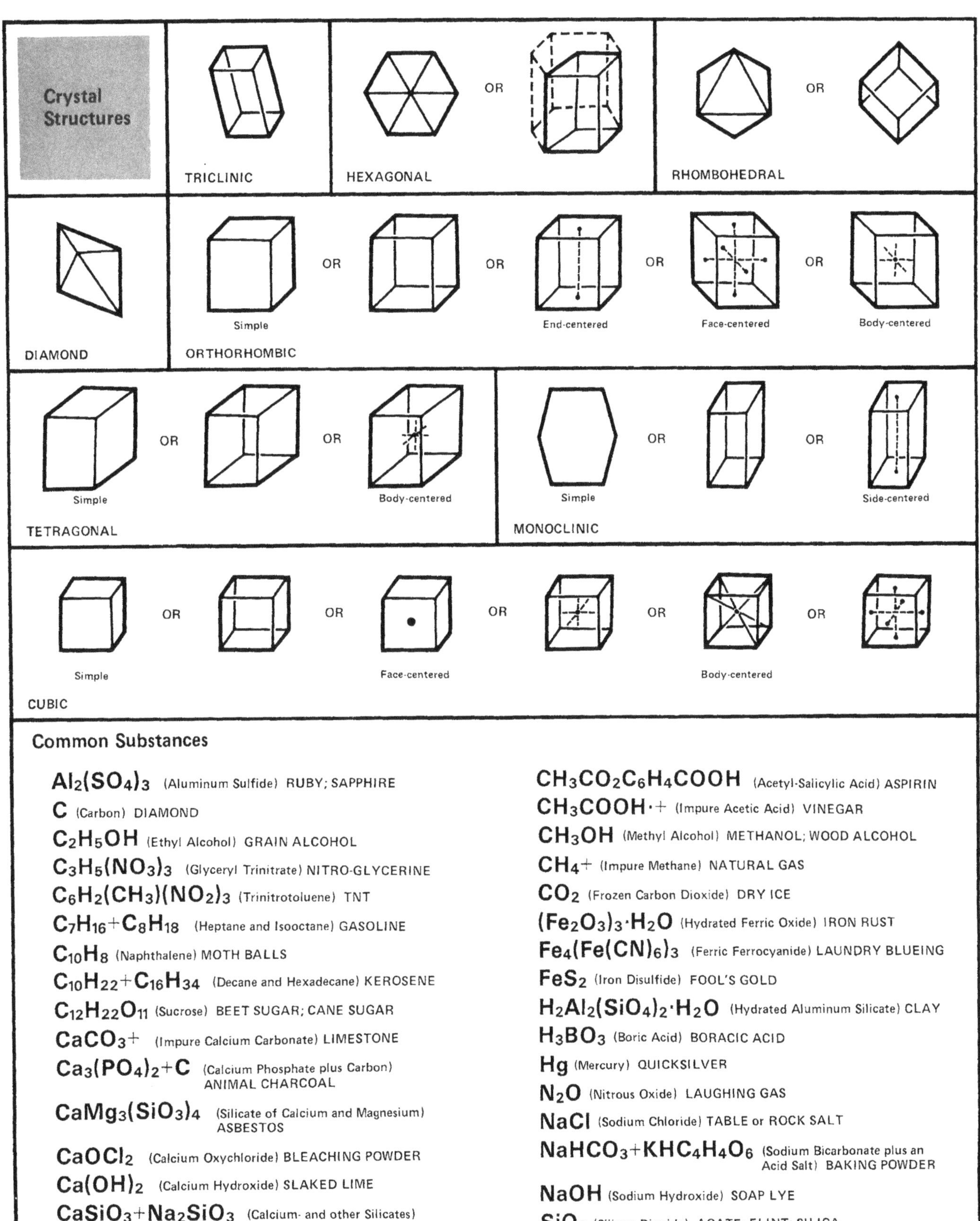
Crystal Structures
TRICLINIC
OR
HEXAGONAL
OR
RHOMBOHEDRAL
DIAMOND
OR
OR
OR
OR
Simple
End-centered
Face-centered
Body-centered
ORTHORHOMBIC
OR
OR
Simple
Body-centered
TETRAGONAL
OR
OR
Simple
Side-centered
MONOCLINIC
OR
OR
OR
OR
OR
Simple
Face-centered
Body-centered
CUBIC

Common Substances

$Al_2(SO_4)_3$ (Aluminum Sulfide) RUBY; SAPPHIRE

C (Carbon) DIAMOND

C_2H_5OH (Ethyl Alcohol) GRAIN ALCOHOL

$C_3H_5(NO_3)_3$ (Glyceryl Trinitrate) NITRO-GLYCERINE

$C_6H_2(CH_3)(NO_2)_3$ (Trinitrotoluene) TNT

$C_7H_{16}+C_8H_{18}$ (Heptane and Isooctane) GASOLINE

$C_{10}H_8$ (Naphthalene) MOTH BALLS

$C_{10}H_{22}+C_{16}H_{34}$ (Decane and Hexadecane) KEROSENE

$C_{12}H_{22}O_{11}$ (Sucrose) BEET SUGAR; CANE SUGAR

$CaCO_3+$ (Impure Calcium Carbonate) LIMESTONE

$Ca_3(PO_4)_2+C$ (Calcium Phosphate plus Carbon) ANIMAL CHARCOAL

$CaMg_3(SiO_3)_4$ (Silicate of Calcium and Magnesium) ASBESTOS

$CaOCl_2$ (Calcium Oxychloride) BLEACHING POWDER

$Ca(OH)_2$ (Calcium Hydroxide) SLAKED LIME

$CaSiO_3+Na_2SiO_3$ (Calcium- and other Silicates) COMMON GLASS

$CH_3CO_2C_6H_4COOH$ (Acetyl-Salicylic Acid) ASPIRIN

$CH_3COOH\cdot+$ (Impure Acetic Acid) VINEGAR

CH_3OH (Methyl Alcohol) METHANOL; WOOD ALCOHOL

CH_4+ (Impure Methane) NATURAL GAS

CO_2 (Frozen Carbon Dioxide) DRY ICE

$(Fe_2O_3)_3\cdot H_2O$ (Hydrated Ferric Oxide) IRON RUST

$Fe_4(Fe(CN)_6)_3$ (Ferric Ferrocyanide) LAUNDRY BLUEING

FeS_2 (Iron Disulfide) FOOL'S GOLD

$H_2Al_2(SiO_4)_2\cdot H_2O$ (Hydrated Aluminum Silicate) CLAY

H_3BO_3 (Boric Acid) BORACIC ACID

Hg (Mercury) QUICKSILVER

N_2O (Nitrous Oxide) LAUGHING GAS

$NaCl$ (Sodium Chloride) TABLE or ROCK SALT

$NaHCO_3+KHC_4H_4O_6$ (Sodium Bicarbonate plus an Acid Salt) BAKING POWDER

$NaOH$ (Sodium Hydroxide) SOAP LYE

SiO_2 (Silicon Dioxide) AGATE; FLINT; SILICA

COMMUNICATIONS

MAILING STAMPS
OR
OR
MAILBOX;
POST OFFICE
MAIL SENDING
MAIL RECEIVING
MONEY ORDERS
R
REGISTERED MAIL
INSURED MAIL
PARCEL POST
INTERNATIONAL
PARCEL POST
A-Z
GENERAL
DELIVERY
WRAPPING of
SMALL PACKAGES
WRAPPING of
LARGE PACKAGES
OR
OR
TELEGRAMS
SWITCHBOARD
and SOUND
TELEPHONE
TELEPHONE, local
TELEPHONE, long
distance (International)
Television
and Radio
PRESS ROOM
PRESS
INTERVIEW ROOM
GROUP ROOM
OR
TELEVISION
CAMERA
TELEVISION
CAMERA, OFF
SIZE, SMALL
SIZE, LARGE
CONTRAST, LOW
CONTRAST, HIGH
HEIGHT, LOW
HEIGHT, HIGH
TELEVISION
MONITOR
0
MAXI
LOUDSPEAKER
VOLUME
VOLUME, LOW
VOLUME, HIGH
Studio
STUDIO
MICROPHONE
LINK PARABOLE
FILM CAMERA

▲ A symbol for one of the various types of mail can be combined with the "Sending Mail" or "Receiving Mail" symbols. **Example:** indicates Sending Parcel Post.

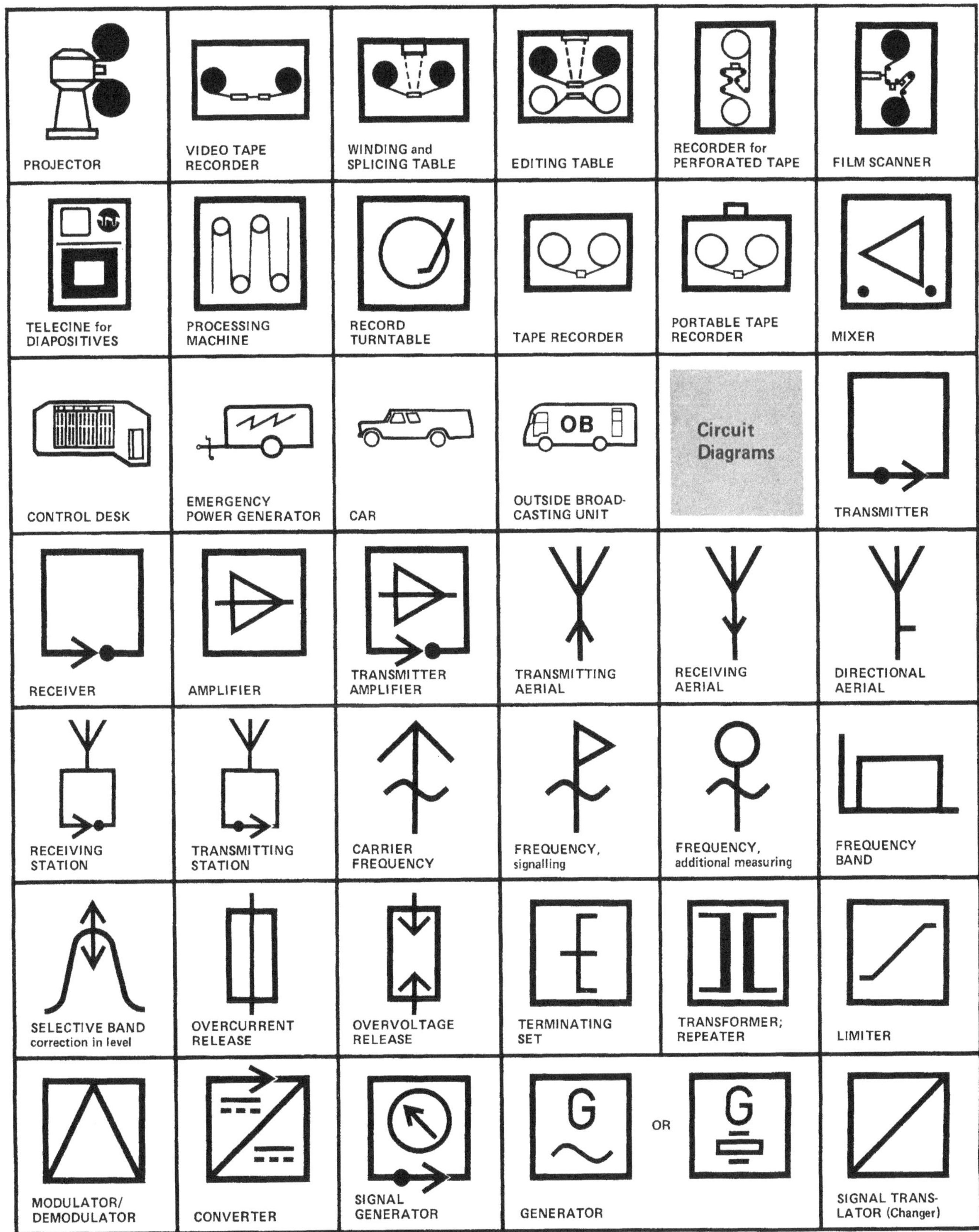
PROJECTOR
VIDEO TAPE RECORDER
WINDING and SPLICING TABLE
EDITING TABLE
RECORDER for PERFORATED TAPE
FILM SCANNER
TELECINE for DIAPOSITIVES
PROCESSING MACHINE
RECORD TURNTABLE
TAPE RECORDER
PORTABLE TAPE RECORDER
MIXER
CONTROL DESK
EMERGENCY POWER GENERATOR
CAR
OB
OUTSIDE BROAD-CASTING UNIT
Circuit Diagrams
TRANSMITTER
RECEIVER
AMPLIFIER
TRANSMITTER AMPLIFIER
TRANSMITTING AERIAL
RECEIVING AERIAL
DIRECTIONAL AERIAL
RECEIVING STATION
TRANSMITTING STATION
CARRIER FREQUENCY
FREQUENCY, signalling
FREQUENCY, additional measuring
FREQUENCY BAND
SELECTIVE BAND correction in level
OVERCURRENT RELEASE
OVERVOLTAGE RELEASE
TERMINATING SET
TRANSFORMER; REPEATER
LIMITER
MODULATOR/ DEMODULATOR
CONVERTER
SIGNAL GENERATOR
G
OR
G
GENERATOR
SIGNAL TRANS-LATOR (Changer)

COMMUNICATIONS *(continued)*

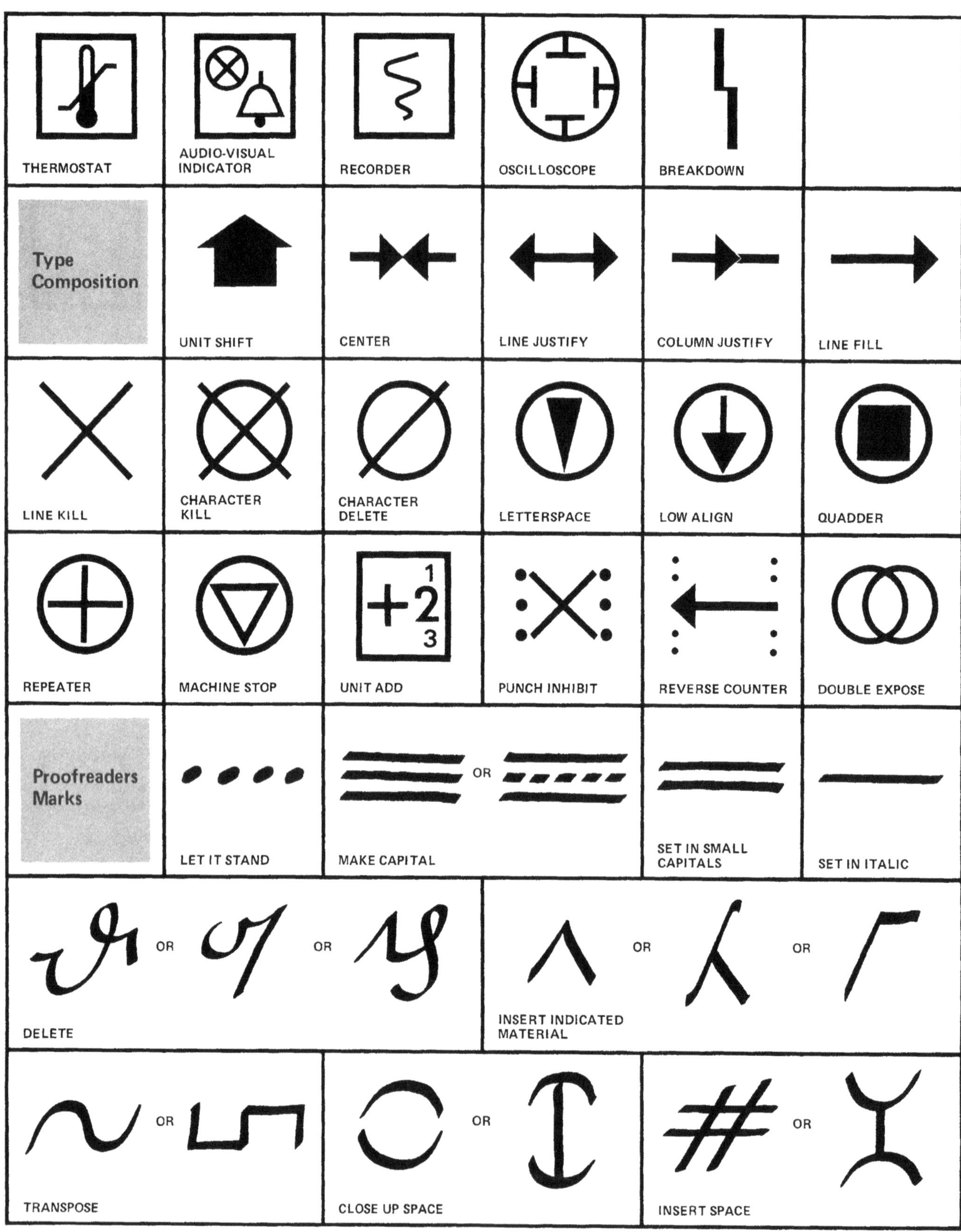

THERMOSTAT
AUDIO-VISUAL INDICATOR
RECORDER
OSCILLOSCOPE
BREAKDOWN
Type Composition
UNIT SHIFT
CENTER
LINE JUSTIFY
COLUMN JUSTIFY
LINE FILL
LINE KILL
CHARACTER KILL
CHARACTER DELETE
LETTERSPACE
LOW ALIGN
QUADDER
REPEATER
MACHINE STOP
+2
1
3
UNIT ADD
PUNCH INHIBIT
REVERSE COUNTER
DOUBLE EXPOSE
Proofreaders Marks
LET IT STAND
OR
MAKE CAPITAL
SET IN SMALL CAPITALS
SET IN ITALIC
OR
OR
DELETE
OR
OR
INSERT INDICATED MATERIAL
OR
TRANSPOSE
OR
CLOSE UP SPACE
OR
INSERT SPACE

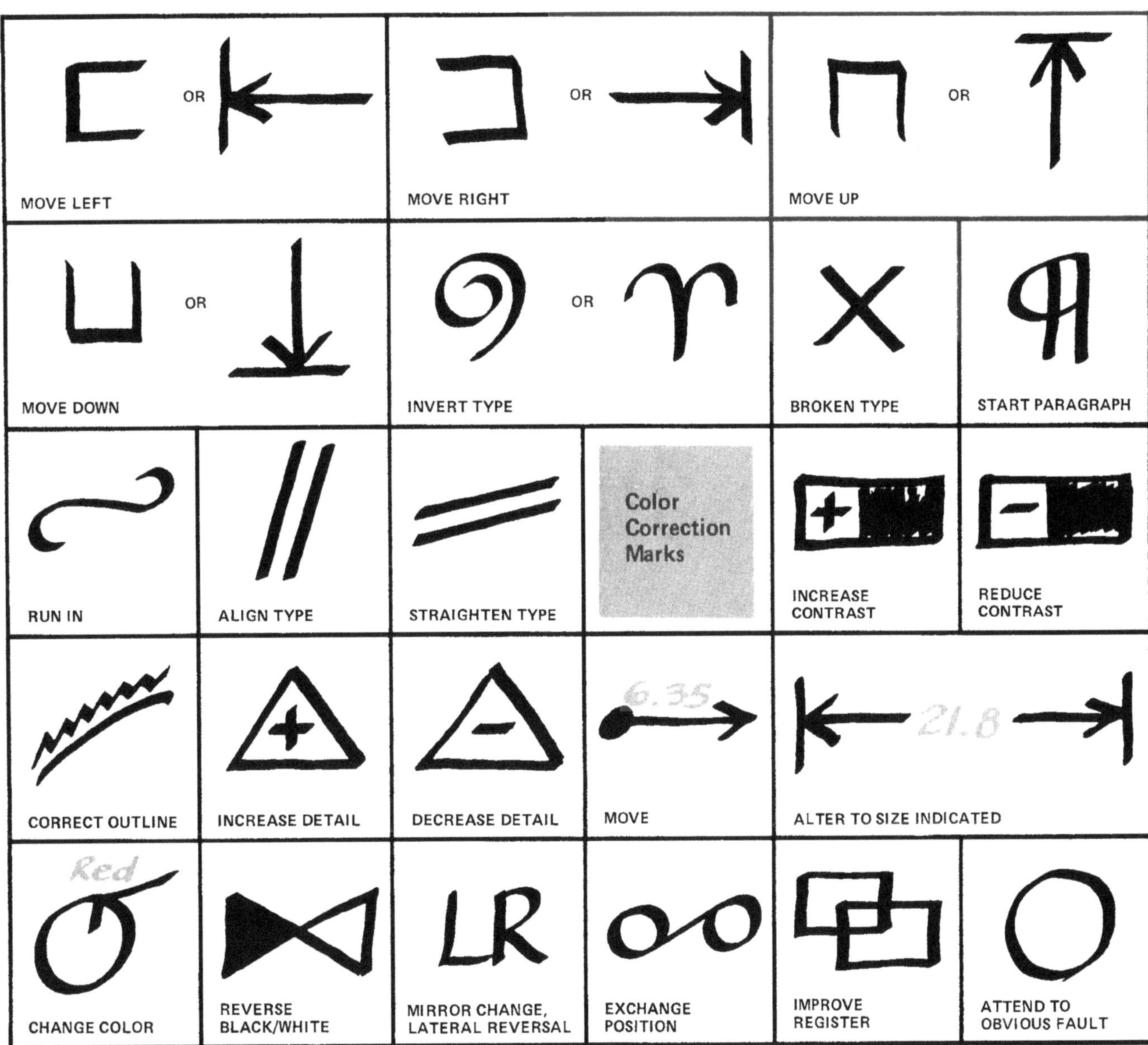
OR
MOVE LEFT
OR
MOVE RIGHT
OR
MOVE UP
OR
MOVE DOWN
OR
INVERT TYPE
BROKEN TYPE
START PARAGRAPH
RUN IN
ALIGN TYPE
STRAIGHTEN TYPE
Color Correction Marks
INCREASE CONTRAST
REDUCE CONTRAST
CORRECT OUTLINE
INCREASE DETAIL
DECREASE DETAIL
6.35
MOVE
21.8
ALTER TO SIZE INDICATED
Red
CHANGE COLOR
REVERSE BLACK/WHITE
LR
MIRROR CHANGE, LATERAL REVERSAL
EXCHANGE POSITION
IMPROVE REGISTER
ATTEND TO OBVIOUS FAULT

THE END IS NEAR

When you pick up a magazine in the dentist's office or on a train or plane, do you ever wonder whether you'll have time to finish an article or story that attracts your attention? One way to quickly match the length of time at your disposal to the length of the printed matter is to look for a symbol sometimes provided at the end of the story or article. These are some commonly used symbols: △ ○ □

Other helpful symbols might show you that the article is continued on the next page. ⊂→ ☞ →

And a variation of this might direct you to a remote page where the reading matter is continued. ⊂ 24 →

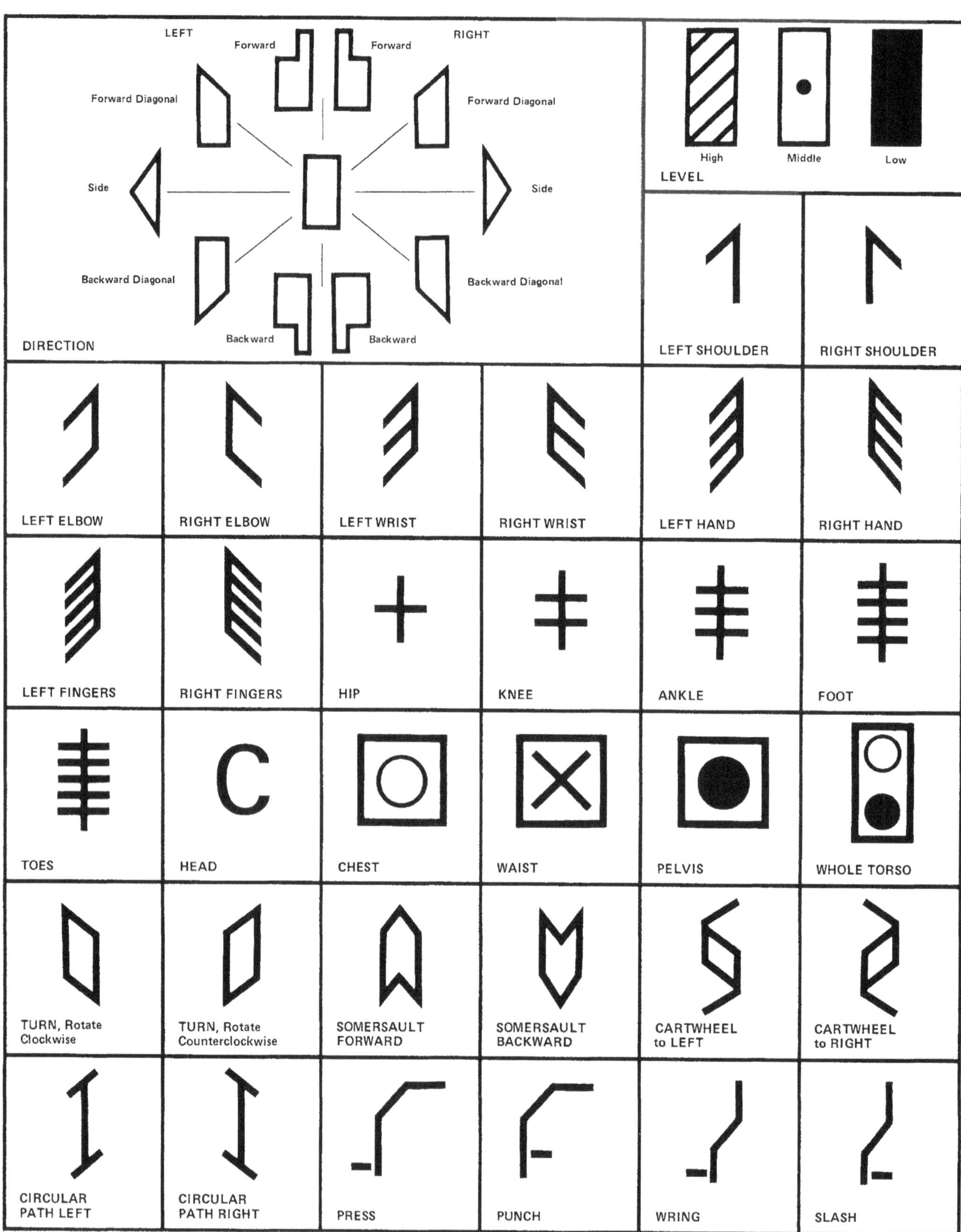
LEFT
Forward
Forward
RIGHT
Forward Diagonal
Forward Diagonal
Side
Side
Backward Diagonal
Backward Diagonal
Backward
Backward
DIRECTION
High
Middle
Low
LEVEL
LEFT SHOULDER
RIGHT SHOULDER
LEFT ELBOW
RIGHT ELBOW
LEFT WRIST
RIGHT WRIST
LEFT HAND
RIGHT HAND
LEFT FINGERS
RIGHT FINGERS
HIP
KNEE
ANKLE
FOOT
TOES
HEAD
CHEST
WAIST
PELVIS
WHOLE TORSO
TURN, Rotate Clockwise
TURN, Rotate Counterclockwise
SOMERSAULT FORWARD
SOMERSAULT BACKWARD
CARTWHEEL to LEFT
CARTWHEEL to RIGHT
CIRCULAR PATH LEFT
CIRCULAR PATH RIGHT
PRESS
PUNCH
WRING
SLASH

Note: "Alphabet of Basic Symbols," copyright 1954 by Rudolf Laban, reproduced by permission of Dance Notation Bureau, Inc.

	Morse Code ▲	International Flags	Semaphore	Manual (Deaf)	Braille
A	• ▬	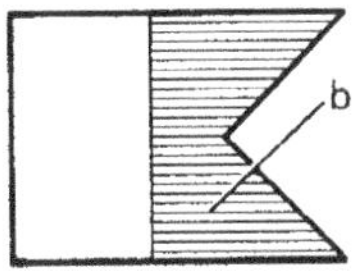 b Speed trial		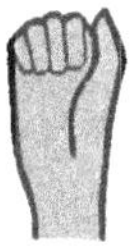	
B	▬ • • •	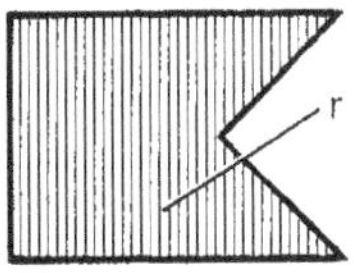 r Explosives	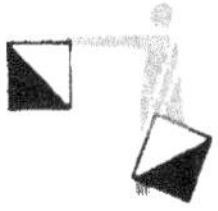	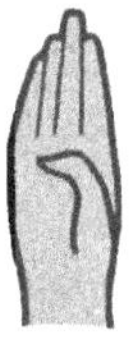	
C	▬ • ▬ •	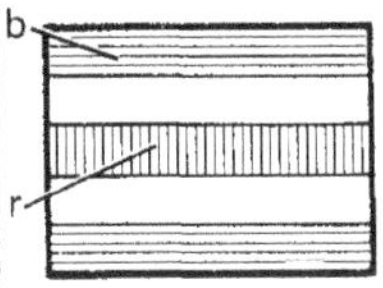 b r Yes		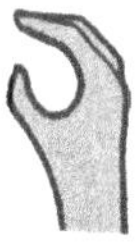	
D	▬ • •	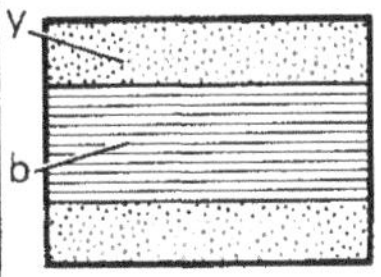 y b Keep clear		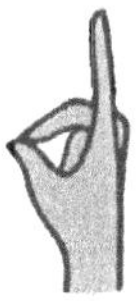	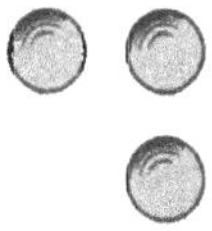
E	•	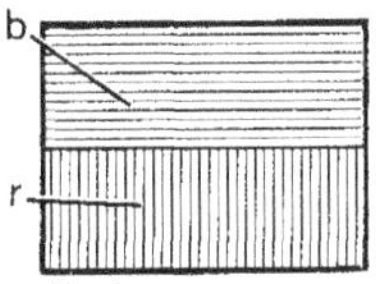 b r Altering course to starboard		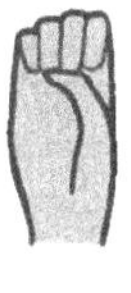	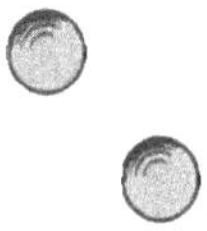
F	• • ▬ •	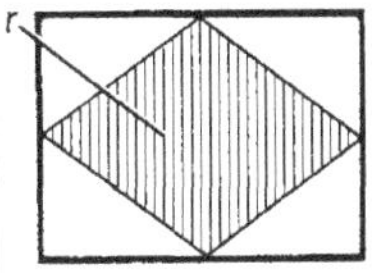 r Disabled	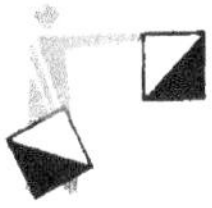		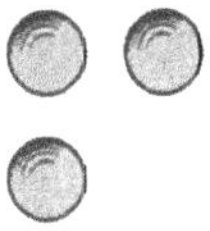
G	▬ ▬ •	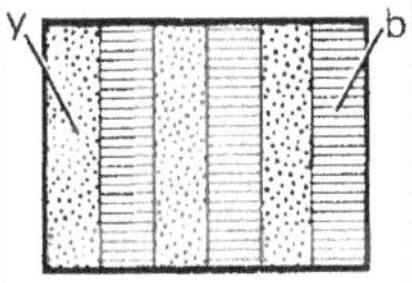 y b Want a pilot		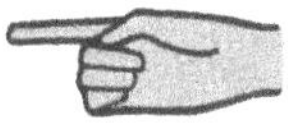	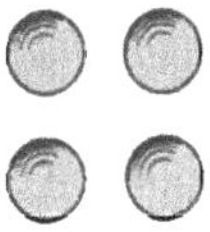
H	• • • •	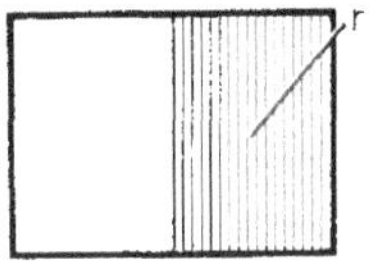 r Pilot on board			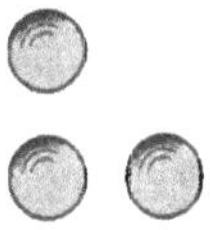

▲ Morse code may also be transmitted by "blinker" lights or by flags.

	Morse Code	International Flags	Semaphore	Manual (Deaf)	Braille
I	• •	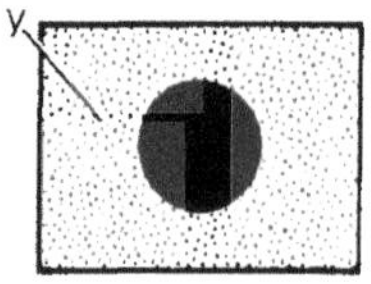 Altering course to port			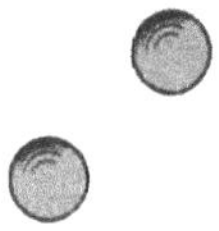
J	• — — —	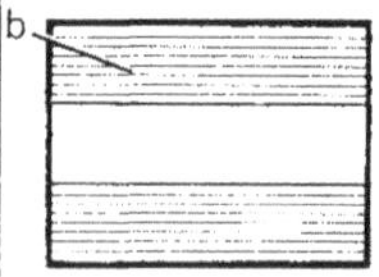 Semaphore	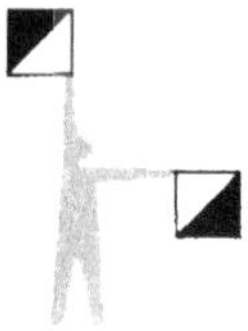	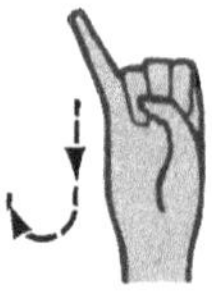	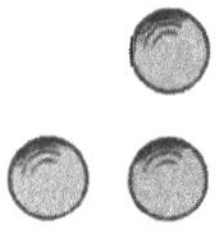
K	— • —	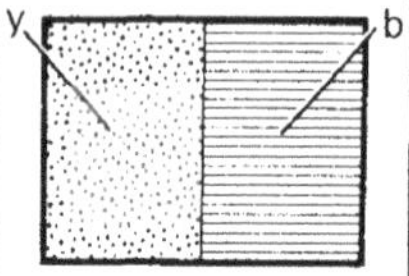 Stop instantly			
L	• — • •	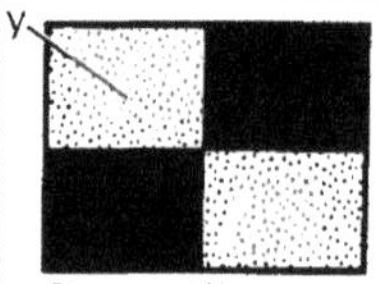 Stop, something to communicate			
M	— —	 Doctor on board		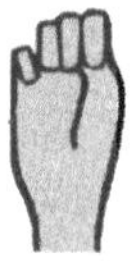	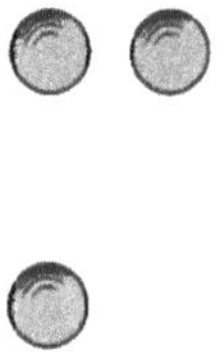
N	— •	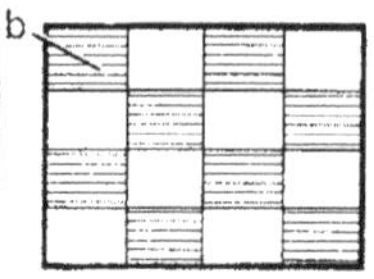 No	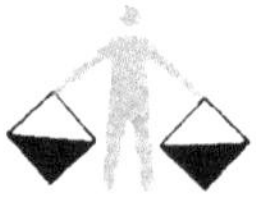		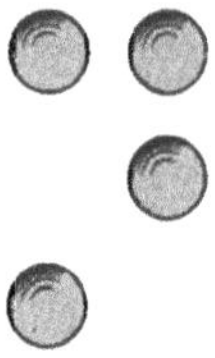
O	— — —	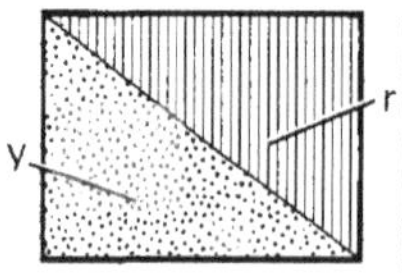 Man overboard			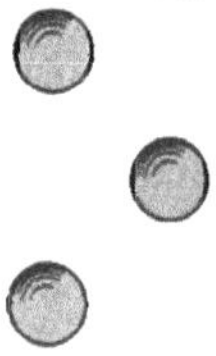
P	• — — •	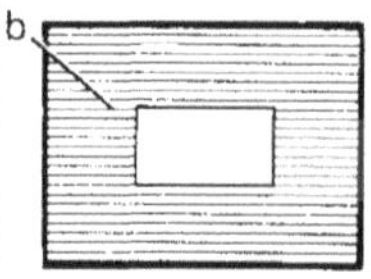 About to sail (lights out)	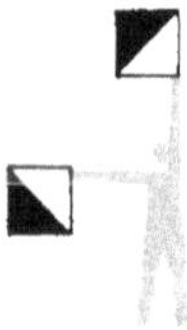		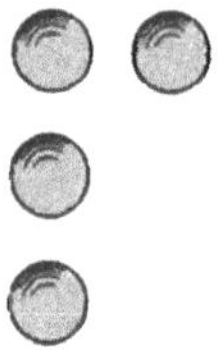

	Morse Code	International Flags	Semaphore	Manual (Deaf)	Braille
Q	— — • —	Request pratique			
R	• — •	Way is off my ship			
S	• • •	Going full speed astern			
T	—	Do not pass ahead of me			
U	• • —	Standing into danger			
V	• • • —	Require assistance			
W	• — —	Require medical assistance			
X	— • • —	Stop your intention			

	Morse Code	International Flags	Semaphore ▲	Manual (Deaf)	Braille ▲
Y	— • — —	y, r Carrying mails			
Z	— — • •	y, r, b Shore stations			
1	• — — — —	r, y			
2	• • — — —	y, r			
3	• • • — —	b, r			
4	• • • • —	r			
5	• • • • •	b, y			
6	— • • • •	b			

▲ In Semaphore and Braille, the first ten letters also stand for numerals. The Numeral sign (in Semaphore, in Braille) must precede any numeral symbol.

	Morse Code	International Flags	Semaphore	Manual (Deaf)	Braille
7	— — • • •	r			
8	— — — • •	y, b			
9	— — — — •	b			
0	— — — — —	b			

LEFT AND RIGHT ARE IN THE EYE OF THE BEHOLDER

In South Africa, most of the men who work in the mines are illiterate. The miners, therefore, are given instructions and warnings in the form of symbols rather than words.

In an effort to enlist the miners' help in keeping mine tracks clear of rock, the South African Chamber of Mines posted this pictorial message:

But the campaign failed miserably. More and more rocks blocked the tracks.

The reason was soon discovered. Miners were indeed reading the message, but from right to left. They obligingly dumped their rocks on the tracks.

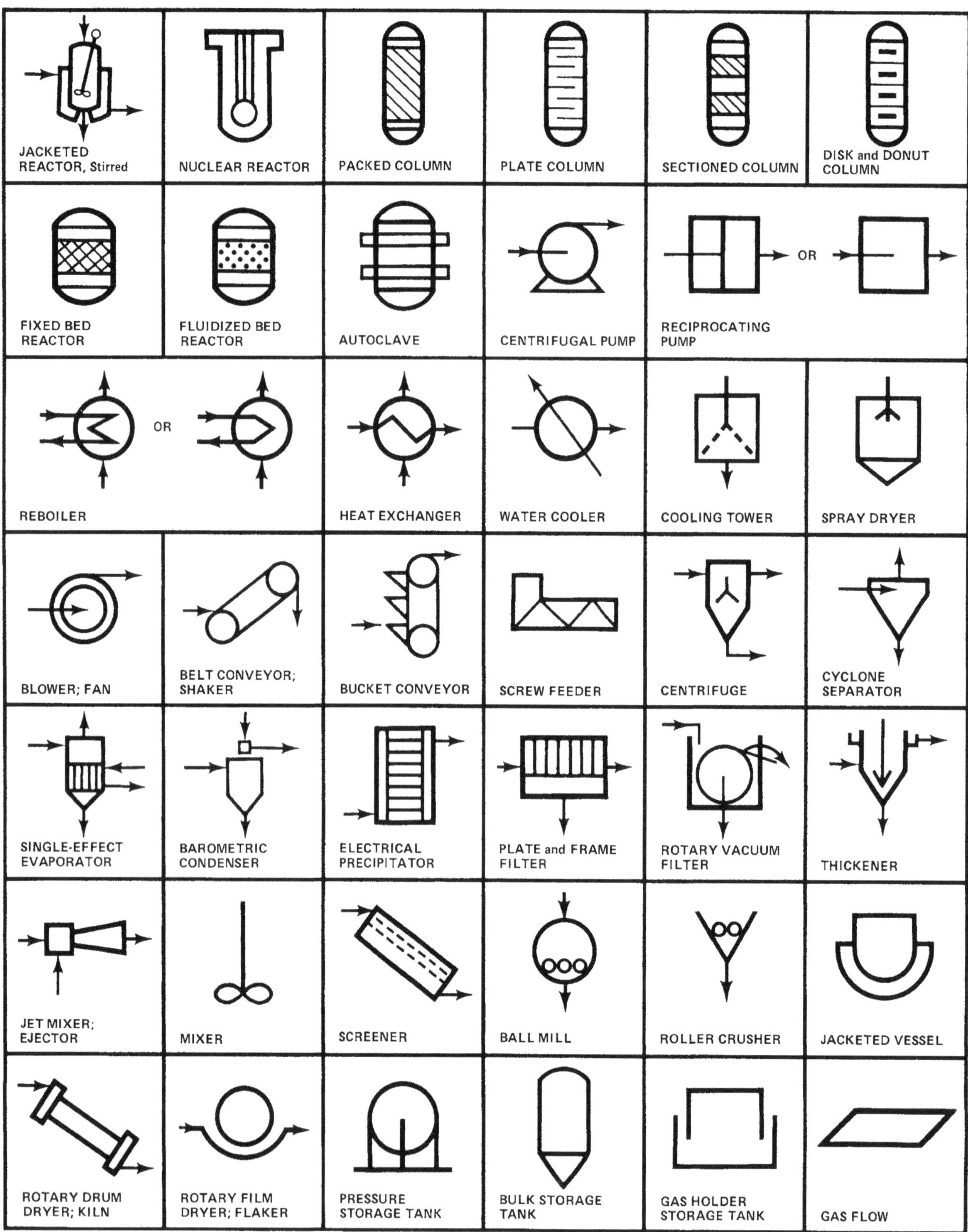
JACKETED REACTOR, Stirred
NUCLEAR REACTOR
PACKED COLUMN
PLATE COLUMN
SECTIONED COLUMN
DISK and DONUT COLUMN
FIXED BED REACTOR
FLUIDIZED BED REACTOR
AUTOCLAVE
CENTRIFUGAL PUMP
OR
RECIPROCATING PUMP
OR
REBOILER
HEAT EXCHANGER
WATER COOLER
COOLING TOWER
SPRAY DRYER
BLOWER; FAN
BELT CONVEYOR; SHAKER
BUCKET CONVEYOR
SCREW FEEDER
CENTRIFUGE
CYCLONE SEPARATOR
SINGLE-EFFECT EVAPORATOR
BAROMETRIC CONDENSER
ELECTRICAL PRECIPITATOR
PLATE and FRAME FILTER
ROTARY VACUUM FILTER
THICKENER
JET MIXER; EJECTOR
MIXER
SCREENER
BALL MILL
ROLLER CRUSHER
JACKETED VESSEL
ROTARY DRUM DRYER; KILN
ROTARY FILM DRYER; FLAKER
PRESSURE STORAGE TANK
BULK STORAGE TANK
GAS HOLDER STORAGE TANK
GAS FLOW

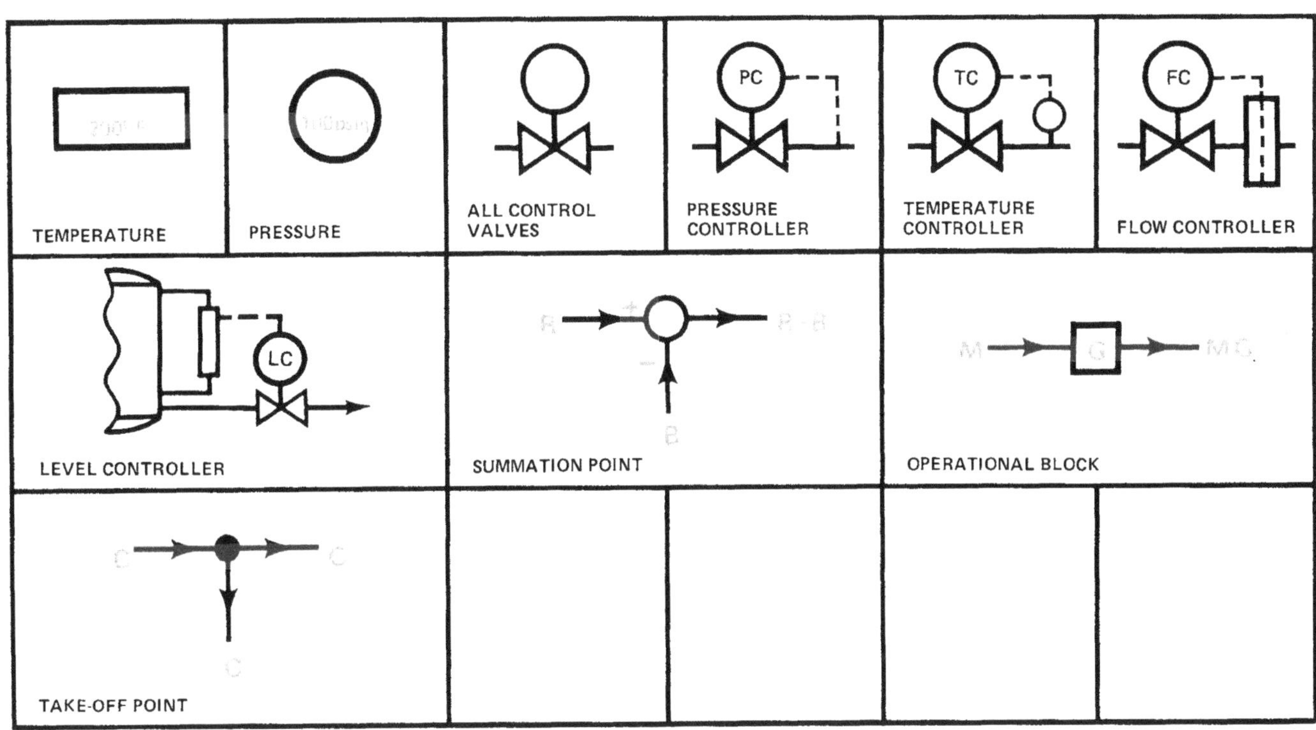

TEMPERATURE
PRESSURE
ALL CONTROL VALVES
PC
PRESSURE CONTROLLER
TC
TEMPERATURE CONTROLLER
FC
FLOW CONTROLLER
LC
LEVEL CONTROLLER
SUMMATION POINT
OPERATIONAL BLOCK
TAKE-OFF POINT

Electrical

DIRECT CURRENT (DC) ¶¶	ALTERNATING CURRENT (AC) ¶¶	AUDIO FREQUENCY AC ¶¶	SUPERAUDIO FREQUENCY AC ¶¶	CROSSED CONDUCTORS ¶¶	JOINED CONDUCTORS ¶¶
SINGLE-PHASE ¶¶	2-PHASE 3-WIRE ¶¶	2-PHASE 4-WIRE ¶¶	3-PHASE 3-WIRE (Delta) ¶¶	3-PHASE 3-WIRE (Star) ¶¶	3-PHASE 4-WIRE (Star) ¶¶
2 and 3-PHASE TEE CONNECTED ¶¶	3-PHASE, 3-WIRE VEE CONNECTED ¶¶	6-PHASE; FORK with NEUTRAL ¶¶	START of WINDING ¶¶	VARIABLE CONTROL ¶¶	VARIABLE CONTROL by STEPS ¶¶

¶¶ Draft ISO Recommendation

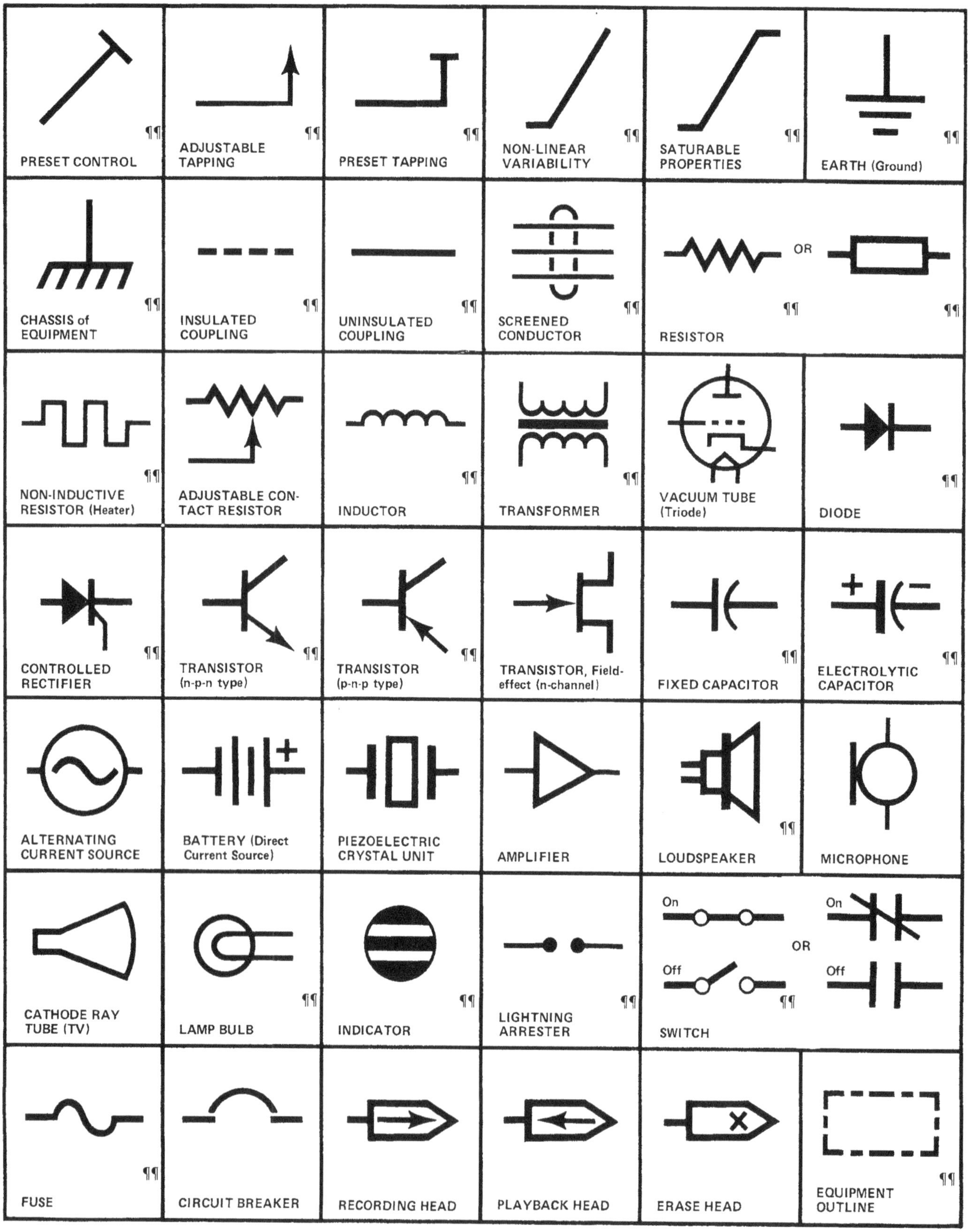

¶¶ PRESET CONTROL	¶¶ ADJUSTABLE TAPPING	¶¶ PRESET TAPPING	¶¶ NON-LINEAR VARIABILITY	¶¶ SATURABLE PROPERTIES	¶¶ EARTH (Ground)
¶¶ CHASSIS of EQUIPMENT	¶¶ INSULATED COUPLING	¶¶ UNINSULATED COUPLING	¶¶ SCREENED CONDUCTOR	¶¶ RESISTOR	OR ¶¶
¶¶ NON-INDUCTIVE RESISTOR (Heater)	ADJUSTABLE CONTACT RESISTOR	¶¶ INDUCTOR	¶¶ TRANSFORMER	VACUUM TUBE (Triode)	¶¶ DIODE
¶¶ CONTROLLED RECTIFIER	¶¶ TRANSISTOR (n-p-n type)	¶¶ TRANSISTOR (p-n-p type)	TRANSISTOR, Field-effect (n-channel)	¶¶ FIXED CAPACITOR	¶¶ ELECTROLYTIC CAPACITOR
ALTERNATING CURRENT SOURCE	BATTERY (Direct Current Source)	PIEZOELECTRIC CRYSTAL UNIT	AMPLIFIER	¶¶ LOUDSPEAKER	MICROPHONE
CATHODE RAY TUBE (TV)	¶¶ LAMP BULB	¶¶ INDICATOR	¶¶ LIGHTNING ARRESTER	On / Off ¶¶ SWITCH	OR On / Off
¶¶ FUSE	CIRCUIT BREAKER	RECORDING HEAD	PLAYBACK HEAD	ERASE HEAD	¶¶ EQUIPMENT OUTLINE

¶¶ Draft ISO Recommendation

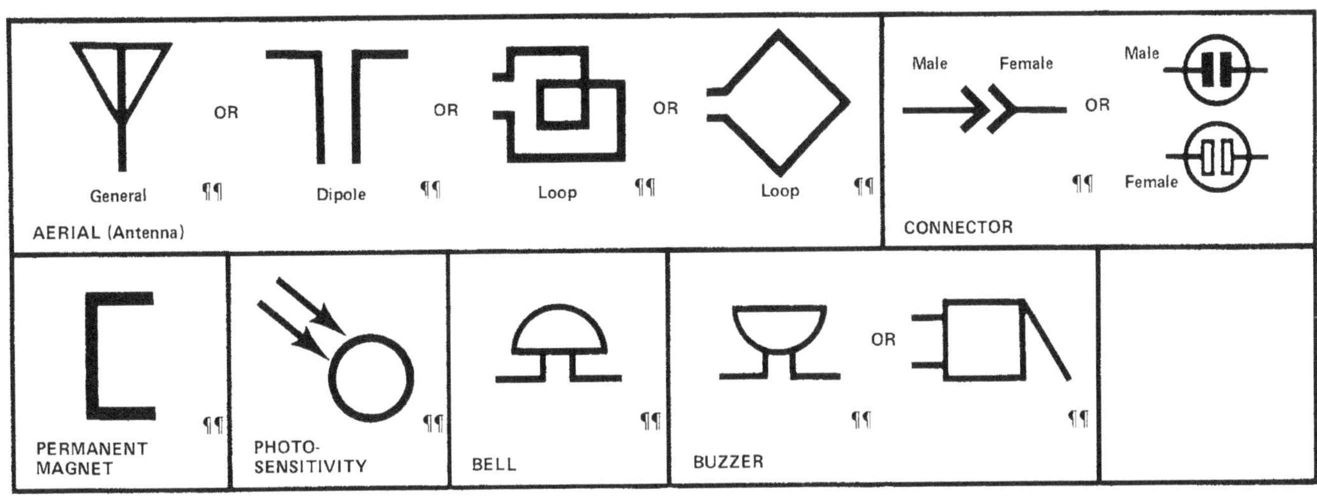

OR
OR
OR
General ¶¶
Dipole ¶¶
Loop ¶¶
Loop ¶¶
AERIAL (Antenna)
Male
Female
OR
Male
Female
¶¶
CONNECTOR
¶¶ PERMANENT MAGNET
¶¶ PHOTO-SENSITIVITY
¶¶ BELL
OR
¶¶ ¶¶ BUZZER

Mechanical *

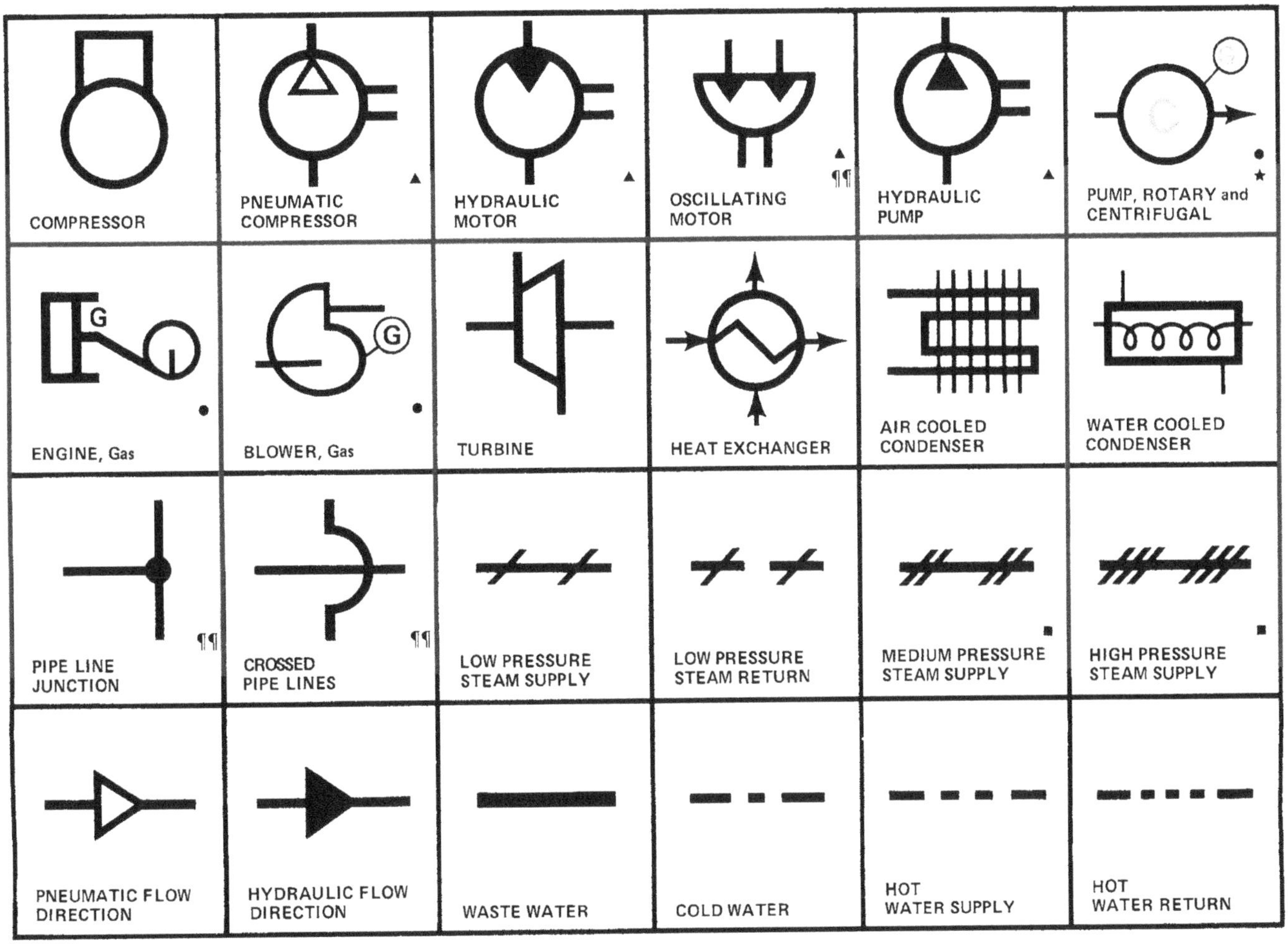

COMPRESSOR	PNEUMATIC COMPRESSOR ▲	HYDRAULIC MOTOR ▲	OSCILLATING MOTOR ▲ ¶¶	HYDRAULIC PUMP ▲	PUMP, ROTARY and CENTRIFUGAL ● ★
ENGINE, Gas ●	BLOWER, Gas ●	TURBINE	HEAT EXCHANGER	AIR COOLED CONDENSER	WATER COOLED CONDENSER
PIPE LINE JUNCTION ¶¶	CROSSED PIPE LINES ¶¶	LOW PRESSURE STEAM SUPPLY	LOW PRESSURE STEAM RETURN	MEDIUM PRESSURE STEAM SUPPLY ■	HIGH PRESSURE STEAM SUPPLY ■
PNEUMATIC FLOW DIRECTION	HYDRAULIC FLOW DIRECTION	WASTE WATER	COLD WATER	HOT WATER SUPPLY	HOT WATER RETURN

▲ Pneumatic machinery is indicated by △ , hydraulic machinery by ▲

● G indicates Gas. Different initial may be substituted to indicate other type of machine; e. g. D (diesel), M (motor), T (turbine), E (steam). **Exception:** (see Engine, Gas) Steam Engine is indicated by symbol without initial.

★ C indicates Circulating Water. Different initial indicates other type of machine or service; e. g. D (concentrate), F (boiler feed), O (oil), S (service), V (air).

■ "Return" indicated by broken line, as illustrated in Low Pressure Steam Return.

¶¶ Draft ISO Recommendation

* FOR MECHANICAL DRAWINGS, SEE **ARCHITECTURE: Drafting,** PAGE 48.

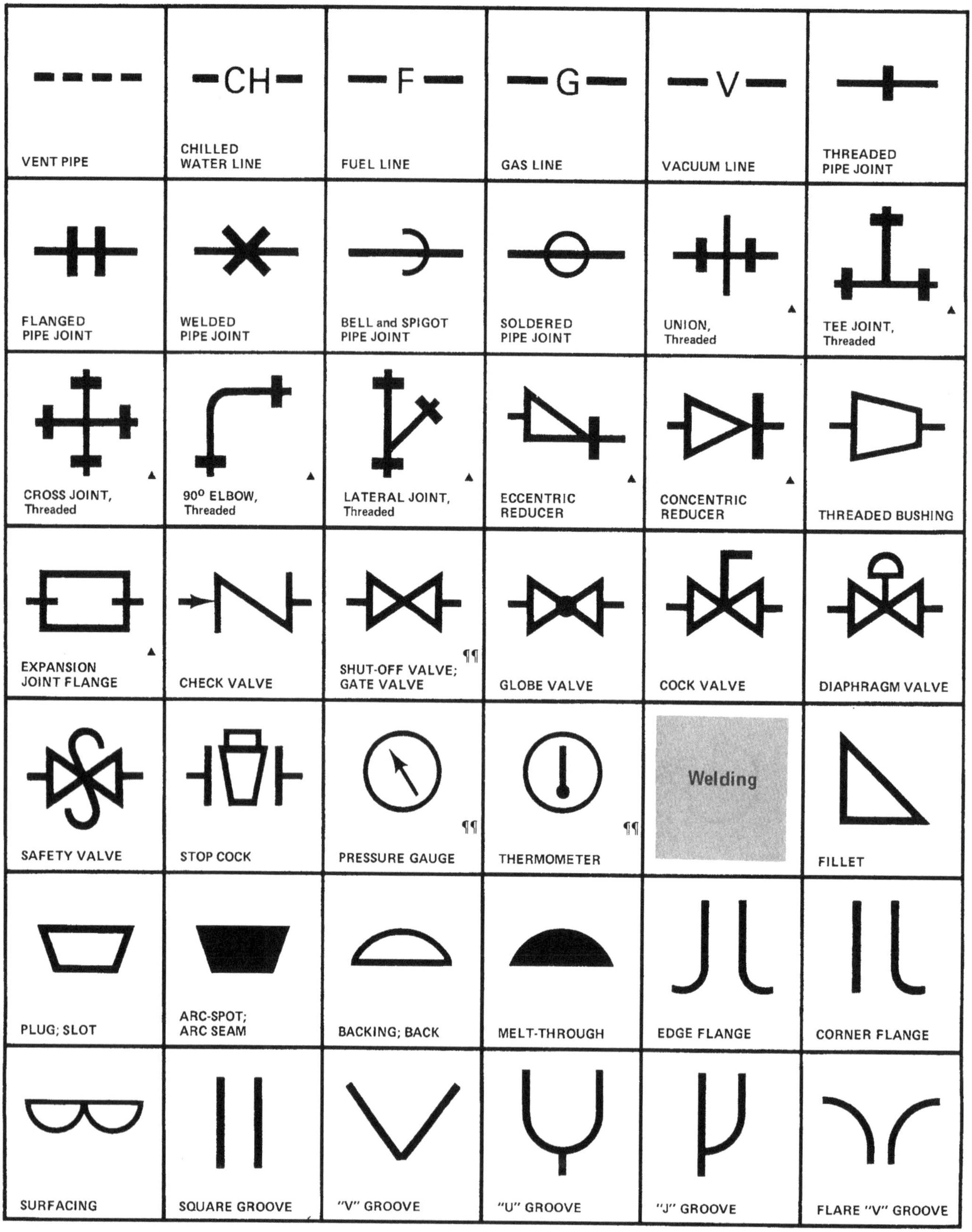

ENGINEERING

Mechanical *(continued)*

—CH—	—F—	—G—	—V—		
VENT PIPE	CHILLED WATER LINE	FUEL LINE	GAS LINE	VACUUM LINE	THREADED PIPE JOINT
FLANGED PIPE JOINT	WELDED PIPE JOINT	BELL and SPIGOT PIPE JOINT	SOLDERED PIPE JOINT	UNION, Threaded ▲	TEE JOINT, Threaded ▲
CROSS JOINT, Threaded ▲	90° ELBOW, Threaded ▲	LATERAL JOINT, Threaded ▲	ECCENTRIC REDUCER ▲	CONCENTRIC REDUCER ▲	THREADED BUSHING
EXPANSION JOINT FLANGE ▲	CHECK VALVE	SHUT-OFF VALVE; GATE VALVE ¶¶	GLOBE VALVE	COCK VALVE	DIAPHRAGM VALVE
SAFETY VALVE	STOP COCK	PRESSURE GAUGE ¶¶	THERMOMETER ¶¶	**Welding**	FILLET
PLUG; SLOT	ARC-SPOT; ARC SEAM	BACKING; BACK	MELT-THROUGH	EDGE FLANGE	CORNER FLANGE
SURFACING	SQUARE GROOVE	"V" GROOVE	"U" GROOVE	"J" GROOVE	FLARE "V" GROOVE

▲ Flanged, Welded, Bell and Spigot, or Soldered Union indicated by substituting appropriate markings (see Joints). **Example:** ✕|✕ Welded Union.
¶¶ Draft ISO Recommendation

FLARE BEVEL GROOVE	BEVEL GROOVE	WELD ALL AROUND	FIELD WELD	FLUSH CONTOUR	CONVEX CONTOUR
Geometric Tolerances	STRAIGHTNESS ¶	FLATNESS ¶	FLATNESS and STRAIGHTNESS	CIRCULARITY (Roundness) ¶	CYLINDRICITY ¶
PROFILE of any LINE ¶	PROFILE of any SURFACE ¶	PARALLELISM ¶	SQUARENESS (Perpendicularity) ¶	ANGULARITY ¶	POSITION ¶
COAXIALITY; CONCENTRICITY ¶	SYMMETRY ¶	RUN-OUT ¶	SURFACE ROUGHNESS	SURFACE to be FINISHED (Machined)	

¶ ISO Recommendation

EASY COME

We all know where our dollars come from, although we are seldom quite sure where they go. But few of us can say where the dollar symbol itself came from.

Zealous patriots erroneously speculate that it was derived by superimposing the first letter of United over the first letter of States, and that through usage over the years the bottom of the U was dropped off.

Historically, the Spaniards in the 16th century brought their peso to the New World. They had abbreviated the peso to a "P" and pluralized it by placing an S above and to its right; eventually the P was simplified to a single long stroke, and the S placed astride it. Those fancifully inclined can imagine a decorative monogram of an S for Spanish, intertwined with a P for peso.

In the 1700s, young America patterned its dollar after the peso and adopted the peso mark – but this mark somehow, and with no explanation whatsoever, now appears with a second oblique line added to its configuration.

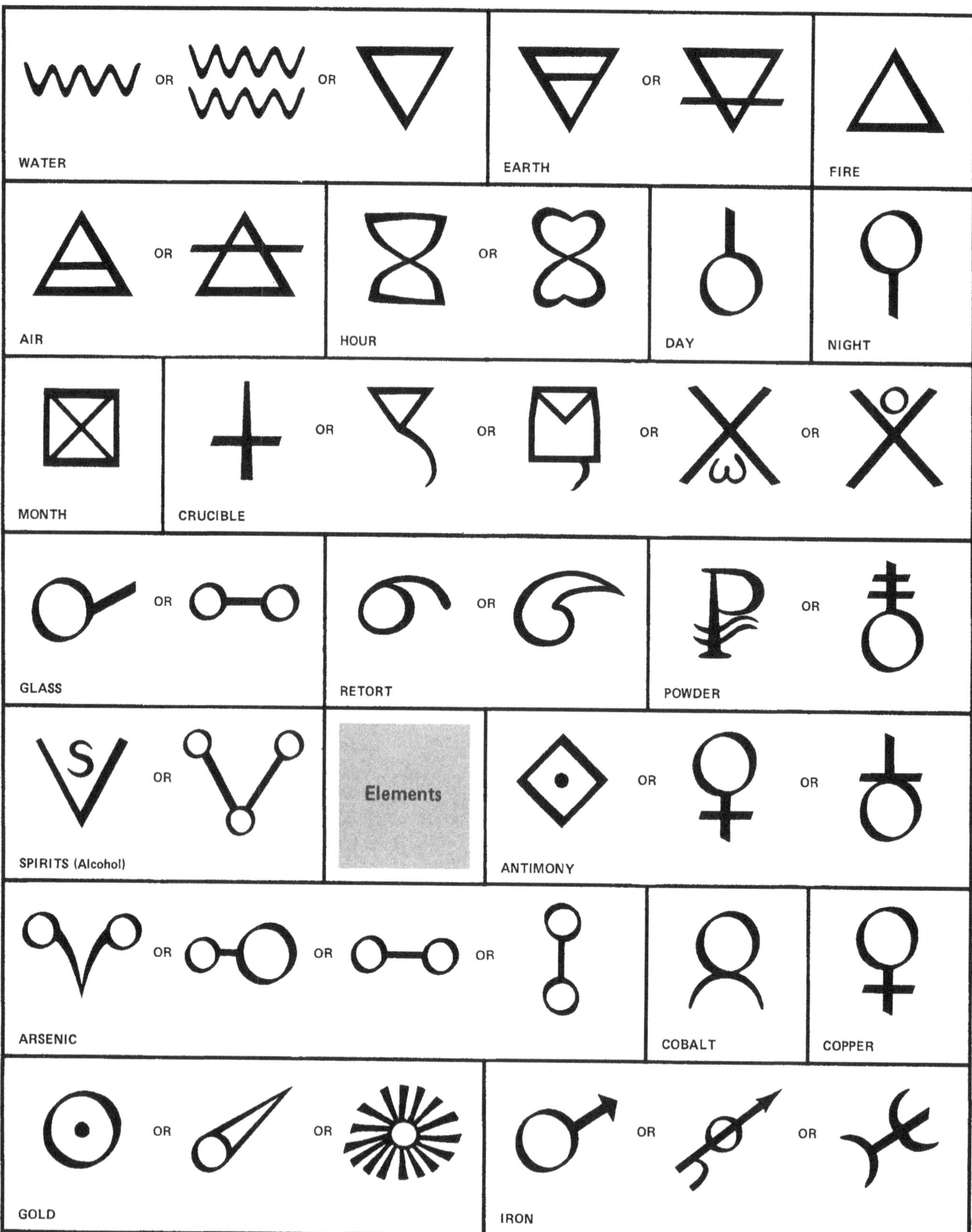
WATER
OR
OR
EARTH
OR
FIRE
AIR
OR
HOUR
OR
DAY
NIGHT
MONTH
CRUCIBLE
OR
OR
OR
OR
GLASS
OR
RETORT
OR
POWDER
OR
SPIRITS (Alcohol)
OR
Elements
ANTIMONY
OR
OR
ARSENIC
OR
OR
OR
COBALT
COPPER
GOLD
OR
OR
IRON
OR
OR

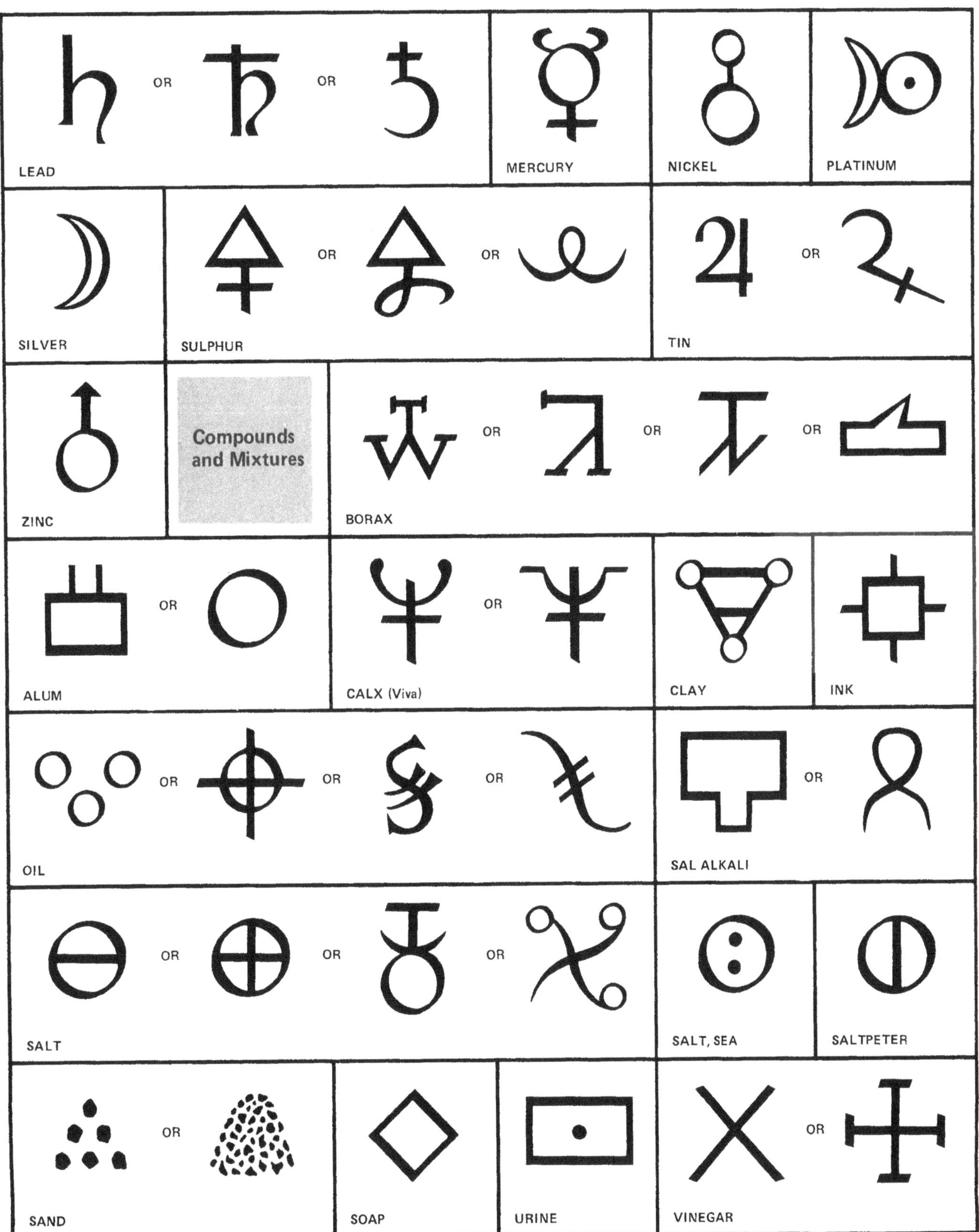

OR
OR
LEAD
MERCURY
NICKEL
PLATINUM
OR
OR
SILVER
SULPHUR
OR
TIN
Compounds and Mixtures
OR
OR
OR
ZINC
BORAX
OR
OR
ALUM
CALX (Viva)
CLAY
INK
OR
OR
OR
OR
OIL
SAL ALKALI
OR
OR
OR
SALT
SALT, SEA
SALTPETER
OR
OR
SAND
SOAP
URINE
VINEGAR

FOLKLORE

Alchemy *(continued)*

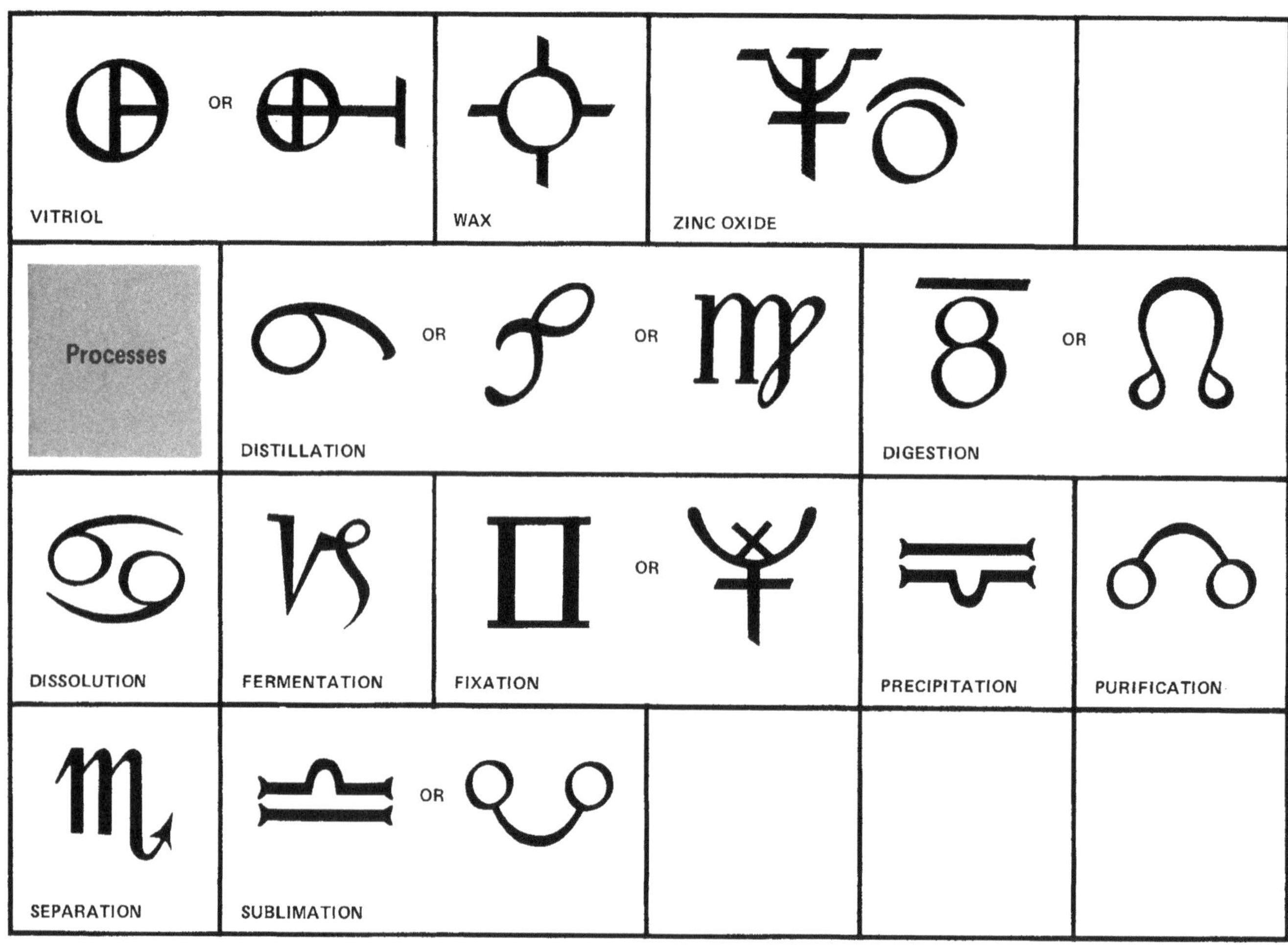
OR
VITRIOL
WAX
ZINC OXIDE
Processes
OR
OR
DISTILLATION
OR
DIGESTION
DISSOLUTION
FERMENTATION
OR
FIXATION
PRECIPITATION
PURIFICATION
SEPARATION
OR
SUBLIMATION

Astrology

OR ARIES	OR TAURUS	OR GEMINI
OR CANCER	OR LEO	OR VIRGO

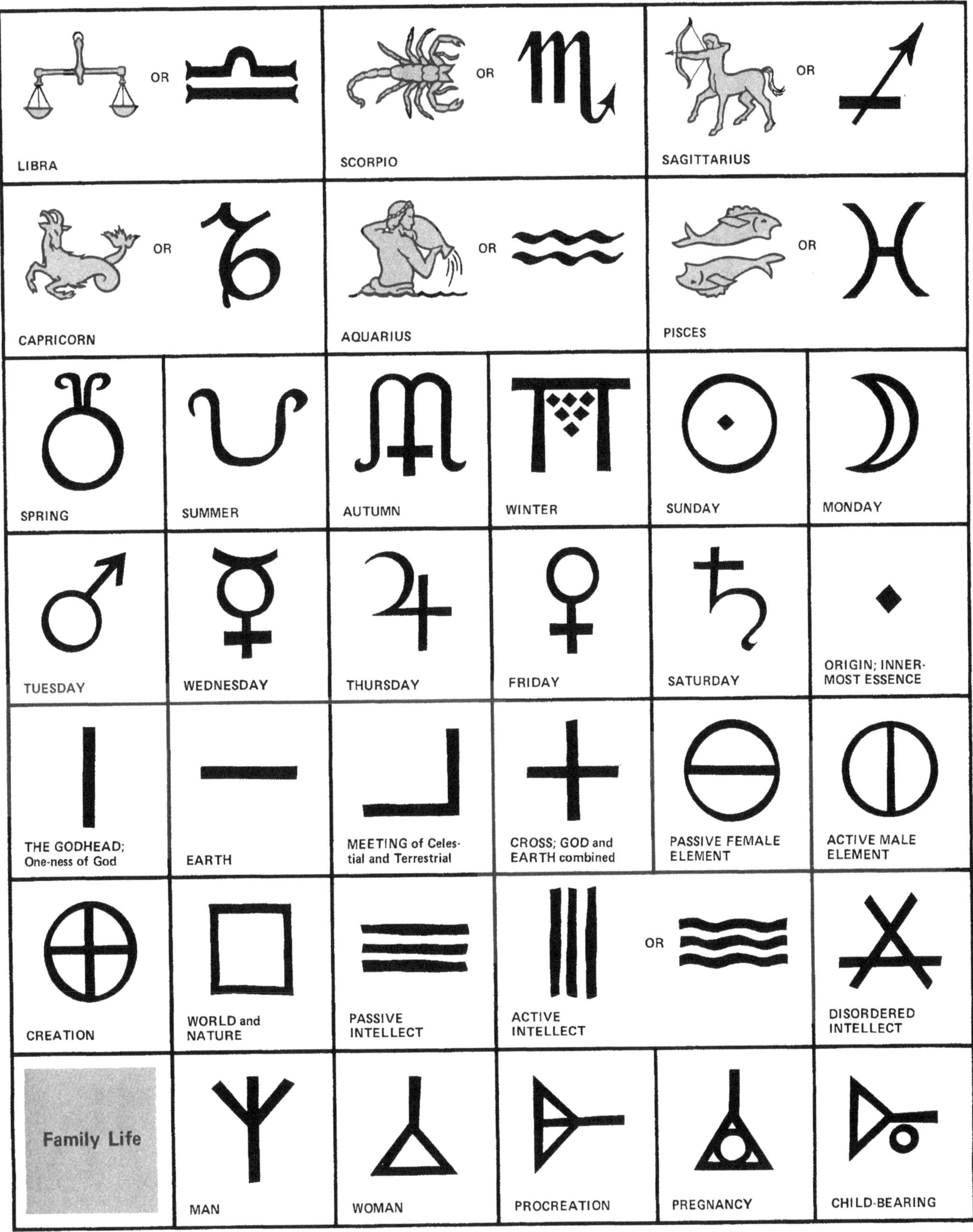

OR
LIBRA
OR
SCORPIO
OR
SAGITTARIUS
OR
CAPRICORN
OR
AQUARIUS
OR
PISCES
SPRING
SUMMER
AUTUMN
WINTER
SUNDAY
MONDAY
TUESDAY
WEDNESDAY
THURSDAY
FRIDAY
SATURDAY
ORIGIN; INNER-MOST ESSENCE
THE GODHEAD; One-ness of God
EARTH
MEETING of Celes-tial and Terrestrial
CROSS; GOD and EARTH combined
PASSIVE FEMALE ELEMENT
ACTIVE MALE ELEMENT
CREATION
WORLD and NATURE
PASSIVE INTELLECT
ACTIVE INTELLECT
OR
DISORDERED INTELLECT
Family Life
MAN
WOMAN
PROCREATION
PREGNANCY
CHILD-BEARING

Astrology *(continued)*

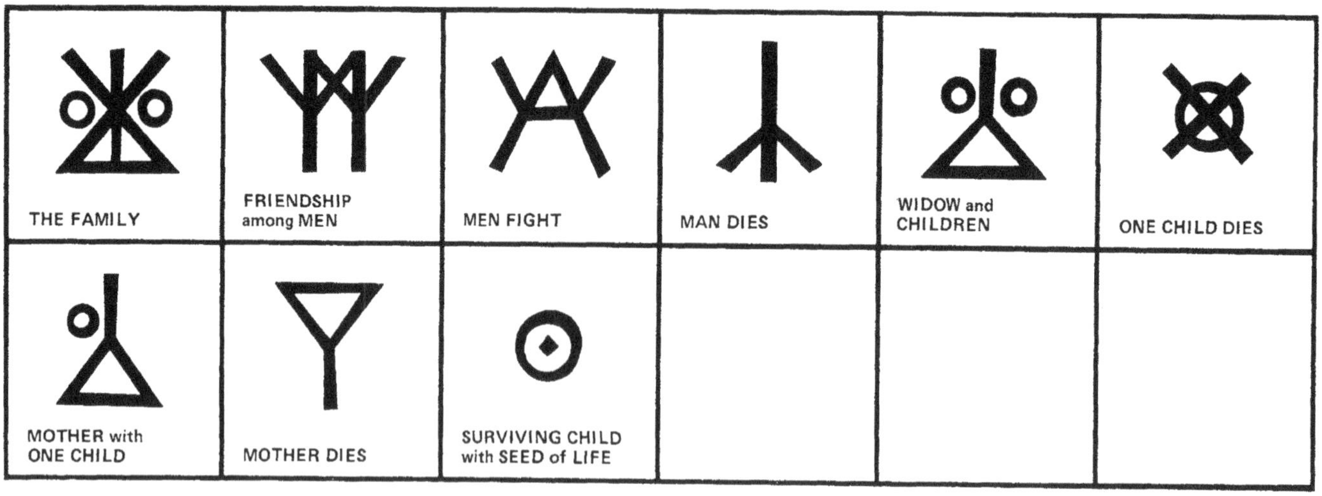

THE FAMILY	FRIENDSHIP among MEN	MEN FIGHT	MAN DIES	WIDOW and CHILDREN	ONE CHILD DIES
MOTHER with ONE CHILD	MOTHER DIES	SURVIVING CHILD with SEED of LIFE			

Hobo Signs

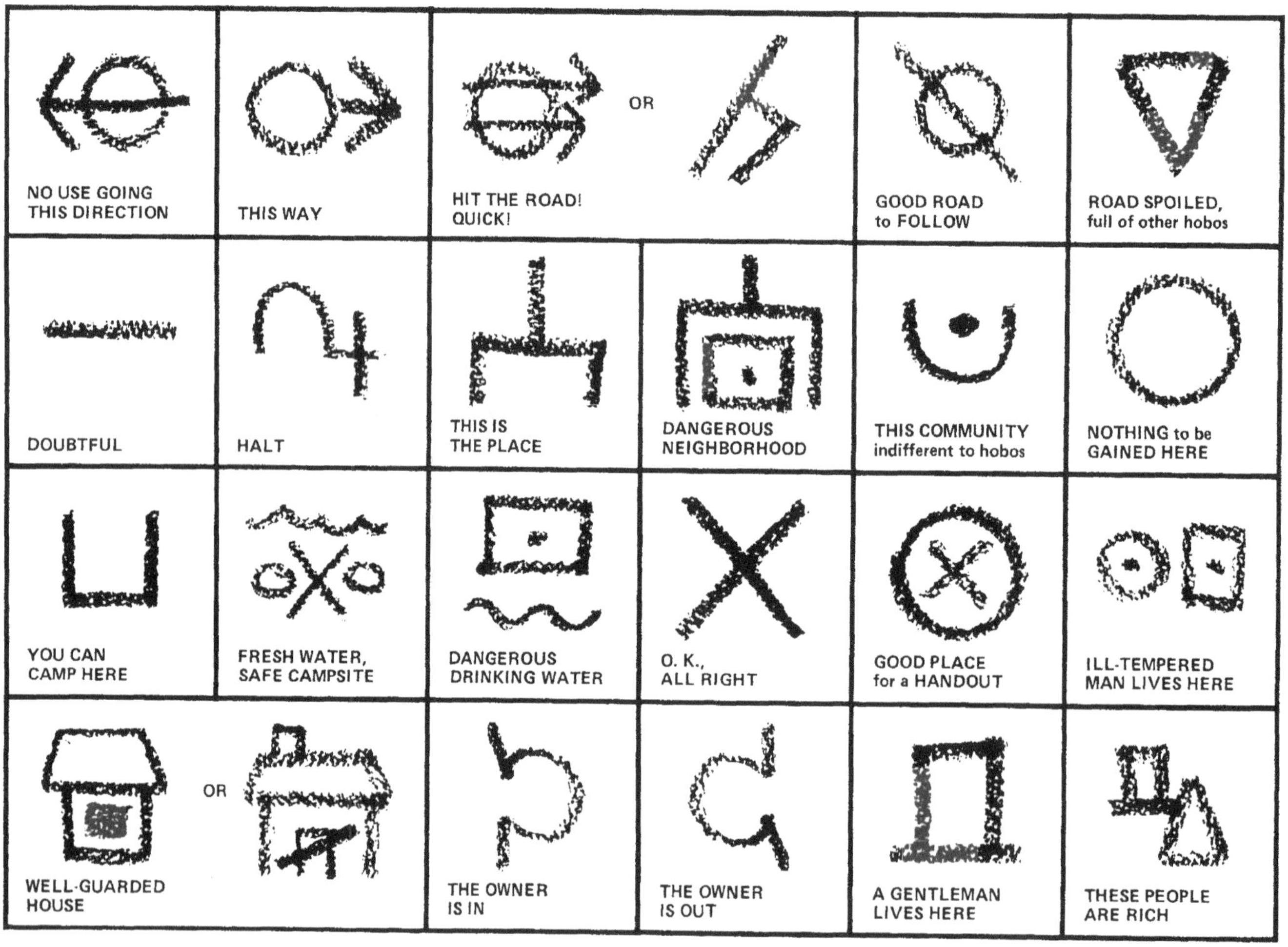

NO USE GOING THIS DIRECTION	THIS WAY	HIT THE ROAD! QUICK! (OR)		GOOD ROAD to FOLLOW	ROAD SPOILED, full of other hobos
DOUBTFUL	HALT	THIS IS THE PLACE	DANGEROUS NEIGHBORHOOD	THIS COMMUNITY indifferent to hobos	NOTHING to be GAINED HERE
YOU CAN CAMP HERE	FRESH WATER, SAFE CAMPSITE	DANGEROUS DRINKING WATER	O. K., ALL RIGHT	GOOD PLACE for a HANDOUT	ILL-TEMPERED MAN LIVES HERE
WELL-GUARDED HOUSE (OR)		THE OWNER IS IN	THE OWNER IS OUT	A GENTLEMAN LIVES HERE	THESE PEOPLE ARE RICH

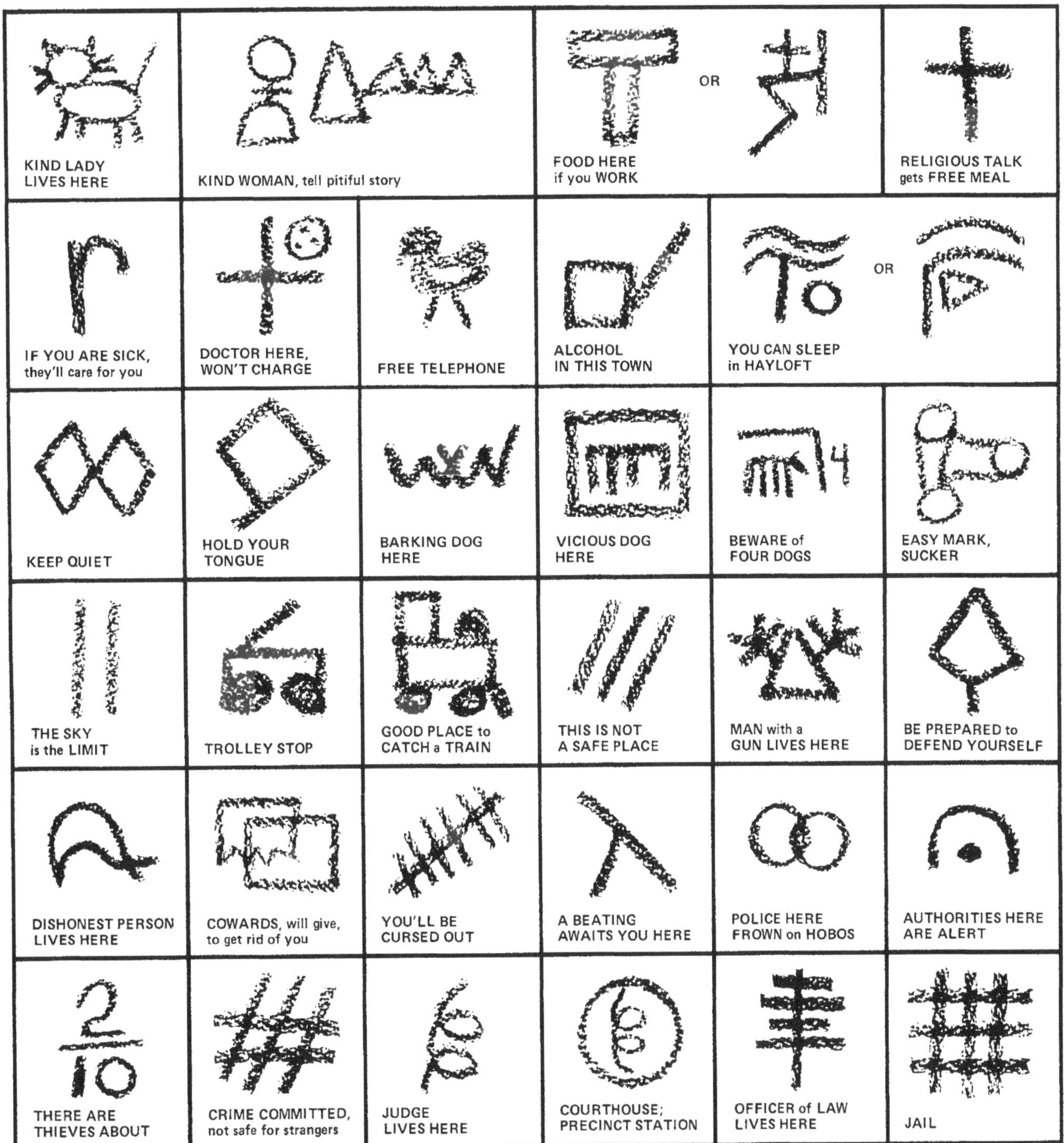

KIND LADY LIVES HERE
KIND WOMAN, tell pitiful story
FOOD HERE if you WORK
OR
RELIGIOUS TALK gets FREE MEAL
IF YOU ARE SICK, they'll care for you
DOCTOR HERE, WON'T CHARGE
FREE TELEPHONE
ALCOHOL IN THIS TOWN
YOU CAN SLEEP in HAYLOFT
OR
KEEP QUIET
HOLD YOUR TONGUE
BARKING DOG HERE
VICIOUS DOG HERE
BEWARE of FOUR DOGS
EASY MARK, SUCKER
THE SKY is the LIMIT
TROLLEY STOP
GOOD PLACE to CATCH a TRAIN
THIS IS NOT A SAFE PLACE
MAN with a GUN LIVES HERE
BE PREPARED to DEFEND YOURSELF
DISHONEST PERSON LIVES HERE
COWARDS, will give, to get rid of you
YOU'LL BE CURSED OUT
A BEATING AWAITS YOU HERE
POLICE HERE FROWN on HOBOS
AUTHORITIES HERE ARE ALERT
THERE ARE THIEVES ABOUT
CRIME COMMITTED, not safe for strangers
JUDGE LIVES HERE
COURTHOUSE; PRECINCT STATION
OFFICER of LAW LIVES HERE
JAIL

Note: Hobo signs are drawn as they usually appear – in chalk, on a rough wood fence, post or sidewalk.

GEOGRAPHY

Roads and Railroads	r SUPERHIGHWAY	r SUPERHIGHWAY under construction	r FULL INTERCHANGE	r PARTIAL INTERCHANGE	r ACCESS DENIED
r DUAL HIGHWAY ▲	r MAIN ROAD ▲	r SECONDARY ROAD ▲	r TRACK; PATH	r b BRIDGE and ROAD ●	r b DRAWBRIDGE and ROAD ●
r TUNNEL and ROAD ●	RAILROAD TRACK, single ▲	RAILROAD TRACKS, two or more ▲	RAILROAD STATION	NARROW GAUGE TRACK ▲	
Boundaries	r INTERNATIONAL	r UNDEMARCATED INTERNATIONAL	r UNDEFINED INTERNATIONAL	PROVINCIAL or STATE	COUNTY
TOWNSHIP	INCORPORATED VILLAGE	RESERVATION, national or state	r LAND GRANT	SMALL PARK, CEMETERY	BOUNDARY BEACON
Settlements	pink URBAN AREA	r METROPOLIS	r CITY	r TOWN	CITY of administrative importance
CITY of no administrative importance	CAPITAL CITY	NAMED TOWN within larger urban area	VILLAGE	HAMLET	VILLAGE, permanently inhabited

▲ Line may be broken or interrupted to indicate "under construction," as shown in Superhighway under Construction.
● Bridge, Drawbridge, and Tunnel shown here with Dual Highway; may also be used in combination with other road or railroad symbols.

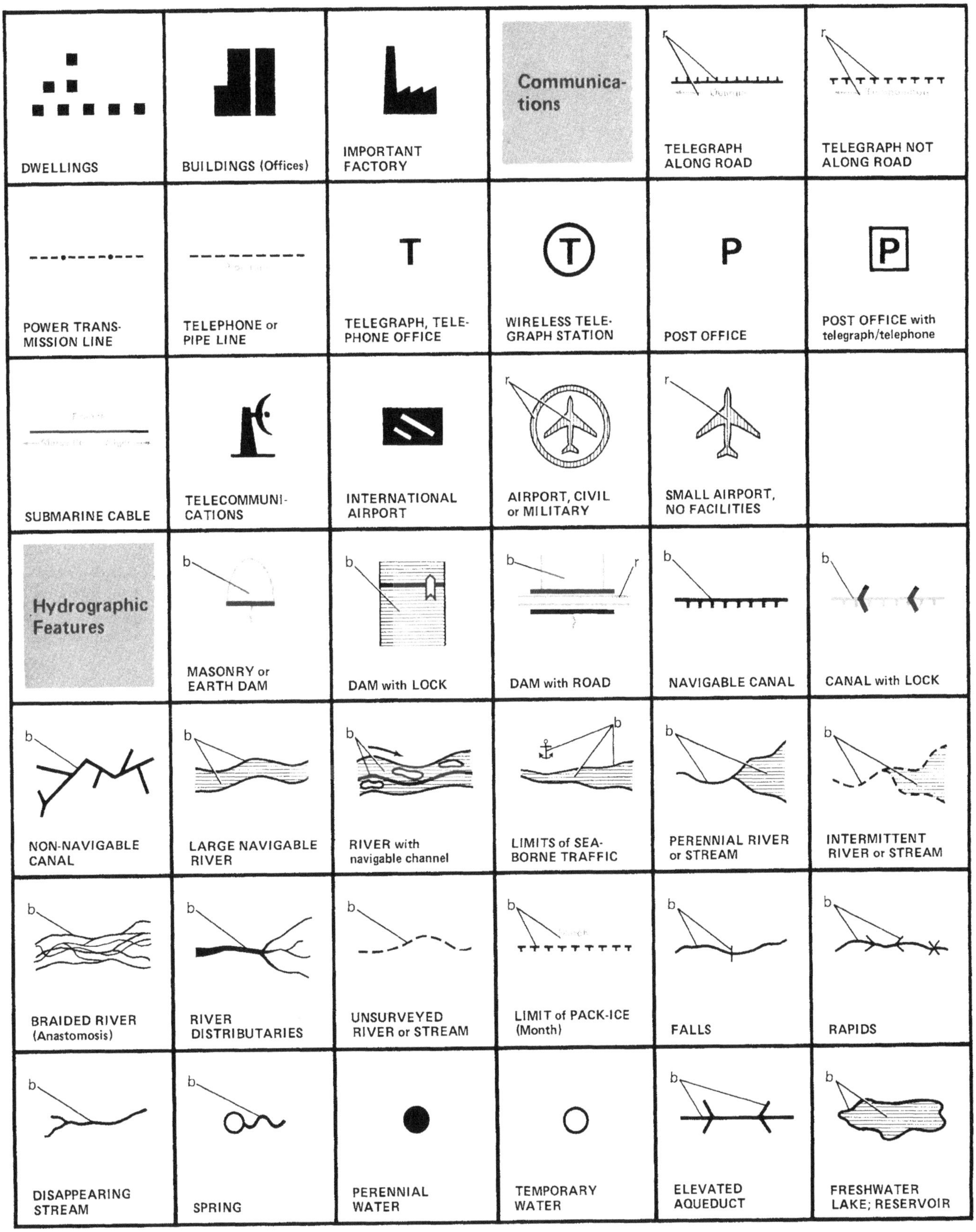

DWELLINGS	BUILDINGS (Offices)	IMPORTANT FACTORY	**Communications**	TELEGRAPH ALONG ROAD	TELEGRAPH NOT ALONG ROAD
POWER TRANSMISSION LINE	TELEPHONE or PIPE LINE	T TELEGRAPH, TELEPHONE OFFICE	(T) WIRELESS TELEGRAPH STATION	P POST OFFICE	[P] POST OFFICE with telegraph/telephone
SUBMARINE CABLE	TELECOMMUNICATIONS	INTERNATIONAL AIRPORT	AIRPORT, CIVIL or MILITARY	SMALL AIRPORT, NO FACILITIES	
Hydrographic Features	MASONRY or EARTH DAM	DAM with LOCK	DAM with ROAD	NAVIGABLE CANAL	CANAL with LOCK
NON-NAVIGABLE CANAL	LARGE NAVIGABLE RIVER	RIVER with navigable channel	LIMITS of SEA-BORNE TRAFFIC	PERENNIAL RIVER or STREAM	INTERMITTENT RIVER or STREAM
BRAIDED RIVER (Anastomosis)	RIVER DISTRIBUTARIES	UNSURVEYED RIVER or STREAM	LIMIT of PACK-ICE (Month)	FALLS	RAPIDS
DISAPPEARING STREAM	SPRING	PERENNIAL WATER	TEMPORARY WATER	ELEVATED AQUEDUCT	FRESHWATER LAKE; RESERVOIR

GEOGRAPHY *(continued)*

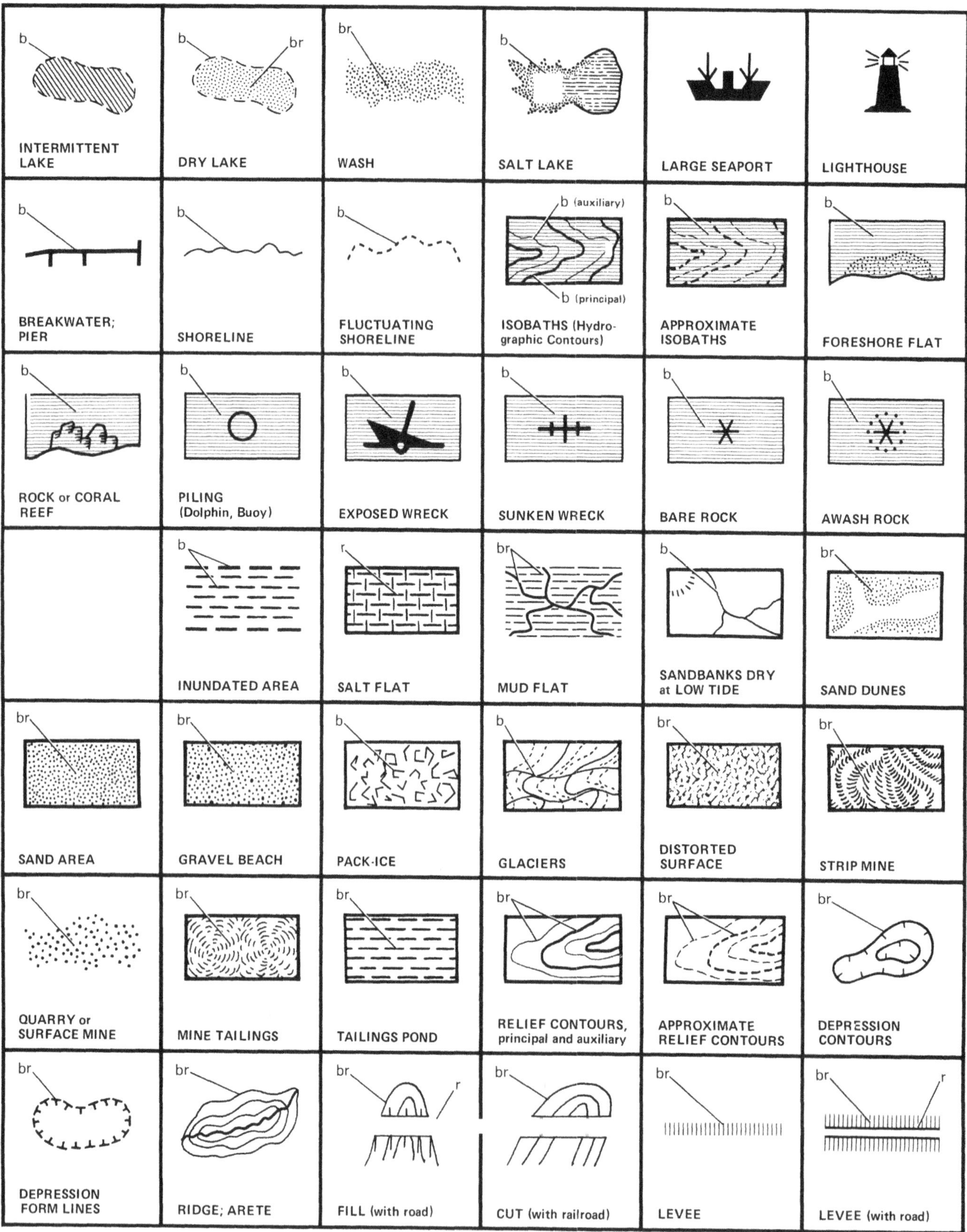

b
br
INTERMITTENT LAKE
DRY LAKE
WASH
SALT LAKE
LARGE SEAPORT
LIGHTHOUSE
b (auxiliary)
b (principal)
BREAKWATER; PIER
SHORELINE
FLUCTUATING SHORELINE
ISOBATHS (Hydrographic Contours)
APPROXIMATE ISOBATHS
FORESHORE FLAT
ROCK or CORAL REEF
PILING (Dolphin, Buoy)
EXPOSED WRECK
SUNKEN WRECK
BARE ROCK
AWASH ROCK
r
INUNDATED AREA
SALT FLAT
MUD FLAT
SANDBANKS DRY at LOW TIDE
SAND DUNES
SAND AREA
GRAVEL BEACH
PACK-ICE
GLACIERS
DISTORTED SURFACE
STRIP MINE
QUARRY or SURFACE MINE
MINE TAILINGS
TAILINGS POND
RELIEF CONTOURS, principal and auxiliary
APPROXIMATE RELIEF CONTOURS
DEPRESSION CONTOURS
DEPRESSION FORM LINES
RIDGE; ARETE
FILL (with road)
CUT (with railroad)
LEVEE
LEVEE (with road)

Vegetation	g WOODS; BRUSHWOODS	g SCRUB	g MANGROVE	g ORCHARD	OASIS
g VINEYARD	b SALT MARSH	b FRESH-WATER MARSH ▲	Cultural and Natural Features	MOUNTAIN PASS	TRIGONOMETRICAL POINT, 1st order ●
ELEVATION ABOVE SEA LEVEL ★	HIGHEST POINT in COUNTRY ■	RANGER STATION	MINING PROSPECT	r ROUTE of EXPLORERS	r EXPLORER ROUTE FROM REPORTS
r POINT of INTEREST	SCHOOL	r COLLEGE; UNIVERSITY	MOHAMMEDAN MOSQUE	SYNAGOGUE	PAGODA (Temple)
CHRISTIAN MISSION	CATHEDRAL; CHURCH	CEMETERY of geographical importance	LARGE HOSPITAL	HEALTH CENTER	RUINS
r CASTLE	BATTLEFIELD	r MILITARY INSTALLATION	NON-CONIFEROUS TREES	CONIFEROUS TREES	REDWOOD GROVES
g PARK with BOUNDARIES	GOLF COURSE	WINDMILL	NATIONAL WILD-LIFE REFUGE	TANK (Oil, Water)	

▲ Blue background would indicate submerged marsh; green background would indicate wooded marsh or swamp.
● Refers to quality of survey.
★ Also indicates 2nd Order Trigonometrical Point.
■ ▼ indicates Lowest Point in Country.

GEOLOGY *

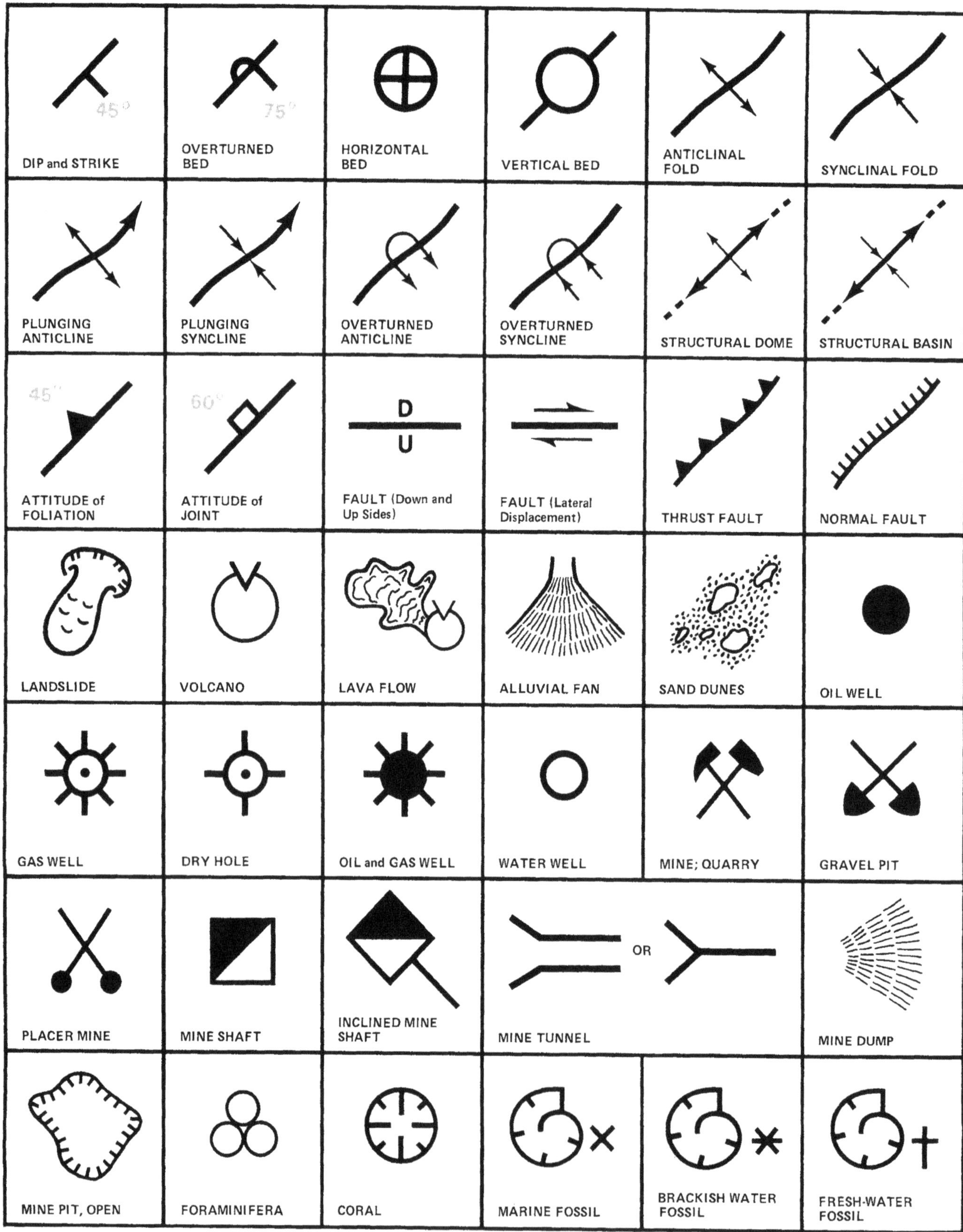

45°
DIP and STRIKE
75°
OVERTURNED BED
HORIZONTAL BED
VERTICAL BED
ANTICLINAL FOLD
SYNCLINAL FOLD
PLUNGING ANTICLINE
PLUNGING SYNCLINE
OVERTURNED ANTICLINE
OVERTURNED SYNCLINE
STRUCTURAL DOME
STRUCTURAL BASIN
45°
ATTITUDE of FOLIATION
60°
ATTITUDE of JOINT
D
U
FAULT (Down and Up Sides)
FAULT (Lateral Displacement)
THRUST FAULT
NORMAL FAULT
LANDSLIDE
VOLCANO
LAVA FLOW
ALLUVIAL FAN
SAND DUNES
OIL WELL
GAS WELL
DRY HOLE
OIL and GAS WELL
WATER WELL
MINE; QUARRY
GRAVEL PIT
PLACER MINE
MINE SHAFT
INCLINED MINE SHAFT
OR
MINE TUNNEL
MINE DUMP
MINE PIT, OPEN
FORAMINIFERA
CORAL
MARINE FOSSIL
BRACKISH WATER FOSSIL
FRESH-WATER FOSSIL

* FOR CARTOGRAPHY, SEE **GEOGRAPHY**, PAGE 92.

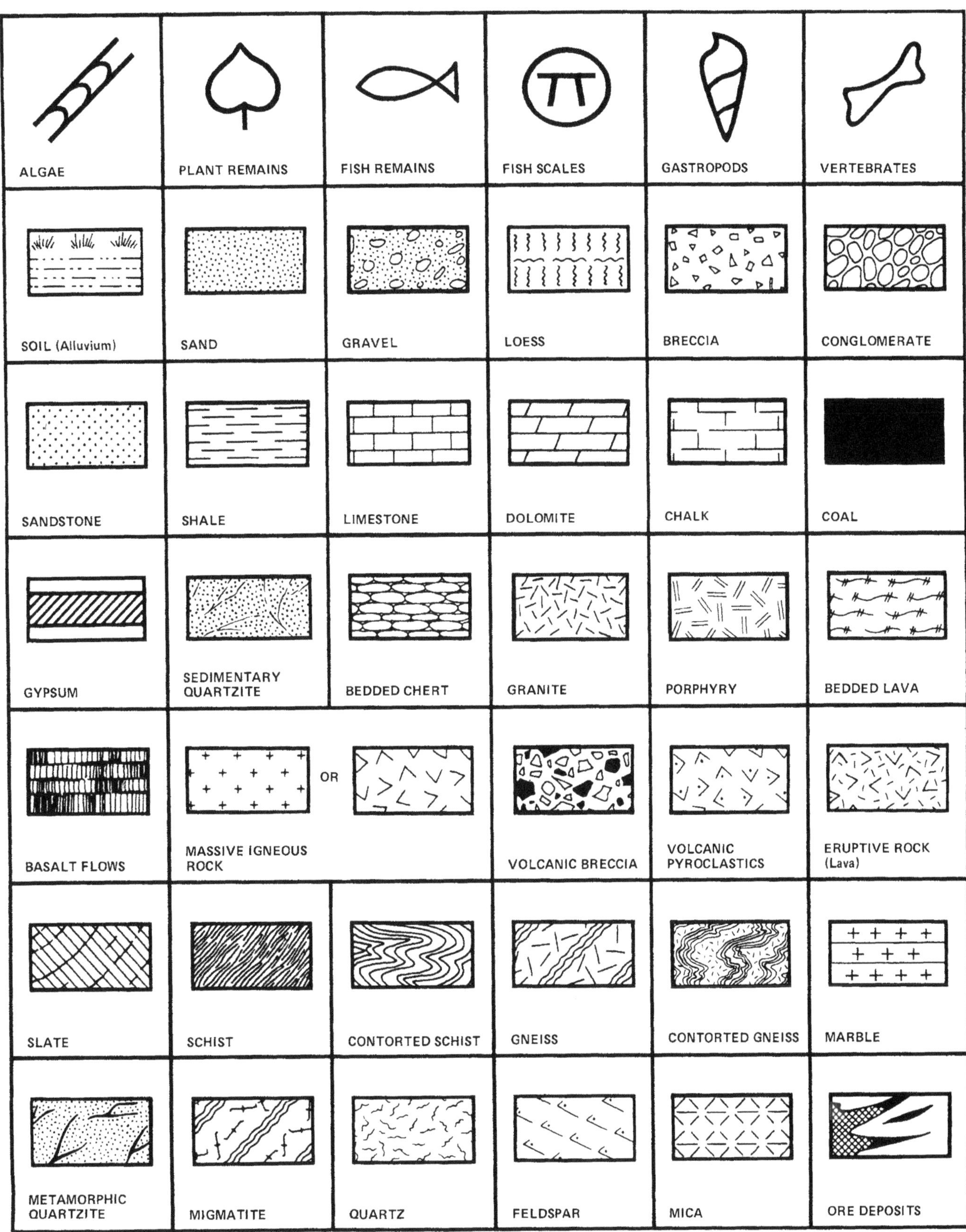
ALGAE
PLANT REMAINS
FISH REMAINS
FISH SCALES
GASTROPODS
VERTEBRATES
SOIL (Alluvium)
SAND
GRAVEL
LOESS
BRECCIA
CONGLOMERATE
SANDSTONE
SHALE
LIMESTONE
DOLOMITE
CHALK
COAL
GYPSUM
SEDIMENTARY QUARTZITE
BEDDED CHERT
GRANITE
PORPHYRY
BEDDED LAVA
BASALT FLOWS
OR
MASSIVE IGNEOUS ROCK
VOLCANIC BRECCIA
VOLCANIC PYROCLASTICS
ERUPTIVE ROCK (Lava)
SLATE
SCHIST
CONTORTED SCHIST
GNEISS
CONTORTED GNEISS
MARBLE
METAMORPHIC QUARTZITE
MIGMATITE
QUARTZ
FELDSPAR
MICA
ORE DEPOSITS

HANDLING OF GOODS

OR
OR
OR
FRAGILE
OR
HANDLE with CARE
OR
OR
KEEP DRY
PROTECT from HEAT
KEEP FROZEN
PROTECT against COLD
THIS WAY UP
SLING HERE
USE NO HOOKS
STACKING LIMIT
DO NOT STACK
INSERT LIFT CART HERE
LIFT HERE
PULL
OPEN HERE
OR
OR
DO NOT TUMBLE
OR
DO NOT ROLL
GROSS WEIGHT
NET WEIGHT
CONTENT in LITERS
DIMENSIONS
TOP-HEAVY
OR
HEAVY WEIGHT THIS END
OR
BALANCE (Center of Gravity)
POISON
POISON
orange
EXPLOSIVE
EXPLOSIVE
RADIOACTIVE
RADIOACTIVITY, Low Level
INFLAMMABLE LIQUID
INFLAMMABLE LIQUID
INFLAMMABLE SOLID
INFLAMMABLE SOLID
SPONTANEOUSLY COMBUSTIBLE
SPONTANEOUSLY COMBUSTIBLE
DANGEROUS when WET
DANGEROUS when WET

▲ This label is also made with the title Poison Gas.
● Vertical bars indicate progressive levels of radioactivity: (II) means Medium, (III) means High.
★ This label is also made with the title Inflammable Gas.
¶ ISO Recommendation

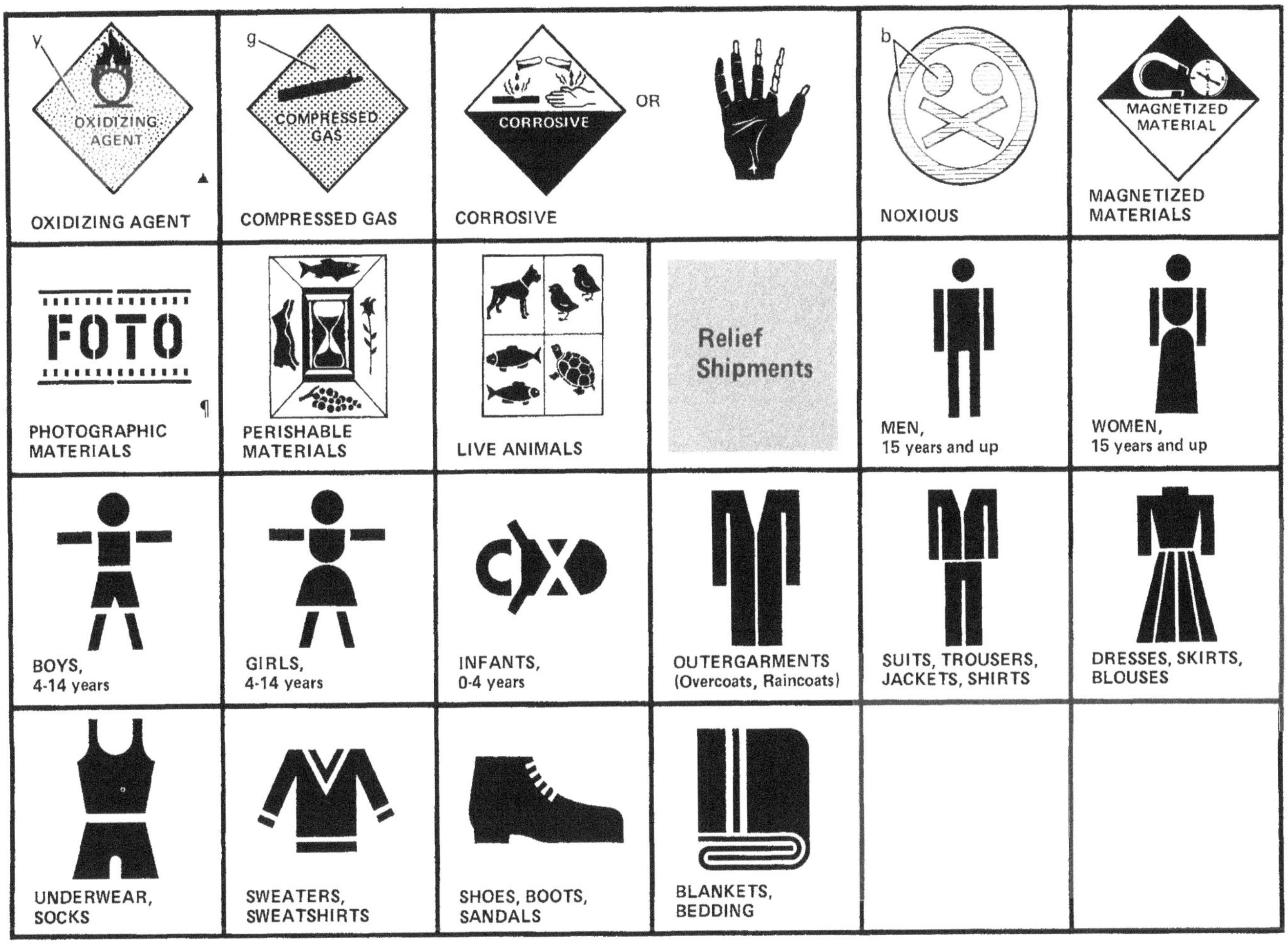

y OXIDIZING AGENT ▲ OXIDIZING AGENT	g COMPRESSED GAS COMPRESSED GAS	CORROSIVE OR CORROSIVE		b NOXIOUS	MAGNETIZED MATERIAL MAGNETIZED MATERIALS
FOTO ¶ PHOTOGRAPHIC MATERIALS	PERISHABLE MATERIALS	LIVE ANIMALS	Relief Shipments	MEN, 15 years and up	WOMEN, 15 years and up
BOYS, 4-14 years	GIRLS, 4-14 years	INFANTS, 0-4 years	OUTERGARMENTS (Overcoats, Raincoats)	SUITS, TROUSERS, JACKETS, SHIRTS	DRESSES, SKIRTS, BLOUSES
UNDERWEAR, SOCKS	SWEATERS, SWEATSHIRTS	SHOES, BOOTS, SANDALS	BLANKETS, BEDDING		

▲ This label is also made with the title Organic Peroxide.
¶ ISO Recommendation

MOSCOW TO NEW YORK

During a visit to the Soviet Union, I shipped a carton of toys home to the United States. Other than the address of destination, it had stencilled on it just three symbol directions:

2 arrows (this side up)
a goblet (fragile)
an umbrella (keep dry)

Considering that the shipment might be routed from Moscow via Constantinople, Piraeus, Genoa, and Lisbon before it reached the United States, and that the handlers in each port perhaps would not read any language other than their own, the message "spoke" in six tongues.

HOME ECONOMICS

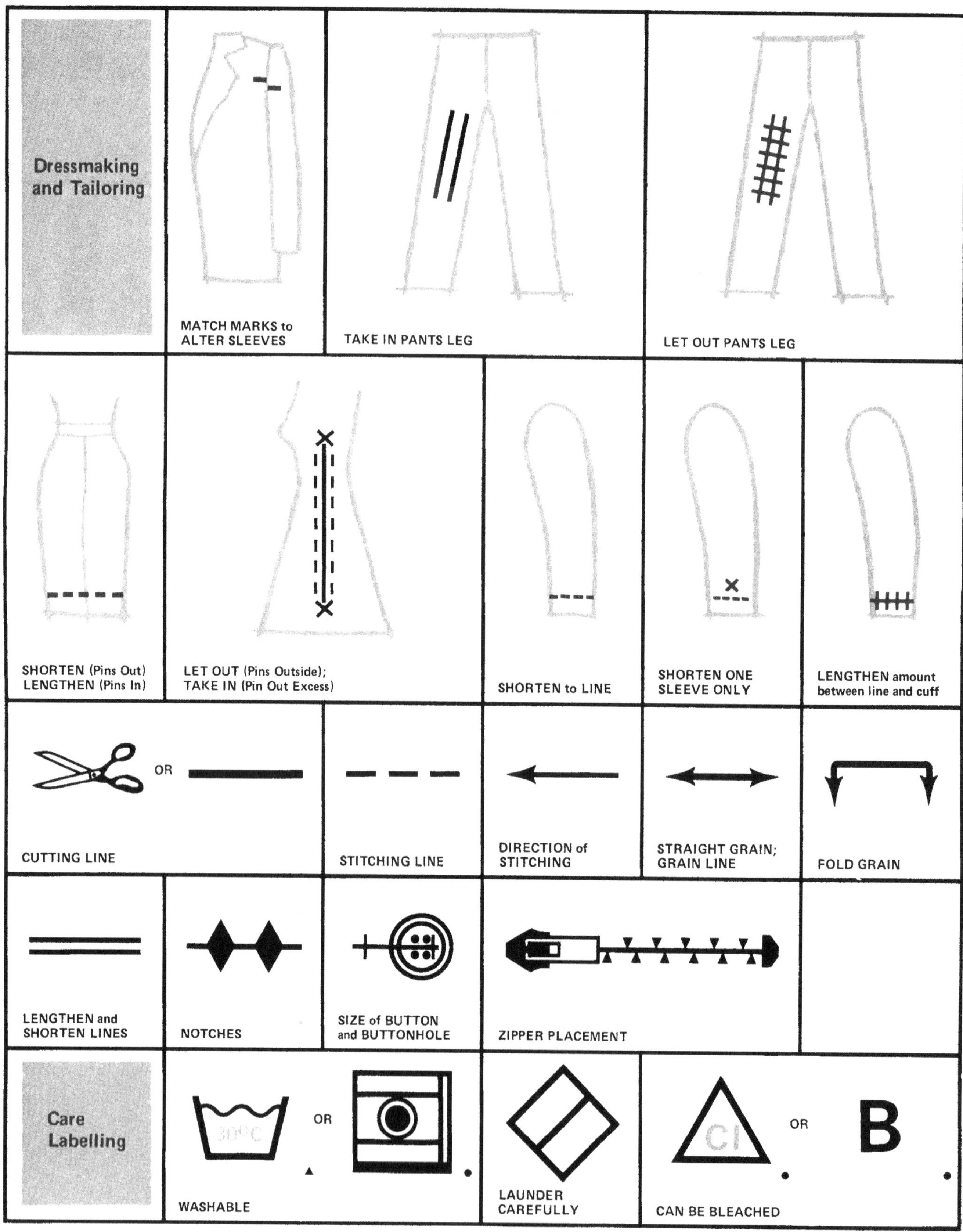

Dressmaking and Tailoring
MATCH MARKS to ALTER SLEEVES
TAKE IN PANTS LEG
LET OUT PANTS LEG
SHORTEN (Pins Out) LENGTHEN (Pins In)
LET OUT (Pins Outside); TAKE IN (Pin Out Excess)
SHORTEN to LINE
SHORTEN ONE SLEEVE ONLY
LENGTHEN amount between line and cuff
OR
CUTTING LINE
STITCHING LINE
DIRECTION of STITCHING
STRAIGHT GRAIN; GRAIN LINE
FOLD GRAIN
LENGTHEN and SHORTEN LINES
NOTCHES
SIZE of BUTTON and BUTTONHOLE
ZIPPER PLACEMENT
Care Labelling
30°C
OR
WASHABLE ▲
LAUNDER CAREFULLY ●
CI
OR
B
CAN BE BLEACHED ●

▲ Number in symbol indicates temperature in degrees Centigrade (Celsius) for washing garment.
● An X or / across the symbol negates its original meaning. **Example:** , Can Not Be Bleached.

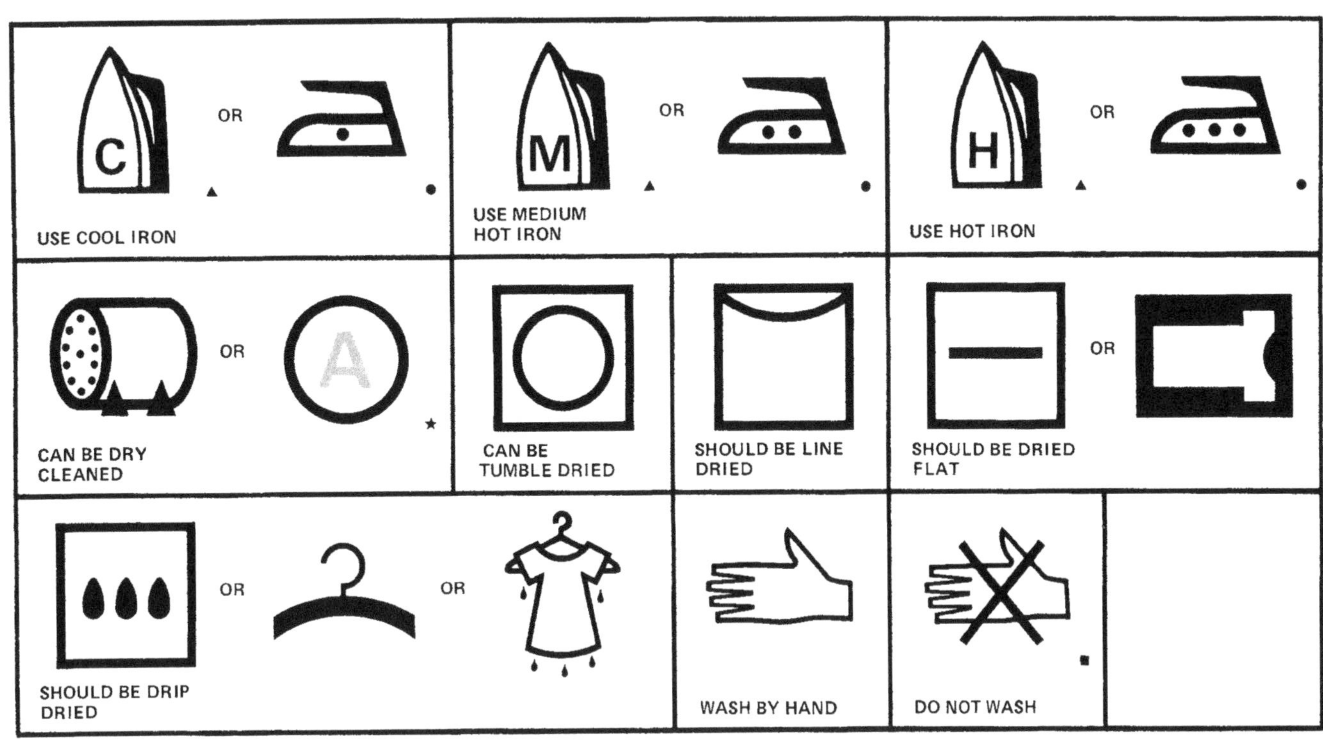
C
OR
USE COOL IRON
M
OR
USE MEDIUM
HOT IRON
H
OR
USE HOT IRON
A
OR
CAN BE DRY
CLEANED
CAN BE
TUMBLE DRIED
SHOULD BE LINE
DRIED
OR
SHOULD BE DRIED
FLAT
OR
OR
SHOULD BE DRIP
DRIED
WASH BY HAND
DO NOT WASH

Appliances

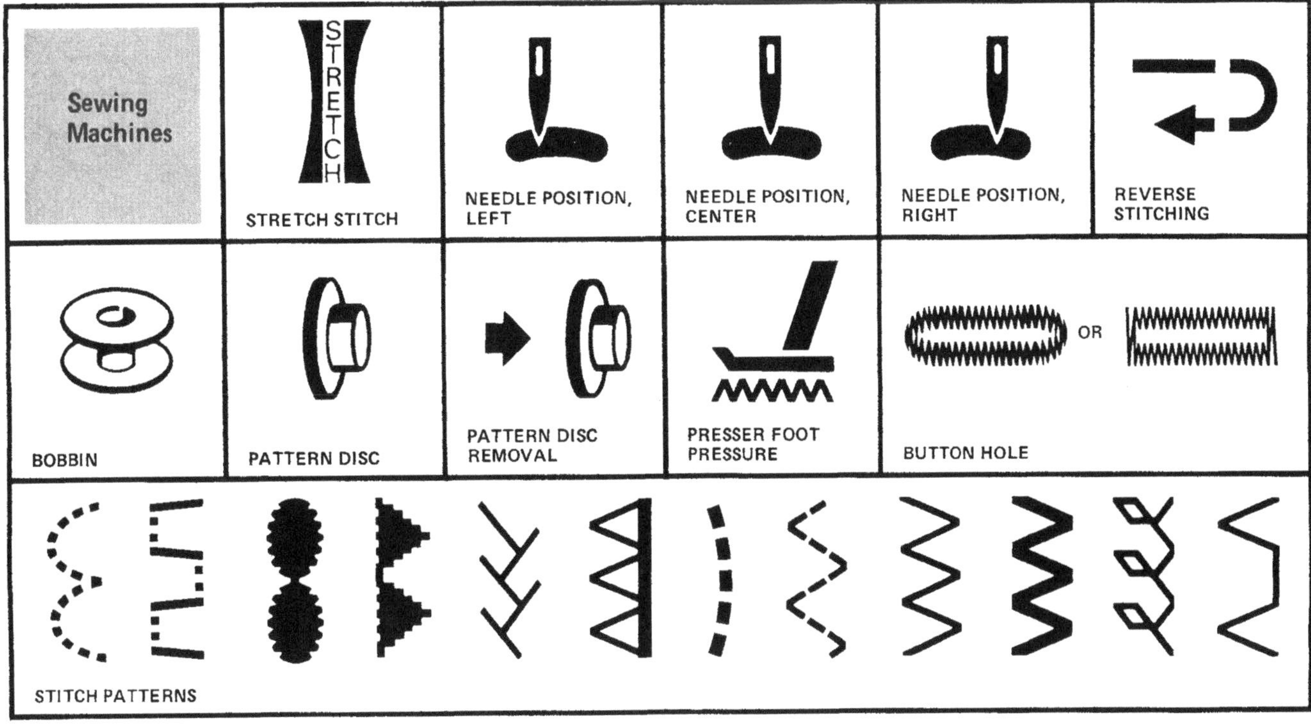
Sewing
Machines
STRETCH
STRETCH STITCH
NEEDLE POSITION,
LEFT
NEEDLE POSITION,
CENTER
NEEDLE POSITION,
RIGHT
REVERSE
STITCHING
BOBBIN
PATTERN DISC
PATTERN DISC
REMOVAL
PRESSER FOOT
PRESSURE
OR
BUTTON HOLE
STITCH PATTERNS

▲ The letters **S** for Steam and **L** for Little may also be used.
● One dot (•) indicates 120°C; two dots (••), 150°C; three dots (•••), 200°C.
★ Circle may include a letter indicating type of dry cleaning agent to be used. **Example:** **A** any solvent; **P** perchloroethylene or white spirit; **F** white spirit only.
■ A **/** or **X**, used to negate, may also be used on other symbols. **Example:** ✗, Do Not Iron.

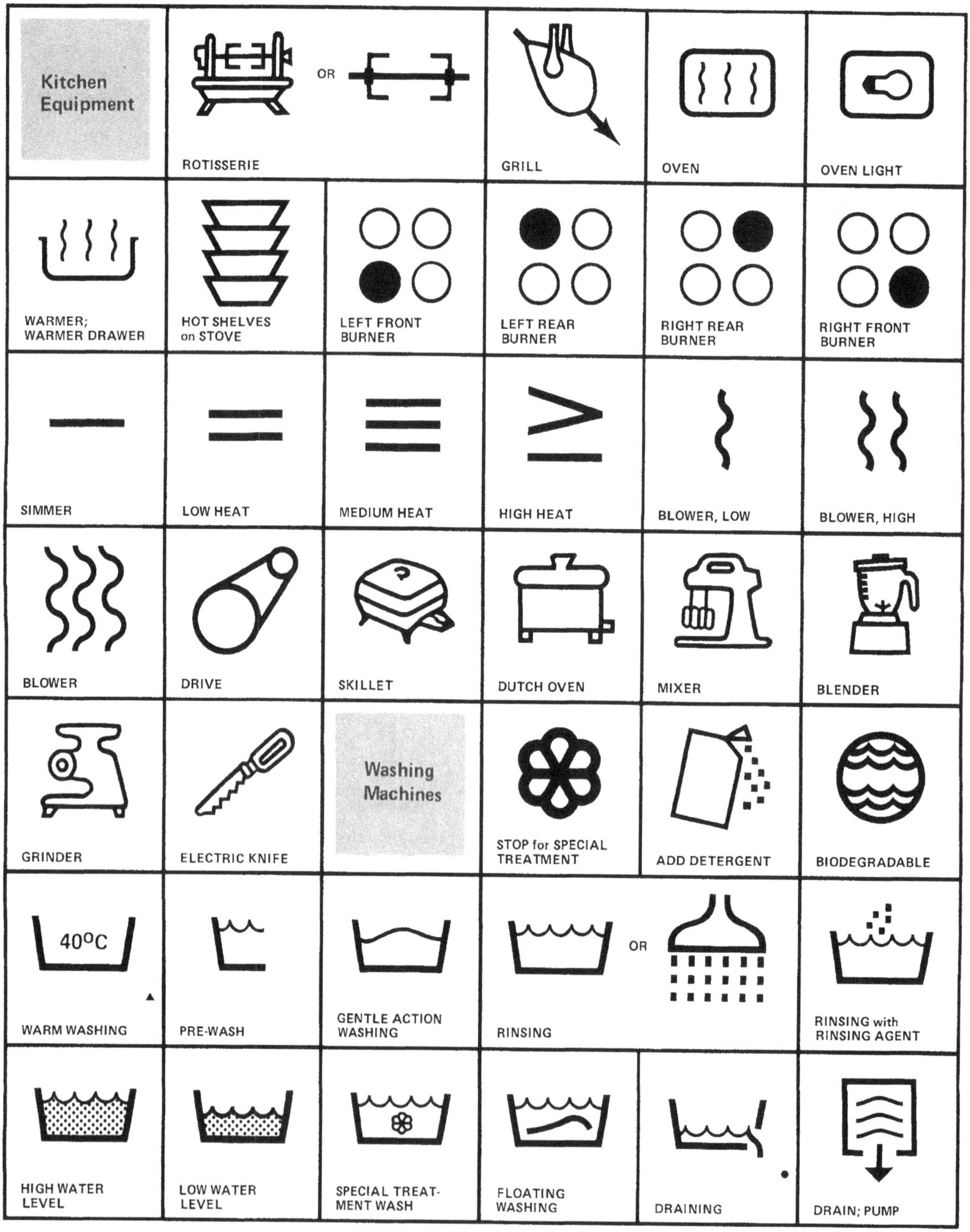

HOME ECONOMICS

Appliances *(continued)*

Kitchen Equipment	ROTISSERIE (OR)		GRILL	OVEN	OVEN LIGHT
WARMER; WARMER DRAWER	HOT SHELVES on STOVE	LEFT FRONT BURNER	LEFT REAR BURNER	RIGHT REAR BURNER	RIGHT FRONT BURNER
SIMMER	LOW HEAT	MEDIUM HEAT	HIGH HEAT	BLOWER, LOW	BLOWER, HIGH
BLOWER	DRIVE	SKILLET	DUTCH OVEN	MIXER	BLENDER
GRINDER	ELECTRIC KNIFE	**Washing Machines**	STOP for SPECIAL TREATMENT	ADD DETERGENT	BIODEGRADABLE
40°C ▲ WARM WASHING	PRE-WASH	GENTLE ACTION WASHING	RINSING (OR)		RINSING with RINSING AGENT
HIGH WATER LEVEL	LOW WATER LEVEL	SPECIAL TREATMENT WASH	FLOATING WASHING	● DRAINING	DRAIN; PUMP

▲ Temperature shown in degrees Centigrade (Celsius).
● An X or / across the symbol negates its original meaning. **Example:** , Not Draining.

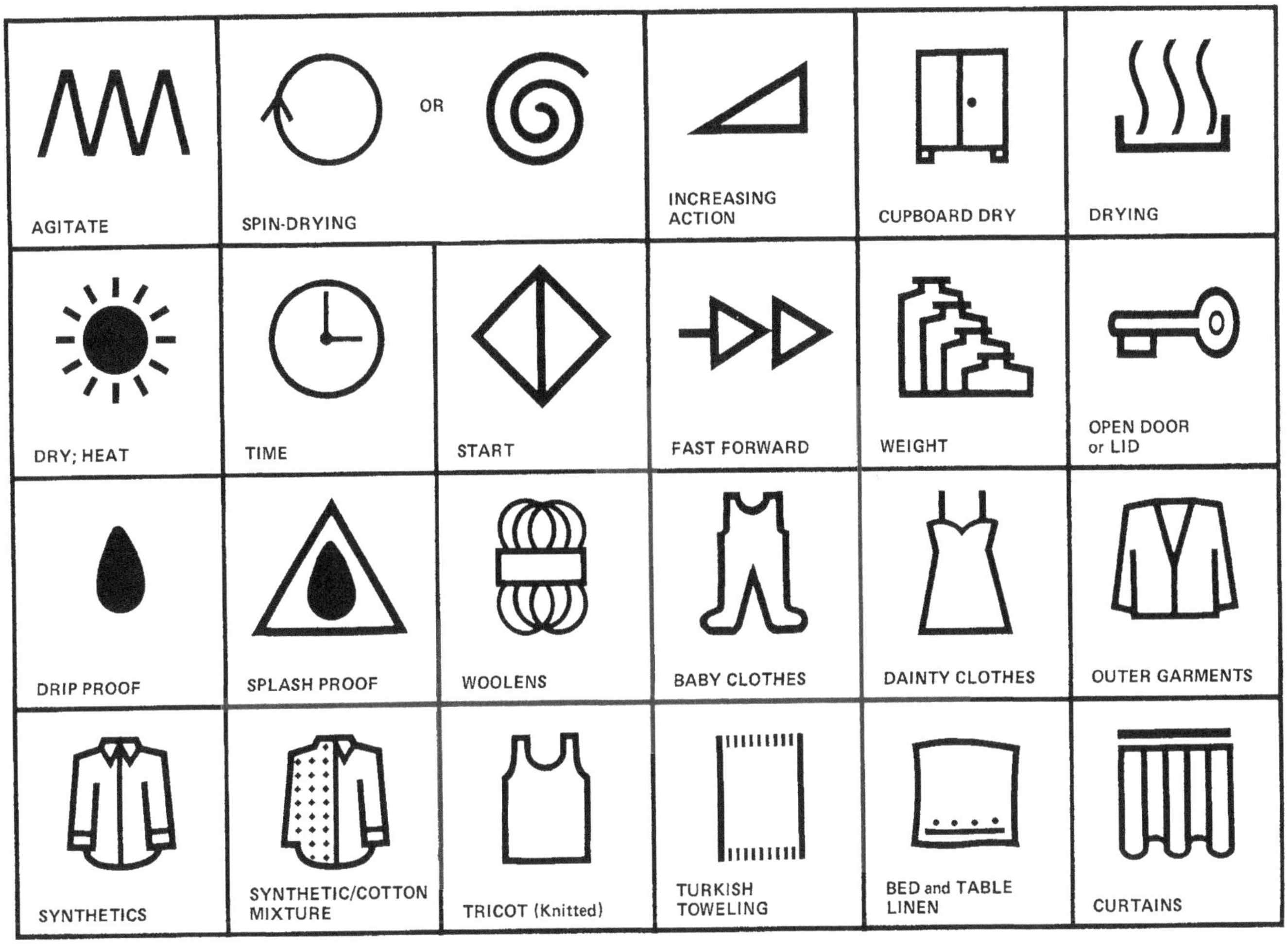

AGITATE	SPIN-DRYING (OR)		INCREASING ACTION	CUPBOARD DRY	DRYING
DRY; HEAT	TIME	START	FAST FORWARD	WEIGHT	OPEN DOOR or LID
DRIP PROOF	SPLASH PROOF	WOOLENS	BABY CLOTHES	DAINTY CLOTHES	OUTER GARMENTS
SYNTHETICS	SYNTHETIC/COTTON MIXTURE	TRICOT (Knitted)	TURKISH TOWELING	BED and TABLE LINEN	CURTAINS

FROM TRADEMARK INTO SYMBOL

It is a rare occurrence when a trademark sheds its strictly commercial usage as a logo and emerges as a widely used symbol. But this is exactly what happened to the Woolmark symbol identifying "Pure New Wool."

Reminiscent of a sleek skein of yarn, this unique design is easily remembered. And it has been so expertly publicized and protected that it has become internationally accepted as a symbol for fine wool products.

(Woolmark registered by International Wool Secretariat and usable only by their licensees. Reproduced here by special permission.)

MANUFACTURING

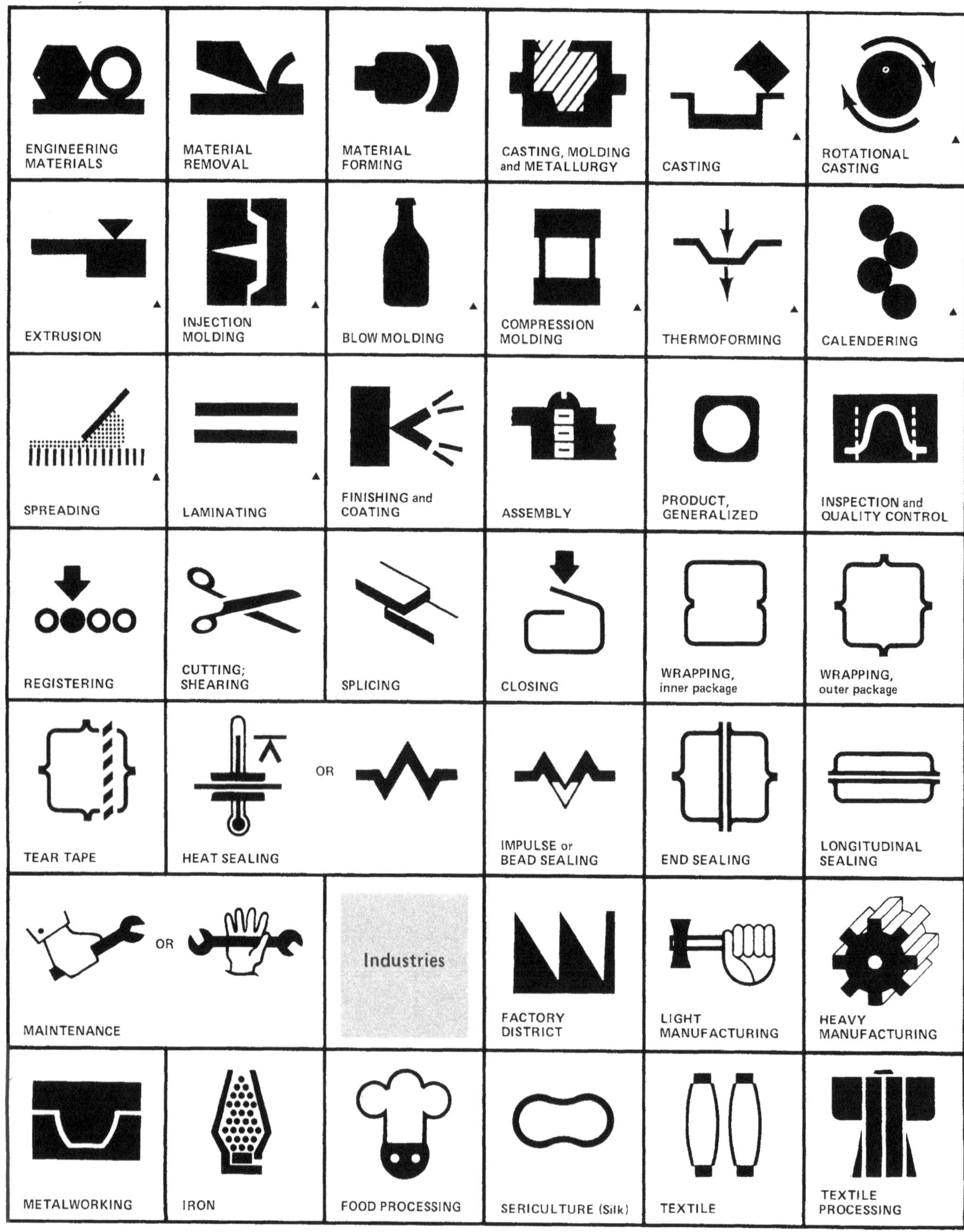

ENGINEERING MATERIALS
MATERIAL REMOVAL
MATERIAL FORMING
CASTING, MOLDING and METALLURGY
CASTING ▲
ROTATIONAL CASTING ▲
EXTRUSION ▲
INJECTION MOLDING ▲
BLOW MOLDING ▲
COMPRESSION MOLDING ▲
THERMOFORMING ▲
CALENDERING ▲
SPREADING ▲
LAMINATING ▲
FINISHING and COATING
ASSEMBLY
PRODUCT, GENERALIZED
INSPECTION and QUALITY CONTROL
REGISTERING
CUTTING; SHEARING
SPLICING
CLOSING
WRAPPING, inner package
WRAPPING, outer package
TEAR TAPE
HEAT SEALING
OR
IMPULSE or BEAD SEALING
END SEALING
LONGITUDINAL SEALING
MAINTENANCE
OR
Industries
FACTORY DISTRICT
LIGHT MANUFACTURING
HEAVY MANUFACTURING
METALWORKING
IRON
FOOD PROCESSING
SERICULTURE (Silk)
TEXTILE
TEXTILE PROCESSING

▲ These symbols were originally designed for the plastics industry, but can also be used in other manufacturing processes.

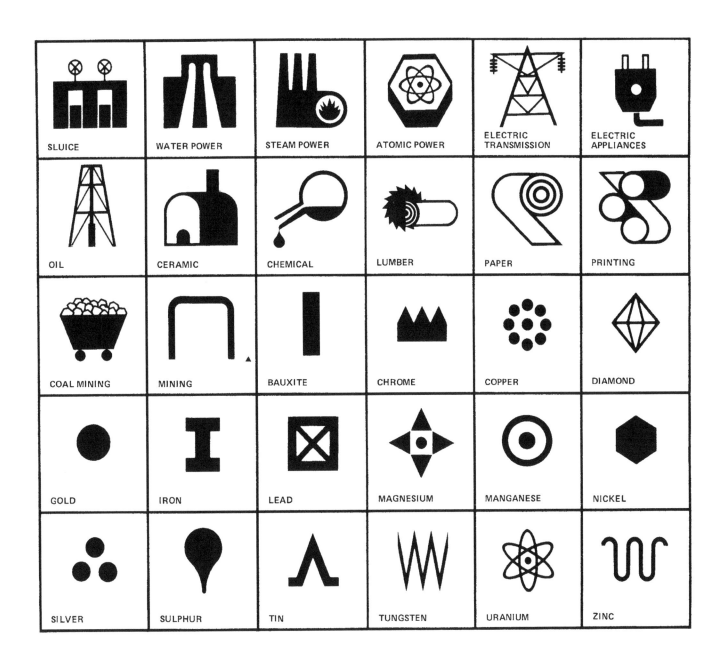

SLUICE	WATER POWER	STEAM POWER	ATOMIC POWER	ELECTRIC TRANSMISSION	ELECTRIC APPLIANCES
OIL	CERAMIC	CHEMICAL	LUMBER	PAPER	PRINTING
COAL MINING	MINING ▲	BAUXITE	CHROME	COPPER	DIAMOND
GOLD	IRON	LEAD	MAGNESIUM	MANGANESE	NICKEL
SILVER	SULPHUR	TIN	TUNGSTEN	URANIUM	ZINC

Heavy Duty Machinery

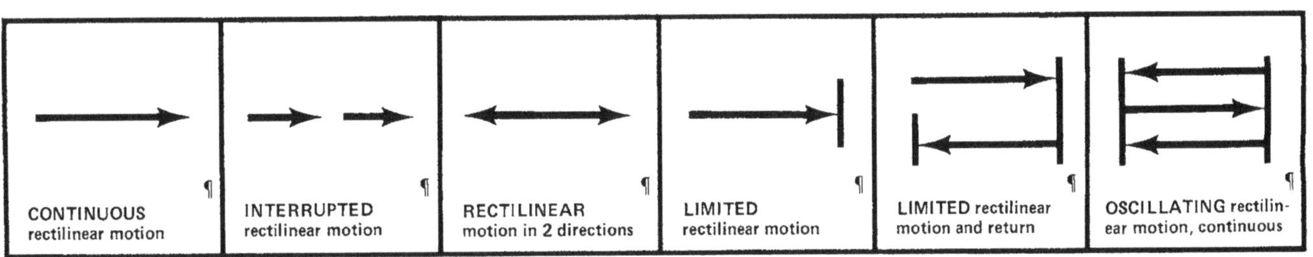
CONTINUOUS rectilinear motion ¶
INTERRUPTED rectilinear motion ¶
RECTILINEAR motion in 2 directions ¶
LIMITED rectilinear motion ¶
LIMITED rectilinear motion and return ¶
OSCILLATING rectilinear motion, continuous ¶

▲ Specific type of mining indicated by inserting a symbol. **Example:** [•] indicates Gold Mining; [I], Iron Mining.
¶ ISO Recommendation

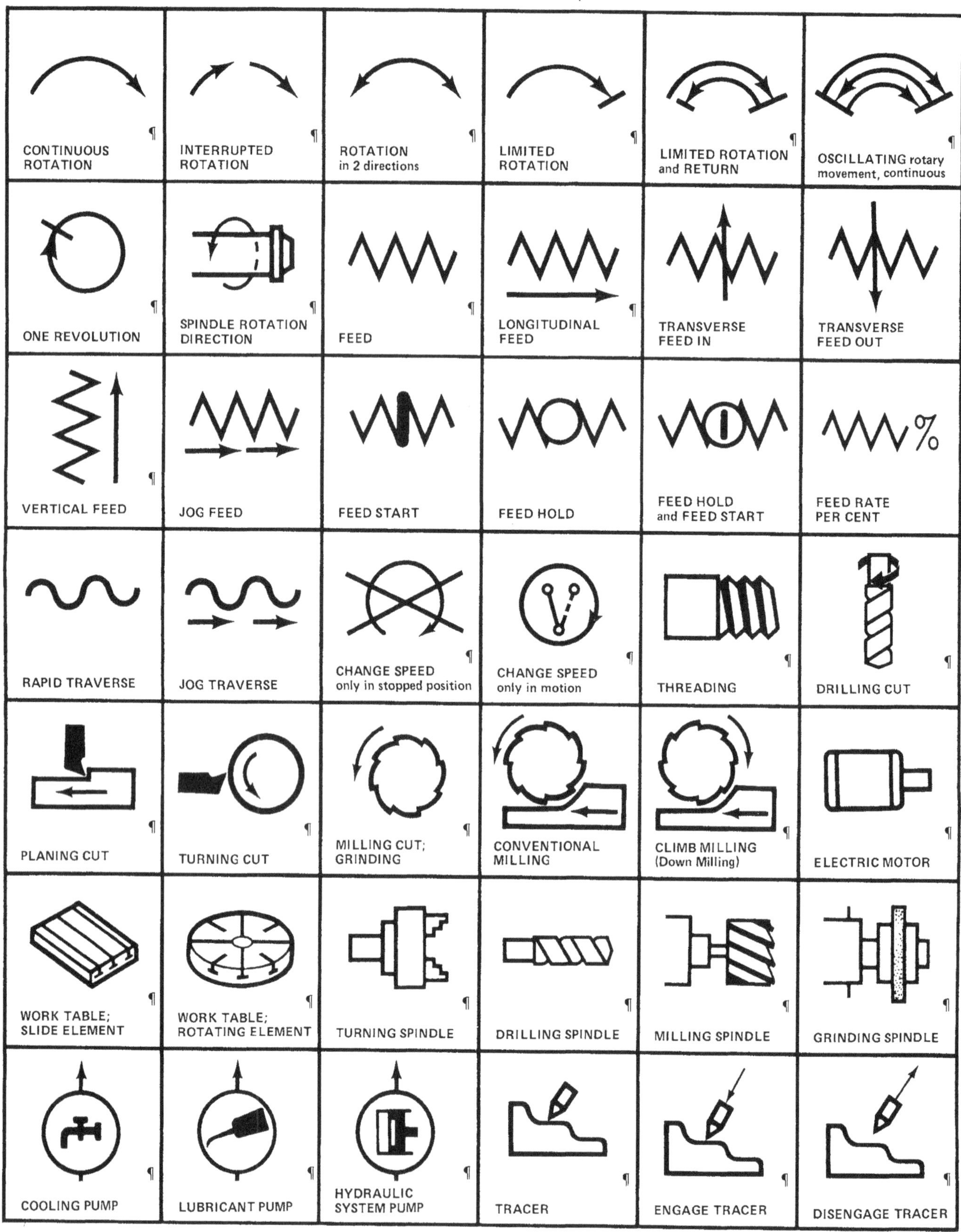
CONTINUOUS ROTATION ¶
INTERRUPTED ROTATION ¶
ROTATION in 2 directions ¶
LIMITED ROTATION ¶
LIMITED ROTATION and RETURN ¶
OSCILLATING rotary movement, continuous ¶
ONE REVOLUTION ¶
SPINDLE ROTATION DIRECTION ¶
FEED ¶
LONGITUDINAL FEED ¶
TRANSVERSE FEED IN
TRANSVERSE FEED OUT
VERTICAL FEED ¶
JOG FEED
FEED START
FEED HOLD
FEED HOLD and FEED START
FEED RATE PER CENT
%
RAPID TRAVERSE
JOG TRAVERSE
CHANGE SPEED only in stopped position ¶
CHANGE SPEED only in motion ¶
THREADING ¶
DRILLING CUT ¶
PLANING CUT ¶
TURNING CUT ¶
MILLING CUT; GRINDING ¶
CONVENTIONAL MILLING
CLIMB MILLING (Down Milling) ¶
ELECTRIC MOTOR ¶
WORK TABLE; SLIDE ELEMENT ¶
WORK TABLE; ROTATING ELEMENT ¶
TURNING SPINDLE ¶
DRILLING SPINDLE ¶
MILLING SPINDLE ¶
GRINDING SPINDLE ¶
COOLING PUMP ¶
LUBRICANT PUMP ¶
HYDRAULIC SYSTEM PUMP ¶
TRACER ¶
ENGAGE TRACER ¶
DISENGAGE TRACER ¶

¶ ISO Recommendation

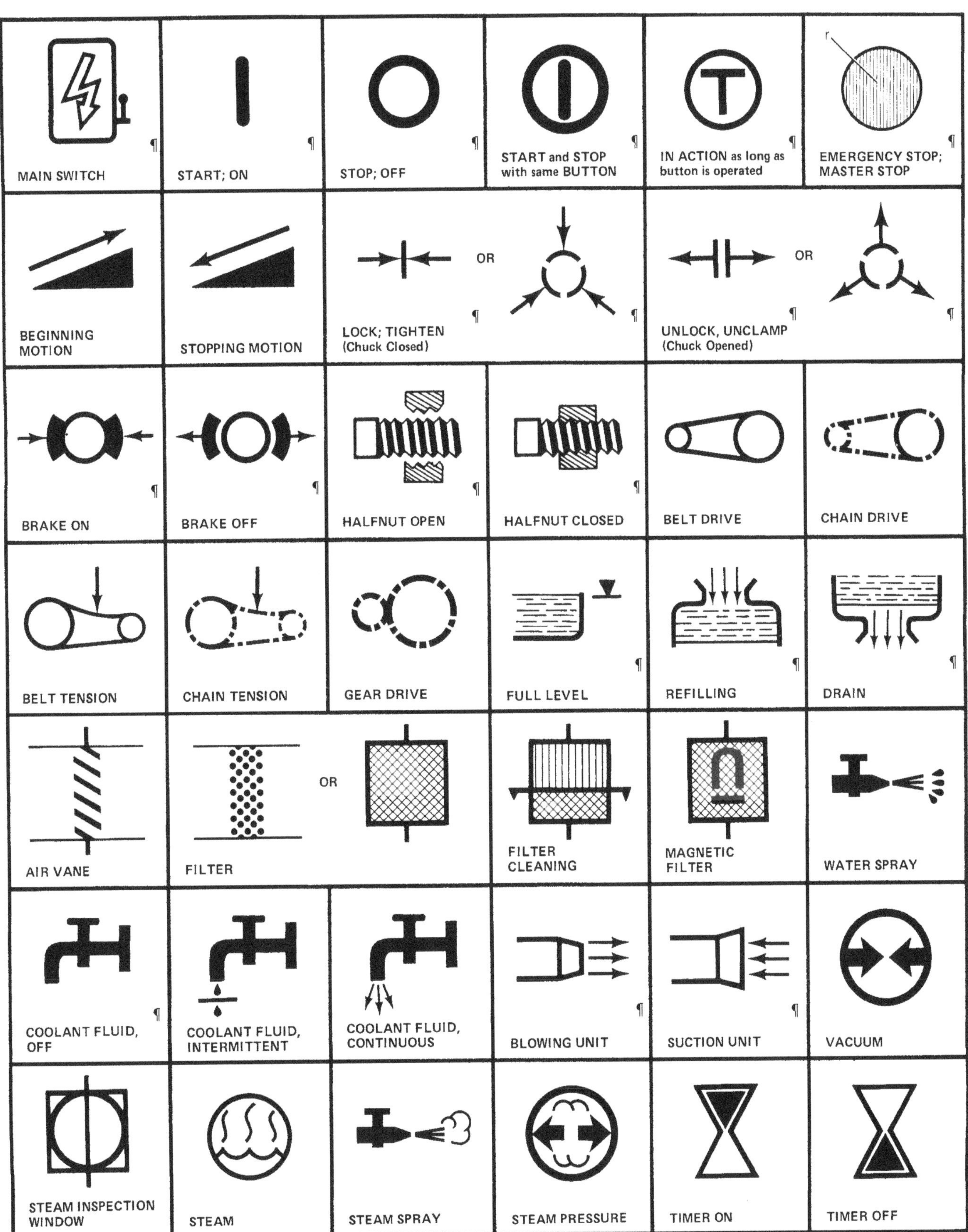

MAIN SWITCH ¶
START; ON ¶
STOP; OFF ¶
START and STOP with same BUTTON ¶
IN ACTION as long as button is operated ¶
r
EMERGENCY STOP; MASTER STOP ¶
BEGINNING MOTION
STOPPING MOTION
LOCK; TIGHTEN (Chuck Closed) ¶
OR ¶
UNLOCK, UNCLAMP (Chuck Opened) ¶
OR ¶
BRAKE ON ¶
BRAKE OFF ¶
HALFNUT OPEN ¶
HALFNUT CLOSED ¶
BELT DRIVE
CHAIN DRIVE
BELT TENSION
CHAIN TENSION
GEAR DRIVE
FULL LEVEL ¶
REFILLING ¶
DRAIN ¶
AIR VANE
FILTER
OR
FILTER CLEANING
MAGNETIC FILTER
WATER SPRAY
COOLANT FLUID, OFF ¶
COOLANT FLUID, INTERMITTENT
COOLANT FLUID, CONTINUOUS
BLOWING UNIT ¶
SUCTION UNIT ¶
VACUUM
STEAM INSPECTION WINDOW
STEAM
STEAM SPRAY
STEAM PRESSURE
TIMER ON
TIMER OFF

¶ ISO Recommendation

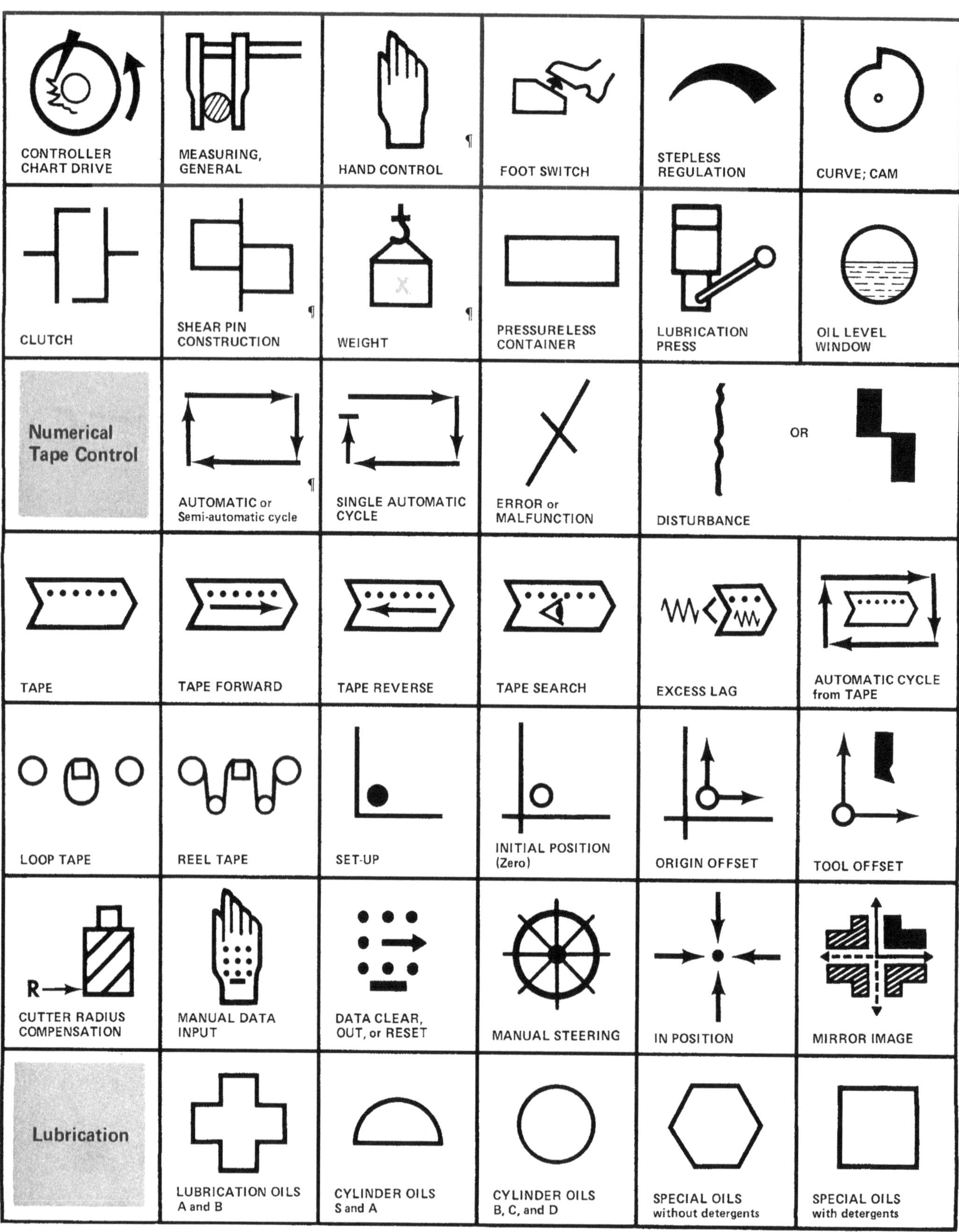
CONTROLLER CHART DRIVE
MEASURING, GENERAL
HAND CONTROL ¶
FOOT SWITCH
STEPLESS REGULATION
CURVE; CAM
CLUTCH
SHEAR PIN CONSTRUCTION ¶
WEIGHT ¶
PRESSURELESS CONTAINER
LUBRICATION PRESS
OIL LEVEL WINDOW
Numerical Tape Control
AUTOMATIC or Semi-automatic cycle ¶
SINGLE AUTOMATIC CYCLE
ERROR or MALFUNCTION
OR
DISTURBANCE
TAPE
TAPE FORWARD
TAPE REVERSE
TAPE SEARCH
EXCESS LAG
AUTOMATIC CYCLE from TAPE
LOOP TAPE
REEL TAPE
SET-UP
INITIAL POSITION (Zero)
ORIGIN OFFSET
TOOL OFFSET
R
CUTTER RADIUS COMPENSATION
MANUAL DATA INPUT
DATA CLEAR, OUT, or RESET
MANUAL STEERING
IN POSITION
MIRROR IMAGE
Lubrication
LUBRICATION OILS A and B
CYLINDER OILS S and A
CYLINDER OILS B, C, and D
SPECIAL OILS without detergents
SPECIAL OILS with detergents

¶ ISO Recommendation

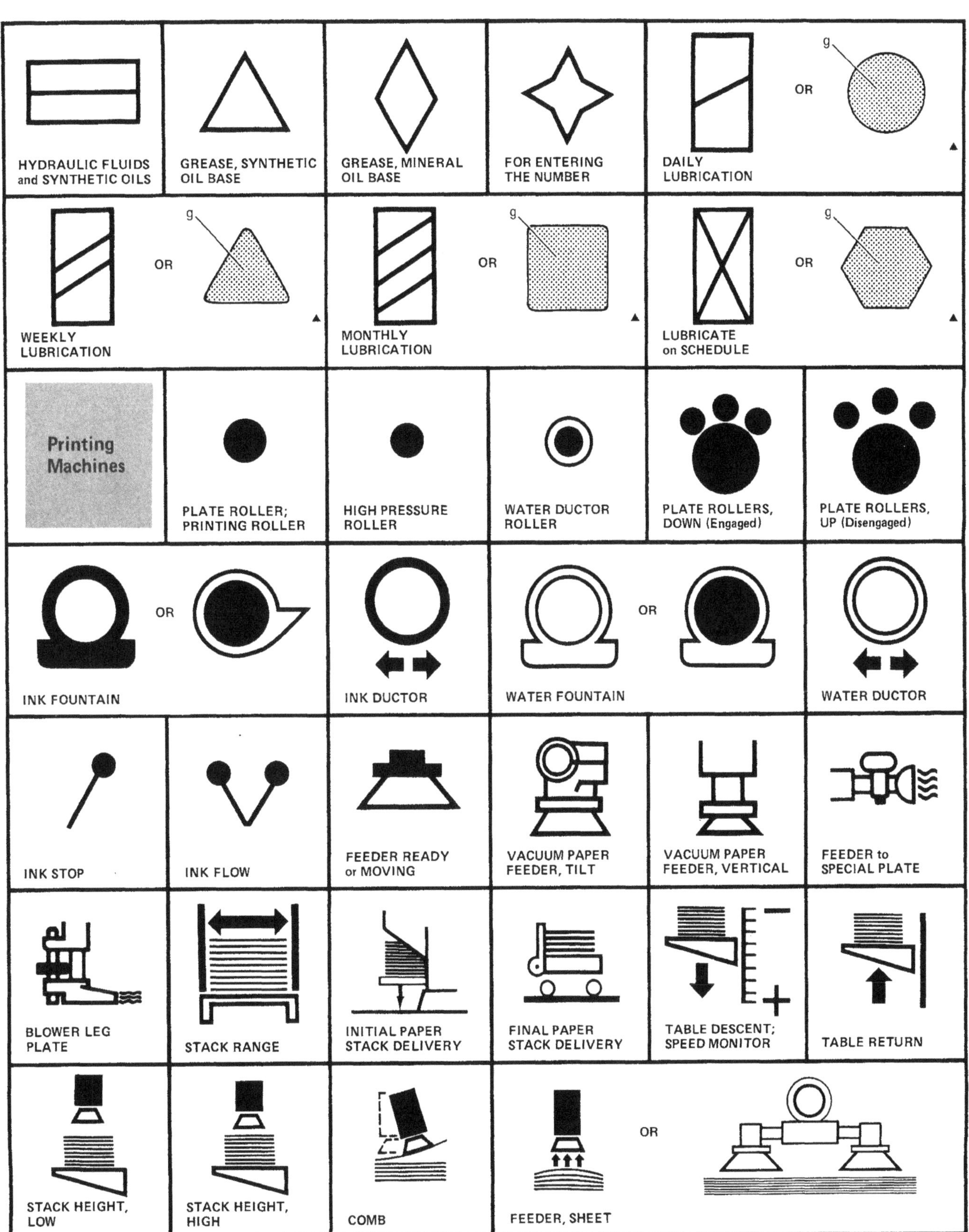
HYDRAULIC FLUIDS and SYNTHETIC OILS
GREASE, SYNTHETIC OIL BASE
GREASE, MINERAL OIL BASE
FOR ENTERING THE NUMBER
DAILY LUBRICATION
OR
g
▲
WEEKLY LUBRICATION
MONTHLY LUBRICATION
LUBRICATE on SCHEDULE
Printing Machines
PLATE ROLLER; PRINTING ROLLER
HIGH PRESSURE ROLLER
WATER DUCTOR ROLLER
PLATE ROLLERS, DOWN (Engaged)
PLATE ROLLERS, UP (Disengaged)
INK FOUNTAIN
INK DUCTOR
WATER FOUNTAIN
WATER DUCTOR
INK STOP
INK FLOW
FEEDER READY or MOVING
VACUUM PAPER FEEDER, TILT
VACUUM PAPER FEEDER, VERTICAL
FEEDER to SPECIAL PLATE
BLOWER LEG PLATE
STACK RANGE
INITIAL PAPER STACK DELIVERY
FINAL PAPER STACK DELIVERY
TABLE DESCENT; SPEED MONITOR
TABLE RETURN
STACK HEIGHT, LOW
STACK HEIGHT, HIGH
COMB
FEEDER, SHEET

▲ Color indicates type of grease or oil. For grease: green, lime grease (shown); yellow, lithium; pink, soda. For oil: red, light weight; black, medium weight; orange, heavy weight; blue, hydraulic; white, slideway; red stripes on white, special purpose. A number within the figure indicates grade of grease or oil. Higher numbers mean higher viscosities. This does not apply on "special purpose" grease or oil where sequence numbers indicate the special type to be used.

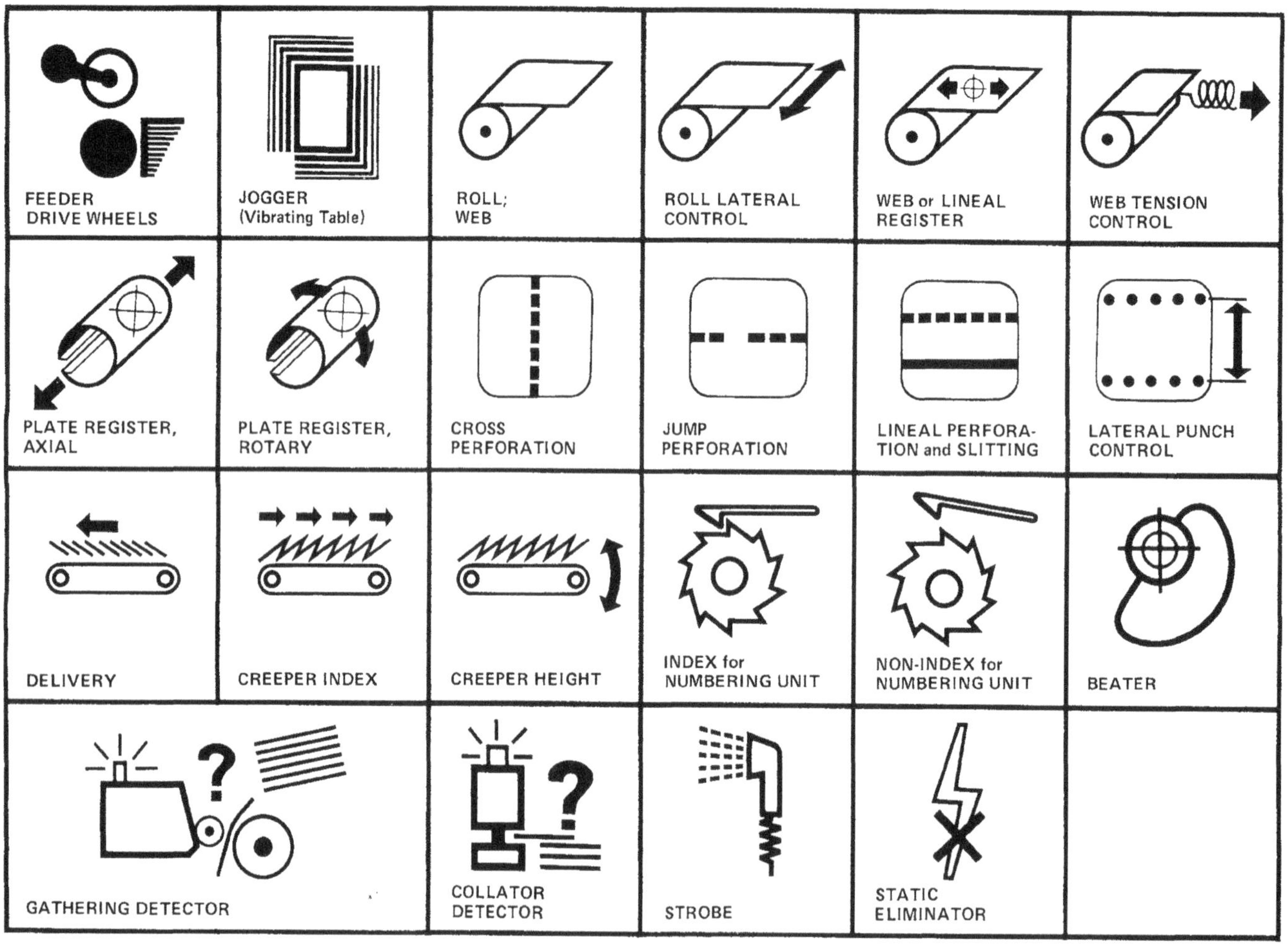

FEEDER DRIVE WHEELS	JOGGER (Vibrating Table)	ROLL; WEB	ROLL LATERAL CONTROL	WEB or LINEAL REGISTER	WEB TENSION CONTROL
PLATE REGISTER, AXIAL	PLATE REGISTER, ROTARY	CROSS PERFORATION	JUMP PERFORATION	LINEAL PERFORATION and SLITTING	LATERAL PUNCH CONTROL
DELIVERY	CREEPER INDEX	CREEPER HEIGHT	INDEX for NUMBERING UNIT	NON-INDEX for NUMBERING UNIT	BEATER
GATHERING DETECTOR		COLLATOR DETECTOR	STROBE	STATIC ELIMINATOR	

HOW TO AVOID A RASPBERRY CREAM

Do you open a box of chocolates – and hesitate?

You want a chewy caramel. But short of poking your finger into the bottom of each piece, how do you know what you will get?

Try selecting by symbols!

You stand a good chance of getting what you are after if you correctly decipher the "squiggle" code with which most chocolates are marked.

But beware, this method isn't infallible: not all candy makers use the same symbols. You might still end up with that raspberry cream!

MATHEMATICS

∞ ¶	INFINITY
$+$ ¶	PLUS
$-$ ¶	MINUS
$\pm$	PLUS or MINUS
$\times$ ▲ ¶ OR $\cdot$ ¶	MULTIPLIED BY
$\div$ OR $/$ ¶	DIVIDED BY
$=$ ¶	EQUAL TO
$\neq$ ¶	NOT EQUAL TO
$\equiv$ ¶	IDENTICALLY EQUAL TO
$\approx$ ¶	APPROXIMATELY EQUAL TO
$\sim$ ¶ OR $\propto$	PROPORTIONAL TO
$<$ ¶	SMALLER THAN
$>$ ¶	LARGER THAN
$\nless$	NOT SMALLER THAN
$\ngtr$	NOT LARGER THAN
$\leqq$ ¶	SMALLER THAN or EQUAL TO
$\geqq$ ¶	LARGER THAN or EQUAL TO
$\ll$ ¶	MUCH SMALLER THAN
$\gg$ ¶	MUCH LARGER THAN
∂	PARTIAL DERIVATIVE
$\int$ ¶	INDEFINITE INTEGRAL
$\triangle$	TRIANGLE (Geom.); LAPLACIAN (Vector)
Δ	INCREMENT (Calculus)
∇	DEL (Vector)
$\square$	d' ALEMBERTIAN
$\angle$	ANGLE
$\perp$	PERPENDICULAR TO
$\parallel$	PARALLEL TO
$\cong$	CONGRUENT
$\stackrel{m}{=}$	MEASURED BY
$\therefore$	THEREFORE
$\exists$	THERE EXISTS
$\forall$	FOR ALL
$\cup$	UNION
$\cap$	INTERSECTION
$\subset$	INCLUDED IN
$\supset$	CONTAINS
$\Rightarrow$	IMPLIES
$\Leftrightarrow$	IF and ONLY IF

▲ When X in bold face (**X**), means Vector Product (Vector).
¶ ISO Recommendation

MATHEMATICS *(continued)*

$\ni$	$\in$	$\notin$	$\sum$ ¶	log ¶	ln ¶
SUCH THAT	BELONGS TO	DOES NOT BELONG TO	SUM	LOGARITHM	NATURAL LOGARITHM
e	π	$\sqrt[n]{a}$ ¶	$n!$ ¶	$\lvert x \rvert$ ¶	$\langle x \rangle$ ¶
"e" (2.71828...)	PI (3.1416...)	n'th ROOT OF a	FACTORIAL n	MAGNITUDE OF x	MEAN VALUE OF x

THE RHYTHM OF LIFE

In ancient times, the Chinese believed that the world was created by the spontaneous separation of an amorphous ether into heaven and earth, the Yin and the Yang – and that everything originated with them.

A flowing S line divides the circle into two equal areas. The dark shape is the female Yin, the light one is the male Yang; the light spot in the Yin is the male germ in the female, and conversely the dark spot in the Yang is the female germ in the male. Thus each of these opposites carries the essence of the other.

Countless qualities are attributed to each form.

YIN

YIN	YANG
Female	Male
Passive	Active
Moon	Sun
Earth	Heaven
Black in color	Red in color
Ox	Horse
Even numbers	Odd numbers
Cold	Warm
Dark	Bright
Valleys and Streams	Hills and Mountains

YANG

Yin and Yang when interlocked, represent perfect unity, the universe, eternity.

Sometimes the combined Yin-Yang is surrounded by trigrams, an arrangement of cabalistic lines which have definite characteristics and meanings. Yang is represented by an unbroken line, Yin by a broken one. One such arrangement is shown here.

- ☷ K'UN: Southwest, mother, earth, black, ox, afternoon, late summer
- ☴ SUN: Southeast, eldest daughter, wind, white, cock, forenoon, late spring
- ☲ LI: South, middle daughter, lightning, sun, fire, pheasant, noon, mid-summer
- ☱ TUI: West, youngest daughter, lake or marsh, sheep, evening, mid-autumn
- ☰ CH'IEN: Northwest, father, heaven, deep crimson, horse, night, late autumn
- ☳ CHÊN: East, eldest son, thunder, yellow-green, dragon, dawn, spring
- ☵ K'AN: North, middle son, moon, rain, clouds, bright red, pig, midnight, mid-winter
- ☶ KÊN: Northeast, youngest son, mountain, dog, pre-dawn, late winter

MEDICINE

CADUCEUS; Staff of Hermes (Mercury)	STAFF of AESCULAPIUS	MEDICAL ALERT	r ▲ RED CROSS	r ▲ RED LION and SUN	r ▲ RED CRESCENT
r ● RED STAR of DAVID	Ψ PSYCHOLOGY	VETERINARY SERVICES	α IN RELATION TO	$\bar{C}$ CUM (With)	$\bar{S}$ SINE (Without)
INJECTIONS; VACCINATION	(h) BY HYPODERMIC	(iv) INTRAVENEOUSLY	(im) INTRAMUSCULARLY	(o) ORALLY	(r) RECTALLY
(m) MURMUR	→ DISTAL	← PROXIMAL	/ MILD LIMITATION	// MODERATE LIMITATION	/// SEVERE LIMITATION
+ MILD	++ NORMAL; Moderate	+++ INCREASED; Moderately Severe	++++ MARKEDLY INCREASED; Severe	✶ BIRTH	† DEATH
••• NO DATA	△ CHANGE	CIRCUMDUCTION	[ ] CONCENTRATION	TRIPLE ARTHRODESIS	ROTATION
℞ PRESCRIPTION; TREATMENT	M̶ MISCE (Mix)	/ EXTENSOR; EXTENSION	✓ FLEXOR; URINE	•/• DEFECATION	URINE and DEFECATION

▲ Members of the League of Red Cross Societies. The Red Crescent is used in some predominantly Moslem countries; the Red Lion and Sun is used in Iran.
● Sign of Magen David Adom, the humanitarian relief organization in Israel.

MEDICINE *(continued)*

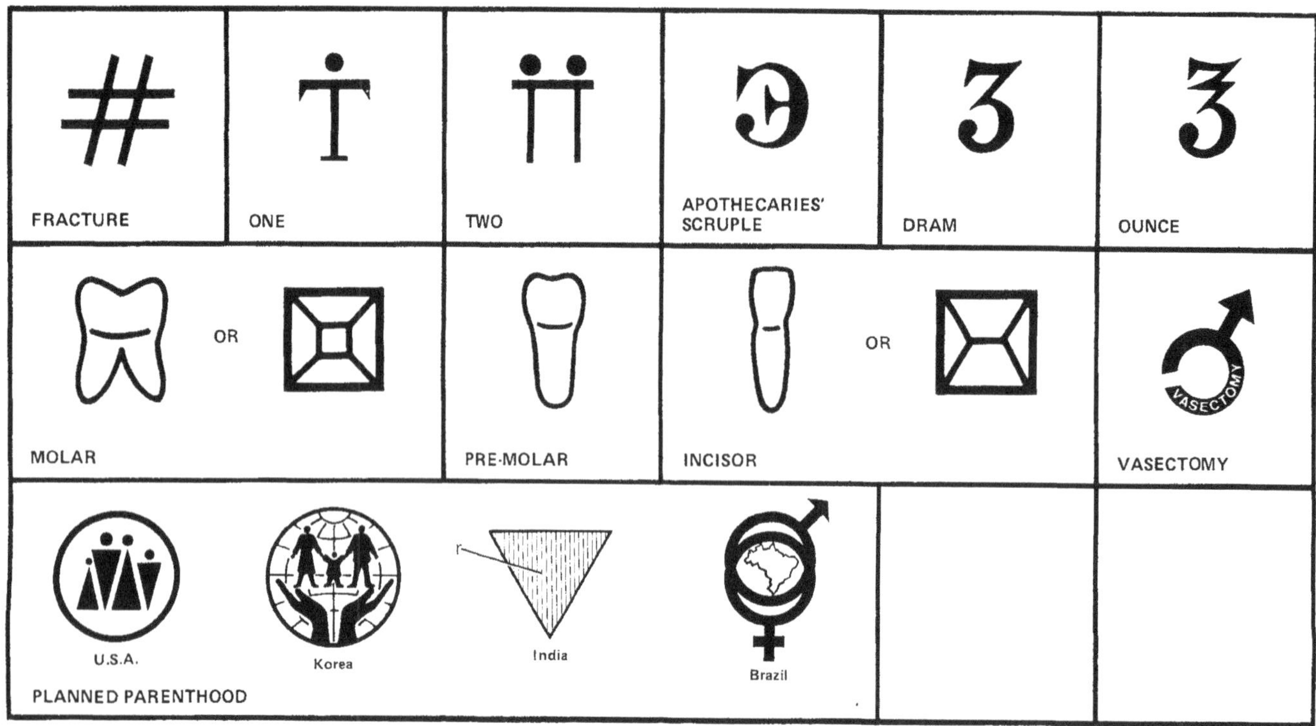
FRACTURE
ONE
TWO
APOTHECARIES' SCRUPLE
DRAM
OUNCE
MOLAR
OR
PRE-MOLAR
INCISOR
OR
VASECTOMY
VASECTOMY
U.S.A.
Korea
India
Brazil
PLANNED PARENTHOOD

Equipment

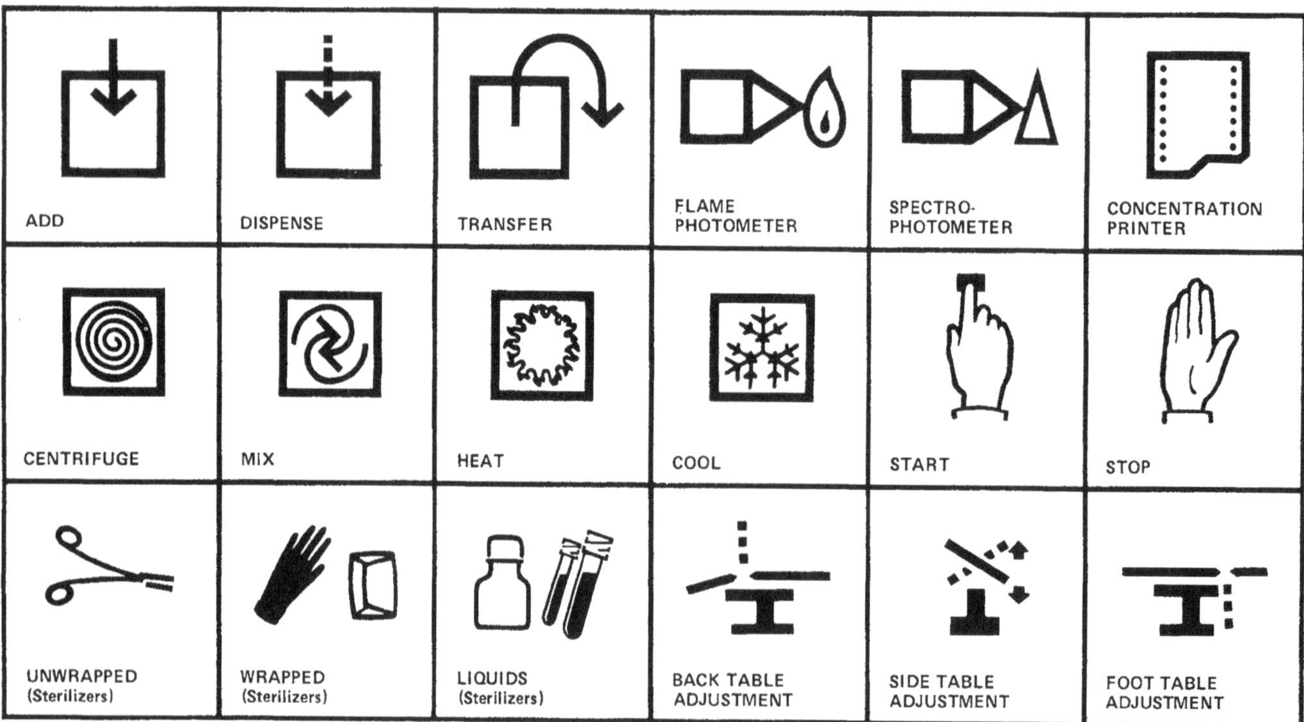
ADD
DISPENSE
TRANSFER
FLAME PHOTOMETER
SPECTRO-PHOTOMETER
CONCENTRATION PRINTER
CENTRIFUGE
MIX
HEAT
COOL
START
STOP
UNWRAPPED (Sterilizers)
WRAPPED (Sterilizers)
LIQUIDS (Sterilizers)
BACK TABLE ADJUSTMENT
SIDE TABLE ADJUSTMENT
FOOT TABLE ADJUSTMENT

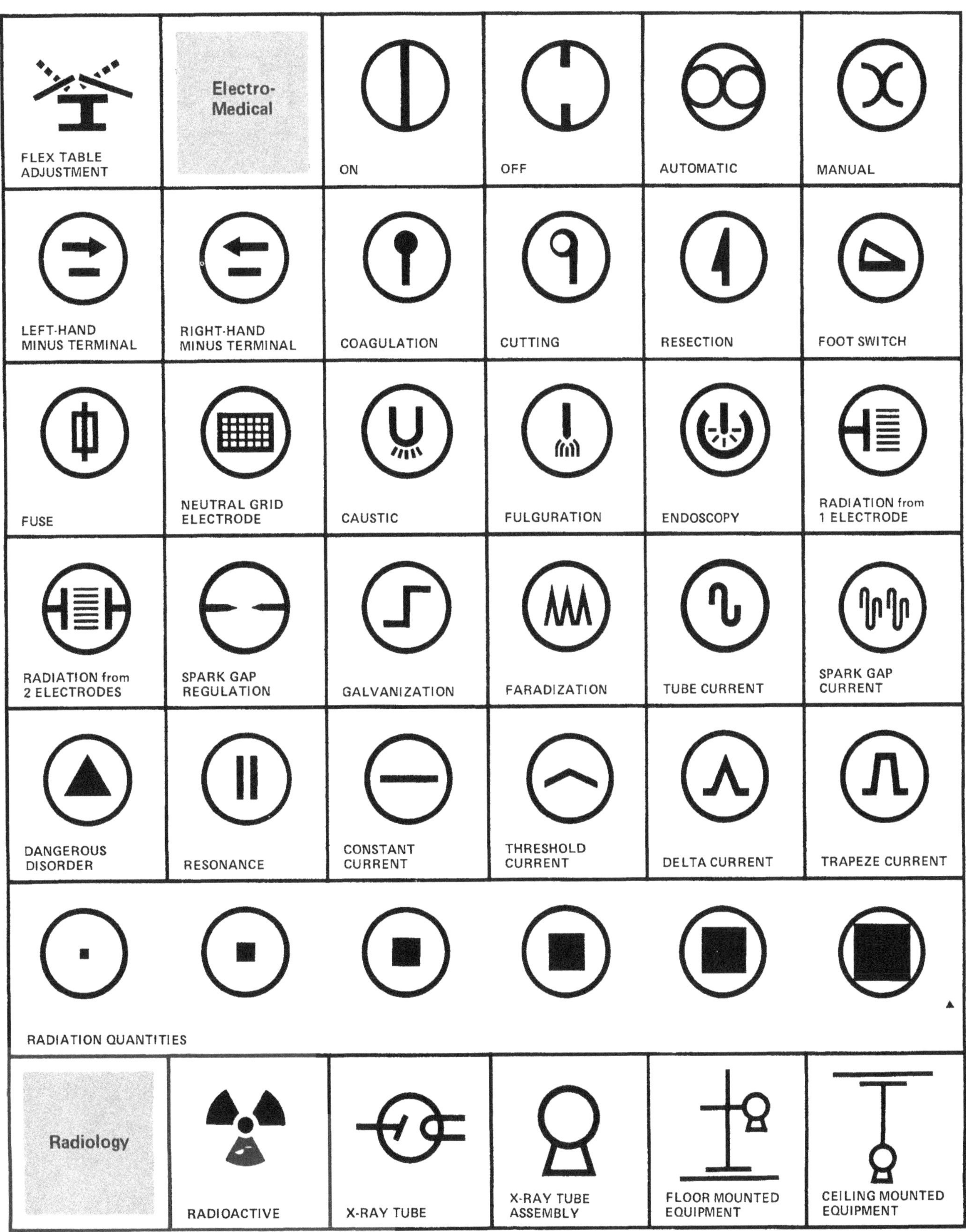
FLEX TABLE ADJUSTMENT
Electro-Medical
ON
OFF
AUTOMATIC
MANUAL
LEFT-HAND MINUS TERMINAL
RIGHT-HAND MINUS TERMINAL
COAGULATION
CUTTING
RESECTION
FOOT SWITCH
FUSE
NEUTRAL GRID ELECTRODE
CAUSTIC
FULGURATION
ENDOSCOPY
RADIATION from 1 ELECTRODE
RADIATION from 2 ELECTRODES
SPARK GAP REGULATION
GALVANIZATION
FARADIZATION
TUBE CURRENT
SPARK GAP CURRENT
DANGEROUS DISORDER
RESONANCE
CONSTANT CURRENT
THRESHOLD CURRENT
DELTA CURRENT
TRAPEZE CURRENT
RADIATION QUANTITIES ▲
Radiology
RADIOACTIVE
X-RAY TUBE
X-RAY TUBE ASSEMBLY
FLOOR MOUNTED EQUIPMENT
CEILING MOUNTED EQUIPMENT

▲ Radiation intensity is shown increasing from left to right.

Equipment *(continued)*

BODY SECTION RADIOGRAPHY	FILM CHANGER	RADIOGRAPHY	FLUOROGRAPHY CAMERA	IMAGE AMPLIFIER	FLUOROSCOPY
MOTION PICTURES (Fluoroscopic)	FILM FEED	SPOT FILM DEVICE	KYMOGRAPH	MOVEABLE GRID	LAYER LEVEL (Body Adjustment)
X-RAY TELEVISION	NORMAL FIELD	ENLARGED FIELD	BRIGHTNESS	ILLUMINATION LIGHT	RED LIGHT
DIAPHRAGM OPEN	DIAPHRAGM CLOSED	AUTOMATIC EX-POSURE CONTROL	CONSOLE SWITCH	HAND SWITCH	FOOT SWITCH
CONTRAST	BLACKENING	FINE FOCAL SPOT	SMALL FOCAL SPOT	LARGE FOCAL SPOT	STEREO FOCAL SPOT
LONGITUDINAL MOTION	TRANSVERSE MOTION	VERTICAL MOTION	ROTARY MOTION	SLOW MOTION	RAPID MOTION
LOCK	UNLOCK	COMPRESSION	DECOMPRESSION	FOOTPLATE MOTION	TABLE TILT

HOSPITAL
CLINIC
AMBULANCE
EMERGENCIES
OR
EMERGENCY
CHILDREN'S EMERGENCY
APPOINTMENTS
REGISTRATION
OR
ADMISSIONS
MEDICAL RECORDS
PRAYER; MEDITATION
ACCESS for the HANDICAPPED
OR
VISITORS
VOLUNTEERS
CLINICAL ROOM
OUT-PATIENT DEPARTMENT
TEMPORARY HOSPITALIZATION
PHYSICAL THERAPY
OR
OR
OCCUPATIONAL THERAPY
CHILD CARE
PEDIATRIC CLINIC
PEDIATRICS
NURSES
SENIOR NURSE
NURSES' WORKING ROOM
DRESSING ROOMS
DRESSING ROOMS, NURSES
DRESSING ROOMS, female technicians
DRESSING ROOMS and BATHROOMS
CLEAN CLOTHING
SOILED CLOTHING
TRASH
BLOOD DONORS
OR
HEMATOLOGY
BLOOD BANK
SERUM LABORATORIES
LABORATORY

EXPERIMENTAL SURGERY
PATHOLOGY
FRIGORIFICS
REFRIGERATION of CADAVERS
RECEPTION of CADAVERS
GENERAL MEDICINE
OPHTHALMOLOGY
OTORHINO-LARYNGOLOGY
DERMATOLOGY
DENTIST
OR
PROSTHETICS
NEUROLOGY
NEUROSURGERY
NEPHROLOGY
ORTHOPEDICS
OR
MENTAL HYGIENE
CHEST CARE
CARDIOLOGY
PULMONARY PHYSIOLOGY
BRONCHO-ESOPHAGOLOGY
ONCOLOGY
CASTS
SPEECH and HEARING
PHONIATRICS
HEAD of PHONIATRICS
HYDROTHERAPY
X-RAYS
X-RAY INTERPRETATION
ENDOSCOPY
RADIOTHERAPY
ELECTRO-CARDIOGRAMS
ELECTROENCEPH-ALOGRAPHY
ELECTROTHERAPY
TAKING of SPECIMENS
MATERNITY
NURSERY
MILK LABORATORY
ANTHROPOMETRY
PERINATHOLOGY
OR

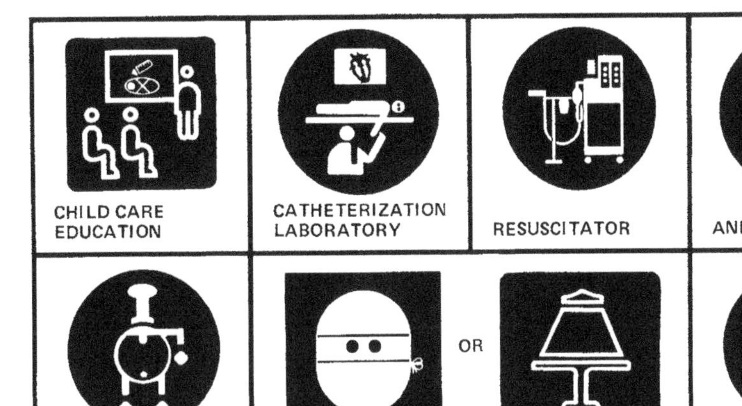
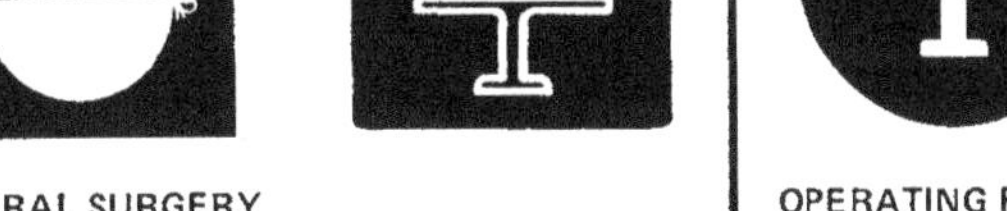
CHILD CARE EDUCATION
CATHETERIZATION LABORATORY
RESUSCITATOR
ANESTHESIOLOGY
STERILIZATION and EQUIPMENT
OR
SEPTIC ROOM
GENERAL SURGERY
OR
OPERATING ROOM
OBSERVATION ROOM
RECOVERY ROOM

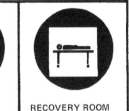

TWO SNAKES, OR ONE?

Aesculapius, the mythological god of medicine, carried a knotty wooden staff entwined with a *single* snake representing life-giving powers. In 1910 the American Medical Association adopted this staff as its insignia. The British and French armies, World Health Organization, U.S. Air Force Medical Service, and other groups the world over, also use this staff and single snake to identify their medical professionals.

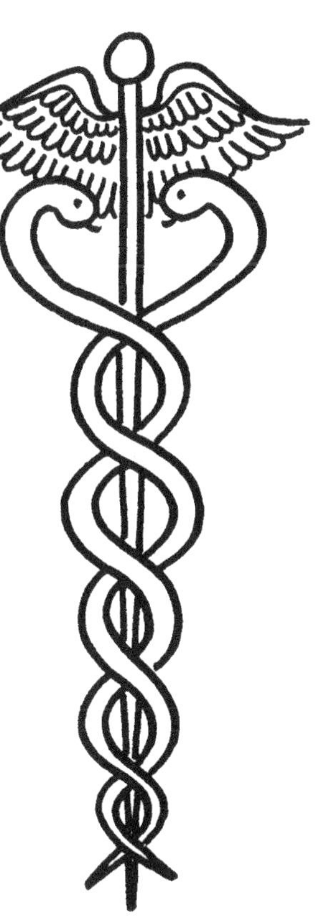

But to confuse the situation, the Caduceus, a staff with *two* snakes coiled around it, is the official symbol of the U.S. Army Medical Corps, Navy Pharmacy Division, and Public Health Service.

This two-snake design dates back some 4,000 years to Babylon. It reappeared in Greek mythology with a pair of wings added, as Hermes' wand, and called the Caduceus, a name derived from the Greek word meaning herald's wand or staff.

In ancient Rome the name for Hermes was Mercury and messengers carried his symbol as a sign of neutrality. And so their medicos, searching battlefields for the wounded, carried the Caduceus to establish their noncombatant status.

This doubtless is the justification for the U.S. Army's and Navy's use of the two-snake insignia. Traditionalists hold out for the single snake of Aesculapius to mark the medical profession, contending that the Greek Hermes or the Roman Mercury had little to do with medicine. Indeed, they say he did quite the reverse, for it was he who accompanied the dead from earth to Hades — hardly a healing process.

METEOROLOGY

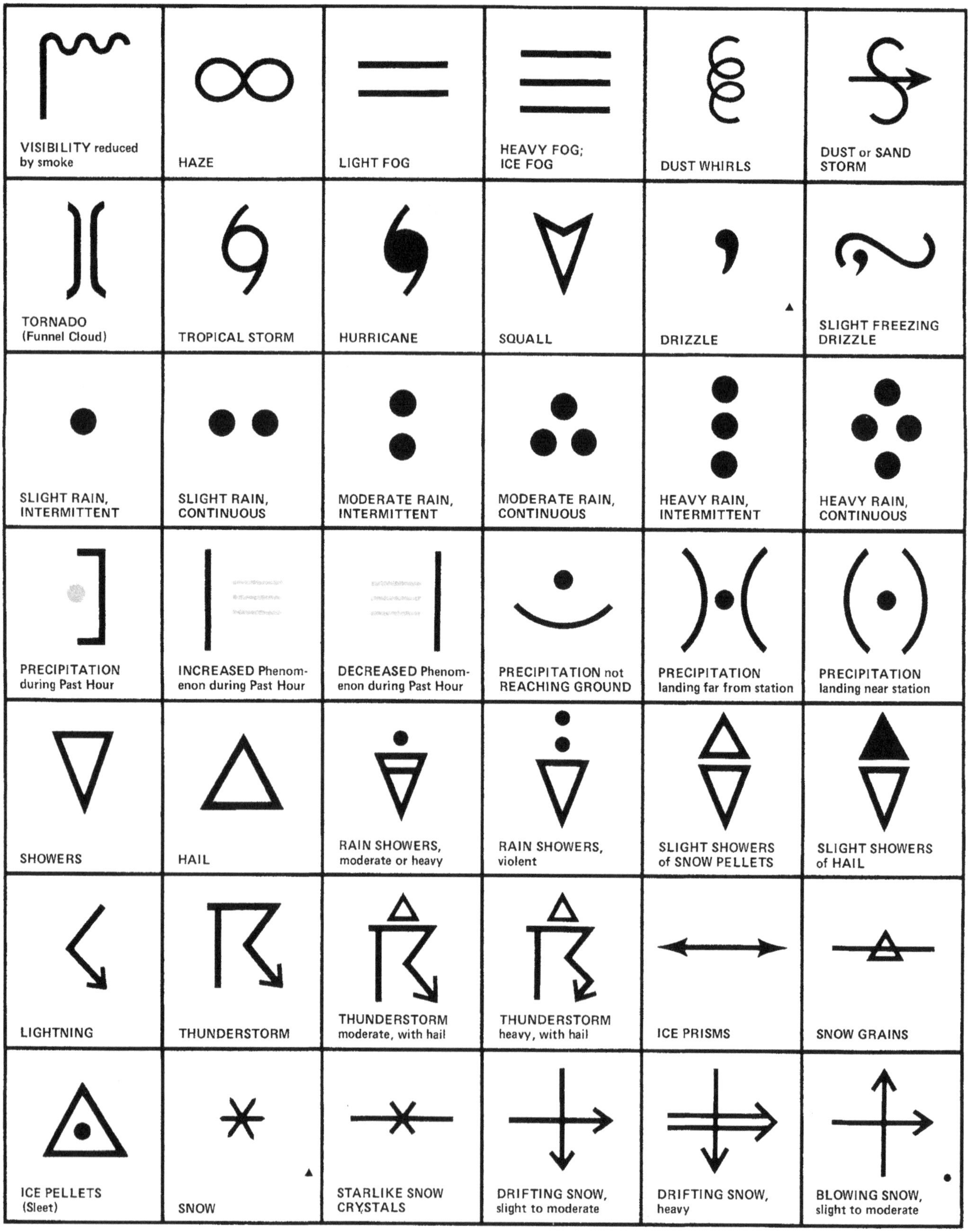

VISIBILITY reduced by smoke	HAZE	LIGHT FOG	HEAVY FOG; ICE FOG	DUST WHIRLS	DUST or SAND STORM
TORNADO (Funnel Cloud)	TROPICAL STORM	HURRICANE	SQUALL	DRIZZLE ▲	SLIGHT FREEZING DRIZZLE
SLIGHT RAIN, INTERMITTENT	SLIGHT RAIN, CONTINUOUS	MODERATE RAIN, INTERMITTENT	MODERATE RAIN, CONTINUOUS	HEAVY RAIN, INTERMITTENT	HEAVY RAIN, CONTINUOUS
PRECIPITATION during Past Hour	INCREASED Phenomenon during Past Hour	DECREASED Phenomenon during Past Hour	PRECIPITATION not REACHING GROUND	PRECIPITATION landing far from station	PRECIPITATION landing near station
SHOWERS	HAIL	RAIN SHOWERS, moderate or heavy	RAIN SHOWERS, violent	SLIGHT SHOWERS of SNOW PELLETS	SLIGHT SHOWERS of HAIL
LIGHTNING	THUNDERSTORM	THUNDERSTORM moderate, with hail	THUNDERSTORM heavy, with hail	ICE PRISMS	SNOW GRAINS
ICE PELLETS (Sleet)	SNOW ▲	STARLIKE SNOW CRYSTALS	DRIFTING SNOW, slight to moderate	DRIFTING SNOW, heavy	BLOWING SNOW, slight to moderate ●

▲ Progression of precipitation intensity may be indicated as in Rain.
● Heavy Blowing Snow is indicated by ⇸
Note: Weather symbols can be combined. **Example:** means Moderate or Heavy Freezing Rain; Slight Rain Showers.

Wind Speed	WIND calm	WIND approx. 1mph (1 Knot) ▲	WIND approx. 6mph (5 Knots) ▲	WIND approx. 12mph (10 Knots) ▲	WIND approx. 58mph (50 Knots) ▲
Weather Fronts	WARM FRONT, ALOFT	WARM FRONT, SURFACE	COLD FRONT, ALOFT	COLD FRONT, SURFACE	OCCLUDED FRONT, SURFACE
STATIONARY FRONT, SURFACE	Sky Coverage	CLEAR SKY ●	SCATTERED CLOUDS, 0.1 or less ●	SCATTERED CLOUDS, 0.2 or 0.3	SCATTERED CLOUDS, 0.4
SCATTERED CLOUDS, 0.5	BROKEN CLOUDS, 0.6 - 0.9 ●	BROKEN CLOUDS, 0.6	BROKEN CLOUDS, 0.7 or 0.8	BROKEN CLOUDS, 0.9	OVERCAST ●
OVERCAST, COMPLETE	OVERCAST; SKY OBSCURED	Clouds	STRATUS and/or FRACTOSTRATUS	FRACTOSTRATUS, Fractocumulus (Scud)	ALTOSTRATUS, thin, semi-transparent
ALTOSTRATUS, thick	STRATOCUMULUS, spreading from cumulus	STRATOCUMULUS, not from cumulus	CUMULUS, little vertical development	CUMULUS and STRATOCUMULUS	CUMULUS, considerable development
CUMULONIMBUS, clear-cut tops lacking	CUMULONIMBUS clear top	ALTOCUMULUS, thin, semi-transparent	ALTOCUMULUS, thin, patches	ALTOCUMULUS, in bands and thickening	ALTOCUMULUS, double-layered

▲ Line drawn in direction from which wind is blowing, toward station circle; half barb, barbs and pennants may be combined. **Example:** means 75 knots north westerly wind.

● Used in aviation weather reports (however, means 0.1 to 0.5 in aviation).

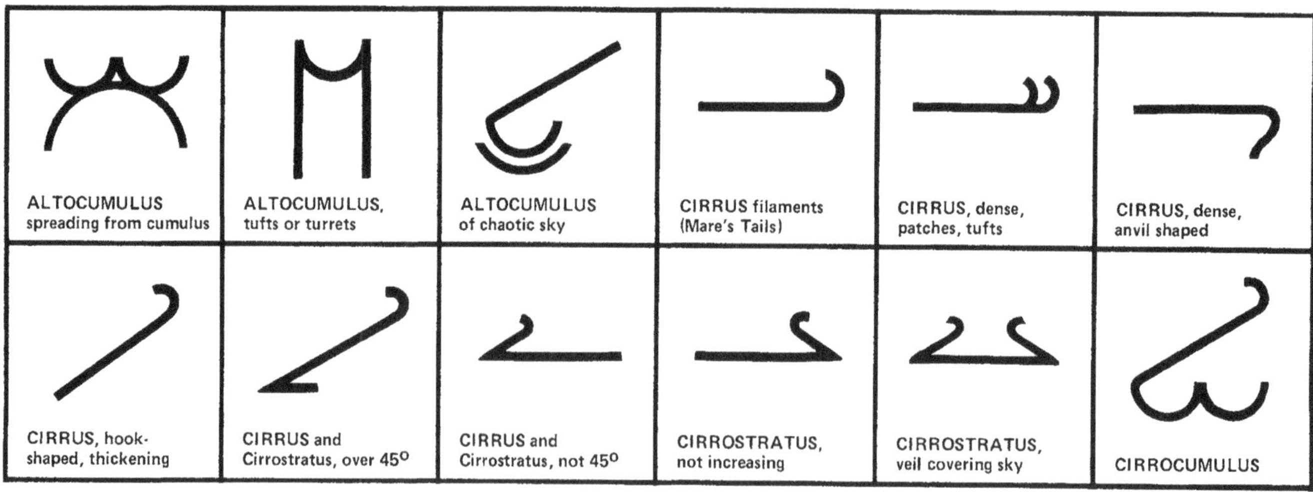
ALTOCUMULUS spreading from cumulus
ALTOCUMULUS, tufts or turrets
ALTOCUMULUS of chaotic sky
CIRRUS filaments (Mare's Tails)
CIRRUS, dense, patches, tufts
CIRRUS, dense, anvil shaped
CIRRUS, hook-shaped, thickening
CIRRUS and Cirrostratus, over 45°
CIRRUS and Cirrostratus, not 45°
CIRROSTRATUS, not increasing
CIRROSTRATUS, veil covering sky
CIRROCUMULUS

CLOUD 9

When we say that someone is on Cloud 9, it indicates that he is in a state of euphoria.

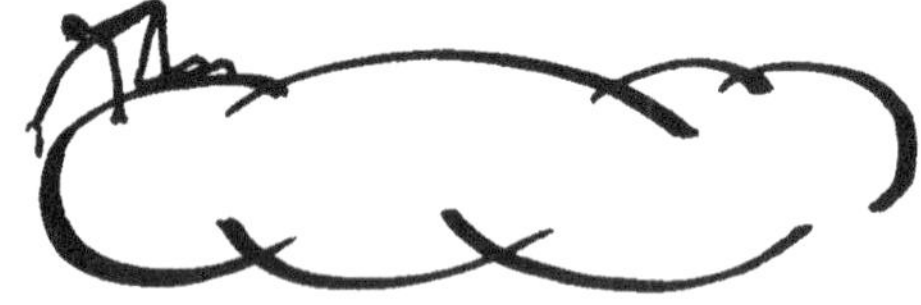

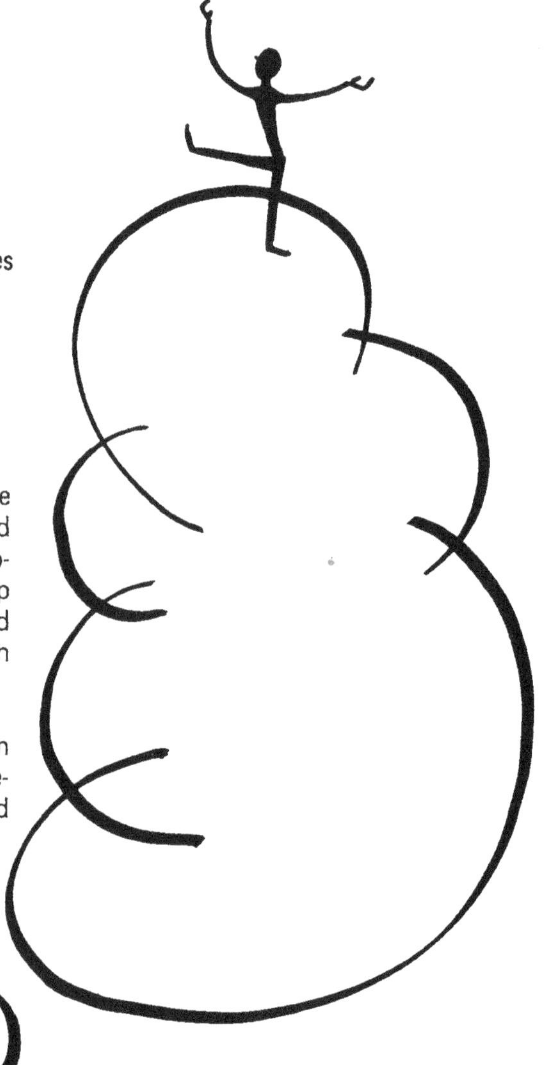

In all probability the expression is derived from the fact that in the meteorological synoptic code, cloud types are assigned numbers. Cloud 9 is the cumulonimbus cloud – billowy, with a flat base, its top often extending up to 40,000 feet or more. To avoid this cloud, airplane pilots must indeed fly high, which in the vernacular might suggest exuberance.

But the paradox is this: Cloud 9 is a violent storm cloud, a thunderhead, and extremely unstable – representing anything but the kind of state any of us would like to be in.

MUSIC

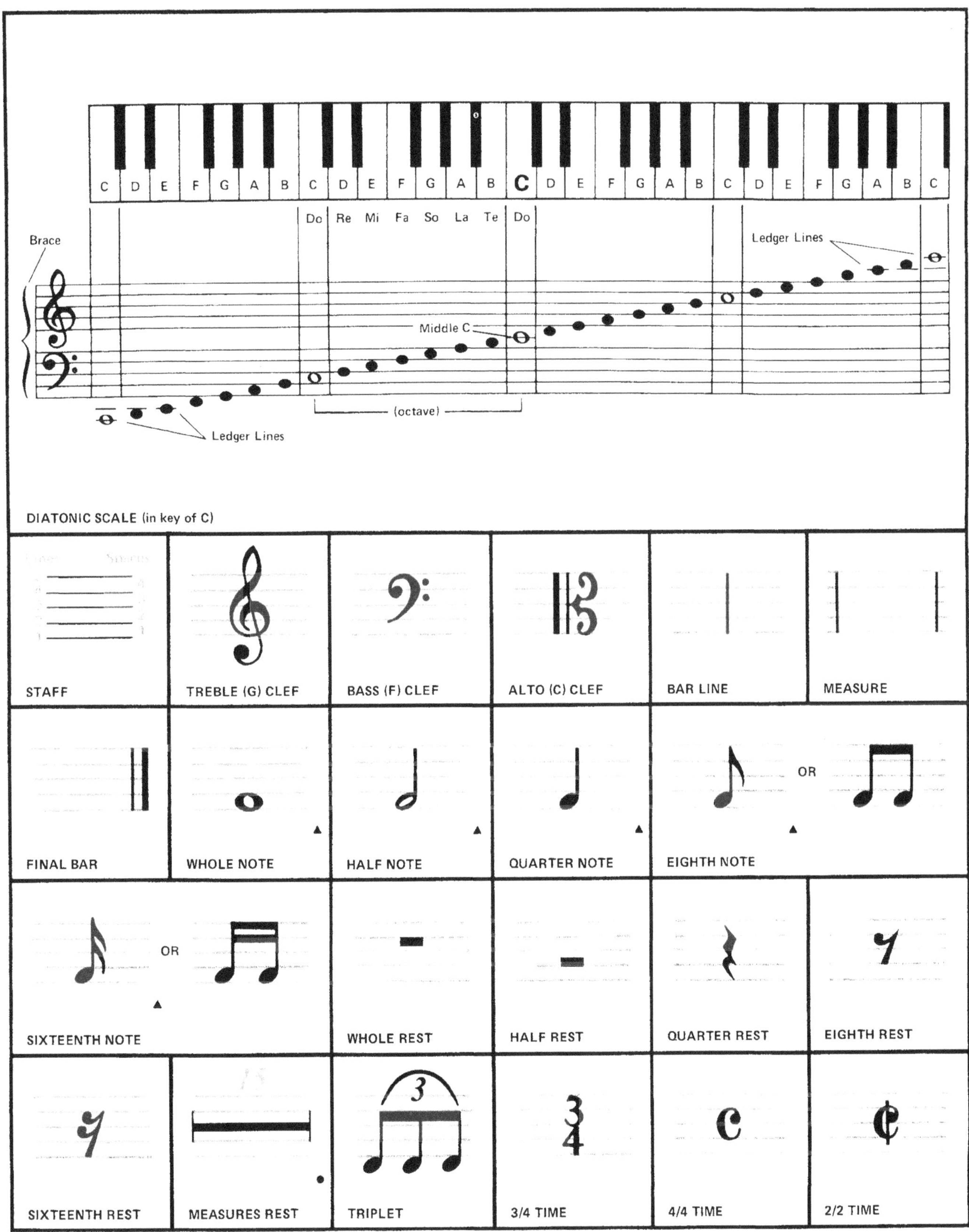

C D E F G A B C D E F G A B C D E F G A B C D E F G A B C
Do Re Mi Fa So La Te Do
Brace
Ledger Lines
Middle C
(octave)
Ledger Lines
DIATONIC SCALE (in key of C)
STAFF
TREBLE (G) CLEF
BASS (F) CLEF
ALTO (C) CLEF
BAR LINE
MEASURE
FINAL BAR
WHOLE NOTE ▲
HALF NOTE ▲
QUARTER NOTE ▲
EIGHTH NOTE ▲
OR
SIXTEENTH NOTE ▲
OR
WHOLE REST
HALF REST
QUARTER REST
EIGHTH REST
SIXTEENTH REST
MEASURES REST ●
TRIPLET
3
3/4 TIME
4/4 TIME
2/2 TIME

▲ A single dot (•) after the note increases its value by one-half. **Example:**
● Number of measures of rest shown above staff.

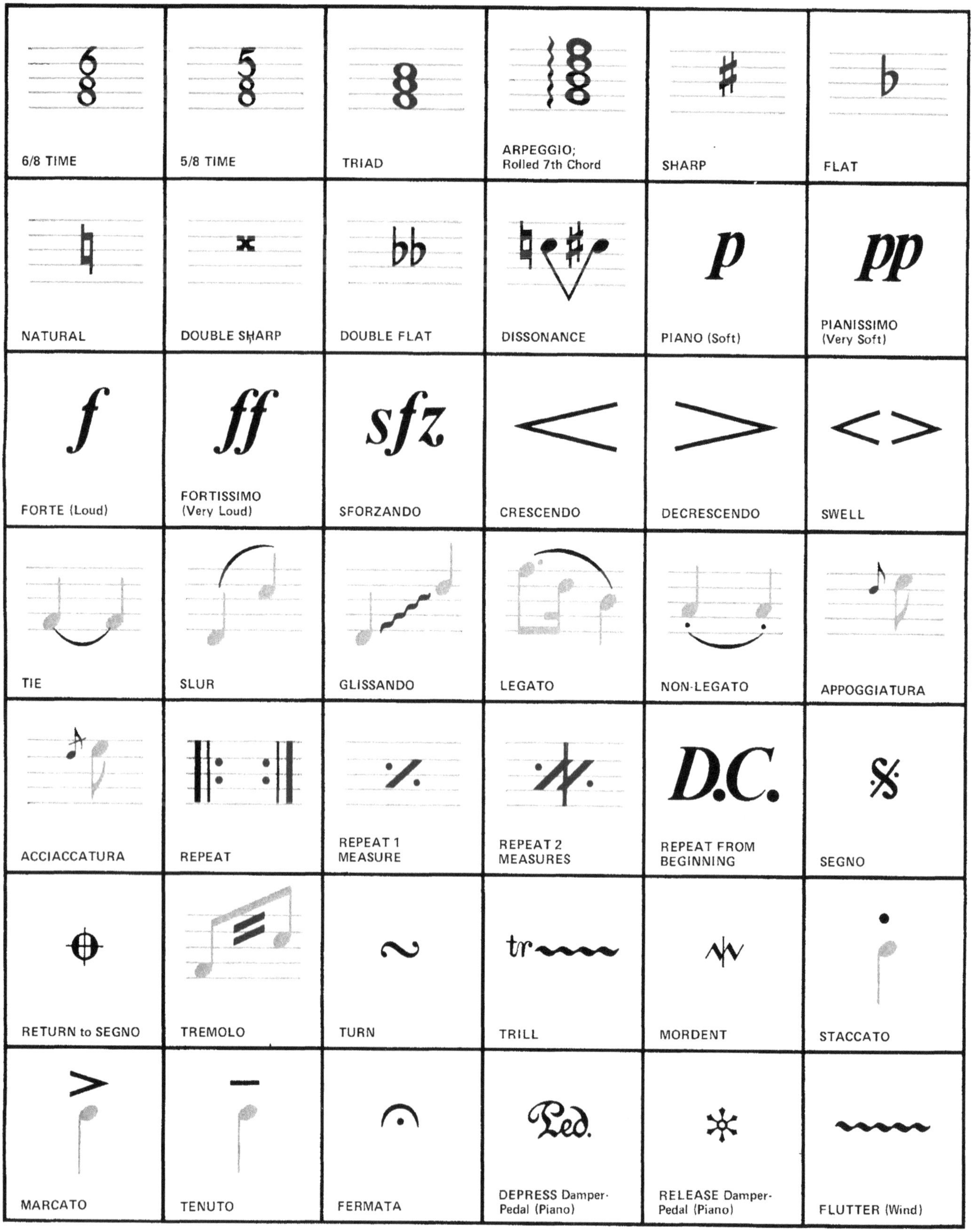

MUSIC *(continued)*

6/8 TIME	5/8 TIME	TRIAD	ARPEGGIO; Rolled 7th Chord	SHARP	FLAT
NATURAL	DOUBLE SHARP	DOUBLE FLAT	DISSONANCE	*p* PIANO (Soft)	*pp* PIANISSIMO (Very Soft)
f FORTE (Loud)	*ff* FORTISSIMO (Very Loud)	*sfz* SFORZANDO	CRESCENDO	DECRESCENDO	SWELL
TIE	SLUR	GLISSANDO	LEGATO	NON-LEGATO	APPOGGIATURA
ACCIACCATURA	REPEAT	REPEAT 1 MEASURE	REPEAT 2 MEASURES	*D.C.* REPEAT FROM BEGINNING	SEGNO
RETURN to SEGNO	TREMOLO	TURN	tr TRILL	MORDENT	STACCATO
MARCATO	TENUTO	FERMATA	Ped. DEPRESS Damper-Pedal (Piano)	RELEASE Damper-Pedal (Piano)	FLUTTER (Wind)

STOPPED TONE (Horn)	UP BOW	DOWN BOW	Key Signatures	G major; E minor	D major; B minor
A major; F - sharp minor	E major; C - sharp minor	B major; G - sharp minor	F - sharp major; D - sharp minor		
C - sharp major; A - sharp minor	F major; D minor	B - flat major; G minor	E - flat major; C minor	A - flat major; F minor	
D - flat major; B - flat minor	G - flat major E - flat minor	C - flat major; A - flat minor			

A 15th-CENTURY ROUND

No matter if it be "Sumer is icumen in" as sung in the 14th century or "Row, row, row your boat" which was introduced several centuries later, the round has great appeal.

In a round, one singer starts a song and at a prescribed time a second singer joins in with the same song, then a third, etc. Thus, a kind of counterpoint results.

A 15th-century calligrapher took the term "round" literally and wrote his tune in disc-like fashion and, I daresay, spun it around so the proper note came in front of the singer when it was his turn to join in.

(Drawing reproduced by permission of Musée Chantilly. Photo by Giraudon.)

PHOTOGRAPHY

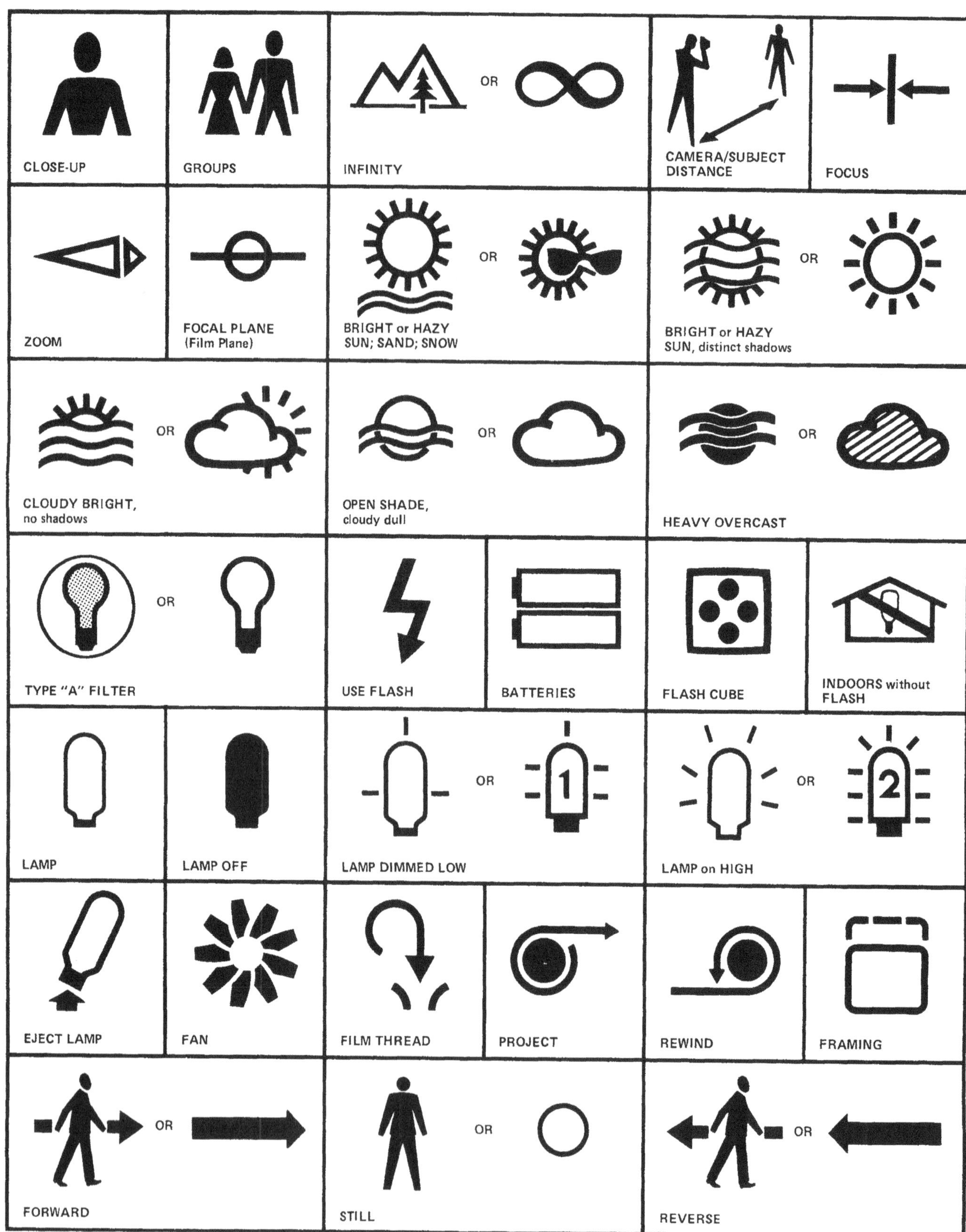
CLOSE-UP
GROUPS
OR
INFINITY
CAMERA/SUBJECT DISTANCE
FOCUS
ZOOM
FOCAL PLANE (Film Plane)
OR
BRIGHT or HAZY SUN; SAND; SNOW
OR
BRIGHT or HAZY SUN, distinct shadows
OR
CLOUDY BRIGHT, no shadows
OR
OPEN SHADE, cloudy dull
OR
HEAVY OVERCAST
OR
TYPE "A" FILTER
USE FLASH
BATTERIES
FLASH CUBE
INDOORS without FLASH
LAMP
LAMP OFF
OR
1
LAMP DIMMED LOW
OR
2
LAMP on HIGH
EJECT LAMP
FAN
FILM THREAD
PROJECT
REWIND
FRAMING
OR
FORWARD
OR
STILL
OR
REVERSE

ELEVATE
LEVEL
LOCK
UNLOCK
PROCESS
LOAD
LIGHTEN; DARKEN
DOCUMENTARY FILM
OR
PROJECTION ROOM

WHIRLIGIG

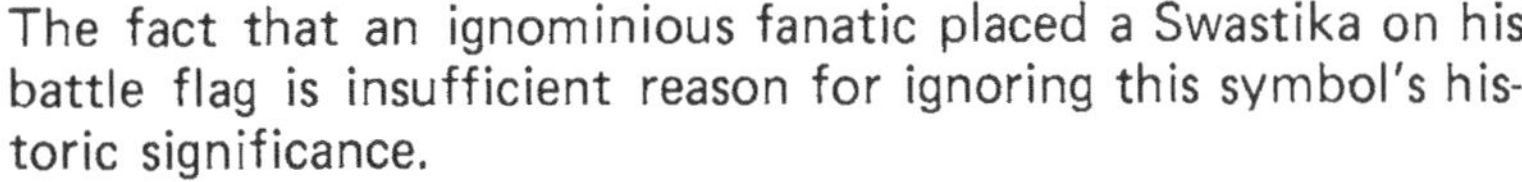

The fact that an ignominious fanatic placed a Swastika on his battle flag is insufficient reason for ignoring this symbol's historic significance.

The Swastika has been whirling around since prehistory and used in widely separated cultures as a favorable symbol representing many things to many people: the supreme diety, infinity, the sun's power, the four winds, well being, the succession of generations. Long before the white man appeared in the Western Hemisphere, the Swastika showed up on pre-Columbian artifacts, and many a Navajo wove it into blankets and baskets.

Yet no one can trace the origin of the Swastika.

Did sun worshippers create it by cutting into the perimeter of the sun circle?

It is related to the anatomical three-legged triskelion, which indeed races around showing movement as well as any symbol we know?

Was it reborn in the Greek gammadion, by joining four gamma letters together?

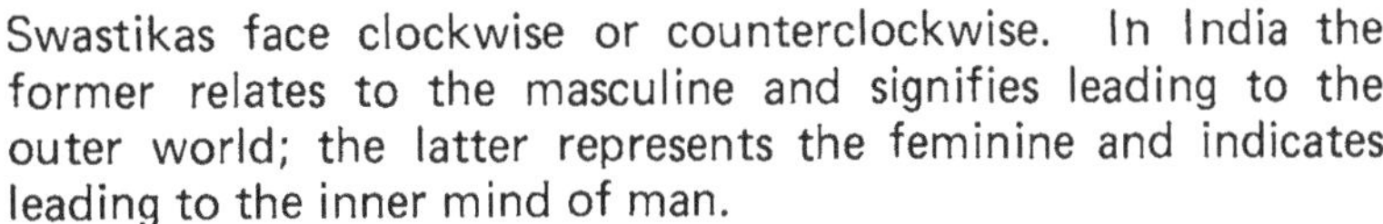

Swastikas face clockwise or counterclockwise. In India the former relates to the masculine and signifies leading to the outer world; the latter represents the feminine and indicates leading to the inner mind of man.

Time is bound to erase the association of the Swastika with the Nazi holocaust. Then one of the most distinctive of graphic symbols will be absolved of its latter-day stigma and its early meanings will again be known.

PHYSICS

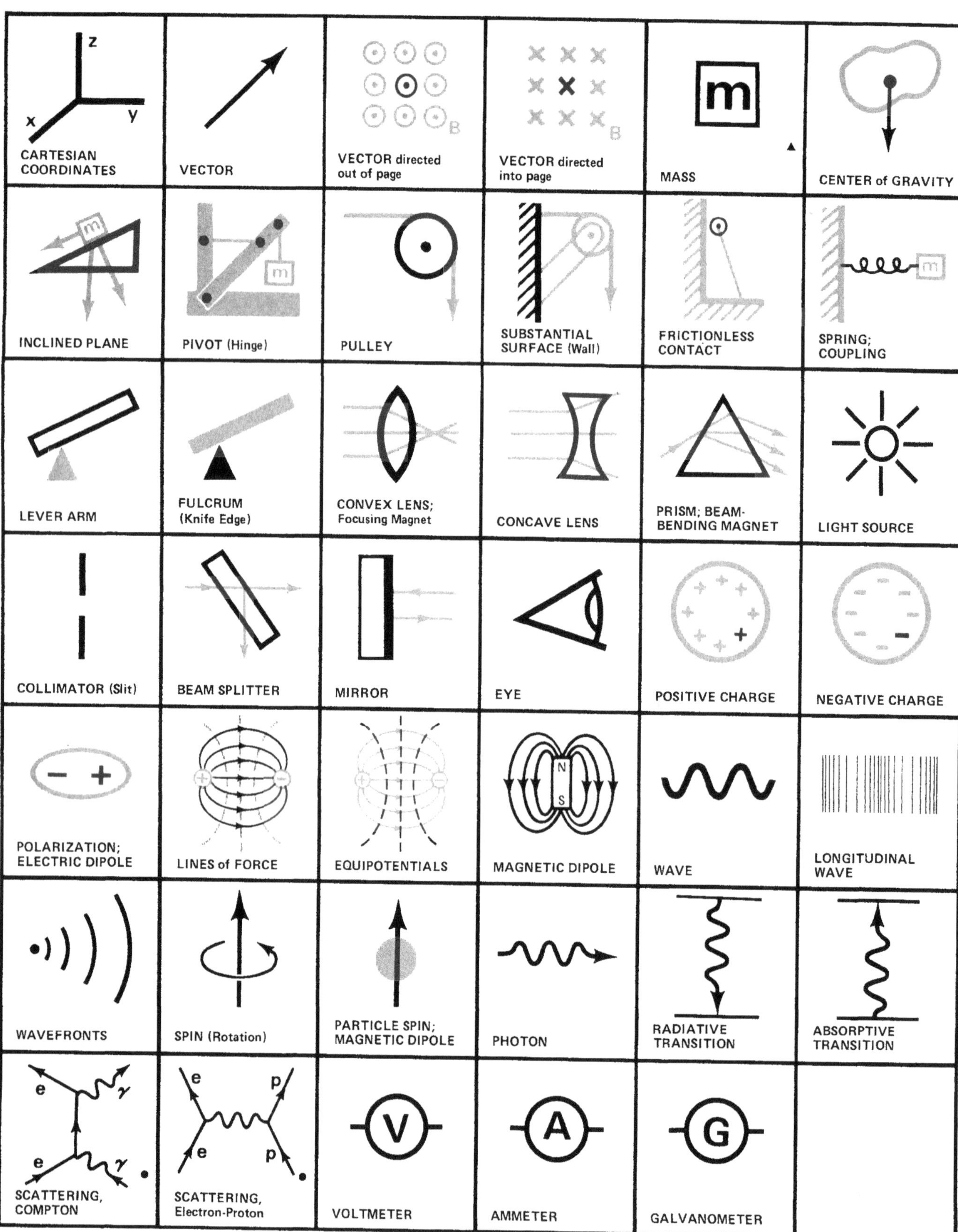

z
x
y
CARTESIAN COORDINATES
VECTOR
B
VECTOR directed out of page
B
VECTOR directed into page
m
MASS ▲
CENTER of GRAVITY
m
INCLINED PLANE
m
PIVOT (Hinge)
PULLEY
SUBSTANTIAL SURFACE (Wall)
FRICTIONLESS CONTACT
m
SPRING; COUPLING
LEVER ARM
FULCRUM (Knife Edge)
CONVEX LENS; Focusing Magnet
CONCAVE LENS
PRISM; BEAM-BENDING MAGNET
LIGHT SOURCE
COLLIMATOR (Slit)
BEAM SPLITTER
MIRROR
EYE
POSITIVE CHARGE
NEGATIVE CHARGE
− +
POLARIZATION; ELECTRIC DIPOLE
LINES of FORCE
EQUIPOTENTIALS
N
S
MAGNETIC DIPOLE
WAVE
LONGITUDINAL WAVE
WAVEFRONTS
SPIN (Rotation)
PARTICLE SPIN; MAGNETIC DIPOLE
PHOTON
RADIATIVE TRANSITION
ABSORPTIVE TRANSITION
e
γ
e
γ
SCATTERING, COMPTON ●
e
p
e
p
SCATTERING, Electron-Proton ●
V
VOLTMETER
A
AMMETER
G
GALVANOMETER

▲ Also shown as (m)
● Feynman Diagram

Letter Symbols

A AMPERE; AREA; MASS NUMBER
B MAGNETIC FLUX DENSITY
C COULOMB; CAPACITANCE; COMPTON WAVELENGTH
E ENERGY; ELECTRIC FIELD STRENGTH
F FARAD; FORCE
G GAUSS; GIGA; GRAVITATIONAL CONSTANT
H HENRY; MAGNETIC FIELD STRENGTH
I ELECTRIC CURRENT; MOMENT of INERTIA
J JOULE
K KELVIN; K-MESON
L ANGULAR MOMENTUM; SELF-INDUCTANCE
M MEGA
N NEWTON; NUMBER of MOLECULES; NEUTRON NUMBER
P POWER
Q ELECTRIC CHARGE; QUALITY FACTOR
R RESISTANCE
T TESLA; TERA; PERIOD
V VOLT; ELECTRIC POTENTIAL; VOLUME
W WATT; WORK
Z IMPEDANCE; ATOMIC NUMBER
b BARN; BREADTH
c CENTI; SPEED of LIGHT in a VACUUM; MOLECULAR VELOCITY
d DECI; DISTANCE BETWEEN LATTICE PLANES; THICKNESS; DIAMETER; DEUTERON
e ELECTRON; PROTON CHARGE
f FEMTO; FREQUENCY
g GRAM; ACCELERATION of FREE FALL
h HECTO; PLANCK CONSTANT; HEIGHT
k KILO; BOLTZMANN CONSTANT
l LITER; LENGTH; MEAN FREE PATH
m METER; MILLI
n NANO; NEUTRON; REFRACTIVE INDEX; NUMBER DENSITY of MOLECULES
p PICO; PROTON; MOMENTUM
r RADIUS
s SECOND
t TON; TRITON; TIME
V or $\boldsymbol{v}$ VELOCITY
a_0 BOHR RADIUS
atm ATMOSPHERE
cd CANDELA
Ci CURIE
da DEKA
eV ELECTRONVOLT
Hz HERTZ
lm LUMEN
lx LUX
m_H HYDROGEN ATOMIC MASS
mmHg MILLIMETER of MERCURY
mol MOLE
N_A AVOGADRO CONSTANT
R RYDBERG CONSTANT
rad RADIAN
r_e ELECTRON RADIUS
sr STERADIAN
Wb WEBER
(h k l) LATTICE PLANE
[h k l] DIRECTION in LATTICE
Å ANGSTRÖM
°C DEGREE CELSIUS
°F DEGREE FAHRENHEIT
Ω OHM; SOLID ANGLE
μ MICRO; MUON; PEMEABILITY; MAGNETIC MOMENT OF PARTICLE; ATTENUATION COEFFICIENT
Λ LAMBDA PARTICLE
Σ SIGMA PARTICLE
Ξ XI PARTICLE
α ALPHA PARTICLE; FINE STRUCTURE CONSTANT
π PION
γ PHOTON; TIME DILATION FACTOR
ν NEUTRINO; FREQUENCY;
ω SOLID ANGLE; ANGULAR VELOCITY; ANGULAR FREQUENCY
λ WAVELENGTH; MEAN FREE PATH; DECAY CONSTANT
τ RELAXATION TIME; TIME CONSTANT
ρ DENSITY
β PARTICLE SPEED DIVIDED BY SPEED OF LIGHT
ϕ PHASE DISPLACEMENT
ϵ PERMITTIVITY
Θ CHARACTERISTIC TEMPERATURE
σ STEFAN-BOLTZMANN CONSTANT; CROSS SECTION
Ψ WAVE FUNCTION
θ BRAGG ANGLE

A GLOBAL WORD

In the language of the American Indian Choctaw tribe, OKEH translates into "it is so."

Bostonians contend OK stems from an illiterate spelling – "Oll Korrect."

Perhaps the most authoritative explanation refers to the O.K. Club, formed in 1840 by the partisans of Martin Van Buren, then President of the United States. This alluded to his nickname "Old Kinderhook" which came from his birthplace, Kinderhook, New York.

OK (and spelled out okay, okey, or okeh) knows no geographical boundaries – it is used in Kenya or Greenland.

Its meaning is clear, but its origin is controversial and anyone's guess. OK?

OK.

RECREATION

REPORT FIRES
USE YOUR ASHTRAY
CRUSH SMOKES
BREAK MATCHES
CAMPFIRES
DROWN CAMPFIRES
NO FIRES
NO FIREWORKS
SMOKEY
SMOKEY the BEAR (Forest Fire Prevention)
SPARKY the FIRE DOG (Fire Protection)
RANGER STATION
LOOKOUT TOWER
OR
LODGINGS
HOSTEL; PIONEER CABIN
TRAILER SANITARY STATION
TRAILER SITES
UTILITY OUTLET
DISHWASHING
COLD SPRING
WASHING FACILITY
BATH and SHOWER
DOGS ALLOWED
NO DOGS
KENNEL
PLAYGROUND
AMPHITHEATER
COUNCIL RING
OR
VIEW or CAMERA POINT
CAMPGROUND
GROUP CAMPING
OR
PICNIC AREA
PICNIC SHELTER
SLEEPING SHELTER
TRAIL SHELTER
FOOT BRIDGE
FORDING PLACE
OR
HIKING TRAIL
NATURE TRAIL

SELF-GUIDING NATURE TRAIL
AUTO NATURE TRAIL
DEER AREA
BEAR AREA
FISH HATCHERY
TRAMWAY
BICYCLE TRAIL
TRAIL BIKE TRAIL
JEEP TRAIL
VEHICLE FERRY
TOURIST ACTIVITIES
HISTORIC PLAQUE
CAVERNS
DAM
LIGHTHOUSE
CULTURAL MONUMENT
MUSEUM
MINERAL SPRING
AUDITORIUM
THEATER
BAND
Sports
WATER SPORTS AREA
FISHING
b
GUARD on DUTY
BEACH
SCUBA DIVING
DIVING
CAUTION: DEEP WATER (Drop-off)
CAUTION: ROCKS
OR
b
b
WATER SKIING
DOCK
MARINA
LAUNCHING RAMP
MOTOR BOATING
ROW BOATING
BOATING (Sail)
OR
OR
HORSE TRAIL
STABLE

RECREATION *(continued)*

FIREARMS
HUNTING
ARCHERY
SHOOTING RANGE
FOOTBALL
SOFTBALL
BASEBALL
LITTLE LEAGUE
GOLF
OR
POOL (Billiards)
SHUFFLEBOARD
PING-PONG
TENNIS
OR
WINTER SPORTS AREA
WINTER RECREATION AREA
SKI TRACK
LIGHTED SKI TRACK
TOWLIFT; T-BAR
CHAIR LIFT
OR
tan
TRAIL CLOSED
r
TRAILS MERGE
r
orange
CLOSED: AVALANCHE AREA
r
EXTRA CAUTION AREA
g
EASIER SKI RUN
tan
MORE DIFFICULT SKI RUN
b
MOST DIFFICULT SKI RUN
r
NO SCHUSSBOOMING
y
r
CONGESTED AREA
y
r
WARMING HUT
r
EMERGENCY TELEPHONE
SLEDDING
SKI BOBBING
SNOW PLAY
SNOWMOBILING
g
SNOWMOBILE TRAIL
r
SNOWMOBILES PROHIBITED
r
SNOWMOBILE TRAIL, DIRECTION
y
SNOWMOBILE CROSSING
y
THIN ICE (Snowmobile)

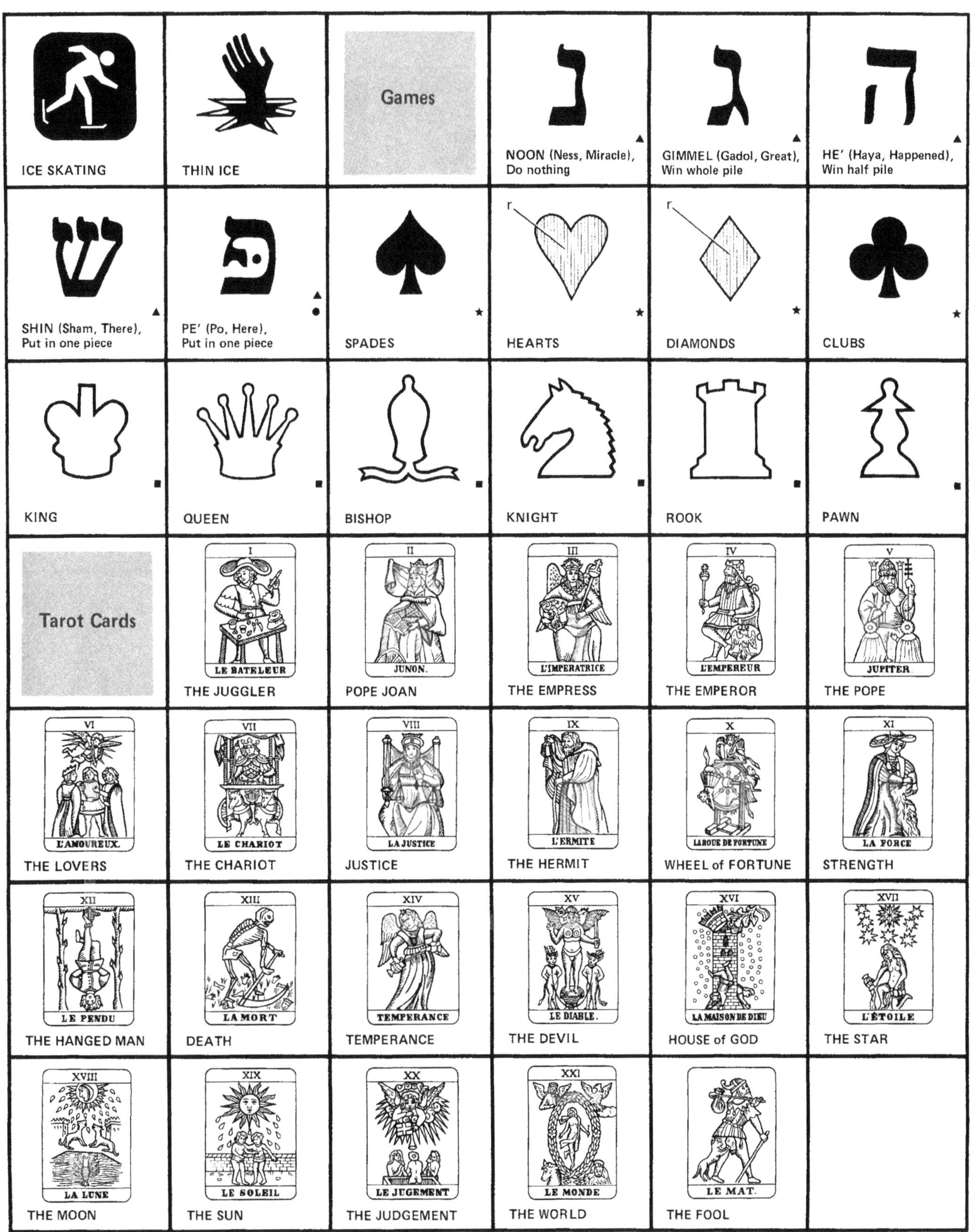
ICE SKATING
THIN ICE
Games
NOON (Ness, Miracle), Do nothing
GIMMEL (Gadol, Great), Win whole pile
HE' (Haya, Happened), Win half pile
SHIN (Sham, There), Put in one piece
PE' (Po, Here), Put in one piece
SPADES
r
HEARTS
r
DIAMONDS
CLUBS
KING
QUEEN
BISHOP
KNIGHT
ROOK
PAWN
Tarot Cards
I
LE BATELEUR
THE JUGGLER
II
JUNON.
POPE JOAN
III
L'IMPERATRICE
THE EMPRESS
IV
L'EMPEREUR
THE EMPEROR
V
JUPITER.
THE POPE
VI
L'AMOUREUX.
THE LOVERS
VII
LE CHARIOT
THE CHARIOT
VIII
LA JUSTICE
JUSTICE
IX
L'ERMITE
THE HERMIT
X
LA ROUE DE FORTUNE
WHEEL of FORTUNE
XI
LA FORCE
STRENGTH
XII
LE PENDU
THE HANGED MAN
XIII
LA MORT
DEATH
XIV
TEMPERANCE
TEMPERANCE
XV
LE DIABLE.
THE DEVIL
XVI
LA MAISON DE DIEU
HOUSE of GOD
XVII
L'ÉTOILE
THE STAR
XVIII
LA LUNE
THE MOON
XIX
LE SOLEIL
THE SUN
XX
LE JUGEMENT
THE JUDGEMENT
XXI
LE MONDE
THE WORLD
LE MAT.
THE FOOL

▲ Symbol is a Hebrew letter which appears on a four-sided top used in the game of Dreydle. For example, נ is the letter Noon, standing for the word Ness, which means Miracle in English. When this turns up on the top, the player does nothing.
● Pe' is used instead of Shin when playing the game in Israel.
★ Suits of playing cards.
■ Pieces used in chess.

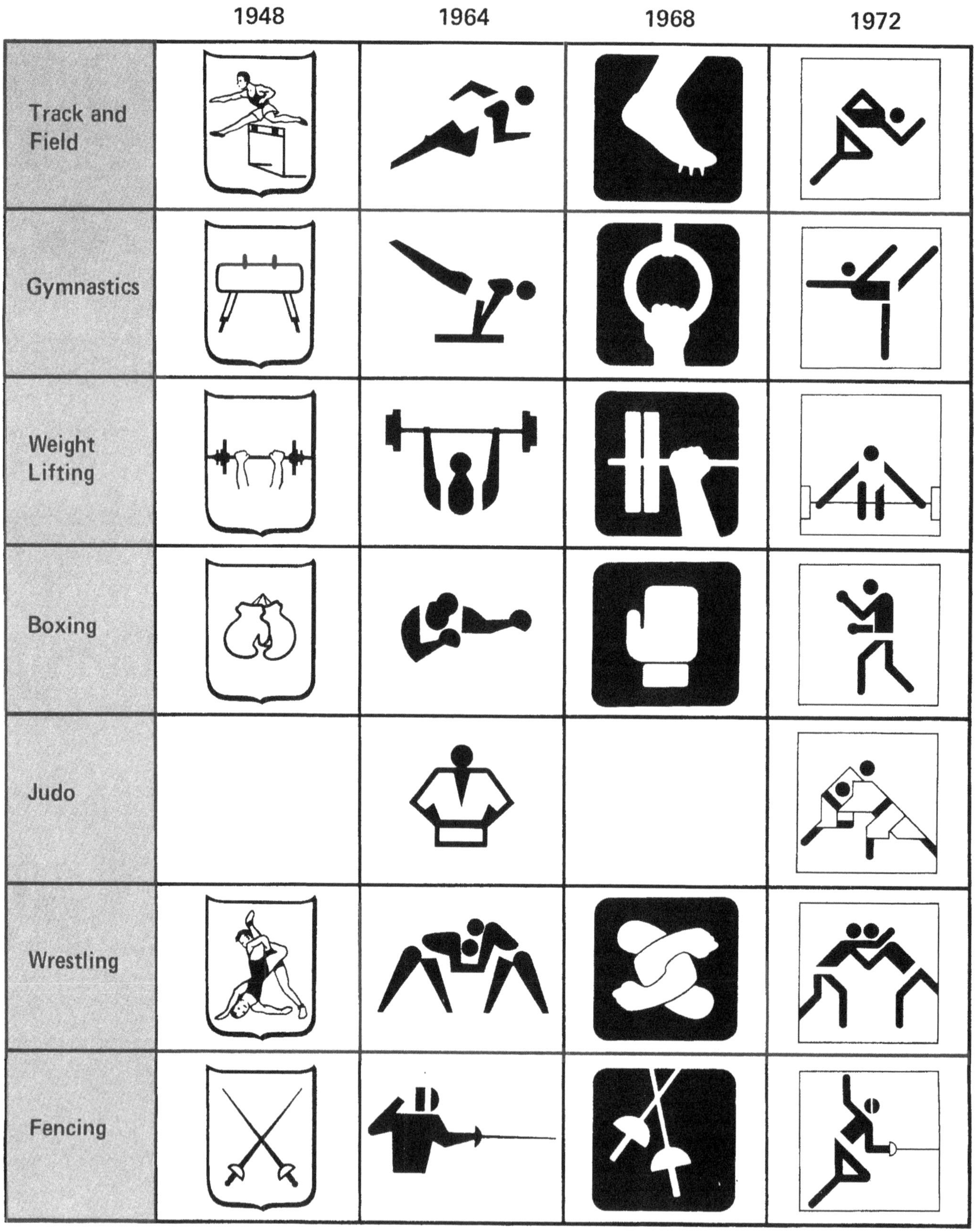

	1948	1964	1968	1972
Track and Field				
Gymnastics				
Weight Lifting				
Boxing				
Judo				
Wrestling				
Fencing				

	1948	1964	1968	1972
Swimming				
Sailing				
Canoeing				
Rowing				
Water Polo				
Volleyball				
Basketball				

RECREATION

Olympics *(continued)*

	1948	1964	1968	1972
Soccer				
Hockey				
Wall Contact Sports			▲	
Shooting				
Cycling				
Equestrian				
Modern Pentathlon●				

▲ Handball, Jai Alai, Squash, Tennis.
● Equestrian, Fencing, Pistol Shooting, Swimming, Track and Field.

Winter Olympics / GIANT SLALOM	SLALOM (OR)	DOWN HILL SKIING (OR)
SKI JUMPING (OR)	CROSS-COUNTRY SKIING (OR)	BIATHLON (OR)
ICE HOCKEY (OR)	SPEED SKATING (OR)	FIGURE SKATING (OR)
BOBSLEIGH (OR)	LUGE (OR)	

SMOKEY IS ALIVE AND WELL

In 1950, high in the Lincoln National Forest of New Mexico, there was a tremendous fire. A fire fighter stumbled upon a badly singed and frightened little bear cub. The local Game Warden adopted the cub and he and his wife nursed it back to health. They called him Smokey.

The U.S. Forest Service selected Smokey as the national symbol for forest fire prevention. Shortly thereafter the United States Congress unanimously passed the Smokey Bear law to protect Smokey's name and character, and thus maintain his status.

Today the original Smokey lives happily in Washington, D.C.'s National Zoological Park. He is never lonely, for he has four million visitors a year.

SMOKEY

RELIGION

BUDDHISM Buddha	BUDDHISM Buddha's Footprint	BUDDHISM Lotus
BUDDHISM Wheel of Law	BUDDHISM, Tibetan The Path of Universality	BUDDHISM, Zen Eternal State of Buddha
CHRISTIANITY Latin Cross	CHRISTIANITY Celtic Cross	CHRISTIANITY Orthodox Cross
CHRISTIANITY Christ Victorious	CHRISTIANITY Chi Rho	CHRISTIANITY Triquetra
CHRISTIANITY The Fish	CHRISTIANITY Agnus Dei	CHRISTIANITY Descending Dove; Holy Spirit
CHRISTIANITY Anchor; St. Clement	CHRISTIANITY Ten Commandments	CHRISTIANITY, Church of Christ, Scientist Cross and Crown ▲
CONFUCIANISM Confucius	CONFUCIANISM Conjugal Bliss	HINDUISM Mandala

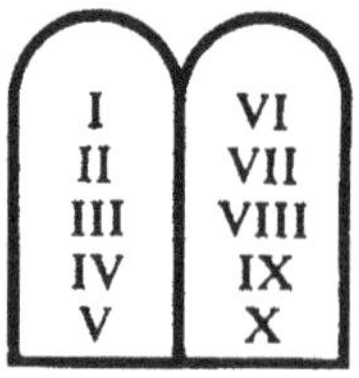

▲ The design of the Cross and Crown seal is a trademark of the Trustees under the Will of Mary Baker G. Eddy, registered in the United States and other countries. Used by permission.

HINDUISM
Shiva
HINDUISM
Vishnu
HINDUISM
Aum; Brahman-Atman
ISLAM
Star and Crescent
ISLAM
Holy Qur-an
JAINISM
Brush and Bowl
JUDAISM
Star of David
JUDAISM
Menorah
JUDAISM
Ten Commandments
SHINTO
Torii
SIKHISM
Kirpan
TAOISM
Water; Life-giving Source
TAOISM
Yin-Yang
ZOROASTRIANISM
Sacred Fire

PALM SUNDAY

In Jerusalem, where the palm tree flourishes, Christ's triumphal entry was celebrated by the waving of palm fronds. Hence the Western world's traditional symbol for the Sunday before Easter. But in Russia where palms are scarce, the substitute symbol is *pussy-willow*!

SAFETY

g
LOOK OUT!
(Safety Alert)
r
FIRST AID
r
NO ENTRY
r
NO ENTRY to
PEDESTRIANS
EMERGENCY EXIT
(Escape Route)
b
FIRE ALARM
ACCESS for the
HANDICAPPED
ACCESS for the
AMBULANT
KEEP AWAY
from CHILDREN
WATCH for
WORK VEHICLES
orange
r
SLOW MOVING
VEHICLE
r
DO NOT START
r
DO NOT TOUCH
r
DO NOT LUBRICATE
r
NO SITTING
r
NO STANDING
r
NO RIDING
r
LADDER
OFF LIMITS
y
OR
SLIPPERY
y
OPEN PIT
y
OR
r
ELECTRICAL
DANGER
ELECTRIC
FACILITIES
y
SHARP
y
MACHINERY
HAZARD
y
SUSPENDED LOAD
OVERHEAD
y
FALLING OBJECTS
OR
POISON
r
CAUTION
LASER
CAUTION: LASER
OR
y
¶
IONIZING RAYS
(Radiation Warning)
y
FALLOUT SHELTER
(Civil Defense)
BIOHAZARD
WARNING
OR
SMOKING
PERMITTED
r
OR
r
OR
r
OR
r
NO SMOKING

¶ ISO Recommendation

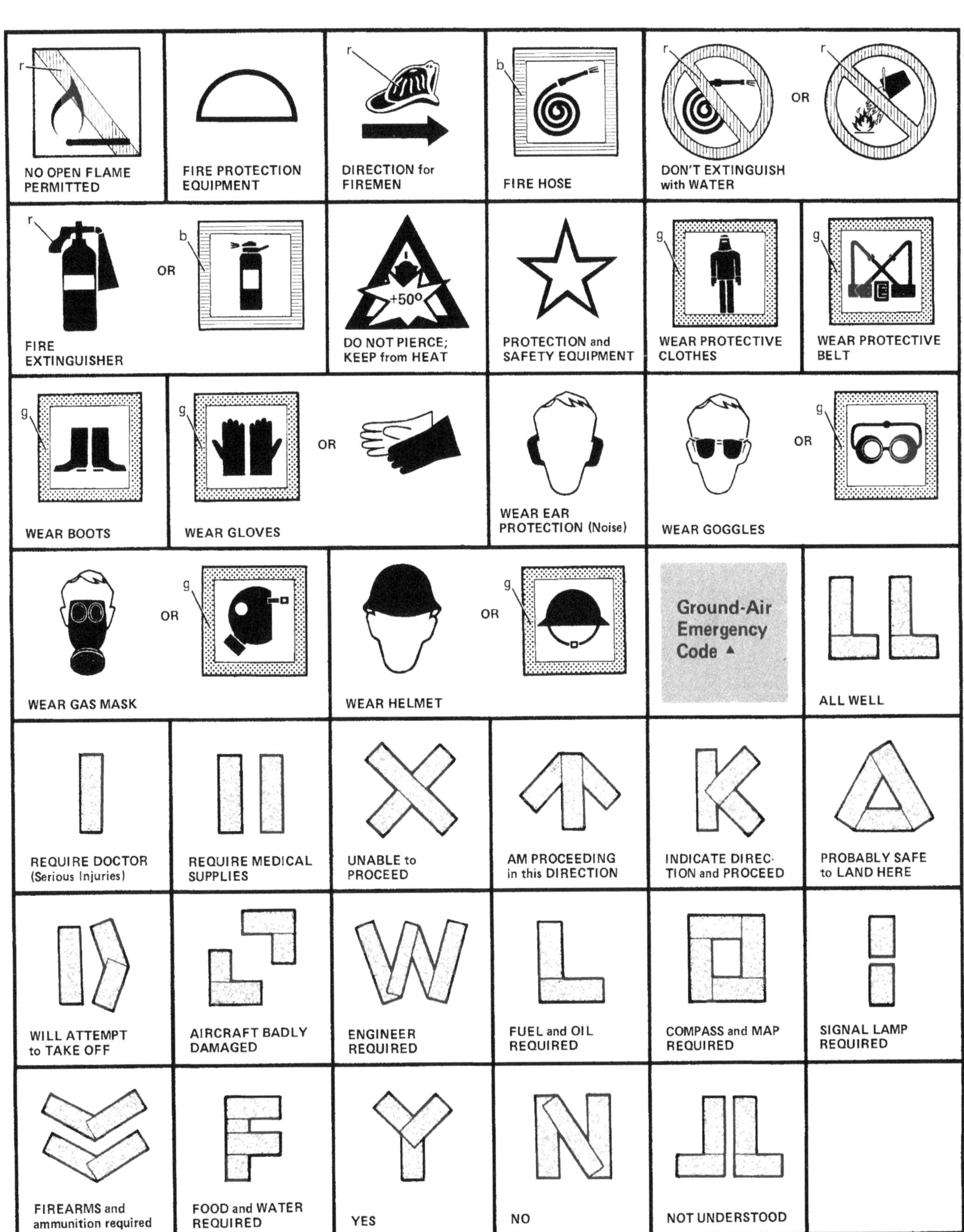
r
NO OPEN FLAME PERMITTED
FIRE PROTECTION EQUIPMENT
r
DIRECTION for FIREMEN
b
FIRE HOSE
r
OR
r
DON'T EXTINGUISH with WATER
r
OR
b
FIRE EXTINGUISHER
+50°
DO NOT PIERCE; KEEP from HEAT
PROTECTION and SAFETY EQUIPMENT
g
WEAR PROTECTIVE CLOTHES
g
WEAR PROTECTIVE BELT
g
WEAR BOOTS
g
OR
WEAR GLOVES
WEAR EAR PROTECTION (Noise)
OR
g
WEAR GOGGLES
OR
g
WEAR GAS MASK
OR
g
WEAR HELMET
Ground-Air Emergency Code ▲
ALL WELL
REQUIRE DOCTOR (Serious Injuries)
REQUIRE MEDICAL SUPPLIES
UNABLE to PROCEED
AM PROCEEDING in this DIRECTION
INDICATE DIREC-TION and PROCEED
PROBABLY SAFE to LAND HERE
WILL ATTEMPT to TAKE OFF
AIRCRAFT BADLY DAMAGED
ENGINEER REQUIRED
FUEL and OIL REQUIRED
COMPASS and MAP REQUIRED
SIGNAL LAMP REQUIRED
FIREARMS and ammunition required
FOOD and WATER REQUIRED
YES
NO
NOT UNDERSTOOD

▲ Symbols may be made of strips of fabric or parachutes, pieces of wood, tree branches, stones or any other available material.

SAFETY *(continued)*

Traffic Accidents	MATERIAL DAMAGE	INJURY, NON-FATAL	INJURY, FATAL	▲ PARKED BUS, TRUCK, or TRACTOR	OTHER OBJECTS
INTENDED MOVEMENT	● MOVING CAR, VAN or MOTORCYCLE	● STOPPED CAR, VAN or MOTORCYCLE	MOVING BUS, TRUCK or TRACTOR	STOPPED BUS, TRUCK or TRACTOR	★ TOWED and TOWING VEHICLE
HEAVY TRUCK and TRAILER	REVERSING	OUT of CONTROL	SKIDDING	VEHICLE OVERTURNED	COLLISION, BROADSIDE
COLLISION, OVERTAKING TURN	COLLISION, TURN	COLLISION, HEAD-ON	COLLISION, REAR END	SIDESWIPE, HEAD-ON	SIDESWIPE, OVERTAKING

▲ Solid line drawing ( ) indicates Parked Car, Van, or Motorcycle.
● A letter P above arrow indicates Pedestrian; **A**, Animal; **PC**, Pedal Cycle.
★ A letter **A** above arrow indicates Animal-drawn Vehicle.

BEFORE ABC'S

Youngsters below reading age can be protected by graphic symbols.

In the framework of traffic signs for "grown-ups" that sanction or forbid, various do's and don'ts are quickly recognized and remembered by children.

Caution: *Sharp*

Forbid: *Hot*

The importance of symbols in context was never more clearly shown than when we ran a specially designed test at a nursery school. A drawing of the skull and crossbones was displayed to a group of three-year-olds. "PIRATES!" they screamed. But when I drew the outline of a bottle around the symbol, they immediately shouted "POISON!"

TRAFFIC

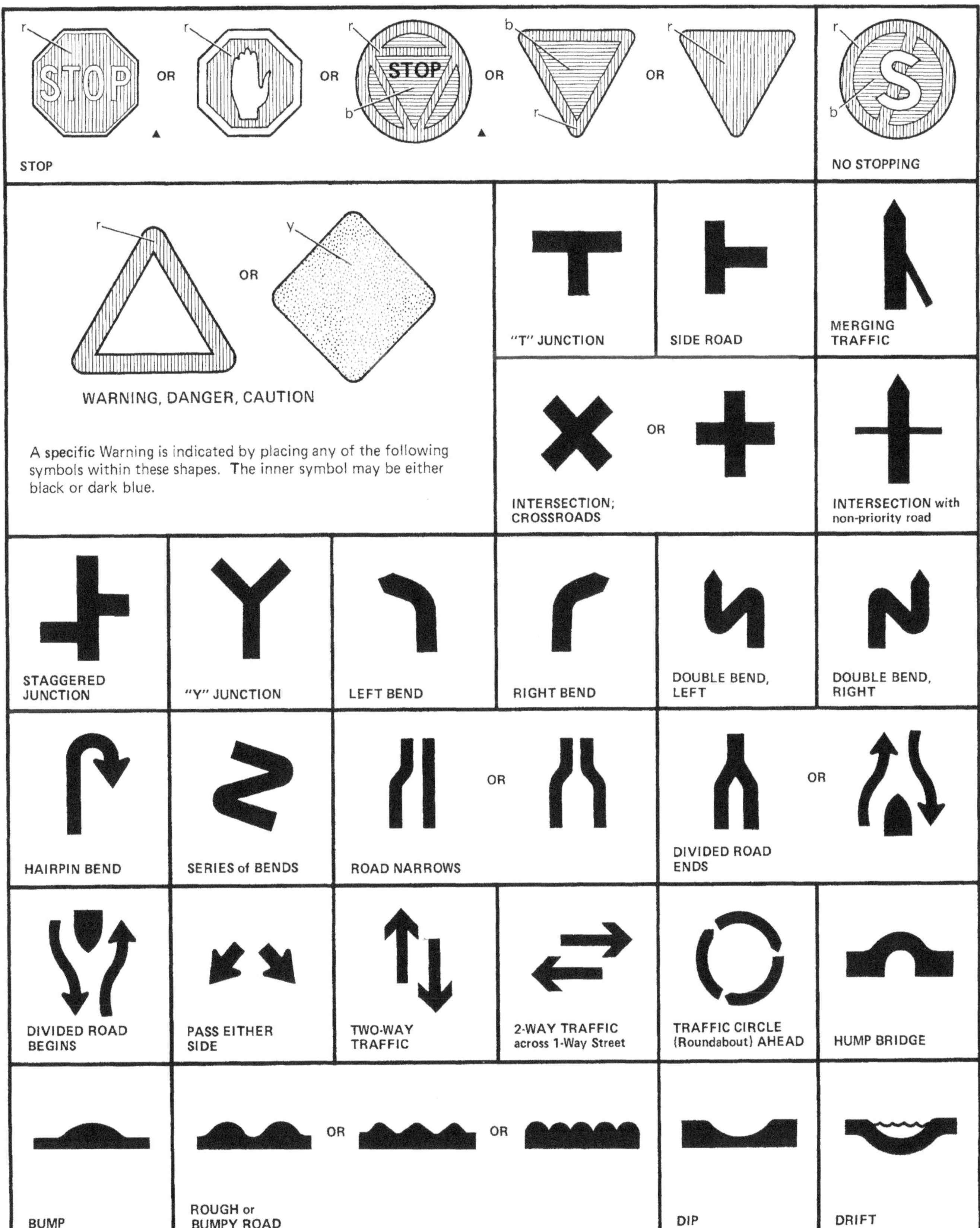
r
STOP
OR
r
OR
r
STOP
b
OR
b
r
OR
r
r
b
STOP
NO STOPPING
r
y
OR
WARNING, DANGER, CAUTION
A specific Warning is indicated by placing any of the following symbols within these shapes. The inner symbol may be either black or dark blue.
"T" JUNCTION
SIDE ROAD
MERGING TRAFFIC
OR
INTERSECTION; CROSSROADS
INTERSECTION with non-priority road
STAGGERED JUNCTION
"Y" JUNCTION
LEFT BEND
RIGHT BEND
DOUBLE BEND, LEFT
DOUBLE BEND, RIGHT
OR
OR
HAIRPIN BEND
SERIES of BENDS
ROAD NARROWS
DIVIDED ROAD ENDS
DIVIDED ROAD BEGINS
PASS EITHER SIDE
TWO-WAY TRAFFIC
2-WAY TRAFFIC across 1-Way Street
TRAFFIC CIRCLE (Roundabout) AHEAD
HUMP BRIDGE
OR
OR
BUMP
ROUGH or BUMPY ROAD
DIP
DRIFT

▲ "STOP" often translated into language of country.

STEEP ASCENT
OR
10%
STEEP DESCENT
OR
10%
GRADE CROSSING
r
Blinking Light
OR
r
Alternately Blinking Lights
STOP AHEAD
OR
TRAFFIC SIGNAL AHEAD
r
y
g
OR
STOP - GO CONTROL AHEAD
r
SCHOOL PATROL AHEAD
r
YIELD SIGN AHEAD
FALLING ROCKS
LOOSE GRAVEL
SLIPPERY ROAD
NARROW BRIDGE
NARROW STRUCTURE
QUAYSIDE or RIVER BANK
DRAWBRIDGE
GATE
MOTOR GATE
GRADE CROSSING (Railroad)
FLASHING LIGHT AHEAD (Railroad)
GRADE CROSSING without GATES
GRADE CROSSING with GATES
GRADE CROSSING, automatic half-barriers
ROAD WORK AHEAD
OR
TRUCK CROSSING
CHILDREN CROSSING
OR
PEDESTRIAN CROSSING
ANIMAL CROSSING
WILD ANIMAL CROSSING
LOW FLYING AIRCRAFT
TUNNEL
OR
SOFT SHOULDER
CROSS WIND
OVERHEAD CABLE
OTHER DANGERS

▲ Amount of grade may also be expressed as a ratio. **Example:** 1:10.

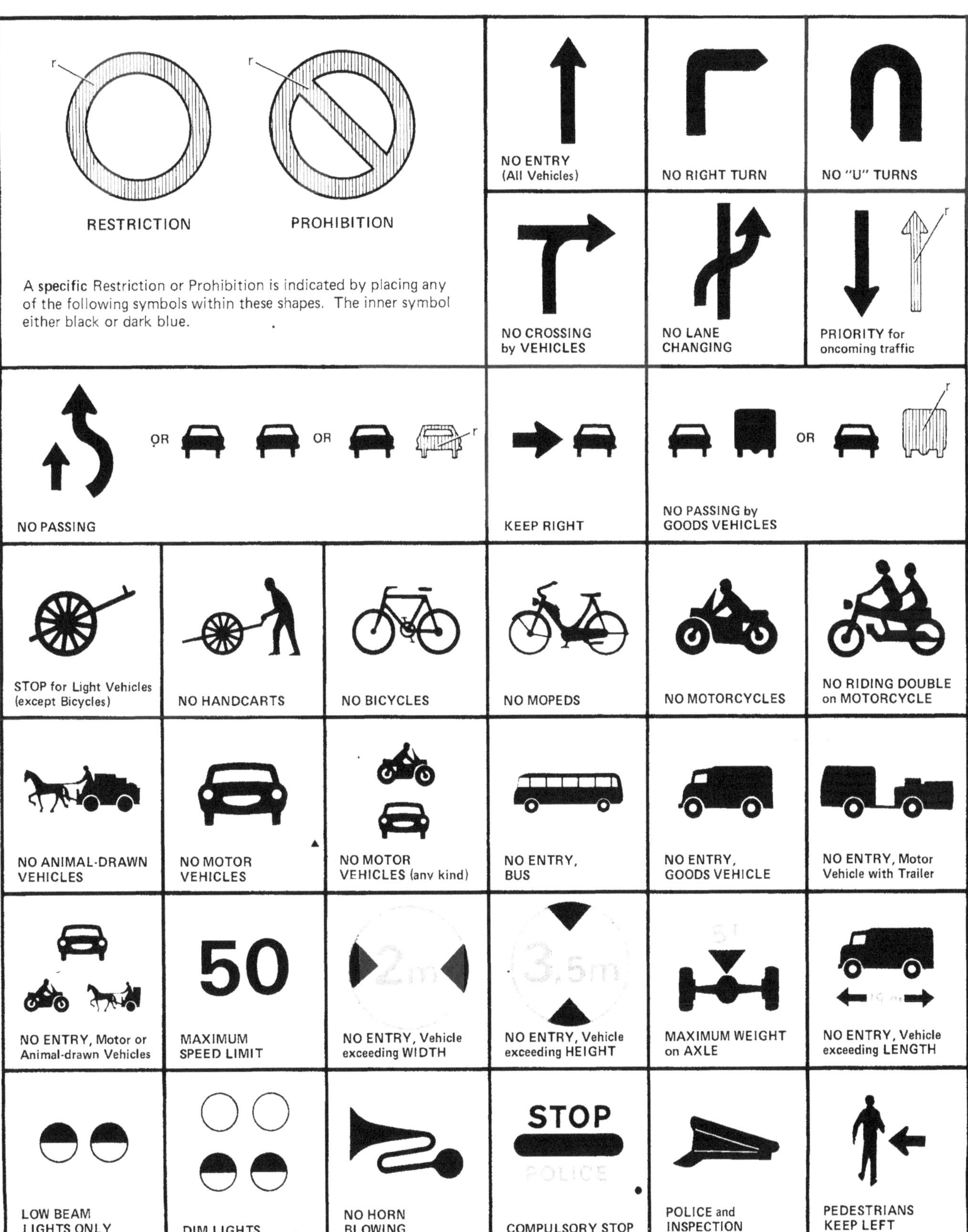
RESTRICTION
PROHIBITION
A specific Restriction or Prohibition is indicated by placing any of the following symbols within these shapes. The inner symbol either black or dark blue.
NO ENTRY (All Vehicles)
NO RIGHT TURN
NO "U" TURNS
NO CROSSING by VEHICLES
NO LANE CHANGING
PRIORITY for oncoming traffic
OR
OR
NO PASSING
KEEP RIGHT
OR
NO PASSING by GOODS VEHICLES
STOP for Light Vehicles (except Bicycles)
NO HANDCARTS
NO BICYCLES
NO MOPEDS
NO MOTORCYCLES
NO RIDING DOUBLE on MOTORCYCLE
NO ANIMAL-DRAWN VEHICLES
NO MOTOR VEHICLES
NO MOTOR VEHICLES (any kind)
NO ENTRY, BUS
NO ENTRY, GOODS VEHICLE
NO ENTRY, Motor Vehicle with Trailer
NO ENTRY, Motor or Animal-drawn Vehicles
50
MAXIMUM SPEED LIMIT
NO ENTRY, Vehicle exceeding WIDTH
NO ENTRY, Vehicle exceeding HEIGHT
MAXIMUM WEIGHT on AXLE
NO ENTRY, Vehicle exceeding LENGTH
LOW BEAM LIGHTS ONLY
DIM LIGHTS
NO HORN BLOWING
STOP
COMPULSORY STOP
POLICE and INSPECTION
PEDESTRIANS KEEP LEFT

▲ **Exception**: Two-wheeled motor vehicles without side-cars.

● Other reasons for stopping may be indicated. **Example:** STOP - CHILDREN; STOP - WEIGHT CHECK.

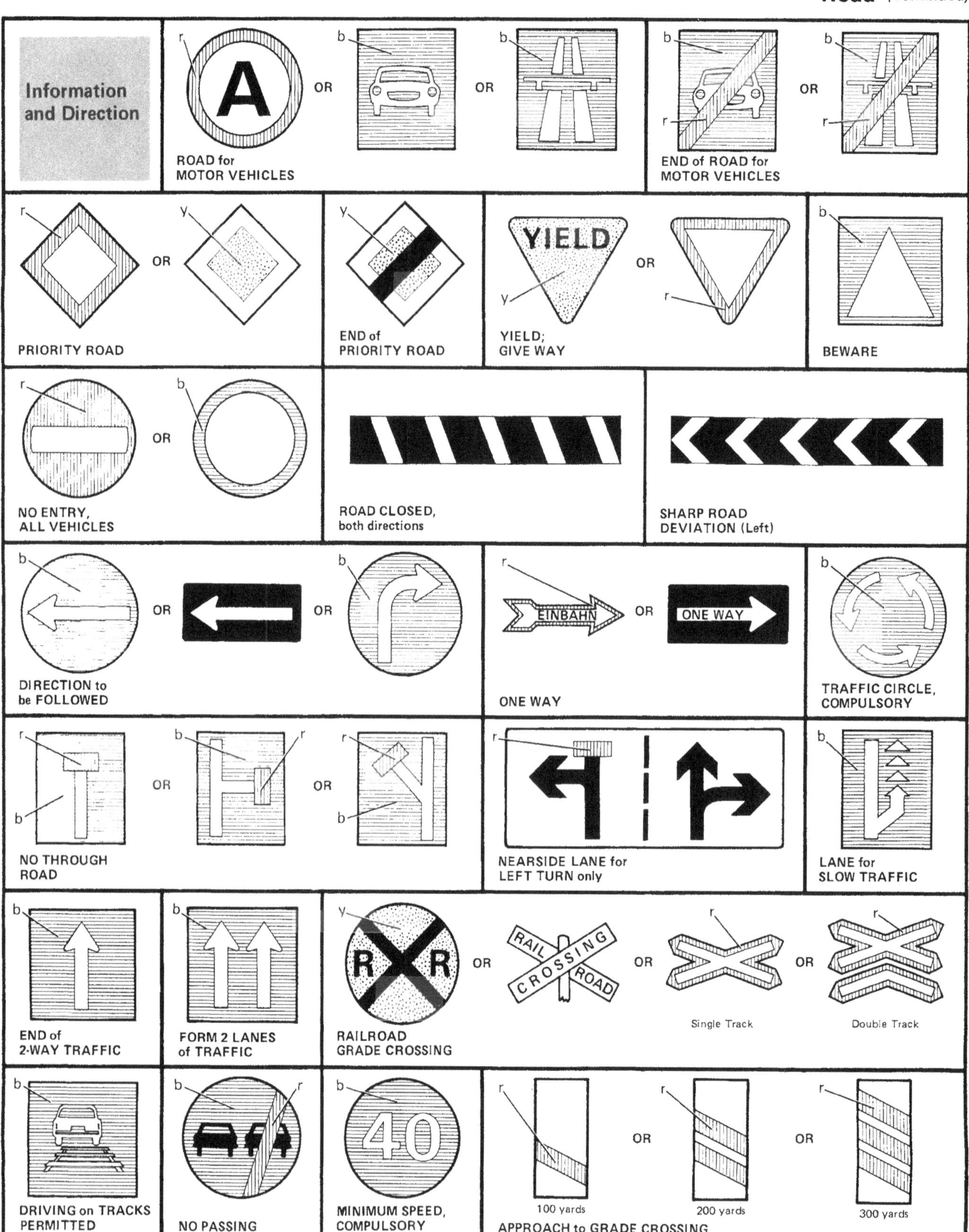
Information and Direction
r
A
OR
b
OR
b
ROAD for MOTOR VEHICLES
b
b
r
OR
r
END of ROAD for MOTOR VEHICLES
r
OR
y
PRIORITY ROAD
y
END of PRIORITY ROAD
YIELD
y
OR
r
YIELD; GIVE WAY
b
BEWARE
r
OR
b
NO ENTRY, ALL VEHICLES
ROAD CLOSED, both directions
SHARP ROAD DEVIATION (Left)
b
OR
OR
b
DIRECTION to be FOLLOWED
r
EINBAHN
OR
ONE WAY
ONE WAY
b
TRAFFIC CIRCLE, COMPULSORY
r
b
OR
b
r
OR
r
b
NO THROUGH ROAD
r
NEARSIDE LANE for LEFT TURN only
b
LANE for SLOW TRAFFIC
b
END of 2-WAY TRAFFIC
b
FORM 2 LANES of TRAFFIC
y
R R
OR
RAIL ROAD CROSSING
OR
r
OR
r
RAILROAD GRADE CROSSING
Single Track
Double Track
b
DRIVING on TRACKS PERMITTED
b
r
NO PASSING
b
40
MINIMUM SPEED, COMPULSORY
r
OR
r
OR
r
100 yards
200 yards
300 yards
APPROACH to GRADE CROSSING

ROUTE MARKER, INTERSTATE
40
ROUTE MARKER, ASSEMBLY
40
ROUTE MARKER, U. S. (State)
P
OR
PARKING
P
PARKING OFF ROAD
P
METERED PARKING
P
PARKING DISC COMPULSORY
P
OR
NO PARKING
NO PARKING on ODD DATES
NO PARKING on EVEN DATES
NO PARKING on LEFT
NO PARKING on RIGHT
I
II
NO PARKING (Odd days, Left; Even, Right)
NO STOPPING
OR
END of PROHIBITION
COMPULSORY BICYCLE TRAIL
PARALLEL Riding Permitted
UNDERPASS or BRIDGE
COMPULSORY WAY for PEDESTRIANS
CROSSING
OR
PEDESTRIAN CROSSING
CHILDREN CROSSING
CHILDREN CAN PLAY in STREET
NO PEDESTRIAN CROSSING
NO PEDESTRIANS
SAFETY ISLAND
BRIDLE PATH
H
OR
HOSPITAL
OR
HOSPITAL
SOUND HORN
PARKING LIGHTS Required at NIGHT
STOP and CHECK BRAKES
DON'T POLLUTE WATER
TRAMWAY STOP
OR
BUS STOP or STATION
FERRY
FIRE AREA (Potential)

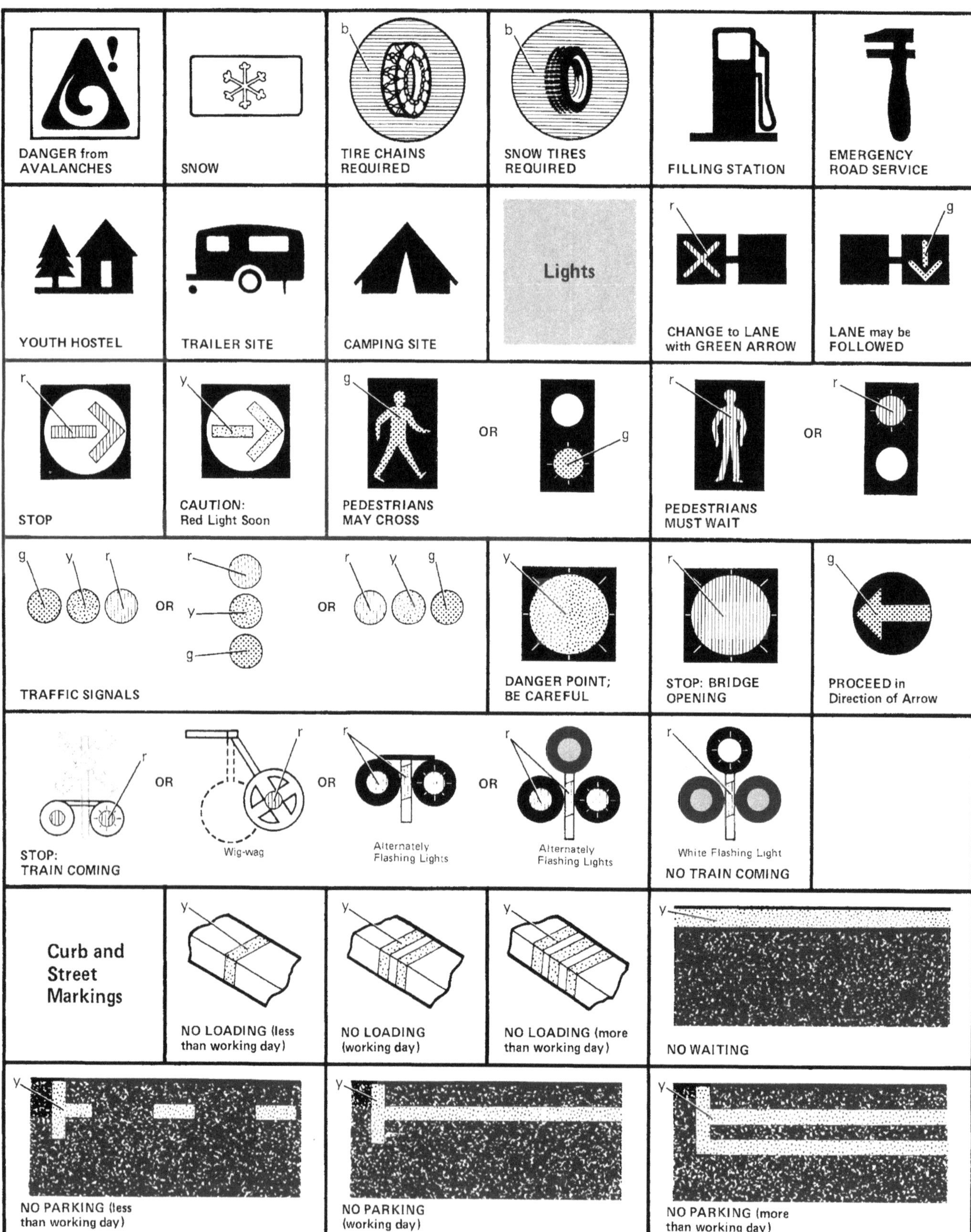
DANGER from AVALANCHES
SNOW
b
TIRE CHAINS REQUIRED
b
SNOW TIRES REQUIRED
FILLING STATION
EMERGENCY ROAD SERVICE
YOUTH HOSTEL
TRAILER SITE
CAMPING SITE
Lights
r
CHANGE to LANE with GREEN ARROW
g
LANE may be FOLLOWED
r
STOP
y
CAUTION: Red Light Soon
g
OR
g
PEDESTRIANS MAY CROSS
r
OR
r
PEDESTRIANS MUST WAIT
g
y
r
OR
r
y
g
OR
r
y
g
TRAFFIC SIGNALS
y
DANGER POINT; BE CAREFUL
r
STOP: BRIDGE OPENING
g
PROCEED in Direction of Arrow
r
OR
r
Wig-wag
OR
r
Alternately Flashing Lights
OR
r
Alternately Flashing Lights
STOP: TRAIN COMING
r
White Flashing Light
NO TRAIN COMING
Curb and Street Markings
y
NO LOADING (less than working day)
y
NO LOADING (working day)
y
NO LOADING (more than working day)
y
NO WAITING
y
NO PARKING (less than working day)
y
NO PARKING (working day)
y
NO PARKING (more than working day)

PAVED SHOULDERS
OR
No Motor Vehicles
Motor Vehicles Permitted
CYCLING LANE
OR
CENTER LINE
LANE LINE
WARNING LINE
NO CROSSING if solid line on your side
NO CROSSING (either side)
STOP
STOP Controlled by Sign
STOP
STOP Controlled by Traffic Signal
R R
RAILROAD CROSSING
YIELD Controlled without Sign
YIELD Controlled with Sign
DO NOT ENTER MARKED AREA

▲ Solid Line(s) may also be shown in yellow.

TRAFFIC

Road *(continued)*

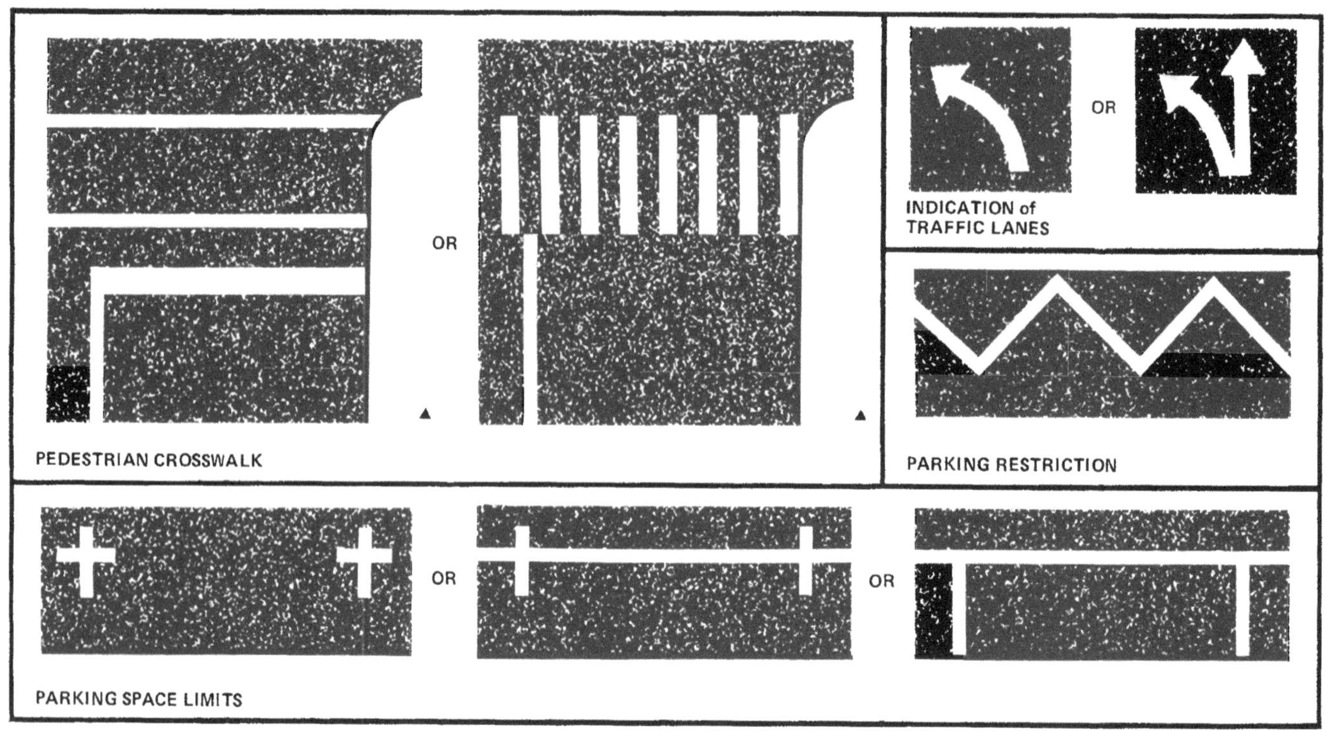
OR
PEDESTRIAN CROSSWALK
OR
INDICATION of TRAFFIC LANES
PARKING RESTRICTION
OR
OR
PARKING SPACE LIMITS

Air

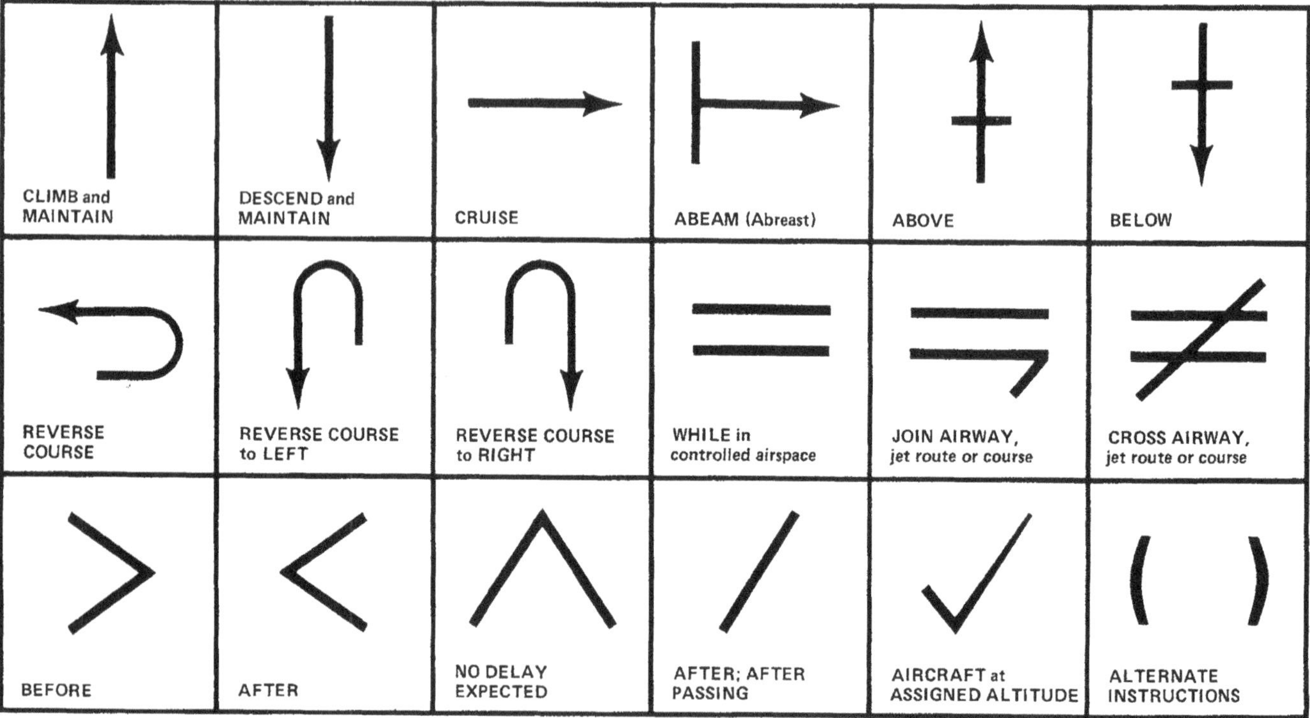
CLIMB and MAINTAIN
DESCEND and MAINTAIN
CRUISE
ABEAM (Abreast)
ABOVE
BELOW
REVERSE COURSE
REVERSE COURSE to LEFT
REVERSE COURSE to RIGHT
WHILE in controlled airspace
JOIN AIRWAY, jet route or course
CROSS AIRWAY, jet route or course
BEFORE
AFTER
NO DELAY EXPECTED
AFTER; AFTER PASSING
AIRCRAFT at ASSIGNED ALTITUDE
ALTERNATE INSTRUCTIONS

▲ Solid Line(s) may also be shown in yellow.

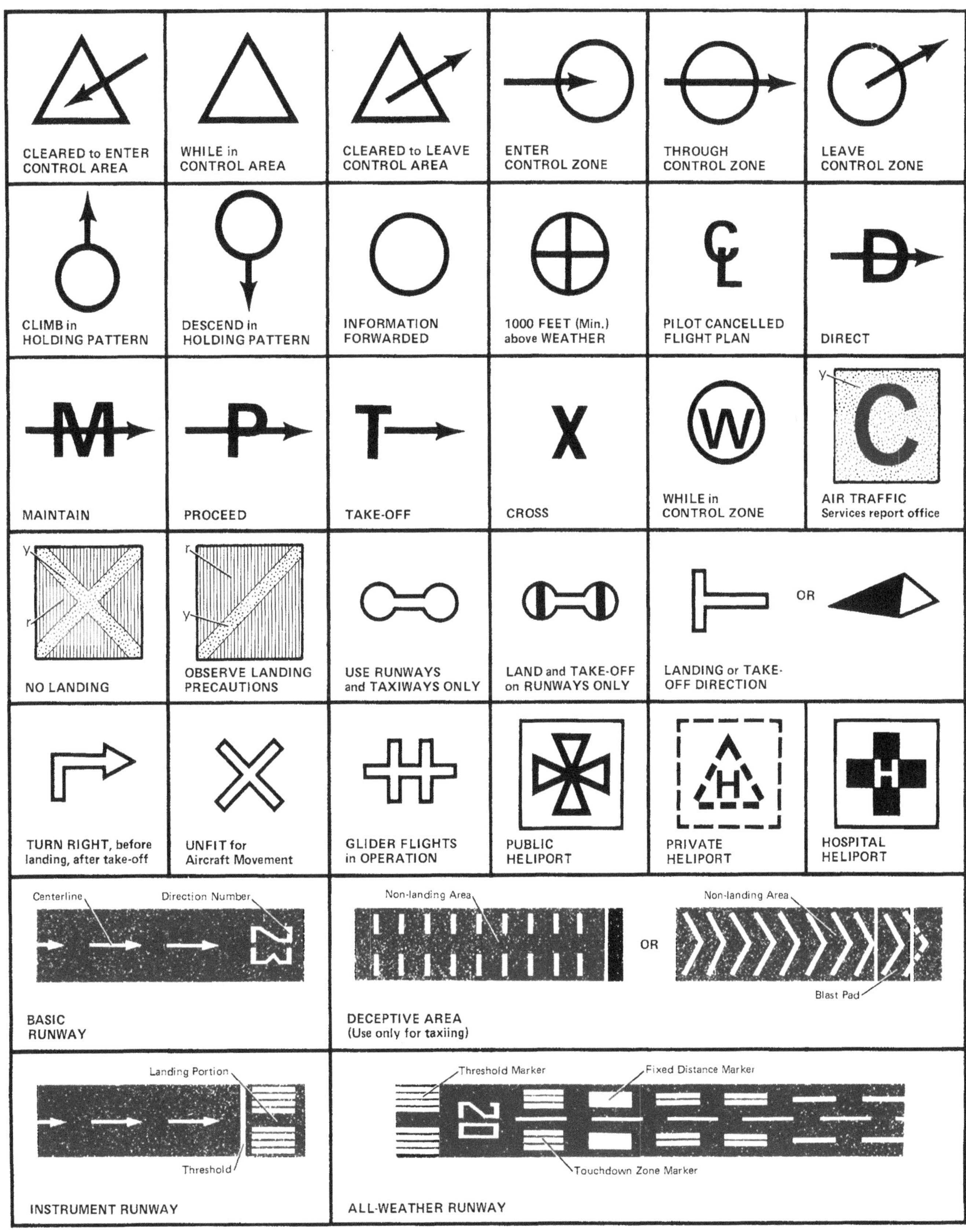
CLEARED to ENTER CONTROL AREA
WHILE in CONTROL AREA
CLEARED to LEAVE CONTROL AREA
ENTER CONTROL ZONE
THROUGH CONTROL ZONE
LEAVE CONTROL ZONE
CLIMB in HOLDING PATTERN
DESCEND in HOLDING PATTERN
INFORMATION FORWARDED
1000 FEET (Min.) above WEATHER
PILOT CANCELLED FLIGHT PLAN
DIRECT
M
MAINTAIN
P
PROCEED
T
TAKE-OFF
X
CROSS
W
WHILE in CONTROL ZONE
y
C
AIR TRAFFIC Services report office
y
r
NO LANDING
r
y
OBSERVE LANDING PRECAUTIONS
USE RUNWAYS and TAXIWAYS ONLY
LAND and TAKE-OFF on RUNWAYS ONLY
OR
LANDING or TAKE-OFF DIRECTION
TURN RIGHT, before landing, after take-off
UNFIT for Aircraft Movement
GLIDER FLIGHTS in OPERATION
PUBLIC HELIPORT
H
PRIVATE HELIPORT
H
HOSPITAL HELIPORT
Centerline
Direction Number
BASIC RUNWAY
Non-landing Area
OR
Non-landing Area
Blast Pad
DECEPTIVE AREA (Use only for taxiing)
Landing Portion
Threshold
INSTRUMENT RUNWAY
Threshold Marker
Fixed Distance Marker
20
Touchdown Zone Marker
ALL-WEATHER RUNWAY

Marshalling Signals	PROCEED; WATCH SIGNALS	THIS WAY	PROCEED to NEXT SIGNALMAN	TURN LEFT ▲	TURN RIGHT ▲
MOVE AHEAD	STOP ▲	START ENGINES	INSERT CHOCKS	PULL CHOCKS	CUT ENGINES
SLOW DOWN	SLOW DOWN LEFT ENGINES	SLOW DOWN RIGHT ENGINES	MOVE BACK	BACK UP, Tail to STARBOARD	BACK UP, Tail to PORT
ALL CLEAR	HOVER	MOVE UPWARDS ●	MOVE DOWNWARDS ●	MOVE HORIZONTALLY	LAND

Marine

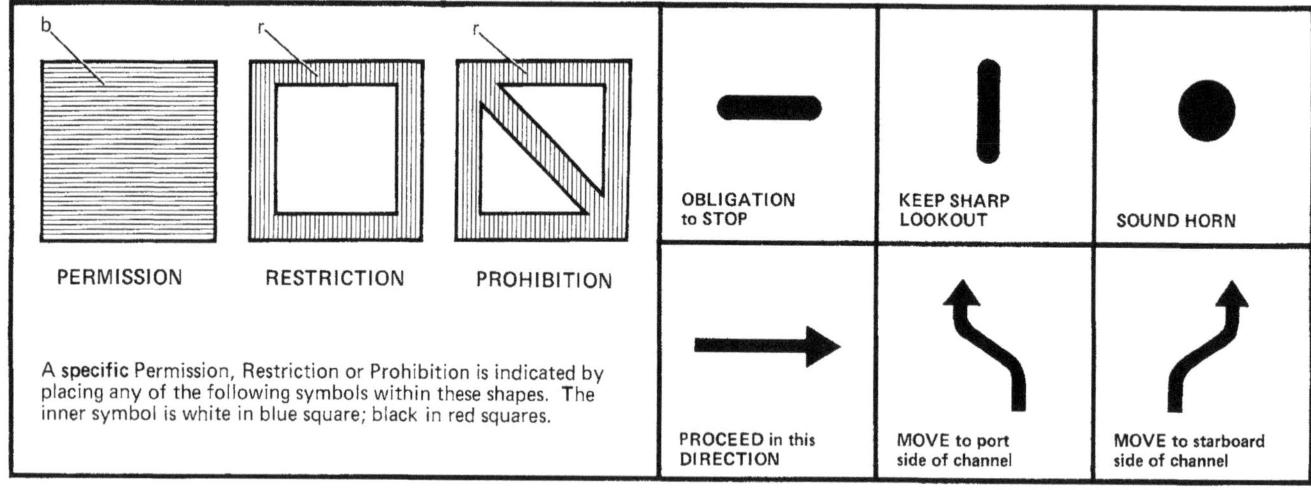

b
r
r
PERMISSION
RESTRICTION
PROHIBITION
A specific Permission, Restriction or Prohibition is indicated by placing any of the following symbols within these shapes. The inner symbol is white in blue square; black in red squares.
OBLIGATION to STOP
KEEP SHARP LOOKOUT
SOUND HORN
PROCEED in this DIRECTION
MOVE to port side of channel
MOVE to starboard side of channel

▲ The signalman is shown facing the aircraft. Signals may also be made with illuminated wands, bats or torchlights.

● The speed of the signalman's arm movement indicates the speed of the action to be taken by the pilot.

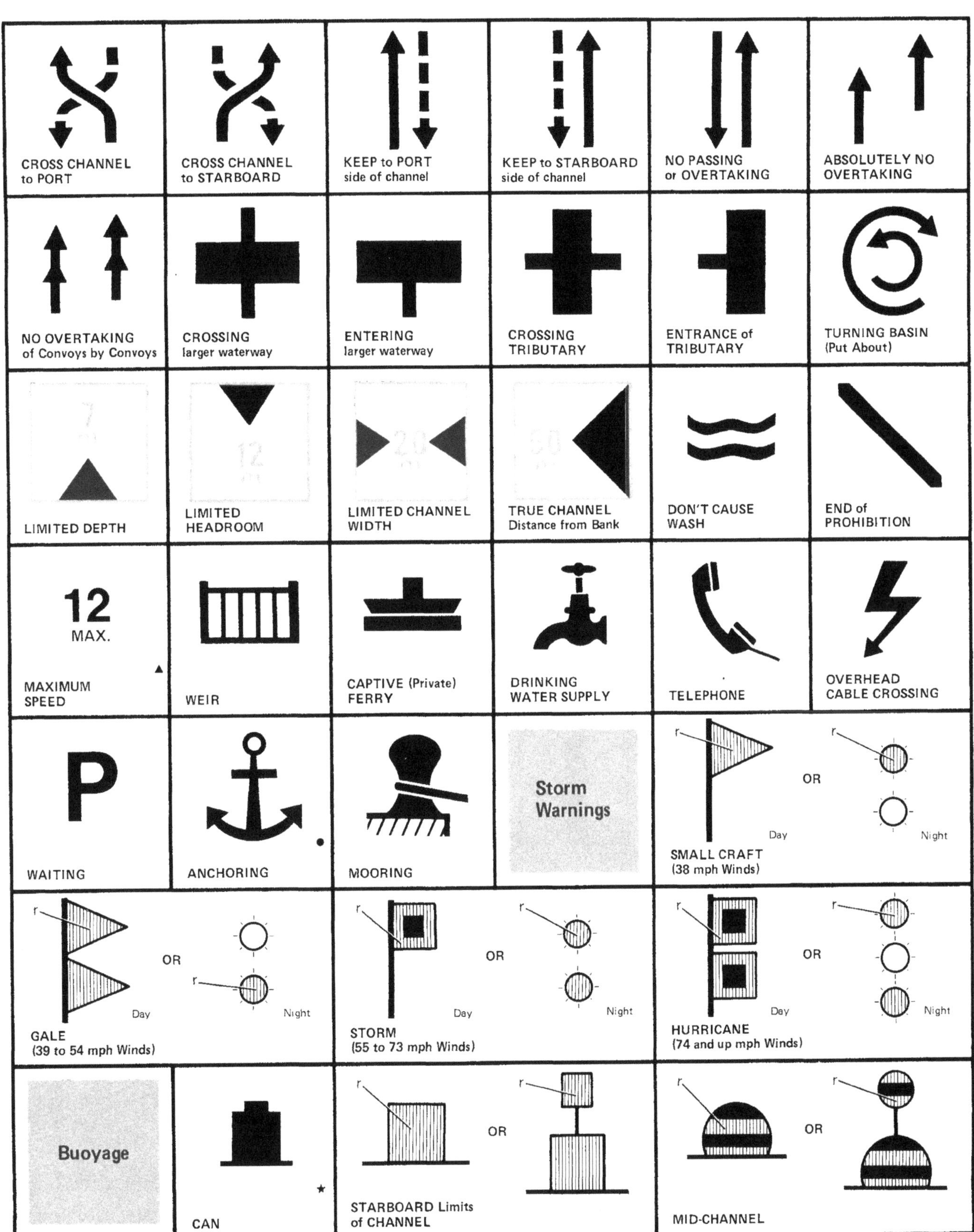

CROSS CHANNEL to PORT
CROSS CHANNEL to STARBOARD
KEEP to PORT side of channel
KEEP to STARBOARD side of channel
NO PASSING or OVERTAKING
ABSOLUTELY NO OVERTAKING
NO OVERTAKING of Convoys by Convoys
CROSSING larger waterway
ENTERING larger waterway
CROSSING TRIBUTARY
ENTRANCE of TRIBUTARY
TURNING BASIN (Put About)
LIMITED DEPTH
LIMITED HEADROOM
LIMITED CHANNEL WIDTH
TRUE CHANNEL Distance from Bank
DON'T CAUSE WASH
END of PROHIBITION
12
MAX.
MAXIMUM SPEED ▲
WEIR
CAPTIVE (Private) FERRY
DRINKING WATER SUPPLY
TELEPHONE
OVERHEAD CABLE CROSSING
P
WAITING
ANCHORING ●
MOORING
Storm Warnings
r
OR
Day
Night
SMALL CRAFT (38 mph Winds)
GALE (39 to 54 mph Winds)
STORM (55 to 73 mph Winds)
HURRICANE (74 and up mph Winds)
Buoyage
CAN ★
STARBOARD Limits of CHANNEL
MID-CHANNEL

▲ May be any prescribed kilometers per hour.
● Anchor inverted when used in Prohibition square.
★ Color of buoy structure indicates location of channel: black for port side; black and white, mid-channel; red, starboard. Numbers may also be added: odd for port side; none, mid-channel; even, starboard.

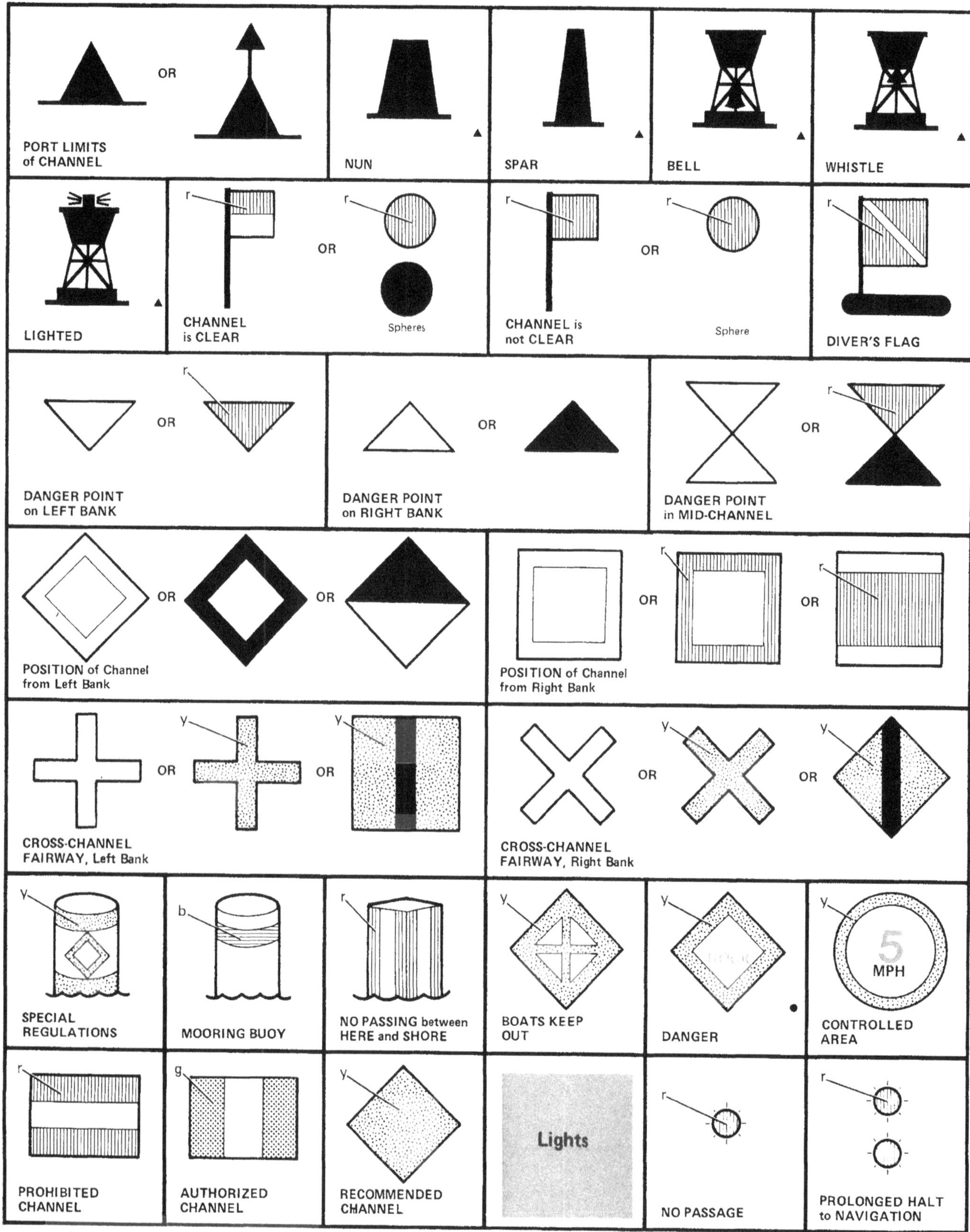

OR
PORT LIMITS of CHANNEL
NUN
SPAR
BELL
WHISTLE
LIGHTED
r
CHANNEL is CLEAR
OR
Spheres
CHANNEL is not CLEAR
Sphere
DIVER'S FLAG
DANGER POINT on LEFT BANK
DANGER POINT on RIGHT BANK
DANGER POINT in MID-CHANNEL
POSITION of Channel from Left Bank
POSITION of Channel from Right Bank
y
CROSS-CHANNEL FAIRWAY, Left Bank
CROSS-CHANNEL FAIRWAY, Right Bank
SPECIAL REGULATIONS
b
MOORING BUOY
NO PASSING between HERE and SHORE
BOATS KEEP OUT
DANGER
5
MPH
CONTROLLED AREA
g
PROHIBITED CHANNEL
AUTHORIZED CHANNEL
RECOMMENDED CHANNEL
Lights
NO PASSAGE
PROLONGED HALT to NAVIGATION

▲ Color of buoy structure indicates location of channel: black for port side; black and white, mid-channel; red, starboard. Numbers may also be added: odd for port side; none, mid-channel; even, starboard.

● Specific danger may be indicated inside. **Example:** Wreck, Shoal, Dam.

r

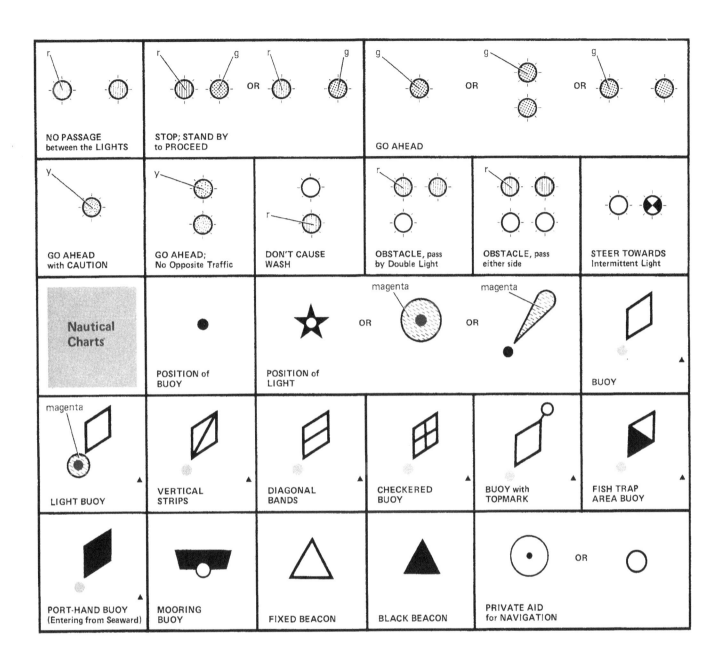

NO PASSAGE between the LIGHTS

r g OR r g

STOP; STAND BY to PROCEED

g OR g OR g

GO AHEAD

y

GO AHEAD with CAUTION

y

GO AHEAD; No Opposite Traffic

r

DON'T CAUSE WASH

r

OBSTACLE, pass by Double Light

r

OBSTACLE, pass either side

STEER TOWARDS Intermittent Light

Nautical Charts

POSITION of BUOY

magenta OR magenta

POSITION of LIGHT

BUOY ▲

magenta

LIGHT BUOY ▲

VERTICAL STRIPS ▲

DIAGONAL BANDS ▲

CHECKERED BUOY ▲

BUOY with TOPMARK ▲

FISH TRAP AREA BUOY ▲

PORT-HAND BUOY (Entering from Seaward) ▲

MOORING BUOY

FIXED BEACON

BLACK BEACON

OR

PRIVATE AID for NAVIGATION

Rail

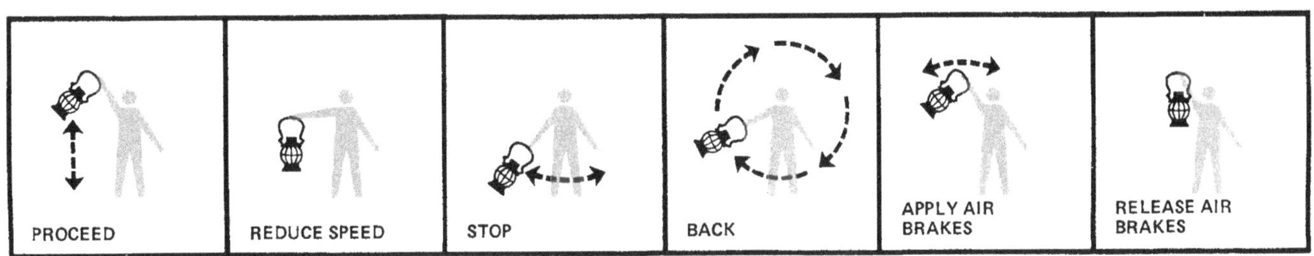
PROCEED
REDUCE SPEED
STOP
BACK
APPLY AIR BRAKES
RELEASE AIR BRAKES

▲ Words or initials are often used with symbol to identify a specific type of buoy. **Example:** C means Can Buoy, BELL, Bell Buoy.

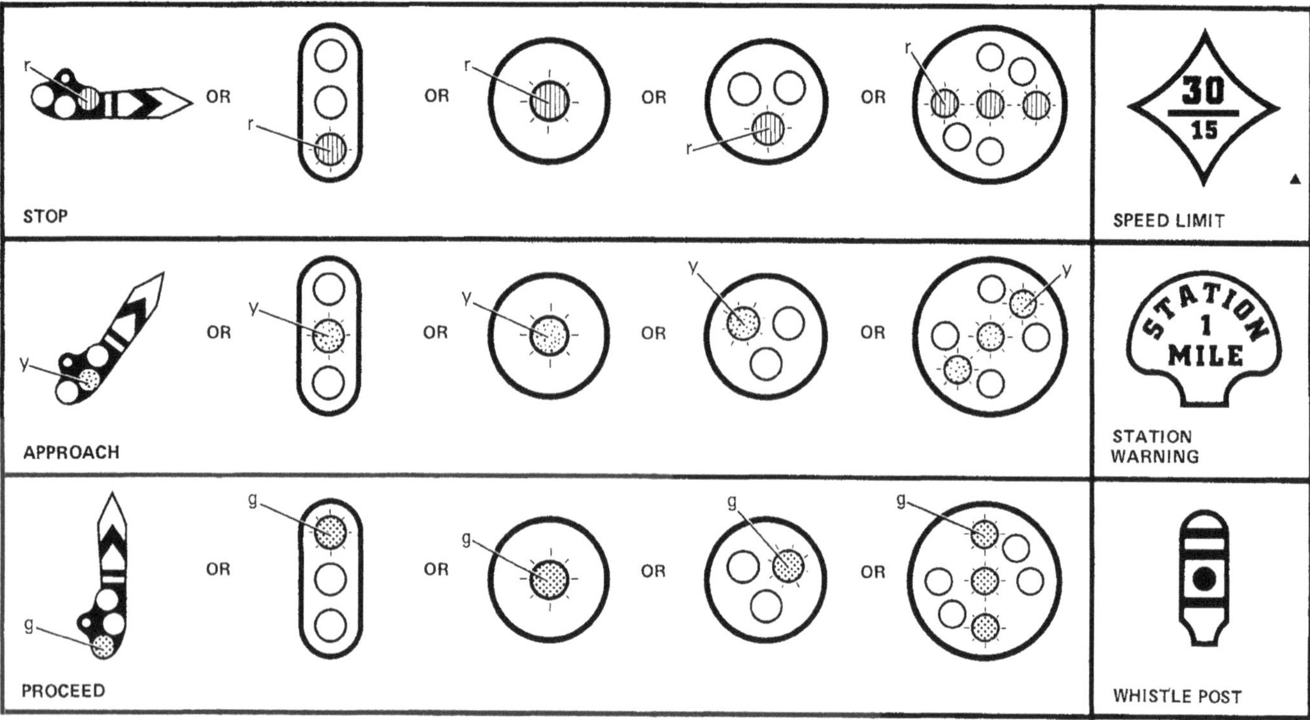
r
OR
r
OR
r
OR
r
OR
r
30
15
STOP
SPEED LIMIT
y
OR
y
OR
y
OR
y
OR
y
STATION
1
MILE
APPROACH
STATION WARNING
g
OR
g
OR
g
OR
g
OR
g
PROCEED
WHISTLE POST

▲ Top number is for Passenger Train; bottom, Freight Train.

KNIGHTS OF THE ROAD

Nonchalant and carefree as they may appear, the hoboes are sufficiently sophisticated to have produced a system of graphic symbols all their own. What is more, it is international, and gypsies around the world can translate it into their mother tongues.

If you should come upon a country wall and find this message chalked on it, could *you* read it?

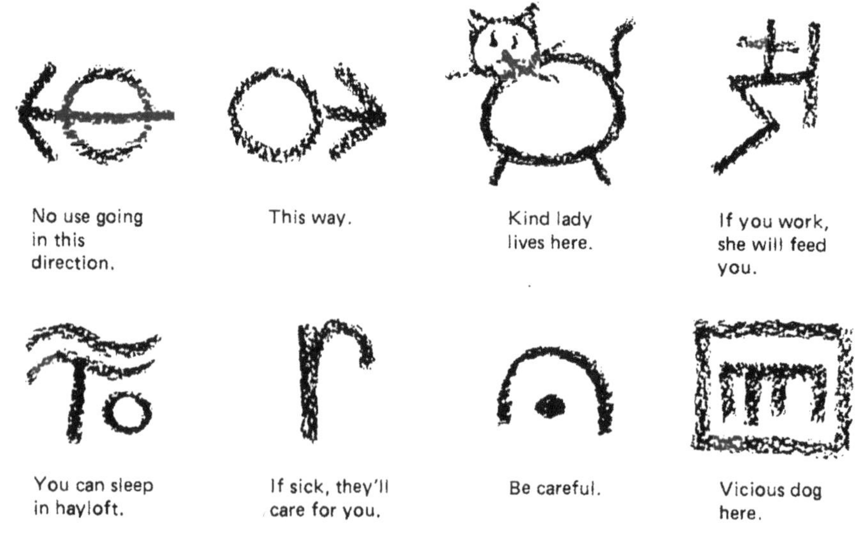
No use going in this direction.
This way.
Kind lady lives here.
If you work, she will feed you.
You can sleep in hayloft.
If sick, they'll care for you.
Be careful.
Vicious dog here.

VEHICLE CONTROLS

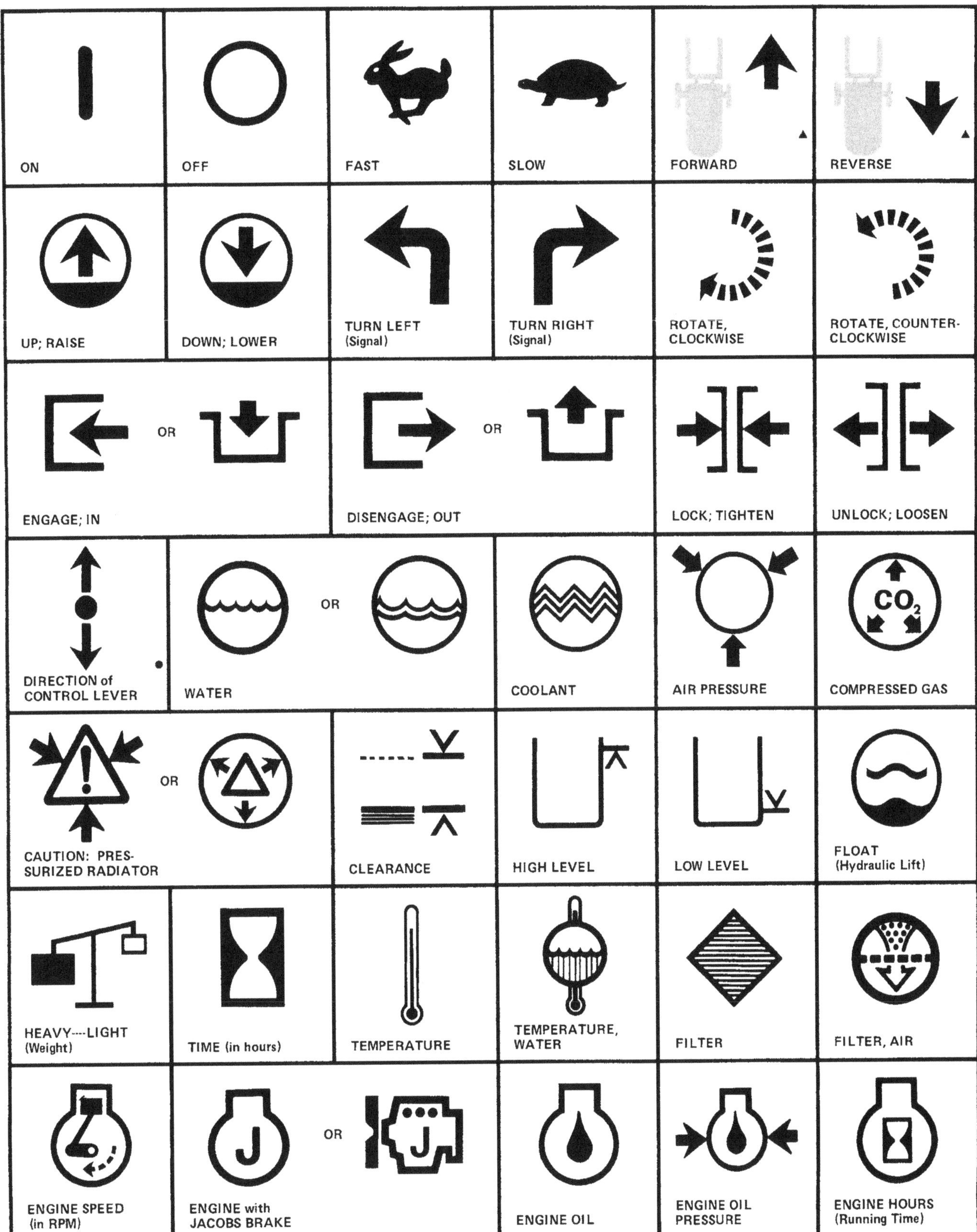

ON
OFF
FAST
SLOW
FORWARD ▲
REVERSE ▲
UP; RAISE
DOWN; LOWER
TURN LEFT (Signal)
TURN RIGHT (Signal)
ROTATE, CLOCKWISE
ROTATE, COUNTER-CLOCKWISE
OR
ENGAGE; IN
OR
DISENGAGE; OUT
LOCK; TIGHTEN
UNLOCK; LOOSEN
DIRECTION of CONTROL LEVER ●
OR
WATER
COOLANT
AIR PRESSURE
CO_2
COMPRESSED GAS
OR
CAUTION: PRESSURIZED RADIATOR
CLEARANCE
HIGH LEVEL
LOW LEVEL
FLOAT (Hydraulic Lift)
HEAVY----LIGHT (Weight)
TIME (in hours)
TEMPERATURE
TEMPERATURE, WATER
FILTER
FILTER, AIR
ENGINE SPEED (in RPM)
J
OR
J
ENGINE with JACOBS BRAKE
ENGINE OIL
ENGINE OIL PRESSURE
ENGINE HOURS (Running Time)

▲ Any vehicle, correctly oriented to arrow, may be used.
● May be used in conjunction with other symbols to designate lever motion.

VEHICLE CONTROLS *(continued)*

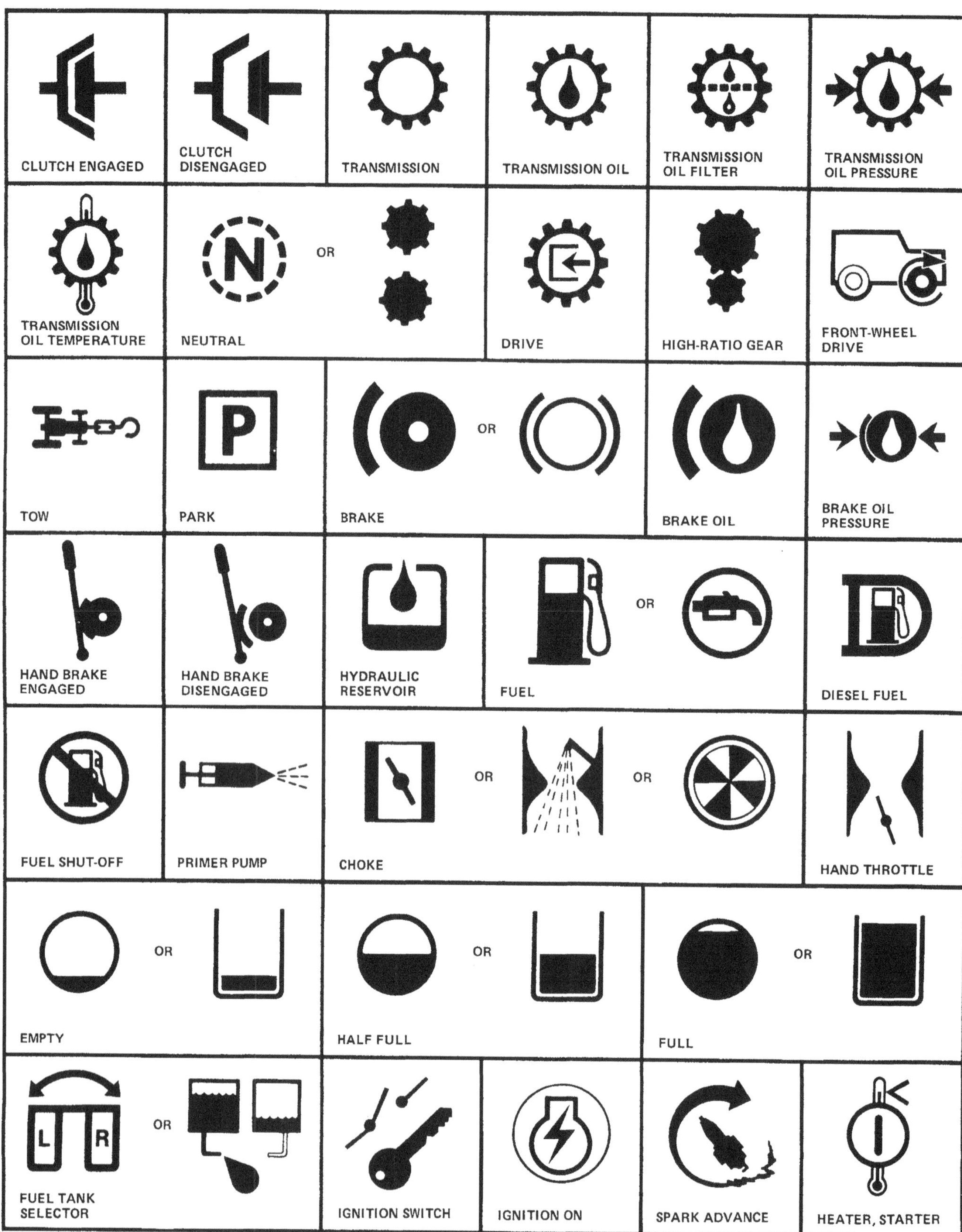

CLUTCH ENGAGED
CLUTCH DISENGAGED
TRANSMISSION
TRANSMISSION OIL
TRANSMISSION OIL FILTER
TRANSMISSION OIL PRESSURE
TRANSMISSION OIL TEMPERATURE
N
OR
NEUTRAL
DRIVE
HIGH-RATIO GEAR
FRONT-WHEEL DRIVE
TOW
P
PARK
OR
BRAKE
BRAKE OIL
BRAKE OIL PRESSURE
HAND BRAKE ENGAGED
HAND BRAKE DISENGAGED
HYDRAULIC RESERVOIR
OR
FUEL
DIESEL FUEL
FUEL SHUT-OFF
PRIMER PUMP
OR
OR
CHOKE
HAND THROTTLE
OR
EMPTY
OR
HALF FULL
OR
FULL
L
R
OR
FUEL TANK SELECTOR
IGNITION SWITCH
IGNITION ON
SPARK ADVANCE
HEATER, STARTER

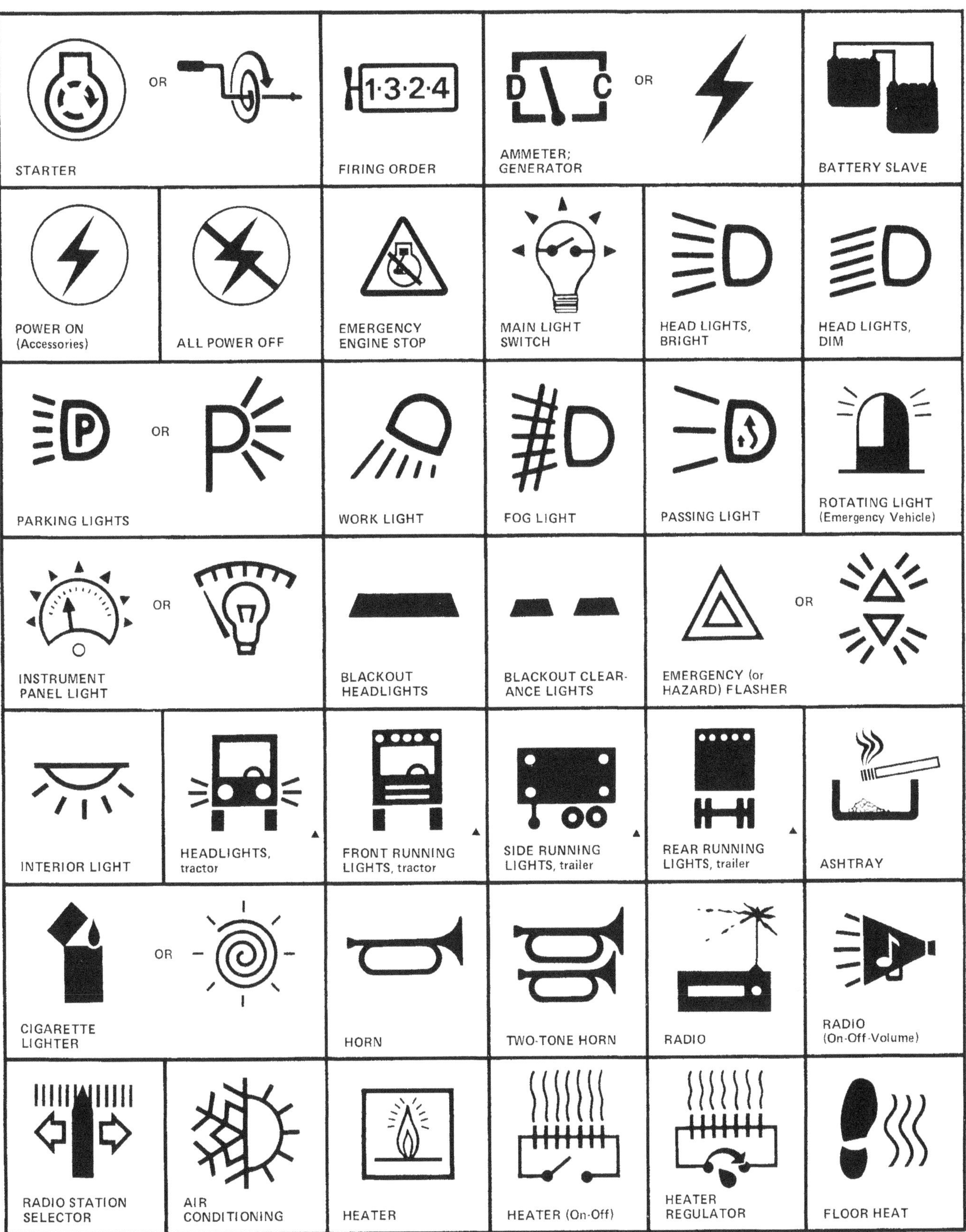

STARTER
OR
FIRING ORDER
1·3·2·4
AMMETER; GENERATOR
D
C
OR
BATTERY SLAVE
POWER ON (Accessories)
ALL POWER OFF
EMERGENCY ENGINE STOP
MAIN LIGHT SWITCH
HEAD LIGHTS, BRIGHT
HEAD LIGHTS, DIM
PARKING LIGHTS
P
OR
P
WORK LIGHT
FOG LIGHT
PASSING LIGHT
ROTATING LIGHT (Emergency Vehicle)
INSTRUMENT PANEL LIGHT
OR
BLACKOUT HEADLIGHTS
BLACKOUT CLEARANCE LIGHTS
EMERGENCY (or HAZARD) FLASHER
OR
INTERIOR LIGHT
HEADLIGHTS, tractor ▲
FRONT RUNNING LIGHTS, tractor ▲
SIDE RUNNING LIGHTS, trailer ▲
REAR RUNNING LIGHTS, trailer ▲
ASHTRAY
CIGARETTE LIGHTER
OR
HORN
TWO-TONE HORN
RADIO
RADIO (On-Off-Volume)
RADIO STATION SELECTOR
AIR CONDITIONING
HEATER
HEATER (On-Off)
HEATER REGULATOR
FLOOR HEAT

▲ Applies to semi tractor-trailer (truck).

VEHICLE CONTROLS *(continued)*

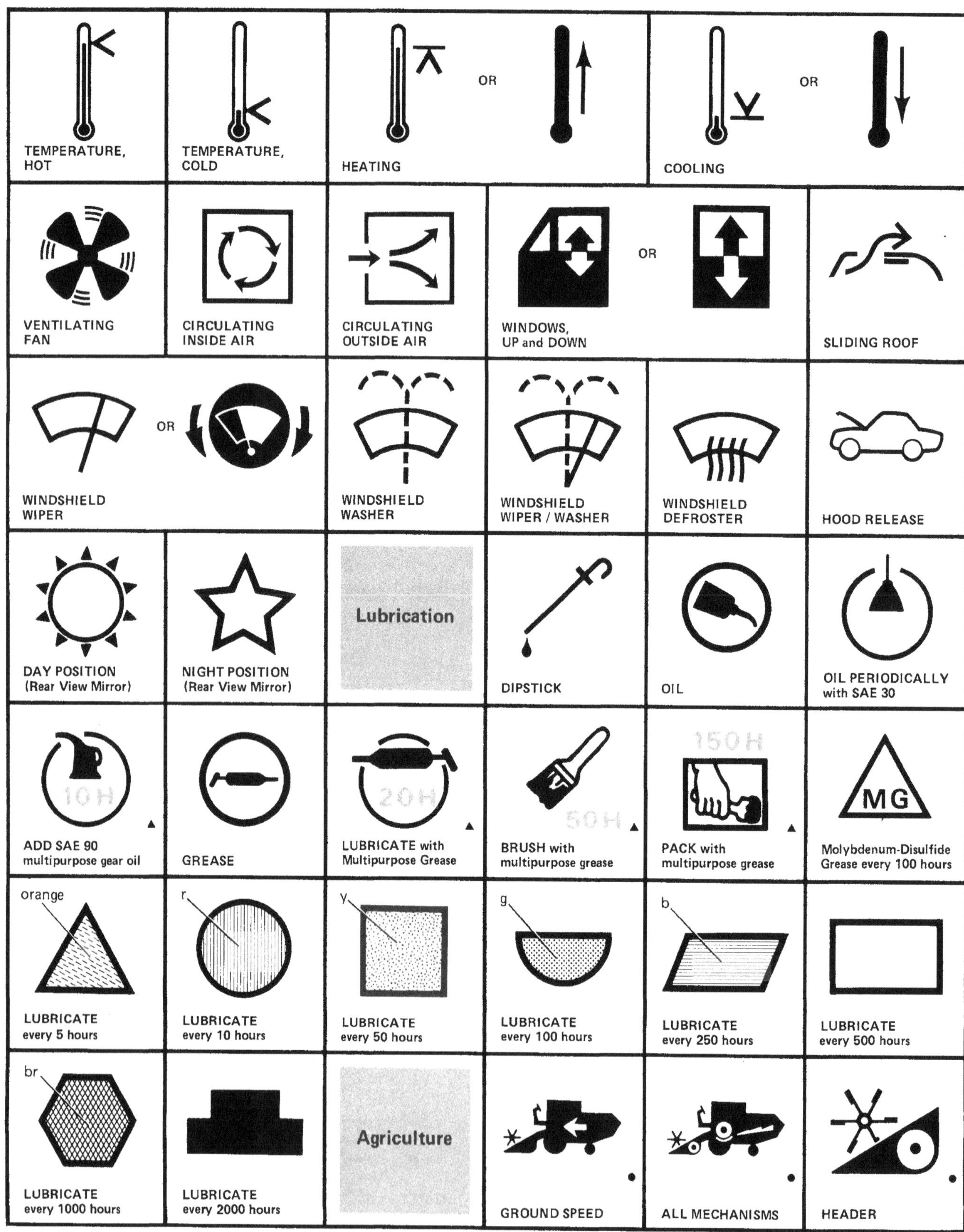

TEMPERATURE, HOT
TEMPERATURE, COLD
OR
HEATING
OR
COOLING
VENTILATING FAN
CIRCULATING INSIDE AIR
CIRCULATING OUTSIDE AIR
OR
WINDOWS, UP and DOWN
SLIDING ROOF
OR
WINDSHIELD WIPER
WINDSHIELD WASHER
WINDSHIELD WIPER / WASHER
WINDSHIELD DEFROSTER
HOOD RELEASE
DAY POSITION (Rear View Mirror)
NIGHT POSITION (Rear View Mirror)
Lubrication
DIPSTICK
OIL
OIL PERIODICALLY with SAE 30
10 H
ADD SAE 90 multipurpose gear oil ▲
GREASE
20 H
LUBRICATE with Multipurpose Grease ▲
50 H
BRUSH with multipurpose grease ▲
150 H
PACK with multipurpose grease ▲
MG
Molybdenum-Disulfide Grease every 100 hours
orange
LUBRICATE every 5 hours
r
LUBRICATE every 10 hours
y
LUBRICATE every 50 hours
g
LUBRICATE every 100 hours
b
LUBRICATE every 250 hours
LUBRICATE every 500 hours
br
LUBRICATE every 1000 hours
LUBRICATE every 2000 hours
Agriculture
GROUND SPEED ●
ALL MECHANISMS ●
HEADER ●

▲ Number refers to frequency of lubrication (in hours).
● Applies to combines.

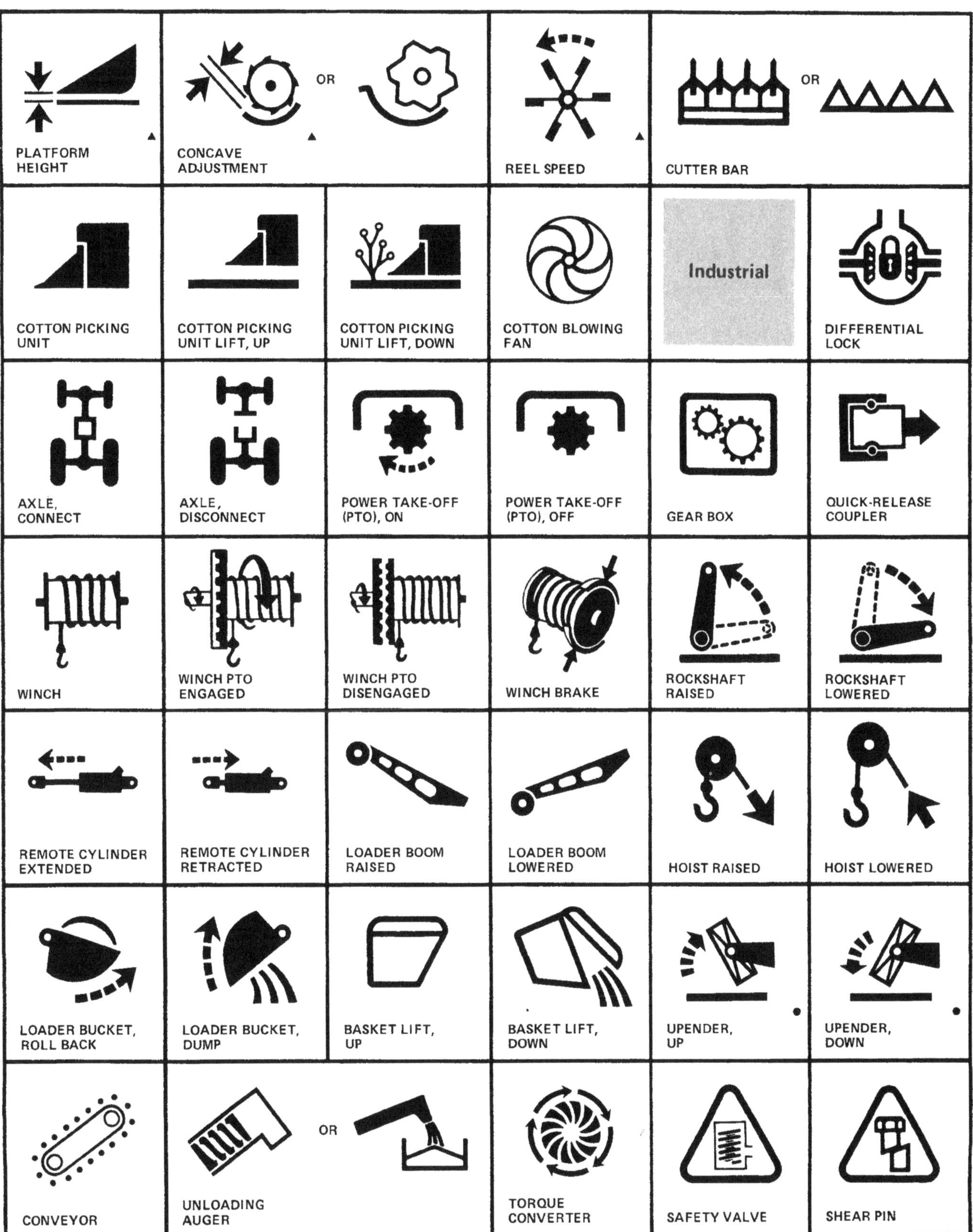
PLATFORM HEIGHT ▲
OR
CONCAVE ADJUSTMENT ▲
REEL SPEED ▲
OR
CUTTER BAR
COTTON PICKING UNIT
COTTON PICKING UNIT LIFT, UP
COTTON PICKING UNIT LIFT, DOWN
COTTON BLOWING FAN
Industrial
DIFFERENTIAL LOCK
AXLE, CONNECT
AXLE, DISCONNECT
POWER TAKE-OFF (PTO), ON
POWER TAKE-OFF (PTO), OFF
GEAR BOX
QUICK-RELEASE COUPLER
WINCH
WINCH PTO ENGAGED
WINCH PTO DISENGAGED
WINCH BRAKE
ROCKSHAFT RAISED
ROCKSHAFT LOWERED
REMOTE CYLINDER EXTENDED
REMOTE CYLINDER RETRACTED
LOADER BOOM RAISED
LOADER BOOM LOWERED
HOIST RAISED
HOIST LOWERED
LOADER BUCKET, ROLL BACK
LOADER BUCKET, DUMP
BASKET LIFT, UP
BASKET LIFT, DOWN
UPENDER, UP ●
UPENDER, DOWN ●
CONVEYOR
OR
UNLOADING AUGER
TORQUE CONVERTER
SAFETY VALVE
SHEAR PIN

▲ Applies to combines.
● Applies to fork lift vehicles.

VEHICLE CONTROLS *(continued)*

▲ LIFT, RAISED	▲ LIFT, LOWERED	▲ TILT, REARWARD	▲ TILT, FORWARD	▲ REACH, RETRACT	▲ REACH, EXTEND
▲ SIDESHIFT, RIGHT	▲ SIDESHIFT, LEFT	▲ FORK SPREAD, CLOSE	▲ FORK SPREAD, OPEN	▲ SWING (or PIVOT) RIGHT	▲ SWING (or PIVOT) LEFT
▲ LOAD STABILIZER, RELEASE	▲ LOAD STABILIZER, CLAMP	▲ PULL	▲ PUSH	▲ CLAMP, CLOSE	▲ CLAMP, RELEASE
LEFT STABILIZER, UP	LEFT STABILIZER, DOWN	RIGHT STABILIZER, UP	RIGHT STABILIZER, DOWN		

▲ Applies to fork lift vehicles.

ALERT

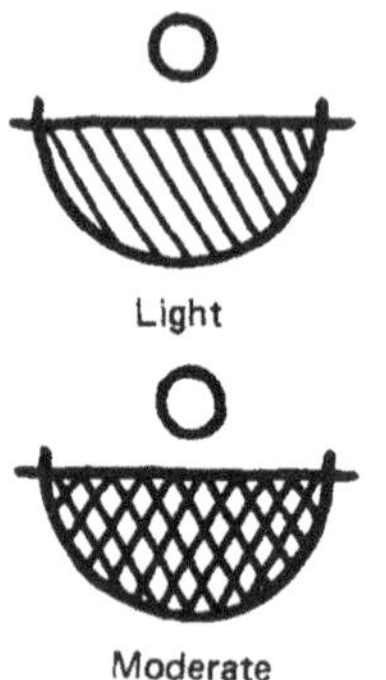

Light

Moderate

Heavy

While arranging the meteorology symbols we came upon one listed as "visibility reduced by smoke." We suggested a synonym: SMOG. But our consultant at the National Weather Service told us that the two terms are not synonymous and that no symbol for smog exists.

It seemed absurd to have no graphic symbol for so prevalent and dangerous a nuisance. So, we went to Dr. Arie Haagen-Smit, that eminent authority who served as Chairman of the President's Task Force on Air Pollution and is known as Mr. Smog-control himself.

Over a lunch table this symbol was developed.

It represents a valley or basin that holds varying degrees of pollutants caused by the effects of the sun, and suspended in the atmosphere.

Would simply a skull and crossbones be more appropriate?

Three-dimensional shapes also can serve as *touch symbols*. Like two-dimensional graphics, they may be visual symbols, often reinforced by color differentiation – but more importantly, they can also be recognized by touch instead of sight.

The U.S. Air Force uses shape codes on its complex of aircraft mechanisms. Thus a pilot whose eyes are needed to guide his plane quickly learns the function indicated by each shape and can delegate vital controls to his fingers. The U.S. Army and Navy also make use of shape codes for controls on vehicles and radar equipment, but each has its own individual system.

The farmer, confronted by a multitude of levers, knobs, and buttons, yet needing to keep his eye on the furrow, finds an essential safety factor in being able to recognize by *feel* the shape of each control.

How unfortunate that we have no standard system which would permit *any* user of *any* piece of equipment – be it kitchen range or helicopter – to know beyond a doubt, that a particular shape always serves the same particular function.

But even before we achieve this utopia, it should not be too much to hope that in the interest of *safety,* all airplanes, all automobiles, and all farm and industrial equipment will be fitted with identical controls for identical functions. This must and will be accomplished through the efforts of manufacturing associations and national and international standards organizations, with the cooperation of government agencies.

Standardization will then have conquered confusion in an area vital to us all.

VEHICLE CONTROLS

Agriculture

Seat Adjust

Gearshift

Platform Lift; Reel Lift

Throttle

Aircraft

Supercharger

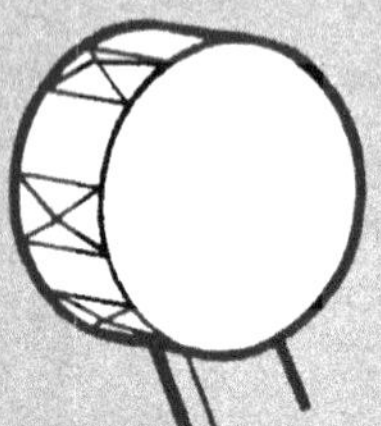
Mixture

Power (Throttle)

Landing Gear

Army Vehicle

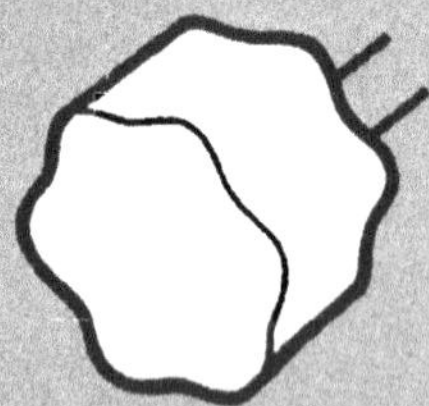
Fuel System

Lighting System

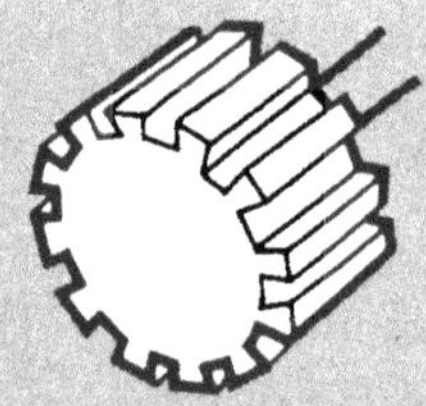
Power Train

Automotive

Finger-operated,
continuous, multi-turn

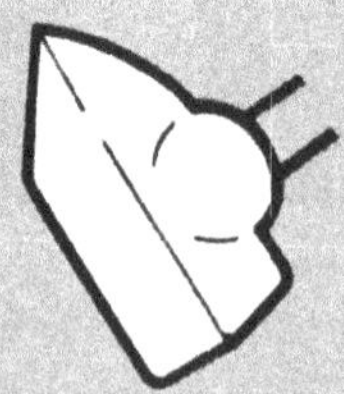
Detented
(more than 2 steps)

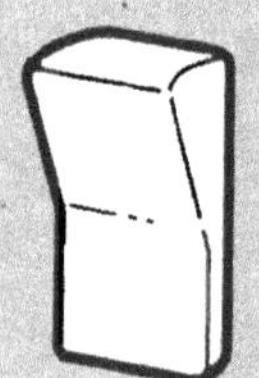
OR

2-Position
(discrete switching only)

Navy Radar

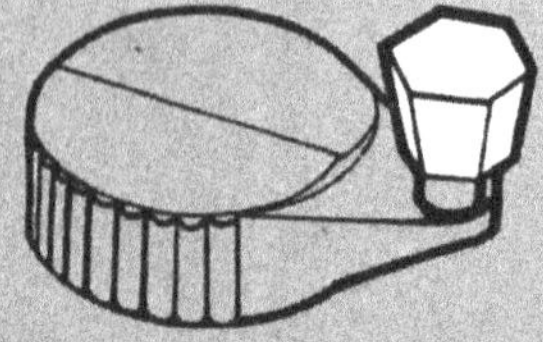
Bearing

Tuning

Gain

Dimmer

Auger

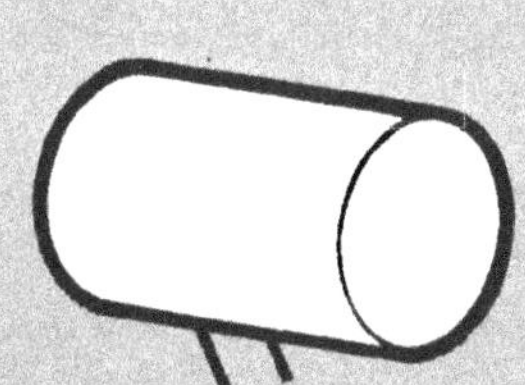
Ground Speed

Separator;
Ratchet

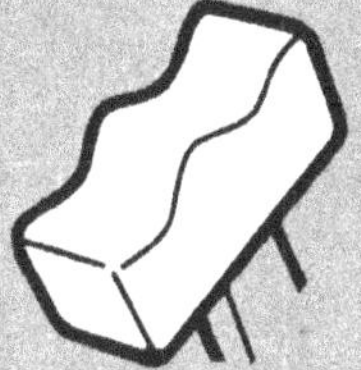
RPM

Landing Flap

Carburetor Air

Reverse Power

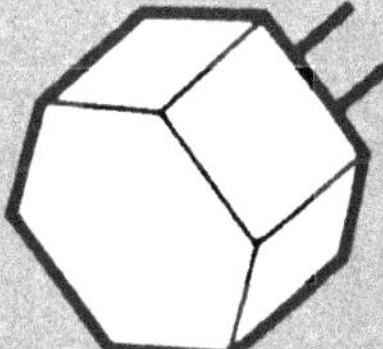
Special Purpose
Equipment

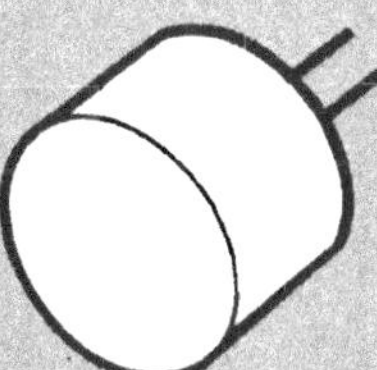
Ignition System

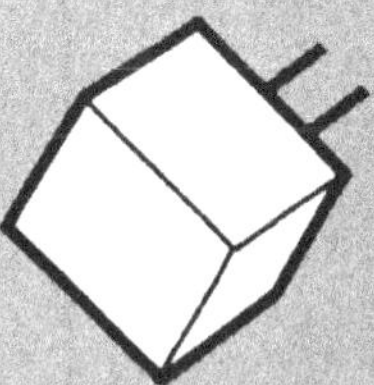
Accessory Equipment

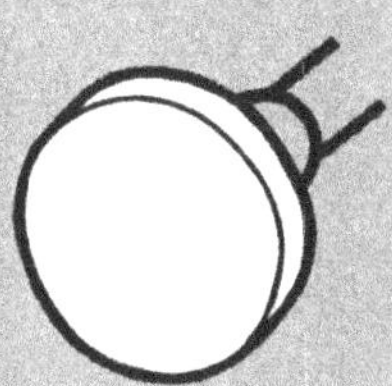
Finger-operated,
very light force

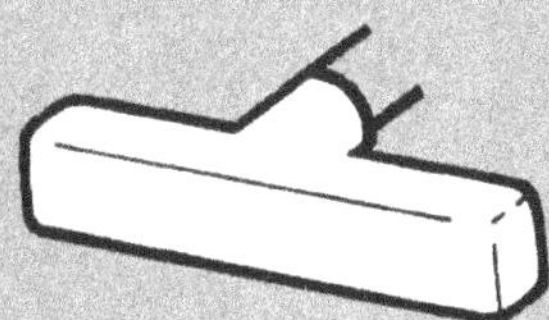
Push/Pull,
heavy force

Slide Action,
light force

Intensity

Focus

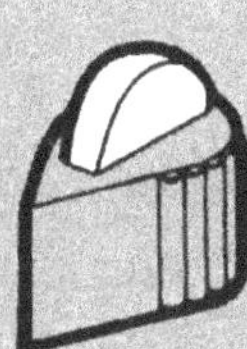
Range

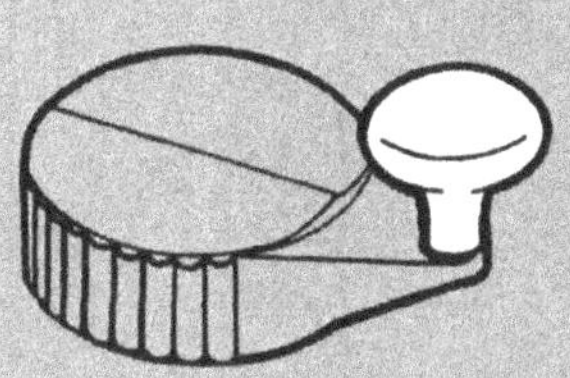
Marker

GRAPHIC FORM SECTION

This section permits identification of symbols out of context. It also establishes the meanings of a given graphic form, and directs to the appropriate Discipline by page number. So it serves as a visual reference for the designer of a new symbol and provides a basis of comparison for standardization.

No computer or other mechanical or exact parameters could be used to define how a designer might see various forms. The overall classification and arrangement of the symbols is therefore of necessity a purely personal judgment, based only on an individual "eye" for the determination of graphic form.

GROUPING of SYMBOLS – is by *form only*, without regard to meaning. We have extracted from the Discipline section those symbols which lend themselves to classification by the Key Form system we established.

Key Forms in the page margin introduce each major classification and subclassification, arranged in a consistent pattern. Within each grouping, the symbols are sequenced from simple to complex.

p. 168
p. 175
p. 177
p. 182
p. 186
p. 190
p. 193

When a symbol is composed of several distinct forms, the complete symbol or its individual components are entered under each classification. However, when one form is clearly subordinated to another, only the major form is entered.

TEXT – Often the same graphic form has different meanings in different Disciplines. In these cases, all such meanings are listed with the symbol, each with its reference page number.

When two or more symbols are basically similar in graphic form, differing only in relative size, line weight, or modification of their graphic components, we have illustrated only *one typical symbol* and have established the following guide:

v following a page number (for example, 143v) indicates a *graphic variation* of the illustrated symbol.

+ following a page number (for example, 154+) indicates that *additional* symbols, with *closely related meanings* (not listed) and similar graphic form, appear on the same page, usually adjacent to one another.

p. 199
p. 201
p. 203
p. 208
p. 215
p. 221
p. 224
p. 229

GRAPHIC FORM

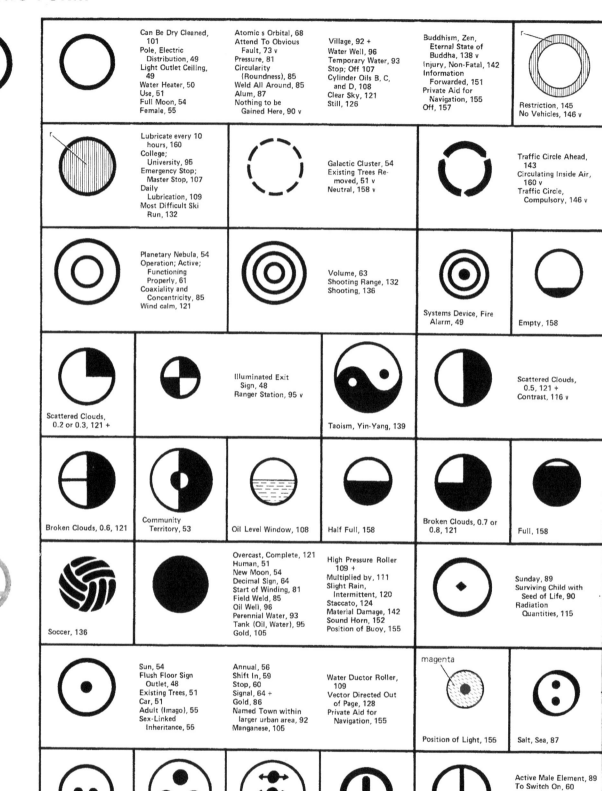

Can Be Dry Cleaned, 101
Pole, Electric Distribution, 49
Light Outlet Ceiling, 49
Water Heater, 50
Use, 51
Full Moon, 54
Female, 55

Atomic s Orbital, 68
Attend To Obvious Fault, 73 v
Pressure, 81
Circularity (Roundness), 85
Weld All Around, 85
Alum, 87
Nothing to be Gained Here, 90 v

Village, 92 +
Water Well, 96
Temporary Water, 93
Stop; Off 107
Cylinder Oils B, C, and D, 108
Clear Sky, 121
Still, 126

Buddhism, Zen, Eternal State of Buddha, 138 v
Injury, Non-Fatal, 142
Information Forwarded, 151
Private Aid for Navigation, 155
Off, 157

r

Restriction, 145
No Vehicles, 146 v

r

Lubricate every 10 hours, 160
College; University, 95
Emergency Stop; Master Stop, 107
Daily Lubrication, 109
Most Difficult Ski Run, 132

Galactic Cluster, 54
Existing Trees Removed, 51 v
Neutral, 158 v

Traffic Circle Ahead, 143
Circulating Inside Air, 160 v
Traffic Circle, Compulsory, 146 v

Planetary Nebula, 54
Operation; Active; Functioning Properly, 61
Coaxiality and Concentricity, 85
Wind calm, 121

Volume, 63
Shooting Range, 132
Shooting, 136

Systems Device, Fire Alarm, 49

Empty, 158

Scattered Clouds, 0.2 or 0.3, 121 +

Illuminated Exit Sign, 48
Ranger Station, 95 v

Taoism, Yin-Yang, 139

Scattered Clouds, 0.5, 121 +
Contrast, 116 v

Broken Clouds, 0.6, 121

Community Territory, 53

Oil Level Window, 108

Half Full, 158

Broken Clouds, 0.7 or 0.8, 121

Full, 158

Soccer, 136

Overcast, Complete, 121
Human, 51
New Moon, 54
Decimal Sign, 64
Start of Winding, 81
Field Weld, 85
Oil Well, 96
Perennial Water, 93
Tank (Oil, Water), 95
Gold, 105

High Pressure Roller 109 +
Multiplied by, 111
Slight Rain, Intermittent, 120
Staccato, 124
Material Damage, 142
Sound Horn, 152
Position of Buoy, 155

Sunday, 89
Surviving Child with Seed of Life, 90
Radiation Quantities, 115

Sun, 54
Flush Floor Sign Outlet, 48
Existing Trees, 51
Car, 51
Adult (Imago), 55
Sex-Linked Inheritance, 55

Annual, 56
Shift In, 59
Stop, 60
Signal, 64 +
Gold, 86
Named Town within larger urban area, 92
Manganese, 105

Water Ductor Roller, 109
Vector Directed Out of Page, 128
Private Aid for Navigation, 155

magenta

Position of Light, 155

Salt, Sea, 87

Biennial, 56

Core Service Adjacencies, 52

Community Projects Two-Sided, 53

Start and Stop, 107
Odd; Bit Information, 61

Active Male Element, 89
To Switch On, 60
Start, 63
Saltpeter, 87
On, 115
Scattered Clouds, 0.1 or less, 121

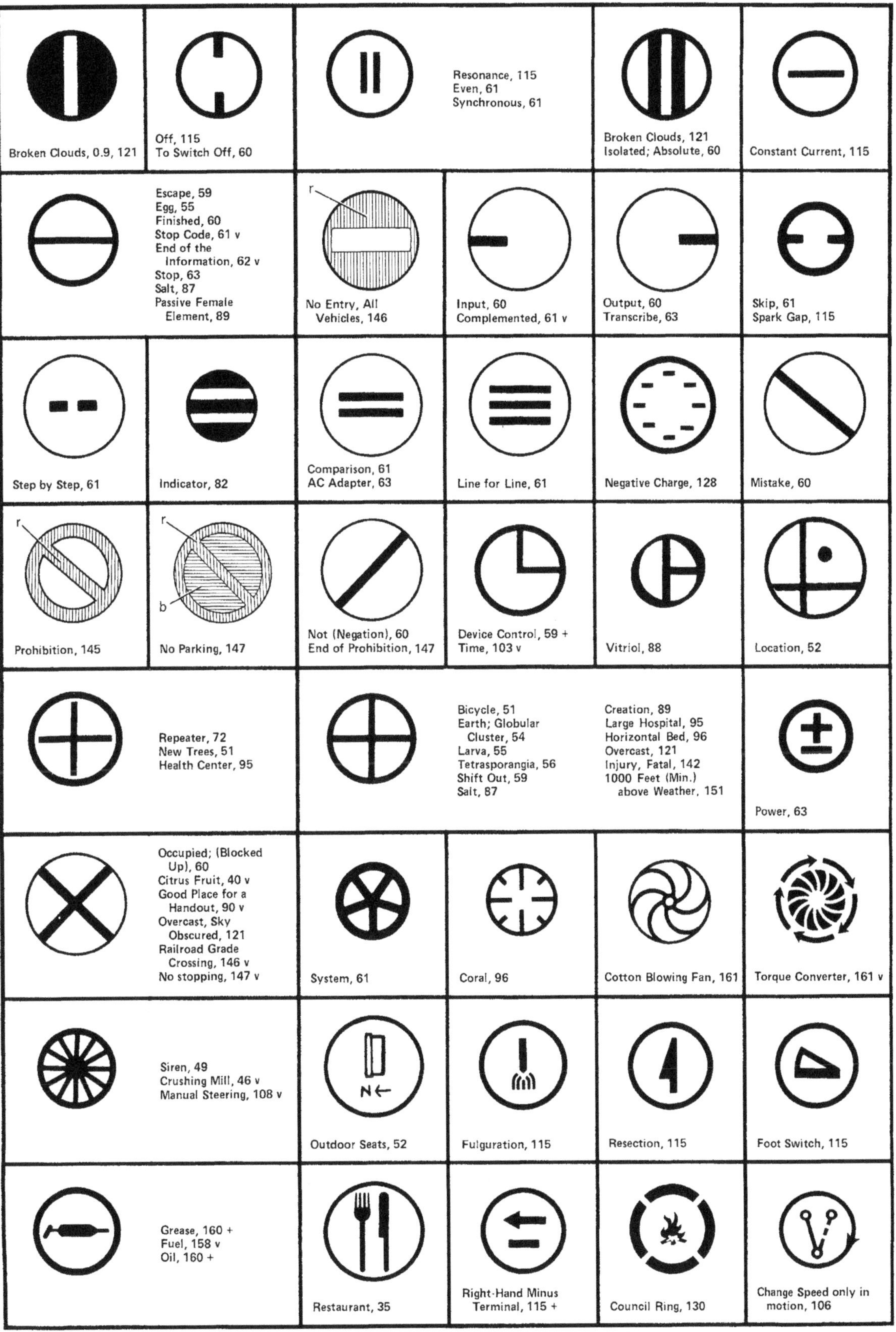

Broken Clouds, 0.9, 121
Off, 115
To Switch Off, 60
Resonance, 115
Even, 61
Synchronous, 61
Broken Clouds, 121
Isolated; Absolute, 60
Constant Current, 115
Escape, 59
Egg, 55
Finished, 60
Stop Code, 61 v
End of the Information, 62 v
Stop, 63
Salt, 87
Passive Female Element, 89
r
No Entry, All Vehicles, 146
Input, 60
Complemented, 61 v
Output, 60
Transcribe, 63
Skip, 61
Spark Gap, 115
Step by Step, 61
Indicator, 82
Comparison, 61
AC Adapter, 63
Line for Line, 61
Negative Charge, 128
Mistake, 60
r
Prohibition, 145
r
b
No Parking, 147
Not (Negation), 60
End of Prohibition, 147
Device Control, 59 +
Time, 103 v
Vitriol, 88
Location, 52
Repeater, 72
New Trees, 51
Health Center, 95
Bicycle, 51
Earth; Globular Cluster, 54
Larva, 55
Tetrasporangia, 56
Shift Out, 59
Salt, 87
Creation, 89
Large Hospital, 95
Horizontal Bed, 96
Overcast, 121
Injury, Fatal, 142
1000 Feet (Min.) above Weather, 151
Power, 63
Occupied; (Blocked Up), 60
Citrus Fruit, 40 v
Good Place for a Handout, 90 v
Overcast, Sky Obscured, 121
Railroad Grade Crossing, 146 v
No stopping, 147 v
System, 61
Coral, 96
Cotton Blowing Fan, 161
Torque Converter, 161 v
Siren, 49
Crushing Mill, 46 v
Manual Steering, 108 v
N←
Outdoor Seats, 52
Fulguration, 115
Resection, 115
Foot Switch, 115
Grease, 160 +
Fuel, 158 v
Oil, 160 +
Restaurant, 35
Right-Hand Minus Terminal, 115 +
Council Ring, 130
Change Speed only in motion, 106

GRAPHIC FORM

(continued)

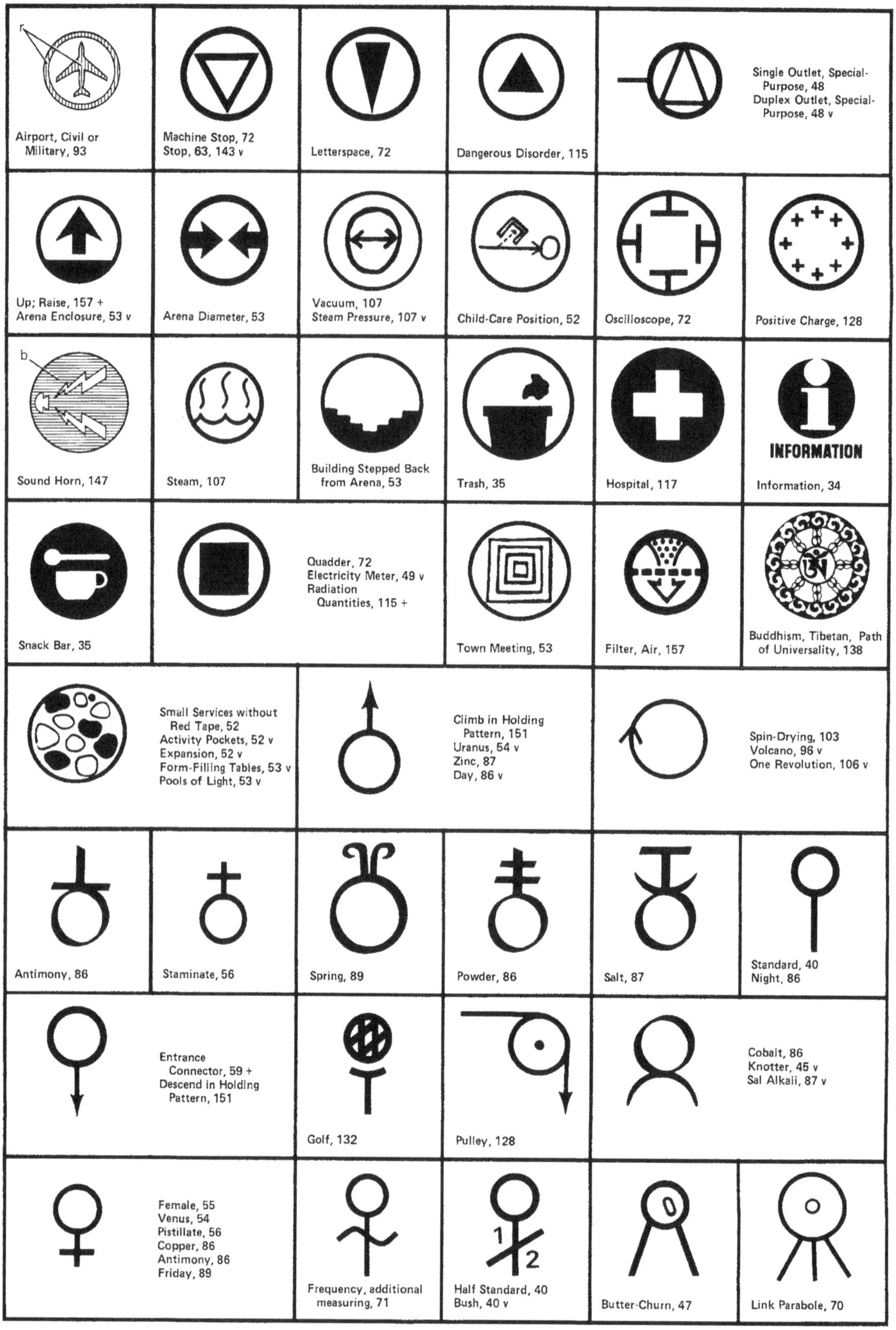

Airport, Civil or Military, 93

Machine Stop, 72
Stop, 63, 143 v

Letterspace, 72

Dangerous Disorder, 115

Single Outlet, Special-Purpose, 48
Duplex Outlet, Special-Purpose, 48 v

Up; Raise, 157 +
Arena Enclosure, 53 v

Arena Diameter, 53

Vacuum, 107
Steam Pressure, 107 v

Child-Care Position, 52

Oscilloscope, 72

Positive Charge, 128

Sound Horn, 147

Steam, 107

Building Stepped Back from Arena, 53

Trash, 35

Hospital, 117

INFORMATION

Information, 34

Snack Bar, 35

Quadder, 72
Electricity Meter, 49 v
Radiation Quantities, 115 +

Town Meeting, 53

Filter, Air, 157

Buddhism, Tibetan, Path of Universality, 138

Small Services without Red Tape, 52
Activity Pockets, 52 v
Expansion, 52 v
Form-Filling Tables, 53 v
Pools of Light, 53 v

Climb in Holding Pattern, 151
Uranus, 54 v
Zinc, 87
Day, 86 v

Spin-Drying, 103
Volcano, 96 v
One Revolution, 106 v

Antimony, 86

Staminate, 56

Spring, 89

Powder, 86

Salt, 87

Standard, 40
Night, 86

Entrance Connector, 59 +
Descend in Holding Pattern, 151

Golf, 132

Pulley, 128

Cobalt, 86
Knotter, 45 v
Sal Alkali, 87 v

Female, 55
Venus, 54
Pistillate, 56
Copper, 86
Antimony, 86
Friday, 89

Frequency, additional measuring, 71

Half Standard, 40
Bush, 40 v

Butter-Churn, 47

Link Parabole, 70

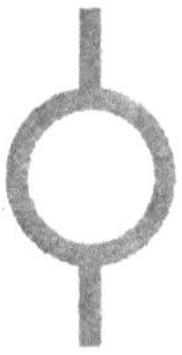

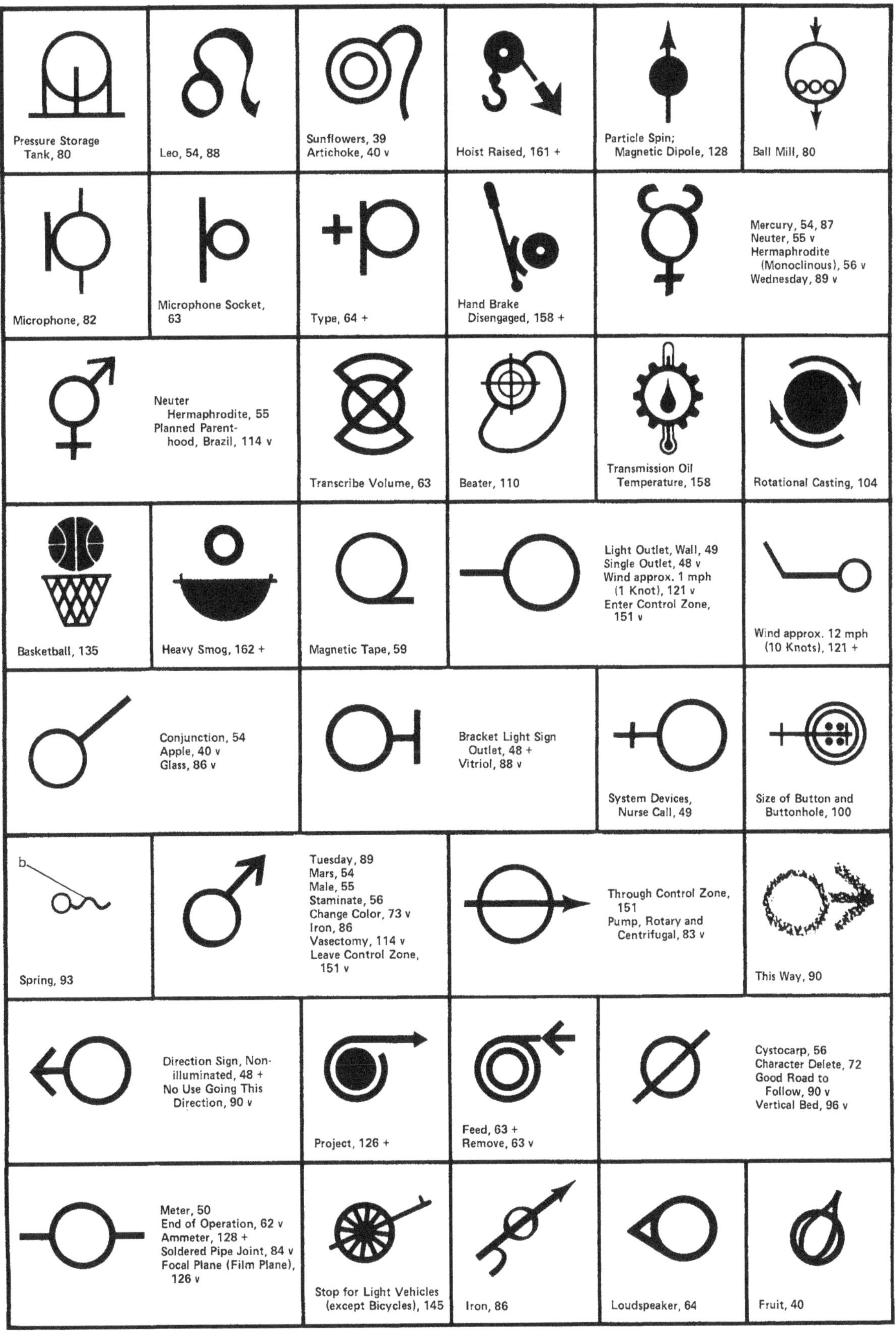
Pressure Storage Tank, 80
Leo, 54, 88
Sunflowers, 39
Artichoke, 40 v
Hoist Raised, 161 +
Particle Spin; Magnetic Dipole, 128
Ball Mill, 80
Microphone, 82
Microphone Socket, 63
Type, 64 +
Hand Brake Disengaged, 158 +
Mercury, 54, 87
Neuter, 55 v
Hermaphrodite (Monoclinous), 56 v
Wednesday, 89 v
Neuter Hermaphrodite, 55
Planned Parent-hood, Brazil, 114 v
Transcribe Volume, 63
Beater, 110
Transmission Oil Temperature, 158
Rotational Casting, 104
Basketball, 135
Heavy Smog, 162 +
Magnetic Tape, 59
Light Outlet, Wall, 49
Single Outlet, 48 v
Wind approx. 1 mph (1 Knot), 121 v
Enter Control Zone, 151 v
Wind approx. 12 mph (10 Knots), 121 +
Conjunction, 54
Apple, 40 v
Glass, 86 v
Bracket Light Sign Outlet, 48 +
Vitriol, 88 v
System Devices, Nurse Call, 49
Size of Button and Buttonhole, 100
b
Spring, 93
Tuesday, 89
Mars, 54
Male, 55
Staminate, 56
Change Color, 73 v
Iron, 86
Vasectomy, 114 v
Leave Control Zone, 151 v
Through Control Zone, 151
Pump, Rotary and Centrifugal, 83 v
This Way, 90
Direction Sign, Non-illuminated, 48 +
No Use Going This Direction, 90 v
Project, 126 +
Feed, 63 +
Remove, 63 v
Cystocarp, 56
Character Delete, 72
Good Road to Follow, 90 v
Vertical Bed, 96 v
Meter, 50
End of Operation, 62 v
Ammeter, 128 +
Soldered Pipe Joint, 84 v
Focal Plane (Film Plane), 126 v
Stop for Light Vehicles (except Bicycles), 145
Iron, 86
Loudspeaker, 64
Fruit, 40

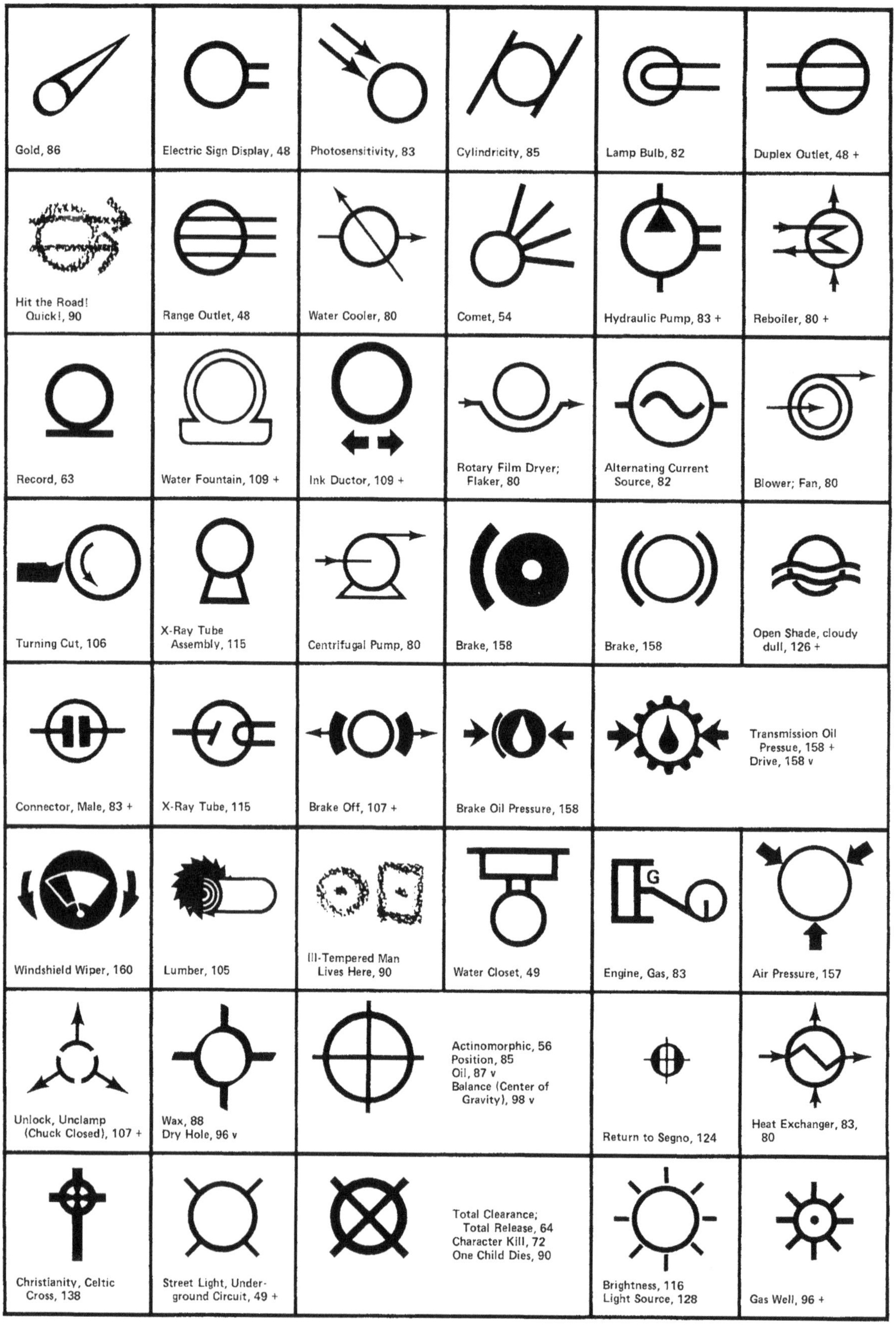

GRAPHIC FORM

Gold, 86	Electric Sign Display, 48	Photosensitivity, 83	Cylindricity, 85	Lamp Bulb, 82	Duplex Outlet, 48 +
Hit the Road! Quick!, 90	Range Outlet, 48	Water Cooler, 80	Comet, 54	Hydraulic Pump, 83 +	Reboiler, 80 +
Record, 63	Water Fountain, 109 +	Ink Ductor, 109 +	Rotary Film Dryer; Flaker, 80	Alternating Current Source, 82	Blower; Fan, 80
Turning Cut, 106	X-Ray Tube Assembly, 115	Centrifugal Pump, 80	Brake, 158	Brake, 158	Open Shade, cloudy dull, 126 +
Connector, Male, 83 +	X-Ray Tube, 115	Brake Off, 107 +	Brake Oil Pressure, 158		Transmission Oil Pressue, 158 + Drive, 158 v
Windshield Wiper, 160	Lumber, 105	Ill-Tempered Man Lives Here, 90	Water Closet, 49	Engine, Gas, 83	Air Pressure, 157
Unlock, Unclamp (Chuck Closed), 107 +	Wax, 88 Dry Hole, 96 v		Actinomorphic, 56 Position, 85 Oil, 87 v Balance (Center of Gravity), 98 v	Return to Segno, 124	Heat Exchanger, 83, 80
Christianity, Celtic Cross, 138	Street Light, Under-ground Circuit, 49 +		Total Clearance; Total Release, 64 Character Kill, 72 One Child Dies, 90	Brightness, 116 Light Source, 128	Gas Well, 96 +

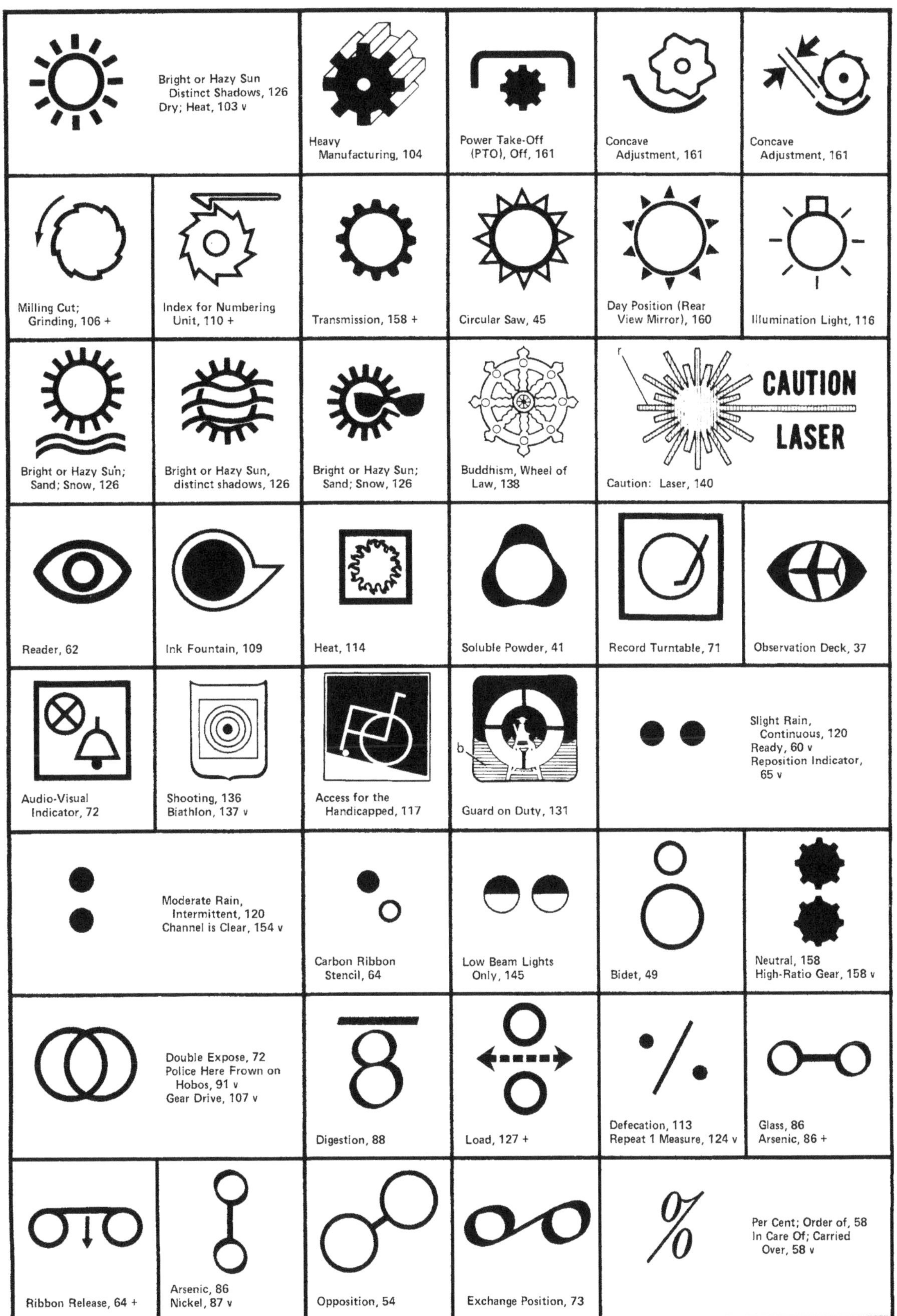

Bright or Hazy Sun
Distinct Shadows, 126
Dry; Heat, 103 v
Heavy
Manufacturing, 104
Power Take-Off
(PTO), Off, 161
Concave
Adjustment, 161
Concave
Adjustment, 161
Milling Cut;
Grinding, 106 +
Index for Numbering
Unit, 110 +
Transmission, 158 +
Circular Saw, 45
Day Position (Rear
View Mirror), 160
Illumination Light, 116
Bright or Hazy Sun;
Sand; Snow, 126
Bright or Hazy Sun,
distinct shadows, 126
Bright or Hazy Sun;
Sand; Snow, 126
Buddhism, Wheel of
Law, 138
CAUTION
LASER
Caution: Laser, 140
Reader, 62
Ink Fountain, 109
Heat, 114
Soluble Powder, 41
Record Turntable, 71
Observation Deck, 37
Audio-Visual
Indicator, 72
Shooting, 136
Biathlon, 137 v
Access for the
Handicapped, 117
Guard on Duty, 131
Slight Rain,
Continuous, 120
Ready, 60 v
Reposition Indicator,
65 v
Moderate Rain,
Intermittent, 120
Channel is Clear, 154 v
Carbon Ribbon
Stencil, 64
Low Beam Lights
Only, 145
Bidet, 49
Neutral, 158
High-Ratio Gear, 158 v
Double Expose, 72
Police Here Frown on
Hobos, 91 v
Gear Drive, 107 v
Digestion, 88
Load, 127 +
Defecation, 113
Repeat 1 Measure, 124 v
Glass, 86
Arsenic, 86 +
Ribbon Release, 64 +
Arsenic, 86
Nickel, 87 v
Opposition, 54
Exchange Position, 73
Per Cent; Order of, 58
In Care Of; Carried
Over, 58 v

GRAPHIC FORM

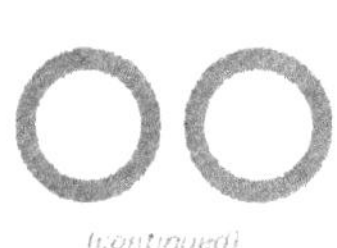

(continued)

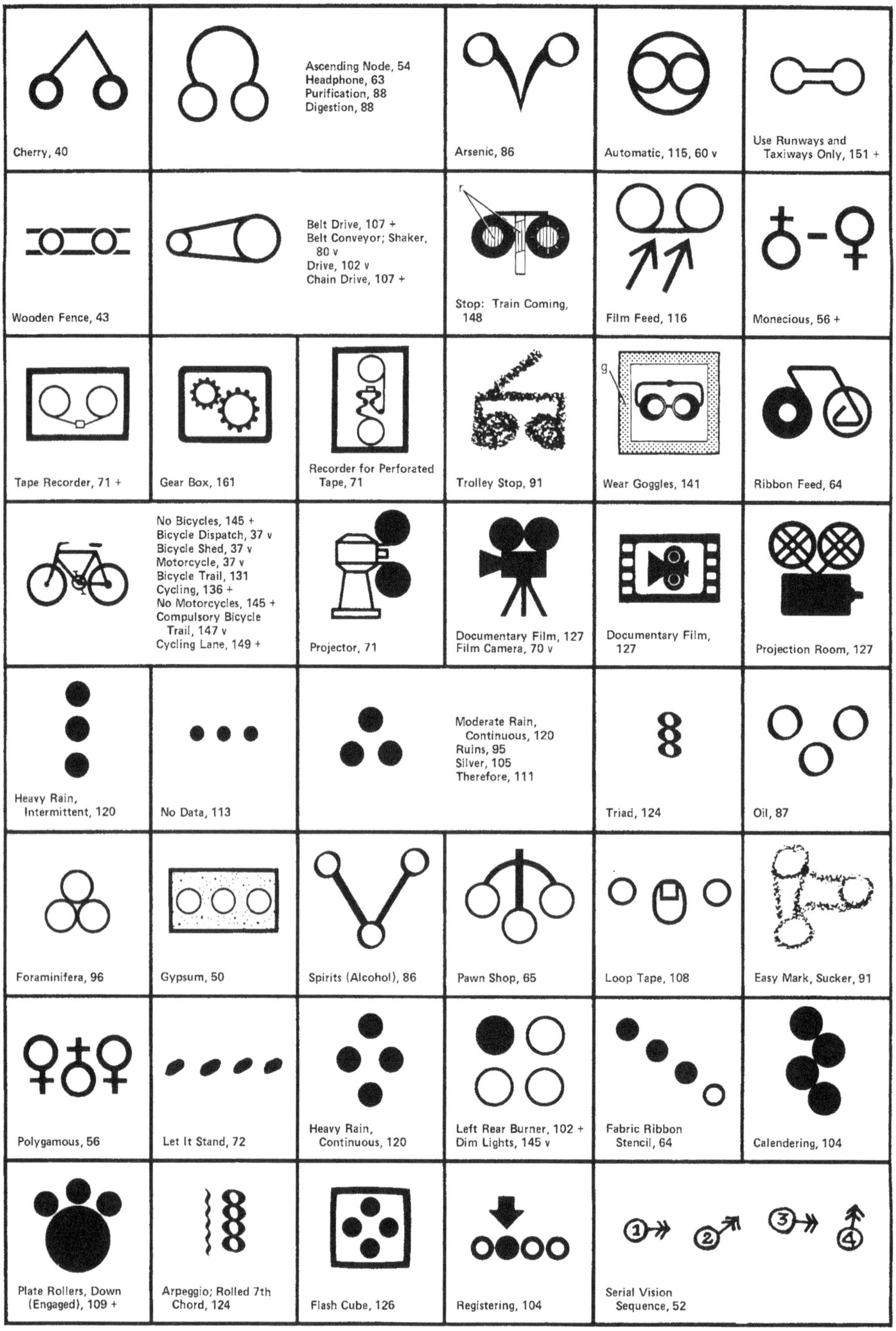

Cherry, 40	Ascending Node, 54 Headphone, 63 Purification, 88 Digestion, 88		Arsenic, 86	Automatic, 115, 60 v	Use Runways and Taxiways Only, 151 +
Wooden Fence, 43	Belt Drive, 107 + Belt Conveyor; Shaker, 80 v Drive, 102 v Chain Drive, 107 +		Stop: Train Coming, 148	Film Feed, 116	Monecious, 56 +
Tape Recorder, 71 +	Gear Box, 161	Recorder for Perforated Tape, 71	Trolley Stop, 91	Wear Goggles, 141	Ribbon Feed, 64
	No Bicycles, 145 + Bicycle Dispatch, 37 v Bicycle Shed, 37 v Motorcycle, 37 v Bicycle Trail, 131 Cycling, 136 + No Motorcycles, 145 + Compulsory Bicycle Trail, 147 v Cycling Lane, 149 +	Projector, 71	Documentary Film, 127 Film Camera, 70 v	Documentary Film, 127	Projection Room, 127
Heavy Rain, Intermittent, 120	No Data, 113	Moderate Rain, Continuous, 120 Ruins, 95 Silver, 105 Therefore, 111		Triad, 124	Oil, 87
Foraminifera, 96	Gypsum, 50	Spirits (Alcohol), 86	Pawn Shop, 65	Loop Tape, 108	Easy Mark, Sucker, 91
Polygamous, 56	Let It Stand, 72	Heavy Rain, Continuous, 120	Left Rear Burner, 102 + Dim Lights, 145 v	Fabric Ribbon Stencil, 64	Calendering, 104
Plate Rollers, Down (Engaged), 109 +	Arpeggio; Rolled 7th Chord, 124	Flash Cube, 126	Registering, 104	Serial Vision Sequence, 52	

Switch On, 82 +	Mechanical Barn Cleaner, 43	Chain Harrow, Weeder, 46	Reel Tape, 108	Editing Table, 71	Loose Fertilizer, Granulated, 41
Manually (Key Board), 60	Sand, 87	Chaff, 39	Stop, 156	Data Clear, Out, or Reset, 108	Orchard, 95 Scrub, 95 v
Copper, 105	Telegrams, 70	Filter, 107			

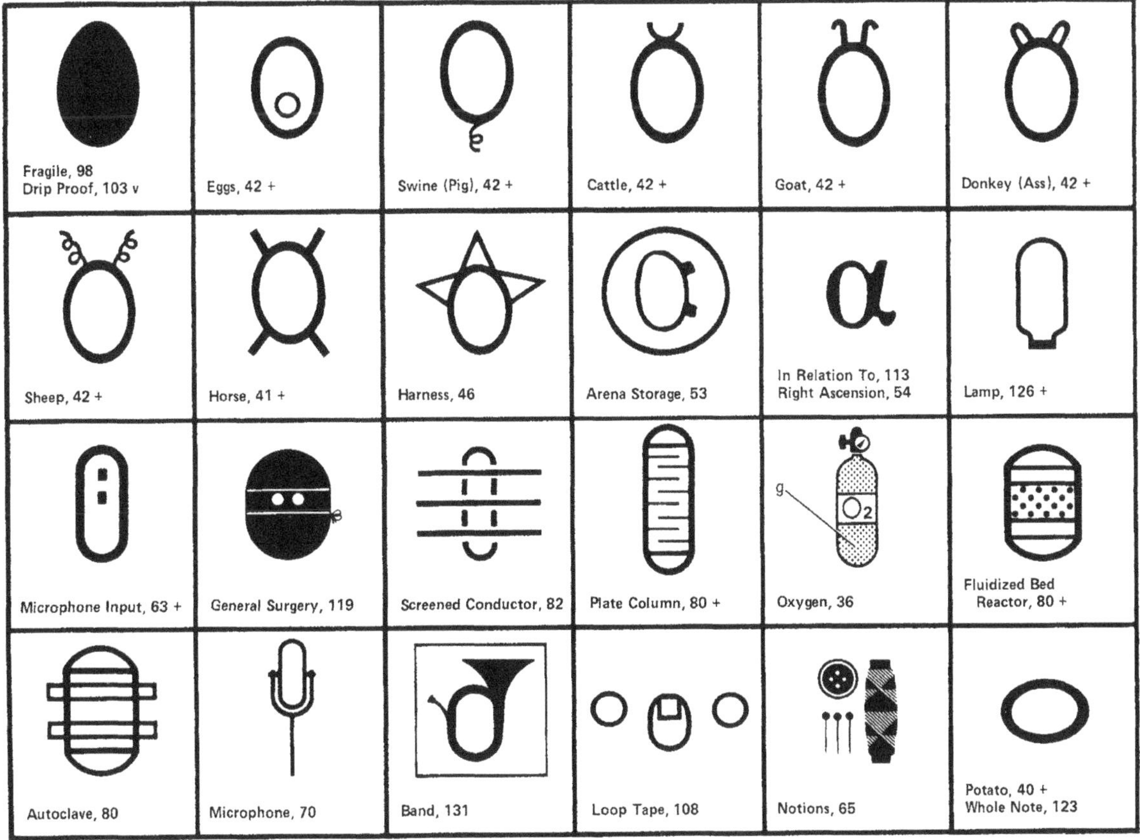

Fragile, 98
Drip Proof, 103 v
Eggs, 42 +
Swine (Pig), 42 +
Cattle, 42 +
Goat, 42 +
Donkey (Ass), 42 +
Sheep, 42 +
Horse, 41 +
Harness, 46
Arena Storage, 53
In Relation To, 113
Right Ascension, 54
Lamp, 126 +
Microphone Input, 63 +
General Surgery, 119
Screened Conductor, 82
Plate Column, 80 +
Oxygen, 36
Fluidized Bed Reactor, 80 +
Autoclave, 80
Microphone, 70
Band, 131
Loop Tape, 108
Notions, 65
Potato, 40 +
Whole Note, 123

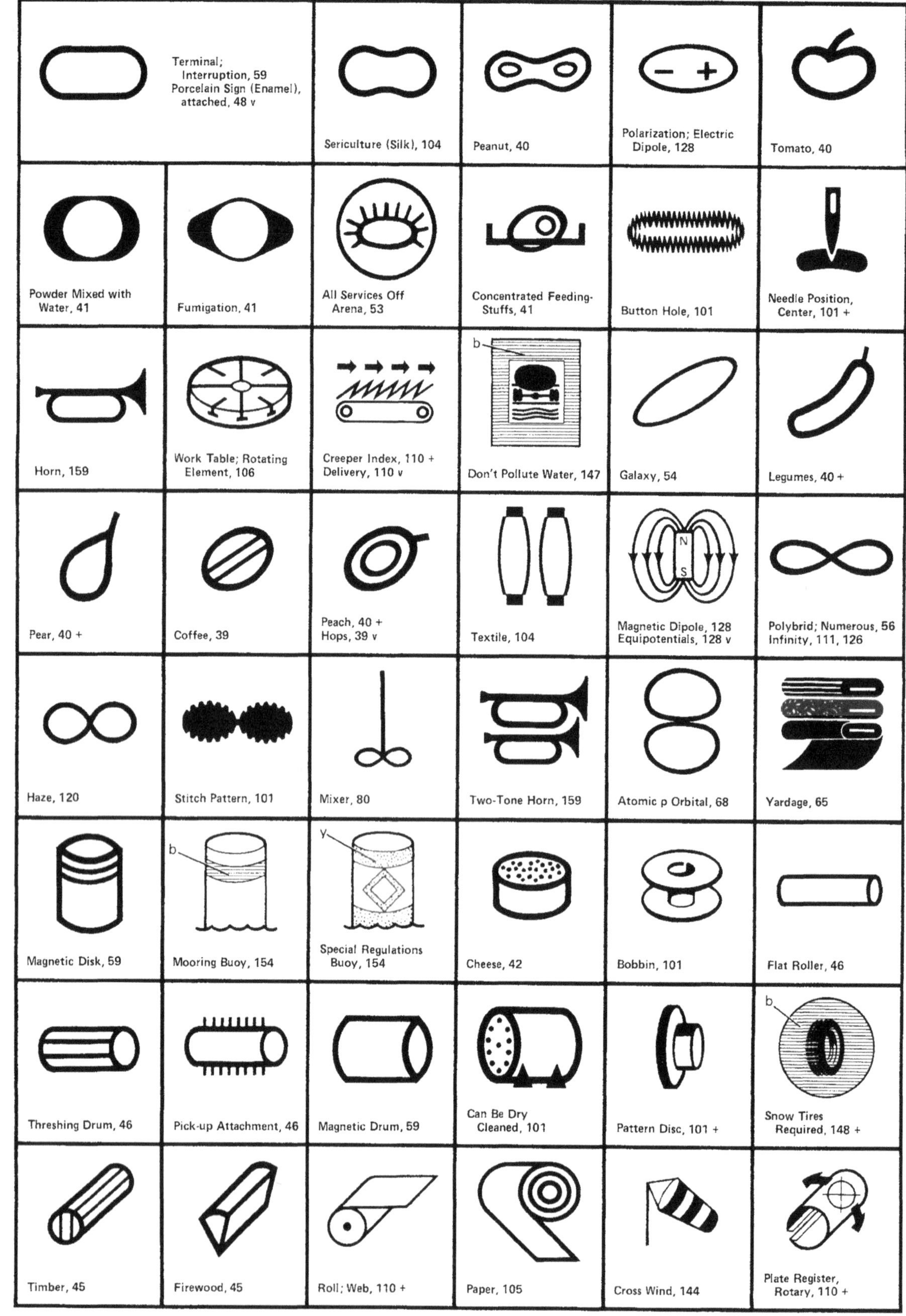
Terminal;
Interruption, 59
Porcelain Sign (Enamel), attached, 48 v
Sericulture (Silk), 104
Peanut, 40
Polarization; Electric Dipole, 128
Tomato, 40
Powder Mixed with Water, 41
Fumigation, 41
All Services Off Arena, 53
Concentrated Feeding-Stuffs, 41
Button Hole, 101
Needle Position, Center, 101 +
Horn, 159
Work Table; Rotating Element, 106
Creeper Index, 110 +
Delivery, 110 v
b
Don't Pollute Water, 147
Galaxy, 54
Legumes, 40 +
Pear, 40 +
Coffee, 39
Peach, 40 +
Hops, 39 v
Textile, 104
N
S
Magnetic Dipole, 128
Equipotentials, 128 v
Polybrid; Numerous, 56
Infinity, 111, 126
Haze, 120
Stitch Pattern, 101
Mixer, 80
Two-Tone Horn, 159
Atomic p Orbital, 68
Yardage, 65
Magnetic Disk, 59
b
Mooring Buoy, 154
y
Special Regulations Buoy, 154
Cheese, 42
Bobbin, 101
Flat Roller, 46
Threshing Drum, 46
Pick-up Attachment, 46
Magnetic Drum, 59
Can Be Dry Cleaned, 101
Pattern Disc, 101 +
b
Snow Tires Required, 148 +
Timber, 45
Firewood, 45
Roll; Web, 110 +
Paper, 105
Cross Wind, 144
Plate Register, Rotary, 110 +

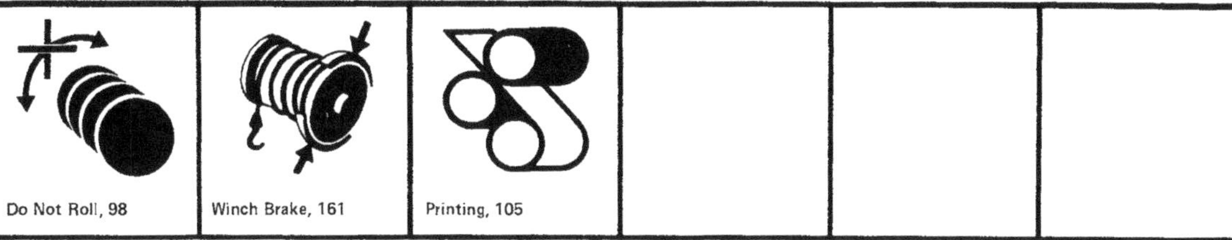
Do Not Roll, 98
Winch Brake, 161
Printing, 105

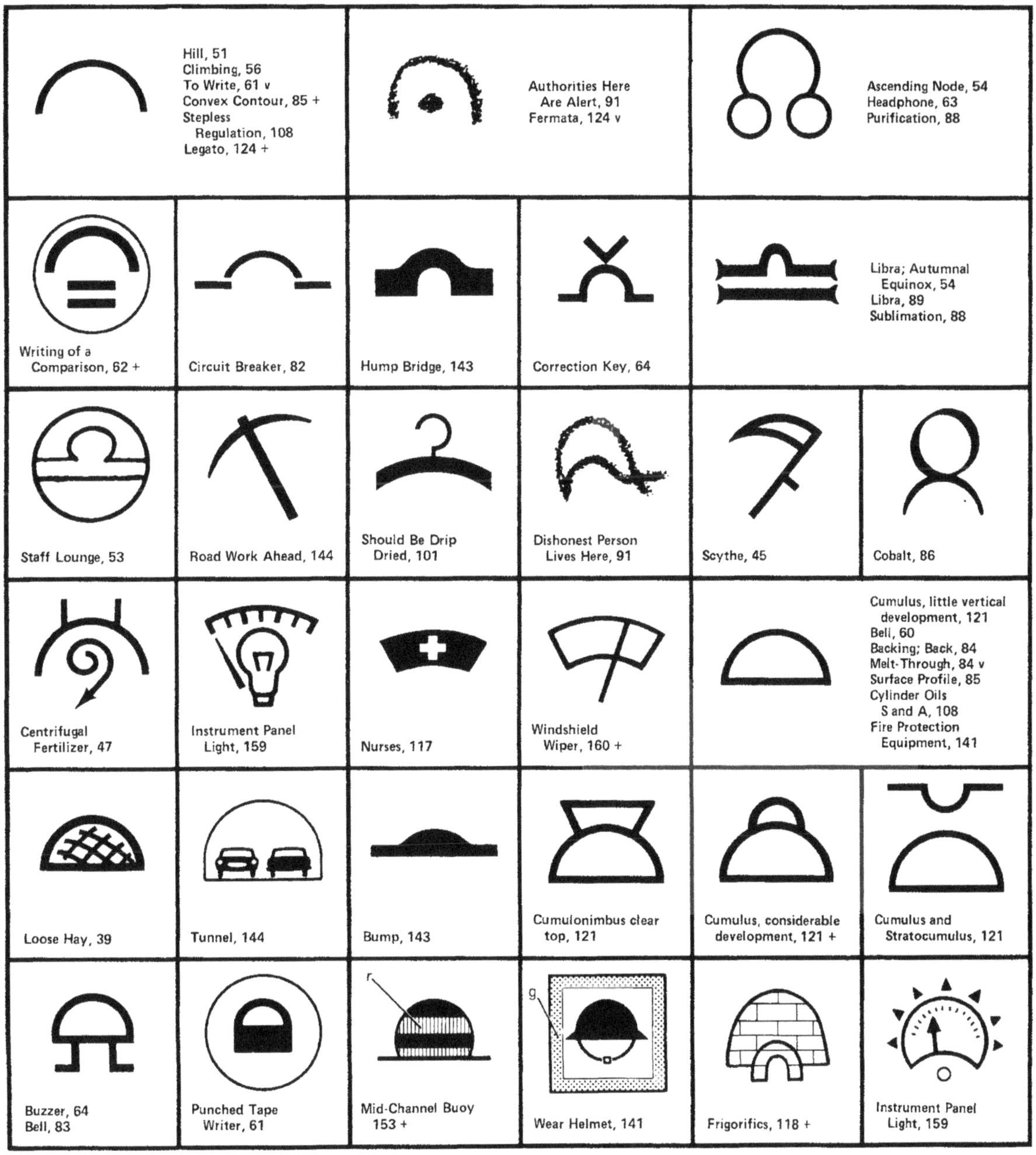

Hill, 51 Climbing, 56 To Write, 61 v Convex Contour, 85 + Stepless Regulation, 108 Legato, 124 +	Authorities Here Are Alert, 91 Fermata, 124 v	Ascending Node, 54 Headphone, 63 Purification, 88

Writing of a Comparison, 62 +	Circuit Breaker, 82	Hump Bridge, 143	Correction Key, 64	Libra; Autumnal Equinox, 54 Libra, 89 Sublimation, 88	
Staff Lounge, 53	Road Work Ahead, 144	Should Be Drip Dried, 101	Dishonest Person Lives Here, 91	Scythe, 45	Cobalt, 86
Centrifugal Fertilizer, 47	Instrument Panel Light, 159	Nurses, 117	Windshield Wiper, 160 +	Cumulus, little vertical development, 121 Bell, 60 Backing; Back, 84 Melt-Through, 84 v Surface Profile, 85 Cylinder Oils S and A, 108 Fire Protection Equipment, 141	
Loose Hay, 39	Tunnel, 144	Bump, 143	Cumulonimbus clear top, 121	Cumulus, considerable development, 121 +	Cumulus and Stratocumulus, 121
Buzzer, 64 Bell, 83	Punched Tape Writer, 61	r Mid-Channel Buoy 153 +	g Wear Helmet, 141	Frigorifics, 118 +	Instrument Panel Light, 159

GRAPHIC FORM

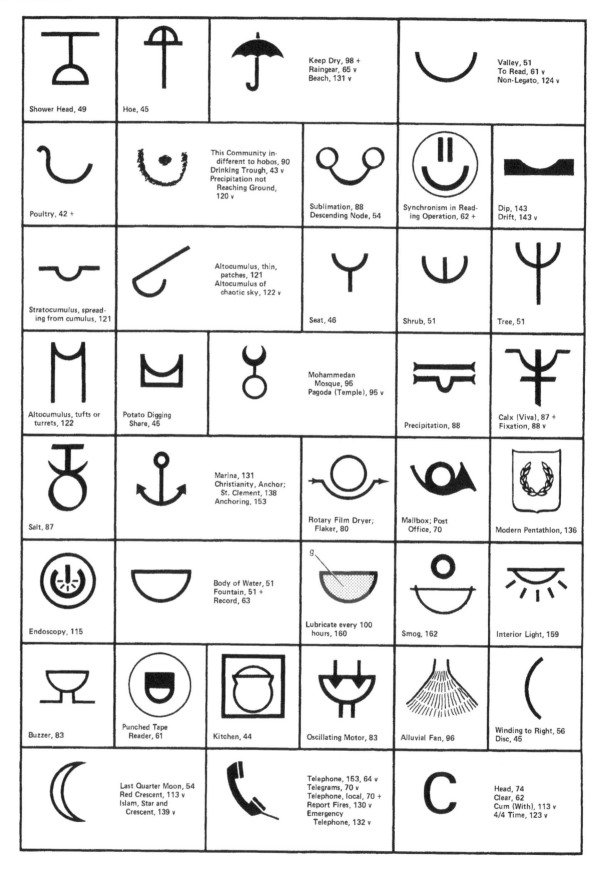

Shower Head, 49

Hoe, 45

Keep Dry, 98 +
Raingear, 65 v
Beach, 131 v

Valley, 51
To Read, 61 v
Non-Legato, 124 v

Poultry, 42 +

This Community indifferent to hobos, 90
Drinking Trough, 43 v
Precipitation not Reaching Ground, 120 v

Sublimation, 88
Descending Node, 54

Synchronism in Reading Operation, 62 +

Dip, 143
Drift, 143 v

Stratocumulus, spreading from cumulus, 121

Altocumulus, thin, patches, 121
Altocumulus of chaotic sky, 122 v

Seat, 46

Shrub, 51

Tree, 51

Altocumulus, tufts or turrets, 122

Potato Digging Share, 45

Mohammedan Mosque, 95
Pagoda (Temple), 95 v

Precipitation, 88

Calx (Viva), 87 +
Fixation, 88 v

Salt, 87

Marina, 131
Christianity, Anchor; St. Clement, 138
Anchoring, 153

Rotary Film Dryer; Flaker, 80

Mailbox; Post Office, 70

Modern Pentathlon, 136

Endoscopy, 115

Body of Water, 51
Fountain, 51 +
Record, 63

g

Lubricate every 100 hours, 160

Smog, 162

Interior Light, 159

Buzzer, 83

Punched Tape Reader, 61

Kitchen, 44

Oscillating Motor, 83

Alluvial Fan, 96

Winding to Right, 56
Disc, 45

Last Quarter Moon, 54
Red Crescent, 113 v
Islam, Star and Crescent, 139 v

Telephone, 153, 64 v
Telegrams, 70 v
Telephone, local, 70 +
Report Fires, 130 v
Emergency Telephone, 132 v

C

Head, 74
Clear, 62
Cum (With), 113 v
4/4 Time, 123 v

Copyright, 58 Air Traffic Service report office, 151 v Clock Hanger Outlet, 48 v	The Owner is Out, 90	Proportional To, 111	Exit, 34	Belongs To, 112 +
Flare Bevel Groove, 85	Disc Drill Colter, 45	Center Line, 48 Clone, 56 v Pilot Cancelled Flight Plan, 151 v	Cent(s), 58 Colon, 58 v 2/2 Time, 123 v	
Brake, 158 Brake Oil Pressure, 158	Winding to Left, 56 To Receive, 61	First Quarter Moon, 54 Pupa, 55 Silver, 87 Monday, 89	Rake Tine, 45	Cultivator Tine, 45 Subsoiler, 45 v
Rotate, Clockwise, 157 +	The Owner Is In, 90	Entrance, 34	Such That, 112 Apothecaries' Scruple, 114 v	Bell and Spigot Pipe Joint, 84
Crossed Pipe Lines, 83	Lead, 87	Mine Dump, 96	Material Forming, 104	Platinum, 87	Spotlight, Reflector, 49
Wear Gas Mask, 141	Delete Code, 61	Air Conditioning, 159	Altocumulus, thin, semi-transparent, 121 + Cirrocumulus, 122 v	Sulphur, 87
Altocumulus spreading from cumulus, 122	You Can Sleep in Hayloft, 91	Hockey, 136	Mountain, 51	Stitch Pattern, 101	Mountain Pass, 95
Hatchet; Axe, 45	Close Up Space, 72	Insert Space, 72	Iron, 86	Close Up Space, 72	Stratocumulus, not from cumulus, 121

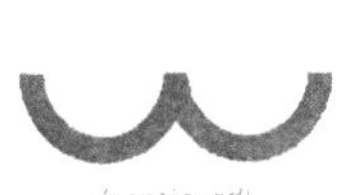

(continued)

Edge Flange, 84 +	Flare "V" Groove, 84 Pigeon, 43 v	Relationships, 52 Precipitation landing near station, 120 v Alternate Instructions, 150 v		Turning Basin (Put About), 153	Manual, 115
Pisces, 54, 89 Tunnel and Road, 92 Precipitation landing far from station, 120 Lines of Force, 128		Concave Lens, 128	Stretch Stitch, 101	Pharmacy, 65	Amphitheater; 130
Wavefronts, 128	Brake Off, 107	Biohazard Warning, 140	Judaism, Menorah, 139	Deciduous Forest, 44	Rough or Bumpy Road, 143 +
Warm Front, Aloft, 121 +	Surfacing, 84 Altocumulus, double-layered, 121 v		Conference, 64	Transcribe, 63	Intersection, 111 No "U" Turns, 145 v
Reverse Course to Right, 150 + Hairpin Bend, 143 v		Apparent Magnitude, 54 Chain Harrow, Spiked, 46 v Virgo, 54, 88 v Distillation, 88 v Murmur, 113 v Mass, 128 v Mineral Spring, 131 v		Headphone, 63	Digestion, 88
Horse Trail, 131	Change Speed, only in stopped position, 106	Rotary Motion, 116	Inspection and Quality Control, 104	Selective Band correction in level, 71	Transfer, 114
Refilling, 107	Magnetic Filter, 107	Stack Silo, 43	Bee Colony, 42	Meteorological Station, 44 Incubator, 47 v	
Rotating Light (Emergency Vehicle, 159	Well, 43	Bulk Storage Tank, 80	Lamp Dimmed Low, 126 +	Grain in Sack, 39 Fertilizer in Bags, 41 v	Whistle Post, 156

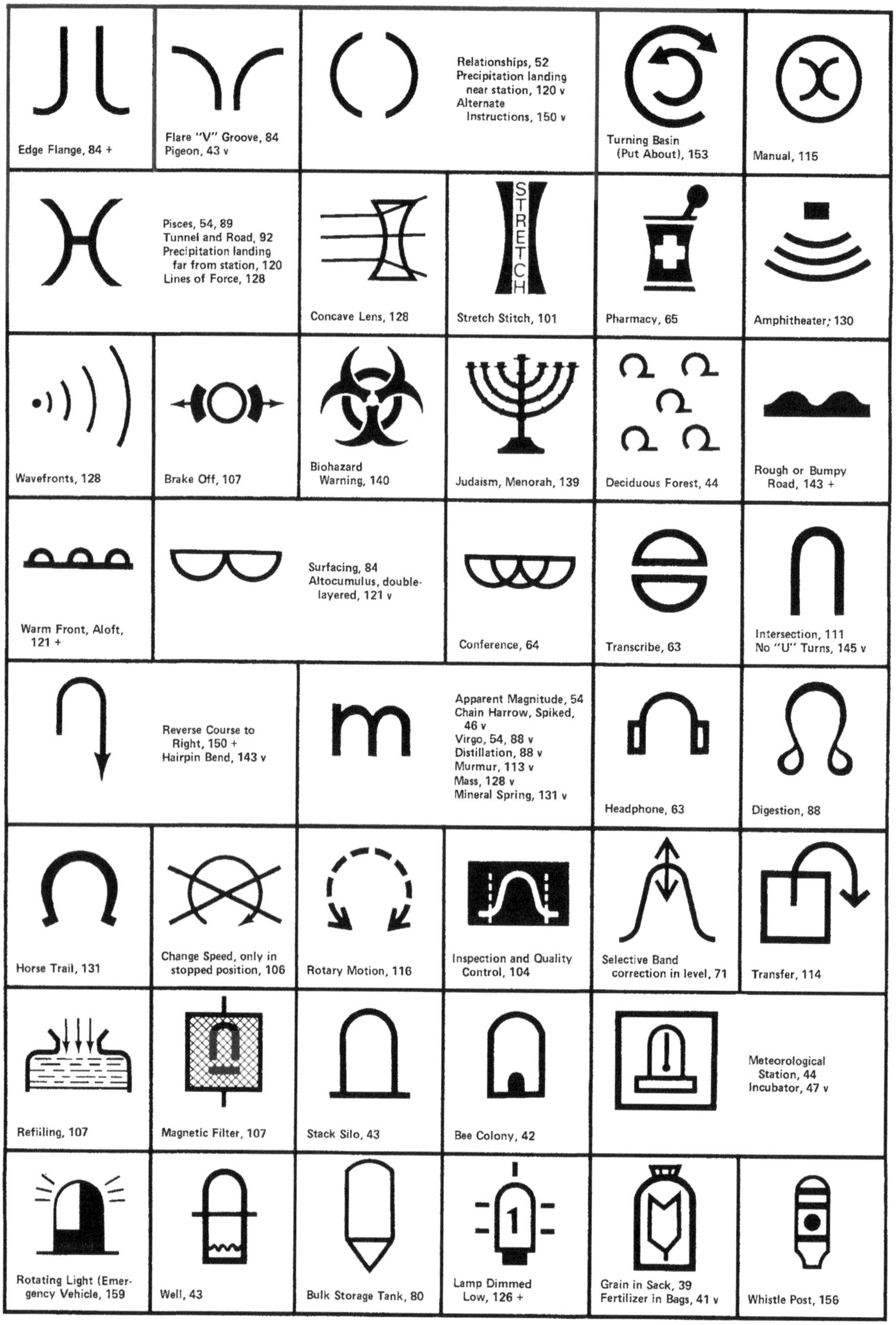

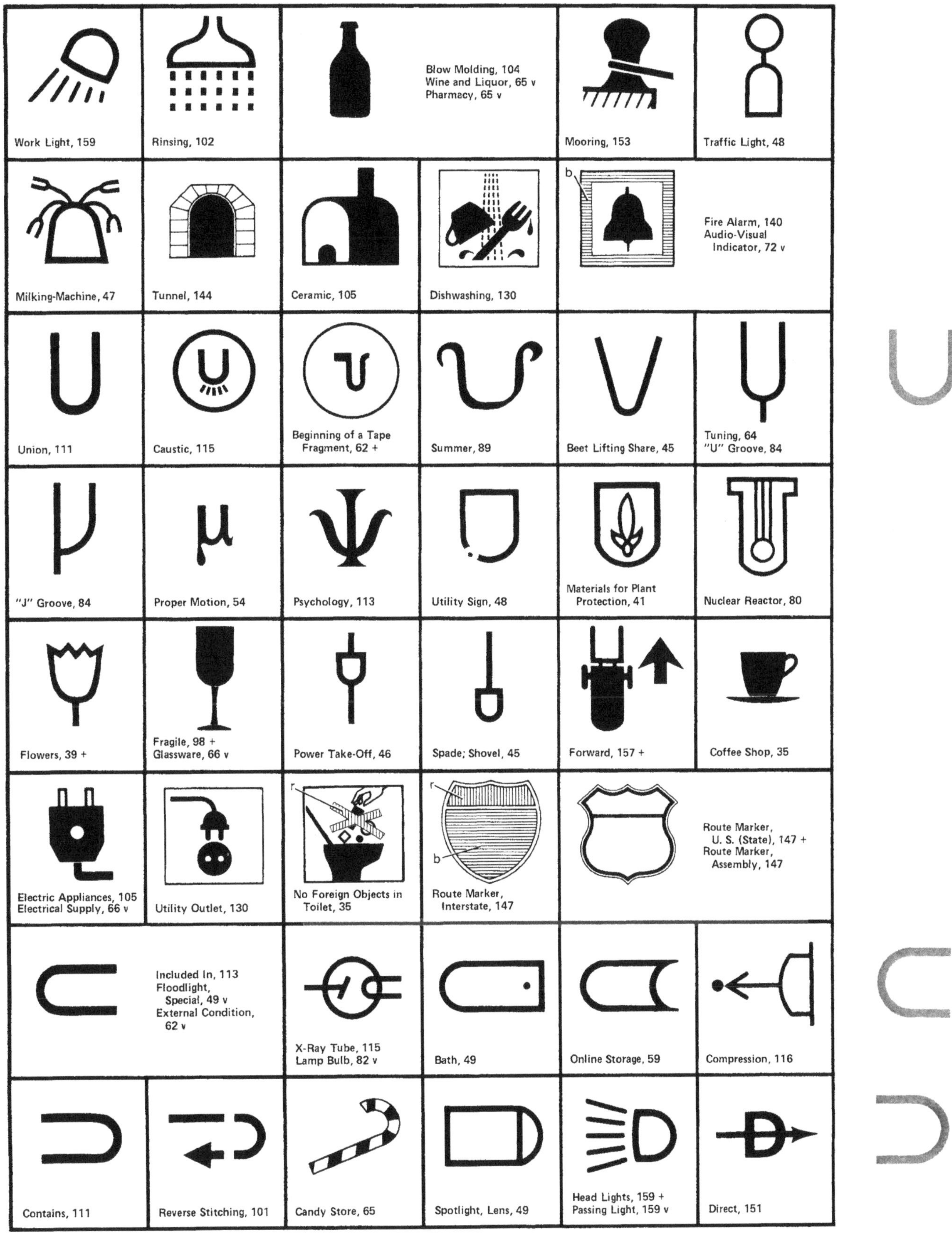
Work Light, 159
Rinsing, 102
Blow Molding, 104
Wine and Liquor, 65 v
Pharmacy, 65 v
Mooring, 153
Traffic Light, 48
Milking-Machine, 47
Tunnel, 144
Ceramic, 105
Dishwashing, 130
b
Fire Alarm, 140
Audio-Visual Indicator, 72 v
Union, 111
Caustic, 115
Beginning of a Tape Fragment, 62 +
Summer, 89
Beet Lifting Share, 45
Tuning, 64
"U" Groove, 84
"J" Groove, 84
Proper Motion, 54
Psychology, 113
Utility Sign, 48
Materials for Plant Protection, 41
Nuclear Reactor, 80
Flowers, 39 +
Fragile, 98 +
Glassware, 66 v
Power Take-Off, 46
Spade; Shovel, 45
Forward, 157 +
Coffee Shop, 35
Electric Appliances, 105
Electrical Supply, 66 v
Utility Outlet, 130
r
No Foreign Objects in Toilet, 35
r
b
Route Marker, Interstate, 147
Route Marker, U. S. (State), 147 +
Route Marker, Assembly, 147
Included In, 113
Floodlight, Special, 49 v
External Condition, 62 v
X-Ray Tube, 115
Lamp Bulb, 82 v
Bath, 49
Online Storage, 59
Compression, 116
Contains, 111
Reverse Stitching, 101
Candy Store, 65
Spotlight, Lens, 49
Head Lights, 159 +
Passing Light, 159 v
Direct, 151

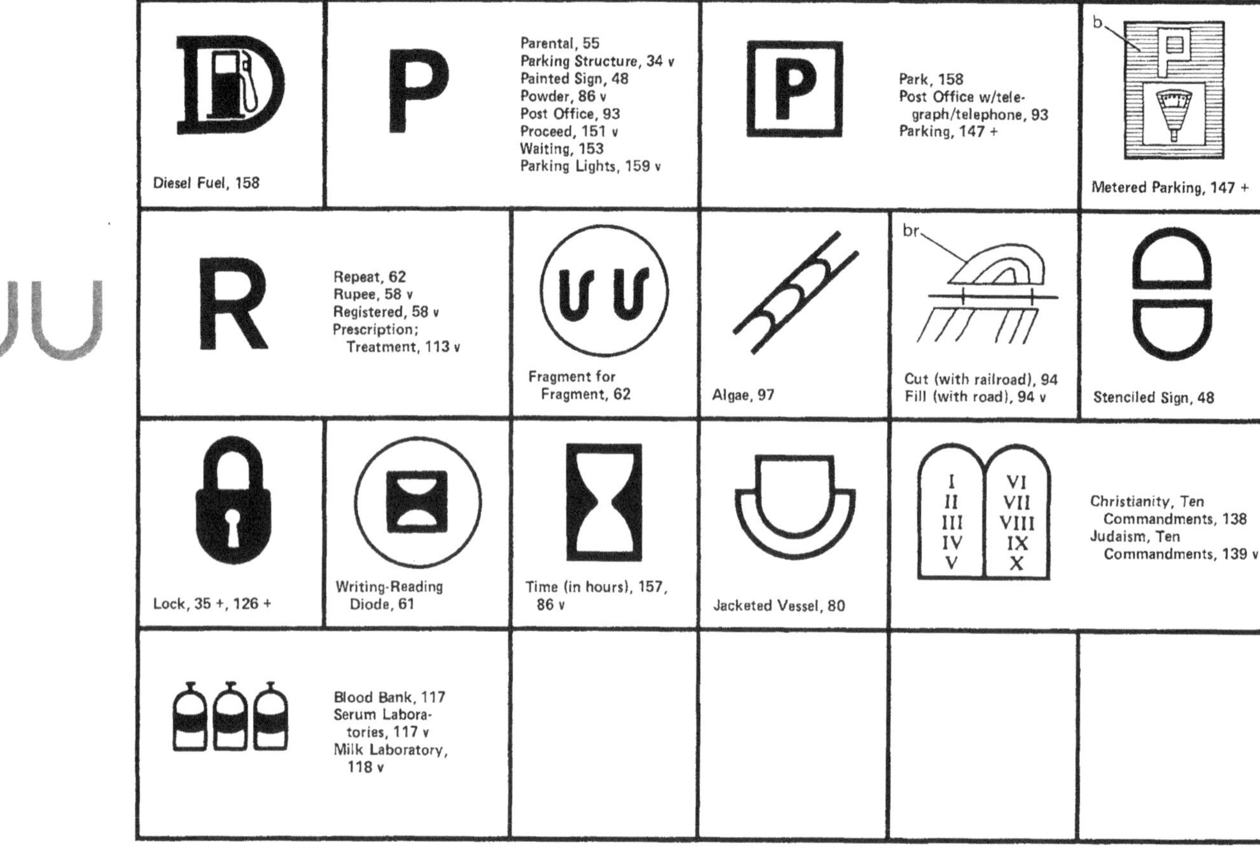
Diesel Fuel, 158
Parental, 55
Parking Structure, 34 v
Painted Sign, 48
Powder, 86 v
Post Office, 93
Proceed, 151 v
Waiting, 153
Parking Lights, 159 v
Park, 158
Post Office w/tele-graph/telephone, 93
Parking, 147 +
b
Metered Parking, 147 +
Repeat, 62
Rupee, 58 v
Registered, 58 v
Prescription; Treatment, 113 v
Fragment for Fragment, 62
Algae, 97
br
Cut (with railroad), 94
Fill (with road), 94 v
Stenciled Sign, 48
Lock, 35 +, 126 +
Writing-Reading Diode, 61
Time (in hours), 157, 86 v
Jacketed Vessel, 80
I II III IV V
VI VII VIII IX X
Christianity, Ten Commandments, 138
Judaism, Ten Commandments, 139 v
Blood Bank, 117
Serum Laboratories, 117 v
Milk Laboratory, 118 v

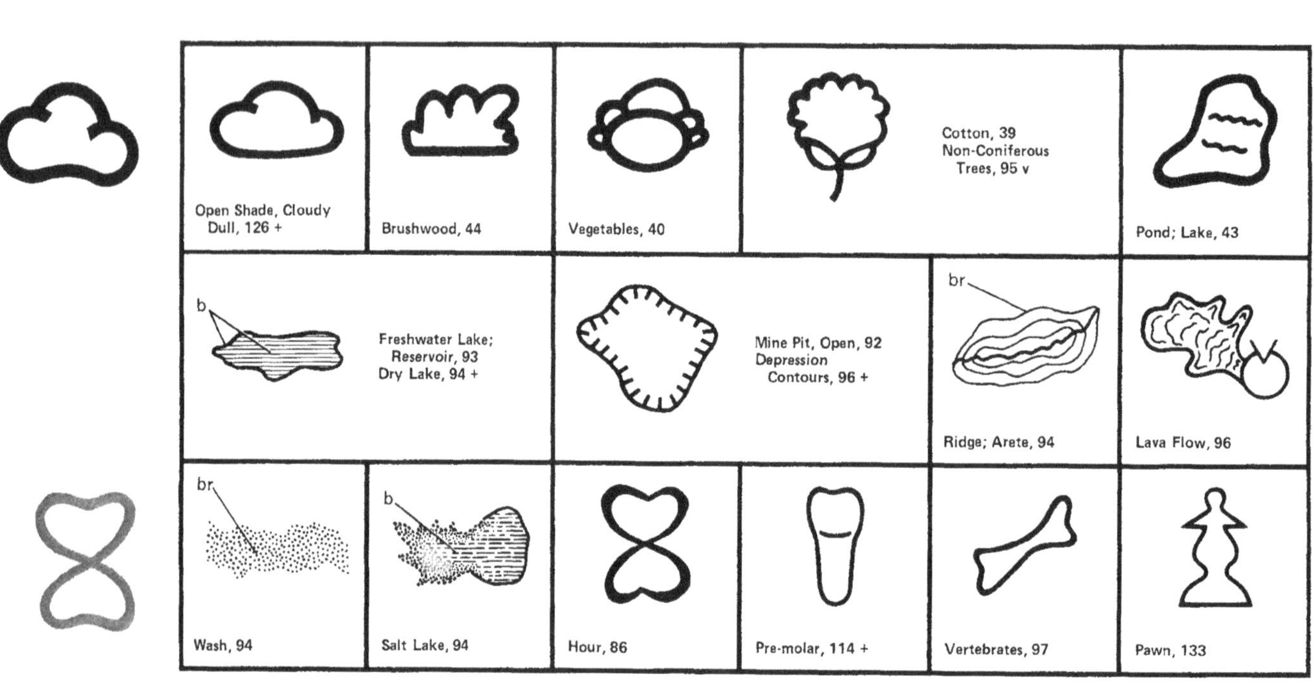
Open Shade, Cloudy Dull, 126 +
Brushwood, 44
Vegetables, 40
Cotton, 39
Non-Coniferous Trees, 95 v
Pond; Lake, 43
b
Freshwater Lake; Reservoir, 93
Dry Lake, 94 +
Mine Pit, Open, 92
Depression Contours, 96 +
br
Ridge; Arete, 94
Lava Flow, 96
br
Wash, 94
b
Salt Lake, 94
Hour, 86
Pre-molar, 114 +
Vertebrates, 97
Pawn, 133

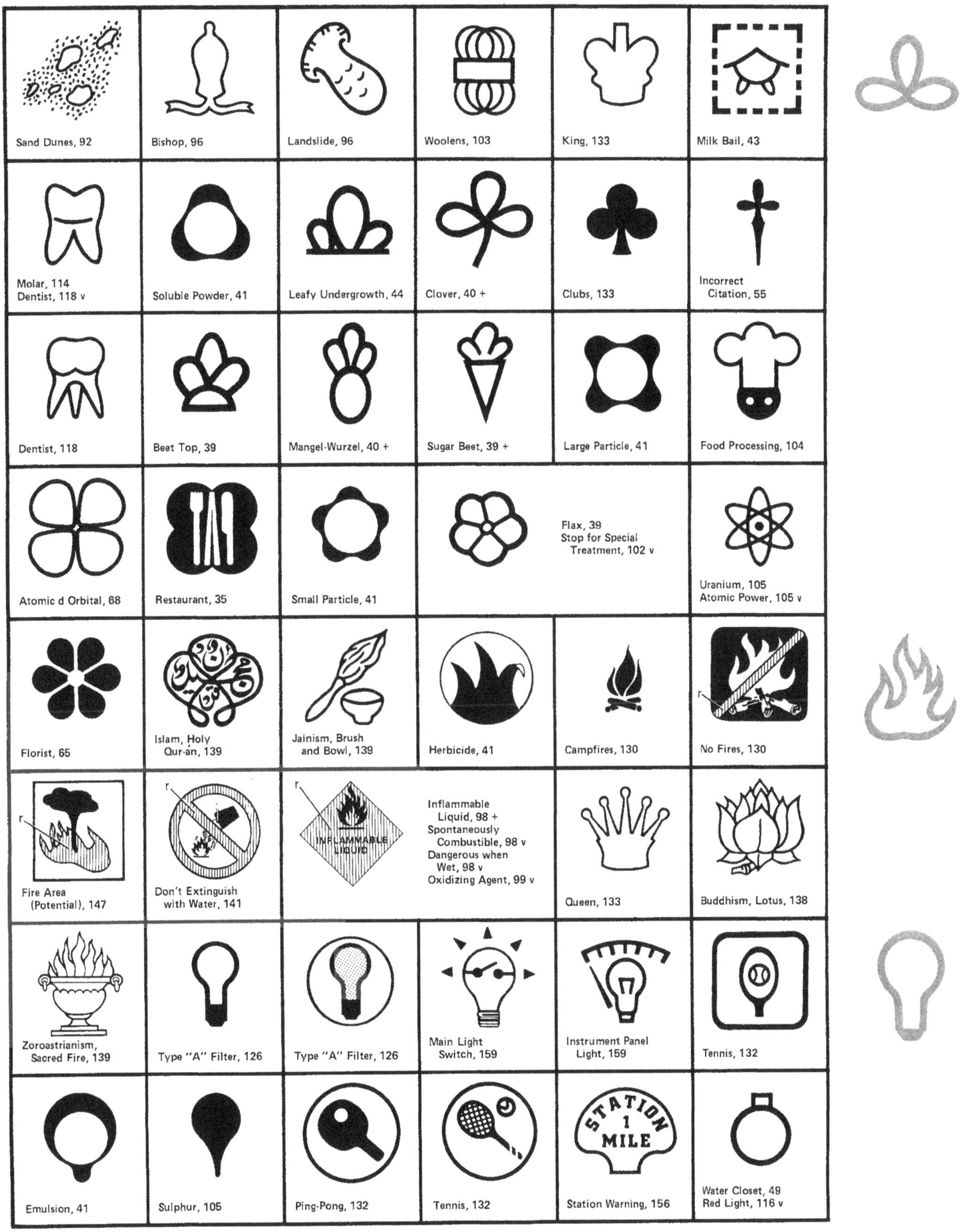

Sand Dunes, 92	Bishop, 96	Landslide, 96	Woolens, 103	King, 133	Milk Bail, 43
Molar, 114 Dentist, 118 v	Soluble Powder, 41	Leafy Undergrowth, 44	Clover, 40 +	Clubs, 133	Incorrect Citation, 55
Dentist, 118	Beet Top, 39	Mangel-Wurzel, 40 +	Sugar Beet, 39 +	Large Particle, 41	Food Processing, 104
Atomic d Orbital, 68	Restaurant, 35	Small Particle, 41		Flax, 39 Stop for Special Treatment, 102 v	Uranium, 105 Atomic Power, 105 v
Florist, 65	Islam, Holy Qur-án, 139	Jainism, Brush and Bowl, 139	Herbicide, 41	Campfires, 130	No Fires, 130
Fire Area (Potential), 147	Don't Extinguish with Water, 141		Inflammable Liquid, 98 + Spontaneously Combustible, 98 v Dangerous when Wet, 98 v Oxidizing Agent, 99 v	Queen, 133	Buddhism, Lotus, 138
Zoroastrianism, Sacred Fire, 139	Type "A" Filter, 126	Type "A" Filter, 126	Main Light Switch, 159	Instrument Panel Light, 159	Tennis, 132
Emulsion, 41	Sulphur, 105	Ping-Pong, 132	Tennis, 132	Station Warning, 156	Water Closet, 49 Red Light, 116 v

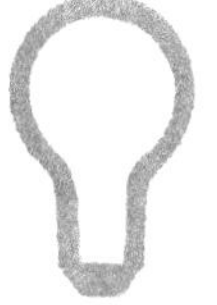

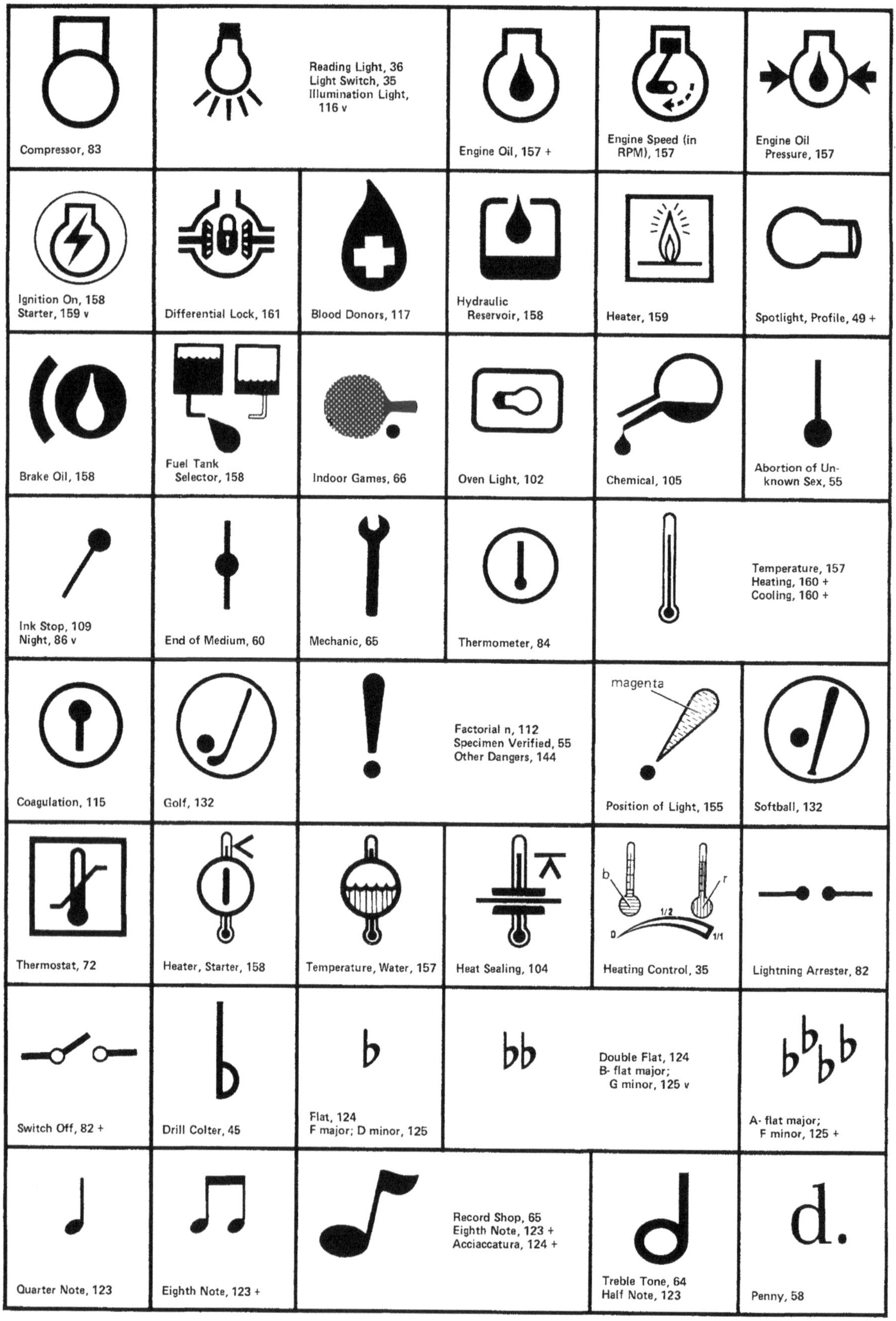

GRAPHIC FORM

Compressor, 83	Reading Light, 36 Light Switch, 35 Illumination Light, 116 v		Engine Oil, 157 +	Engine Speed (in RPM), 157	Engine Oil Pressure, 157
Ignition On, 158 Starter, 159 v	Differential Lock, 161	Blood Donors, 117	Hydraulic Reservoir, 158	Heater, 159	Spotlight, Profile, 49 +
Brake Oil, 158	Fuel Tank Selector, 158	Indoor Games, 66	Oven Light, 102	Chemical, 105	Abortion of Unknown Sex, 55
Ink Stop, 109 Night, 86 v	End of Medium, 60	Mechanic, 65	Thermometer, 84	Temperature, 157 Heating, 160 + Cooling, 160 +	
Coagulation, 115	Golf, 132	Factorial n, 112 Specimen Verified, 55 Other Dangers, 144		magenta Position of Light, 155	Softball, 132
Thermostat, 72	Heater, Starter, 158	Temperature, Water, 157	Heat Sealing, 104	b r 1/2 0 1/1 Heating Control, 35	Lightning Arrester, 82
Switch Off, 82 +	Drill Colter, 45	Flat, 124 F major; D minor, 125	Double Flat, 124 B- flat major; G minor, 125 v		A- flat major; F minor, 125 +
Quarter Note, 123	Eighth Note, 123 +	Record Shop, 65 Eighth Note, 123 + Acciaccatura, 124 +		Treble Tone, 64 Half Note, 123	d. Penny, 58

Partial Derivative, 111	Declination, 54	Curve; Cam, 108	Bass Tone, 64	Piano (Soft), 124 + Quiet Area, 52 v	Pluto, 54
Oak, 44 +	Mature Forest, 44 Thicket, 44 v Polewood, 44 v Regeneration, 44 v Reserve, 44 v		Clearing, 45 + Thinning, 45 v	To Plant, 44 + Regeneration Husbandry, 44 v Soil Cultivation, 44 v Repair Planting, 44 v	
Copse (Coppice), 44	Open Door or Lid, 103	Ignition Switch, 158	Car Rental (Car Hire), 37	Cutting, 115	Paragraph, 58 Paragraph, 73 v
Drizzle, 120 Decimal Sign, 64	Tropical Storm, 120 +	Aries; Vernal Equinox, 54, 88 Tea, 39 v Invert Type, 73 v		Bass (F) Clef, 123	Doubtful Citation, 55 Substitute, 60
Lost and Found, 34	Ink Fountain, 109	Retort, 86	Retort, 85 Distillation, 88	Cancer, 54, 88 Dissolution, 88	Blower, Gas, 83 Marine Fossil, 92 +
Lead, 87 + Saturn, 54 v Plant with Woody Stem, 56 Shrub, 56 v Tree, 56 v Saturday, 89 v		Perennial, 56 Jupiter, 54 Tin, 86, 87 v Thursday, 89 v Halt, 90 v		Delete, 72	Dram, 114 Ounce, 114 v
Delete, 72 +	Pound Sterling, 58	Ampersand (And), 58	Subgenus; Section, 56	Capricornus, 54, 89	Shin (Sham, There), Put in one piece, 133
Per, 58	Alto (C) Clef, 123	Hinduism, Aum; Brahman-Atman, 139	Tobacco, 39 + Medicinal Plants, 39 v	Gastropods, 97	Cane, 40

GRAPHIC FORM

(continued)

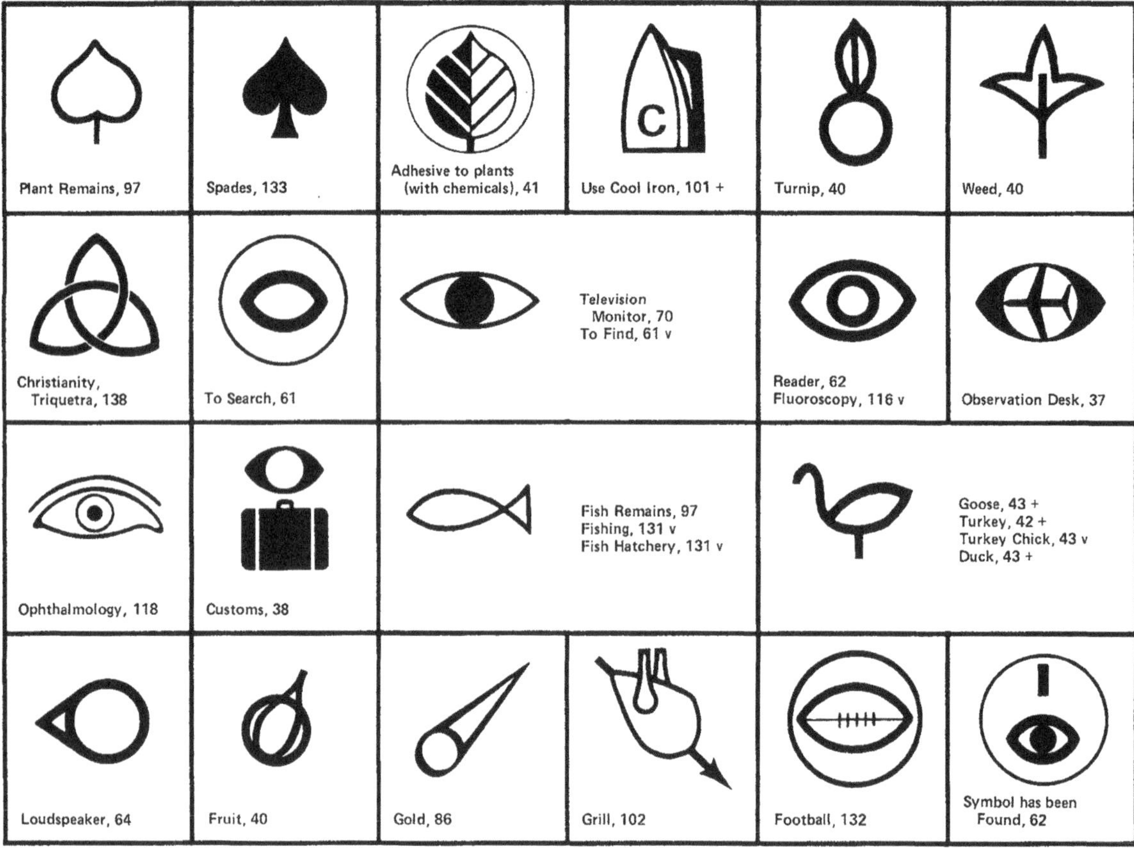

Plant Remains, 97
Spades, 133
Adhesive to plants (with chemicals), 41
C
Use Cool Iron, 101 +
Turnip, 40
Weed, 40
Christianity, Triquetra, 138
To Search, 61
Television Monitor, 70
To Find, 61 v
Reader, 62
Fluoroscopy, 116 v
Observation Desk, 37
Ophthalmology, 118
Customs, 38
Fish Remains, 97
Fishing, 131 v
Fish Hatchery, 131 v
Goose, 43 +
Turkey, 42 +
Turkey Chick, 43 v
Duck, 43 +
Loudspeaker, 64
Fruit, 40
Gold, 86
Grill, 102
Football, 132
Symbol has been Found, 62

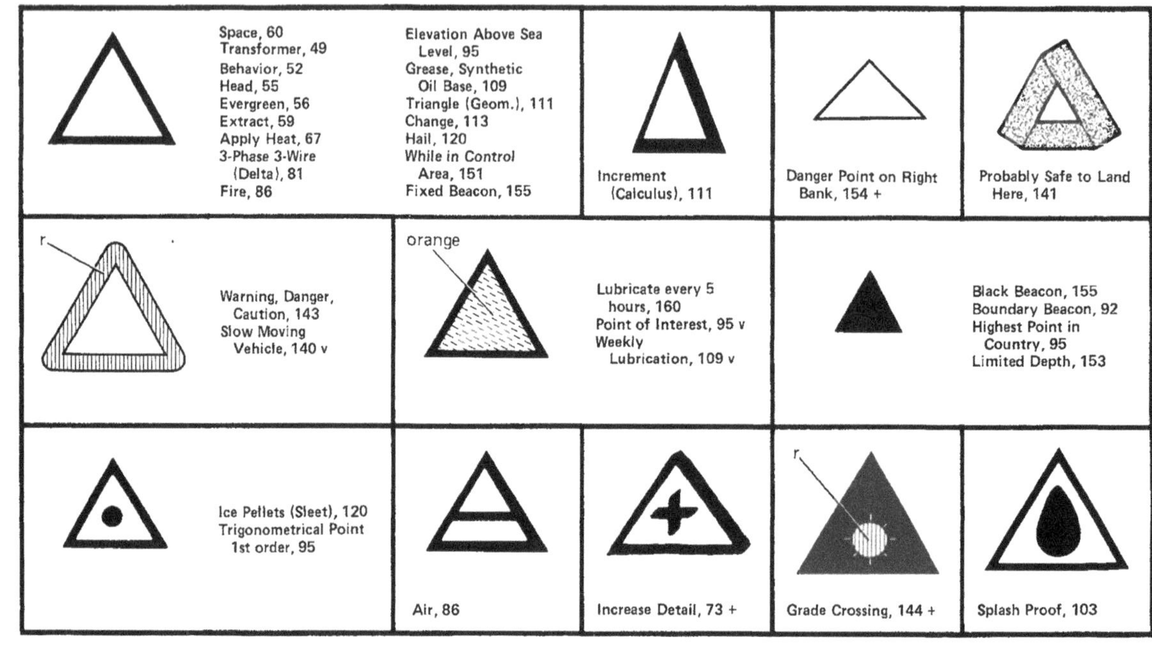

Space, 60
Transformer, 49
Behavior, 52
Head, 55
Evergreen, 56
Extract, 59
Apply Heat, 67
3-Phase 3-Wire (Delta), 81
Fire, 86
Elevation Above Sea Level, 95
Grease, Synthetic Oil Base, 109
Triangle (Geom.), 111
Change, 113
Hail, 120
While in Control Area, 151
Fixed Beacon, 155
Increment (Calculus), 111
Danger Point on Right Bank, 154 +
Probably Safe to Land Here, 141
r
Warning, Danger, Caution, 143
Slow Moving Vehicle, 140 v
orange
Lubricate every 5 hours, 160
Point of Interest, 95 v
Weekly Lubrication, 109 v
Black Beacon, 155
Boundary Beacon, 92
Highest Point in Country, 95
Limited Depth, 153
Ice Pellets (Sleet), 120
Trigonometrical Point 1st order, 95
Air, 86
Increase Detail, 73 +
r
Grade Crossing, 144 +
Splash Proof, 103

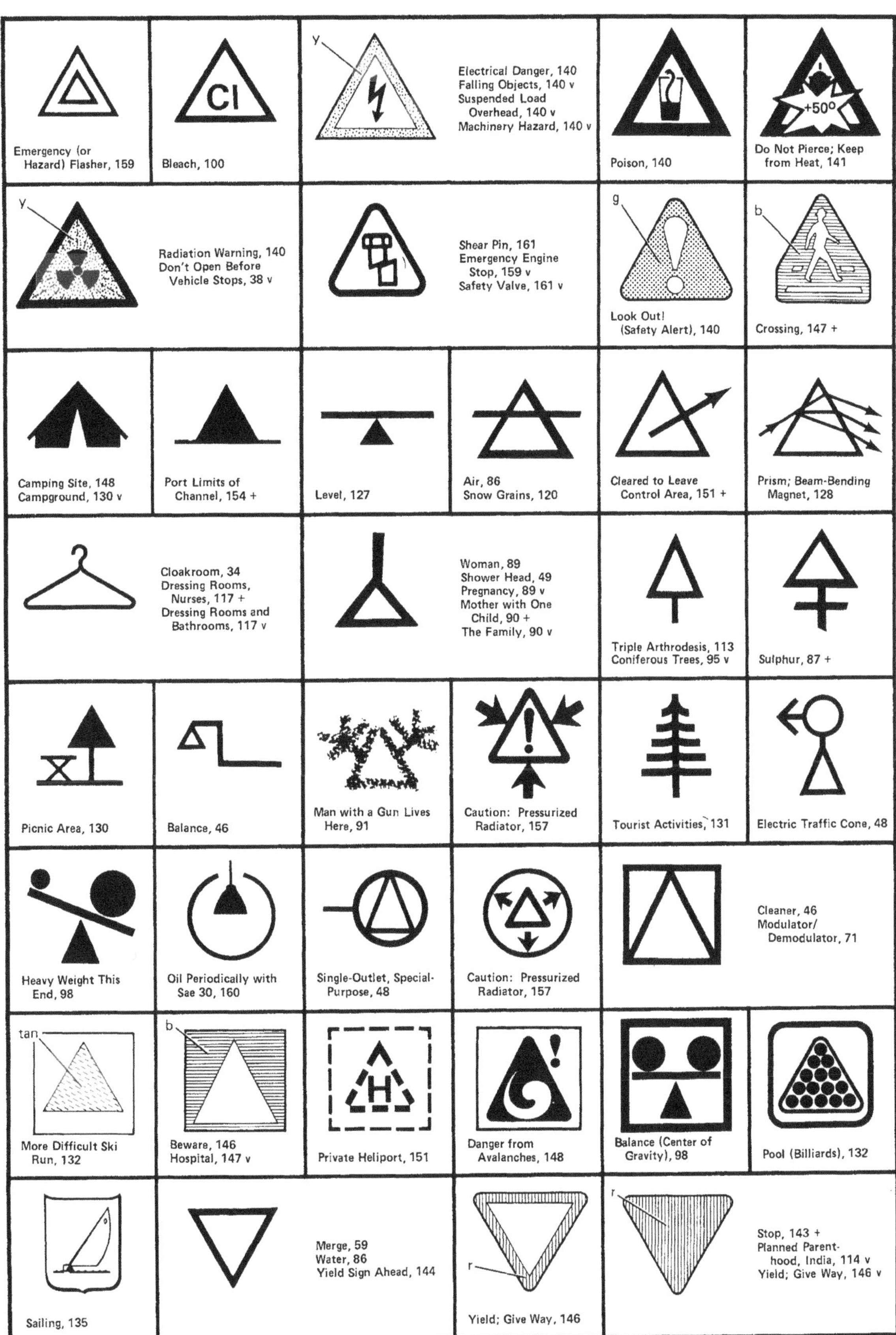
Emergency (or Hazard) Flasher, 159
Cl
Bleach, 100
y
Electrical Danger, 140
Falling Objects, 140 v
Suspended Load Overhead, 140 v
Machinery Hazard, 140 v
Poison, 140
+50°
Do Not Pierce; Keep from Heat, 141
y
Radiation Warning, 140
Don't Open Before Vehicle Stops, 38 v
Shear Pin, 161
Emergency Engine Stop, 159 v
Safety Valve, 161 v
g
Look Out! (Safety Alert), 140
b
Crossing, 147 +
Camping Site, 148
Campground, 130 v
Port Limits of Channel, 154 +
Level, 127
Air, 86
Snow Grains, 120
Cleared to Leave Control Area, 151 +
Prism; Beam-Bending Magnet, 128
Cloakroom, 34
Dressing Rooms, Nurses, 117 +
Dressing Rooms and Bathrooms, 117 v
Woman, 89
Shower Head, 49
Pregnancy, 89 v
Mother with One Child, 90 +
The Family, 90 v
Triple Arthrodesis, 113
Coniferous Trees, 95 v
Sulphur, 87 +
Picnic Area, 130
Balance, 46
Man with a Gun Lives Here, 91
Caution: Pressurized Radiator, 157
Tourist Activities, 131
Electric Traffic Cone, 48
Heavy Weight This End, 98
Oil Periodically with Sae 30, 160
Single-Outlet, Special-Purpose, 48
Caution: Pressurized Radiator, 157
Cleaner, 46
Modulator/ Demodulator, 71
tan
More Difficult Ski Run, 132
b
Beware, 146
Hospital, 147 v
H
Private Heliport, 151
Danger from Avalanches, 148
Balance (Center of Gravity), 98
Pool (Billiards), 132
Sailing, 135
Merge, 59
Water, 86
Yield Sign Ahead, 144
r
Yield; Give Way, 146
r
Stop, 143 +
Planned Parenthood, India, 114 v
Yield; Give Way, 146 v

(continued)

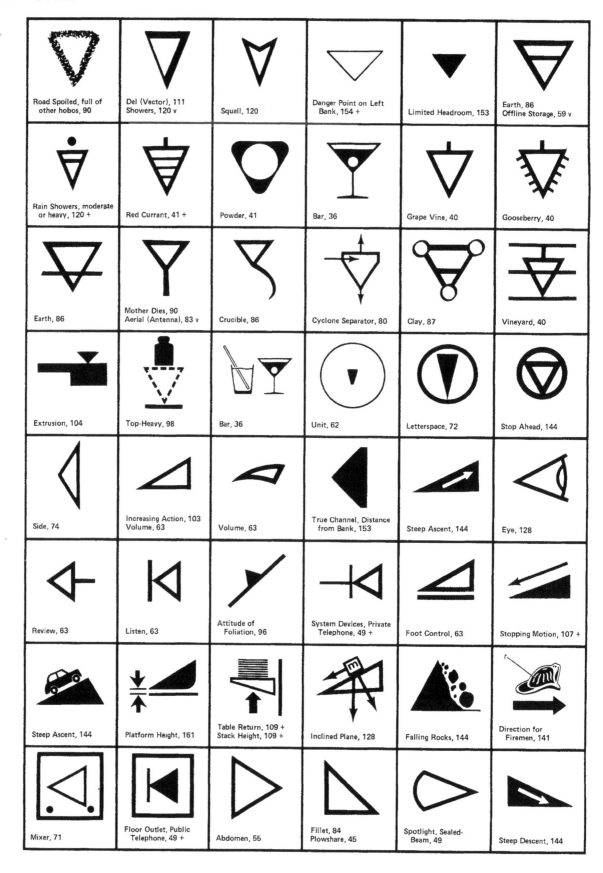

Road Spoiled, full of other hobos, 90	Del (Vector), 111 Showers, 120 v	Squall, 120	Danger Point on Left Bank, 154 +	Limited Headroom, 153	Earth, 86 Offline Storage, 59 v
Rain Showers, moderate or heavy, 120 +	Red Currant, 41 +	Powder, 41	Bar, 36	Grape Vine, 40	Gooseberry, 40
Earth, 86	Mother Dies, 90 Aerial (Antenna), 83 v	Crucible, 86	Cyclone Separator, 80	Clay, 87	Vineyard, 40
Extrusion, 104	Top-Heavy, 98	Bar, 36	Unit, 62	Letterspace, 72	Stop Ahead, 144
Side, 74	Increasing Action, 103 Volume, 63	Volume, 63	True Channel, Distance from Bank, 153	Steep Ascent, 144	Eye, 128
Review, 63	Listen, 63	Attitude of Foliation, 96	System Devices, Private Telephone, 49 +	Foot Control, 63	Stopping Motion, 107 +
Steep Ascent, 144	Platform Height, 161	Table Return, 109 + Stack Height, 109 +	Inclined Plane, 128	Falling Rocks, 144	Direction for Firemen, 141
Mixer, 71	Floor Outlet, Public Telephone, 49 +	Abdomen, 55	Fillet, 84 Plowshare, 45	Spotlight, Sealed-Beam, 49	Steep Descent, 144

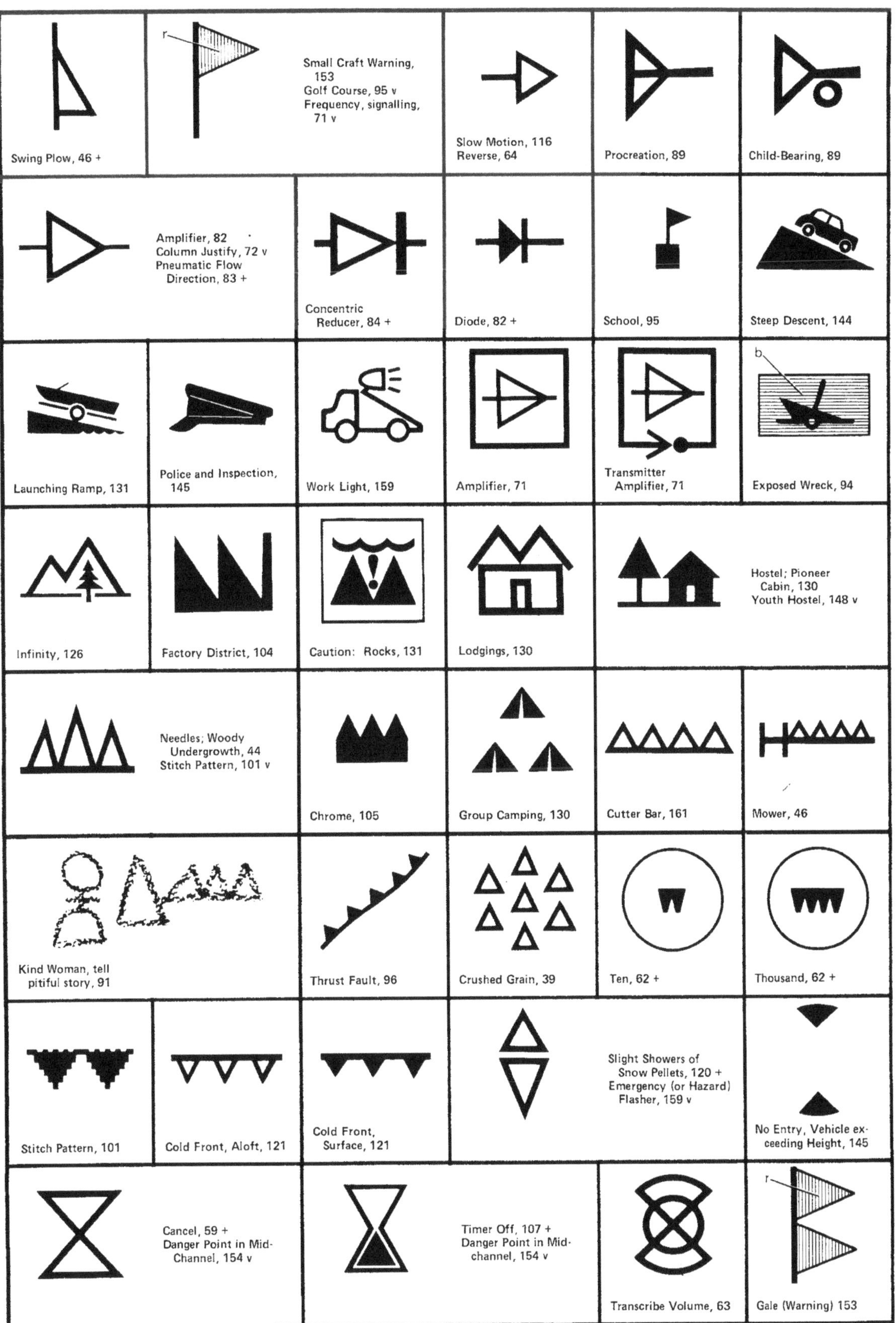

Swing Plow, 46 +
r
Small Craft Warning, 153
Golf Course, 95 v
Frequency, signalling, 71 v
Slow Motion, 116
Reverse, 64
Procreation, 89
Child-Bearing, 89
Amplifier, 82
Column Justify, 72 v
Pneumatic Flow Direction, 83 +
Concentric Reducer, 84 +
Diode, 82 +
School, 95
Steep Descent, 144
Launching Ramp, 131
Police and Inspection, 145
Work Light, 159
Amplifier, 71
Transmitter Amplifier, 71
b
Exposed Wreck, 94
Infinity, 126
Factory District, 104
Caution: Rocks, 131
Lodgings, 130
Hostel; Pioneer Cabin, 130
Youth Hostel, 148 v
Needles; Woody Undergrowth, 44
Stitch Pattern, 101 v
Chrome, 105
Group Camping, 130
Cutter Bar, 161
Mower, 46
Kind Woman, tell pitiful story, 91
Thrust Fault, 96
Crushed Grain, 39
Ten, 62 +
Thousand, 62 +
Stitch Pattern, 101
Cold Front, Aloft, 121
Cold Front, Surface, 121
Slight Showers of Snow Pellets, 120 +
Emergency (or Hazard) Flasher, 159 v
No Entry, Vehicle exceeding Height, 145
Cancel, 59 +
Danger Point in Mid-Channel, 154 v
Timer Off, 107 +
Danger Point in Mid-channel, 154 v
Transcribe Volume, 63
r
Gale (Warning) 153

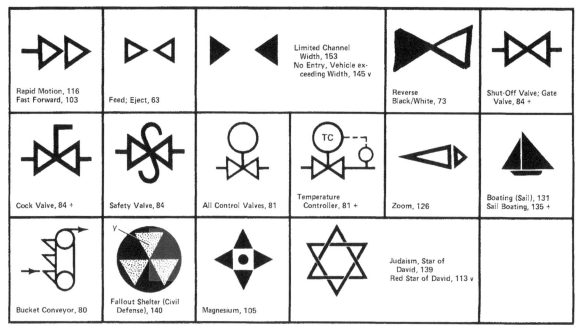

Rapid Motion, 116
Fast Forward, 103

Feed; Eject, 63

Limited Channel Width, 153
No Entry, Vehicle exceeding Width, 145 v

Reverse Black/White, 73

Shut-Off Valve; Gate Valve, 84 +

Cock Valve, 84 +

Safety Valve, 84

All Control Valves, 81

TC

Temperature Controller, 81 +

Zoom, 126

Boating (Sail), 131
Sail Boating, 135 +

Bucket Conveyor, 80

y

Fallout Shelter (Civil Defense), 140

Magnesium, 105

Judaism, Star of David, 139
Red Star of David, 113 v

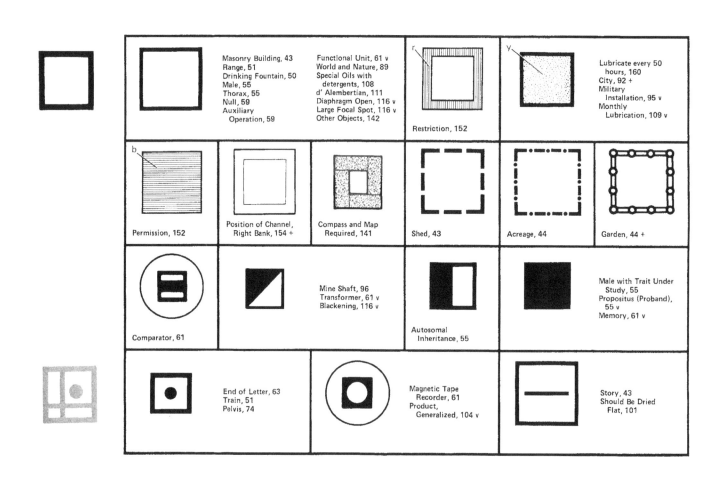

Masonry Building, 43
Range, 51
Drinking Fountain, 50
Male, 55
Thorax, 55
Null, 59
Auxiliary Operation, 59
Functional Unit, 61 v
World and Nature, 89
Special Oils with detergents, 108
d' Alembertian, 111
Diaphragm Open, 116 v
Large Focal Spot, 116 v
Other Objects, 142

r

Restriction, 152

y

Lubricate every 50 hours, 160
City, 92 +
Military Installation, 95 v
Monthly Lubrication, 109 v

b

Permission, 152

Position of Channel, Right Bank, 154 +

Compass and Map Required, 141

Shed, 43

Acreage, 44

Garden, 44 +

Comparator, 61

Mine Shaft, 96
Transformer, 61 v
Blackening, 116 v

Autosomal Inheritance, 55

Male with Trait Under Study, 55
Propositus (Proband), 55 v
Memory, 61 v

End of Letter, 63
Train, 51
Pelvis, 74

Magnetic Tape Recorder, 61
Product, Generalized, 104 v

Story, 43
Should Be Dried Flat, 101

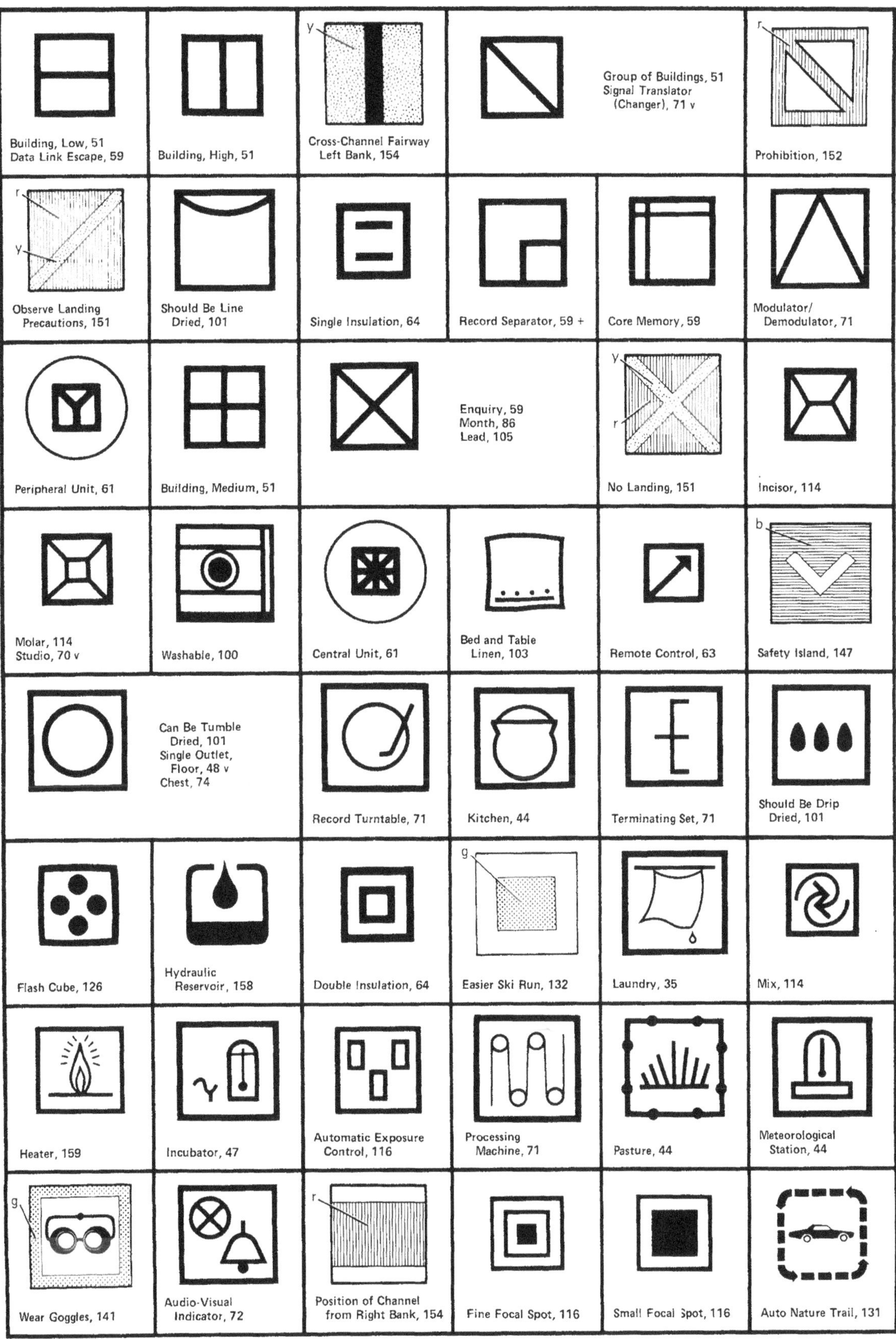
Building, Low, 51
Data Link Escape, 59
Building, High, 51
y
Cross-Channel Fairway
Left Bank, 154
Group of Buildings, 51
Signal Translator
(Changer), 71 v
r
Prohibition, 152
r
y
Observe Landing
Precautions, 151
Should Be Line
Dried, 101
Single Insulation, 64
Record Separator, 59 +
Core Memory, 59
Modulator/
Demodulator, 71
Peripheral Unit, 61
Building, Medium, 51
Enquiry, 59
Month, 86
Lead, 105
y
r
No Landing, 151
Incisor, 114
Molar, 114
Studio, 70 v
Washable, 100
Central Unit, 61
Bed and Table
Linen, 103
Remote Control, 63
b
Safety Island, 147
Can Be Tumble
Dried, 101
Single Outlet,
Floor, 48 v
Chest, 74
Record Turntable, 71
Kitchen, 44
Terminating Set, 71
Should Be Drip
Dried, 101
Flash Cube, 126
Hydraulic
Reservoir, 158
Double Insulation, 64
g
Easier Ski Run, 132
Laundry, 35
Mix, 114
Heater, 159
Incubator, 47
Automatic Exposure
Control, 116
Processing
Machine, 71
Pasture, 44
Meteorological
Station, 44
g
Wear Goggles, 141
Audio-Visual
Indicator, 72
r
Position of Channel
from Right Bank, 154
Fine Focal Spot, 116
Small Focal Spot, 116
Auto Nature Trail, 131

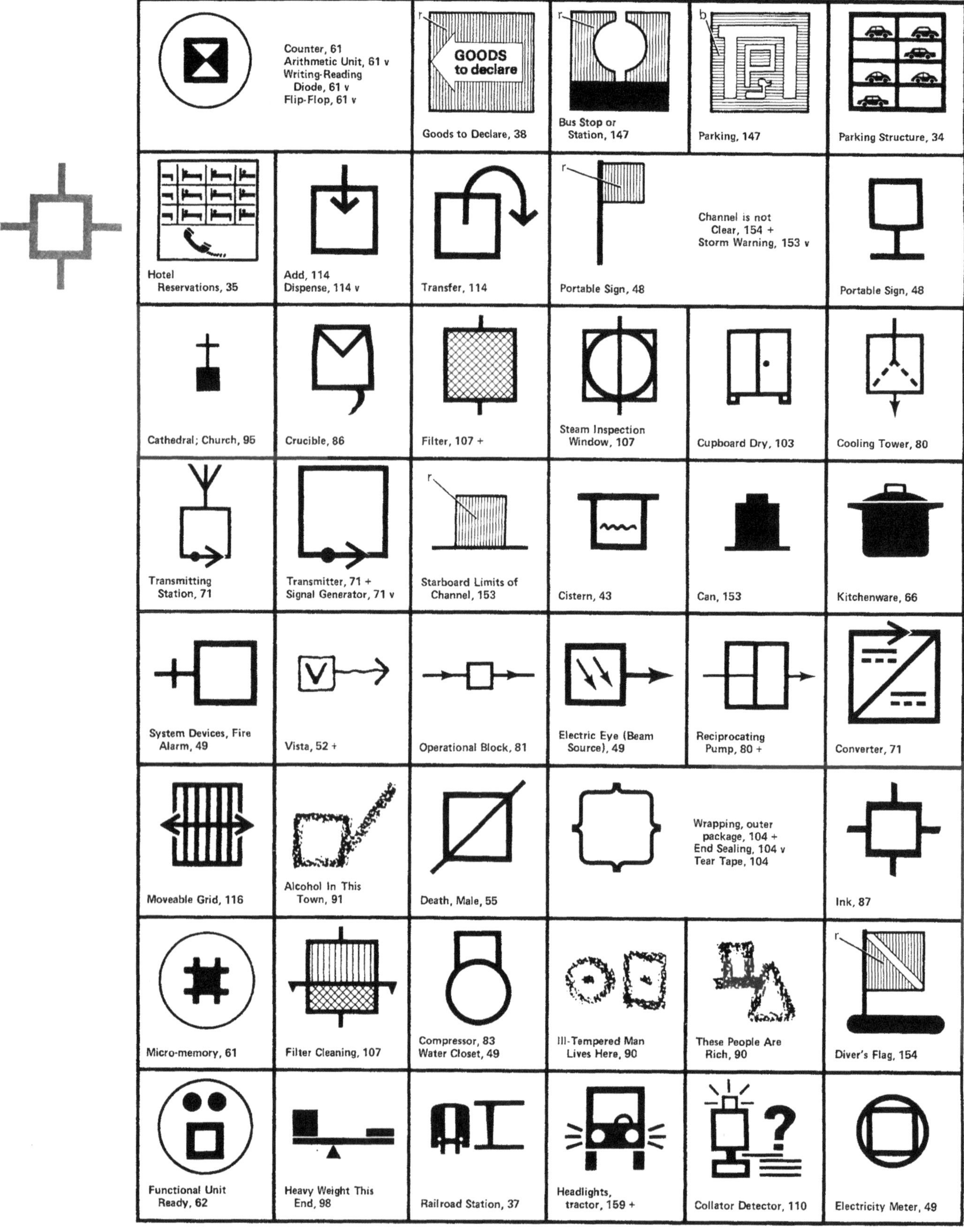
Counter, 61
Arithmetic Unit, 61 v
Writing-Reading Diode, 61 v
Flip-Flop, 61 v
r
GOODS
to declare
Goods to Declare, 38
r
Bus Stop or Station, 147
b
Parking, 147
Parking Structure, 34
Hotel Reservations, 35
Add, 114
Dispense, 114 v
Transfer, 114
r
Portable Sign, 48
Channel is not Clear, 154 +
Storm Warning, 153 v
Portable Sign, 48
Cathedral; Church, 95
Crucible, 86
Filter, 107 +
Steam Inspection Window, 107
Cupboard Dry, 103
Cooling Tower, 80
Transmitting Station, 71
Transmitter, 71 +
Signal Generator, 71 v
r
Starboard Limits of Channel, 153
Cistern, 43
Can, 153
Kitchenware, 66
System Devices, Fire Alarm, 49
V
Vista, 52 +
Operational Block, 81
Electric Eye (Beam Source), 49
Reciprocating Pump, 80 +
Converter, 71
Moveable Grid, 116
Alcohol In This Town, 91
Death, Male, 55
Wrapping, outer package, 104 +
End Sealing, 104 v
Tear Tape, 104
Ink, 87
Micro-memory, 61
Filter Cleaning, 107
Compressor, 83
Water Closet, 49
Ill-Tempered Man Lives Here, 90
These People Are Rich, 90
r
Diver's Flag, 154
Functional Unit Ready, 62
Heavy Weight This End, 98
Railroad Station, 37
Headlights, tractor, 159 +
?
Collator Detector, 110
Electricity Meter, 49

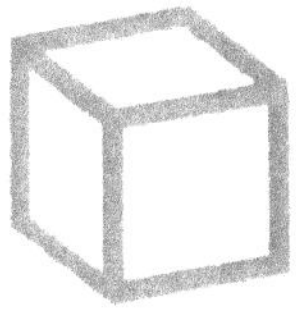

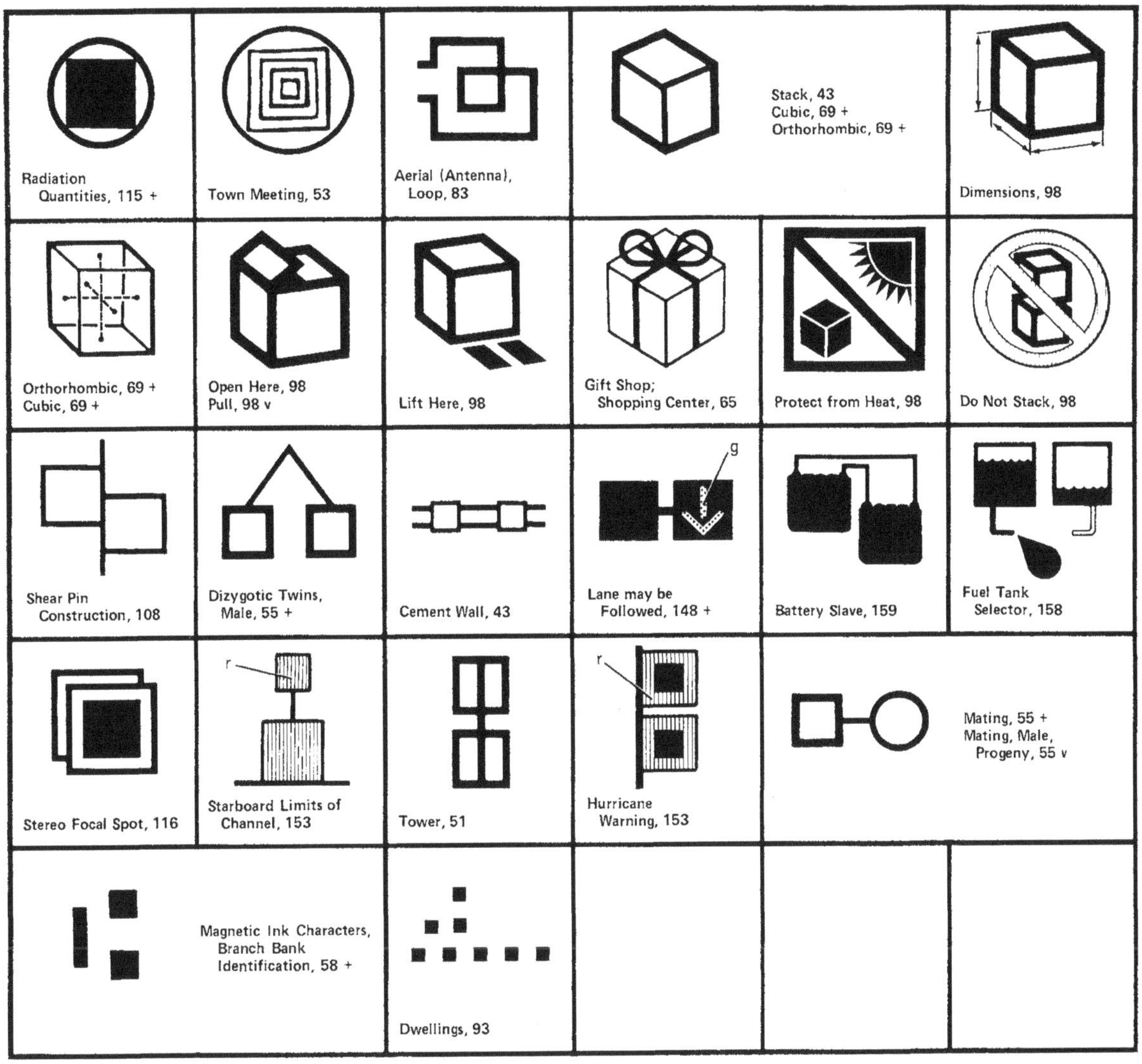

Radiation Quantities, 115 +

Town Meeting, 53

Aerial (Antenna), Loop, 83

Stack, 43
Cubic, 69 +
Orthorhombic, 69 +

Dimensions, 98

Orthorhombic, 69 +
Cubic, 69 +

Open Here, 98
Pull, 98 v

Lift Here, 98

Gift Shop;
Shopping Center, 65

Protect from Heat, 98

Do Not Stack, 98

Shear Pin Construction, 108

Dizygotic Twins, Male, 55 +

Cement Wall, 43

g

Lane may be Followed, 148 +

Battery Slave, 159

Fuel Tank Selector, 158

Stereo Focal Spot, 116

r

Starboard Limits of Channel, 153

Tower, 51

r

Hurricane Warning, 153

Mating, 55 +
Mating, Male,
Progeny, 55 v

Magnetic Ink Characters, Branch Bank Identification, 58 +

Dwellings, 93

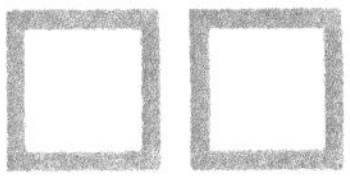

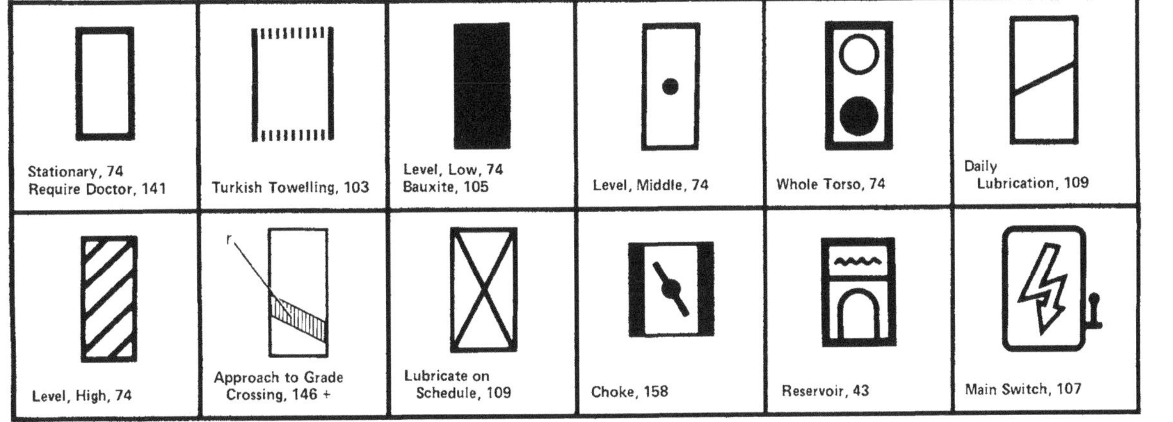
Stationary, 74
Require Doctor, 141
Turkish Towelling, 103
Level, Low, 74
Bauxite, 105
Level, Middle, 74
Whole Torso, 74
Daily Lubrication, 109
Level, High, 74
r
Approach to Grade Crossing, 146 +
Lubricate on Schedule, 109
Choke, 158
Reservoir, 43
Main Switch, 107

GRAPHIC FORM

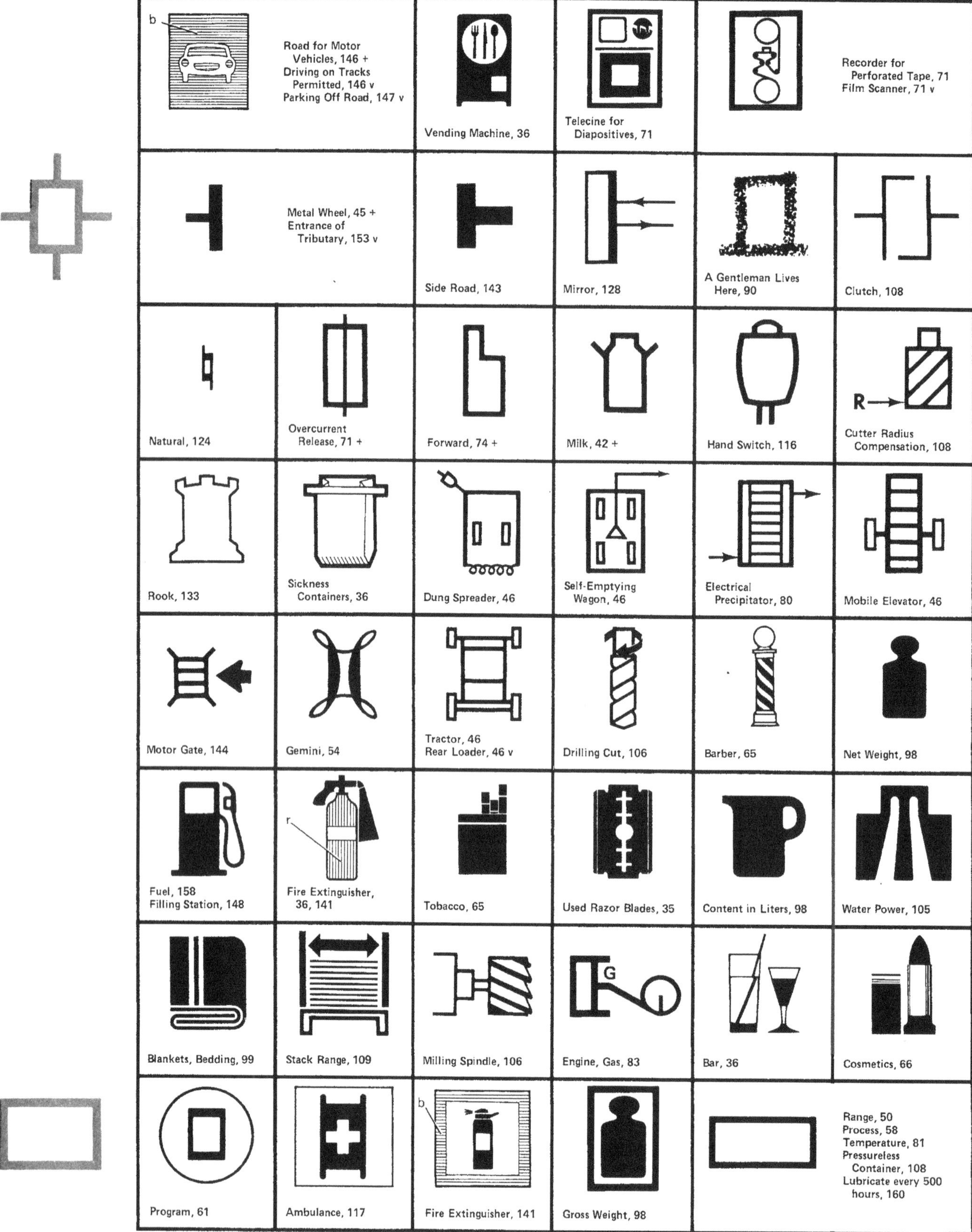

b
Road for Motor Vehicles, 146 +
Driving on Tracks Permitted, 146 v
Parking Off Road, 147 v
Vending Machine, 36
Telecine for Diapositives, 71
Recorder for Perforated Tape, 71
Film Scanner, 71 v
Metal Wheel, 45 +
Entrance of Tributary, 153 v
Side Road, 143
Mirror, 128
A Gentleman Lives Here, 90
Clutch, 108
Natural, 124
Overcurrent Release, 71 +
Forward, 74 +
Milk, 42 +
Hand Switch, 116
R
Cutter Radius Compensation, 108
Rook, 133
Sickness Containers, 36
Dung Spreader, 46
Self-Emptying Wagon, 46
Electrical Precipitator, 80
Mobile Elevator, 46
Motor Gate, 144
Gemini, 54
Tractor, 46
Rear Loader, 46 v
Drilling Cut, 106
Barber, 65
Net Weight, 98
Fuel, 158
Filling Station, 148
r
Fire Extinguisher, 36, 141
Tobacco, 65
Used Razor Blades, 35
Content in Liters, 98
Water Power, 105
Blankets, Bedding, 99
Stack Range, 109
Milling Spindle, 106
G
Engine, Gas, 83
Bar, 36
Cosmetics, 66
Program, 61
Ambulance, 117
b
Fire Extinguisher, 141
Gross Weight, 98
Range, 50
Process, 58
Temperature, 81
Pressureless Container, 108
Lubricate every 500 hours, 160

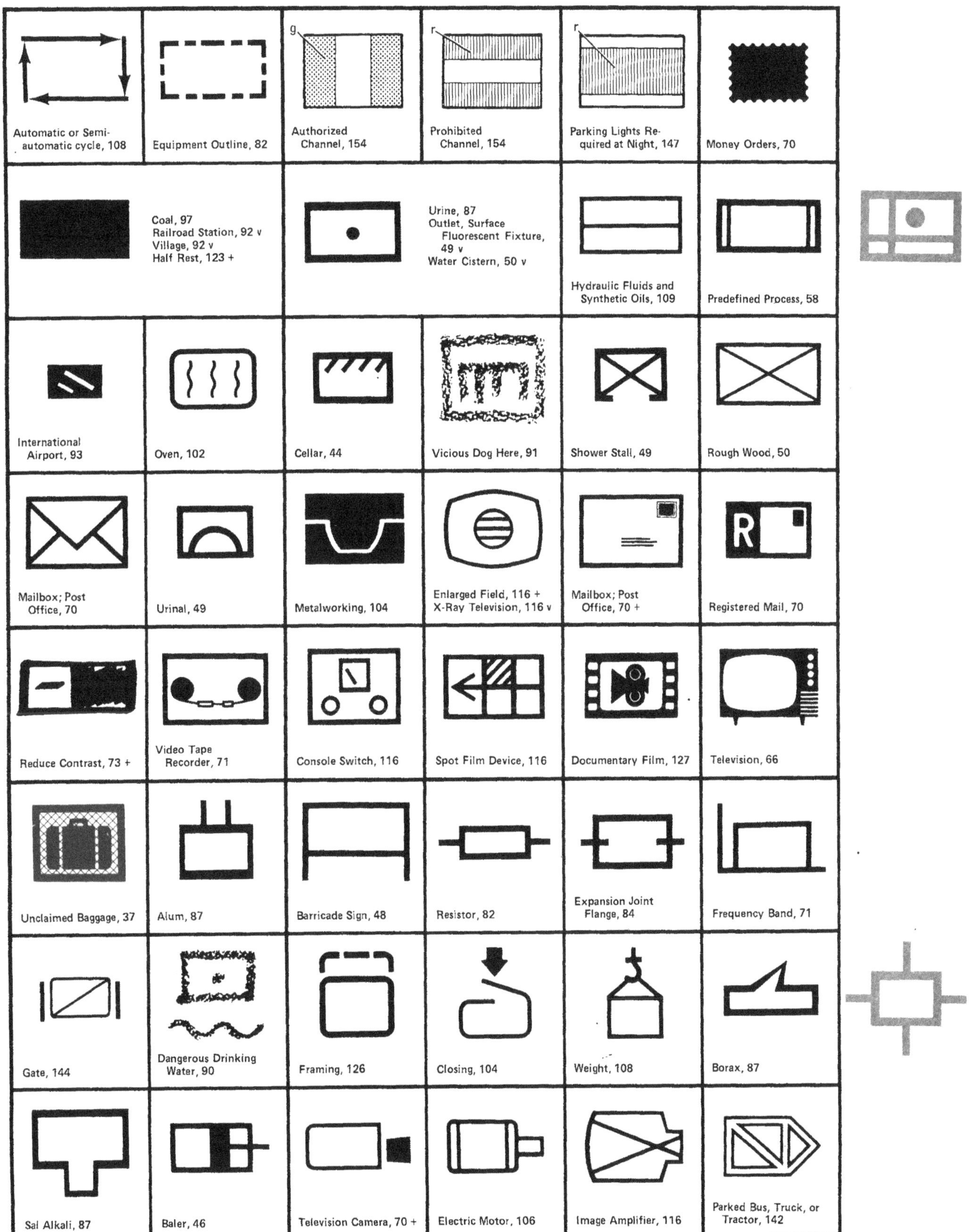

Automatic or Semi-automatic cycle, 108
Equipment Outline, 82
g
Authorized Channel, 154
r
Prohibited Channel, 154
r
Parking Lights Required at Night, 147
Money Orders, 70
Coal, 97
Railroad Station, 92 v
Village, 92 v
Half Rest, 123 +
Urine, 87
Outlet, Surface Fluorescent Fixture, 49 v
Water Cistern, 50 v
Hydraulic Fluids and Synthetic Oils, 109
Predefined Process, 58
International Airport, 93
Oven, 102
Cellar, 44
Vicious Dog Here, 91
Shower Stall, 49
Rough Wood, 50
Mailbox; Post Office, 70
Urinal, 49
Metalworking, 104
Enlarged Field, 116 +
X-Ray Television, 116 v
Mailbox; Post Office, 70 +
R
Registered Mail, 70
Reduce Contrast, 73 +
Video Tape Recorder, 71
Console Switch, 116
Spot Film Device, 116
Documentary Film, 127
Television, 66
Unclaimed Baggage, 37
Alum, 87
Barricade Sign, 48
Resistor, 82
Expansion Joint Flange, 84
Frequency Band, 71
Gate, 144
Dangerous Drinking Water, 90
Framing, 126
Closing, 104
Weight, 108
Borax, 87
Sal Alkali, 87
Baler, 46
Television Camera, 70 +
Electric Motor, 106
Image Amplifier, 116
Parked Bus, Truck, or Tractor, 142

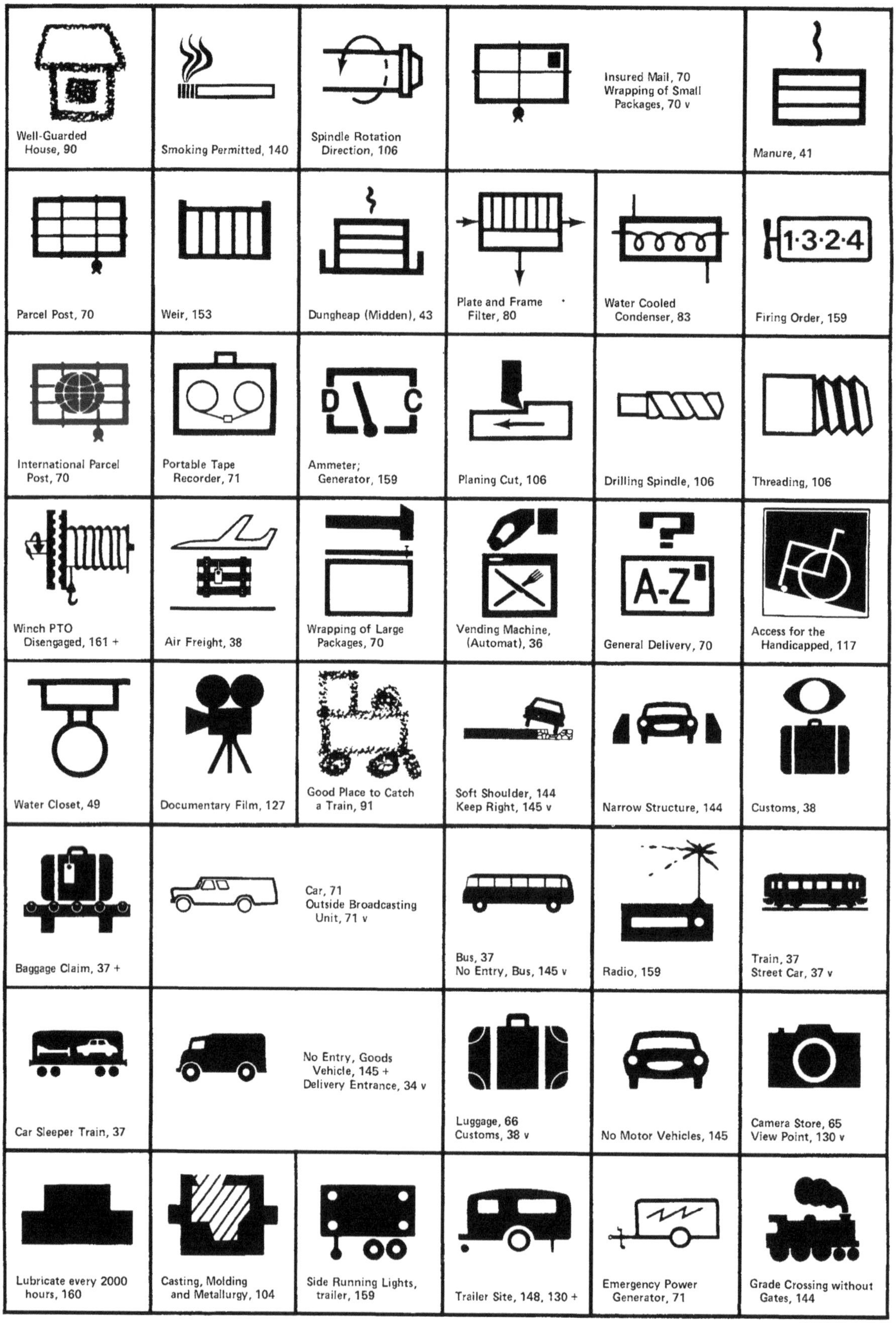

GRAPHIC FORM

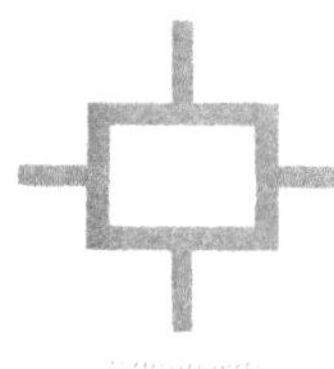

Well-Guarded House, 90	Smoking Permitted, 140	Spindle Rotation Direction, 106	Insured Mail, 70 Wrapping of Small Packages, 70 v		Manure, 41
Parcel Post, 70	Weir, 153	Dungheap (Midden), 43	Plate and Frame Filter, 80	Water Cooled Condenser, 83	Firing Order, 159
International Parcel Post, 70	Portable Tape Recorder, 71	Ammeter; Generator, 159	Planing Cut, 106	Drilling Spindle, 106	Threading, 106
Winch PTO Disengaged, 161 +	Air Freight, 38	Wrapping of Large Packages, 70	Vending Machine, (Automat), 36	General Delivery, 70	Access for the Handicapped, 117
Water Closet, 49	Documentary Film, 127	Good Place to Catch a Train, 91	Soft Shoulder, 144 Keep Right, 145 v	Narrow Structure, 144	Customs, 38
Baggage Claim, 37 +	Car, 71 Outside Broadcasting Unit, 71 v		Bus, 37 No Entry, Bus, 145 v	Radio, 159	Train, 37 Street Car, 37 v
Car Sleeper Train, 37	No Entry, Goods Vehicle, 145 + Delivery Entrance, 34 v		Luggage, 66 Customs, 38 v	No Motor Vehicles, 145	Camera Store, 65 View Point, 130 v
Lubricate every 2000 hours, 160	Casting, Molding and Metallurgy, 104	Side Running Lights, trailer, 159	Trailer Site, 148, 130 +	Emergency Power Generator, 71	Grade Crossing without Gates, 144

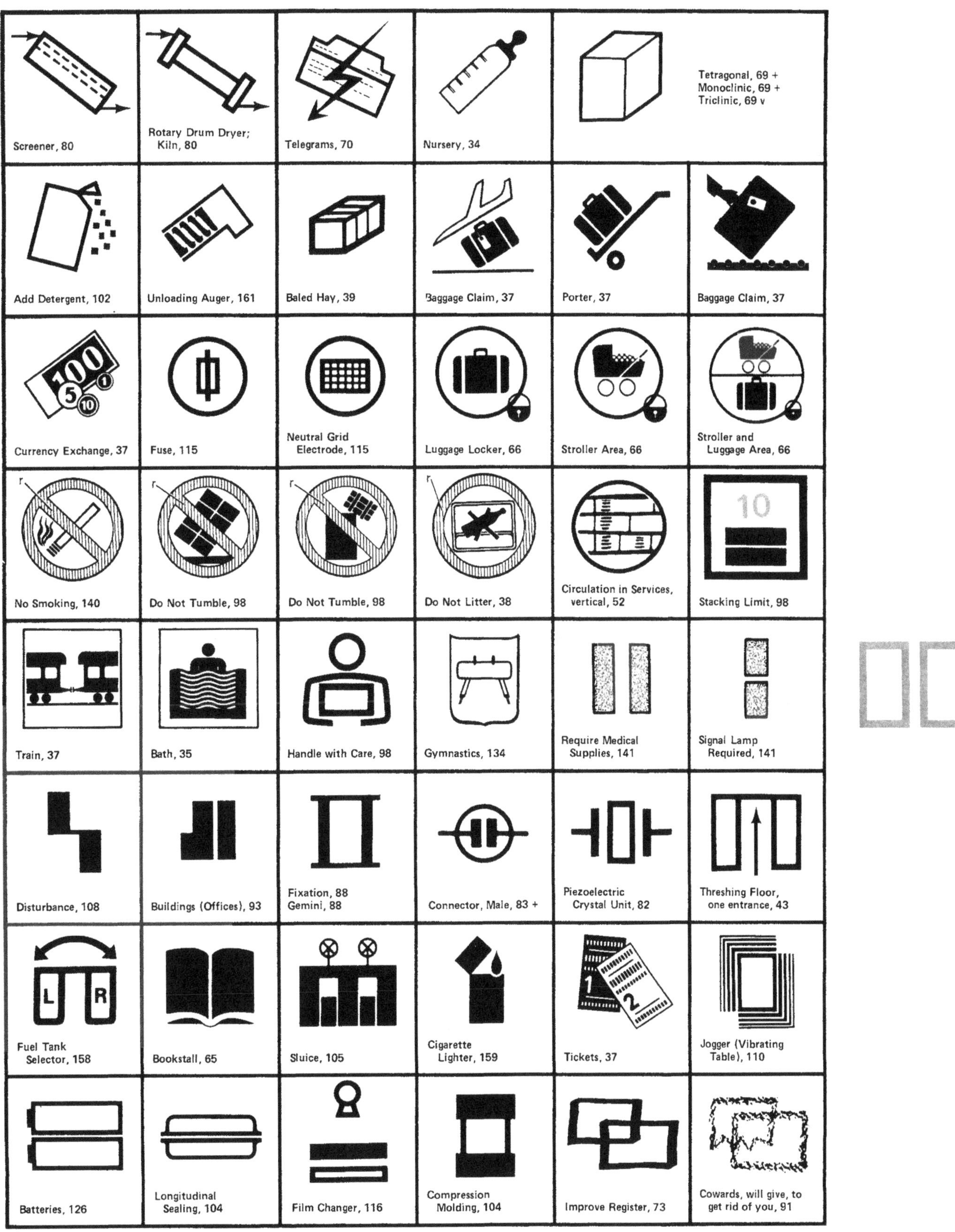
Screener, 80
Rotary Drum Dryer; Kiln, 80
Telegrams, 70
Nursery, 34
Tetragonal, 69 +
Monoclinic, 69 +
Triclinic, 69 v
Add Detergent, 102
Unloading Auger, 161
Baled Hay, 39
Baggage Claim, 37
Porter, 37
Baggage Claim, 37
100
5
10
1
Currency Exchange, 37
Fuse, 115
Neutral Grid Electrode, 115
Luggage Locker, 66
Stroller Area, 66
Stroller and Luggage Area, 66
No Smoking, 140
Do Not Tumble, 98
Do Not Tumble, 98
Do Not Litter, 38
Circulation in Services, vertical, 52
10
Stacking Limit, 98
Train, 37
Bath, 35
Handle with Care, 98
Gymnastics, 134
Require Medical Supplies, 141
Signal Lamp Required, 141
Disturbance, 108
Buildings (Offices), 93
Fixation, 88
Gemini, 88
Connector, Male, 83 +
Piezoelectric Crystal Unit, 82
Threshing Floor, one entrance, 43
L
R
Fuel Tank Selector, 158
Bookstall, 65
Sluice, 105
Cigarette Lighter, 159
1
2
Tickets, 37
Jogger (Vibrating Table), 110
Batteries, 126
Longitudinal Sealing, 104
Film Changer, 116
Compression Molding, 104
Improve Register, 73
Cowards, will give, to get rid of you, 91

(continued)

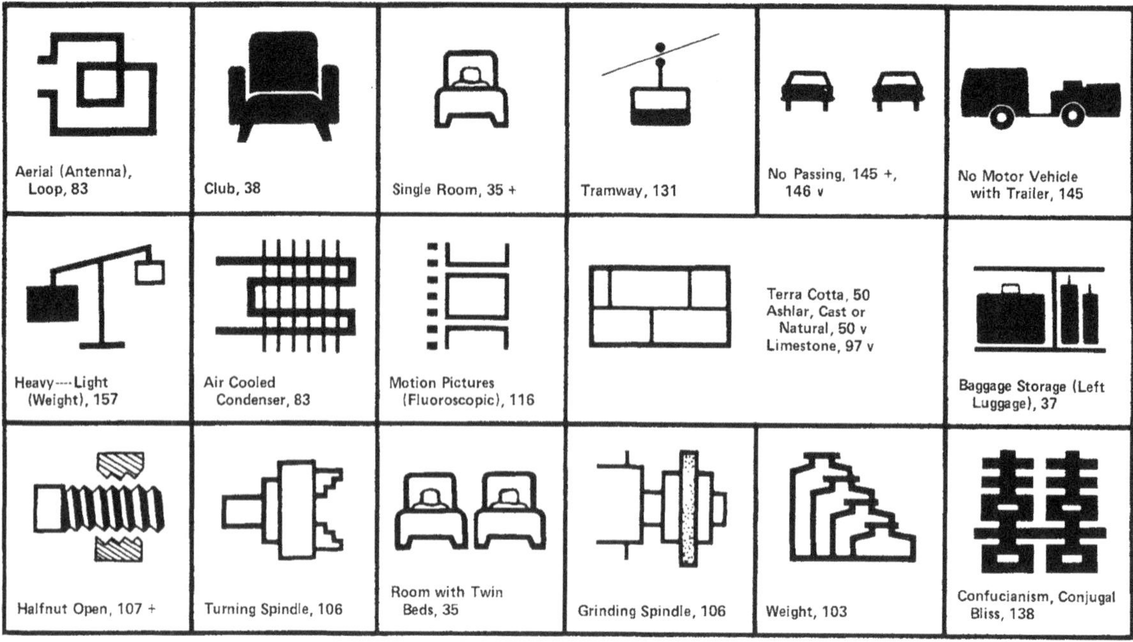
Aerial (Antenna), Loop, 83
Club, 38
Single Room, 35 +
Tramway, 131
No Passing, 145 +, 146 v
No Motor Vehicle with Trailer, 145
Heavy----Light (Weight), 157
Air Cooled Condenser, 83
Motion Pictures (Fluoroscopic), 116
Terra Cotta, 50
Ashlar, Cast or Natural, 50 v
Limestone, 97 v
Baggage Storage (Left Luggage), 37
Halfnut Open, 107 +
Turning Spindle, 106
Room with Twin Beds, 35
Grinding Spindle, 106
Weight, 103
Confucianism, Conjugal Bliss, 138

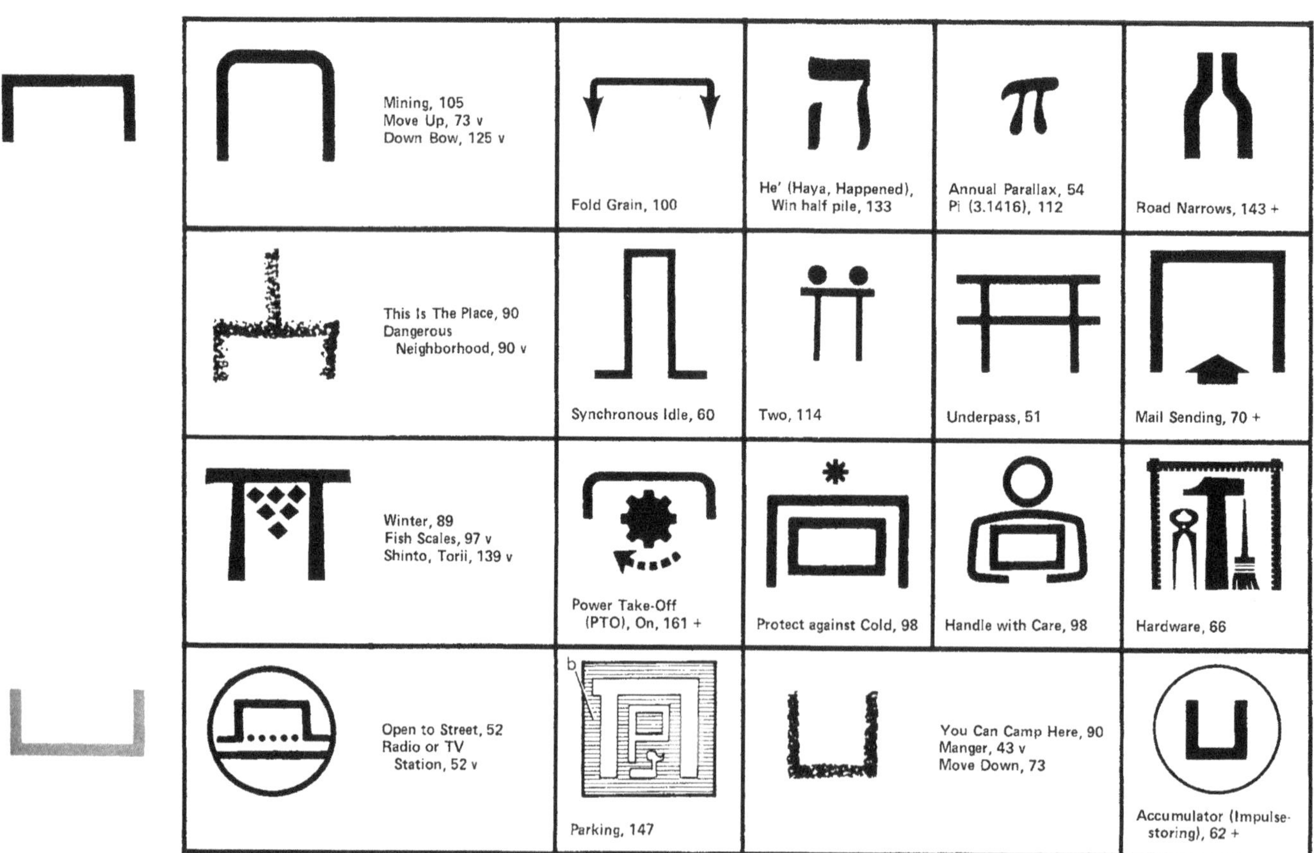
Mining, 105
Move Up, 73 v
Down Bow, 125 v
Fold Grain, 100
He' (Haya, Happened), Win half pile, 133
Annual Parallax, 54
Pi (3.1416), 112
Road Narrows, 143 +
This Is The Place, 90
Dangerous Neighborhood, 90 v
Synchronous Idle, 60
Two, 114
Underpass, 51
Mail Sending, 70 +
Winter, 89
Fish Scales, 97 v
Shinto, Torii, 139 v
Power Take-Off (PTO), On, 161 +
Protect against Cold, 98
Handle with Care, 98
Hardware, 66
Open to Street, 52
Radio or TV Station, 52 v
b
Parking, 147
You Can Camp Here, 90
Manger, 43 v
Move Down, 73
Accumulator (Impulse-storing), 62 +

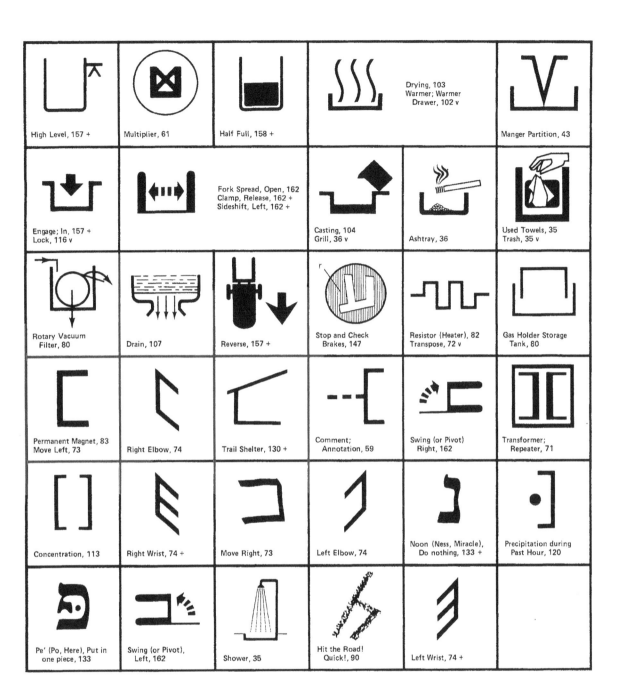

High Level, 157 +	Multiplier, 61	Half Full, 158 +	Drying, 103 Warmer; Warmer Drawer, 102 v		Manger Partition, 43
Engage; In, 157 + Lock, 116 v	Fork Spread, Open, 162 Clamp, Release, 162 + Sideshift, Left, 162 +		Casting, 104 Grill, 36 v	Ashtray, 36	Used Towels, 35 Trash, 35 v
Rotary Vacuum Filter, 80	Drain, 107	Reverse, 157 +	Stop and Check Brakes, 147	Resistor (Heater), 82 Transpose, 72 v	Gas Holder Storage Tank, 80
Permanent Magnet, 83 Move Left, 73	Right Elbow, 74	Trail Shelter, 130 +	Comment; Annotation, 59	Swing (or Pivot) Right, 162	Transformer; Repeater, 71
Concentration, 113	Right Wrist, 74 +	Move Right, 73	Left Elbow, 74	Noon (Ness, Miracle), Do nothing, 133 +	Precipitation during Past Hour, 120
Pe' (Po, Here), Put in one piece, 133	Swing (or Pivot), Left, 162	Shower, 35	Hit the Road! Quick!, 90	Left Wrist, 74 +	

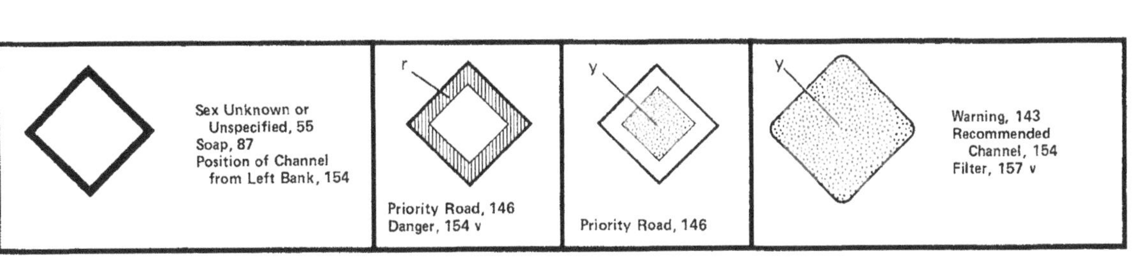

Sex Unknown or Unspecified, 55
Soap, 87
Position of Channel from Left Bank, 154
r
Priority Road, 146
Danger, 154 v
y
Priority Road, 146
y
Warning, 143
Recommended Channel, 154
Filter, 157 v

GRAPHIC FORM

(continued)

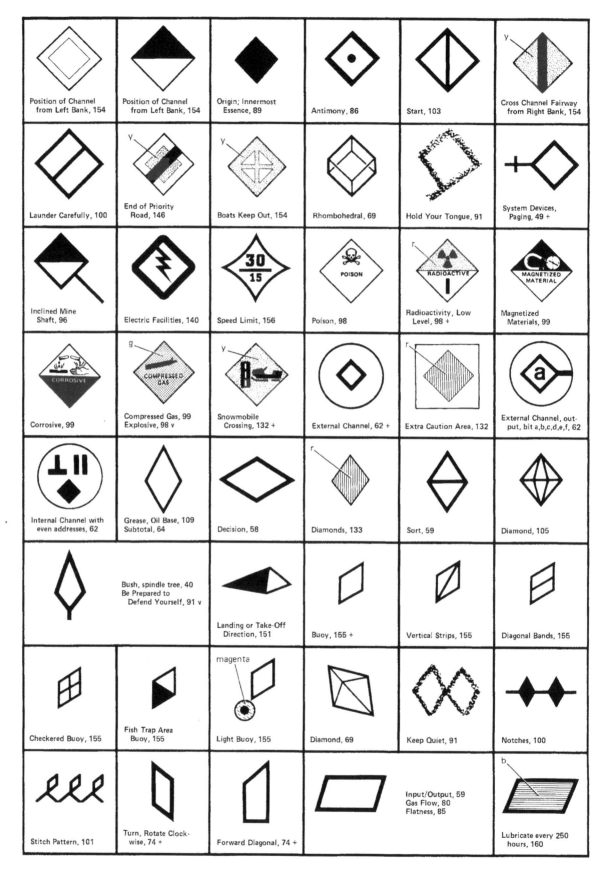

Position of Channel from Left Bank, 154	Position of Channel from Left Bank, 154	Origin; Innermost Essence, 89	Antimony, 86	Start, 103	y Cross Channel Fairway from Right Bank, 154
Launder Carefully, 100	y End of Priority Road, 146	y Boats Keep Out, 154	Rhombohedral, 69	Hold Your Tongue, 91	System Devices, Paging, 49 +
Inclined Mine Shaft, 96	Electric Facilities, 140	30 15 Speed Limit, 156	POISON Poison, 98	r RADIOACTIVE Radioactivity, Low Level, 98 +	MAGNETIZED MATERIAL Magnetized Materials, 99
CORROSIVE Corrosive, 99	g COMPRESSED GAS Compressed Gas, 99 Explosive, 98 v	y Snowmobile Crossing, 132 +	External Channel, 62 +	r Extra Caution Area, 132	a External Channel, output, bit a,b,c,d,e,f, 62
Internal Channel with even addresses, 62	Grease, Oil Base, 109 Subtotal, 64	Decision, 58	r Diamonds, 133	Sort, 59	Diamond, 105
	Bush, spindle tree, 40 Be Prepared to Defend Yourself, 91 v	Landing or Take-Off Direction, 151	Buoy, 155 +	Vertical Strips, 155	Diagonal Bands, 155
Checkered Buoy, 155	Fish Trap Area Buoy, 155	magenta Light Buoy, 155	Diamond, 69	Keep Quiet, 91	Notches, 100
Stitch Pattern, 101	Turn, Rotate Clockwise, 74 +	Forward Diagonal, 74 +		Input/Output, 59 Gas Flow, 80 Flatness, 85	b Lubricate every 250 hours, 160

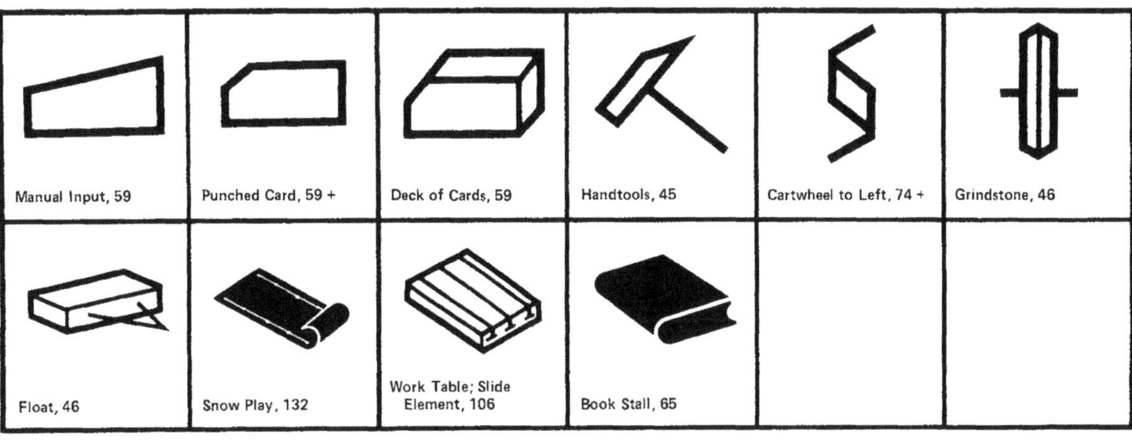

Manual Input, 59
Punched Card, 59 +
Deck of Cards, 59
Handtools, 45
Cartwheel to Left, 74 +
Grindstone, 46
Float, 46
Snow Play, 132
Work Table; Slide Element, 106
Book Stall, 65

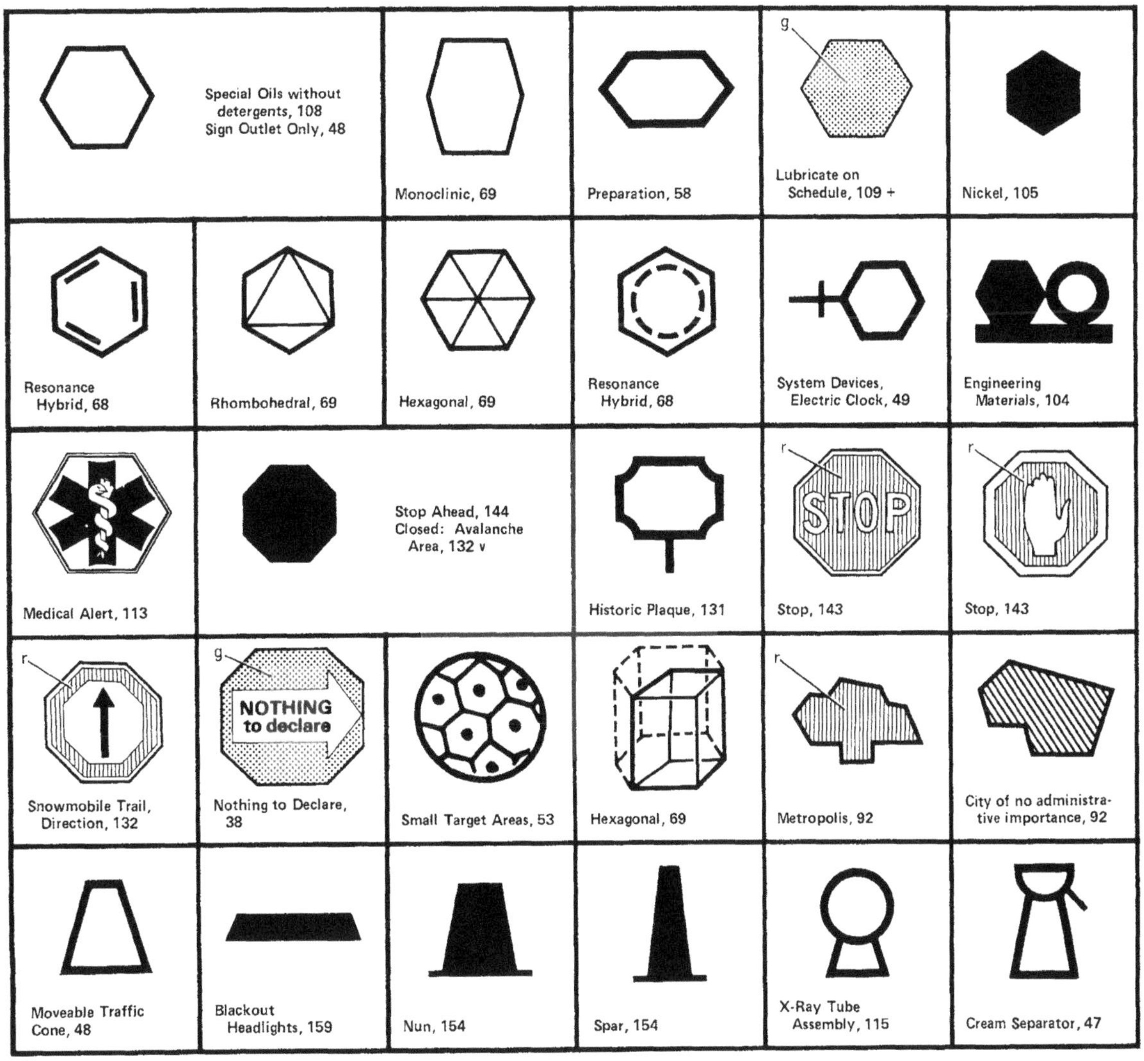

Special Oils without detergents, 108 Sign Outlet Only, 48		Monoclinic, 69	Preparation, 58	g Lubricate on Schedule, 109 +	Nickel, 105
Resonance Hybrid, 68	Rhombohedral, 69	Hexagonal, 69	Resonance Hybrid, 68	System Devices, Electric Clock, 49	Engineering Materials, 104
Medical Alert, 113	Stop Ahead, 144 Closed: Avalanche Area, 132 v		Historic Plaque, 131	r STOP Stop, 143	r Stop, 143
r Snowmobile Trail, Direction, 132	g NOTHING to declare Nothing to Declare, 38	Small Target Areas, 53	Hexagonal, 69	r Metropolis, 92	City of no administrative importance, 92
Moveable Traffic Cone, 48	Blackout Headlights, 159	Nun, 154	Spar, 154	X-Ray Tube Assembly, 115	Cream Separator, 47

GRAPHIC FORM

Castle, 95	Cultural Monument, 131	Lighthouse, 131, 94	Lookout Tower, 130	Picnic Area, 130	Oil, 105
Telecommunications, 93	Windmill, 95	Projector, 71	Use Cool Iron, 101 +	Feeder Ready or Moving, 109	Well-Guarded House, 90 +
General Surgery, 119 +	Vacuum Paper Feeder, Vertical, 109	Vacuum Paper Feeder, Tilt, 109	Loader Bucket, Dump, 161	Quayside or River Bank, 144	Blackout Clearance Lights, 159
City of administrative importance, 92	Manual Operation, 58 Plug; Slot, 84	Arc-Spot; Arc Seam, 84	Scoop for Front Loader, 46	Mooring Buoy, 155	Filling Station, 43
Sprayer, 47 +	Atomizer, 47	Basket Lift, Up, 161	Trench Silo, 43	Duster, 47	Coal Mining, 105
Loader Bucket, Roll Back, 161	Bath, 35	Motor Boating, 131	Ferry, 36	Large Seaport, 94	Ship, 36
Truck Crossing, 144	Bath, 35	Market; Grocery, 65	Whistle Buoy, 154	Hot Shelves on Stove, 102	Basketball, 135
Comb, 109 Feeder, Sheet, 109 v	Feeder, Sheet, 109		Threaded Bushing, 84	Clutch Engaged, 158 +	Radiography, 116

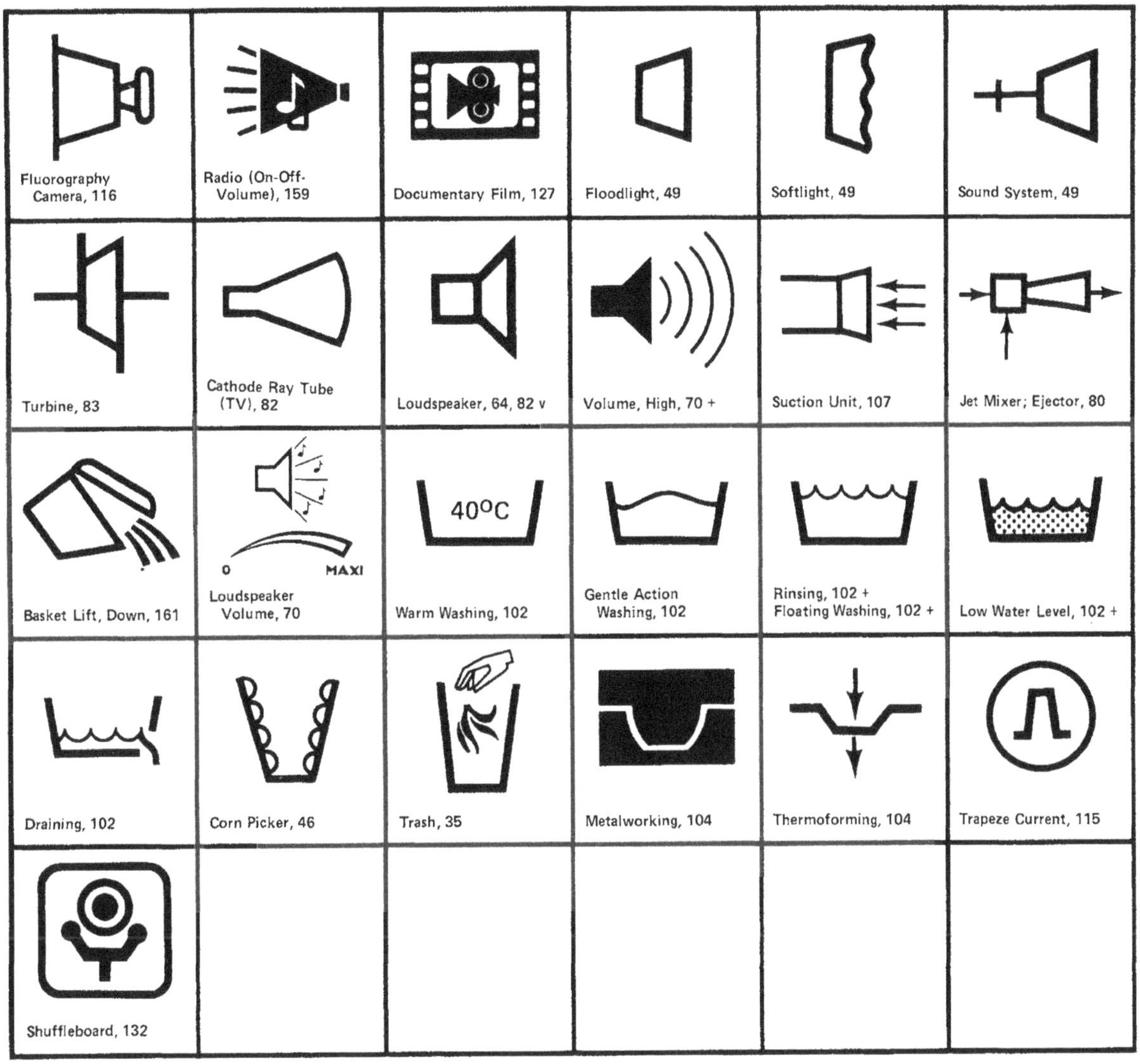

Fluorography Camera, 116	Radio (On-Off-Volume), 159	Documentary Film, 127	Floodlight, 49	Softlight, 49	Sound System, 49
Turbine, 83	Cathode Ray Tube (TV), 82	Loudspeaker, 64, 82 v	Volume, High, 70 +	Suction Unit, 107	Jet Mixer; Ejector, 80
Basket Lift, Down, 161	0 MAXI Loudspeaker Volume, 70	40°C Warm Washing, 102	Gentle Action Washing, 102	Rinsing, 102 + Floating Washing, 102 +	Low Water Level, 102 +
Draining, 102	Corn Picker, 46	Trash, 35	Metalworking, 104	Thermoforming, 104	Trapeze Current, 115
Shuffleboard, 132					

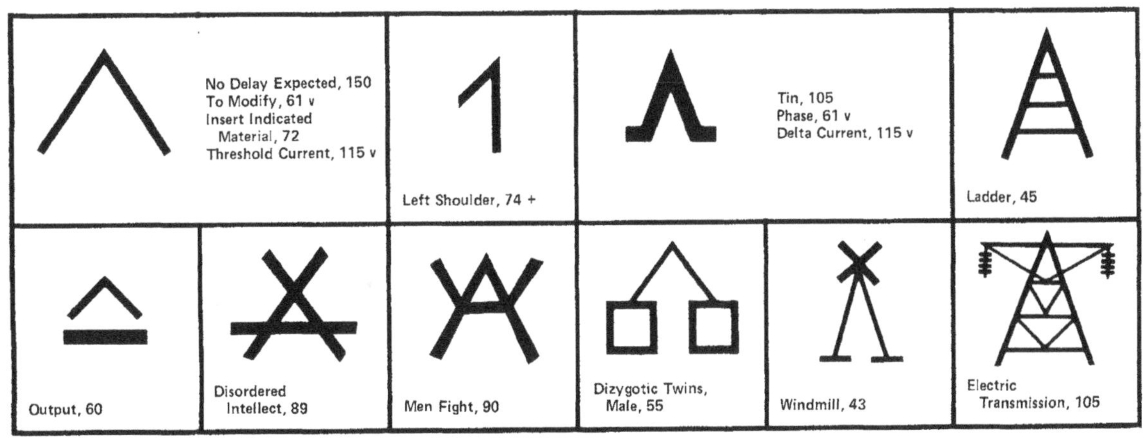

No Delay Expected, 150
To Modify, 61 v
Insert Indicated Material, 72
Threshold Current, 115 v
Left Shoulder, 74 +
Tin, 105
Phase, 61 v
Delta Current, 115 v
Ladder, 45
Output, 60
Disordered Intellect, 89
Men Fight, 90
Dizygotic Twins, Male, 55
Windmill, 43
Electric Transmission, 105

GRAPHIC FORM

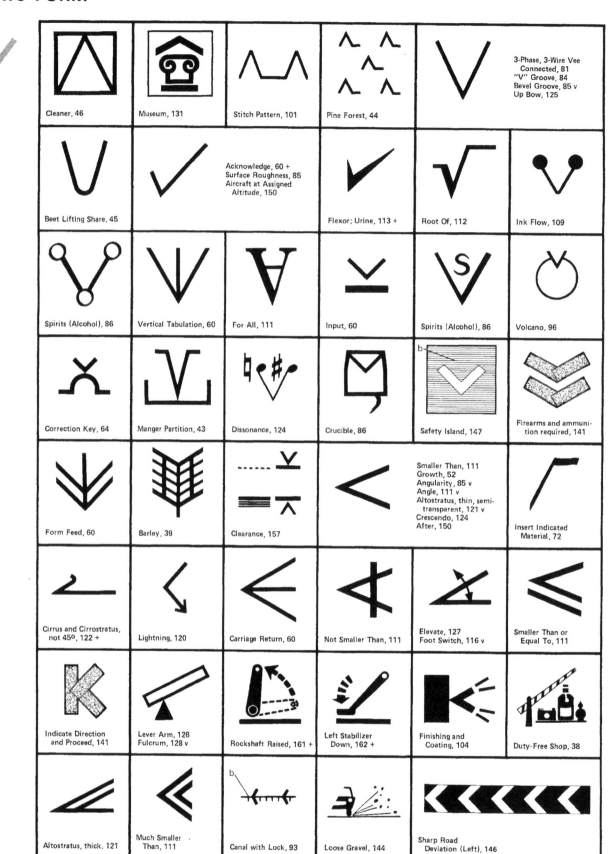

Cleaner, 46	Museum, 131	Stitch Pattern, 101	Pine Forest, 44	3-Phase, 3-Wire Vee Connected, 81 "V" Groove, 84 Bevel Groove, 85 v Up Bow, 125	
Beet Lifting Share, 45	Acknowledge, 60 + Surface Roughness, 85 Aircraft at Assigned Altitude, 150		Flexor; Urine, 113 +	Root Of, 112	Ink Flow, 109
Spirits (Alcohol), 86	Vertical Tabulation, 60	For All, 111	Input, 60	Spirits (Alcohol), 86	Volcano, 96
Correction Key, 64	Manger Partition, 43	Dissonance, 124	Crucible, 86	b Safety Island, 147	Firearms and ammunition required, 141
Form Feed, 60	Barley, 39	Clearance, 157	Smaller Than, 111 Growth, 52 Angularity, 85 v Angle, 111 v Altostratus, thin, semi-transparent, 121 v Crescendo, 124 After, 150		Insert Indicated Material, 72
Cirrus and Cirrostratus, not 45°, 122 +	Lightning, 120	Carriage Return, 60	Not Smaller Than, 111	Elevate, 127 Foot Switch, 116 v	Smaller Than or Equal To, 111
Indicate Direction and Proceed, 141	Lever Arm, 128 Fulcrum, 128 v	Rockshaft Raised, 161 +	Left Stabilizer Down, 162 +	Finishing and Coating, 104	Duty-Free Shop, 38
Altostratus, thick, 121	Much Smaller Than, 111	b Canal with Lock, 93	Loose Gravel, 144	Sharp Road Deviation (Left), 146	

Feldspar, 97

Larger Than, 111
Decrescendo, 124
Marcato, 124
Before, 150

Non-Linear Variability, 82

Horizontal Tabulation, 60

Not Larger Than, 111

Larger Than or Equal To, 111
High Heat, 102 v

Will Attempt to Take Off, 141

Right Stabilizer, Down, 162 +

Presser Foot Pressure, 101

Material Removal, 104

Pawn Shop, 65

Record Turntable, 71

X-Ray Tube, 115

Much Larger Than, 111

Non-landing Area
Blast Pad
Deceptive Area, 151

Mean Value, 112

Swell, 124

Chute, 43

Cirrostratus, veil covering sky, 122

Saturable Properties, 82
Cart Rental, 37 v

Jump, 61

Limiter, 71

Jump when there is a comparison, 62 +

Circular Path Left, 74 +

Balance, 46

Body Section Radiography, 116

Massive Igneous Rock, 97 +

Rack, 45
3-Phase 3-Wire (Star), 81
"Y" Junction, 143

Yes, 141

3-Phase 4-Wire (Star), 81

Hemp, 39

Roller Crusher, 80

Sprinkler, 47

Departing Flights, 37 +

Man, 89

Directional Aerial, 71 +

Lateral Joint, Threaded, 84

Yen, 58

Receiving Station, 71 +

r
b
No Thru Road, 146

Peripheral Unit, 61

Friendship among Men, 90

6-Phase; Fork with Neutral, 81

To Select, 61

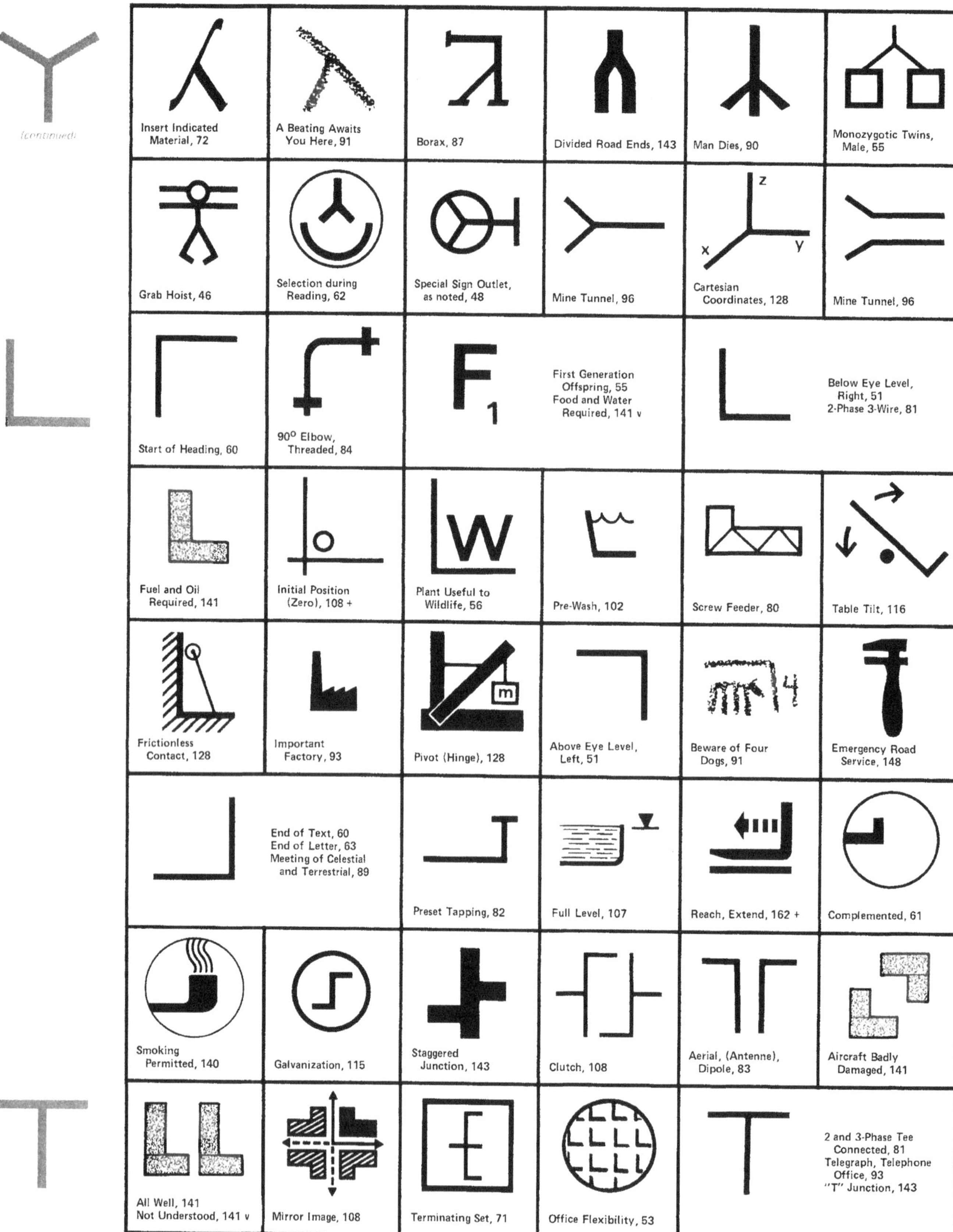
(continued)
Insert Indicated Material, 72
A Beating Awaits You Here, 91
Borax, 87
Divided Road Ends, 143
Man Dies, 90
Monozygotic Twins, Male, 55
Grab Hoist, 46
Selection during Reading, 62
Special Sign Outlet, as noted, 48
Mine Tunnel, 96
z
x
y
Cartesian Coordinates, 128
Mine Tunnel, 96
Start of Heading, 60
90° Elbow, Threaded, 84
F
1
First Generation Offspring, 55
Food and Water Required, 141 v
Below Eye Level, Right, 51
2-Phase 3-Wire, 81
Fuel and Oil Required, 141
Initial Position (Zero), 108 +
W
Plant Useful to Wildlife, 56
Pre-Wash, 102
Screw Feeder, 80
Table Tilt, 116
Frictionless Contact, 128
Important Factory, 93
m
Pivot (Hinge), 128
Above Eye Level, Left, 51
4
Beware of Four Dogs, 91
Emergency Road Service, 148
End of Text, 60
End of Letter, 63
Meeting of Celestial and Terrestrial, 89
Preset Tapping, 82
Full Level, 107
Reach, Extend, 162 +
Complemented, 61
Smoking Permitted, 140
Galvanization, 115
Staggered Junction, 143
Clutch, 108
Aerial, (Antenne), Dipole, 83
Aircraft Badly Damaged, 141
All Well, 141
Not Understood, 141 v
Mirror Image, 108
Terminating Set, 71
Office Flexibility, 53
2 and 3-Phase Tee Connected, 81
Telegraph, Telephone Office, 93
"T" Junction, 143

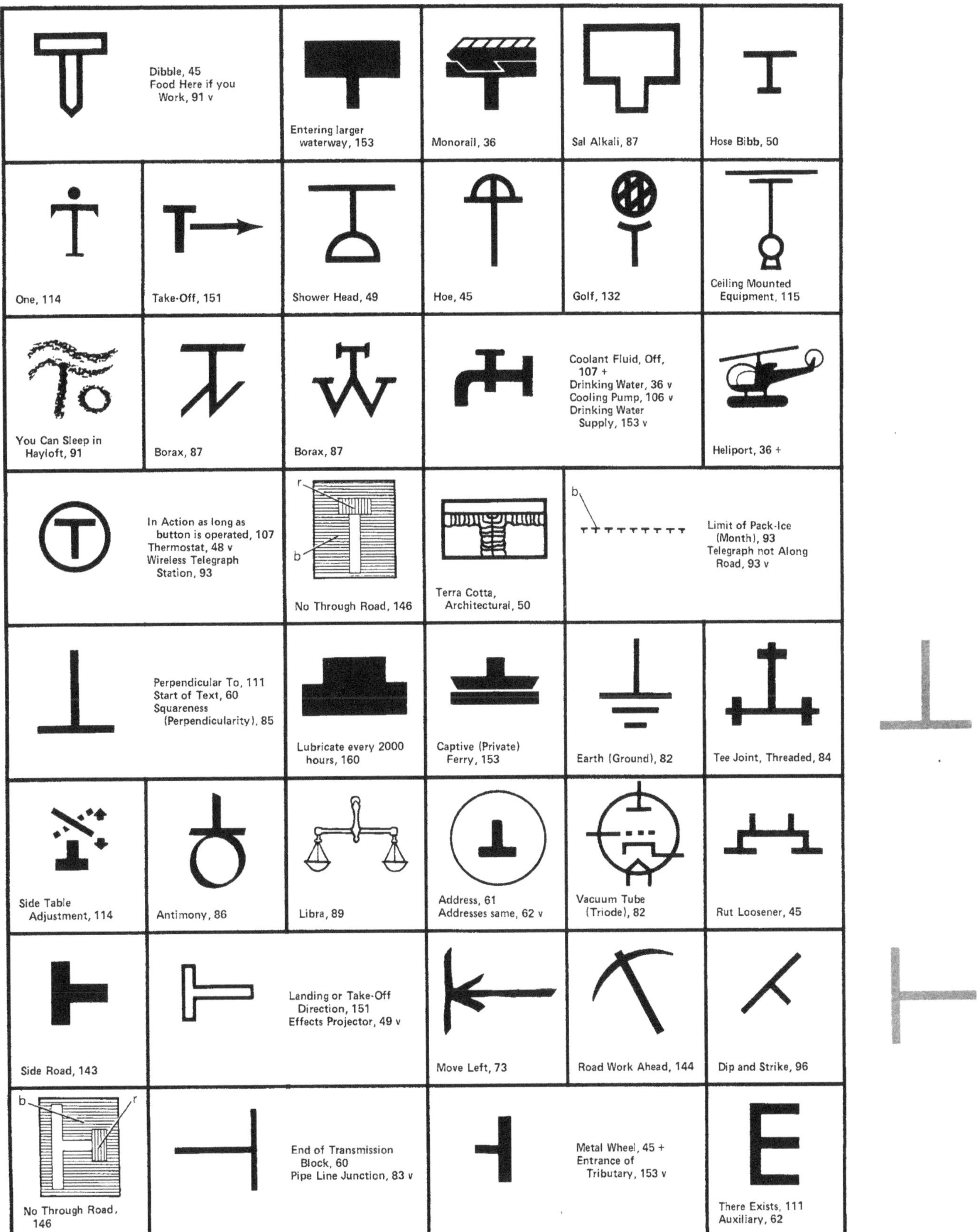

Dibble, 45
Food Here if you Work, 91 v
Entering larger waterway, 153
Monorail, 36
Sal Alkali, 87
Hose Bibb, 50
One, 114
Take-Off, 151
Shower Head, 49
Hoe, 45
Golf, 132
Ceiling Mounted Equipment, 115
You Can Sleep in Hayloft, 91
Borax, 87
Borax, 87
Coolant Fluid, Off, 107 +
Drinking Water, 36 v
Cooling Pump, 106 v
Drinking Water Supply, 153 v
Heliport, 36 +
In Action as long as button is operated, 107
Thermostat, 48 v
Wireless Telegraph Station, 93
r
b
No Through Road, 146
Terra Cotta, Architectural, 50
b
Limit of Pack-Ice (Month), 93
Telegraph not Along Road, 93 v
Perpendicular To, 111
Start of Text, 60
Squareness (Perpendicularity), 85
Lubricate every 2000 hours, 160
Captive (Private) Ferry, 153
Earth (Ground), 82
Tee Joint, Threaded, 84
Side Table Adjustment, 114
Antimony, 86
Libra, 89
Address, 61
Addresses same, 62 v
Vacuum Tube (Triode), 82
Rut Loosener, 45
Side Road, 143
Landing or Take-Off Direction, 151
Effects Projector, 49 v
Move Left, 73
Road Work Ahead, 144
Dip and Strike, 96
b
r
No Through Road, 146
End of Transmission Block, 60
Pipe Line Junction, 83 v
Metal Wheel, 45 +
Entrance of Tributary, 153 v
There Exists, 111
Auxiliary, 62

GRAPHIC FORM

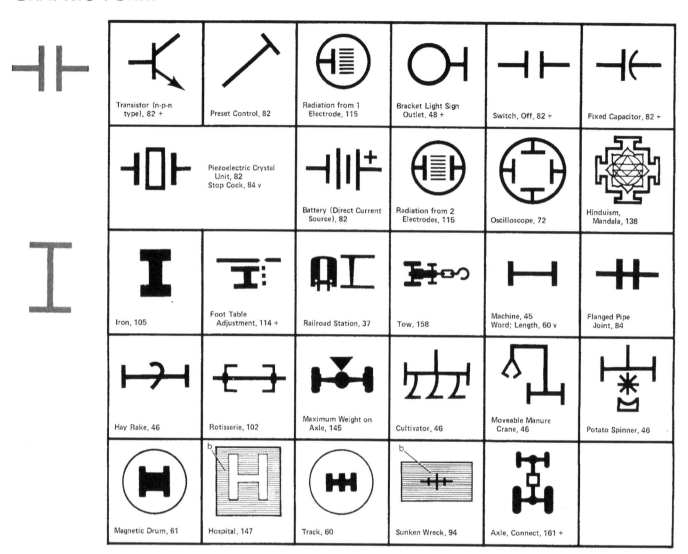

Transistor (n-p-n type), 82 +	Preset Control, 82	Radiation from 1 Electrode, 115	Bracket Light Sign Outlet, 48 +	Switch, Off, 82 +	Fixed Capacitor, 82 +
Piezoelectric Crystal Unit, 82 Stop Cock, 84 v		Battery (Direct Current Source), 82	Radiation from 2 Electrodes, 115	Oscilloscope, 72	Hinduism, Mandala, 138
Iron, 105	Foot Table Adjustment, 114 +	Railroad Station, 37	Tow, 158	Machine, 45 Word; Length, 60 v	Flanged Pipe Joint, 84
Hay Rake, 46	Rotisserie, 102	Maximum Weight on Axle, 145	Cultivator, 46	Moveable Manure Crane, 46	Potato Spinner, 46
Magnetic Drum, 61	Hospital, 147	Track, 60	Sunken Wreck, 94	Axle, Connect, 161 +	

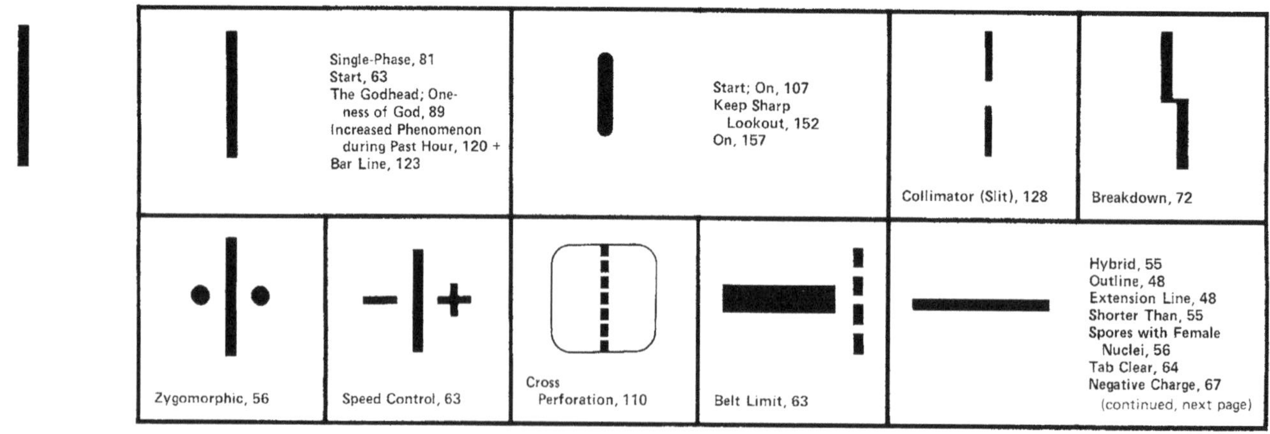

Single-Phase, 81
Start, 63
The Godhead; Oneness of God, 89
Increased Phenomenon during Past Hour, 120 +
Bar Line, 123
Start; On, 107
Keep Sharp Lookout, 152
On, 157
Collimator (Slit), 128
Breakdown, 72
Zygomorphic, 56
Speed Control, 63
Cross Perforation, 110
Belt Limit, 63
Hybrid, 55
Outline, 48
Extension Line, 48
Shorter Than, 55
Spores with Female Nuclei, 56
Tab Clear, 64
Negative Charge, 67
(continued, next page)

(continued) Set In Italic, 72; Direct Current (DC), 81; Negative Polarity, 81; Uninsulated Coupling, 82; Waste Water, 83; Straightness, 85; Flush Contour, 85; Earth, 89; Doubtful, 90; Main Road, 92; Submarine Cable, 93; Cutting Line, 100; Simmer, 102; Minus, 111; Stratus and/or Fractostratus, 121	Obligation to Stop, 152	Cirrus filaments, 122 +; Dipstick, 160 v	Center Line, 48; Cold Water, 83; Provincial or State, 92 v; Incorporated Village, 92 v	
Phantom Line, 48; Hot Water Supply, 83; International, 92 +; County, 92 v	Hot Water Return, 83; Township, 92 v	Vent Pipe, 84; Hidden Line, 48; Insulated Coupling, 82; Track; Path, 92 v; Small Park, Cemetery, 92	Telephone or Pipe Line, 93; Stitching Line, 100; Shorten to Line, 100 +; Stitch Pattern, 101 v; Fractostratus, 121	
Measures Rest, 123	Fault (Lateral Displacement), 92	Finished, 60	Jump Perforation, 110 +	Threaded Pipe Joint, 84; Union, Threaded, 84 v; Plus or Minus, 111 v
Divided By, 111	Wire Fence, 43	Morse Code, 75 +	Reservation, national or state, 92; Route of Explorers, 95 v	Power Transmission Line, 93
Land Grant, 92	Explorer Route From Reports, 95	Lateral Punch Control, 110	Drawbar, 45; Narrow Gauge Track, 92 v	Telegraph Along Road, 93
Navigable Canal, 93	Breakwater; Pier, 94	Railroad Track, single, 92 +	Outlet, Bare-lamp Fluorescent Strip, 49; Lengthen amount between line and cuff, 100 v	Medium Pressure Steam Supply, 83 +
Expand, 65; Fork for Front Loader, 46 v; Half Space, 65 v	Barbed Wire Fence, 43	End of Prohibition, 153	Shilling, 58; Divided By, 111; Extensor; Extension, 113; After; After Passing, 150	
Attitude of Joint, 92	Normal Fault, 92	Hand Brake Engaged, 158 +	Insert Lift Cart Here, 98	Non-Linear Variability, 82
Not (Negation), 60				

GRAPHIC FORM

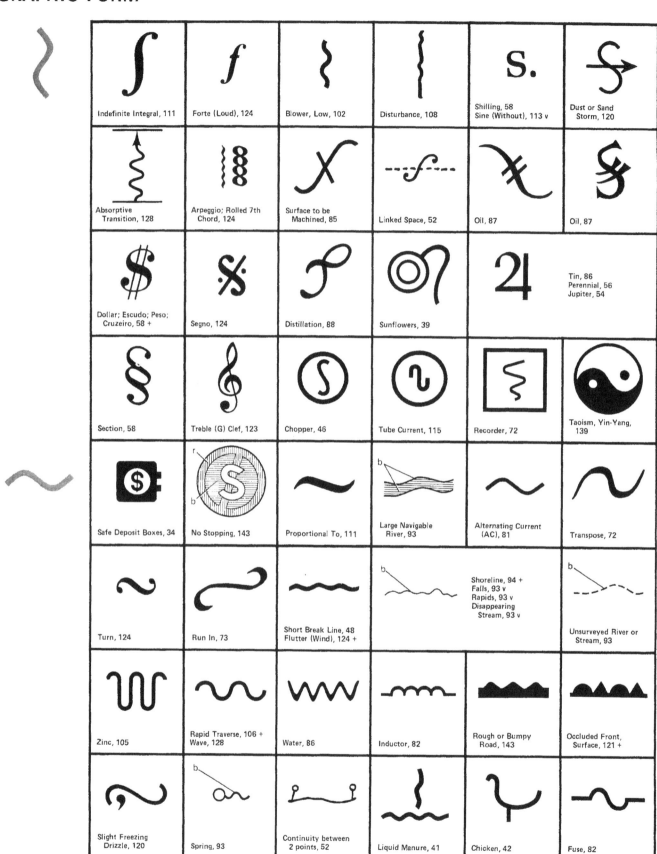

Indefinite Integral, 111	Forte (Loud), 124	Blower, Low, 102	Disturbance, 108	Shilling, 58 Sine (Without), 113 v	Dust or Sand Storm, 120
Absorptive Transition, 128	Arpeggio; Rolled 7th Chord, 124	Surface to be Machined, 85	Linked Space, 52	Oil, 87	Oil, 87
Dollar; Escudo; Peso; Cruzeiro, 58 +	Segno, 124	Distillation, 88	Sunflowers, 39		Tin, 86 Perennial, 56 Jupiter, 54
Section, 58	Treble (G) Clef, 123	Chopper, 46	Tube Current, 115	Recorder, 72	Taoism, Yin-Yang, 139
Safe Deposit Boxes, 34	No Stopping, 143	Proportional To, 111	Large Navigable River, 93	Alternating Current (AC), 81	Transpose, 72
Turn, 124	Run In, 73	Short Break Line, 48 Flutter (Wind), 124 +		Shoreline, 94 + Falls, 93 v Rapids, 93 v Disappearing Stream, 93 v	Unsurveyed River or Stream, 93
Zinc, 105	Rapid Traverse, 106 + Wave, 128	Water, 86	Inductor, 82	Rough or Bumpy Road, 143	Occluded Front, Surface, 121 +
Slight Freezing Drizzle, 120	Spring, 93	Continuity between 2 points, 52	Liquid Manure, 41	Chicken, 42	Fuse, 82

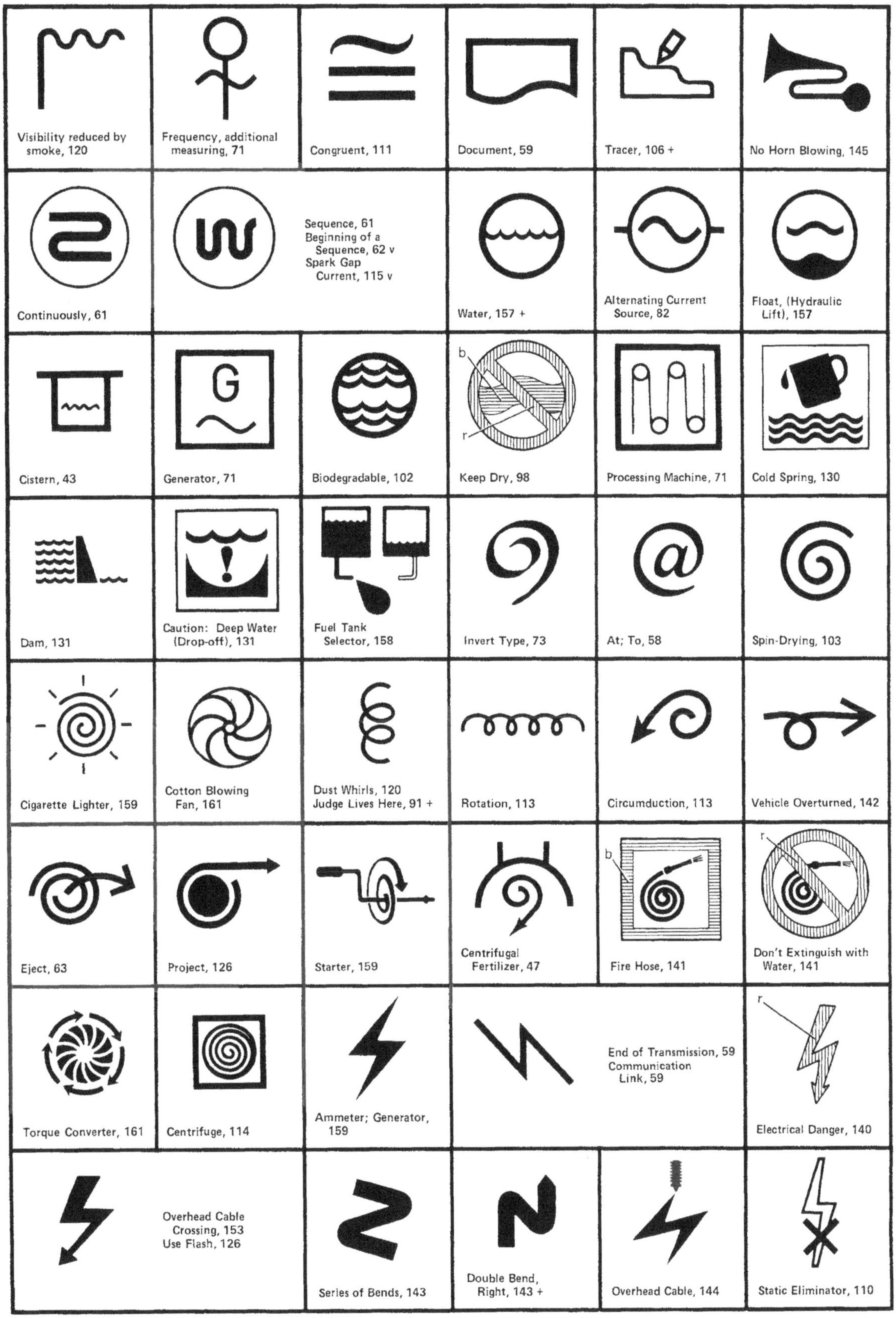

Visibility reduced by smoke, 120	Frequency, additional measuring, 71	Congruent, 111	Document, 59	Tracer, 106 +	No Horn Blowing, 145
Continuously, 61	Sequence, 61 Beginning of a Sequence, 62 v Spark Gap Current, 115 v		Water, 157 +	Alternating Current Source, 82	Float, (Hydraulic Lift), 157
Cistern, 43	Generator, 71	Biodegradable, 102	Keep Dry, 98	Processing Machine, 71	Cold Spring, 130
Dam, 131	Caution: Deep Water (Drop-off), 131	Fuel Tank Selector, 158	Invert Type, 73	At; To, 58	Spin-Drying, 103
Cigarette Lighter, 159	Cotton Blowing Fan, 161	Dust Whirls, 120 Judge Lives Here, 91 +	Rotation, 113	Circumduction, 113	Vehicle Overturned, 142
Eject, 63	Project, 126	Starter, 159	Centrifugal Fertilizer, 47	Fire Hose, 141	Don't Extinguish with Water, 141
Torque Converter, 161	Centrifuge, 114	Ammeter; Generator, 159	End of Transmission, 59 Communication Link, 59		Electrical Danger, 140
Overhead Cable Crossing, 153 Use Flash, 126		Series of Bends, 143	Double Bend, Right, 143 +	Overhead Cable, 144	Static Eliminator, 110

GRAPHIC FORM

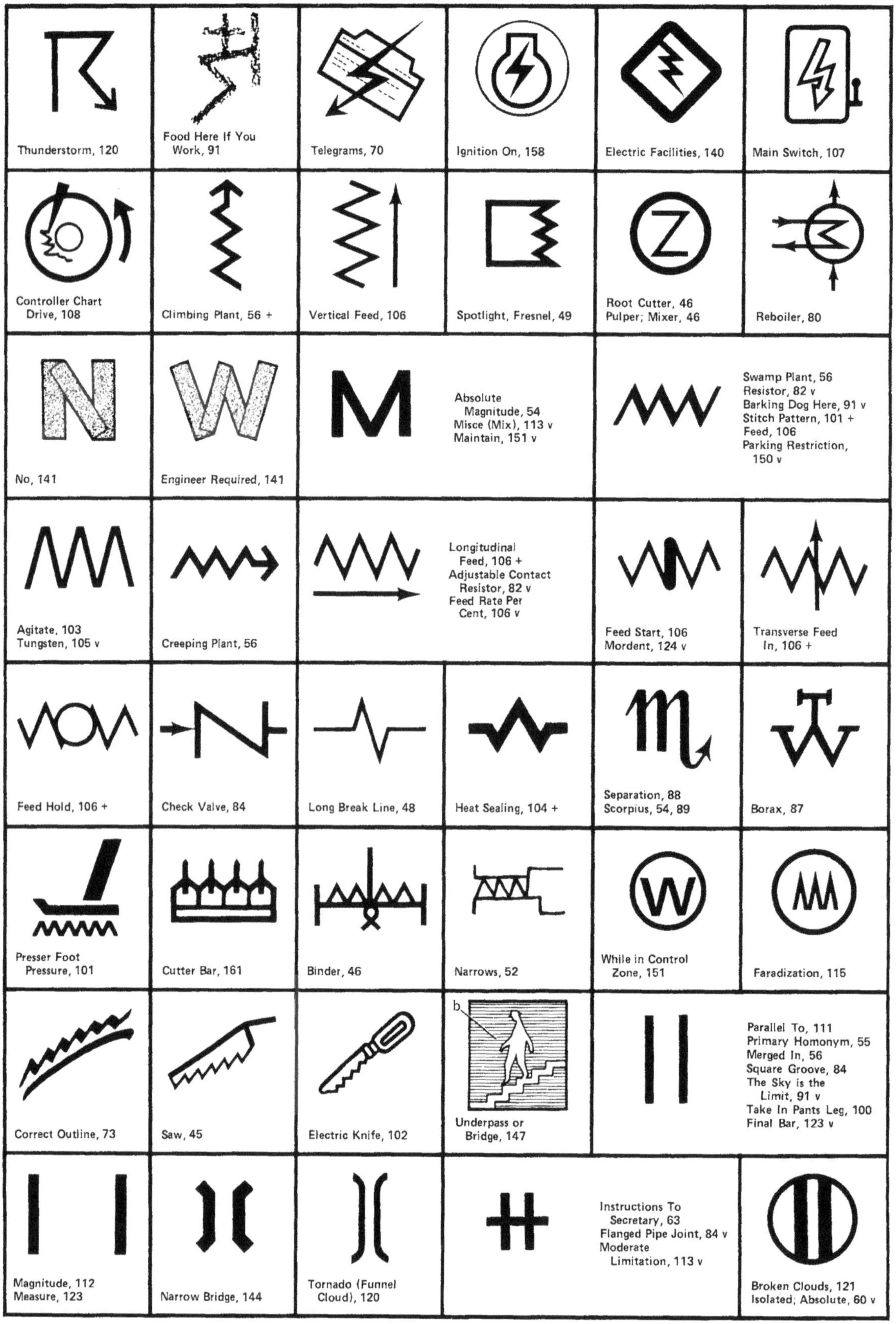

Thunderstorm, 120	Food Here If You Work, 91	Telegrams, 70	Ignition On, 158	Electric Facilities, 140	Main Switch, 107
Controller Chart Drive, 108	Climbing Plant, 56 +	Vertical Feed, 106	Spotlight, Fresnel, 49	Root Cutter, 46 Pulper; Mixer, 46	Reboiler, 80
No, 141	Engineer Required, 141		Absolute Magnitude, 54 Misce (Mix), 113 v Maintain, 151 v		Swamp Plant, 56 Resistor, 82 v Barking Dog Here, 91 v Stitch Pattern, 101 + Feed, 106 Parking Restriction, 150 v
Agitate, 103 Tungsten, 105 v	Creeping Plant, 56		Longitudinal Feed, 106 + Adjustable Contact Resistor, 82 v Feed Rate Per Cent, 106 v	Feed Start, 106 Mordent, 124 v	Transverse Feed In, 106 +
Feed Hold, 106 +	Check Valve, 84	Long Break Line, 48	Heat Sealing, 104 +	Separation, 88 Scorpius, 54, 89	Borax, 87
Presser Foot Pressure, 101	Cutter Bar, 161	Binder, 46	Narrows, 52	While in Control Zone, 151	Faradization, 115
Correct Outline, 73	Saw, 45	Electric Knife, 102	b. Underpass or Bridge, 147		Parallel To, 111 Primary Homonym, 55 Merged In, 56 Square Groove, 84 The Sky is the Limit, 91 v Take In Pants Leg, 100 Final Bar, 123 v
Magnitude, 112 Measure, 123	Narrow Bridge, 144	Tornado (Funnel Cloud), 120		Instructions To Secretary, 63 Flanged Pipe Joint, 84 v Moderate Limitation, 113 v	Broken Clouds, 121 Isolated; Absolute, 60 v

b Water Skiing, 131	Active Intellect, 89	Magnetic Ink Characters, Customer Account Number, 58 Amount of Check, 58 v Dash, 58 v		Let Out (Pins Outside); Take In (Pin Out Excess), 100	
Loose Straw, 39 + Sheaf, 39 v	Crumbroll, 46	Chaff, 39	Repeat, 124	Furrow Press, 46 Rotary Hoe, 46 v	Rake, 45 + Chassis, Equip., 82 v
Windrower, 46	Fence, 51	Harrow, 46	Chain Harrow, Weeder, 46	Railing, 51 Weir, 153 v	Moveable Grid, 116
Longitudinal Wave, 128	br r Levee (with road), 94 Access Denied, 92 v	Spreading, 104	While in controlled airspace, 150 Identical With, 55 Set In Small Capitals, 72 Dam with Road, 93 v	Lengthen and Shorten Lines, 100 Low Heat, 102 Laminating, 104 Equal To, 111 Light Fog, 120	
m Measured By, 111	Knee, 74 Not Equal To, 111 v Cross Airway, jet route or course, 150 v		Heavy Fog; Ice Fog, 120 Line Feed, 60 Make Capital, 72 Symmetry, 85 v Passive Intellect, 89 Medium Heat, 102 Identically Equal To, 111		Make Capital, 72
Ankle, 74	Line Spacing Key, 65	Layer Level (Body Adjustment), 116	Mechanical Barn Cleaner, 43	Screened Conductor, 82	Line for Line, 61
Paved Area, 51	Staff, 123	Brick, 50 Shingles; Siding, 51 v	Foot, 74 Officer of Law, 91 v	Toes, 74	Kymograph, 116
Negative Charge, 128	Silage, 39	b Inundated Area, 94	Parallelism, 85 Align Type, 73	Straighten Type, 73	Tremolo, 124

GRAPHIC FORM

(continued)

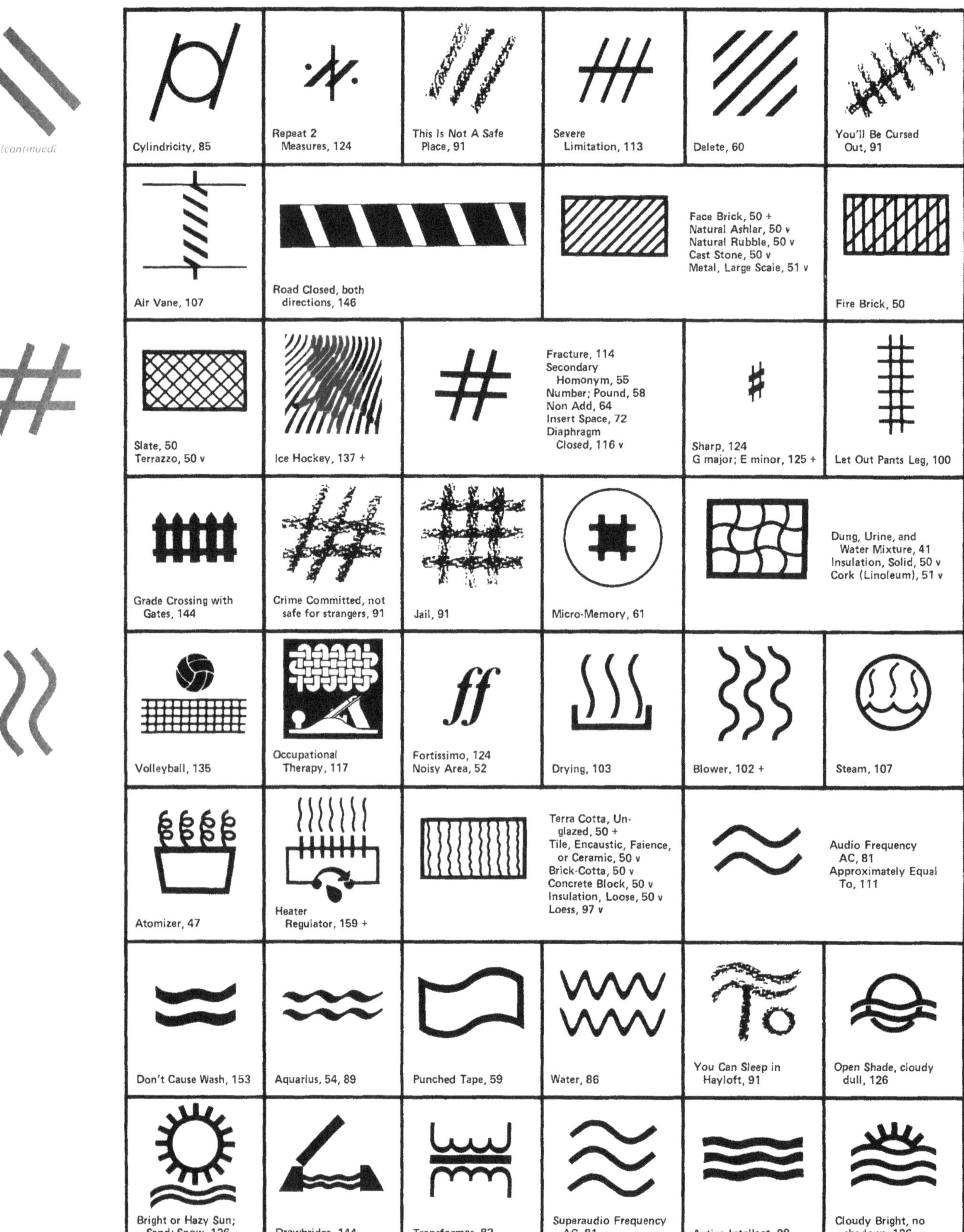

Cylindricity, 85
Repeat 2 Measures, 124
This Is Not A Safe Place, 91
Severe Limitation, 113
Delete, 60
You'll Be Cursed Out, 91
Air Vane, 107
Road Closed, both directions, 146
Face Brick, 50 +
Natural Ashlar, 50 v
Natural Rubble, 50 v
Cast Stone, 50 v
Metal, Large Scale, 51 v
Fire Brick, 50
Slate, 50
Terrazzo, 50 v
Ice Hockey, 137 +
Fracture, 114
Secondary Homonym, 55
Number; Pound, 58
Non Add, 64
Insert Space, 72
Diaphragm Closed, 116 v
Sharp, 124
G major; E minor, 125 +
Let Out Pants Leg, 100
Grade Crossing with Gates, 144
Crime Committed, not safe for strangers, 91
Jail, 91
Micro-Memory, 61
Dung, Urine, and Water Mixture, 41
Insulation, Solid, 50 v
Cork (Linoleum), 51 v
Volleyball, 135
Occupational Therapy, 117
ff
Fortissimo, 124
Noisy Area, 52
Drying, 103
Blower, 102 +
Steam, 107
Atomizer, 47
Heater Regulator, 159 +
Terra Cotta, Unglazed, 50 +
Tile, Encaustic, Faience, or Ceramic, 50 v
Brick-Cotta, 50 v
Concrete Block, 50 v
Insulation, Loose, 50 v
Loess, 97 v
Audio Frequency AC, 81
Approximately Equal To, 111
Don't Cause Wash, 153
Aquarius, 54, 89
Punched Tape, 59
Water, 86
You Can Sleep in Hayloft, 91
Open Shade, cloudy dull, 126
Bright or Hazy Sun; Sand; Snow, 126
Drawbridge, 144
Transformer, 82
Superaudio Frequency AC, 81
Active Intellect, 89
Cloudy Bright, no shadows, 126

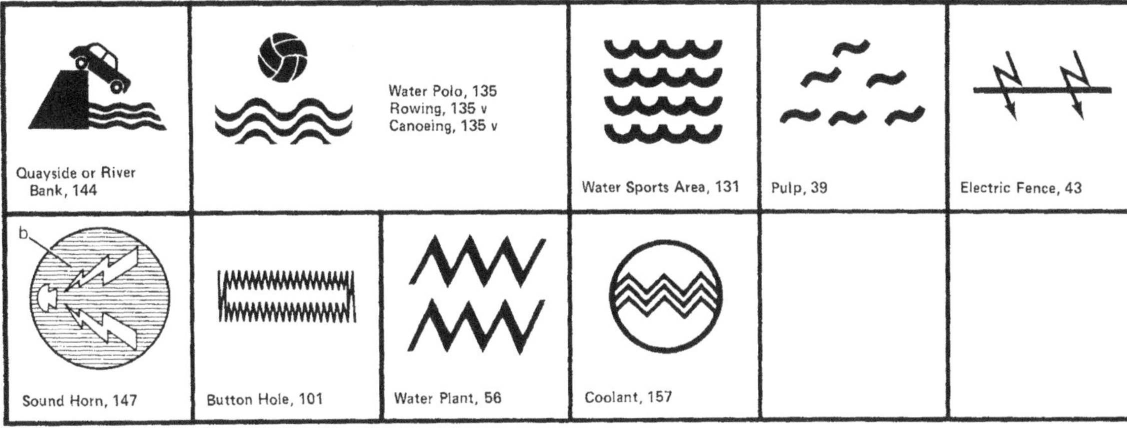

Quayside or River Bank, 144
Water Polo, 135
Rowing, 135 v
Canoeing, 135 v
Water Sports Area, 131
Pulp, 39
Electric Fence, 43
b
Sound Horn, 147
Button Hole, 101
Water Plant, 56
Coolant, 157

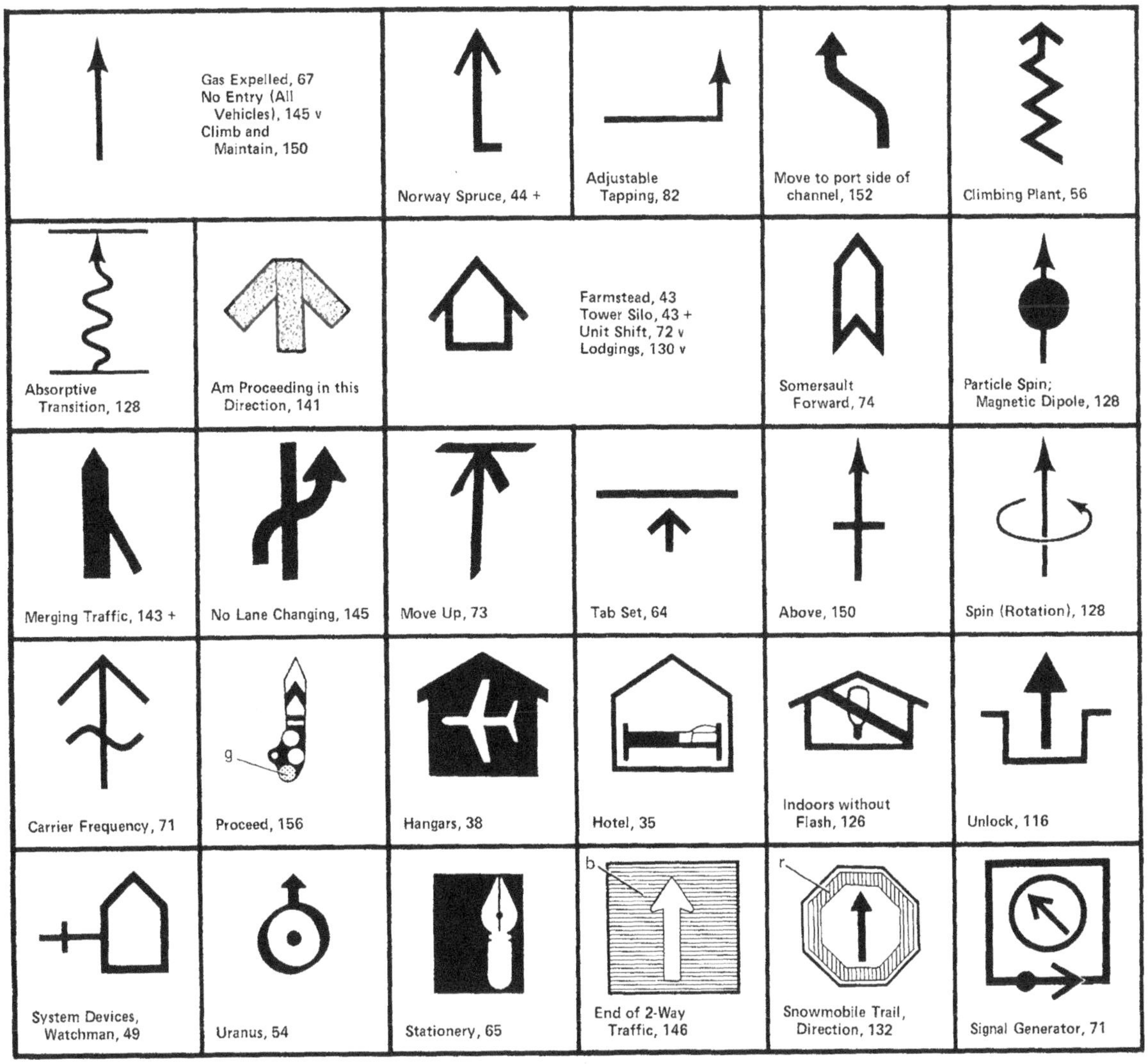

Gas Expelled, 67 No Entry (All Vehicles), 145 v Climb and Maintain, 150		Norway Spruce, 44 +	Adjustable Tapping, 82	Move to port side of channel, 152	Climbing Plant, 56
Absorptive Transition, 128	Am Proceeding in this Direction, 141	Farmstead, 43 Tower Silo, 43 + Unit Shift, 72 v Lodgings, 130 v		Somersault Forward, 74	Particle Spin; Magnetic Dipole, 128
Merging Traffic, 143 +	No Lane Changing, 145	Move Up, 73	Tab Set, 64	Above, 150	Spin (Rotation), 128
Carrier Frequency, 71	g Proceed, 156	Hangars, 38	Hotel, 35	Indoors without Flash, 126	Unlock, 116
System Devices, Watchman, 49	Uranus, 54	Stationery, 65	b End of 2-Way Traffic, 146	r Snowmobile Trail, Direction, 132	Signal Generator, 71

GRAPHIC FORM

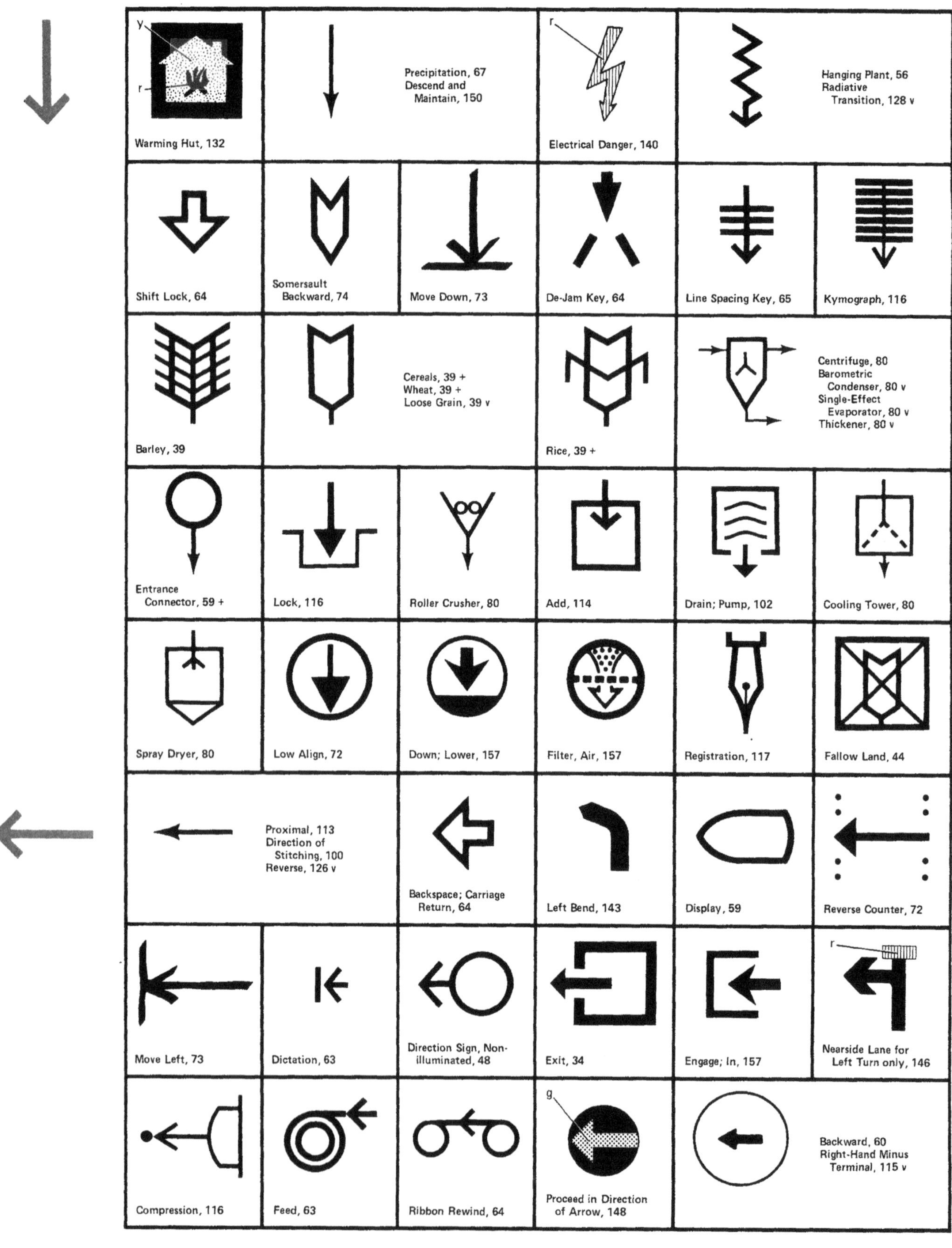

y
r
Warming Hut, 132
Precipitation, 67
Descend and Maintain, 150
r
Electrical Danger, 140
Hanging Plant, 56
Radiative Transition, 128 v
Shift Lock, 64
Somersault Backward, 74
Move Down, 73
De-Jam Key, 64
Line Spacing Key, 65
Kymograph, 116
Barley, 39
Cereals, 39 +
Wheat, 39 +
Loose Grain, 39 v
Rice, 39 +
Centrifuge, 80
Barometric Condenser, 80 v
Single-Effect Evaporator, 80 v
Thickener, 80 v
Entrance Connector, 59 +
Lock, 116
Roller Crusher, 80
Add, 114
Drain; Pump, 102
Cooling Tower, 80
Spray Dryer, 80
Low Align, 72
Down; Lower, 157
Filter, Air, 157
Registration, 117
Fallow Land, 44
Proximal, 113
Direction of Stitching, 100
Reverse, 126 v
Backspace; Carriage Return, 64
Left Bend, 143
Display, 59
Reverse Counter, 72
Move Left, 73
Dictation, 63
Direction Sign, Non-illuminated, 48
Exit, 34
Engage; In, 157
r
Nearside Lane for Left Turn only, 146
Compression, 116
Feed, 63
Ribbon Rewind, 64
g
Proceed in Direction of Arrow, 148
Backward, 60
Right-Hand Minus Terminal, 115 v

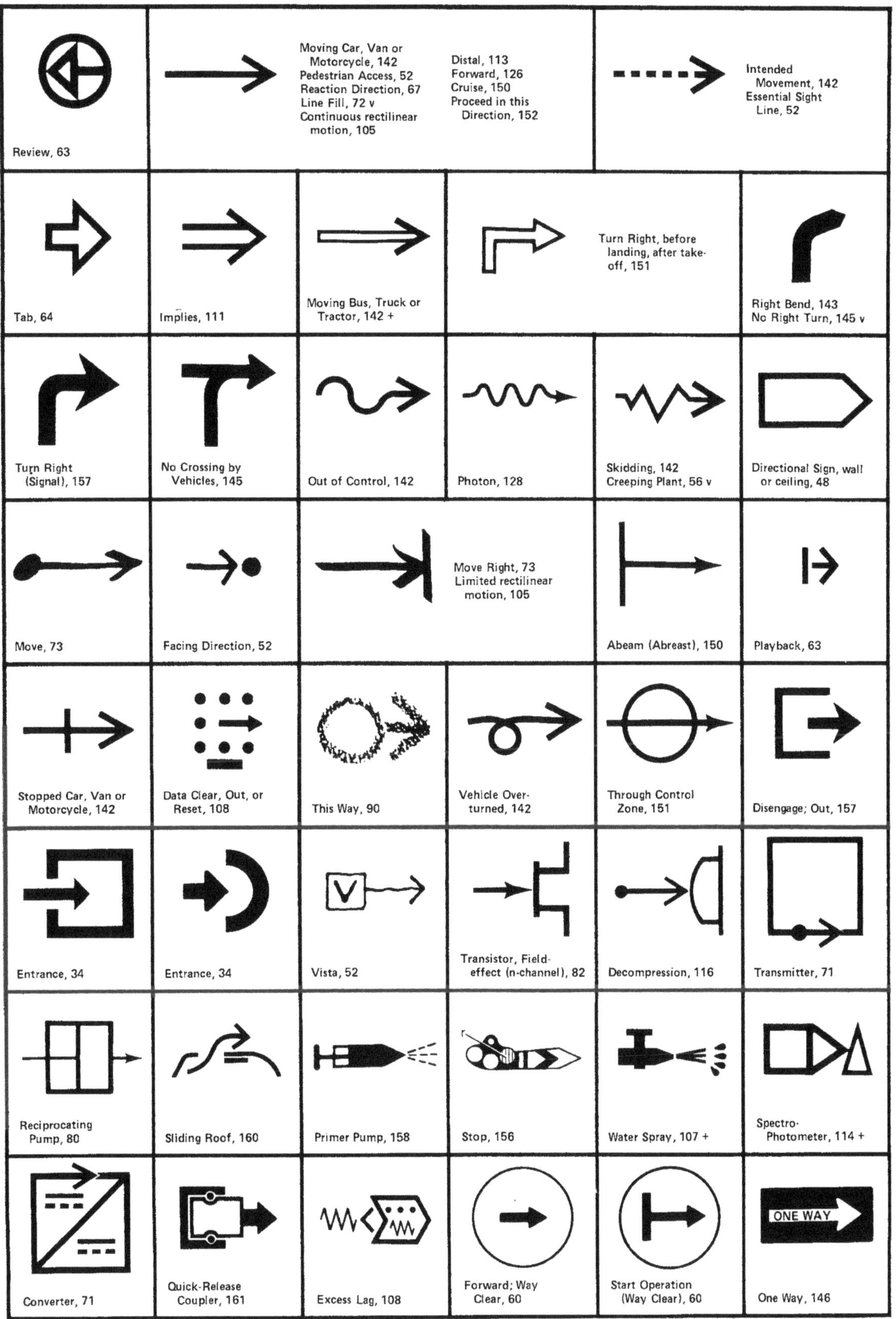

Review, 63
Moving Car, Van or Motorcycle, 142
Pedestrian Access, 52
Reaction Direction, 67
Line Fill, 72 v
Continuous rectilinear motion, 105
Distal, 113
Forward, 126
Cruise, 150
Proceed in this Direction, 152
Intended Movement, 142
Essential Sight Line, 52
Tab, 64
Implies, 111
Moving Bus, Truck or Tractor, 142 +
Turn Right, before landing, after take-off, 151
Right Bend, 143
No Right Turn, 145 v
Turn Right (Signal), 157
No Crossing by Vehicles, 145
Out of Control, 142
Photon, 128
Skidding, 142
Creeping Plant, 56 v
Directional Sign, wall or ceiling, 48
Move, 73
Facing Direction, 52
Move Right, 73
Limited rectilinear motion, 105
Abeam (Abreast), 150
Playback, 63
Stopped Car, Van or Motorcycle, 142
Data Clear, Out, or Reset, 108
This Way, 90
Vehicle Overturned, 142
Through Control Zone, 151
Disengage; Out, 157
Entrance, 34
Entrance, 34
V
Vista, 52
Transistor, Field-effect (n-channel), 82
Decompression, 116
Transmitter, 71
Reciprocating Pump, 80
Sliding Roof, 160
Primer Pump, 158
Stop, 156
Water Spray, 107 +
Spectro-Photometer, 114 +
Converter, 71
Quick-Release Coupler, 161
Excess Lag, 108
Forward; Way Clear, 60
Start Operation (Way Clear), 60
ONE WAY
One Way, 146

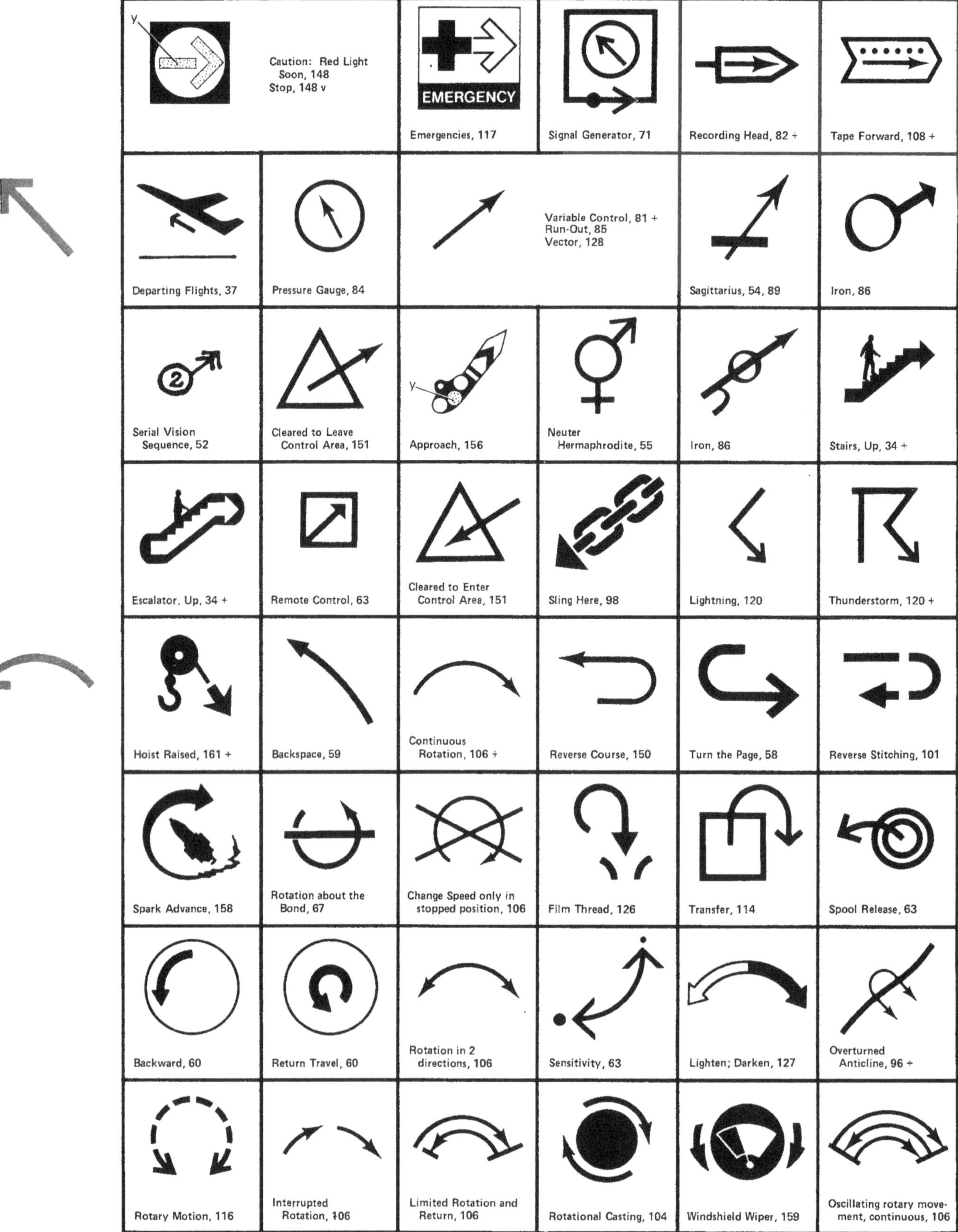
Caution: Red Light Soon, 148
Stop, 148 v
EMERGENCY
Emergencies, 117
Signal Generator, 71
Recording Head, 82 +
Tape Forward, 108 +
Departing Flights, 37
Pressure Gauge, 84
Variable Control, 81 +
Run-Out, 85
Vector, 128
Sagittarius, 54, 89
Iron, 86
Serial Vision Sequence, 52
Cleared to Leave Control Area, 151
Approach, 156
Neuter Hermaphrodite, 55
Iron, 86
Stairs, Up, 34 +
Escalator, Up, 34 +
Remote Control, 63
Cleared to Enter Control Area, 151
Sling Here, 98
Lightning, 120
Thunderstorm, 120 +
Hoist Raised, 161 +
Backspace, 59
Continuous Rotation, 106 +
Reverse Course, 150
Turn the Page, 58
Reverse Stitching, 101
Spark Advance, 158
Rotation about the Bond, 67
Change Speed only in stopped position, 106
Film Thread, 126
Transfer, 114
Spool Release, 63
Backward, 60
Return Travel, 60
Rotation in 2 directions, 106
Sensitivity, 63
Lighten; Darken, 127
Overturned Anticline, 96 +
Rotary Motion, 116
Interrupted Rotation, 106
Limited Rotation and Return, 106
Rotational Casting, 104
Windshield Wiper, 159
Oscillating rotary movement, continuous, 106

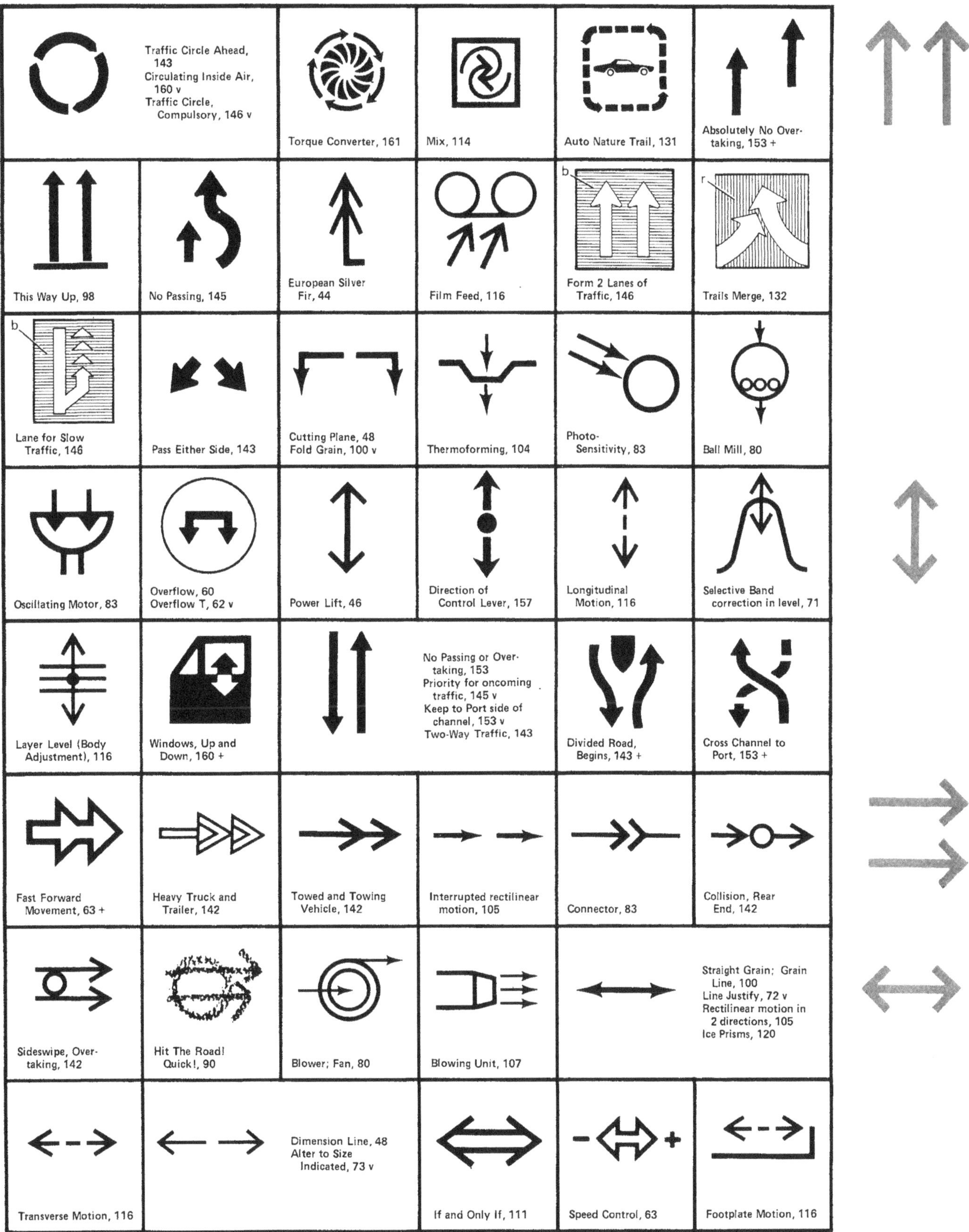

Traffic Circle Ahead, 143
Circulating Inside Air, 160 v
Traffic Circle, Compulsory, 146 v
Torque Converter, 161
Mix, 114
Auto Nature Trail, 131
Absolutely No Over-taking, 153 +
This Way Up, 98
No Passing, 145
European Silver Fir, 44
Film Feed, 116
b
Form 2 Lanes of Traffic, 146
r
Trails Merge, 132
b
Lane for Slow Traffic, 146
Pass Either Side, 143
Cutting Plane, 48
Fold Grain, 100 v
Thermoforming, 104
Photo-Sensitivity, 83
Ball Mill, 80
Oscillating Motor, 83
Overflow, 60
Overflow T, 62 v
Power Lift, 46
Direction of Control Lever, 157
Longitudinal Motion, 116
Selective Band correction in level, 71
Layer Level (Body Adjustment), 116
Windows, Up and Down, 160 +
No Passing or Over-taking, 153
Priority for oncoming traffic, 145 v
Keep to Port side of channel, 153 v
Two-Way Traffic, 143
Divided Road, Begins, 143 +
Cross Channel to Port, 153 +
Fast Forward Movement, 63 +
Heavy Truck and Trailer, 142
Towed and Towing Vehicle, 142
Interrupted rectilinear motion, 105
Connector, 83
Collision, Rear End, 142
Sideswipe, Over-taking, 142
Hit The Road! Quick!, 90
Blower; Fan, 80
Blowing Unit, 107
Straight Grain; Grain Line, 100
Line Justify, 72 v
Rectilinear motion in 2 directions, 105
Ice Prisms, 120
Transverse Motion, 116
Dimension Line, 48
Alter to Size Indicated, 73 v
If and Only If, 111
Speed Control, 63
Footplate Motion, 116

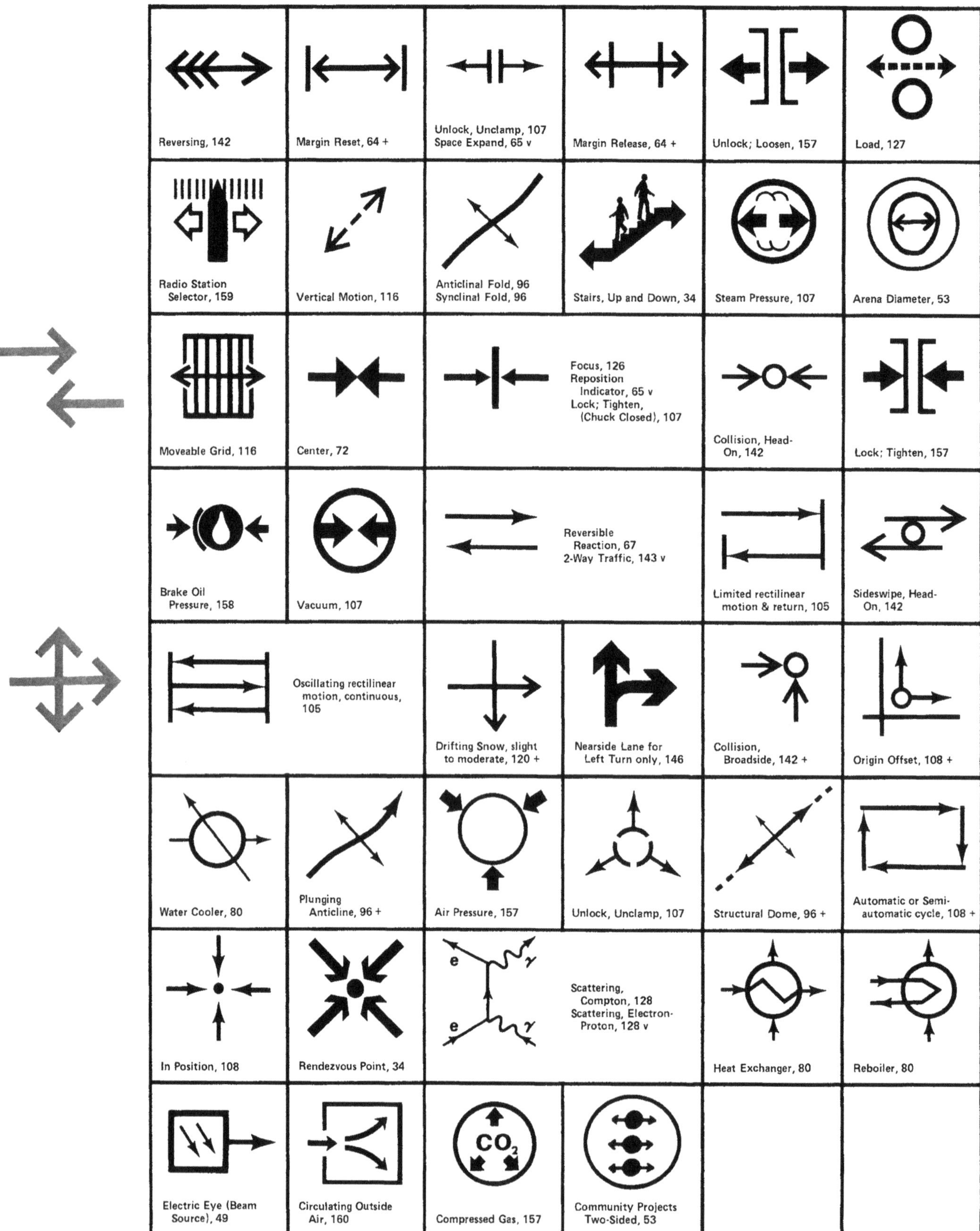

Reversing, 142
Margin Reset, 64 +
Unlock, Unclamp, 107
Space Expand, 65 v
Margin Release, 64 +
Unlock; Loosen, 157
Load, 127
Radio Station Selector, 159
Vertical Motion, 116
Anticlinal Fold, 96
Synclinal Fold, 96
Stairs, Up and Down, 34
Steam Pressure, 107
Arena Diameter, 53
Moveable Grid, 116
Center, 72
Focus, 126
Reposition Indicator, 65 v
Lock; Tighten, (Chuck Closed), 107
Collision, Head-On, 142
Lock; Tighten, 157
Brake Oil Pressure, 158
Vacuum, 107
Reversible Reaction, 67
2-Way Traffic, 143 v
Limited rectilinear motion & return, 105
Sideswipe, Head-On, 142
Oscillating rectilinear motion, continuous, 105
Drifting Snow, slight to moderate, 120 +
Nearside Lane for Left Turn only, 146
Collision, Broadside, 142 +
Origin Offset, 108 +
Water Cooler, 80
Plunging Anticline, 96 +
Air Pressure, 157
Unlock, Unclamp, 107
Structural Dome, 96 +
Automatic or Semi-automatic cycle, 108 +
In Position, 108
Rendezvous Point, 34
e
γ
e
γ
Scattering, Compton, 128
Scattering, Electron-Proton, 128 v
Heat Exchanger, 80
Reboiler, 80
Electric Eye (Beam Source), 49
Circulating Outside Air, 160
CO2
Compressed Gas, 157
Community Projects Two-Sided, 53

Plus, 111 Longer Than, 55 Graft Hybrid, 56 Spores with Male Nuclei, 56 On, 64 Tab Set, 64 Positive Charge, 67 Hip, 74 v	Crossed Conductors, 81 + Cross; God and Earth combined, 89 Mild, 113 Stopped Tone (Horn), 125 Intersection; Cross-roads, 143 v	Crucible, 86	Christianity, Latin Cross, 138 Religious Talk gets Free Meal, 91 v		
Crossing Tributary, 153 + Intersection with non-priority road, 143 v	Cross-Channel Fairway, Left Bank, 154 + Lubrication Oils A and B, 108 v Red Cross, 113 v	Vinegar, 87 Cross Joint, Threaded, 84 v			
Airport, 36 Small Airport, No Facilities, 93 v Low Flying Aircraft, 144	Obscure Species, 56 Incorrect Citation, 55 Dagger (Footnote), 58 Death, 113	Sikhism, Kirpan, 139	Staggered Junction, 143		
Christianity, Orthodox Cross, 138	Christianity, Celtic Cross, 138	Reception of Cadavers, 118	Injections; Vaccination, 113	Pharmacy, 65	g NOTHING to declare Nothing to Declare, 38
Mirror Image, 108	Hinduism, Mandala, 138	Doctor Here, Won't Charge, 91	Above, 150 +	Larch, 44	Return to Segno, 124
Position, 85	Lead, 87	Cathedral; Church, 95 +	Antimony, 86	System Devices, Electric Clock, 49 +	Powder, 86
Mercury, 87	Neuter Hermaphrodite, 55	Food Here If You Work, 91	Floor Mounted Equipment, 115	Autumn, 89	Calx (Viva), 87 +
Neptune, 54	Size of Button and Buttonhole, 100	IC XC NI KA Christianity, Christ Victorious, 138	Volunteers, 117	Injury, Fatal, 142	Building, Medium, 51

GRAPHIC FORM

Hospital, 117
Quarantine, 44
Hospital Heliport, 151 v
r
Airport, Civil or Military, 93
Power, 63
Observation Desk, 37
r
Clinic, 117
Jerusalem Artichoke, 40
Ambulance, 117
EMERGENCY
Emergencies, 117
b
r
Hospital, 147
HEAL·THE·SICK·RAISE·THE·DEAD
CLEANSE·THE·LEPERS·CAST·OUT·DEMONS
Christianity, Church of Christ, Scientist, Cross and Crown, 138
Double Dagger (Footnote), 58
Normal; Moderate, 113
Low Pressure Steam Return, 83
Glider Flights in Operation, 151
Parking Space Limits, 150
Increased; Moderately Severe, 113
Barbed Wire Fence, 43
Markedly Increased, Severe, 113
Loose Fertilizer, Non-Granulated, 41
Fertilizer in Bags, 41
Positive Charge, 128
Marble, 97
Massive Igneous Rock, 97
Hybrid, 56
Mated With, 55
Off, 64
Line Kill, 72
Broken Type, 73
2-Phase 4-Wire, 81
Vinegar, 87
O. K., All Right, 90 v
Mining Prospect, 95 v
Multiplied By, 111
Intersection; Cross-roads, 143 v
Cross, 151 v
Double Sharp, 124
Unable to Proceed, 141
Unfit for Aircraft Movement, 151 v
Cross-Channel Fairway, Right Bank, 154 +
Error; Malfunction, 108
Mild Limitation, 113 v
r
Railroad Grade Crossing, 146 +
Welded Pipe Joint, 84
Starlike Snow Crystals, 120
Grade Crossing (Railroad), 144
Crucible, 86 +
Placer Mine, 96
Cutting; Shearing, 104
Cutting Line, 100 v
Unwrapped (Sterilizers), 114 v
Salt, 87
Punch Inhibit, 72
Fresh Water, Safe Campsite, 90
Flashing Light Ahead (Railroad), 144
The Family, 90
Mine; Quarry, 96
Scissors, 45 v
Battlefield, 95 v

Gravel Pit, 96
Fencing, 134 +
Restaurant, 35
Silverware, 66
Character Kill, 72
RAIL CROSSING ROAD
Railroad Grade Crossing, 146
Barber, 65
No Smoking, 36, 140
Half Standard, 40
Christianity, Chi Rho, 138
Use No Hooks, 98
Poison, 140
Windmill, 95, 43 v
Fixation, 88
Waist, 74
Code, 61 v
Lead, 105 v
Overcast, Sky Obscured, 121
Baseball, 132 +
Noxious, 99
Magnetic Tape Unit Occupied, 62
Rowing, 135
Hockey, 136
Canoeing, 135
Trail Closed, 132
Audio-Visual Indicator, 72
Total, 64
Star, 54 v
Described Well in this Source, 56 v
Asterisk (Footnote), 58 v
Snow, 120
Release Damper-Pedal (Piano), 124 v
Instruction to Secretary, 63
Digging Reel, 45
Point of Reference, 52
Biohazard Warning, 140
Fan, 126
Gold, 86
Winter Sports Area, 132 +
Air Conditioning, 159
Panorama, 52
Grasses, 40
New World, 56 +
So. Hemisphere, 56 +
Ventilator, 43
Header, 160
Reel Speed, 161 v
Bare Rock, 94 +
Snow, 148
Taoism, Water; Life-giving Source, 139
Cool, 114
Medical Alert, 113
Radioactive, 115
Ionizing Rays (Radiation Warning), 140
Ventilating Fan, 160
0 MAXI
Ventilation Control, 35
Fallout Shelter (Civil Defense), 140

GRAPHIC FORM

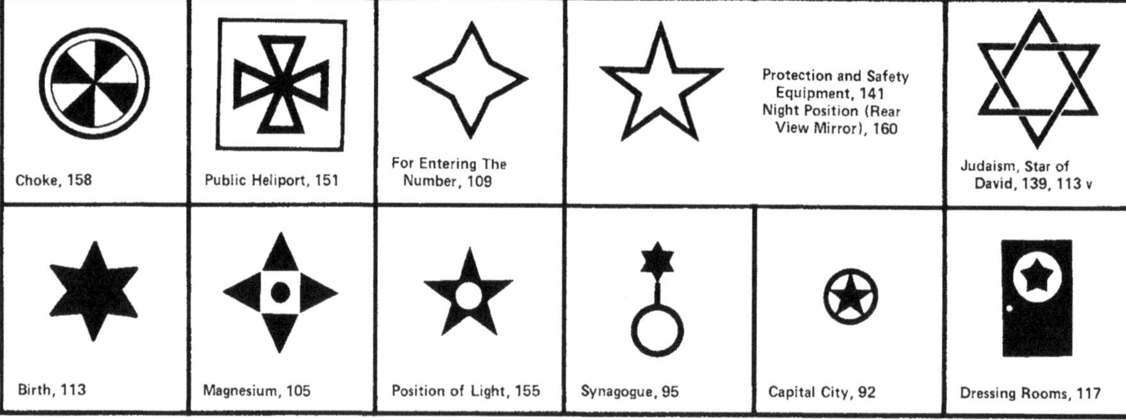

Choke, 158
Public Heliport, 151
For Entering The Number, 109
Protection and Safety Equipment, 141
Night Position (Rear View Mirror), 160
Judaism, Star of David, 139, 113 v
Birth, 113
Magnesium, 105
Position of Light, 155
Synagogue, 95
Capital City, 92
Dressing Rooms, 117

Men's Toilet, 34 Men's Suits, 66 v Men, 15 years and up, 99 v Still, 126		Women's Toilet, 34 Stewardess Call, 36 Women's Wear, 66 v Women, 15 years and up, 99 v Dresses, Skirts, Blouses, 99 v		Men's Work Clothes, 66	Suits, Trousers, Jackets, Shirts, 99 +
Girls' Clothing, 66	Lost Child, 34	Boys, 4-14 years, 99	Girls, 4-14 years, 99	Casts, 118	Pedestrian Crossing, 144
Boxing, 134 Fencing, 134 v	Confucianism, Confucius, 138	Figure Skating, 137 Gymnastics, 134 + Track and Field, 134 v		Hinduism, Shiva, 139	Weight Lifting
Track and Field, 134 + Basketball, 135 v Hockey, 136 v		Speed Skating, 137 Soccer, 136 v Biathlon, 137 v Ski Jumping, 137 v		Swimming, 135	Stop- Go Control Ahead, 144 +
Men's Cloakroom, 34 + Public Health, 38 v Access for the Ambulant, 140 v		Ranger Station, 130	Sundries, 65 Baggage Claim, 37 + Oversize Luggage, 37 v		View or Camera Point, 130

Virgo, 88
Hiking Trail, 130
Barman, 35
Forward, 126 +
Pedestrians Keep Left, 145 v
Pedestrians May Cross, 148 v
Return to Seat, 36
Fording Place, 130
Foot Bridge, 130 v
Hinduism, Vishnu, 139
No Handcarts, 145
Porter, 37
Physical Therapy, 117
Sagittarius, 89
Buddhism, Buddha, 138
Road Work Ahead, 144
Cycling, 136 +
Physical Therapy, 117 v
Ski Bobbing, 132 v
Ski Track, 132 +
Ice Skating, 133 v
Cross-Country Skiing, 137 v
Soccer, 136
Canoeing, 135 v
Volleyball, 135 v
Wall Contact Sports, 136 v
Slalom, 137 +
Towlift; T-Bar, 132 v
Hockey, 136 v
Ice Hockey, 137 v
Down Hill Skiing, 137 v
Diving, 131
Scuba Diving, 131 v
Sledding, 132 v
Slippery, 140
Rowing, 135
Canoeing, 135 v
Sailing, 135 v
Luge, 137 v
Access for the Handicapped, 140, 117
Chair Lift, 132 +
Water Skiing, 131 v
Switchboard and Sound, 70
Blood Donors, 117
Waiting Room, 37
Watch for Work Vehicles, 140
Place Luggage on Floor, 36 +
Seat Occupied, 36
Maid, 35
Room Service, 35
Bellboy, 35
No Entry (Keep Out), 34 +
No Entry (Keep Out), 34
Passengers Only, 37 v
No Entry to Pedestrians, 140 v
Ladder Off Limits, 140
No Riding, 140 v
Men's Toilet, 34 +
Men's Shower, 35 +
Connecting Flights, Domestic, 37 +
Open Pit, 140
Slippery, 140 v
Wear Protective Clothes, 141
No Pedestrians, 147 +

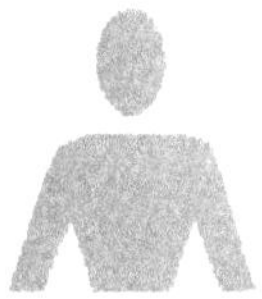

GRAPHIC FORM

Sauna Bath, 35	Self-Guiding Nature Trail, 131	Pedestrians Must Wait, 148	Children Can Play in Street, 147	Caverns, 131	Emergency Exit (Escape Route), 140
Groups, 126	Child Care, 117	Pediatrics, 117	Maternity, 118	Observation Room, 119	Gemini, 88
Children Crossing, 144 +	Swimming, 135 Rowing, 135 v	Wrestling, 134 + Judo, 134 v	Rendezvous Point, 34	Passenger Check-In, 37	Toilets, 34 Toilets Occupied, 36 v
Children's Emergency, 117	Basketball, 135 Wrestling, 134 v	Camera/Subject Distance, 126	Playground, 130	Information, 34	Clinical Room, 117
	Compartment, Mothers and Children, 38 Waiting Room, Mothers and Children, 37 v	Visitors, 117	Taking of Specimens, 118	Nursery, 118	Auditorium, 131
Child Care Education, 119	Out-Patient Department, 117	Registration, 117	Admissions, 117	Keep Away from Children, 140	Compulsory Way for Pedestrians, 147
Parallel Riding Permitted, 147	Elevator, 34 +	No Standing, 140 +	Planned Parenthood, U.S.A., 114	Close-Up, 126	Physical Therapy, 117
Judo, 134	Broncho-esophagology, 118		Height, High, 70 + Size, Large, 70 + Contrast, High, 70 +	Chest Care, 118	Neurology, 118

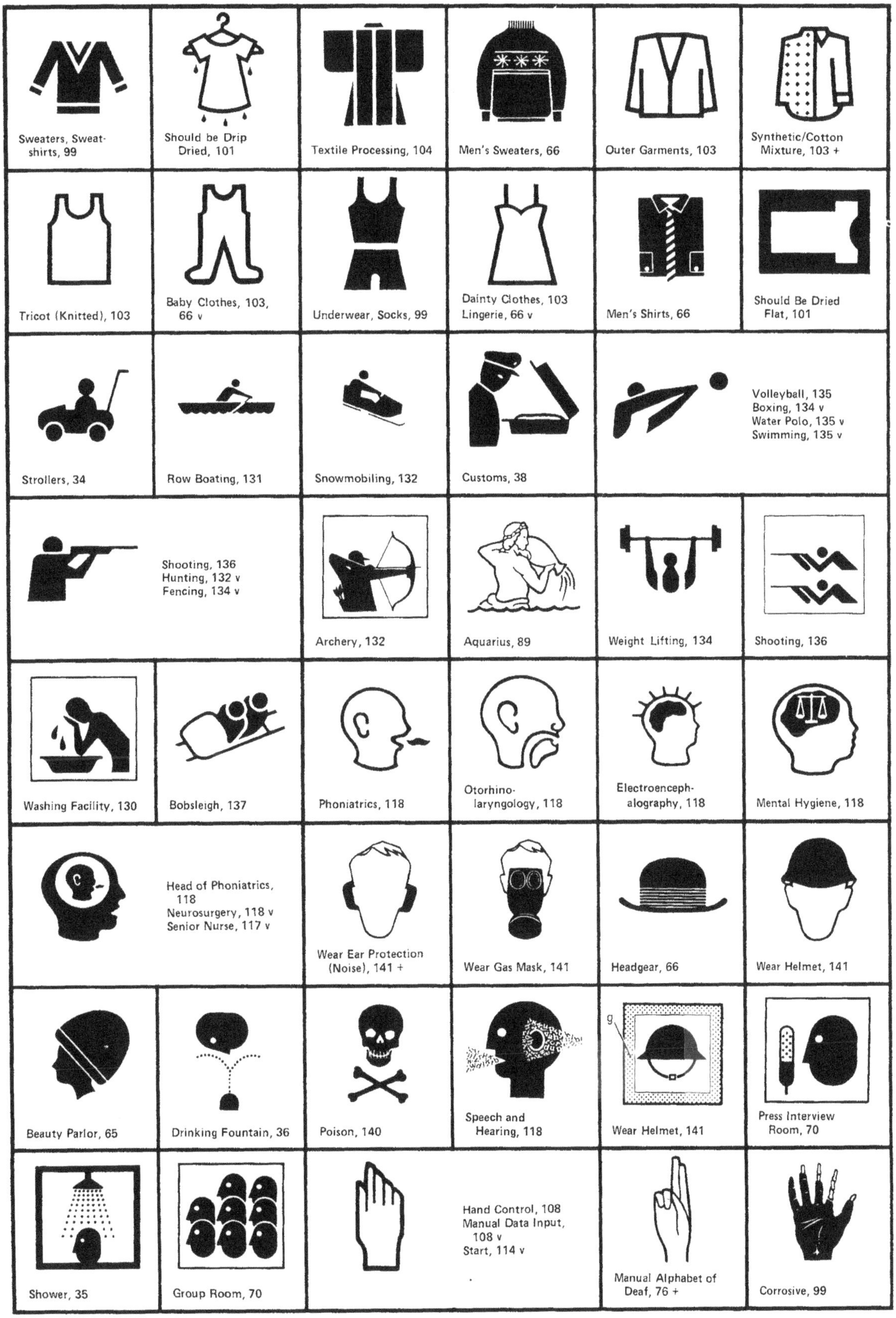

Sweaters, Sweat-shirts, 99	Should be Drip Dried, 101	Textile Processing, 104	Men's Sweaters, 66	Outer Garments, 103	Synthetic/Cotton Mixture, 103 +
Tricot (Knitted), 103	Baby Clothes, 103, 66 v	Underwear, Socks, 99	Dainty Clothes, 103 Lingerie, 66 v	Men's Shirts, 66	Should Be Dried Flat, 101
Strollers, 34	Row Boating, 131	Snowmobiling, 132	Customs, 38	Volleyball, 135 Boxing, 134 v Water Polo, 135 v Swimming, 135 v	
Shooting, 136 Hunting, 132 v Fencing, 134 v		Archery, 132	Aquarius, 89	Weight Lifting, 134	Shooting, 136
Washing Facility, 130	Bobsleigh, 137	Phoniatrics, 118	Otorhino-laryngology, 118	Electroenceph-alography, 118	Mental Hygiene, 118
Head of Phoniatrics, 118 Neurosurgery, 118 v Senior Nurse, 117 v		Wear Ear Protection (Noise), 141 +	Wear Gas Mask, 141	Headgear, 66	Wear Helmet, 141
Beauty Parlor, 65	Drinking Fountain, 36	Poison, 140	Speech and Hearing, 118	g Wear Helmet, 141	Press Interview Room, 70
Shower, 35	Group Room, 70	Hand Control, 108 Manual Data Input, 108 v Start, 114 v		Manual Alphabet of Deaf, 76 +	Corrosive, 99

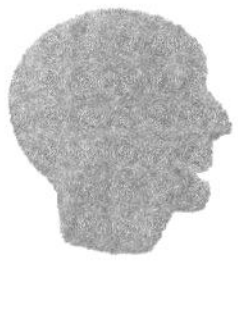

GRAPHIC FORM

No Entry (Keep Out), 34 Stop, 114 v First Aid, 140 v		Boxing, 134	Continued; Index, 58	Wash By Hand, 101 + Dermatology, 118 v	Gloves, 66
Thin Ice, 133	Light Manufacturing, 104	Customs, 38	Gymnastics, 134	Maintenance, 104	Maintenance, 104
Wrapped (Sterilizers), 114	Washroom, 34	Used Cups, 35 + Sanitary Napkins, 35 v	Stop, 143	No Entry, 140	Quiet, 35
Do Not Touch, 140	Pack with multipurpose grease, 160	Break Matches, 130 +	Press Room, 70	Sharp, 140	Do Not Start, 140
Prayer; Meditation, 117	Currency Exchange, 37	Wear Gloves, 141	Fasten Seat Belts, 36		Wear Gloves, 141
Handle with Care, 98	Travel Insurance, 37	Planned Parenthood, Korea, 114	Information, 34	Orthopedics, 118	Swimming, 135
Weight Lifting, 134	Wall Contact Sports, 136	Wrestling, 134	Weight Lifting, 134	Socks, 66	Track and Field, 134
Shoes, Boots, Sandals, 99	Orthopedics, 118	Men's Shoes, 66	Ladies' Shoes, 66	Remove Shoes on Evacuation Slide, 36	Foot Switch, 108

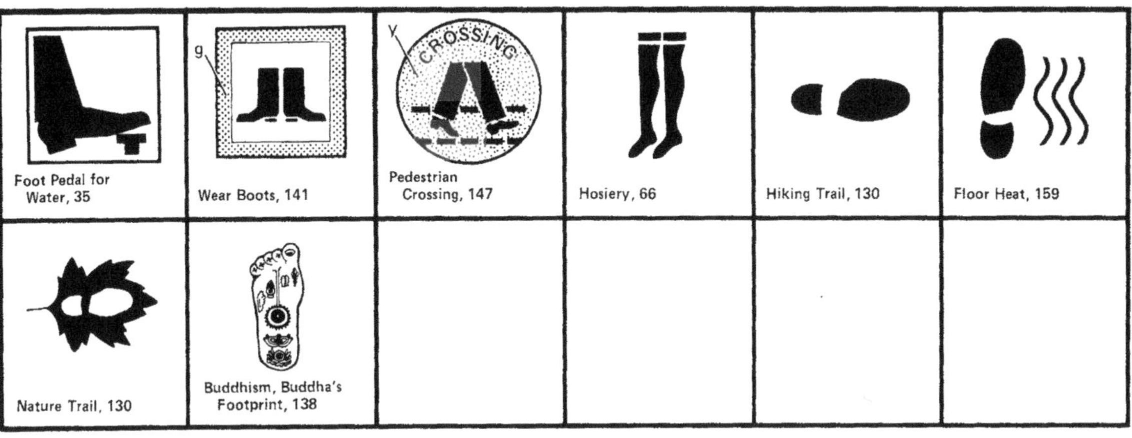
CROSSING
g
y
Foot Pedal for Water, 35
Wear Boots, 141
Pedestrian Crossing, 147
Hosiery, 66
Hiking Trail, 130
Floor Heat, 159
Nature Trail, 130
Buddhism, Buddha's Footprint, 138

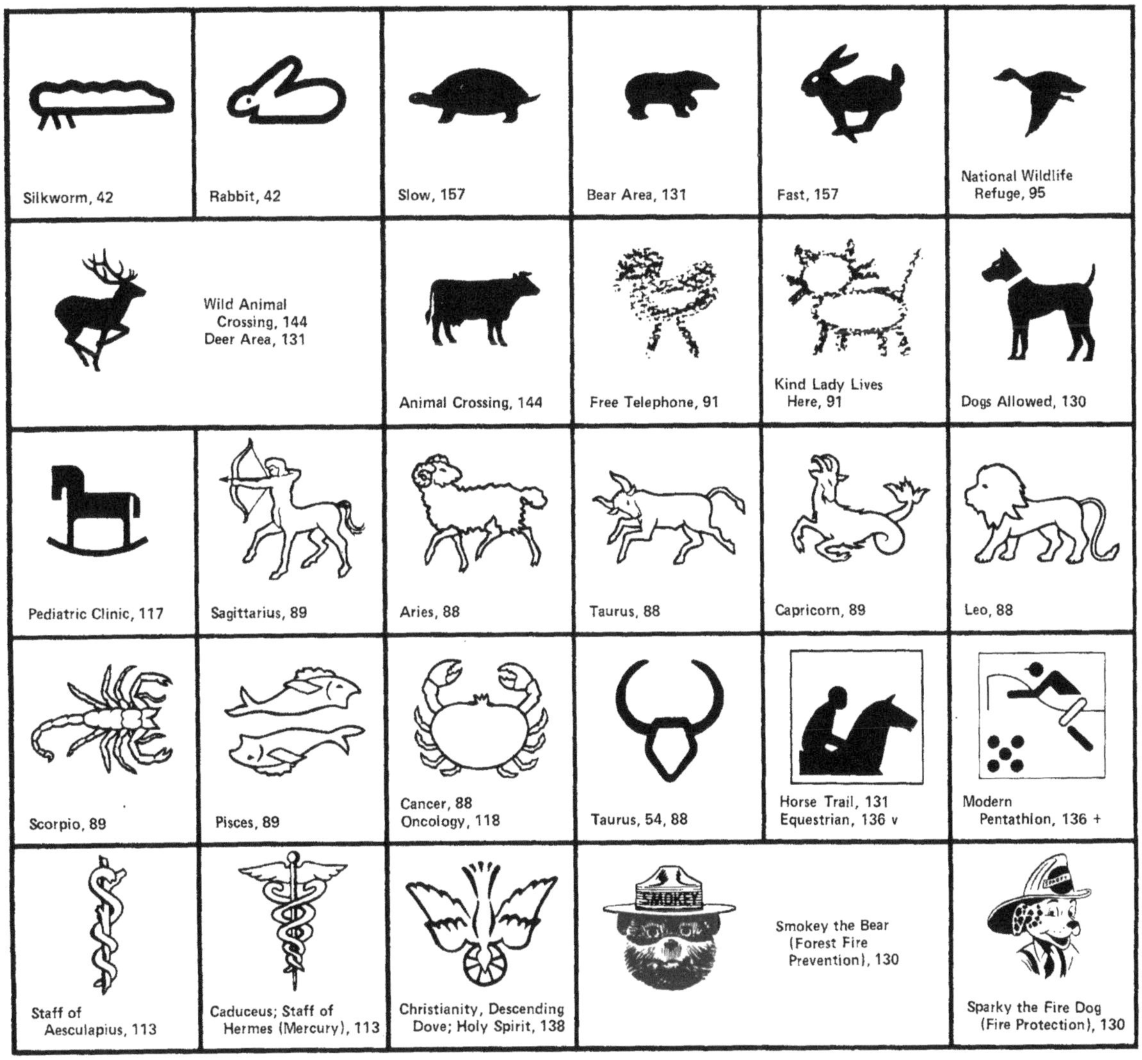

Silkworm, 42	Rabbit, 42	Slow, 157	Bear Area, 131	Fast, 157	National Wildlife Refuge, 95
Wild Animal Crossing, 144 Deer Area, 131		Animal Crossing, 144	Free Telephone, 91	Kind Lady Lives Here, 91	Dogs Allowed, 130
Pediatric Clinic, 117	Sagittarius, 89	Aries, 88	Taurus, 88	Capricorn, 89	Leo, 88
Scorpio, 89	Pisces, 89	Cancer, 88 Oncology, 118	Taurus, 54, 88	Horse Trail, 131 Equestrian, 136 v	Modern Pentathlon, 136 +
Staff of Aesculapius, 113	Caduceus; Staff of Hermes (Mercury), 113	Christianity, Descending Dove; Holy Spirit, 138	Smokey the Bear (Forest Fire Prevention), 130		Sparky the Fire Dog (Fire Protection), 130

IXΘYC
Horse Trail, 131
Knight, 133
Equestrian, 136

Christianity, Agnus Dei, 138
Christianity, The Fish, 138
Red Lion and Sun, 113
Nursery, 34
Veterinary Services, 113
No Animal-Drawn Vehicles, 145
Stable, 131
Bridle Path, 147
Kennel, 130
No Dogs, 130
Keep Frozen, 98
Insecticide, 41

COLOR SECTION

Although this book is primarily a collection of *graphic symbols,* color often plays a vital role in their message. Consequently we have deviated from our premise and have included a glossary of the symbology of *color*.

Graphic symbols often make use of colors to intensify their meaning — in fact in some instances a change of color creates a diametric change of meaning. For example, a red octagon used as a traffic symbol says STOP; but when the British port of entry switches the color to green, it means permission to pass through customs unchallenged (nothing to declare). There are many other examples which show that color takes an important place in international symbolic communication. An obvious one is the red, yellow, and green traffic lights used the world over; and red on road signs always means NO or DON'T, whereas blue means YES or DO.

Color creates instant impact. Whether applied to a three-dimensional form or used graphically, it becomes a vital part of the first impression created; this is true of the exterior color of a skyscraper as well as an artist's painting. Indeed, one's attention is often captured by color before the form or composition is completely distinct.

Industry employs color coding in many areas. The countless wires in a complex cable are instantly traced by their hue; pipes in factories are color-coded to indicate what each contains; the colors of knobs and buttons on vehicles and machinery signify what they control; office filing is simplified by the use of colored forms, folders, and clips. Even trades may be sorted out by color; various colored hard hats are sometimes worn by workers in construction projects to pinpoint their particular occupations – and a spectacular mobile mosaic results as the men climb about the girders.

Although many authoritative studies have been published, we found no single source which explained the traditional and contemporary meanings of specific colors in specific contexts – and these vary widely in different cultures. Nor could we find material divided according to *color*, rather than subject.

The listing on the following pages is presented with real humility; both time and space preclude its being all-inclusive, for the subject clearly deserves many years of research and volumes of its own. But our selection has been made considering primarily the needs of those who have the task of selecting colors for a given environment, structure, product, sign, or other graphic design.

We are indebted to Faber Birren for permission to use his geometric forms to symbolize the first six colors listed and also for the interesting information that, although these geometric forms were original with him, he discovered sometime later that Wassily Kandinsky had made very similar associations of forms and colors – an example of coincidence of ideas so prevalent in basic thinking. As a matter of convenience in organizing this Section we have assigned shapes to the remaining colors as well.

The meaning of color has interested men from all cultures throughout the centuries – from the royal purple robes of ancient Greece to the red carpet we roll out for diplomatic occasions. The robe and the carpet each signals its special message by virtue of its color; take away the color and the message is gone.

POSITIVE ASSOCIATIONS
Day, innocence, purity, perfection, rectitude, wisdom, truth

NEGATIVE ASSOCIATIONS
Spectral, ghostly, cold, blank, void

ALCHEMY
Second stage: Quicksilver, first transmutation

ART
Chinese Art:
Blue on white: Devil's color
Gold on white: Aristocratic
Red on white: Important notice
White on black: Historic
White on blue or black: Lower class mourning
White on red: Good luck
White on yellow: Buddhistic
Yellow on white: Holy

Persian rugs: Purity, light, and peace of the Shah

ASTROLOGY
Temple of Nebuchadnezzar:
Seventh level of building (uppermost), devoted to the Moon

Early Zodiac: Moon, ruling, Cancer

CULTURAL COMPARISONS
American Indian: Feminine, peace, happiness
Arapaho: Male
Cherokee: Peace and happiness

China: Worn by emperor to worship the moon; crystal button was worn on the cap of fourth ranking officials, white by fifth ranking
Seasons: Autumn

French and Russian revolutions: Color of emigrés and legitimists

Rome: Worn by lady as an emblem of virtue and purity

DIRECTION (cardinal points)
Apache, Cherokee: South
China: Face of Mo-li Hai, guardian of the west

C244→

POSITIVE ASSOCIATIONS
Maturity, discretion, humility, penitence, renunciation, retrospection

NEGATIVE ASSOCIATIONS
Neutralization, egoism, depression, inertia, indifference, barrenness, winter, grief, old age, penitence

CULTURAL COMPARISONS
Japan: Soldier

EDUCATION (doctorate hoods)
United States:
Grey: Veterinary Science
Silver grey: Oratory

ELECTRICAL ENGINEERING
Chassis wiring: AC power lines

HANDLING OF GOODS
Gases (Austria): Gases not symbolized by other colors

MEDICINE
Anesthetic gases (Sweden): Carbon dioxide

MUSIC
Instrument tone: Bassoon, Flageolet

KEYS
Alexander Scriabin:
Eb, Bb (steely with the glint of metal)

PSYCHOLOGY
Old, mature, life on even keel

RELIGION
Christianity: Emblem of Christ risen, ashes, humility, and mourning
Order: Franciscans

Judaism:
Kabbalah: Wisdom

SAFETY
Gas-mask canisters (gray stripe):
Particulates (dusts, fumes, mists, fogs, smokes) in combination with other gas

C245→

POSITIVE ASSOCIATIONS
Mighty, dignified, stark, sophistication; regality, without being pompous; fertilized land, grim determination, night, solemnity, humility

NEGATIVE ASSOCIATIONS
Morbidity, nothingness, despair, night, evil, sin, death, sickness, negation

ALCHEMY
First stage: Prime matter, guilt, origin, latent forces

ART
Chinese Art:
Black on blue: Low class
Black on red: Happiness (wedding invitations)
Black on yellow: Religious
Blue on black: Evil spirit
Gold on black: Old man's death
White on black: Historic
White on blue or black: Lower class mourning
Yellow on black: Old man's death

Persian rugs: Sorrow and destruction, sad and somber occasions

ASTROLOGY
Temple of Nebuchadnezzar:
First level of the building, devoted to the planet Saturn

Early Zodiac: Saturn, which ruled Aquarius and Capricorn

CULTURE COMPARISONS
American Indian: Masculine, underworld, mourning, night
Cherokee: Death

China (seasons): Winter

DIRECTION (cardinal points)
Apache: East
Cherokee, Creek: West
China: Face of Mo-li Shou, guardian of the north
Chippewa, Isleta, Navaho: North
Ireland: North
Omaha, Sioux: South

EDUCATION (doctorate hoods)
French Universities: Theology

C245→

RED
(continued)

DIRECTION (cardinal points)

Cherokee, Chippewa, Omaha, Sioux: East
China: Face of Mo-li Hung, the guardian of the south
Creek (red and yellow): North
Hopi, Isleta, Zuni: South
Tibet: West

EDUCATION (doctorate hoods)

United States:
Scarlet: Theology
Crimson: Journalism
France:
Red: Law
Crimson: Medicine
Purplish-red: Science

ELECTRICAL ENGINEERING

Chassis wiring: Power supply B plus (main stem)
Circuits (Switzerland): Power

ELEMENTS

Buddhist, Chinese, Greek (represented spirit), Hindu, Judaic (Josephus): Fire

FOLKLORE

Death:
Africa: Color of mourning
China: Red jade used in burial ceremonies to pay homage to the south
China, India, Scotland: Soldiers carried red amulets as preparation for death
Denmark, Germany, Hungary, Norway, Portugal, Scotland: Red string protected animals from death
Fiji: Islanders painted themselves red after killing a man
Italy: Token of a widow's love and faithfulness
Portugal: Widows not permitted to wear red
Shinto: Used to symbolize giving life to the dead
South Africa: After killing a lion, the hunter painted himself white for four days, then red
Marriage: Marriage colors (red and yellow):
Balkans, Egypt, Orient, Russia
China: Brides wore red and were carried in a red marriage chair with a red parasol; a red card tied the caps of the bride and groom together; red fire-crackers were exploded
Dutch East Indies: Red (or yellow) rice was sprinkled over the bridegroom to keep his soul from flying away; if names of a boy and girl were written on white paper with the blood of a red hen, the girl would become infatuated when she touched it
Ireland: Knotted red handkerchief at marriage ceremony meant curse on the wedding
India: Red paint and blood used in the marriage ceremony
Japan: Red (and white) girdles were protection during pregnancy
Medicine:
China (ribbon): Long life
Egypt: Red and white cake eaten for constipation; vermillion ink, goat's fat, and honey used to salve a wound
England: Protection against smallpox
Red string: Teething
Breath of red ox: Convulsions
Ireland (red wool): Sore throat
Red flannel: Scarlet fever
Japan: Nightmares, smallpox
Macedonia (yarn): Childbirth
Malay: Buffalo covered with red pigment was chased out of town, carrying the town's diseases with him
Perisa: Long life
Russia (flannel): Scarlet fever
Scotland (red wool): Sprains
Medieval magicians' vestments: Red on Tuesday, day of operations of vengeance; scarlet on Thursday, day of great religious or political operations
Superstition:
China: Red and yellow paper used against demons
Egypt: Red amulets prevented disease and protection for wearer from thunder and lightning
India, Ireland, Mexico, Turkey: "Red hand" painted on dwellings shielded inhabitants from harm
Japan: Red cats are bad luck
Syria: Painted on dwellings for good luck

GEMS

Agate: Protected against fire and scorpions
Bloodstone: Happiness and remembrance
Carbuncle: Charity, cured heart ailments
Carnelian: Good luck, cure of voice and speech impediments, restrained hemorrhage and removed blotches
Coral: Cured heart ailments
Garnet: Power, grace, victoriousness, high esteem, good luck; cured heart ailments, skin eruptions; birthstone of January
Ruby: Divine power, dignity, charity, high esteem, remembrance; cured heart ailments; dipped in water for stomach remedy; ground into powder to stop bleeding; birthstone for July
Rings for professions (Brazil): Lawyer

GEOGRAPHY

Roads, telegraph lines

HANDLING OF GOODS

Gases (Austria): Flammable
Inter-Governmental Maritime Consultative Organization shipping labels: Flammable gas or liquid
One-half red, one-half white: Spontaneously combustible
Red and white striped: Flammable solid
League of Red Cross Societies relief shipments: Foodstuffs

HERALDRY

Crusades: French wore red crosses on their shoulders
Tinctures:
Gules: Courage and zeal

HOLIDAYS

Christmas, St. Valentine's Day, Fourth of July, Mother's Day: Red carnation if mother living

LANGUAGE

Colloquialisms:
Reds: Communists
Red herring: Diverts attention
Red letter day: Memorable or happy day
Paint the town red: Wild time
Sees red: Gets angry
Scarlet letter: Adultery
Scarlet woman: Prostitute
In the red: In debt
Red tape: Excessive forms, records, procedures before action can be taken
Russian: Red means beauty

MEDICINE

Doctor call: Red flag displayed outside homes in early Massachusetts to summon doctor on his rounds

Hygiene markings (Sweden):
Unsterile and dirty
England: Physicians wore red cloak

METEOROLOGY

Coast Guard flags: Storm or hurricane (red flag with black center)
Weatherfront markings on maps:
Warm fronts
Red and blue: Quasistationary fronts
Red and green: Intertropical discontinuity

MUSIC

Instruments:
Trumpet (Goethe), strings (Wagner)
Keys:
Alexander Scriabin
C: Red
F: Dark red
Notes:
American Taylor System:
C: Red
C#: Red-orange
Louis Bertrand Castel:
G: Red
G#: Crimson
George Field:
E: Red
Alexander Hector:
G#: Red-violet
A: Red
A#: Red-orange
A. B. Klein:
C: Dark red
C#: Red
D: Red-orange
Isaac Newton:
C: Red
A. Wallace Rimington:
C: Deep red
C#: Crimson
D: Orange-crimson

PRIZES

Second

PSYCHOLOGY

Warm, extroverted, fiery, aggressive, vigorous, impulsive, sympathetic, abrupt, crude, rude, optimistic
Color Preferences:
Child: Fourth
Adult: Second

RECREATION

Sports:
Auto racing: Come to complete stop
British athletic teams: Welsh

RELIGION

Aztec: Used in human sacrifices
Buddhism: Worn by Buddha when pondering the vicissitudes of man
Christianity: Blood of Christ, charity and martyrdom for faith, hell, love, youth, fervor, sin and atonement
Liturgical: From and with vespers of the Saturday before Whitsunday to the vespers of the Saturday before the festival of the Holy Trinity to signify fiery tongues; on all Apostles' and Evangelists' Days (except St. John) to show their passage to heaven in blood; on days of martyrs, on all church anniversaries; the festival of the Harvest, on Thanksgiving Day
Threefold aspect of man: The body
Trinity: God the Holy Ghost
Confucianism: Red disliked by Confucius
Egyptian: Shu, god who separated the earth from the sky
Greek: Token of human love and sacrifice; worn when reciting the Iliad to signify the bloody encounters; Ceres' flower was the red poppy
Hindu (also gold): Brahma
Caste: Kshatriyas, second, soldiers
Islam: Mohammed swore oaths by the "redness of the sky at sunset"
Judaism:
Hebrew color of God: Red fire for love, sacrifice, and sin
Kabbalah: Strength
Twelve tribes of Israel: Judah, Reuben
Shinto: Chief color of the religion; symbolizes life to dead ancestors

SAFETY

Stop, stop harmful activity, fire fighting equipment, danger, flammable
Gas-mask canisters:
Red with gray stripe: All atmospheric contaminants
Piping: Fire protection water or fluids
Nautical:
Green with red stripe: Fire prevention water
Surf: Heavy, dangerous

TRAFFIC

Highway Color Code: Stop, prohibition
Rail: Stop

TRAVEL

Signs in terminals: Danger

PINK

POSITIVE ASSOCIATIONS

Color of the flesh, sensuality, emotions

CULTURE COMPARISONS

Japan: Happy
United States: Baby girl

EDUCATION (doctorate hoods)

United States:
Light rose: Statistics
Pink: Music
Salmon pink: Public Health
Rose: Textiles

GEMS

Pink tourmaline:
Rings worn by professions (Brazil): Businessman

HOLIDAYS

Easter

MUSIC

Instrument tone:
Oboe (Goethe)

PSYCHOLOGY

Color Preferences:
Child: Third
Adult: Fifth

ORANGE

(continued)

Keys:
Alexander Scriabin:
G: Orange
Notes:
American Taylor System:
C#: Red-orange
D: Orange
D#: Orange yellow
Louis Bertrand Castel:
F#: Orange
F: Yellow-orange
George Field:
F: Orange
Alexander Hector:
A#: Red-orange
B: Orange
A. B. Klein
D: Red-orange
D#: Orange
Isaac Newton
D: Orange

A. Wallace Rimington:
D: Orange-crimson
D#: Orange

PSYCHOLOGY

Social, "Hail fellow well met," fickle, unsteady, vacillating, defer to others opinions, agreeable, good natured, gregarious, appeals to Northern Irish

Color preferences:
Child: Fifth
Adult: Seventh

RECREATION

Sports:
Auto racing (flag with blue center): One car attempting to pass another

RELIGION

Judaism:
Kabbalah: Mercy

SAFETY

Dangerous parts of machines or energized equipment which may cut, crush, or shock

TRAFFIC

Highway Color Code: Construction or maintenance warning

YELLOW
(continued)

Creek, Hopi, Zuni: North
Tibet: North

EDUCATION (doctorate hoods)

United States:
Citron: Social Work
Cream: Social Science
Golden yellow: Science
Lemon: Library Science

ELECTRICAL ENGINEERING

Chassis wiring: Cathodes and transistor emitters
Circuits (Switzerland): Heating
Yellow-green: Separately installed electrical conductors

ELEMENTS

Aristotle: Fire
Buddhist: Earth
Chinese: Earth
Greek: Air (represented the person)

FOLKLORE

Death:
China: Yellow tube used in burial ceremonies to pay homage to the earth
Guatemala: Some widows paint their bodies yellow

Marriage: Red and yellow are marriage colors in Egypt, the Orient, Russia, and the Balkans
Dutch East Indies: Red or yellow sprinkled over the bridegroom to keep his soul from flying away
India: Bride wore tattered yellow garments six days before the wedding to drive away evil spirits; also wore yellow at the ceremony

Medicine:
Color for quarantine
Jaundice cures:
England: Yellow spiders rolled in butter
Germany: Turnips, gold coins, saffron
Malay: Disease driven away in a yellow ship
Russia: Gold beads

Superstition:
China: Red and yellow paper used against demons
Theaters in west: Bad luck

GEMS

Beryl: Cured jaundice and bad liver
Saffron: Sleeping potion and tranquilizer
Yellow sapphire: Charity

HANDLING OF GOODS

Inter-Governmental Maritime Consultative Organization shipping labels: Oxidizing agent, organic peroxide
League of Red Cross Societies relief shipments: Medical supplies and equipment

HERALDRY

Tinctures:
Or: Honor and loyalty

HOLIDAYS

Easter (with purple)

LANGUAGE

Colloquialisms:
Contracts: Anti-socialist, trade union
Yellow dog: Scoundrel
Yellow journalism: Sensationalism
Yellow stripe: Coward

Mexico: Word for god who supported the sky was Kan, yellow

MEDICINE

Hygiene markings (Sweden):
Unsterile: Infectious and unsterilized

MUSIC

Instruments:
Clarinet (Goethe)
Oboe (Philip Hale)

Keys:
Alexander Scriabin:
D: Yellow

Notes:
American Taylor System:
D#: Orange-yellow
E: Yellow
F: Yellow-green
Louis Bertrand Castel:
F: Yellow-orange
E: Yellow
D#: Yellow-green
George Field:
G: Yellow
A: Yellow-green
Alexander Hector:
C: Yellow
C#: Yellow-green
A. B. Klein:
E: Yellow
F: Yellow-green
Isaac Newton:
E: Yellow
A. Wallace Rimington:
E: Yellow
F: Yellow-green

PRIZES

Third

PSYCHOLOGY

Imagination, novelty, self-fulfillment, intellectual, idealistic; cultists, reformers; depth of introspection and contemplation; controlled temper; warmth and joy

Color preferences:
Child: First
Adult: Eighth

RECREATION

Sports:
Auto racing (flag): Caution

RELIGION

Buddhism: Buddha's color, color of robes worn in ordination of Buddhist priest

Christianity: Power and the glory, nimbus of Saints, gates of heaven, hue of confessors (saffron), hue of Judas
Dingy yellow: Infernal light, degradation, jealousy, treason and deceit
Threefold aspect of man: Mind

Trinity: God the Son
Confucianism: Sacred to Confucius
Egyptian: Ra (sun)
Hindu: Vishnu, the Preserver, universal understanding
Caste: Vaisyas, third, mercantile
Judaism:
Kabbalah: Beauty
Twelve Tribes of Israel: Simeon

SAFETY

Warning of danger, caution signs, insides of machinery guards; designates striking against, stumbling, falling, tripping, and "caught in between" hazards; often used with black stripes or checks
Yellow lettering on red: Flammable liquid
Yellow and purple: Used for radiation hazards
Gas-mask canisters:
Yellow: Acid gases and organic vapors
Yellow with blue stripe: Hydrocyanic acid gas and chloropicrin vapor
White with yellow stripe: Chlorine
Piping: Dangerous materials (i.e., gases, acids)
Nautical:
Ochre: Gases in gaseous or liquified condition (except air)
With black stripe: Danger
Surf: Caution, rip tides

TRAFFIC

Highway Color Code: General warning
Rail: Proceed with caution and at reduced speed

TRAVEL

Signs in terminals: Information

GREEN
(continued)

plates, and first transistor bases
Circuits (Switzerland):
Green: Telephone and telediffusion
Yellow-green: Separately installed protective conductor

ELEMENTS

Buddhist: Wood
Chinese: Wood
Greek: Water (represented the world)

FOLKLORE

Medicine: Indigestion in Ireland relieved by measuring the waist with green thread in the name of the Trinity, then eating three dandelion leaves on a piece of bread and butter for three consecutive mornings
Medieval magicians' vestments: Green on Wednesday, day favorable to science

GEMS

Alexandrite: Everlasting life and friendship, faith and powers of endearment
Beryl: Happiness and eternal youth, cured eye ailments, birthstone for March (aquamarine)
Chrysolite: Banishes the hidden terrors of night
Chrysoprase: If a thief to be hanged were to put one in his mouth, he would escape
Emerald: Immortality, friendship, happiness, high esteem, powers of endearment, good luck, memory, faith, brought wisdom, struck terror into the viper and cobra to make their eyes burst from their heads, cured eye ailments, heart ailments, birthstone for May
Rings worn by professions (Brazil): Physicians
Feldspar (green): Used when reciting Chapter 27 of the *Egyptian Book of the Dead*
Heliotrope: Power
Jade: Good fortune, good luck, brought rain and frightened wild beasts and evil spirits, used in burial ceremonies in China, assisted in child birth, cured dropsy, quenched thirst, relieved heart palpitation
Peridot: Birthstone for August
Serpentine: Protects against venomous bites
Tourmaline (green):
Rings worn by professions (Brazil): Professors

HANDLING OF GOODS

Gases (Austria): Nitrogen
Inter-Governmental Maritime Consultative Organization shipping labels: Compressed gas
League of Red Cross Societies relief shipments: Blankets and bedding

HERALDRY

Tinctures:
Vert: Youth and hope
Crusades: Flemish wore green crosses on their shoulders

HOLIDAYS

St. Patrick's Day, Christmas

LANGUAGE

Colloquialisms:
Green for jealousy and envy
Greenbacks: Paper currency
Green goose: Harlot
Green, greenhorn: Inexperienced

MEDICINE

Hygiene markings (Sweden): Sterile

METEOROLOGY

Weatherfront markings on maps: Intertropical discontinuity

MUSIC

Instruments:
French horn, woodwinds (Wagner)
Keys:
Alexander Scriabin
A: Green
Notes:
American Taylor System:
F: Yellow-green
F#: Green
G: Blue-green
Louis Bertrand Castel:
D#: Yellow-green
D: Green
C#: Blue-green
George Field:
A: Yellow-green
B: Green
Alexander Hector:
C#: Yellow-green
D: Green
D#: Blue-green
A. B. Klein:
F: Yellow-green
F#: Green
G: Blue-green
Isaac Newton:
F: Green
A. Wallace Rimington:
F: Yellow-green
F#: Green
G: Bluish-green
G#: Blue-green

PRIZES

Special Awards

PSYCHOLOGY

Civility and the good citizen, sensitive to social customs and etiquette, bourgeois, abundance and good health
Color preferences:
Child: Seventh
Adult: Third

RECREATION

Sports:

Auto racing (flag): Start

RELIGION

Christianity:

Holy Grail: Color of God, faith, immortality, contemplation, everlasting as nature, hue of baptism, hope, peace, spring, triumph of life over death, charity, regeneration of the soul through good works

Liturgical: Epiphany and Trinity seasons

Used on days (except Saint's Day) from Trinity Sunday until Advent and from Octave of the Epiphany to Septuagesima, exclusively

Druidism:

Division of Ovates (lowest): Color of learning, members expected to be versed in medicine and astrology

Egyptian: Osiris, god of vegetation and death, material aspect of solar divinity

Hindu: Color of the horse with seven heads that drew Om, the sun, across the sky

Islam: The most sacred color, the banner of Mohammed

Judaism:

Kabbalah: Victory

Twelve tribes of Israel: Ephraim, Benjamin, Dan

SAFETY

Escape routes and refuges, clear or go signals for persons and vehicles, first aid and rescue stations and equipment and their location, gas masks and stretchers, stands for safety itself; water

Gas-mask canisters:

Green: Ammonia gas

Green with white stripe: Acid gases and ammonia

White with green stripe: Hydrocyanic acid gas

Piping: Safe materials

Nautical: Water in liquid state

Surf: Average

TRAFFIC

Highway Color Code: Indicated movement permitted, direction guidance

Rail:

Green: Track is clear

Green and white: Stop train only at flag stations on its schedule

TRAVEL

Signs in terminals: Identification

BLUE

(continued)

EDUCATION (doctorate hoods)

United States:

Dark blue: Philosophy

Light blue: Education

Peacock blue: Public Administration

ELECTRICAL ENGINEERING

Chassis wiring: Plates (anodes) and transistor collectors

Circuits (Switzerland): Lighting

ELEMENTS

Greek: Earth (represented man)

Jewish (Josephus): Air

FOLKLORE

Death:

Blue amulet as preparation: England

Fertility:

Blue beads: East Central Africa

Blue and white girdles: Protection during pregnancy in France

Marriage: Blue spot behind groom's ear thwarted powers of evil in Morocco

Medicine: Blue thread cured croup in Ireland

Medieval magicians' vestments: Sky blue on Friday, day of amorous operations

Mourning: Borneo, Mexico, Chaldee, Germany

Superstition:

Blue string around necks of animals protected them from death: Afghanistan, Syria, Macedonia

Blue hand painted on doors and walls for protection: Jerusalem

GEMS

Hyacinth: Second sight

Lapis Lazuli: Used when reciting Chapter 26 of the *Egyptian Book of the Dead*

Sapphire: Guardian of chastity, true love, friendship, memory, and life everlasting; royal stone; powers of endearment; brought mental and physical well being; prevented disease and plague; cured eye ailments and heart ailments; birthstone for September

Rings worn by professions (Brazil): Engineers

Turquoise: Powers of endearment, warded off evil eye, marital harmony, protects against injury from falling, poisons, reptile bites, eye disease; dipped in water to make cure for retention of urine, warned of death by changing color; birthstone for December

GEOGRAPHY-CARTOGRAPHY

Hydrographic features

HANDLING OF GOODS

Gases (Austria): Oxygen

Inter-Governmental Maritime Consultative Organization shipping labels: Dangerous (combustion may occur) when wet

League of Red Cross Societies relief shipments: Clothing

HERALDRY

Tinctures:

Azure: Piety and sincerity

LANGUAGE

Colloquialisms:

Feeling blue, have the blue devils: Depression

Blues: Music of American Negro origin usually using a major scale with the third and seventh notes flatted

Blue laws: Puritanical laws

Blue blood: Aristocracy

MEDICINE

Anesthetics (Sweden): Nitrous oxide (laughing gas)

Hygiene markings (Sweden): Clean, but not sterilized

METEOROLOGY

Weatherfront markings on maps:

Blue: Cold front

Red and blue: Quasistationary front

Coast Guard: Rain or snow

MUSIC

Instruments:

Cello: Indigo (Goethe)

Flute (Philip Hale)

Violin: Ultramarine

Keys:

Alexander Scriabin:

E: Blue

F#: Bright blue

B: "Pearly blue, "the shimmer of moonshine

Notes:

American Taylor System:

G: Blue-green

G#: Blue

A: Blue-violet
Louis Bertrand Castel:
C#: Blue-green
C: Blue
B: Indigo
George Field:
C: Blue
Alexander Hector:
D#: Blue-green
E: Blue
F: Indigo
F#: Blue-violet
A. B. Klein:
G: Blue-green
G#: Blue
A: Blue-violet
Isaac Newton:
G: Blue
A: Indigo
A. Wallace Rimington:
G: Bluish-green
G#: Blue-green
A: Indigo
A#: Deep blue

PRIZES

First

PSYCHOLOGY

Deliberation and introspection, conservatism, acceptance of obligations, higher education, culture, income, spirituality and thought, relaxing

Color preferences:
Child: Sixth
Adult: First

RECREATION

Sports:
Auto racing:
Blue flag: Last lap
Orange flag with blue center: One car attempting to pass another
British athletic teams: Scots

RELIGION

Christianity:
Virgin Mary, love of divine and good works, heavenly love, hope, sincerity, piety, peace, prudence, serene conscience
Liturgical: Advent and pre-Lenten Gesima Sundays (English only)
Threefold aspect of man: Spirit
Trinity: God the Father

Druidism: Division of Bards (Middle); color of harmony and truth; members were poets and musicians

Egyptian: Amen, god of life and reproduction

Greek: Conception of good and sign of truth

Hindu: Associated with the origin of the gods in the sea

Judaism: Sacred to God, blue fire of of God means glory

Kabbalah: Mercy
Twelve tribes of Israel: Issachar, Naphthal

SAFETY

Designates caution, particularly against the starting of, use of, or the movement of equipment under repair or being worked upon; an auxiliary color for purposes of organization, instruction, or information

Gas-mask canisters:
Blue: Carbon monoxide
Yellow with blue stripe: Hydrocyanic acid gas and chloropicrin vapor

Piping: Protective materials (i.e. antidote gases)
Nautical:
Green with blue stripe: Fresh water, potable or nonpotable
Light blue: Air

TRAFFIC

Highway Color Code: Motorist services guidance

Rail: Workmen are about or under an engine, car, or train

TRAVEL

Signs in terminals: Information and instruction

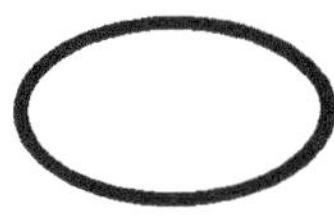

PURPLE

(continued)

HERALDRY

Tinctures:
Murrey: Sacrifice
Purpure: Royalty and rank

HOLIDAYS

Easter (with yellow)

LANGUAGE

Colloquialisms:
Purple with rage

MEDICINE

Anesthetics (Sweden): Ethelyne

METEOROLOGY

Weatherfront markings on maps: Occluded fronts

MUSIC

Instruments:
Oboe (Christopher Ward)
Trombone (Philip Hale)
Goethe:
Purple: French horn
Violet: Flageolet

Keys
Alexander Scriabin:
Db: Purple
Ab: Violet

Notes:
American Taylor System:
A: Blue-violet
A#: Violet
B: Violet-red
Louis Bertrand Castel:
A: Violet
A#: Pale-violet
George Field:
D: Violet-purple
Alexander Hector:
F#: Blue-violet
G: Violet
G#: Red-violet
A. B. Klein:
A#: Violet
B: Dark-violet
Isaac Newton
B: Violet-purple
A. Wallace Rimington:
B: Violet-purple

PRIZES

Winner over all classes

PSYCHOLOGY

Vanity, good mind and wit

Color preferences:
Child: Eighth
Adult: Sixth

RELIGION

Christianity: Purple robes worn by Christ before crucifixion; suffering and endurance, the hue of the penitent, the self-sacrificing god, repentance, royalty, imperial power, passion
Liturgical: From vespers on the Saturday before Advent Sunday to vespers on the eve of the Nativity; from the vespers of the day before Ash Wednesday throughout Lent (excepting Good Friday) to vespers of the Eve of Easter; ember and Rogation days, funerals, Holy Innocents (unless on Sunday, then red)

Confucianism: Purple disliked intensely by Confucius

Greek: Worn when reciting the Odyssey to signify the sea wanderings of Odys.

Judaism:
Hebrew color of God: Purple fire for splendor and dignity; divine condescension
Kabbalah: Foundation-basis of all there is
Twelve Tribes of Israel: Zebulon, Asher

SAFETY
Used for radiation hazards (with yellow); valuable materials, caution against waste
Gas-mask canisters: Radioactive materials, excepting tritium and noble gases
Piping:
Nautical: Acids and alkalis

TRAFFIC
Highway Color Code: Children's crossing
Rail: "Dwarf signal" – stop

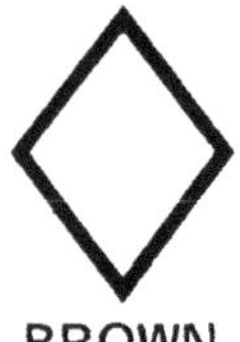

BROWN
(continued)

Topaz: Friendship and fidelity, powers of endearment, faith; birthstone for November
Rings worn by professions (Brazil): Dentist

HERALDRY
Used by lesser nobility

HOLIDAYS
Thanksgiving

LANGUAGE
Colloquialisms:
Done brown: victim of a genteel swindle

MEDICINE
Anesthetic gases (Sweden): Helium

MUSIC
Instrument tone:
Trombone, French horn
Bass (Christopher Ward)

PSYCHOLOGY
Conscientious performance of duty, parsimony, and shrewdness with money; obstinacy of habits and convictions; reliability

RELIGION
Christianity: Penitence, renunciation, monasticism, spiritual death, degradation
Magi: Brown King (incense)
Orders: Reformed branch of Franciscans
White over brown: The Carmelites

SAFETY
Gas-mask canisters: Acid gases, organic vapors, ammonia gases
Piping:
Nautical: Mineral, vegetable, and animal oil; combustible liquids

TRAFFIC
Highway Color Code: Public recreation and scenic guidance

GOLD
(continued)

FOLKLORE
Marriage (Judaic): Ceremony under golden robe
Superstition:
Bavaria: Sower wore gold ring to endow his grain with a rich color

HERALDRY
British royalty: Crown of England fashioned of gold and purple; reserved for higher nobility

RELIGION
Greek: Robe worn by Athena
Hindu: Brahma (also red), the Creator

WHITE
(continued)

Chippewa, Creek, Hopi, Isleta, Navaho, Zuni: East
Ireland: South
Tibet: East

EDUCATION (doctorate hoods)
United States: Arts and letters

ELECTRICAL ENGINEERING
Chassis wiring: Bias supply, B or C minus, AVC and AGC

ELEMENTS
Buddhist: Metal
Chinese: Metal
Greek: Sphere of the deity
Hindu (white color of fire): Water
Judaic (Josephus): Flax

FOLKLORE
Death:
Borneo: White (or dark blue) used in mourning
China: Accepted color of mourning, white jade used in burial ceremonies to pay respects to the west
England: Widows wore white band with black
Japan: Accepted color of mourning; when worn by Japanese bride it means she is dead to her family and belongs solely to her husband

Marriage:
In Japan, the daughter of a man who fed 1,000 white hares in his house would marry a prince; white (and red) girdles were protection during pregnancy
France: Blue and white girdles were protection during pregnancy

Medicine:
Brittany: The milk of a white hare cured fever
Egypt: Red on white cake cured constipation
Greece and Rome: White garments worn to cause pleasant dreams
Plutarch: White reed found on banks of a river while one journeyed to a dawn sacrifice; is strewn in a wife's bedroom, drove an adulterer mad and forced him to confess his sin.

Medieval magicians' vestments: White on Monday (no particular function)
Superstition:
Egypt: White amulets protected bearer from evil eye and other perils
England: Yorkshire fishermen fear white
India: Sacrificing white beasts brought the sun
Spain: White insect was good luck, but white moth was a harbinger of death in Castile and Spanish Galicia

GEMS

Crystal: Divination; in powder form it cured swellings of glands, diseased eyes, heart ailments, fever, and intestinal pains; mixed with honey it increased the milk of a mother
- Australia: Brought rain
- Mexico: Stones were the dwellings for souls of the living and dead
- Scotland: Stone of victory

Diamond: High esteem, powers of endearment, friendship, good luck; fortified mind and body and cured almost everything; dipped in water and wine, it formed an elixir that cured gout, jaundice, and apoplexy; birthstone for April
- Pliny: Rendered poisons harmless; drove away madness, the evil eye, demons, and wild beasts

Jasper: Wisdom and courage
Moonstone: Produced abundant crops and fruit, lucky stone in the Orient
Quartz (Iris Stone): Epilepsy
Zircon: Everlasting life

HANDLING OF GOODS

Gases (Austria): Acetylene
Inter-Governmental Maritime Consultative Organization shipping labels:
- Black and white: Corrosive, poison, poison gas, radioactive
- One-half red and one-half white: Spontaneously combustible
- Red and white striped: Flammable solid

HERALDRY

Crusades: English soldiers wore white crosses on their shoulders
English royalty:
- Lancastrians: White and blue
- Stuarts: White
- Tudors: White and green

LANGUAGE

Colloquialisms:
- To be white: Noble human (as contrasted by Caucasians with non-Aryans such as Indian and Negro)
- White feather, white flag: Surrender, symbol of peace, truce

MEDICINE

Anesthetics (Sweden): Oxygen
- Black and white: Air

METEOROLOGY

Coast Guard weather flags:
- Fair weather
- White flag with square black center: Cold wave

PRIZES

Fourth

PSYCHOLOGY

Simplicity, willingness to live, honest, noninvolved
Color preferences:
- Child: Second
- Adult: Fourth

RECREATION

Sports:
- Auto racing (flag): Stop for consultation
- Black and white checkered: The finish
- British athletic teams: English

RELIGION

Christianity: Chastity, innocence, purity, baptism, light, faith, divinity, virginity, angels, confessions, virgins, the spotless Lamb of God, holiness of life
- Liturgical: From and with vespers of the Eve of Nativity, through the Epiphany season (except St. Stephen's Day), from Easter Day to the vespers of the Saturday before Whitsunday; on the festival of Transfiguration, the presentation; festival of the Holy Trinity and its octave, days of Annunciation and Visitation, day of St. Michael and All Angels
- Magi:
  - White king: Gold
- Orders: Reformed branch of the Benedictines, Cistercians, the Order of the Holy Cross
  - Black over white: The Dominicans
  - White over brown: The Carmelites

Confuscianism: Sacred to Confucius
Druidism: Division of Ministers
Egypt: Horus (masculinity and femininity)
Greek: Emblem of divinity; white robes worn by temple priests
Hindu:
- Caste: Brahman, first class, priests

Islam: Chief color worn by Mohammed
Judaism: White fire of God symbolized purity, joy, victory
- Kabbalah: Concentration of divine light
- Twelve Tribes of Israel: Gad

SAFETY

Black and white: Used for traffic and housekeeping markers (stairs, trash cans)
Gas-mask canisters:
- White: Acid gases
- White with green stripe: Hydrocyanic acid gas
- White with yellow stripe: Chlorine

TRAFFIC

Highway Color Code: Regulation
Rail (with green): Used to stop train only at flag station on its schedule

GRAY
(continued)

Piping:
- Nautical: Steam

BLACK
(continued)

ELECTRICAL ENGINEERING

Chassis wiring: Grounds, grounded elements, and returns

ELEMENTS

Buddhist: Water
Chinese: Water
Hindu (black color of burning fire): Earth

FOLKLORE

Death:
- China: Black jade used in burial ceremonies to pay respects to the north
- West: Universal color of mourning

Fertility:
- Africa (East-Central): Wife wore black hen on her back
- Algeria: Black hens sacrificed

Medicine: Black snails cured warts; black fowl, if buried where caught, cured epilepsy
- Egypt: Blood of black cat used for various ailments
- England and South Africa: Blood of a black cat prescribed for pneumonia
- France: The limbs of black animals applied warm to the limbs of the body relieved rheumatism
- Ireland, England, and Vermont: Black wool cured earache
- Russia: Cured jaundice

Medieval magicians' vestments: Black on Saturday, day of funeral operations

Superstition:
England: Northumberland fishermen fear black
India: Crops were saved from rain and hail damage by a twin standing in the direction of the wind with his right buttock painted black and his left some other color; sacrifice of black animals brought rain
Ireland: Pelt of a black dog buried to quell storms
Japan: Black cat had divine powers and could foretell the weather
Spain: Black insect was bad omen, black cat was good luck
United States: Black cat is generally bad luck, but success for a theatrical production

GEMS

Jet: Nullified spells, drove away snakes, quelled thunderstorms, gave safety to the traveler and kept him free of the evil eye, healed epilepsy, toothache, headache, glandular swellings

GEOGRAPHY

Contours (sea and land), heights and soundings, railways, submarine cables

HANDLING OF GOODS

Inter-Governmental Maritime Consultative Organization shipping labels (with white): Corrosive, poison, radioactivity
League of Red Cross Societies relief shipments: Toilet and comfort articles

HERALDRY

Tinctures:
Sable: Grief and penitence

HOLIDAYS

Halloween

LANGUAGE

Colloquialisms: Synonym for evil and despair
Blackball: Ostracism, negative vote
Blackmail: Extortion
Black sheep: Disgrace of the family

MEDICINE

Anesthetic gases (Sweden): Nitrogen
Black and white: Air

METEOROLOGY

Weatherfront markings on maps: Instability lines, shear lines, axis of trough, axis of ridges
Coast Guard weather:
White flag with square black center: Cold wave
Red flag with black center: Hurricane
Black pennant above weather flag: Temperatures will get warmer
Black pennant below weather flag: Temperatures will get cold

MUSIC

Instrument tone:
Bassoon (grayish-black) (Philip Hale)
Brass (Wagner)
Keys:
Beethoven:
B minor

PSYCHOLOGY

Morbid, despairing, gloom, sophistication, regal without being pompous

RECREATION

Sports:
Auto racing (black and white checkered): Finish

RELIGION

Christianity: Death and regeneration, black rose a symbol of silence, Protestant dress of students and ministers, mourning.
Liturgical: Good Friday and Day of Humiliation
Magi: Black king brought myrrh
Orders: Benedictines, Augustinians, Jesuits, Cowley Fathers
Black over white: Dominicans
Confucianism: Sacred to Confucius
Egypt: Set, god of evil and darkness
Hindu: Shiva, the destroyer and reproducer
Caste: Sudras, lowest, servile class
Islam: Color of "Blackstone," turned black by sins of man; Moslems pray for its return to whiteness
Judaism:
Kabbalah: Understanding (absorbs all light)

SAFETY

Physical hazards, used with yellow (*see under* Yellow)
Black and white: Traffic and housekeeping markings (stairways and trash cans)
Gas-mask canisters: Organic vapors
Piping:
Nautical: Other liquids

TRAFFIC

Highway Color Code: Regulation

ACKNOWLEDGMENTS
BIBLIOGRAPHY
INDEX

ACKNOWLEDGMENTS

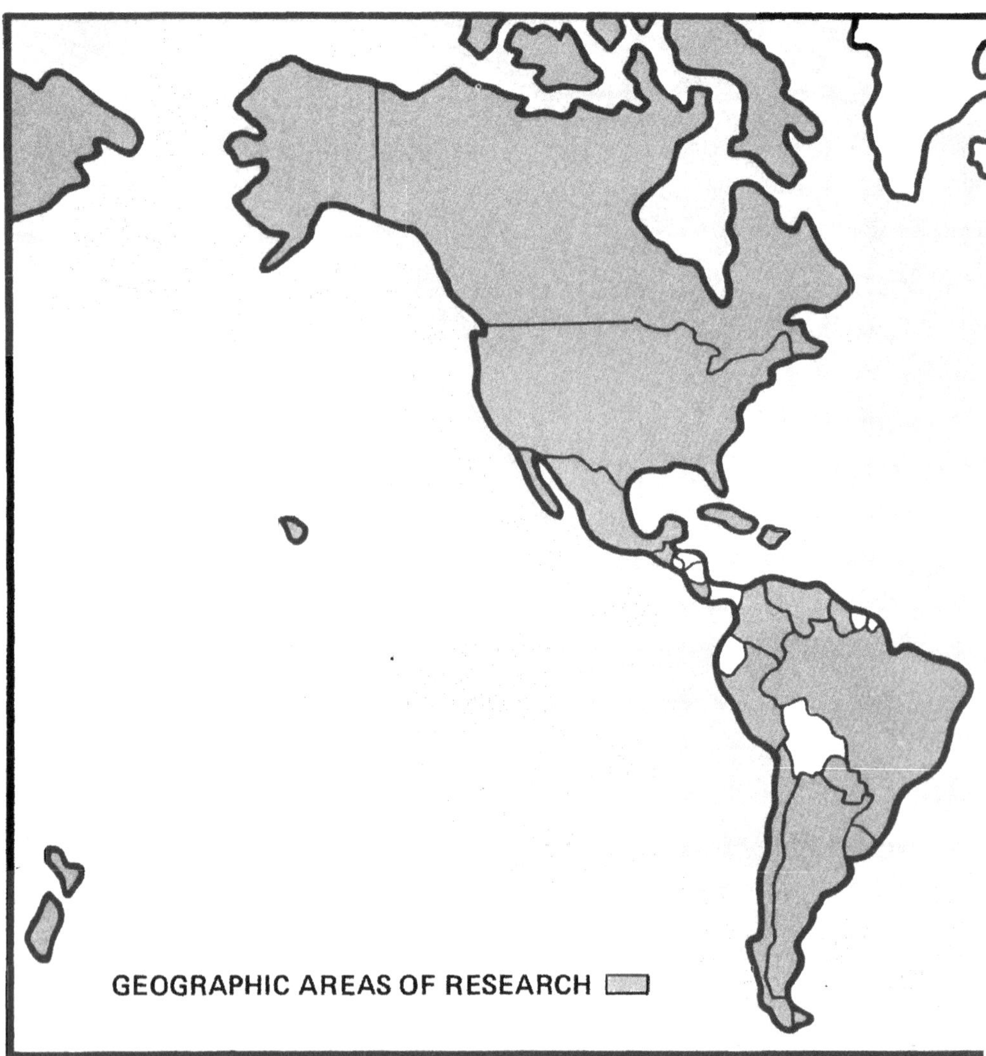
GEOGRAPHIC AREAS OF RESEARCH

Accumulating material for this book has been the work of many heads and hands in many places. There were literally thousands who contributed invaluable material; and to all of them, my gratitude. But among these are a few organizations and individuals to whom I must express special thanks for their exceptional cooperation in developing our Data Bank of symbols on which this Sourcebook is based.

The first concrete step toward the concept of the Sourcebook came in the form of a feasibility study grant from the National Endowment for the Humanities, administered by the California Institute of Technology with the authorization of Lee A. DuBridge, its president. It was their faith that permitted me to explore the subject and move ahead.

The official standards organizations in many countries have given us excellent advice and cooperation. Donald Peyton, Managing Director of the American National Standards Institute (ANSI), was one of my first champions; he has advised and constantly encouraged our efforts. Olle Sturen, Secretary-General of the International Organization for Standards (ISO), and his staff received me in Geneva, opening their files to me, and at all times keeping my staff and me

informed on current developments. In Berlin, Deutscher Normenausschuss (DNA), through Nikolaus Ludwig and Karl-Heinz Bergner, put their research at our disposal and have kept us up to date on all their activities. Major cooperation has been extended to us by many other standards organizations including Association Francaise de Normalisation, British Standards Institution, Canadian Standards Association, Indian Standards Institution, Sveriges Standardiseringskommission, and the Zentral-institut (DAMW) of East Germany.

UNESCO's U.S. National Commission unanimously endorsed our symbol program, and through the efforts of their Executive Secretary, L. A. Minnich, obtained important data from its affiliates throughout the world. This Commission was chaired by Alvin C. Eurich, whose enthusiastic recognition of the international need for symbols has spurred me on for many years.

The U.S. Department of Commerce, whose National Bureau of Standards endorsed our project, as well as the U.S. Departments of Transportation, Agriculture (Forest Service), and Interior (National Park Service) have cooperated with us wholeheartedly.

The Sourcebook was also officially endorsed by the American Institute of Architects (AIA), American Institute of Graphic Arts (AIGA), American Society of Agricultural Engineers (ASAE), Industrial Designers Society of America (IDSA), International Council of Graphic Design Associations (ICOGRADA), and the International Council of Societies of Industrial Design (ICSID). These groups proved to be of great assistance to us in our research by circulating our symbol questionnaire to their entire membership and thus stimulating contributions to our Data Bank.

My colleagues here and abroad cooperated to the fullest, gathering data and granting us permission to include their symbols in our book. For this, my very special thanks. Dr. Margaret Mead and Rudolf Modley of Glyphs Inc. have worked with us throughout the project (and it was Dr. Mead who gave us the inspiration for the Graphic Forms Section); Masaru Katzumie gave us constant cooperation and provided us with the Expo '70 and Japan Olympic symbols; Ramirez Vazquez advised us and gave permission to use the Mexico Olympic symbols, as well as others he personally designed; Paul Arthur contributed the symbols for Expo '67, Vermont Travel Information, and others; Faber Birren was generous with his help on color; Yuri Soloviev of the All Union Research Institute of Industrial Design established contacts for us in the U.S.S.R.; and Martin Krampen gave us his International Survey on Pictographs. Much help was also given us by Christopher Alexander, Saul Bass, Ivan Chermayeff, Mildred Constantine, Josine des Cressonnieres, R. S. Easterby, Michael Farr, Thomas Geismar, Rex Goode, Lawrence Halprin, Isamu Kenmochi, Christopher Klumb, Peter Kneebone, and Tomas Maldonado.

There are many groups working on standardization of symbols in their own fields, most of whom I have worked with directly, who have generously helped us with our collection. Among those to whom particular thanks are due are the Air Transport Association (ATA), American Airlines, American Society of Mechanical Engineers (ASME), Deere & Company, Hyster Company, International Civil Aviation Organization (ICAO), Industrial Truck Association (ITA), and the Society of Automotive Engineers (SAE).

Appreciation is due to Alcan Aluminum Limited and Gordon Cullen for their unique architectural symbols; Arthur Crapsey of Eastman Kodak Company; Henry Dreyfuss Associates; International Business Machines Corporation and Paul Rand for their symbols in the Business discipline; Herbert Kummel and Muriel Topaz of the Dance Notation Bureau, Inc., for their selection of the Movement and Dance symbols; Peter Kyropoulos of General Motors; Max-Planck Institute for "Symbola" material; N. V. Philips' Gloeilampenfabrieken, Netherlands; Olivetti, and Herbert Lindinger; Siemens Aktiengesellschaft of West Germany; G. Dean Smith for his ecology symbols; Kenneth Stager and Roy Snelling of the Los Angeles County Museum of Natural History for their help in our search for zoology symbols; and Sveriges Radio of Stockholm.

From abroad, we also received invaluable material and permission to reproduce symbols from the Japan Association for 1970 World Exposition, Industrial Design Centre Scientific Group on Visual Communication in Bulgaria, N. V. Nederlandse Spoorwegen, South African Bureau of Mines, and Union International des Chemins de Fer.

Our expert consultants in academic and technical disciplines gave us expertise and enthusiasm beyond all possible expectation. They not only advised us on the selection of symbols, but also concerned themselves with sequence, layout, and detail captions. To each of them we are indebted, and with the following list express our gratitude:

Robert M. Benbow – Pre-Doctoral Fellow, CIT.* *Biology*
Stephen H. Caine – President, Caine, Farber & Gordon, Inc., Pasadena. *Computers*
Francis H. Clauser – Professor, CIT. *Engineering*
Donald S. Cohen – Associate Professor, CIT. *Mathematics*
James G. Edinger – Associate Professor, UCLA.† *Meteorology*
Harry B. Gray – Professor of Chemistry, CIT. *Alchemy*
Shirley B. Gray – *Alchemy*
James E. Gunn – Assistant Professor, CIT. *Astronomy*
R. Stewart Harrison, M.D. – Chief Radiologist, Huntington Memorial Hospital, Pasadena. *Medicine*
Franklyn D. Josselyn – Associate Professor, Occidental College, Los Angeles. *Religion*
George W. Kalstrom – Chief Meteorologist, National Weather Service, Los Angeles. *Meteorology*
Robert B. Leighton – Professor, CIT. *Astronomy, Chemistry, Mathematics, Physics*
R. David Middlebrook – Professor, CIT. *Electrical Engineering*
Richard C. Nielsen – Pre-Doctoral Fellow, CIT. *Mechanical Engineering*
Elma G. Schonbach – Faculty, Westridge School, Pasadena. *Music*
Frederick H. Shair – Associate Professor, CIT. *Chemical Engineering*
Robert P. Sharp – Professor, CIT. *Geology*
Robert L. Sinsheimer – Professor, CIT. *Biology*
Walter F. Starkie – Hon. Fellow, Trinity College, Dublin. *Folklore (Tarot Cards)*
Edward C. Stone – Assistant Professor, CIT. *Physics*
Norman J. W. Thrower – Professor, UCLA. *Geography*

*CIT – California Institute of Technology, Pasadena
†UCLA – University of California, Los Angeles

Finally, though first in importance, I express deepest thanks to my dedicated and tireless staff. Under the guidance of Paul Clifton, major responsibilities were carried by Kathryn Bray, and by George Ball, Pamela Holaday, and Jeanette MacFarland. The total staff worked diligently and efficiently in spite of chaotic pressures, and I am sincerely grateful. The South Pasadena Library staff, almost as part of our own group, helped us with unlimited patience.

BIBLIOGRAPHY

The Bibliography is divided into three separate parts: General, Disciplines, and Color.

GENERAL – Composed of references not limited to any one Discipline.

A discussion of the publications of standards organizations is also included here.

DISCIPLINES – Includes all bibliographic sources from which symbols have been selected, as well as additional material to provide more extensive research in any given Discipline.

It should be noted that many enthusiastic individuals were kind enough to send us printed material and photographs which were, unfortunately, not sufficiently identified to permit proper bibliographic entry in spite of their clear authenticity.

In academic areas where vast numbers of references exist, we have followed the advice of our consultants in noting only a few publications selected to give the reader the extended knowledge he may seek.

COLOR – This subject is one of great scope and interest and a vast amount of material on various phases of color studies exists. Our Bibliography is, of necessity, limited to the sources actually used in developing our listings.

General

Since the role played by various national and international standards organizations is so significant in the universal acceptance of symbols, a brief description of these organizations may be helpful to the reader.

ISO (International Organization for Standardization) promotes and coordinates worldwide standards, in all areas except those covered by IEC, through its national member bodies. The standardization work of ISO is handled in its Technical Committees (chaired by individual member bodies). A full list of ISO Recommendations and Draft ISO Recommendations, under the title "ISO CATALOG," is published annually by:

ISO Central Secretariat
1, rue de Varembe
1211 Geneva 20, Switzerland

IEC (International Electrotechnical Commission) promotes and coordinates international electrotechnical standards in the fields of power, electronics, and telecommunications. Countries participate in the IEC through National Committees. Standardization is handled by Technical Committees with participation from the National Committees. A full list of IEC Recommendations, under the title "Publications of the International Electrotechnical Commission," is published annually by:

Central Office of the IEC
1, rue de Varembé
1211 Geneva 20, Switzerland

ANSI (American National Standards Institute) is the national member body representing the United States in ISO. ANSI acts within the United States as the agent and information center for all other ISO national member bodies, and publishes an annual catalog, with bimonthly supplements, of its own standards, as well as those of ISO and IEC. This catalog is available from:

American National Standards Institute
1430 Broadway
New York, New York 10018

Other countries have equivalent organizations which, as member bodies of ISO, offer similar services.

DNA (Deutscher Normenausschuss), the national member body representing Germany in ISO, has the ISO Technical Committee Secretariat for developing recommendations for international standardization of *signs* and *symbols*. The work of this Technical Committee, ISO/TC

145 "Graphic Symbols," is currently being coordinated as Proposals, Drafts and Standards. Information may be obtained from:

Deutscher Normenausschuss
4-7 Burggrafenstrasse
1 Berlin 30, Germany

NOTE: Symbols recommended by official standards institutes and associations are subject to revision or withdrawal at any time. Current information may be obtained by contacting the official group concerned.

"The American Heritage Dictionary," American Heritage Publishing Co., Boston, 1969.

Arnell, Alvin: "Standard Graphical Symbols: A Comprehensive Guide for Use in Industry, Engineering, and Science," McGraw-Hill Book Company, New York, 1963.

Bliss, Charles K.: "Semantography (Blissymbolics)," 2d enlarged edition, Semantography (Blissymbolics) Publications, 2 Vicar Street, Coogee 2034, Sydney, Australia.

Cirlot, J. E.: "A Dictionary of Symbols," translated from the Spanish "Diccionario de Simbolos Tradicionales" by Jack Sage, Philosophical Library, New York, 1962.

Crosby, Theo (ed.): "Uppercase 5," Whitefriars, London, 1961.

Crosby/Fletcher/Forbes: "A Sign Systems Manual," Praeger Publishers, New York, 1970.

Deutscher Normenausschuss (DNA): "Bildzeicheń," DIN 30 600, Berlin, 1969–.

Diethelm, Walter: "Signet, Signal, Symbol: Handbook of International Signs," ABC Verlag, Zurich, 1970.

Dreyfuss, Henry: Case Study: Symbols for Industrial Use, in Gyorgy Kepes (ed.), "Sign, Image, Symbol," George Braziller, New York, 1966.

Feddersen, Martin: "Chinese Decorative Art: A Handbook for Collectors and Connoisseurs," Faber & Faber, London, 1961.

Goff, Beatrice Laura: "Symbols of Prehistoric Mesopotamia," Yale University Press, New Haven and London, 1963.

Goldsmith, Elisabeth: "Ancient Pagan Symbols," G. P. Putnam's Sons, New York, 1929.

Hammond, Natalie Hays: "Anthology of Pattern," William Helburn, New York, 1949.

Hangen, Eva C.: "Symbols: Our Universal Language," McCormick-Armstrong, Wichita, Kansas, 1962.

Helfman, Elizabeth S.: "Signs and Symbols Around the World," Lothrop, Lee & Shepard Co., New York, 1967.

Hogben, Lancelot: "From Cave Painting to Comic Strip," Chanticleer Press, New York, 1949.

Hornung, Clarence Pearson: "Handbook of Designs and Devices: 1836 Geometric Elements Drawn by the Author," Dover Publications, New York, 1946.

International Council of Graphic Design Associations (ICOGRADA): "Sign Information Sheets," A1/A6.1, working papers, Amsterdam, 1967.

Jung, Carl G., et al.: "Man and His Symbols," Dell Publishing Co., Laurel Edition, New York, 1968.

Kamekura, Yusaku: "Trademarks and Symbols of the World," Reinhold Publishing Corporation, New York, 1965.

Katzumie, Masaru: "Towards an International Sign Language," paper presented to Second ICOGRADA Congress, Bled, 1966.

Kepes, Gyorgy (ed.): "Sign, Image, Symbol," George Braziller, New York, 1966.

Kneebone, Peter (ed.): International Signs and Symbols: Special ICOGRADA Issue, *Print*, vol. 23, no. 6, November/December, 1969.

Koch, Rudolf: "The Book of Signs: Which Contains All Manner of Symbols Used from the Earliest Times to the Middle Ages by Primitive People and Early Christians," reprint, translated from the German by Vyuyan Holland, Dover Publications, New York [n.d.].

Krampen, Martin: Signs and Symbols in Graphic Communication, *Design Quarterly*, vol. 62, 1965.

Lehner, Ernst (comp.): "American Symbols: A Pictorial History," Wm. Penn Publishing Corporation, New York, 1966.

Lehner, Ernst: "The Picture Book of Symbols," Wm. Penn Publishing Corporation, New York, 1956.

Lehner, Ernst: "Symbols, Signs & Signets," Dover Publications, New York, 1969.

Mead, Margaret, and Rudolf Modley: Communication Among All People Everywhere, *Natural History*, August/September, 1968.

Modley, Rudolf: "The Challenge of Symbology," Fourth Annual Communications Conference of the Art Directors Club of New York, Fund for the Advancement of Education (Ford Foundation), New York, 1959.

Modley, Rudolf: Graphic Symbols for Worldwide Communication, in "Sign, Image, Symbol," edited by Gyorgy Kepes, George Braziller, New York, 1966.

Neurath, Otto: "BASIC by ISOTYPE," Psyche Miniatures General Series, Kegan Paul, Trench, Trubner & Co., London, 1937.

Neurath, Otto: "International Picture Language: The First Rules of ISOTYPE," Psyche Miniatures General Series, Kegan Paul, Trench, Trubner & Co., London, 1936.

"Odyssey Scientific Library," 12 vols., The Odyssey Press, New York, 1965.

"The Random House Dictionary of the English Language," pp. 1665–1666, Random House, New York, 1966.

Reiser, Oliver L.: "Unified Symbolism for World Understanding in Science: Including Bliss Symbols (Semantography) and Logic, Cybernetics and Semantics," Semantography Publishing Company, Sydney, Australia, 1955.

Ruesch, Jurgen, and Weldon Kees: "Nonverbal Communication: Notes on the Visual Perception of Human Relations," University of California Press, Berkeley and Los Angeles, 1956.

Whitney, Elwood (ed.): "Symbology: The Use of Symbols in Visual Communications," a report on the Fourth Communications Conference of the Art Directors Club of New York, Hastings House, New York, 1960.

Whittick, Arnold: "Symbols, Signs, and Their Meaning," Charles T. Branford Company, Newton, Mass., 1960.

Wildbur, Peter: "Trademarks: A Handbook of International Designs," Studio Vista, London, 1966.

Williams, C. A. S.: "Encyclopedia of Chinese Symbolism and Art Motives," The Julian Press, New York, 1960.

Disciplines

Accommodations and Travel

Aeropuertos y Servicios Auxiliares (ASA), Centro de Diseño, Teuscher-Aceves: Poster, (Impreso por) Signos de Mexico, S.A. de C.V. [1970?].

Air Transport Association, Airline Airport Technical Group: "Signs of the Jet Age," prepared by Arnold Thompson Associates, New York [n.d.].

International Air Transport Association (IATA): "Airport Terminals," 4th ed., Montreal, December, 1966.

International Air Transport Association (IATA): "Airport Terminals Reference Manual," [Montreal?] 1970.

International Civil Airport Association (ICAA): "Signs and Symbols on Airports," Technical DOC 6802-TEC./01 terminal buildings, Paris, October, 1968.

International Civil Aviation Organization: "ICAO System of International Signs to Facilitate Passengers Using International Airports," [Montreal?] December, 1969.

International Committee for Travel Signs and Symbols: "International Survey on Pictographs," draft report, prepared by Martin Krampen and B. Sevray, Paris, 1969.

International Union of Railways (UIC, Union Internationale des Chemins de Fer): "Measures to Facilitate Travel by Rail (1)," 413 OR, 5th ed., Paris, 1968.

N. V. Nederlandse Spoorwegen: Pictogrammen Aanduidingen in de Stations, NS-normblad O-11A, Utrecht, 1968.

Print: "International Signs and Symbols: Special ICOGRADA Issue," vol. 23, no. 6, November/December, 1969.

Short-term Housing for a Long-term Problem, *Progressive Architecture*, pp. 167–172, May, 1966.

Agriculture

Chu-gai Pharmatical [sic] Company: Packaging Manual, [n.p.], pp. 3.1–3.3 [n.d.].

Dupont, Robert, Jean Piel-Deruisseaux, Gerhardt Preuschen, and Johannes Röhner: "Symbols in Agriculture (Symbola)," 4th ed., Heft 29 der Schriftenreine "Landarbeit und Technik," Max-Planck Institutes für Landarbeit und Landtechnick, Bad Kreuznach, 1962.

Architecture

Alexander, Christopher, Sara Ishikawa, and Murray Silverstein: "A Pattern Language Which Generate Multi-Service Centers," Center for Environmental Structure, Berkeley, California, 1968.

American National Standards Institute (ANSI): "Graphic Electrical Wiring Symbols for Architectural and Electrical Layout Drawings," Y32.9–1962, New York, 1962.

American National Standards Institute (ANSI): "Graphic Symbols for Plumbing," Y32.4–1955, New York, 1955.

Constantine, Mildred, and Egbert Jacobson: "Sign Language: For Buildings and Landscape," Reinhold Publishing Corporation, New York, 1961.

Goode, Rex: Symbols for Signage, *Sourcebook*, vol. 16, p. 33, October, 1968.

Halprin, Lawrence: Motation, *Progressive Architecture*, pp. 126–133, July, 1965.

Halprin, Lawrence: "The RSVP Cycles: Creative Processes in the Human Environment," George Braziller, New York, 1969.

Montgomery, Roger: Pattern Language, *The Architectural Forum*, vol. 132, no. 1, pp. 55-59, January/February, 1970.

Ramsey, Charles George, and Harold Reeve Sleeper: "Architectural Graphical Standards for Architects, Engineers, Decorators, Builders, Draftsmen, and Students," 5th ed., John Wiley & Sons, New York, 1956.

A Town Called Alcan, *The Architectural Review*, vol. CXII, no. 844, pp. 33-36, June, 1967.

Astronomy

Allen, Clabon Walter: "Astrophysical Quantities," 2d ed., University of London, Athlone Press, London, 1963.

Becvar, Antonin: "Atlas Coeli 1950," Czechoslovakia and Academy Press, Prague, 1950.

Biology

Dayhoff, Margaret O.: "Atlas of Protein Sequence and Structure 1965-," National Biomedical Research Foundation, Silver Spring, Maryland, 1965-.

Deutscher Normenausschuss (DNA): "Pflanzenbeschreibungen im gärtnerischen Schrifttum," DIN 11530, Berlin, 1956.

Engler, Adolf: "Syllabus der Pflanzenfamilien mit besonderer Berücksichtigung der Nutzpflanzen nebst einer Übersicht über die Florenreiche und Florengebiete der Erde," 12 vollig neugestalte Aufl von Hans Melchior und Erich Wendermann, Gebrüder Borntraeger, Berlin-Nikolasse, 1954.

Hockling, George MacDonald (comp.): "A Dictionary of Terms in Pharmacognosy and Other Divisions of Economic Botany," Charles C Thomas, Springfield, Illinois, 1955.

Jackson, Benjamin Daydon: "A Glossary of Botanic Terms with Their Derivation and Accent," 4th ed., Gerald Duckworth & Co., London, 1928, reprinted 1960.

Kelsey, Harlan P., and William A. Dayton (eds.): "Standardized Plant Names," J. Horace McFarland, Harrisburg, Pennsylvania, 1942.

Mahler, Henry R., and Eugene H. Cordes: "Biological Chemistry," Harper and Row, New York, 1966.

Rieger, Rigomar, Arnd Michaelis, and Melvin M. Green: "A Glossary of Genetics and Cytogenetics: Classical and Molecular," 3d ed. (previous editions titled Genetisches und Cytogenetisches Wörterbach), Springer-Verlag, New York, 1968.

Tanford, Charles: "Physical Chemistry of Macromolecules," John Wiley & Sons, New York, 1961.

"Webster's New International Dictionary of the English Language," 2d ed., G. & C. Merriam Company, Springfield, Massachusetts, 1950.

Willis, John Christopher: "A Dictionary of the Flowering Plants and Ferns," 7th ed., revised by H. K. Airy Shaw, Cambridge University Press, Cambridge, 1966.

Business

Aeropuertos y Servicios Auxiliares (ASA), Centro de Diseño, Teuscher-Aceves: Poster, (Impreso por) Signos de Mexico, S.A. de C.V. [1970?].

American National Standards Institute (ANSI): "Flowchart Symbols and Their Usage in Information Processing," X3.5-1968, New York, 1970.

American National Standards Institute: "Graphic Representation of the Control Characters of ASCII," X3.2/960 (Draft), [New York?] April, 1970.

Chapin, Ned: Flowcharting with the ANSI Standard: A Tutorial, *Computing Surveys*, vol. 2, no. 2, June, 1970.

Deutscher Normenausschuss (DNA): "Büromaschinen: Funktions symbole für Buchungsmaschinen," DIN 9764, Berlin, 1966.

European Computer Manufacturers Association (ECMA): "Graphic Representation of Control Characters of the ECMA 7 Bit Coded Character Set for Information Interchange," ECMA-17, Geneva, November, 1968.

IBM Corporation: "Flowcharting Techniques," C20-8152, New York, 1964.

International Organization for Standardization (ISO): "Flowchart Symbols for Information Processing," ISO Recommendation R1028, 1st ed., March, 1969.

International Organization for Standardization (ISO): "Function Key Symbols on Typewriters," ISO Recommendation R1090, 1st ed., June, 1969.

International Organization for Standardization (ISO): "Keytop and Printed or Displayed Symbols for Adding Machines and Calculating Machines," ISO Recommendation R1093, 1st ed., June, 1969.

Maldonado, Tomás, and Gui Bonsiepe: Sign System Design for Operative Communication, in "Uppercase 5," edited by Theo Crosby, Whitefriars, London, 1961.

N. V. Nederlandse Spoorwegen: Railway Pictograms (printed sheet), Utrecht, 1969.

Print: "International Signs and Symbols: Special ICOGRADA Issue," vol. 23, no. 6, November/December, 1969.

Chemistry

Christiansen, J. A.: Manual of Physico-Chemical Symbols and Terminology, *Journal of the American Chemical Society,* vol. 82, no. 21, pp. 5517–5584, November 9, 1960.

Dickerson, Richard E., Harry B. Gray, and Gilbert P. Haight: "Chemical Principles," W. A. Benjamin, Inc., New York, 1970.

Ewing, Alfred M.: "Common Substances: Their Common Names, Chemical Names and Formulas," 4 pages, Texas Wesleyan College, Fort Worth, Texas, 1930.

Kosower, Edward M.: "An Introduction to Physical Organic Chemistry," John Wiley & Sons, New York, 1968.

Krebs, H.: "Fundamentals of Inorganic Crystal Chemistry," McGraw-Hill Publishing Company, London, 1968.

Weast, Robert C.: "Handbook of Chemistry and Physics," The Chemical Rubber Co. Ltd., Cleveland, 1969.

Communications

Braille Institute of America, Inc.: Braille Alphabet, card, Los Angeles [n.d.].

British Standards Institution: "Colour Proof Corrections," Draft British Standard, 70/38379, January, 1971.

Dell, Cecily: "A Primer for Movement Description," Dance Notation Bureau, Inc., New York, 1970.

Deutscher Normenausschuss (DNA): "Bildzeichen," DIN 30 600, Berlin, 1969–.

Gelb, I. J.: "A Study of Writing," revised edition, University of Chicago Press, Chicago & London, 1963.

Hutchinson, Ann: "Labanotation: The System of Analyzing and Recording Movement," Theatre Arts Books, New York, 1970.
Jensen, Hans: "Sign, Symbol and Script: An Account of Man's Efforts to Write," 3d ed., translated from the German "Die Schrift in Vergangenheit und Gegenwart" by George Unwin, G. B. Putnam's Sons, New York, 1959.
McGraw-Hill Book Company: "Instructions to Authors (Proofreaders' Marks)," leaflet, New York [n.d.].
The Monotype Corporation Limited: "Monotype Electronic Perforator," *Monotype Bulletin*, no. 76, pp. 2-5, October, 1968.
Ogg, Oscar: "The 26 Letters," Thomas Y. Crowell Company, New York, 1948.
Santelli, M. A.: "Appraisal of a Proposed Set of Symbolic Labels for the MOD II PICTURE-PHONE® Control Unit – Case No. 39320," Bell Telephone Laboratories, Inc., Holmdel, New Jersey, May, 1968.
The System of Visual Information in the Main Post Office in Vellnus, *Technical Esthetics,* U.S.S.R., vol. 7, no. 11, pp. 6-7, November, 1970.
U.S. Bureau of Naval Personnel: International Alphabet Flags, Phonetic Alphabet, Morse Code and Semaphore Alphabet, poster, Washington, D.C., 1968.
World Federation of the Deaf: International Manual Alphabet, post card [n.p., n.d.].

Engineering

American National Standards Institute (ANSI) "Graphic Symbols for Electrical and Electronics Diagrams," Y32.2-1967, New York, 1968.
American National Standards Institute (ANSI): "Graphic Symbols for Fluid Power Diagrams," Y32.10-1967, New York, 1967.
American National Standards Institute (ANSI): "Graphic Symbols for Process Flow Diagrams in the Petroleum and Chemical Industries," Y32.11-1961, New York, 1961.
Arnell, Alvin: "Standard Graphical Symbols: A Comprehensive Guide for Use in Industry, Engineering, and Science," McGraw-Hill Book Company, New York, 1963.
DECHEMA (Deutsche Gesellschaft für Chemisches Apparatewesen E.V.) Erfahrungsaustausch: "Sinnbilder für Apparate," Frankfurt am Main, 1957.
Deutscher Normanausschuss (DNA): "Fliessbilder verfahrenstechnischer Anlagen," DIN 28004 (Blatt 1-4), Berlin, 1969.
Institute of Electrical and Electronics Engineers (IEEE), and American National Standards Institute (ANSI): "Graphic Symbols for Electrical and Electronics Diagrams," (IEEE No. 315, March 1971; ANSI Y32.2-1970), New York, 1970.
Institution of Engineers: "Engineering Drawing Practice," Science House, Sydney, Australia, 1966.
International Electrotechnical Commission (IEC), Technical Committee No. 12 (Radio-communication): "Informative Symbols on Equipment, Part 1: Equipment Symbols for General Use," draft, February, 1968.
International Organization for Standardization (ISO): "Aircraft Electrical Symbols," Draft ISO Recommendation No. 1339, June, 1967.
International Organization for Standardization (ISO): "Graphical Symbols for Hydraulic and Pneumatic Equipment and Accessories for Fluid Power Transmission," Draft ISO Recommendation No. 1219, December, 1966.

International Organization for Standardization (ISO): "Tolerances of Form and Position, Part I: Generalities, Symbols, Indications on Drawings," 1st ed., ISO Recommendation R1101, July, 1969.

N. V. Philips' Gloeilampenfabrieken, Concern Standardization Department: "Graphical Symbols for Electrotechnical Diagrams," Eindhoven, The Netherlands, 1967.

Perry, John H.: "Chemical Engineers' Handbook," McGraw-Hill Book Company, New York, 1950.

Polon, David D. (ed.): "Encyclopedia of Engineering Signs and Symbols (EESS)," The Odyssey Scientific Library, The Odyssey Press, New York, 1965.

Process Flow Diagrams (?), *Oil and Gas Journal*, November 17, 1958.

Simonton, David P. and John T. Milek: Condensed Engineering Language: A Bibliography, *Standards Engineering,* pp. 4-9, April/May, 1969.

Folklore

Allcock, Hubert: "Heraldic Design: Its Origins, Ancient Forms, and Modern Usage," Tudor Publishing Company, New York, 1962.

Ambix: *Journal of the Society for the Study of Alchemy and Early Chemistry*, Vol. I, Taylor and Francis, 1937-1938.

Ferchl, Fritz, and A. Süssenguth: "A Pictorial History of Chemistry," William Heinemann, London, 1939.

Hammond, Natalie Hays: "Anthology of Pattern," William Helburn, New York, 1949.

Howey, M. Oldfield: "The Encircled Serpent: A Study of Serpent Symbolism in All Countries and Ages," Arthur Richmond Co., New York, 1955.

Koch, Rudolf: "The Book of Signs," Dover Publications (reprint), New York [n.d.].

Lehner, Ernst (comp.): "American Symbols: A Pictorial History," Wm. Penn Publishing Corporation, New York, 1966.

Lehner, Ernst: "The Picture Book of Symbols," Wm. Penn Publishing Corporation, New York, 1956.

Lehner, Ernst: "Symbols, Signs, & Signets," Dover Publications, New York, 1969.

Lehner, Ernst, and Johanna Lehner: "Folklore and Symbolism of Flowers, Plants, and Trees," Tudor Publishing Company, New York, 1960.

Read, John: "Through Alchemy to Chemistry," G. Bell & Sons, London, 1957.

Richards, Stan, and Associates: "Hobo Signs," Canterbury Press, Dallas, Texas [n.d.].

Taylor, F. Sherwood: "The Alchemists," Henry Schuman, New York, 1949.

Thompson, C. J. S.: "The Lure and Romance of Alchemy," George G. Harrap & Co., London, 1932.

Geography

Imhof, Eduard (ed.): "International Yearbook of Cartography," C. Bertelsmann Verlag, Gütersloh, Germany, 1961, 1966.

Raisz, Erwin: "Principles of Cartography," McGraw-Hill Book Company, New York, 1962.

Rand McNally: "The International Atlas; Der Internationale Atlas; El Atlas Internacionale; L'Atlas International," Rand McNally & Company, Chicago, 1969.

U.N. Department of Economic and Social Affairs: "World Cartography," volume IV, New York, 1954.

U.S. Geological Survey: "Topographical Map Symbol Sheet," Washington, D.C., November, 1966.

Geology

Compton, Robert R.: "Manual of Field Geology," pp. 334-337, John Wiley & Sons, New York, 1961.

Consejo de Recursos Naturales no Renovables: "Compilación de Símbolos Empleados en la Representación Cartográfica de Accidentes Geológico-Mineros," Publicación 5-E, Centro Regional de Ayuda Técnica, Agencia para el Desarrollo International (A.I.D.), Mexico, D.F., 1963.

Ridgway, John Livesy: "The Preparations of Illustrations for Reports of the United States Geological Survey," Government Printing Office, Washington, D.C., 1920.

Royal Dutch/Shell Group of Companies, Exploration and Production Departments: "Standard Legend," N. V. De Bataafsche Petroleum Maatschappij, The Hague, 1958.

Handling of Goods

Air Transport Board: "Official Air Transport Restricted Articles Tariff No. 6-D Governing the Transport of Restricted Articles by Air," Airline Tariff Publishers, Washington, D.C., 1966.

American National Standards Institute (ANSI): "Pictorial Markings for Handling of Goods," MH6.1-1968, New York, 1968.

Indian Standards Institution: "Pictorial Markings for Handling of Goods in General," IS:1286-1967, New Delhi, 1967.

Inter-Governmental Maritime Consultative Organization: International Maritime Dangerous Goods Code, leaflet, London [n.d.].

International Organization for Standardization (ISO): "Pictorial Markings for Handling of Goods (General Symbols)," ISO Recommendation R780, 1st ed., July, 1968.

Japan Packaging Design Association: "Care Mark," Tokyo [n.d.].

League of Red Cross Societies: "Disaster Relief Manual, Annex 2: Recommended Procedures for Packing and Marking Relief Shipments in International Disasters," Geneva [n.d.].

Lindinger, Herbert: Transport Signs: Olivetti Proposes an International Sign System, *form*, no. 46, pp. 18-21, 1969.

Standards Association of Australia: "Pictorial Markings for the Handling of Packages," AS Z29-1966, Sydney, 1966.

United Nations: "Transport of Dangerous Goods," New York, 1956.

Home Economics

The Butterick Company: Pattern Markings, instructions with patterns, New York, 1970.

Care Labels, *Which?*, published by the Consumers' Association, London, pp. 244-249, August 1970.

Hoover, Ltd.: C.E.C.E.D. Working Group – Washing Machine Symbols, Engineering Department Report No. 6684, Project No. 247, May 30, 1969.

Hoover, Ltd.: C.E.C.E.D. Working Group at A.E.G. Nürnberg, Germany, Report No. 7713, Project No. 247, December 3, 1970.

International Federation of Cotton and Allied Textile Industries: "International Care Labelling Code for Textiles," Zurich.

National Retail Merchants Association: Sure Care Symbols, 1 page, New York [n.d.].

Recipe Symbols, *Woman's Day*, June, 1969.

Simplicity Pattern Company: How to Use Your Simplicity Pattern, instructions with patterns, New York, 1970.

Manufacturing

Bogdanov, Ivan, Dobroljub Peshin, and Milan Nikolov: "Communication Signs for Products of Radioelectronics and Machine-tool Industry," Industrial Design Centre, Sofia, Bulgaria, 1967/1968.

Deutscher Normenausschuss (DNA): "Sinnbilder für textlose Bedienschilder an Werkzeugmaschinen; Grundsinnbilder," DIN 55003, Blatt 2, Berlin, 1964.

Deutscher Normenausschuss (DNA): "Sinnbilder für textlose Bedienschilder an Werkzeugmaschinen; Grundsinnbilder, Ergänzungen und Änderungen zu DIN 55003 Blatt 2," DIN 55003, Blatt 20, Berlin, 1968.

Deutscher Normenausschuss (DNA): "Sinnbilder für textlose Bedienschilder an Werkzeugmaschinen; Schmieranweisungen," DIN 55003, Blatt 4, Berlin, 1967.

Easterby, R. S.: "An Evaluation of the British Standard Symbols for Machine Tool Indicator Plates," MTIRA research report No. 10, The Machine Tool Industry Research Association, Hulley Road, Hurdsfield, Macclesfield, Cheshire, 1966.

Electronic Industries Association (EIA): "Symbols for Use with Numerical Control Systems," RS-379, Washington, D.C., September, 1970.

International Organization for Standardization (ISO): "Symbols for Indications Appearing on Machine Tools," ISO Recommendation R369, 1st ed., April, 1964.

"KURAUN HYAKKA JITEN (Encyclopedia Crown)," 1st ed., Sanseido Company, Tokyo, 1968.

Rose Forgrove Limited: Designer's Manual, December, 1970.

Mathematics

International Organization for Standardization (ISO): "Mathematical Signs and Symbols for Use in Physical Sciences and Technology," ISO Recommendation R31, Part XI, 1st ed., February, 1961.

James, Glenn, and Robert Clarke James: "Mathematics Dictionary," D. Van Nostrand Company, New York, 1949.

Polon, David D. (ed.): "Dictionary of Physics and Mathematics Abbreviations, Signs, and Symbols (DPMA)," The Odyssey Press, New York, 1965.

Medicine

Deutscher Normenausschuss(DNA): "Medizinische Röntgen-Einrichtungen Bildzeichen," DIN 6839, Berlin, 1967.

Industrial Design, No. 11, November, 1965.

Institucion Mexicana de Asistencia a la Niñez: Hospital Infantile, pamphlet, México, D.F., 1970.

Lucas, Andrew: Sacas Simplifies Blood Analysis, *Design*, vol. 249, pp. 46-51, September, 1969.

Michigan Occupational Therapy Association, Special Studies Committee: "Medical Abbreviations: A Cross Reference Dictionary," 2d ed., Ann Arbor, Michigan, 1967.

New York State Health and Mental Hygiene Facilities Improvement Corporation: "Architectural Graphics Manual: Signage Standards for Medical Facilities of the City of New York," prepared by E. Christopher Klumb Associates for New York City Health and Hospitals Corporation: Health S.P.A.C.E., New York, 1970.

Potter, Edwin S., M.D.: "Serpents in Symbolism, Art and Medicine: The Babylonian Caduceus and Aesculapius Club," Schauer Printing Studio, Santa Barbara, 1937.

Stile Industria, September, 1962.

Meteorology

American National Standards Institute (ANSI): "Letter Symbols for Meteorology," Y10.10–1953, New York, 1953.

U.S. Department of Commerce, Environmental Science Services Administration: Explanation of the Weather Map, sheet, Government Printing Office, Washington, D.C., 1969.

U.S. Department of Commerce, Environmental Science Services Administration: A Pilot's Guide to Aviation Weather Services, pamphlet, Government Printing Office, Washington, D.C., 1969.

World Meteorological Organization: "Guide to the Preparation of Synoptic Weather Charts and Diagrams," Geneva, 1964.

Music

Baker, Theo: "Dictionary of Musical Terms," 23d ed., G. Schirmer, New York, 1923.

Boehm, Laszlo: "Modern Music Notation," G. Schirmer, Inc., New York, 1961.

Britten, Benjamin, and Imogen Holst: "The Wonderful World of Music," Doubleday & Company, Garden City, New York, 1968.

Grove, Sir George: "Dictionary of Music and Musicians," 5 vols., 5th ed., edited by Eric Blom, St. Martin's Press, New York, 1954.

Photography

No bibliographic or published reference documented for the material used in this section.

Physics

International Union of Pure and Applied Physics; Commission for Symbols, Units and Nomenclature: "Symbols, Units and Nomenclature in Physics," Document U.I.P. 11 (S.U.N. 65–3), report published with the financial support of UNESCO, 1965.

Polon, David D. (ed.): "Dictionary of Physics and Mathematics Abbreviations, Signs and Symbols (DPMA)," The Odyssey Press, New York, 1965.

Polon, David D. (ed.): "Encyclopedia of Engineering Signs and Symbols (EESS)," The Odyssey Scientific Library, The Odyssey Press, New York, 1965.

Royal Society of London, Symbols Committee: "Symbols, Signs, and Abbreviations Recommended for British Scientific Publications," The Royal Society, London, 1969.

Recreation

Bogdanov, Ivan, and Dimiter Dimitrov: "Communication Signs for Resort Sites," Industrial Design Centre, Sofia, Bulgaria, 1968/1969.

Canadian Corporation for the 1967 World Exhibition: "Standard Sign Manual, Expo 67," prepared by Paul Arthur and Associates, [n.p.], 1963.

Comite Organizador de Los Juegos de La XIX Olimpiada, Programa de Identidad Olimpica, Diseño Urbano: Señalamientos de Servicio, Mexico, 1968.

International Committee on Travel Signs and Symbols: Collection of Existing Pictograms Answering to the Basic List of Informations, working Paper, Paris, 1967.

International Committee on Travel Signs and Symbols: International Survey on Pictographs, draft report, Paris, 1969.

Jacob, Heiner, and Masaru Katzumie: Sign Systems for International Events, Munich, Sapporo, Osaka & Co., *Print,* vol. 23, no. 6, pp. 40–49, November/December, 1969.

Kamekura, Yusaku: "Trademarks and Symbols of the World," Reinhold Publishing Corporation, New York, 1965.

Mexico Departmento de Turismo: Señales Informativas, announcement, [n.p., n.d.].

National Fire Protection Association: "Sparky's Fire Dept. Inspector's Handbook," pamphlet, Boston, 1963.

Province of Quebec, Department of Lands and Forests: Markers and Signs for Snowmobile Trails, announcement, Quebec, 1970.

Sveriges Standardiseringkommission: "Symboler för Friluftsmärken," SIS 03 12 11, Stockholm, 1970.

U.S. Department of Agriculture, Forest Service: Skiing, pamphlet, Government Printing Office, Washington, D.C., 1968.

U.S. Department of Agriculture, Forest Service: Smokey's 1971 Campaign, pamphlet, Government Printing Office, Washington, D.C., 1970.

U.S. Department of the Interior, National Park Service: National Park Service Signs, pamphlet [n.p., n.d.].

U.S. Department of the Interior, National Park Service: "Standard Sign Graphics Report," prepared by Chermayeff & Geismar Associates Inc., [n.p., n.d.].

Vermont Travel Information Council: "Vermont Travel Information Guide," Montpelier, Vermont, [n.d.].

Religion

Ferguson, George: "Signs & Symbols in Christian Art," 2d ed., Oxford University Press, New York, 1955.

Lehner, Ernst: "Symbols, Signs & Signets," Dover Publications, New York, 1969.

"New Larousse Encyclopedia of Mythology," 2d ed., Prometheus Press, Paris, 1968.

Noss, John B.: "Man's Religions," 4th ed., Macmillan & Co., London, 1969.

Post, W. Ellwood: "Saints, Signs and Symbols," Morehouse-Barlow, New York, 1962.

Whittemore, Carroll E.: "Symbols of the Church," Whittemore Associates, Boston, 1959.

"The World's Great Religions," Time-Life Books, New York, 1957.

Safety

American National Standards Institute (ANSI): "Specifications for Accident Prevention Tags," Z35.2-1968, New York, 1968.

Deutscher Normenausschuss (DNA): "Blitzpfeile," DIN 40006, Berlin, 1968.

Deutscher Normenausschuss (DNA): "Sicherheitszeichen und Sicherheitsschider," DIN 4819, Berlin, 1965.

Deutscher Normenausschuss (DNA): "Warnzeichen für ionisierende Strahlung," DIN 25400, Berlin, 1966.

Dow Biohazards Research and Development Team: A Proposed Universal Biohazards Warning Symbol, feasibility study for the National Cancer Institute and National Institutes of Health, [n.p., n.d.].

Föreningen För Arbetarskydd (FFA): "Katalog Prislista," Stockholm, 1970.

Implement and Tractor, p. 19, March 21, 1970.

International Organization for Standardization (ISO): "Basic Ionizing Radiation Symbol," ISO Recommendation R361, 1st ed., December, 1963.

Karapantev, Dontcho: "Production Communication Signs for Industrial Interior and Exterior," Industrial Design Centre, Sofia, Bulgaria, 1970.
O'Keeffe, P. J.: "A Study of Traffic Accidents on the Dublin-Naas Road (1966 and 1967)," An Foras Forbartha Report RS 22, Dublin, May, 1968.
Sveriges Standardiseringkommission: "Bildsymboler for Markning," SIS 03 12 10, Stockholm, 1967.
U.S. Department of Transportation, Federal Aviation Administration: "Airman's Information Manual, Part I, Basic Flight Manual and ATC Procedures," Government Printing Office, Washington, D.C., May, 1970.

Traffic

Association of American Railroads: "American Railway Signaling Principles and Practice, Chapter 2, Symbols, Aspects and Indications," [n.p.] 1956.
California, Resources Agency, Department of Navigation and Ocean Development: ABC's of California Boating Law, pamphlet, Sacramento, 1970.
"Collier's Encyclopedia," Crowell-Collier Educational Corporation, New York, 1968.
Congreso Panamericano de Carreteras, Comisión Técnica de Tránsito Y Seguridad: "Manual Interamericano Dispositivos para el Control del Tránsito en Calles y Carreteras," [n.p., n.d.].
Economic Commission for Europe, Inland Transport Committee: "Signalling Systems on Inland Waterways," text of resolution, March, 1968.
United Kingdom Ministry of Transport: The New Traffic Signs, pamphlet, Her Majesty's Stationery Office, London, 1965.
United Kingdom Ministry of Transport: "Report of the Traffic Signs Committee," Her Majesty's Stationery Office, London, 1963.
United Nations Conference on Road Traffic: "Final Act, Convention on Road Traffic, Convention on Road Signs and Signals," New York, 1969.
U.S. Department of Commerce, Bureau of Public Roads: "Manual on Uniform Traffic Control Devices for Streets and Highways," also ANSI D6.1-1961, Government Printing Office, Washington, D.C., 1961.
U.S. Department of Commerce, Bureau of Public Roads: Standard Traffic Control Signs as defined in the Manual on Uniform Traffic Control Devices, one sheet, Government Printing Office, Washington, D.C., 1965.
U.S. Department of Commerce, Environmental Science Services Administration, Coast and Geodetic Survey: United States of America Nautical Chart Symbols and Abbreviations, pamphlet, Washington, D.C., 1968.
U.S. Department of Transportation, Federal Aviation Administration: "Airman's Information Manual, Part 1, Basic Flight Manual and ATC Procedures," Government Printing Office, Washington, D.C., May, 1970.
"The World Book Encyclopedia," Field Enterprises Educational Corporation, Chicago, 1967.
World Touring and Automobile Organisation (OTA): International Road Signs, leaflet [n.p., n.d.].
NOTE: In addition to the above publications, the national standards for road signs for Australia, West Germany, Israel, Japan, Kuwait, Mexico, The Netherlands, South Africa, and Switzerland were used as source material.

Vehicle Controls

American Society of Agricultural Engineers (ASAE): "Lubrication Charts for Tractors and Farm Machinery," ASAE R232, 1962.

American Society of Agricultural Engineers (ASAE): "Symbols for Operator Controls on Agricultural Tractors and Agricultural Machinery," ASAE S304.3, St. Joseph, Michigan,October, 1970.

British Standards Institution: "Symbols for Control Markings for Agricultural Machines, Implements and Trailers," Doc. 69/6120 draft, London, February, 1969.

Industrial Truck Association (ITA): "ITA Recommended Practices Manual," Pittsburgh, 1970.

International Harvester: Information Symbols for Products, Engineering Standard No. 148.

International Organization for Standardization (ISO), Technical Committee 22; Automobiles: Proposal.

International Organization for Standardization (ISO), Technical Committee 110, Working Group 4: Proposal, ISO/TC 110 WG4 (USA).

John Deere and Company, "Worldwide Symbols for Operator Controls," Design Manual 26, Moline, Illinois [n.d.].

National Highway Safety Bureau: Motor Vehicle Safety Standards, Control Location, Identification and Illumination, Docket No. 1-18, Notice No. 2, 49 CFR Part 571.

Nissan Motors Company, Ltd.: Control Knob Markings for Automobiles, JASO 6805 [n.p., n.d.].

Society of Automotive Engineers (SAE): "Control Symbols Subcommittee – Overall Outline," New York, October, 1969.

Color

Abbott, Arthur G.: "The Color of Life," McGraw-Hill Book Company, New York, 1947.

Air Transport Association, Airline Airport Technical Group: "Signs of the Jet Age," prepared by Arnold Thompson Associates, New York [n.d.].

American National Standards Institute (ANSI): "Color Coding of Chassis Wiring," C83.37-1968, New York, 1968.

American National Standards Institute (ANSI): "Identification of Gas Mask Canisters," K13.1-1967, New York, 1967.

American National Standards Institute (ANSI): "Manual on Uniform Traffic Control Devices for Streets and Highways," D6.1-1961, New York, 1961.

American National Standards Institute (ANSI): "Safety Color Code for Marking Physical Hazards and the Identification of Certain Equipment," Z53.1-1967, New York, 1967.

American National Standards Institute (ANSI): "Scheme for the Identification of Piping Systems," A13.1-1956, New York, 1956.

Bailey, Henry Turner, and Ethel Pool: "Symbolism for Artists: Creative and Appreciative," The Davis Press, Worcester, Massachusetts, 1925.

Birren, Faber: "Color: A Survey in Words and Pictures: From Ancient Mysticism to Modern Science," University Books, New York, 1963.

Birren, Faber: "Selling Color to People," University Books, New York, 1956.

Cirlot, J. E.: "A Dictionary of Symbols," translated from the Spanish "Diccionario de Simbolos Tradicionales," by Jack Sage, Philosophical Library, New York, 1962.

Eisenstein, Sergei: Color and Meaning, Chapter 3 of "Film Form and the Film Sense," pp. 113–153, Meridian Books, New York, 1957.

Hammond, Natalie Hays: "Anthology of Pattern," William Helburn, New York, 1949.

Hangen, Eva C.: "Symbols: Our Universal Language," McCormick-Armstrong Publishing Division, Wichita, Kansas, 1962.

Hodge, Frederick Webb (ed.): "Handbook of American Indians North of Mexico," Bulletin 30, 2 vols., Smithsonian Institution, Bureau of American Ethnology, Washington, D.C., 1907.

Inter-Governmental Maritime Consultative Organization: International Maritime Dangerous Goods Code, leaflet, London [n.d.].

International Organization for Standardization (ISO): "Identification Colours for Pipes Conveying Fluids in Liquid or Gaseous Condition in Land Installations and on Board Ships," ISO Recommendation R508, 1st ed., October, 1966.

International Organization for Standardization (ISO): "Safety Colours," ISO Recommendation R408, 1st ed., December, 1964.

Itten, Johannes: "The Art of Color," Reinhold Publishing Corporation, New York, 1961.

Itten, Johannes: "The Elements of Color," Van Nostrand Reinhold Company, New York, 1970.

Kandinsky, Wassily: "On the Spiritual in Art," Solomon R. Guggenheim Foundation, New York, 1946.

Kandinsky, Wassily: "Point and Line to Plane," Solomon R. Guggenheim Foundation, New York, 1947.

League of Red Cross Societies: "Disaster Relief Manual, Annex 2: Recommended Procedures for Packing and Marking Relief Shipments in International Disasters," Geneva, [n.d.].

Lockmiller, David A.: "Scholars on Parade," Macmillan & Co., London, 1969.

Lüscher, Max: "The Lüscher Color Test," Random House, New York, 1969.

Melville, Herman: The Whiteness of the Whale, chapter 41 of "Moby Dick," pp. 170–178, Dodd, Mead & Company, New York, 1942.

Post, W. Elwood: "Saints, Signs, and Symbols," Morehouse-Barlow, New York, 1962.

Schweizerischer Elektrotechnischer Verein (SEV): "Graphical Symbols for Wiring Plans," SEV 9002.1. 1968, Zurich, 1968.

Spris Publikationscentral: "Hygienmärkning," Spri Specifikation 700 01, Stockholm, 1969.

Spris Publikationscentral: "Narkosmaterial," Spri Specifikation 52301, Stockholm, 1969.

U.N. Department of Economic and Social Affairs: "World Cartography," volume IV, New York, 1954.

Williams, C. A. S.: "Encyclopedia of Chinese Symbolism and Art Motives," The Julian Press, New York, 1960.

World Meteorological Organization: "Guide to the Preparation of Synoptic Weather Charts and Diagrams," Geneva, 1964.

Zephyr Amir, M. K.: "A Concise Guide to Hand-made Oriental Carpets," published as a private edition by M. K. Zephyr Amir, first printed by Tien Wah Press, Singapore, 1968.

INDEX

Our prime concern in creating the Index for this Sourcebook was to make it as easy to use as possible. With this in view, we have developed a system of cross referencing that varies somewhat from the norm. Plus we have made a selection of design concepts and areas of design and put them into one convenient listing we call Design Categories.

CROSS REFERENCING

1. When a cross reference leads the reader to an entry with only one page reference, or to an entry uncomplicated by related subentries, we have included the page number in the cross reference to save the reader the trouble of having to look up yet another entry in the Index.

   For example: Cafe (*see* Coffee shop, 35)

2. We have also included page numbers for references which do not appear in the Index but do appear on a particular page. The reader can thus go directly from the entry in the Index to the page itself.

   For example: *under* Boating: (*See also* Sailing, Canoeing, Rowing, 135)

3. We have used yet another unusual type of cross referencing system with entries directly related to Disciplines within the Sourcebook.

   For example: Constellations, *see* Astronomy, 54. Here, the reader is directed to the Discipline page without having to look for the Discipline itself in the Index.

It is our belief that these cross referencing devices will save the reader time by making it unnecessary for him to go back and forth through the Index to find a particular symbol reference.

DESIGN CATEGORIES

Certain ideas, functions, and physical states are common to many disciplines and have a wide variety of applications. We have grouped these into what we call Design Categories, since they are likely to be referred to most frequently in symbol identification and selection. The complete listing of these Design Categories is shown below, with words in parentheses that further describe each category. Each Design Category appears as a separate entry in normal alphabetical position within the Index.

Building signage (elevators, stairs; retail shops . . .)
Forward and reverse (toward, away; return . . .)
In and out (extend, retract; engage, disengage; arrive, depart . . .)
Increase and decrease (relative change; progression; large, small; multiply, divide . . .)
Male and female (man, woman . . .)
Measurement (linear dimension; amount; near, far; length, height . . .)
On and off (start, stop . . .)
Open and close (lock, unlock; tighten, loosen . . .)
Pressure (of oil, air, etc.; force . . .)
Speed (fast, slow; rate . . .)
Temperature (thermometer; heat; frozen)
Time (frequency; interval; clock . . .)
Up and down (raise, lower; hill, valley; above, below . . .)
Volume (mass, quantity; full, empty; loud, soft; light, dark; weight . . .)

INDEX

Abortion, 55
AC (*see* Alternating current, 81)
Accommodations and travel, 34-38
  lodgings, 130
  terminals, 36-38
Acids, amino, 57
Acknowledge, 60
Active, 89
Add, 114
Adding machines, 64
Address, 61
Admissions, 117
Admittances (*see* Admissions, 117)
Aerials, 71, 83
Aesculapius' staff, 113, 119
After, 150
Age:
  annual, biennial, perennial, 56
  of livestock, 41-43
  mature forest, 44
  old and new world, 56
Agriculture, 39-47
  agronomy, 39-41
  farm structures and lands, 43-44
  forestry, 44-45
  implements, 45-47
  livestock and dairy products, 41-43
  vehicle controls, 160, 164-165
Agronomy, 39-41
Air, 57, 86
  circulating, 160
  conditioning, 159
    (*See also* Fan; Ventilation control)
  cooled condenser, 83
  filter, 157
  freight, 38
  marshalling signals, 152
  pollution, 162
  pressure, 157
  traffic, 150-152
  vane, 107
Aircraft:
  badly damaged, 141
  low-flying, 144
  on-board signs, 36
  three-dimensional controls, 164-165
Airports, 36, 93
Alchemy, 86-88
Alcohol, 86, 91
Algae, 97
All right, 91
Alphabets, non-graphic, 75-79
Alternate instructions, 150
Alternating current, 81
  AC adapter, 63
Alternative instructions (*see* Alternate instructions, 150)
Alum, 87
Ambulance, 117
Amino acids, 57
Ammeter, 128, 159
Ampersand, 58
Amphitheater, 130
Amplifier, 71, 82
  image, 116
Anastomosis, 93
Anchoring, 153
And, 58
Animal:
  crossing, 144
  -drawn vehicles, 145
Animals, 142*n.*
  live, 99
  livestock, 41-43
Ankle, 74
Antenna, 83
  (*See also* Aerials)
Antimony, 86
Appliances, 101-103
  electric, 105
Appointments, 117
Approximately equal to, 111
Aqueduct, 93
Archery, 132
Architectural materials, 50-51
Architecture, 48-53
  drafting, 48-51
  landscaping and planning, 51-53
Arenas, 53
Arsenic, 86
Ascend (*see* Up and down, 26, 157)
Ashlar, 50
Ashtray, 36, 130, 159
Assembly, 104
Asterisk, 58
Astrology, 88-90
  (*See also* Astronomy)
Astronomy, 54
At, 58
Athletics (*see* Sports)
Atomic power, 105
Atomizer, 47
Audio-visual indicator, 72
Auditorium, 131
Auger, 161
Autoclave, 80
Automat, 36
Automatic, 60, 115
  cycle, 108
Automotive service, 65
  (*See also* Car; Vehicles)
Autumn, 89
Avalanches, 132, 148
Axle, 161

Baggage, 37
  (*See also* Luggage)
Balance, 46, 98
  level, 127
Band, 131

Bar, 36
  snack, 35
Barber, 65
Barman, 35
Barometric condenser, 80
Barricade sign, 48
Baseball, 132
Basic symbols, 26-27
Basket lift, 161
Bath, 34-35, 49, 130
  sauna, 35
Bathrooms (*see* Toilets)
Battery, 67, 82, 126
  slave, 159
Battlefield, 95
Bauxite, 105
Beach, 94, 131
Beacon, boundary, 92
Bear area, 131
Beater, 110
Beauty parlor, 65
Bedding, 99
Before, 150
Behavior, 52
Bell, 60, 83
  buoy, 154
Bellboy, 35
Belt, 107
Benzene, 68
Berries, 40-41
Beware, 146
  (*See also* Caution; Danger; Warning)
Bibb, hose, 50
Bicycle, 51, 145
  dispatch, 37
  shed, 37
  trail, 131, 147
  (*See also* Cycling, 136)
Bidet, 49
Billiards, 132
Biodegradable, 102
Biohazard warning, 140
Biology, 55-57
  botany, 56
  molecular, 57
Birth, 113
  control (*see* Planned parenthood, 114)
Black, 237
Blackening, 116
Blankets, 99
Blender, 102
Blood:
  bank, 117
  donors, 117
Blower, 80, 83, 102
  leg plate, 109
  (*See also* Fan)
Blowing unit, 107
Blue, 235
Boating, 131
  (*See also* Canoeing, Rowing, Sailing, 135)
Body (movement), 74
Bonds, 68
Book stall, 65
Boom, loader, 161
Borax, 87
Botany, 56
Boundaries, 92, 95
Braille, 75-79
Brake, 107, 158
  apply, release air, 155
  hand, 158
  Jacobs (engine with), 157
  oil, 158
  pressure, 158
  stop and check, 147
  winch, 161
Brick, 50
Bridge opening, 148
Bridges, 92, 130, 143, 144, 147
Bridle path, 147
  (*See also* Horses)
Brightness, 116
Brown, 236
Bucket, loader, 161
Buddhism, 138
  pagoda, 95
Building signage:
  accommodations and travel, 34-38
  facilities, 34-35
  food and drink, 35-36
  group room, 70
  hospitals, 117-119
  post office, 70
  press room, 70
  recreation, 130-137
  safety, 140-141
  shops and services, 65-66
  studio, 70
  switchboard, 70
  telegram, 70
  telephone, 70
Buildings, 51
  castle, 95
  churches, 95
  farmstead, 43
  hospital, 95
  masonry, 43
  military, 95
  offices, 93
  planning, 53
  ranger station, 95
  schools. 95
  shed, 43
Bulb, lamp, 82
Bump, 143
Buoys, 94, 153-155
Bus, 37, 142
  no entry, 145
  stop, 147
Business, 58-66
  camera store, 65

Business (*cont.*)
  computers, 58-62
  office equipment, 63-65
  office procedure (*see* Hospitals, 117)
  shops and services, 65-66
Button, 100
Buttonhole, 100-101
Buzzer, 64, 83

Cab (*see* Taxi, 37)
Cabin, 130
Cable, 93
  overhead, 144, 153
Caduceus, 113, 119
Cafe (*see* Coffee shop, 35)
Calendering, 104
Calx, 87
Cam, 108
Camera point, 130
Camera store, 65
Cameras, 70
  (*See also* Photography, 126-127)
Campfires, 130
Campground, 130
Camping site, 148
Canals, 93
Cancel, 59
Candy, 110
Candy store, 65
Canoeing, 135
Capacitors, 82
Capital city, 92
Car, 51, 71, 142
  rental, 37
  wash, 65
  (*See also* Automotive service; Vehicles)
Cards:
  computer, 59
  playing, 133*n.*
  tarot, 133
Care:
  handle with, 98
  in care of, 58
  labeling, 100-101
Carried over, 58
Cartesian coordinates, 128
Cartwheel, 74
Casting, 104
Castle, 95
Cathedral, 95
Cathode ray tube (TV), 82
Cattle, 42
Caustic, 115
  (*See also* Corrosive, 99)
Caution, 142, 143
  deep water (drop-off), 131
  pressurized radiator, 157
  red light soon, 148
  rocks, 131
  (*See also* Beware; Danger; Warning)
Caverns, 131
Ceiling:
  heights, 52
  light outlet, 49
  mounted equipment, 115
Cemetery, 95
  boundary, 92
Center, 72
  of gravity, 98
  line, 48, 149
  (*See also* Balance)
Centre (*see* Center)
Centrifugal:
  fertilizer, 47
  pump, 80, 83
Centrifuge, 80, 114
Ceramic industry, 105
Cereals, 39
Chain, 107
Chalk, 97
Change, 113
Channel crossing, 152-154
Chemical:
  engineering, 80-81
  industry, 105
Chemist (*see* Pharmacy, 65)
Chemistry, 67-69
Chess pieces, 133*n.*
Chest, 74
Chickens, 42
Children:
  can play in the street, 147
  child care, 52, 117, 119
  crossing, 144, 147
  keep away from, 140
  lost, 34
  mother and, 38, 90
  offspring, progeny, 55
  pediatrics, 117
  relief shipments, 99
Choke, 158
Christianity, 138
  church, 95
Chrome, 105
Church, 95
Cigarette lighter, 159
Circuit:
  breaker, 82
  diagrams, 71-72
Circumduction, 113
Cistern, 43, 50
Citation, incorrect (*see* Incorrect citation, 55)
City, 92
Civil defense, 140
Clamp, 162
Clay, 87
Cleaner, 46
Clear, 62
Clearance, 157
  total, 64

Climbing plant, 56
Clinic, 117
Cloakroom, 34
Clock:
  electric system devices, 49
  hanger outlet, 48
Clockwise, 74, 157
Closed (*see* Open and close)
Clothing, 66
  care labeling, 100–101
  clean, soiled, 117
  protective, 141
  relief shipments, 99
  washing machines, 103
Clouds, 121–122, 126
Club, 38
Clutch, 108, 158
Coagulation, 115
Coal, 97
  mining, 105
Coatroom (*see* Cloakroom, 34)
Cobalt, 86
Cocktail lounge (*see* Bar, 36)
Code, 61
Coffee, 39
Coffee shop, 35
Cold (*see* Temperature)
Collate, 59
Collator detector, 110
College, 95
Collimator, 128
Color, 231–246
  correction, 73
Colour (*see* Color)
Combines, 160*n.*–161*n.*
Combustible, 98
Comet, 54
Comfort station (*see* Toilets)
Common substances, 69
  (*See also* Compounds and Mixtures, 87–88)
Communications, 70–79, 93
  movement and dance, 74
  non-graphic alphabets, 75–79
Comparator, 61
Comparison, 61
Compass required, 141
Compounds, 87–88
  (*See also* Common substances, 69)
Compressed gas, 99, 157
Compression, 116
  molding, 104
Compressors, 83
  (*See also* Pump)
Computers, 58–62
  numerical tape control, 108
Concentration, 113
Concrete, 50
Condenser:
  air-cooled, 83
  barometric, 80
Condenser (*cont.*):
  electrical (*see* Capacitors, 82)
  water-cooled, 83
Confectionery store (*see* Candystore, 65)
Conference, 64
Confucianism, 138
Conjunction, 54
Connector (electrical), 83
Constellations. see Astronomy, 54
Contains, 111
Continued, 58
Continuity, 52
Continuously, 61
Contours: hydrographic, 94
  relief, 94
Contrast, 70, 116
Control characters (computers), 59–60
Converter, 71
Conveyors, 80, 161
Copper, 86, 105
Copyright, 58
Coral, 96
Cork, 51
Correction key, 64
Corridors, 52
Corrosive, 99
  (*See also* Caustic, 115)
Cosmetics, 66
Cotton, 39
  picking, 161
Counter, 61
Counter-clockwise, 74, 157
County boundary, 92
Coupling, 128
  insulated, uninsulated, 82
Courthouse, 91
Crane, movable manure, 46
Creation, 89
Creeper, 110
Creeping plant, 56
Crime, 91
Crops (*see* Agronomy, 39–41)
Cross, 151
  airway, 150
  channel, 153
Crosses, Christian, 138
Crossings, larger waterway, 153
Crossroads, 143
Crucible, 86
Crusher:
  ball mill, 80
  mill, 46
  roller, 80
Crystal:
  structures, 69
  unit, piezoelectric, 82
Cultural features, 95
Cultural movement, 131
Cum, 113
Curb markings, 148

Currency, see Business, 58
  exchange, 37
Current, 81, 115
Curtains, 103
Curve, 108
Customs, 38
Cuts, 94, 106
Cutter bar, 161
Cutting, 100, 115
  line, 100
Cycling, 136
  lane, 149
  (*See also* Bicycle)
Cylinder, remote, 161

Dagger, 58
Dairy products, 42
Dams, 93, 131
Dance, 74
Danger, 154
  point, 148, 154
  (*See also* Beware; Caution; Warning)
Dangers, 144
Dark and light, 27
Data processing (*see* Computers)
David, Star of, 113, 139
Day, 86, 160
Days of week, see Folklore, 89
DC (*see* Direct current, 81)
Deaf alphabet, 75–78
Death, 55, 90, 113, 133
  character kill, 72
  reception, refrigeration of cadavers, 118
Decimal sign, 64
Decision, 58
Decompression, 116
Decrease (*see* Increase and decrease)
Deer area, 131
Defecation, 113
Delivery entrance, 34
Demons, against, 47
Dentist, 118
  incisors, molars, 114
Dermatology, 118
Descend (*see* Up and down)
Detector, collator, 110
Diamond, 105
Dictating machines, 63
Dictation, 63
Diesel fuel, 158
Differential lock, 161
Digestion, 88
Dip, 143
  and strike, 96
Dipole:
  antenna, 83
  electric, 128
  magnetic, 128
Direct current, 81
Direction, 27, 74
Disabled (*see* Handicapped, 117, 140)
Disciplines, 32–165
Disengage (*see* In and out)
Dispensary (*see* First aid, 140)
Dispense, 114
Dissolution, 88
Distillation, 88
Disturbance, 108
Diver's flag, 154
Divided by, 111
Diving, 131
Dock, 131
Doctor:
  on board, 76
  required (medical assistance), 77, 141
Document, 59
Dog, 91, 130
Dollar, 58, 85
Double expose, 72
Down (*see* Up and down)
Drafting, 48–51
Drain, 107
Draining, 102
Dram, 114
Dressing rooms, 117
Dressmaking, 100
Dreydle, 133*n*.
Drift, 143
Drilling cut, 106
Drink, 35–36
Drinking:
  fountain, 36, 50
  trough, 43
  water, 36, 90, 153
Drive, 102, 158
  belt, 107
  chain, 107
  front-wheel, 158
  gear, 107
  wheels, 110
Drugstore (*see* Pharmacy, 65)
Dry, 98
Dryers (*see* Chemical engineering, 80)
Drying, 101, 103
Duck, 43
Dunes, sand, 94, 96
Dust, 120
Dwellings, 93

Earth, 50, 54, 86, 89
  ground, electrical, 82
  (*See also* World)
Ecology, 57
Egg, 42, 55
Eject, 63
  lamp, 126
Ejector, 80
Elbow, 74
Electric:
  appliances, 105

Electric (*cont.*):
eye, 49
facilities, 140
knife, 102
motor, 106
razor socket, 35
transmission, 105
Electrical:
danger, 140
engineering, 81-83
precipitator, 80
schematic diagrams: architecture, 48-49
circuit, 71-72
electronic, 81-83
supply, 66
Electricity:
electrical engineering, 81-83
meter, 49
physics, 128-129
Electromedical equipment, 115
Electronic schematic diagrams, 81-83
Elements (chemical), 67, 86-87
(*See also* Mining)
Elevation, 95
drawings, 50*n*.-51*n*.
Elevator, 34
mobile, 46
ramp, 52
Eliminator, static, 110
Emergencies, 117
Emergency code, 141
Emergency exit, 140
Empty (*see* Volume)
End (*see* On and off)
Endoscopy, 115, 118
Engage (*see* In and out)
Engine, 83
hours, 157
with Jacobs brake, 157
oil, 157
pressure, 157
speed (in RPM), 157
stop (emergency), 159
Engineer required, 141
Engineering, 80-85
chemical, 80-81
electrical, 81-83
mechanical, 83-85
Entomology, see Biology, 55
Entrance (*see* In and out)
Entry (*see* In and out)
Equal to, 111
Equestrian, 136
Equinox, 54
Equipment:
kitchen, 44
in medicine, 114-116
office, 63-65
X-ray, 115-116
Error, 108
(*See also* Incorrect citation; Mistake)
Escalator, 34
Escape route, 140
Essence, 89
Eternal state of Buddha, 138
Even, 61
Exit (*see* In and out)
Expansion, 52
Explorer routes, 95
Explosive, 75, 98
Extract, 59
Eye, 128
level, 51

Factory, 93
district, 104
Falling objects, 140
Fallout shelter, 140
Family, 90
life, 89-90
Fan, 80, 126, 160
alluvial, 96
cotton blowing, 161
ventilator, 43
(*See also* Air, conditioning; Blower; Ventilation control)
Faradization, 115
Farm (*see* Agriculture)
Farmstead, 43
Fast (*see* Speed)
Fasten seat belt, 36
Fault, 96
Feed, 63, 106
film, 116
form, 60
line, 60
ribbon, 64
Feeder, 109, 110
Female (*see* Male and female)
Fences, 43, 51
Fermentation, 88
Ferry, 36, 147
captive, 153
vehicle, 131
Fertility, 47
Fertilizers, 41
Feynman diagrams, 128*n*.
Fill, 94
Filling station, 148
Film, 70-71, 126-127
(*See also* Motion pictures)
Filter, 107, 157
air, 157
cleaning, 107
magnetic, 107
oil, transmission, 158
plate and frame, 80
rotary vacuum, 80
type "A," 126
Find, 61
Fingers, 74

Fire, 86
  alarm, 140
    system devices, 49
  area, 147
  extinguisher, 36, 165
  prevention, 130
  protection equipment, 141
  sacred, 139
  safety, 140–141
Firearms, 132
  required, 141
First aid, 140
Fish, 97
  hatchery, 131
  trap area buoy, 155
Fishing, 131
Fixation, 88
Flag, diver's, 154
Flags, international, 75–79
Flame photometer, 114
Flats, 94
Float (hydraulic lift), 157
Floodlights, 49
Floor:
  heat, 159
  mounted equipment, 115
  outlets, 48–49
Flow charts (*see* Programming, 58–59)
Flowers, 39
  florist, 65
Fluorescent lamps, 49
Fluoroscopy, 116
Focus, 126, 165
Fog, 120
Foliation, 96
Folklore, 86–91
  alchemy, 86–88
  astrology, 88–90
  hobo signs, 90–91
Food, 35–36
  processing, 104
  required, 141
  (*See also* Agronomy, 39–41; Livestock and dairy products, 41–43)
Foot, 74
  control, 63
  switch, 108, 115, 116
Football, 132
Footnote, 58
Footplate motion, 116
Foraminifera, 96
Forbid, 142
Forest fire prevention, 130
Forestry, 44–45
  (*See also* Vegetation, Natural features, 95)
Fork lifts, 161*n*.–162*n*.
Forward and reverse, 126, 157
  back, 155
  backspace, 59, 64
  carriage return, 60, 64

Forward and reverse (*cont.*):
  dance, 74
  dictation, 63
  fast forward, backward, movement, 63, 103
  fork lifts, 162*n*.
  forward, backward, 60
  longitudinal: feed, 106
    motion, 116
  move ahead, back, 152
  playback, 63
  recording heads, 82
  return travel, 60
  reverse, 64
    counter, 72
    course, 150
    stitching, 101
  reversible reaction, 67
  reversing, 142
  tab, 64
  tape, 108
  three-dimensional structure, 68
Fossils, 96–97
Found (*see* Lost and found, 34)
Fountain, 51
  drinking, 36, 50
  ink, 109
  water, 109
Fragile, 98
Freight, air, 38
Frequency, 71
Frictionless contact, 128
Front-wheel drive, 158
Frozen, 98
Fruits, 40–41
Fuel, 158
  diesel, 158
  required, 141
  shut-off, 158
  system, 164
  tank selector, 158
Fulcrum, 128
Fulguration, 115
Full (*see* Volume)
Fuse, 82, 115

Galvanization, 115
Galvanometer, 128
Games, 133
  indoor, 66
Gammadion, 127
Garbage (*see* Trash)
Garden, 44
Gas:
  compressed, 99, 157
  expelled, 67
  filling station, 148
  flow, 80
  holder, 80
  line, 84
  well, 96

Gastropods, 97
Gate, 144
Gauge:
pressure, 84
thermometer, 84
Gear:
box, 161
drive, 107
high-ratio, 158
Gearshift, 165
Generator, 71, 159
emergency power, 71
signal, 71
Genetics, see Biology, 55
Geography, 92–95
Geology, 96–97
Geometric tolerances, 84–85
Gift shop, 65
Glaciers, 94
Glass, 50, 86
Glider flights, 151
Glimpse, 52
Goats, 42
Godhead, 89
Gold, 86, 105, 236
Golf, 132
Golf course, 95
Good luck, 47
Goods, handling of, 98-99
Grade crossing, 144, 146
Grain, 39
Graphic form, 166–230
Grassed area, 51
Grasses, 40
Gravity, center of, 98
Gray, 237
Grease, 160
Greases, 109, 160
Green, 235
Grill, 36, 102
Grinder, 102
Grinding, 106
Grindstone, 46
Grocery, 65
Ground (electrical), 82
Ground-air emergency code, 141
Group room, 70
Groups, 126
Growth, 52
Guard on duty, 131
Gypsum, 50, 97

Hail, 120
Hairdresser (*see* Barber, 65)
Halfnut, 107
Hamlet, 92
HAMS code, 51*n.*, 52*n.*
Hand, 74
control, 108
Hand (*cont.*):
switch, 116
Hand tools, 45
Handicapped, 117, 140
Handle with care, 98
Handling of goods, 98-99
Hangars, 38
Hanging plant, 56
Hardware, 66
Harness, 46
Haze, 120
Head, 55, 74
Header, 160
Headphone, 63
Heads (recording), 82
Health:
center, 95
public, 38
Hearing, 118
Heat (*see* Temperature)
Heater, 82, 158
Heavy, 157
Heavy-duty machinery, 105-110
Height (*see* Measurement)
Heliport, 36, 151
Hemispheres, 56
Hermes, staff of, 113, 119
Hex signs, 47
Highways, 92
Hill, 51
Hinduism, 138–139
Hinge, 128
Hip, 74
Historic plaque, 131
Hobo signs, 90–91
Hoist:
control, 161
grab, 46
Home economics, 100-103
appliances, 101–103
Hooks, 98
Horizontal:
bed, 96
tabulation, 60
Horn, 159
blowing, 145
sound, 147, 152
Horses, 41, 131
(*See also* Bridle path, 147;
Equestrian, 136)
Horticulture (*see* Botany, 56)
Hose bibb, 50
Hospital, 95, 117, 147
heliport, 151
Hospitals, 117–119
Hostel, youth, 148
Hot (*see* Temperature)
Hotel, 35
reservations, 35
Hour, 86

Household goods, see Shops and Services, 65-66
Houses (*see* Dwellings, 93)
Human, 51
Hunting, 132
Hurricane, 120
Hybrid, 55, 56
  resonance structure, 68
Hydraulic:
  lift (float), 157
  machinery, 83*n*.
  pump, 83
  reservoir, 158
Hydrographic features, 93-94
Hydrotherapy, 118

Ice:
  pack, 93, 94
  skating, 133, 137
Identical with, 55
If and only if, 111
Ignition, 158
  system, 164
Illumination (*see* Light)
Implements (farm), 45-47
Implies, 111
In and out, 27, 157
  absorptive transition, 128
  access denied, 92
  air brakes, 155
  axle connect, 161
  baggage, 37
  data out, 108
  departing, arriving flights, 37
  depress, 124
  dispense, 114
  do not enter, 149
  eject, 63
    lamp, 126
  engage and disengage, 157
    clutch, 158
    hand brake, 158
    plate rollers, 109
    tracer, 106
    winch, 161
  enter, leave control area, 151
  entering larger waterway, 153
  entrance, 34
    connector, 59
    locations, 52
    one, 43
    shape, 52
    tributary, 153
  exit, 34
    connector, 59
    emergency, 140
    illuminated sign, 48
  external, internal channel, 62
  extract, 59
  feed, 63
  film thread, 126

In and out (*cont.*):
  fork lifts, 162*n*.
  in position, 108
  incoming, outgoing, 67
  indoors, 126
  input/output, 59, 60
  insert, pull chocks, 152
  let out, 100
  mail sending, receiving, 70
  manual data input, 108
  merge, 59
  microphone input, output, 63
  no entry, 34, 140, 145, 146
  owner is, 90
  project, 126
  quick release coupler, 161
  radiative transition, 128
  receiver, 71
  release, 124
  remote cylinder (extended and retracted), 161
  remove, 63
  shift in, out, 59
  take in, 100
  three-dimensional structure, 68
  transfer, 114
  transmitter, 71
  transverse: feed, 106
    motion, 116
  vector direction, 128
Included in, 111
Incorrect citation, 55
  (*See also* Error; Mistake)
Increase and decrease, 27
  add, 114
  approach to grade crossing, 146
  blower, 102
  change, 113
  contrast, 70, 73
  coolant fluid, 107
  crescendo, 124
  decrescendo, 124
  delete, 72
  detail, 73
  dim lights, 145
  divided by, 111
  dot (music), 123*n*.
  double expose, 72
  expansion, 52
  flat, 124
  focal spot, 116
  growth, 52
  heat, 102
  heating control, 35
  heavy, light fog, 120
  height, 70
  increasing action, 103
  insert, 72
  lamp, 126
  lengthen, 100
  let out, 100

Increase and decrease (*cont.*):
lighten, darken, 127
merged in, 56
mild .... severe, 113
multiplied by, 111
multiplier, 61
non-linear variability, 82
per cent, 58
phenomenon, 120
radiation, 115
radioactivity, 98
rain, 120
repeat, 62
repeater, 72
road narrows, 143
sensitivity, 63
sharp, 124
shorten, 100
size, 70
space expand, 65
speed control, 63
steam, 83
stepless regulation, 108
by steps, 81
swell, 124
take in, 100
unit add, 72
variable control, 81
ventilation control, 35
Incubator, 47
perinathology, 118
Index, 58, 110
Indicator, 82
Inductor, 82
Industrial vehicle controls, 161
Industries, 104–105
Infinity, 111, 126
Inflammable, 98
Information, 34, 146
Inheritance, 55
Injections, 113
Injury, 142
Ink, 87, 109
Insecticide, 41
Inspection (police), 145
Inspection (quality control), 104
Insulation, 50, 64
Insured mail, 70
Intellect, 89
Interchange, 92
International:
boundary, 92
flags, 75–79
flights, connecting, 37
parcel post, 70
telephone, 70
Intersection, 111, 143
Invert type, 73
Ionizing rays, 140
Iron, 86, 105
industry, 104
Ironing, 101
Islam, 139
mosque, 95
Isobaths, 94

Jacobs brake (engine with), 157
Jail, 91
Jainism, 139
Jeep trail, 131
Jog, 106
Jogger, 110
Join airway, 150
Judaism, 139
synagogue, 95
Jump, 61
Jupiter, 54
Justice, 47, 133

Keep out, 34
access denied, 92
Kennel, 130
Kerb markings (*see* Curb markings)
Key:
board, 60
signatures (music), 125
King, 133
Kitchen, 44
equipment, 102
ware, 66
Knee, 74
Knife:
edge, 128
electric, 102
Kymograph, 116

Laboratory, 117
Ladder, 45
Lakes, 43, 93-94
Laminating, 104
Lamp, 126
bulb, 82
Land, 57
forms, 94
Landscaping, 51
Landslide, 96
Lane line, 149
Large (*see* Measurement)
Larger than, 111
Laser, 140
Latrine (*see* Toilets)
Laundry, 35
(*See also* Home economics, 100–103)
Lava, 96-97
Lavatory (*see* Toilets)
Law, wheel of, 138
Lead, 105
Left, 26
Lenses, 128

Less (*see* Measurement; Volume)
Levee, 94
Level, 74, 127
  crossing (*see* Grade crossing)
  high, low, 157
Lever arm, 128
Lifeguard (*see* Guard on duty, 131)
Lift (*see* Elevator, 34)
  fork, 161*n*.-162*n*.
  here, 98
  hydraulic (float), 157
  insert lift cart here, 98
  power, 46
Light (illumination):
  blinking, 144
  bulb (*see* Lamp bulb, 82)
  and dark, 27
  fluorescent lamp, 49
  illumination, 116
  outlet, 49
  oven, 102
  pools of, 53
  reading, 36
  red, 116
  source, 128
  street, 49
  switch, 35, 159
  traffic, 48
  (*See also* Lights)
Light (weight), 157
Lighted buoy, 154
Lighter, cigarette, 159
Lighthouse, 94, 131
Lighting, 49
  system, 164
Lightning, 120
  against, 47
  arrester, 82
Lights:
  dim, 145
  low beam, 145
  marine, 154-155
  parking, 147
  traffic, 148
  vehicle, 159
  (*See also* Light)
Limit:
  belt, 63
  of seaborne traffic, 93
  stacking, 98
Limited motion, 105, 106
Limiter, 71
Limousine, 37
Lines, drafting, 48
Liquid manure, 41
Liquids, 114
Liquor, 65
Listen, 63
Litter, do not, 38
Livestock, 41-43
Loader bucket, 161
Loading (times), 148
Lock (*see* Open and close)
Locker:
  baggage, 37
  luggage, 66
Lodgings, 130
Logarithm, 112
Longer than, 55
Loosen, 157
  (*See also* Open and close)
Lost:
  child, 34
  and found, 34
Loudspeaker, 64, 82
  volume, 70
Lounge, cocktail (*see* Bar, 36)
Lower, 157
  (*See also* Up and down)
Lubricant pump, 106
Lubricate, do not, 140
Lubrication, 108-109, 160
  press, 108
Luck, 47
Luggage, 37, 66
  locker, 37, 66
Lumber industry, 105

Machine controls (computers), 60-62
Machinery, heavy-duty, 105-110
Machines:
  adding, 64
  dictating, 63
  hydraulic, 83*n*.
  pneumatic, 83*n*.
  printing, 109-110
  sewing, 65, 101
  vending, 36
  washing, 102-103
Magen David Adom, 113*n*.
Magnesium, 105
Magnet:
  beam-bending, 128
  focusing, 128
  permanent, 83
Magnetic:
  filter, 107
  ink characters, 58
Magnetism, see Physics, 128
Magnetized materials, 99
Maid, 35
Mail, 70
  carrying, 78
Mailbox, 70
Maintenance, 104
Male and female, 26, 55
  clothing, 66, 99
  connector (electrical), 83
  dressing rooms, 117
  elements, 89

Male and female (*cont.*):
man, woman, 89
mare, 41
men's, women's cloakroom, 34
men's, women's shower, 35
men's suits, 66
nuclei, 56
stallion, 41
stewardess call, 36
toilets for, 34
women's wear, 66
Malfunction, 108
Man, 89
(*See also* Male and female)
Mandala, 138
Manganese, 105
Mangrove, 95
Manual, 115
alphabet, 75-78
data input, 108
input, 59
operation, 58
steering, 108
Manually, 60
Manufacturing, 104-110
heavy-duty machinery, 105-110
Map:
required, 141
symbols, see Geography, 92-95
Marble, 50, 97
Margins, 64
Marina, 131
Marine traffic, 152-155
Market, 65
Mars, 54
Marsh, 95
swamp plant, 56
Marshalling signals, 152
Masonry, 43
Mass, 128
Maternity, 118
Mathematics, 111-112
Mating, 55
Measurement:
alter to size indicated, 73
amount of check, 58
approach to grade crossing, 146
arena diameter, 53
building, 51
camera/subject distance, 126
channel, 153
clearance, 157
height, width, length, 145
counter, 61
dimensions, 98
drafting lines, 48
elevation, 95
geometric tolerances, 85
height, vehicle, 145
large, small, 26
Measurement (*cont.*):
larger than, 111
or equal to, 111
length, 60
vehicle, 145
lengthen, 100
level, 74
limit, belt, 63
longer than, 55
magnitude, 54, 112
measure, 123
measured by, 111
measuring, 108
much larger (smaller) than, 111
narrow bridge, structure, 144
number, 58
particle, small and large, 41
precipitation far or near station, 120
shorten, 100
shorter than, 55
smaller than, 111
or equal to, 111
stack: height, 109
range, 109
type composition, 72
weight, vehicle, 145
width, vehicle, 145
window height, 53
(*See also* Volume)
Mechanic, 65
Mechanical engineering, 83-85
Medical:
assistance (doctor) required, 77, 141
records, 117
supplies, require, 141
Medicinal plants, 39
Medicine, 113-119
equipment, 114-116
hospitals, 117-119
(*See also* Doctor)
Meditation, 117
Meeting point (*see* Rendezvous point, 34)
Megaphone, 36
Memory, 61
Men's toilet, 34
Mental hygiene, 118
Mercury, 54, 87
staff of, 113, 119
Merge, 59
Metal, 51
Metallurgy, 104
Metalworking, 104
Meteorological station, 44
Meteorology, 120-122
storm warnings, 153
Meter, 50
electricity, 49
Methane, 68
Metropolis, 92

Microphone, 70, 82
  input, output, 63
  socket, 63
Military installation, 95
Milk, 42
Milling, 106
Mincer (*see* Grinder, 102)
Mineral spring, 131
Minerals, see Geology, 97
  (*See also* Architectural materials, 50-51)
Mines, 94, 96
Mining, 105
  prospect, 95
Mirror, 128
  image, 108
Misce, 113
Mission, 95
Mistake, 60
  (*See also* Error; Incorrect citation)
Mix, 113, 114
Mixer, 46, 71, 80, 102
  jet, 80
Mixtures, 87-88
Modify, 61
Modulator, 71
Mohammedan mosque, 95
Molding, 104
Molecular biology, 57
Money:
  dollar, peso, etc., 58
  orders, 70
  (*See also* Currency)
Monorail, 36
Month, 86
Monument, cultural, 131
Moon, 133
Mooring, 153
  buoy, 154, 155
More (*see* Measurement; Volume)
More or less (*see* Plus or minus, 111)
Morse code, 75-79
Mosque, 95
Mother and child, 38, 90
Motion, 27, 105-107, 116
Motion pictures:
  fluoroscopic, 116
  (*See also* Film)
Motor:
  electric, 106
  vehicles, 145
    road for, 146
Motorcycle, 37, 142, 145
Motors, 83
Mountain, 51
  pass, 95
Movement and dance, 74
Moving stairway (*see* Escalator, 34)
Mud flat, 94
Multiplied by, 111
Museum, 131
Music, 123-125
  band, 131
  record shop, 65

Natural features, 95
Nature, 89
Nautical charts, 155
Navigation, 152-155
Negation, 60
  (*See also* Prohibition)
Negative charge, 67, 128
Neptune, 54
Neurology, 118
Neutral, 158
New world, 56
Newsstand, 37
Nickel, 87, 105
Night, 86, 160
No, 76, 141
No passing, 145, 146, 153
No riding, 140
Noise, 57
Noisy area, 52
Non-graphic alphabets, 75-79
Northern hemisphere, 56
Not, 60
Note (music), 123
Notions, 65
Numerals, non-graphic, 78-79
Numerical tape control, 108
Nurse, 117
  call system devices, 49
Nursery, 34, 118

Oasis, 95
Occupational therapy, 117
Occupied:
  seat, 36
  toilets, 36
Odd, 61
Off (*see* On and off)
  limits (*see* In and out, no entry)
Office:
  architectural planning, 51-53
  buildings, 93
  equipment, 63-65
  procedure (*see* Hospitals, 117)
Offspring, 55
Oil, 87, 160
  brake, 158
  engine, 157
  filter (transmission), 158
  industry, 105
  level window, 108
  pressure:
    brake, 158
    engine, 157
    transmission, 158
  required, 141
  temperature (transmission), 158

Oil (*cont.*):
  transmission, 158
  well, 96
Oils, 108–109, 160
O.K., 90, 129
Old world, 56
Olympics, 134–137
On and off, 26, 64, 107, 115, 157
  in action as long as button is operated, 107
  beginning motion, 107
  brake, 107
  end:
    finished, 60
    of letter, 63
    of medium, 60
    of operation, 62
    of text, 60
    of transmission, 59
    of transmission block, 60
  go, 155
  heater, 159
  ignition, 158
  ink flow, stop, 109
  lamp, 126
  moving car, 142
  online, offline storage, 59
  pedestrians may cross, wait, 148
  power, 159
  power take-off, 161
  proceed, 155, 156
  radio, 159
  start, 63, 103, 107, 114
    do not, 140
    engines, 152
    feed, 106
    of heading, 60
    operation, 60
    of text, 60
    of winding, 81
  start and stop with same button, 107
  stop, 60, 63, 107, 114, 143, 148, 149, 152, 155, 156
    ahead, 144
    compulsory, 145
    emergency, 107
    engine (emergency), 159
    final bar, 123
    halt, 90
    instantly, 76
    machine, 72
    master, 107
    obligation to, 152
    train coming, 148
  stopped:
    car, 142
    tone, 125
  stopping motion, 107
  switch, 60, 82
  television camera, 70
  timer, 107
On-board aircraft, 36
One, 114
One way, 146
Open and close:
  chuck, 107
  close-up space, 72
  closed trail, 132
  closing, 104
  diaphragm, 116
  door or lid, 103
  fork lifts, 162*n*.
  halfnut, 107
  load, process (camera), 127
  lock and unlock, 35, 107, 116, 127, 157
    zones, 52
  lock, differential, 161
  margin set, release, 64
  open here, 98
  road closed, 146
  spool release, 63
  stroller and luggage area (locker), 66
  switch (off and on), 82
Operation, 61
Ophthalmology, 118
Opposition, 54
Optics, see Physics, 128
Orally, 113
Orange, 234
Orbitals, 68
Orchard, 44, 95
Order of, 58
Ore deposits, 97
Origin, 89
Orthopedics, 118
Oscillating motion, 105, 106
Oscilloscope, 72
Ounce, 114
Out (*see* In and out)
Outlets, 48–49
Oven, 102
  [*See also* Range (Stove)]
Overturned vehicle, 142
Oxidizing agent, 99
Oxygen, 36

Paging system devices, 49
Pagoda, 95
Panorama, 52
Paper industry, 105
Paragraph, 58
Parcel post, 70
Park, 158
  boundary, 92, 95
Parked, 142
Parking, 147, 148
  restriction, 150
  space limits, 150
  structure, 34
Passing, no, 145, 146, 153
Passive, 89

Path, 92
Pathology, 118
Patterns, 65
  dressmaking (instructions), 100
  stitch, 101
Paved area, 51
Pawn shop, 65, 66
Peace, 53
Pedestrian, 142*n.*, 147
  access, 52
  compulsory way for, 147
  crossing, 144, 147
  crosswalk, 150
  density, 52
  keep left, 145
  may cross, wait, 148
Pediatrics, 117
Pelvis, 74
Per, 58
Per cent, 58
Perforation, 110
Perishable materials, 99
Permission, 27
Peso, 58, 85
Pesticides (*see* Poisons, 41)
Petrol (*see* Gas)
Pharmacy, 65
Phase, 61
Photographic materials, 99
Photography, 126-127
  motion pictures, 116
Photometer, 114
Photon, 128
Photosensitivity, 83
Physical therapy, 117
Physician (*see* Doctor)
Physics, 128-129
Physiotherapy (*see* Physical therapy, 117)
Picnic area, 130
Pier, 94
Piezoelectric crystal unit, 82
Pigs, 42
Pipeline, 93
Piping, 83-84
Pivot, 128
Plan drawing, 50*n.*-51*n.*
Planets, see Astronomy, 54
Planing cut, 106
Planned parenthood, 114
Planning (architectural), 51-53
Planted area, 51
Plants:
  agronomy, 39-41
  botany, 56
  forestry, 44
  fossils, 97
  landscaping, 51
Plastics industry, 104*n.*
Platinum, 87
Playback, 63
Playback (*cont.*):
  head, 82
Playground, 130
Playing cards, 133*n.*
Ploughs (*see* Plows, 46)
Plows, 46
Plumbing, 49
  mechanical engineering, 83-84
Plus or minus, 111
Pluto, 54
Pneumatic machinery, 83*n.*
Point, 95
  of reference, 52
Poisons, 41, 98, 140
Pole, electric distribution, 49
Police, 91, 145
Pool, 132
Population, 57
Porter, 37
Positive charge, 67, 128
Post (*see* Mail)
Post office, 70, 93
Postage stamps (*see* Stamps, mailing, 70)
Postbox (*see* Mailbox, 70)
Poultry, 42-43
Powder, 86
Power, 63, 159
  generator, emergency, 71
  industries, 105
  take-off, 46, 161
  throttle, 165
  train, 165
  transmission line, 93
Prayer, 117
Precipitation, 67, 88
  (*See also* Meteorology, 120)
Precipitator, electrical, 80
Pregnancy, 89
Preparation, 58
Prescription, 113
Press room, 70
Pressure, 81
  air, 157
  blowing unit, 107
  compressed gas, 157
  compression, 116
  controller, 81
  decompression, 116
  gauge, 84
  oil: brake, 158
    engine, 157
    transmission, 158
  radiator, 157
  steam, 107
  steam supply, 83
  suction unit, 107
  vacuum, 107
  vessels (process), see Chemical engineering, 80
Printing:
  industry, 105

Printing (*cont.*):
  machines, 109-110
  proofreader marks, 72-73
  type composition, 72
Priority, 145, 146
Prism, 128
Private telephone, 49
Process, 58
  pressure vessels, see Chemical engineering, 80
Processes (alchemy), 88
Procreation, 89
Product, 104
Progeny, 55
Programming, 58-59
Prohibition, 26, 145, 152
  end of, 153
Projection room, 127
Projector, 71
  effects, 49
Proofreader marks, 72-73
Psychology, 113
Pub (*see* Bar, 36)
Public:
  health, 38
  telephone, 49
Pull, 98, 162
Pulley, 128
Pump, 102
  centrifugal, 80, 83
  cooling, 106
  hydraulic, 83
    system, 106
  lubricant, 106
  primer, 158
  reciprocating, 80
  rotary, 83
Purification, 88
Purple, 235
Push, 162, 164

Quality control, 104
Quarantine, 44
Quayside, 144
Queen, 133
Quiet, 35, 91
  area, 52

Rabbit, 42
Radar, 164-165
Radiation:
  quantities, 115
  warning, 140
  (*See also* Radioactive; Radioactivity)
Radiator, pressurized, 157
Radio, 70-71, 159
  station, 52
    selector, 159
Radioactive, 115
Radioactivity, 98
Radiography, 116
Radiology, 115
Radiotherapy, 118
Railing, 51
Railroad, 92, 144, 146
  crossing, 149
  station, 37, 92
  traffic, 155-156
  (*See also* Grade crossing; Train)
Railway (*see* Railroad)
Rain, 47, 120
Raise, 157
  (*See also* Up and down)
Range (scope), 51, 165
Range (stove), 50
  outlet, 48
  (*See also* Oven)
Ranger station, 95, 130
Razor:
  blades, used, 35
  socket, electric, 35
Reactions, 67
Reactors, 80
Read, 61
Reader, 62
Ready, 60
Receive, 61
Receiver, 71
Reciprocating pump, 80
Record, 63
Record shop, 65
Recorder, 72
Recorders, tape, 71
Recording:
  heads, 82
  machines, 63
Records, medical, 117
Recreation, 130-137
Rectifier, 82
Recycling, 57
Red, 234
  Crescent, 113
  Cross, 113
  Lion and Sun, 113
  Star of David, 113
Reducers, 84
Reef, 94
Reel speed, 161
Reference, point of, 52
Refilling, 107
Refuge, wildlife, 95
Refuse (*see* Trash)
Regeneration, 44
Registered, 58
  mail, 70
Registering, 64, 104
Registration, 117
Regulation, stepless, 108
Relationships, 52
Release, 124
  ribbon, 64

Release (*cont.*):
spool, 63
total, 64
Relief contours, 94
Relief shipments, 99
Religion, 138-139
buildings, 95
Remote control, 63
Remove, 63
Rendezvous point, 34
Rental, car, 37
Repeat, 62, 124
Repeater, 72
Reservation boundary, 92
Reservations, hotel, 35
Reserve, 44
Reservoir, 43, 93
hydraulic, 158
Resistor, 82
Resonance, 115
hybrid structure, 68
Restaurant, 35
Restrooms (*see* Toilets)
Retort, 86
Return to seat, 36
Reverse (*see* Forward and reverse)
Reversible reaction, 67
Review, 63
Revolution, 106
Rewind, 126
ribbon, 64
Rich people, 90
Ridge, 94
Riding, no, 140
Right, 26
Rinsing, 102
River bank, 144
Rivers, 93
Road:
markings (*see* Street markings, 148-150)
service, 148
traffic signs, 143-150
work ahead, 144
Roads, 92
Rocks, 50, 94, 97
falling, 144
Rockshaft, 161
Roll, do not, 98
Rollers, 109
Room service, 35
Rooms, 35, 53
Rotary pump, 83
Rotate, 74, 157
Rotation, 106, 113, 128
about the bond, 67
Rotisserie, 102
Route marker, 147
Routes, explorer, 95
Rowing, 135
RPM (engine speed), 157
Rubbish (*see* Trash)
Ruins, 95
Runways, 151

Safe deposit boxes, 34
Safety, 140-142
water, 131
Sailing, 135
Sal alkali, 87
Salt, 87
Saltpeter, 87
Sand, 50, 87, 94, 97, 120
dunes, 94, 96
Saturn, 54
Sauna, 35
Scale (diatonic), 123
Scattering, 128
School, 95
patrol ahead, 144
Screener, 80
Scrub, 95
Scruple, 114
Scuba diving, 131
Sealing, 104
Seaport, 94
Search, 61
tape, 108
Seasons, see Astrology, 89
Seat belts, fasten, 36
Seats, 46, 52
Section, 56, 58
drawings, 50*n*.-51*n*.
Sectioning, 48
Select, 61
Semaphore, 75-79
Separation, 88
Separator, 47, 59, 80
Sequence, 61
Sericulture, 104
Service, road, 148
Services, 65-66
veterinary, 113
Set-up, 108
Settlements, 92-93
Sewing machines, 65, 101
Sex, see Biology, 55-56
(*See also* Male and female)
Shapes, three-dimensional, 163-165
Sharp, 140
Shear pin, 161
construction, 108
Shearing, 104
Shed, 43
Sheep, 42
Shelter, fallout, 140
Shingles, 51
Shinto, 139
Ship, 36
Shooting, 136
range, 132

Shopping center, 65
Shops, 65-66
food and drink, 35-36
pre-neon, 38
Shoreline, 94
Shorter than, 55
Shoulder, 74
soft, 144
Shower, 34-35, 49, 130
Shrub, 51, 56
Sichi, 66
Siding, 51
Signal, 64
traffic, 144, 148
translator, 71
Signs:
electrical, 48
road traffic, 143-150
Sikhism, 139
Silk, 104
worm, 42
Silver, 87, 105, 236
Sine, 113
Siren, 49
Sitting, no, 140
Size, 70
Skating, ice, 133, 137
Skidding, 142
Skiing, 132, 137
Skillet, 102
Skip, 61
Sky, see Meteorology, 121
Slate, 50, 97
Slippery, 140
Slot machine (*see* Vending machine, 36)
Slow (*see* Speed)
Sluice, 105
Small (*see* Measurement)
Smaller than, 111
Smog, 162
Smoke, visibility reduced by, 120
Smokey the Bear, 130, 137
Smoking, 36, 130, 140
Snack bar, 35, 65
Snow, 120, 148
Snowmobiles, 132
Soap, 87
Soft shoulder, 144
Soil, 97
Solar system, see Astronomy, 54
Somersault, 74
Sort, 59
Sound system, 49
Source:
alternating current, 81
light, 128
Southern hemisphere, 56
Spark:
advance, 158
gap current, 115
Spark (*cont.*):
gap regulation, 115
Sparky the Fire Dog, 130
Speaker (loudspeaker), 82
Specimen verified, 55
Spectrophotometer, 114
Speech, 118
Speed:
change, 106
compulsory minimum, 146
control, 63
engine (in RPM), 157
fast and slow, 27, 157
fast forward, backward, movement, 63, 103
ground, 160
jog traverse, 106
lane for slow traffic, 146
limit, 145, 156
monitor, 109
motion, 116
quick!, 90
rapid traverse, 106
reduce, 155
reel, 161
slow: down, 152
moving vehicle, 140
wind, 121, 153
Spin, 128
Spindle, 106
Spirits, 86
Spirits (liquor), 65
Splicing, 104
Sports, 131-133
golf course, 95
Olympic, 134-137
Spotlights, 49
Spray:
dryer, 80
steam, 107
water, 107
Sprayer, 47
Spring (coil), 128
Spring (season), 89
Spring (water), 93
cold, 130
mineral, 131
Sprinkler, 47
Stabilizer, 162
Stable, 131
Stack range, 109
Stacking limit, 98
Staff register system devices, 49
Stairs, 34
Stamps, mailing, 70
Standing, no, 140
Star, 54, 133
of David, 113, 139
Start (*see* On and off)
Starter, 158, 159

State boundary, 92
Static eliminator, 110
Stationery, 65
Steam, 107
  power, 105
  pressure, 107
  spray, 107
Steering, manual, 108
Stenciled sign, 48
Stencils, 64
Sterilization, 119
Sterilizers, 41, 114
Stewardess call, 36
Stone, 50
Stop (*see* On and off)
Storage tanks, 80
Stores (*see* Shops)
Storm warnings, 153
Storms, 120
Stove [*see* Oven; Range (stove)]
Streams, 93
Street car, 37
  tramway stop, 147
  trolley stop, 91
Street markings, 148–150
Strobe, 110
Stroller area, 66
Structure, three-dimensional, 68
Structures, farm, 43–44
Studio, 70
Sublimation, 88
Substances, common, 69
Substitute, 60
Suction unit, 107
Sulphur, 87, 105
Sum, 112
Summer, 89
Sun, 54, 126, 133
Sunshine, 47
Sundries, 65
Surgery, 119
Suspended load overhead, 140
Swamp:
  marshes, 95
  plant, 56
Swastika, 127
Sweets (*see* Candy, 110)
Swimming, 135
Swine, 42
Switch, 82
  ignition, 158
  light, 35, 159
  main, 107
Switchboard, 70
Synagogue, 95
System, 61

Table:
  adjustment, 114
Table (*cont.*):
  tilt, 116
  vibrating, 110
Tailoring, 100
Tanks, 80, 95
Taoism, 139
Tape, 108
  control, 108
  magnetic, 59
  punched, 59
  recorders, 71
  tear, 104
Tarot cards, 133
Tavern (*see* Bar, 36)
Taxi, 37
Tea, 39
Teeth, see Medicine, 114
Telecommunications, 93
Telegrams, 70
Telegraph, 93
Telephone, 64, 70, 153
  emergency, 132
  free, 91
  international, 70
  line, 93
  private, 49
  public, 49
Television, 66, 70–71
  camera, 70
  tube (*see* Tube, cathode ray, 82)
  TV station, 52
Temperature, 27, 81, 157, 160
  controller, 81
  cool, 114
  coolant, 157
    fluid, 107
  cooling pump, 106
  heat, 103, 114,
    apply, 67
    floor, 159
    protect from, 98
    sealing, 104
    stove, 102
    transfer equipment, see Chemical engineering, 80
  heater, 82, 158
  heating control, 35
  hot and cold, 27
    water supply, 83
  iron, 101
  keep frozen, 98
  oil, transmission, 158
  protect from heat, cold, 98
  refrigeration of cadavers, 118
  stove, 102
  thermometer, 84
  thermostat, 48, 72
  warm front, cold front, 121
  water, 157
  weather fronts, 121

Tension, 107
  control, 110
Terminals, 36-38
Terminuses (*see* Terminals, 36-38)
Terra cotta, 50
Terrazzo, 50
Terskelion, 127
Textile industry, 104
Theater, 131
Therapy, occupational, physical, 117
Therefore, 111
Thermoforming, 104
Thermometer, 84
Thermostat, 48, 72
  heating control, 35
  (*See also* Temperature)
Threading, 106
Three-dimensional shapes, 163-165
Three-dimensional structure, 68
Throttlé, hand, 158, 164
Thunderstorm, 120
Tickets, 37
Tighten, 107, 157
Tile, 50
Timber, 45
Time, 27, 103, 157
  after, 150
  annual, 56
  before, 150
  biennial, 56
  clock, 48, 49
  lubrication, 109, 160
  no parking on odd, even dates, 147
  parking, 148
  past hour, 120
  perennial, 56
  perishable materials, 99
Timer, 107
Tin, 87, 105
Tire chains required, 148
To, 58
Tobacco, 39, 65
Toilets, 34
  accessible bathrooms, 52
  aft, 36
  occupied, 36
  water closet, 49
Tolerances, geometric, 85
Tone, 64
Tools (*see* Implements, 45-47)
Tornado, 120
Torque converter, 161
Total, 64
Touch, do not, 140
Tow, 158
Tower, 51
Towing, 142
Town, 92
Township boundary, 92
Tracer, 106
Track, 60, 92
Tractor, 46, 142
Traffic, 143-156
  accidents, 142
  air, 150-152
  cone, 48
  light, 48
  marine, 152-155
  rail, 155-156
  road, 143-150
  running (engine hours), 157
  signals, 144, 148
  timer, 107
  watches, 66
Trailer:
  no entry, 145
  sites, 130, 148
Trails, 130-131
  bicycle, 131, 147
Train, 37, 51, 91
  coming, 148
  (*See also* Railroad)
Tramp signs (*see* Hobo signs, 90-91)
Tramway, 131
  stop, 147
  (*See also* Street car, 37)
Transfer, 114
Transformer, 49, 61, 71, 82
Transistor, 82
Transition, 128
Translator, signal, 71
Transmission, 158
  oil, 158
    filter, pressure, temperature, 158
Transmitter, 71
Transpose, 72
Trash, 35, 117
Travel, 34-38
Traverse, 106
Treatment, 113
Trees, 51, 56, 95
  forestry, 44-45
  vegetation, 95
Triquetra, 138
Trolly stop, 91
  (*See also* Street car, 37)
Trot (*see* Jog, 106)
Trough, drinking, 43
Truck, 142
  crossing, 144
Tube:
  cathode ray (TV), 82
  current, 115
  vacuum, 82
Tumble, do not, 98
Tungsten, 105
Tuning, 64, 164
Tunnel, 92, 144
Turbine, 83
Turkeys, 42-43

Turn, 124
  signal, 157
Turning, 106
Turntable, record, 71
Twins, 55
Two, 114
Type composition, 72
Typewriters, 64

Unclamp, 107
Underpass, 51, 147
Union, 111
  threaded, 84
Units, computers, 61-62
Universality, the path of, 138
University, 95
Unlock (*see* Open and close)
Unwrapped, 114
Up and down, 26, 157
  above, 150
    eye level, 51
  anticline, syncline, 96
  ascending, descending node, 54
  ascent, descent, 144
  basket lift, 161
  below, 150
    eye level, 51
  bow (music), 125
  climb:
    in holding pattern, 151
    and maintain, 150
  climbing plant, 56
  contours, 94
  cotton picking unit lift, 161
  descend:
    in holding pattern, 151
    and maintain, 150
  distal, 113
  drifting snow, 120
  elevate, 127
  elevator, 34
  escalator, 34
  fault, 96
  fork lifts, 161*n.*-162*n.*
  gas expelled, 67
  hanging plant, 56
  hill, 51
  hoist control (raise, lower), 161
  loader boom (raise, lower), 161
  move upwards, downwards, 152
  northern, southern hemispheres, 56
  plate rollers, 109
  platform height, 161
  power lift, 46
  precipitation, 67
  proximal, 113
  rockshaft (raise, lower), 161
  stairs, 34
  table descent, return, 109
Up and down (*cont.*):
  this way up, 98
  underpass, 51, 147
  valley, 51
  vertical:
    feed, 106
    motion, 116
  weather fronts, 121
  windows, 160
Upender, 161
Uranium, 105
Uranus, 54
Urban area, 92
Urinal, 49
Urine, 87, 113
  with dung and water, 41
Use, 51
Utility outlet, 130

Vaccination, 113
Vacuum, 107
  paper feeder, 109
  tube, 82
Valley, 51
Valves, 81, 84
  safety, 161
Van, 142
Vane, air, 107
Vasectomy, 114
Vector, 128
  product, 111*n.*
Vegetables, 40
Vegetation, 95
  (*See also* Forestry)
Vehicle controls, 157-162
  three-dimensional shapes, 164-165
Vehicle ferry, 131
Vehicles:
  animal drawn, 145
  slow moving, 140
  work, 140
Vending machine, 36
Ventilation control, 35
  (*See also* Air, conditioning; Fan)
Ventilator, 43
Venus, 54
Verified specimen, 55
Vertebrates, 97
Vertical:
  bed, 96
  circulation, 52
  feed, 106
  motion, 116
  tabulation, 60
Vessels, process pressure, see Chemical engineering, 80
Veterinary services, 113
Vibrating table, 110

View point, 130
Village, 92
Vinegar, 87
Vineyard, 95
Visibility (*see* Sky coverage, 121)
  reduced by smoke, 120
Visitors, 117
Vista, 52
Vitriol, 88
Volcano, 96
Voltmeter, 128
Volume, 63, 70
  blackening, 116
  brightness, 116
  contents in liters, 98
  contrast, 116
  empty, 26, 158
  flow controller, 81
  forte, fortissimo, 124
  full, 26, 158
    level, 107
  gas flow, 80
  heavy. . .light, 157
  level, 157
    controller, 81
  lighten, darken, 127
  loudspeaker, 70
  mass, 128
  moon quarters, 54
  noisy, quiet, 52
  piano, pianissimo, 124
  pound, 58
  sky coverage (clouds), 121
  water level, 102
  weight, 103, 108, 157
    gross, net, 98
  (*See also* Measurement)

Waist, 74
Waiting room, 37
Wall light outlet, 49
Warmer, 102
Warning, 26
  biohazard, 140
  line, 149
  radiation, 140
  storm, 153
  (*See also* Beware; Caution; Danger)
Washing:
  facility, 130
  machines, 102-103
Washroom, 34
Waste (*see* Trash)
Watchman system devices, 49
Water, 57, 86, 157
  Aquarius, 54, 89
  cistern, 43, 50
  closet, 49
    (*See also* Toilets)
Water (*cont.*):
  cooled condenser, 83
  cooler, 80
  don't pollute, 147
  drinking, 36, 90, 153
    fountain, 36, 50
  ductor, 109
  on farm lands, 43
  foot pedal for, 35
  fresh, 93, 95, 96
  fountain, 109
  heater, 50
  hydrographic features, 93-94
  hydrotherapy, 118
  landscaping, 51
  level, 102
  life-giving source, 139
  pipes, 83-84
  plant, 56
  polo, 135
  power, 105
  required, 141
  salt (marine), 94-96
  sports, 131
  spray, 107
  temperature, 157
  way, larger, crossing and entering, 153
  well, 96
Wave, 128
Wax, 88
WC (*see* Toilets)
Weather (*see* Meteorology)
Weekdays, see Astrology, 89
Weight (*see* Volume)
Weir, 153
Welding, 84
Well, 43
  gas, 96
  oil, 96
  water, 96
Wheels, 45
Whistle:
  buoy, 154
  post, 156
White, 237
Wildlife refuge, 95
Winch, 161
Winding (moving air):
  cross, 144
  speed, 121, 153
Windmill, 43, 95
Windows, 160
Windscreen (*see* Windshield, 160)
Windshield, 160
Wine, 65
Winter, 89
  Olympics, 137
  sports, 132-133
Wireless (*see* Radio)

Wiring:
architectural, 48-49
electronic, 81-83
Wisdom, 47
With, 113
Without, 113
Woman, 89
(*See also* Male and female)
Women's toilet, 34
Women's wear, 66
Wood, 50
Woods, 95
(*See also* Forestry, 44-45)
Wool, 103
pure new, 103
Woolens, 103
Word, 60
World, 89, 133
hemispheres, 56
old, new, 56
(*See also* Earth)
Wrapped, 114
Wrapping, 104
Wreck, 94
Wrist, 74
Write, 61

X-ray equipment (*see* Radiology, 115-116)
X-rays, 118

Yellow, 234
Yes, 75, 141
Yield, 146, 149
sign ahead, 144
Yin-yang, 112, 139
Youth hostel, 148

Zen Buddhism, 138
Zero, 108
Zinc, 87, 105
oxide, 88
Zip fastener (*see* Zipper, 100)
Zipper, 100
Zodiac:
astrology, 88-90
astronomy, 54
Zoology, see Biology, 55
Zoom, 126
Zoroastrianism, 139

POSITIVE ASSOCIATIONS

Blood (life), fire (warmth), passion, sentiment, valor, patriotism, revolution, Christ, liberty

NEGATIVE ASSOCIATIONS

Blood (spilled), fire (burning), death throes and sublimation, wounds, surging and tearing emotions, passions, war, anarchy, revolution, martyrdom, danger, the devil

ALCHEMY

Third stage: Sulphur, passion

ART

Chinese Art:
Black on red: Happiness
Gold on red: Special happiness
Red on blue: Old mourning
Red on green: Happiness
Red on white: Important notice
Red on yellow: Royal
White on red: Good luck
Persian Rugs: Joy, life, happiness

ASTROLOGY

Temple of Nebuchadnezzar: Third level of building, devoted to Mars
Early Zodiac: Mars, ruling Aries and Scorpio

CULTURE COMPARISONS

American Indian: Masculine, day
Cherokee: Success and triumph
Hopi: Sun god
China: Worn by emperor to worship the sun; coral button on cap worn by first ranking officials; visiting cards traditionally red, color of joy and festive occasions
Season: Summer
England: Color of the livery of the royalty
France: Red kerchiefs worn around necks by aristocrats in post-guillotine days
Japan: Fighting, anger, danger, permissive
Theater: Used as a warm and attractive color (as an opposite to blue)
United States:
Red rose: Love

C238→

POSITIVE ASSOCIATIONS

Fire and flames, marriage, hospitality, benevolence, celestial fruit, pride and ambition, earthly wisdom

NEGATIVE ASSOCIATIONS

Malevolence, Satan

ASTROLOGY

Temple of Nebuchadnezzar: Second level of building devoted to the planet Jupiter

EDUCATION (doctorate hoods)

United States:
Apricot: Nursing
Maize: Agriculture
Orange: Engineering

ELECTRICAL ENGINEERING

Chassis wiring: Screen grids and second transistor bases

GEMS

Jacinth: Modesty, cures heart ailments

HANDLING OF GOODS

Inter-Governmental Maritime Consultative Organization shipping labels: Explosives, fireworks

HERALDRY

Tinctures:
Tenne: Strength and endurance

HOLIDAYS

Thanksgiving, Halloween

MEDICINE

Anesthetics (Sweden): Cyclopropane

METEOROLOGY

Weatherfront markings on maps: Intertropical convergence zone

MUSIC

Instruments:
Brass

C239→

POSITIVE ASSOCIATIONS

The sun, light, illumination, dissemination and comprehensive generalization, magnanimity, intuition, intellect, supreme wisdom, highest values, divinity, ripening grain

NEGATIVE ASSOCIATIONS

Treachery, cowardice
Saffron: Debauchery, malevolence, impure love

ART

Chinese art:
Black on yellow: Religious
Blue on yellow: Old mourning
Gold on yellow: Special happiness
Red on yellow: Royal
White on yellow: Buddhistic
Yellow on black: Old man's death
Yellow on blue: Divine
Yellow on green: First class
Yellow on white: Holy
Chinese, Thai, Vietnamese, and Malaysian rugs: Royalty
Persian rugs (cream): Modesty

ASTROLOGY

Temple of Nebuchadnezzar: Fourth level of building devoted to the Sun
Early Zodiac: Sun, ruling Leo

CULTURE COMPARISONS

American Indian: Masculine
Arapaho: Feminine
China:
Dynasties: Ch'ing (1644–1911)
Only the emperor could wear yellow; worn by the emperor to worship the sky
Earth, honor, imperial dignity
Egypt: Happiness and prosperity
France (10th century): Doors and abodes of criminals, felons, and traitors
Japan: Childish, gay
Jews: Forced to wear yellow by Venetians and Hitler
Spain (medieval): Yellow as part of the executioner's costume stood for the accused's treachery

DIRECTION (cardinal points)

Apache, Navaho, Omaha, Sioux: West

C240→

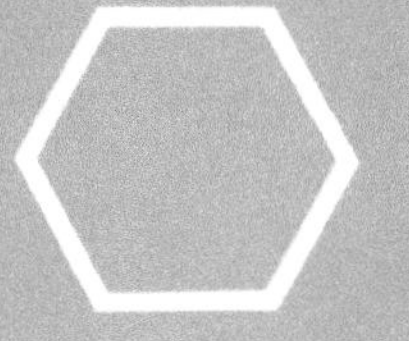

POSITIVE ASSOCIATIONS

Vegetation, nature, fertility of the fields, sympathy, adaptability, prosperity, hope, life, immortality, youth, freshness, auspicious, recognition of soul, wisdom

NEGATIVE ASSOCIATIONS

Death, connecting link between black mineral life and red animal life; lividness, envy, jealousy, disgrace, sinister, opposition, moral degradation, madness

ART

Chinese Art:
Blue on green: Women's colors
Red on green: Happiness
Yellow on green: First class
Persian Rugs: The sacred and holy color

ASTROLOGY

Temple of Nebuchadnezzar:
Fifth level of building, devoted to the planet Venus
Early Zodiac: Venus, ruling Taurus and Libra

CULTURE COMPARISON

American Indian: Feminine
China: Dynasties: Ming (1368–1644)
Egypt: Fertility, vegetation, rain, strength
Japan: Youth, energy, future
Olive green: Dignity

DIRECTIONS

China: Face of Mo-li Ch'ing, guardian of the east
Chippewa: South

EDUCATION (doctorate hoods)

United States:
Green: Medicine
Green: Osteopathy
Nile green: Podiatry
Olive: Pharmacology
Sage green: Physical education
Sea green: Optometry

ELECTRICAL ENGINEERING

Chassis wiring: Control grids, diode

C241→

POSITIVE ASSOCIATIONS

The sky. Light blue connotes day, the calm sea; thinking, religious feeling, devotion, innocence, truth, constancy, justice, charity, cold

NEGATIVE ASSOCIATIONS

Dark blue connotes night and the stormy sea; doubt and discouragement

ART

Chinese Art:
Black on blue: Low class
Blue on black: Evil spirit
Blue on green: Women's color
Blue on white: Devil's color
Blue on yellow: Old mourning
Red on blue: Old mourning
White on blue or black: Lower class mourning
Yellow on blue: Divine
Persian Rugs: The warrior, power and might

ASTROLOGY

Temple of Nebuchadnezzar:
Sixth level of building, devoted to the planet Mercury
Early Zodiac: Jupiter, ruling Sagittarius and Pisces

CULTURE COMPARISONS

American Indian: Feminine
Cherokee: Tribulation and defeat
China: Worn by emperor to worship the sky; blue button on cap worn by second ranking officials
Season: Spring
Egypt: Virtue, faith, truth
Gaul: Worn by slaves
Japan: In theater, color of villains, supernatural creatures, ghosts and fiends
Tibet:
Light blue: Celestial
United States: Baby boy

DIRECTION (cardinal points)

Apache, Cherokee, Omaha,. Sioux: North
Creek, Navaho: South
Hopi, Isleta, Zuni: West
Tibet: South

C242→

POSITIVE ASSOCIATIONS

Power, spirituality, royalty, love of truth, loyalty, empire, patience, humility, nostalgia, memories

NEGATIVE ASSOCIATIONS

Sublimation, martyrdom, mourning, regret, penitence, resignation, humility

CULTURE COMPARISONS

China: Worn by literary and educated figures; purple button on cap worn by third ranking officials
Egypt: Virtue and faith
Japan: Graceful, nobility
Rome: Royal hue of the Caesars

DIRECTION (cardinal points)

Ireland: East

EDUCATION (doctorate hoods)

France:
Purple: Science
Violet: Rector, administration
United States:
Purple: Law
Lilac: Dentistry

ELECTRICAL ENGINEERING

Chassis wiring: Power supply, minus
Circuits (Switzerland): Aerial, electroacoustic

ELEMENTS

Judaic (Josephus): Sea

FOLKLORE

Death:
Preparation for: Egyptian warrior carried amulets of purple stone
Medieval magicians' vestments: Purple on Sunday, works of light

GEMS

Amethyst: Cured and prevented drunkenness; faith, charity, peace and devotion, powers of endearment, cured gout, gave pleasant dreams when placed under pillow; birthstone for February

C243→

POSITIVE ASSOCIATIONS
The earth

NEGATIVE ASSOCIATIONS
Barrenness, poverty

CULTURAL COMPARISONS
China: Sung Dynasty (960–1127A.D.) Chinese visiting cards when in mourning
Japan: Earth, dignity

DIRECTION (cardinal points)
Ireland: West

EDUCATION (doctorate hoods)
United States:
Brown: Fine Arts, including Architecture
Copper: Economics
Drab: Business and Accounting
Russet: Forestry

ELECTRICAL ENGINEERING
Chassis wiring: Heaters or filaments, off ground
Circuits: Low voltage

GEMS
Agate: Health, wealth, longevity, power to warrior, favor to lover, intelligence, happiness, health and long life; drove away fevers, epilepsy, madness; stopped the flow of rheum in the eye; reduced menstruation, dispersed the water of dropsy; warded away evil eye
Amber: Protection against the evil eye, witchcraft, and misfortune; when mixed with honey, cured earache and blindness; in dust form helped pains in the stomach, kidneys, liver, and intestines; burnt amber helped women in labor; a ball of amber reduced fever; beads prevented rheumatism, toothache, headache, rickets, and jaundice; a bit in the nose made it stop bleeding; worn around the neck, goiters vanished; Arab physicians used powdered amber for miscarriage, boils, carbuncles, and ulcers
Sard: Immortality

C244→

GOLD

POSITIVE ASSOCIATIONS
Mystic aspect of the sun, majesty, riches, honor, wisdom

NEGATIVE ASSOCIATIONS
Idolatry

ALCHEMY
Fourth Phase: End product

ART
Chinese Art:
Gold on black: Old man's death
Gold on red: Special happiness
Gold on white: Aristocratic
Gold on yellow: Imperial

CULTURAL COMPARISONS
China: Gold button on cap worn by sixth ranking officials
Japan: Gold thread symbolic of long life

C244→

SILVER

POSITIVE ASSOCIATIONS
Purity, chastity, test of truth, the moon

ART
Persian rugs: When lavishly used, signifies the power, grandeur and riches of the owner

HERALDRY
Tinctures:
Argent: Faith and purity
English nobility: Reserved for the higher

ASTROLOGY
Early Zodiac: Mercury, ruling Virgo and Gemini

GEMS
Cat's eye: Arabs used it to make wearer invisible in battle; overcame witchcraft and sudden death
Onyx: Conjugal felicity, happiness, and remembrance
Opal: Cured diseases of the eye; hope, immortality, happiness, good luck and remembrance; conquered the evil eye and was used in healing; today it is accused of bringing bad luck; birthstone for October
Tourmaline: Friendship, faith, charity

RELIGION
American Indian:
Hopi: Fire god
Egypt: Isis, virgin of the world
Greek: Iris, goddess of the rainbow
Judaism: Union of man and deity (Noah story)
Kabbalah: Kingdom
Twelve Tribes of Israel: Mannasseh